SECOND EDITION

EDUCATING THE ABLEST

a book of readings

on the education of gifted children

Edited by

JOHN CURTIS GOWAN, National Association for Gifted Children

JOE KHATENA, Mississippi State University and National Association for Gifted Children

E. PAUL TORRANCE, University of Georgia

F. E. PEACOCK PUBLISHERS, INC.

Contents

President's Message

The National Association for Gifted Children was founded in 1954 and incorporated as a tax-exempt, nonprofit association, devoted solely to advancing interest in and programs for the gifted, without regard to race, creed, color, or sex. Our purpose is to further the education of the gifted so as to enhance their potential creativity. To this end, the association publishes *The Gifted Child Quarterly*, the only journal of record in the area. The journal is free to all members, and membership is open to all.

The editorial board of *The Gifted Child Quarterly* consists of outstanding experts and researchers in the United States. Through the pages of this journal, you may receive a liberal education about theory, practice, new curriculum, and local and national news about gifted and talented children, book reviews, and many other features. The journal is written so that it may benefit the average parent or adult as well as the professional. Most of the articles in this volume have been taken from its pages. A substantial portion of the royalties will revert to the national association.

In addition to the journal, which is its chief means of communication, the organization holds a national convention once a year in which the latest information, discoveries, new curriculum methods, and other matters pertaining to the gifted are discussed. Membership is $20 per year, and you are cordially invited to join.

The association has been thoroughly revitalized in the past few years and now has a new, young, and prestigious board of directors who are providing leadership for greater service now that interest in the area of the gifted is at an all-time high. The board members represent a truly national constituency and a wide scholastic and academic competence. All have pledged continuing efforts to help the gifted child become more creative. They and I solicit your membership and help in furthering the cause of the education of gifted and talented students as an aid in preparing the next generation for the increasing challenges of the future.

Through the sponsorship of this association, *Educating the Ablest* was produced in 1971 as a guide to those interested in the gifted during a period of rapid expansion of the gifted movement. Increasing demand for the book has led to the production of the second edition, which clearly and effectively reflects advances in thought on the gifted. As president of the National Association for Gifted Children, let me invite you to share with us the stimulating and fertile experiences presented in *Educating the Ablest*.

Joe Khatena
President
National Association for Gifted Children

Preface

As executive director of the National Association for Gifted Children, and as the editor of *The Gifted Child Quarterly*, from whose pages most of the readings in this volume were taken, it is my pleasure to welcome the reader to a consideration of national efforts on behalf of the gifted child.

A pioneer in these efforts is the National Association for Gifted Children, with headquarters at 217 Gregory Dr., Hot Springs, Ark. 71901. This is the only national organization in the field open to the public and the only one to publish a recognized journal. Membership extends throughout the United States and abroad and includes school and business executives, psychiatrists, psychologists, counselors, researchers, teachers, parents, and a variety of civic-minded and forward-looking adults. Membership is open to all.

Over the years, since its founding in 1954 as a nonprofit, tax-deductible agency, the association has had as members, at one time or another, a majority of the leaders important in the fields of education and psychology of the gifted. Perhaps the most famous was Lewis M. Terman, whose monumental work has made him indisputably the father of the gifted child movement.

In the beginning *The Gifted Child Quarterly* was to be a tool for the school administrator and possibly the parent. It was to aid in the development of wise plans for providing, starting, updating, evaluating, and revising programs for the gifted. The intent was to produce a journal which would report new practices and research in the field of education and psychology of the gifted. Through the years readers have found the information in the various issues of *The Gifted Child Quarterly* personally helpful to them as individuals. They have found the research and practices useful in their roles as supervisors, teachers, and parents. To those of us who have worked on the award-winning quarterly, the steady flow of feedback which indicates that the articles are valuable in helping gifted children is more than enough reward.

We are interested in the gifted not because they constitute some elitist group, but because they represent the largest easily identifiable pool of youngsters who have the potential to become verbally creative. Verbal creativity is a necessity for cultural advance, but we could increase the number of such adults four or five times by proper attention and the same kind of facilitation we give to the develop-

ment of youth with athletic potential. The recurrent ecology, pollu-
tion, and energy crises we face indicate the overriding urgency of
more creative solutions if our way of life is to survive. Thus the
education of the gifted is not some elitist frill but is central to the
major educational issue of our times—talent development.

The neglect of gifted children and the consequent loss of their
potential to society is a vital problem in conservation of talent, our
most important natural resource. This is where public support is
needed in the form of local associations for gifted children. Experience has proven that such associations of parents and lay persons are
a vital necessity in developing a sound program for gifted children
in a state or school district. They also are of great assistance in maintaining favorable community attitudes toward gifted children. This
is where you, dear reader, come into the picture. Anyone can start
a local NAGC group in his or her community; information will be
supplied gladly from national headquarters. Only a community that
cares about its gifted children deserves to have them; only one that
fosters their development can expect to see its fruition.

The problem of talent conservation is bound to assume even more
significance in the decades ahead. The executive secretary, the co-
editors of this volume, and many other worthy volunteers have grown
gray in service to this organization and its cause of help for the
uncommon and able children in our midst. We need your help and
assistance—your effort and financial backing for the task at hand.
May this book make clear some of the problems, issues, and solutions
and provide the stimulus for greater efforts to help gifted children of
all races, creeds, and classes in the strenuous years ahead.

J. C. Gowan
Executive Director
National Association for Gifted Children

Chapter One

Introduction and History

Introduction

If the past is prologue, let us start with an expert witness at the bar of history. Speaking of the Declaration of Independence, Abraham Lincoln said in the Lincoln-Douglas debates (Springfield, Illinois, June 26, 1857):

> I think the authors of that notable instrument intended to include *all* men, but they did not intend to declare that all men were equal *in all respects.* They did not mean to say all were equal in color, size, intellect, moral development or social capacity. They defined with tolerable distinctness in what respects they did consider all men equal—equal in "certain inalienable rights, among which are life, liberty and the pursuit of happiness."

Concern for the qualities of exceptional human beings arises out of an exceptional concern for the qualities of all human beings. Physical, mental, and emotional differences constitute a fact of experience, but we must value the differences, not merely tolerate them, if we would hope to use their power to improve the world. Would our life today not be poorer without the individualistic lives of Socrates, Buddha, Jesus, Lao Tze, Copernicus, St. Teresa, da Vinci, Beethoven, Newton, Jefferson, Freud, and Einstein? As Toynbee tells us, it is only a few in each generation who form the creative minority, able to reward society with new responses to challenges of the day.

Lewis M. Terman, the father of gifted child research, concluded his valedictory (1954) by referring to the discovery and encouragement of exceptional talent as follows:

> To identify the internal and external factors that help or hinder the fruition of exceptional talent, and to measure the extent of their influences, are surely among the major problems

of our time. These problems are not new; their existence has been recognized by countless men from Plato to Francis Galton. What is new is the general awareness of them caused by the manpower shortage of scientists, engineers, moral leaders, statesmen, scholars and teachers that the country must have if it is to survive in a threatened world.

The significance of this article by Terman is summed up in an introduction by E. P. Torrance to a reprint in the first edition of E. P. Torrance and W. H. White (eds.), *Issues and Advances in Educational Psychology*, as follows:

In the 1954 paper by Terman, he identifies and discusses some of the major issues concerning the encouragement of exceptionally gifted children. Using Lehman's (1953) study of age and creative productivity, Terman stressed early identification and attacked the strong prejudice against accelerating gifted children in schools. He reported evidence supporting the earlier studies of Keys and Pressey. In 1954, Terman could also cite much progress in the use of intelligence and achievement tests to identify gifted performance in the United States and in other countries. Terman believed, however, that identification and educational provisions alone would be inadequate and cited evidence from both historical and contemporary studies demonstrating the importance of the *Zeitgeist* or "climate."

.....

Our expanding knowledge concerning giftedness has made it clear there is a variety of kinds of intellectual giftedness that should be cultivated in our society that ordinarily do not flourish without special encouragement. It is clear that if we establish a point on any single measure of intellectual giftedness, we eliminate highly gifted children on other measures of giftedness. For example, if we identify as gifted those children scoring in the upper 20 percent on a measure of intelligence such as the *Stanford-Binet*, the *Kuhlmann-Anderson*, or the *California Test of Mental Maturity*, we would eliminate 70 percent of those who would score in the upper 20 percent on the Torrance Tests of Creative Thinking. It is also clear that both intelligence and creative ability (at least as assessed by tests) may increase or decrease, depending upon a variety of physical, psychological, and social factors both within children and within their environment.

The increasing acceptance of a realistically complex view of the human mind is itself a tremendous advance. In moving from an oversimplified view of giftedness to a more complex one, educators should be able to avoid in the future many of the errors of the past. They should be able to provide a more humane kind of education for gifted children—one in which all children will have a better chance to achieve their potentialities. . . .[1]

The articles in this chapter have been selected to provide a historical introduction and resumé of the problems and attitudes surrounding the education of gifted children. They review what has been done in the past and cite both the urgency of the problem and some of the reasons why action has been slow. Together they set the stage for a better understanding of the issues in educating the ablest.

---

[1]E. P. Torrance and W. H. White (eds.), *Issues and Advances in Educational Psychology* (Itasca, Ill.: F. E. Peacock Publishers, Inc., 1969), pp. 174–75.

1 Creativity and the Gifted Child Movement

J. C. GOWAN

Introduction

Those who live through historical experiences or movements are very apt to see them in isolation, especially as they pertain to personal or local interests. It is the task of history to set these developments into their proper place in a larger whole. For example, the American colonists considered the French and Indian War of 1754–59 as just a local conflict, mostly unaware that it was but a small part of a contest between France and England for global supremacy.

It is the task of this paper to set the gifted child movement and the creativity movement into their proper interrelationships and places in the larger gestalt of humanistic psychology. This gestalt appears to be the chief psychosocial motif of the twentieth century, and its latest forms are just now in the process of development. This is unfoldment of the zeitgeist on a grand scale.

Interest in gifted children or in creativity cannot be well understood as separate and independent disciplines. Instead, they, with other components, are a part of a *structure d'ensemble* which can best be subsumed under the heading of humanistic psychology. This constellation of specialties was founded by William James (who, incidentally, was interested in all of its parts), and carried on by his colleagues and their students, notably Hall, Dewey, Jastrow, Kuhlmann, Terman, Gesell, McKinnon, Erikson, McDougall, and Rhine. It consists of seven aspects: (1) a broad humanism, (2) measurement, (3) intelligence, (4) gifted children, (5) creativity, (6) development, and (7) parapsychology. The order in which these aspects are given also indicates the temporal sequence in which psychological interest in each area has been, is being, or will be emphasized.

Protheans all, these men had the stubbornness of the creative

Note: Parts of this article are based on an article by the author which appeared in Julian C. Stanley, William C. George, and Cecilia H. Solano (Eds.), *The Gifted and the Creative: A Fifty Year Perspective*, published and copyrighted 1977 by The Johns Hopkins University Press, Baltimore, Md. 21218. Documentation for statements made in the first section will be found therein.

4

innovator—an unwillingness to bow to the pressure of authority, and a bold, daring thrust which allowed them to explore the unknown. With their razor-sharp minds they made formidable adversaries and often did not suffer fools gladly, thereby incurring the wrath of the establishment. They also often displayed two qualities popularly considered to be contradictory, neither of which was well accepted—a nonorthodox espousal of underdog causes, unpedigreed ideas, and radicalism in thinking, combined with an almost frenzied mathematical desire to quantify and measure what had previously been considered unmeasurable.

James, the founder of psychology in America, subsumes all these categories; even parapsychology is seen in his *Varieties of Religious Experience* (1902). Hall (1923), his first doctorate, absorbed this broad humanism from James and carried it first to Johns Hopkins, where he transmitted it to Cattell, Dewey, and Jastrow, and then to Clark University, where he taught Gesell, Kuhlmann, and Terman.

Components of the Humanistic Psychology Gestalt

As we name the essential ingredients of each component discipline in the humanistic gestalt and identify some of the people most prominent in them, please notice how the defining characteristics bear family relationships. Second, note that a preponderance of the researchers in each field are the students of the students of William James. And last, note how the components open up successively. You may also notice that most of the writers in the area overlap their writing in two or more contiguous fields. This alone suggests that there is some connection among them.

Broad Humanism. Humanistic psychology finds intrinsic value in the *individual,* considered as an end and not a behavioristic means. Thus it is that humanistic psychologists of all types are found to be interested in the rights of men and women. Dewey was an early exponent of these individual rights, as was Rogers later on. Hollingworth, besides her eminence in the gifted child movement, was an early champion of women's rights, as was noted in a recent article in the *American Psychologist* (Shields, 1975). Paul Torrance has been most diligent in championing the right of the uncommon student to be different and has expressed concern for the creative disadvantaged student. This valuing of individual differences, this prizing of the idiosyncratic talents of the uncommon man, is the essence of commonality among this group.

Measurement. If people have individual differences, and if we prize and value those differences, then why not measure them? This is the creed of a group of high-level, mathematically oriented measurement people to which many of us are proud to give our allegiance.

B. S. Pierce is the godfather of this group in the USA, as was Galton in England. It includes Jastrow, Kuhlmann, Cattell, Terman, Kelley, Flanagan, Rulon, Thorndike (father and son), Thurstone, and Guilford in this country; Spearman, Burt, Thomson, and Vernon in England; Binet in France; and many others. Always clearheaded, sometimes monomaniacal and waspish, seldom the bon vivants of our profession, these men have brought academic respectability to behavioral science and have set the stage for much solid advance.

Indeed the adjacent area of intelligence and gifted children can be regarded as no more than the applied aspect of this field. Terman is typical of this group, although he possessed more social grace than many.

Measurement of individual differences involves the belief that human beings have differential talents and that these can be measured, are valuable to society, and should be cultivated. There is a very mathematical flavor to this study, but its ethic was perhaps best enunciated by Terman when he said: "The stage is set for one of the most important educational reforms of this century: a reform that would have for its end the discovery, conservation, and intensive cultivation of every kind of exceptional talent" (1930:474).

Intelligence and Gifted Children. This component is characterized by a change from unifactor to multifactor views of intelligence, from seeing the gifted child as an abnormal genius to seeing the gifted as a pool for potential creativity. There is also a shift from a concept of intelligence as mechanistic and consisting of cognition and memory to a concept which emphasizes transformations, implications, and a more creative consciousness. The most typical researchers in this section were Sir Cyril Burt in England and Lewis Terman in this country.

Creativity. Creativity has gone from a religious to a psychological concept, from an unknown to a turn-on variable. The shift has been from connectedness to psychological openness, as creativity has come to be seen as less of a neurotic trait and more of an early dividend of mental health. It has gone from a curiosity to an end in itself, or a correlate of self-actualization. No one person completely typifies this new field.

Development. This component is also quite new. It shows change from continuous growth concepts to discontinuous developmental concepts; from separate views of development to fused views of concurrent development of psychomotor, affective, and cognitive processes; and from tests which do not measure developmental process to those which do. Piaget and Erikson are typical here.

Parapsychology. Going from quacks, spooks, and psychics to scientific investigation of the unknown, parapsychology has become a recognized component of humanistic psychology. It has gone from unverifiable reports to an examination of physical effects, from superstitious epiphenomena to a niche in humanistic psychology demanded by modern views of the power of man's mind, such as, but not limited to, creativity, biofeedback, self-actualization, peak experience, drug experience, dream analysis, and the like. Finally it has gone from folklore to a belief that all phenomena of whatever kind are natural and can be accounted for, although we may not at present be in possession of all knowledge. William McDougall is typical here.

Common to all these areas are the following overriding characteristics:

1. A sense of the innate dignity, uniqueness, and worth of the human individuality, which is seen as something transcending social groups, laws, restrictions, and generalities. The human being is not merely a reactive creature but an end in himself.

2. A sense of development, of process, of growth, of change, and of becoming or unfoldment. Evolution and man's life are seen as twin aspects of the debut of new powers—an expanding concept of intellect.

3. A flavor, a mathematical measurement, which seeks to quantify data wherever possible but not to reject data which appear unquantified. A scientific rather than a superstitious approach to the unknown which views the universe as subject to natural law but has the modesty to believe that we may not yet understand all there is to know.

4. Concern for the unusual, in persons, things, and events, and particularly concern for an understanding and appreciation and valuing of the unusual, because of the possibility that it is through the examination of the unusual that we have the best chance of gaining greater knowledge about things, events, and ourselves.

Brief History of the Gifted Child Movement

Though intelligence had been recognized since the time of the Romans as the first aspect of personality, no one up to the 20th century had been able to solve the puzzle of measuring it. It was the genius of Alfred Binet, a French psychologist, who perceived that developmental tasks were the answer which could crack the problem. He found out at what ages ordinary children complete certain easy tasks, such as telling points of the compass. He then arranged these developmental minitasks in a serial order by age. Then by measuring a child on this scale, he could tell the child's mental age. Binet's discovery was built upon Lewis M. Terman, who perceived

that what Binet had found was really a method of measuring developmental progress in all children, and a modification could be adapted
for the measurement of gifted children. Furthermore, the rate of
developmental progress with respect to chronological age represents
a ratio which is unity in the average but greater than 1 in the case
of brighter children. Multiplying this rate of intellectual development by 100 to avoid decimals, Terman named it the "intelligence
quotient." In 1916, he brought out the *Stanford-Binet Individual
Intelligence Scale*, and in 1922, he was funded to commence his
epoch-making *Genetic Studies of Genius* (1926, 1930) with 1,500
children whom the Stanford-Binet had identified at 140 IQ or above.
This longitudinal study still continues.

It is only fair, in summary, to describe Terman as the father of the
gifted child movement and its most important adherent to date.
Terman's findings, as detailed in five volumes of *The Genetic Studies
of Genius*, are too well known to need elaboration here. But we
might briefly recap some of the highlights of the most impressive
longitudinal study ever undertaken:

1. The genetic hypothesis is strongly indicated.
2. The gifted are not a homogeneous group but differ among
   themselves.
3. The gifted are not puny, asocial, or prepsychotic.
4. The most intelligent child in class is often the youngest.
5. Superiority in IQ is maintained throughout life.
6. Acceleration at all levels is beneficial.
7. Noncollege gifted have the same mental ability as Ph.D. candidates.
8. Socioeconomic status proved to be the factor discriminating
   between most and least successful gifted men.
9. Mental age of the gifted continues to increase in middle age.
10. The mean IQ of the children of the Terman group was 133.
11. There are several times as many persons with over 150 IQ as
    the normal curve predicts.
12. Males exceed females in the general sample (Gowan, 1977).

With the advantage of hindsight, the major omissions of the Terman study can be described as: (1) consideration of intelligence as
one dimensional, (2) lack of control on the socioeconomic status factor, (3) neglect of creativity, (4) lack of rationale, and (5) failure to
investigate, control, or balance ethnic aspects. Despite these flaws,
the Terman studies awakened education in the United States to the
importance of the gifted child and enlisted the efforts of hundreds
of disciples and followers across the country.

We should note some individuals outside the gifted child field who
have had an important impact on it. The first of these was Robert

Havighurst, whose research on the effects of socioeconomic status on achievement has been very helpful. He is one of the few investigators who has dared to look at IQ in terms of SES levels. A second individual is Calvin Taylor, one of the earliest workers in the creativity area and the sponsor of some famous conferences at Utah in the 1950s, as well as the editor of several books on the subject. The third individual is Sidney Parnes of the Buffalo Creativity Workshop. As the protege of Alex Osborn, Parnes has been identified with the Osborn-Parnes group, started in 1955, which has had a significant and growing impact on techniques for helping gifted children to become creative.

Among these practitioners, there is one who stands out as second only to Terman in the importance of his efforts for the gifted— Charles Bish of the NEA Carnegie Academically Talented Project. He, more than any other person, contrived to bring the present knowledge to the education establishment in general. Charlie's green books approached half a million copies, and his occasional journal, *Accent on Talent*, went to every schoolhouse in America for two years. He spoke the language of administrators and carried the message for the gifted all over the USA. But his most ambitious work was bringing together the leaders in the field for better communication among themselves, for concerted action, and for the rapid dissemination of new ideas. *Productive Thinking in Education* (Aschner & Bish, 1968) grew out of such conferences and popularized the Guilford SOI concepts. In no small part the renaissance in interest in the gifted we are now experiencing belongs to his efforts of ten years ago.

The remarkable thing about all this process in the followers of Terman during the decades from 1920 to 1960 was that so little new was discovered and so little advance was made. One reason why we find so little development in the field is that the gifted child movement is not really a discipline at all but merely the applied area of the measurement of individual differences. It is hence the development section of a larger gestalt which embraces theory and procedures for creative development of all the talents of mankind. It is consequently not complete in itself and is best understood merely as the educational applications consequent on a new way of looking at talent development. It is for this reason that so much emphasis has been put on this presentation of a larger whole of humanistic psychology and developmental process in the individual.

Creativity

It would be redundant to dwell extensively on creativity here, since it is the chief issue in Chapters IX and XII, and has been extensively investigated by all three editors elsewhere (see References at the end of the book). The various theses about creativity can be grouped into a continuum which runs from cognitive, rational, and semantic, through personality and environmental views, to mental health and psychological openness, to preconscious sources. In place of such an unnecessary analysis,[1] we shall examine some of the relationships between giftedness and creativity.

We should point out that the connections made here between giftedness and creativity are the responsibility of the author and not the official views of *The Gifted Child Quarterly* or the Creative Education Foundation. It has been the position of the foundation that creativity is a learned skill which may be taught to anyone, gifted or not. While these views differ somewhat from those of this article, perhaps the difference lies in whether creativity is seen as a *process* of thinking and living or as a *product* which is new not only to the individual but to society as well. In this discussion we shall use the latter definition.

Relationship Between Giftedness and Creativity

While it is obvious both from biographical inspection (e.g., Einstein, Mozart, Picasso, Gauss), as well as from the research of Getzels and Jackson (1962), that most creative persons are gifted, it is by no means true that most gifted persons are creative. Giftedness, then appears to be a necessary but not a sufficient condition for verbal creativity that is new to the culture. To discover what that condition may be, it is necessary to analyze theories about creativity itself.

Those who have investigated the rationale for creativity (Hallman, 1963; Rothenberg & Hausman, 1976; Gowan, 1972) have tended to divide along a continuum from rational problem solving to psychedelic mind expansion. Such an overview goes from the structure of intellect model at the rationale end, through personal and environmental factors, to mental health, Oedipal predispositions, and psychological openness, to preconscious and transpersonal sources. Since these views have been discussed thoroughly elsewhere (Gowan, 1972), we shall not belabor them here.

It is necessary, however, to point out two important clues:

1.   The Wallas (1926) paradigm clearly states that both preparation (rational discipline) and incubation (subconscious cogitation) are necessary for illumination.

---

[1]The reader who wishes recent update on creativity should consult Biondi and Parnes (1976), Parnes, Noller, and Biondi (1977), Guilford (1977) or Rothenberg & Hausman (1976). Also see Gowan (1967, 1972, 1975).

2. Wechsler (1974) has shown that the interpersonal variance on almost all physiological and psychological aspects of individuality cannot exceed the ratio $e/1$ (where $e = 2.8$), but it is obvious that creative production in some geniuses exceeds this level by several magnitudes.

If creativity is the flowering of giftedness due to developmental escalation, we have merely discovered another relationship between adjacent components of humanistic psychology. Should this be true, then the best way to help persons become creative is to help their developmental progress at the same time that we educate them in the specific discipline which preparation demands.

If psychological openness to transpersonal sources is the key to the cave of Aladdin within us all, and if the right cerebral hemisphere is modeled on a radio receiver whereas the left is modeled on a problem-solving computer, then the creative person may be merely the one who can translate and fix the vibrations, images, and emotion in a transcendent experience (or creative spell) into intellectually negotiable forms as in art, music, mathematics, or literature. Many objects may be set in sympathetic vibration by the miniscule waves of a distant radio station, but a good receiver can mute static, amplify without distortion, and finally convert radio frequency to audio and so to intelligible speech.

Not only does such a view underscore the close relationship among creativity, mental health, and individual development to self-actualization, it also sets the stage for a new and far more scientific investigation of those possible higher and more exotic abilities of man which may be involved in parapsychology. Such a vista is completely consistent with the gestalt of humanistic psychology, as well as furnishing a very open-minded model for research and development.

It would be easy and possibly appropriate to introduce here a great deal of evidence pointing to the accuracy of these observations, and particularly to their promise. But since that has been done elsewhere (Gowan, 1974, 1975), we will not do so.

Under these circumstances, we might redefine giftedness as follows: *A gifted child is one who has the potential to become verbally creative; a talented child is one who has the potential to become nonverbally creative.* Such a definition emphasizes the fact that giftedness is *potentiality*, not *performance*, and gets us away from a definition using an arbitrary IQ cutoff score.

A natural question which arises is: Why is it necessary to have an IQ of over 130 (the old definition of giftedness) to become verbally creative? While we do not have definitive research on this point,[2] it

---

[2]For one theory, see Gowan (1972:58).

is probable that there is a cutoff point somewhere in the middle 120s. Perhaps the definition of giftedness depends upon the very inefficient way we teach children to be creative; only the gifted can make the intuitive leaps that poor teaching requires. Before we get closure on this issue, we will have to define more carefully what we mean by creative performance. Is it to be of genius class ($E = mc^2$), or more ordinary types of new discoveries and culturally useful advances? Curiously enough, it seems easier to judge this sort of matter at present (Maslow, 1954; Gowan, 1974:ch. 5), by evidence of self-actualization or other high developmental success than by creative productions solely, although the latter attempt has been made (Arieti, 1976:297, quoting Krober & Gray). Eventually we shall probably be able to reduce the IQ level somewhat, thus further clarifying the relationship between giftedness and creativity.

Development

To understand fully the relationship between giftedness and creativity it is necessary to follow through with a brief discussion of the two subsequent interrelated components of the humanistic psychology gestalt—development and parapsychology. This is especially true of development, which is the component contiguous to creativity and thus closely related to it, as well as the next discipline just opening up.

The concept that there are qualitatively different developmental stages with specific emphases has been voiced by a number of writers, including Sullivan (1953), Maslow (1954), and Gowan (1972). Piaget identified cognitive developmental stages (1962), and Erikson, affective developmental stages (1950). Indeed the concept seems to be one whose time has come. Said Dr. Stephen Bailey (1971):

> It seems to me that the most liberating and viable educational reforms of the next several years will come through the building of curricular and other educative activities around some of the developmental insights of Piaget, Bruner, Erikson, Bloom and Maslow. Although much separates these scholars in terms of analytic style and specific fields of concentration, they all seem to hold the idea that human beings go through fairly discrete stages of development, and that each stage calls for rather special educational treatment. And all of these men seem to be united in their belief that the maximization of human potential within the constraints of each life stage is the best way of preparing for succeeding stages.

Gowan (1972) combined the affective (Eriksonian) stages and the cognitive (Piagetian) stages into a developmental chart having a periodicity of three, and said that there were higher cognitive stages than those discovered by Piaget which fit the last three Eriksonian stages. Kohlberg (Kohlberg & Mayer, 1972) has done similarly for the moral stages, and Simpson (1966) for the psychomotor stages. Since divergent thinking follows convergent thinking in the structure of intellect model, Gowan (1972) also hypothesized that creativity was the name of the cognitive stage next above formal operations. For fuller development of these theories, the reader is referred to the References at the end of this book, but it is necessary to examine the concepts of escalation and dysplasia which follow directly on developmental stage theory.

Developmental stage theory can really be regarded as the carrying over of the discontinuous quantum theory to behavioral science. For if there are jumps between the successive levels, it must take energy from the organism to make them. Escalation is the jump from one riser to the next on a staircase, and it is immediately obvious that guidance is needed to tide the individual over this developmental discontinuity. Escalation, according to Gowan (1972), consists of five interrelated aspects: discontinuity, succession, emergence (the debut of new powers), differentiation, and integration. Each of these again has specific guidance implications.

Dysplasia (Gowan, 1974) means malformation of development. This occurs when one aspect of the psyche (e.g., affective) continues to escalate, although another aspect (e.g., cognitive) becomes arrested at a given stage. This condition produces block, anomie, and eventually neurosis. Since the most common dysplasia is the one that prevents cognitive escalation to creativity in young adulthood, this problem becomes at once a prime focus for guidance for the gifted. Elsewhere Gowan (1972) points out that most counseling problems can be ordered in terms of maladaptations of development. The real function of guidance for the gifted and talented is the escalation of all parts of the psyche beyond the fifth developmental stage (cognitive formal operations, and affective identity period) so that the individual can become fully creative and self-actualizing.

The importance of understanding escalation and dysplasia becomes more apparent when we consider the benefits of full synergistic function. If one compares a solo pianist or violin player with the effect of an orchestra in concert, it is evident the synergistic effect *tout ensemble* is more than additive: interaction between the instruments produces a new level of musical sound. In a similar manner, when the various modes and domains into which we have analyzed the psyche are all operating in harmonious concert, there is an indescribably enhanced effect, and this basis is the necessary

platform for higher levels of achievement, creativity, and self-actualization. Positive guidance for mental health is an objective for all
children, but in the case of the gifted child, such differential guidance may well produce the high-level full functioning which is the
prelude and necessary condition for major creative work, and continued personal development after maturity. We know very little
from a psychological viewpoint about the higher reaches of such
personal development, although both Maslow and Erikson have giv-
en us some hints, but even from the "oceanic experiences" described
by Maslow's investigations (1954), we know that there are spectacular highs and peaks. In former more religious times, these were described as "theophanies" or "openings," and they have been
recorded of saints and religious leaders since Old Testament times.
They were first psychologically described and attributed to high
intelligence by Bucke (1901), and later Maslow (1954). That such
conditions which only occasionally occur "wild" in geniuses can be
domesticated and induced in more ordinary gifted persons by guidance was the theme of Gowan's *Development of the Creative Individual* (1972), and it suggests the very positive nature of differential
guidance for the able.

Finally, it is suspected in some quarters that harmonious total function of the psyche reduces stress and internal resistance. Analogous
to a radio receiver, when this type of static is cleared away, the
instrument can be more finely tuned, and what we previously heard
as a howl now becomes audible as an intelligent signal. This is accomplished in the radio through the property of resonance (or sympathetic vibration)—resonance which would not be possible unless all
systems were "go" and working harmoniously, thus eliminating static
and allowing the minisignals from outside to be received, amplified
and produced without undue distortion or noise. If the human mind
functions in an analogous manner in creative process, the importance
of synergistic development is reinforced.

It is obvious that this view of developmental stage process ties in
and relates to creativity (as it should, if they are contiguous aspects
of a larger gestalt). Creativity is seen as enhanced by certain developmental stages which are critical for its manifestation. Developmental
theory also explains the close association between creativity and
mental health, including the Maslovian observation that among his
self-actualizing people he found none who were not creative.

Parapsychology

The last and least understood component of humanistic psychology is as yet a dimly seen and slowly emerging understanding of the

reach of man's mind, to which has been given the inadequate name of parapyschology. A better name would perhaps be "the expanded abilities of man," and it is becoming evident that creative openness is the vestibule to these expanded abilities. Even evidence now available strongly suggests that some creative and fully developed people have occasional conscious access to a realm of potential action which is outside time and space (cf. Maslow's "Oceanic experience" and his "peak experience"). It is surprising how many scientists and mathematicians, as well as artists and writers, testify to this transpersonal afflatus (Ghiselin, 1952, Gowan, 1974), which, as Socrates observes, is the essence of creative inspiration and from which such spectacular abilities as telepathy, precognition and intuition naturally flow. Superstitiously, we have heretofore considered these abilities supernatural, but they are probably mere extensions of more ordinary powers whose operations will someday be much better understood and hence stimulated. Naturally the genius is in the forefront of this evolutional progression and hence much more apt to possess these powers, as their testimony (Ghiselin, 1952; Gowan, 1975; Prince, 1963) so well indicates. Thus this last component is related to its predecessor, development, and is the one which is the most difficult at present to understand.

Thirty years ago no one could have predicted the spectacularly emergent aspects of the new science of creativity or how it would give new thrust and direction to the gifted child movement and the other earlier components of humanistic psychology. We are in the same position today with regards to development and parapsychology, and it would be equally foolish to try to foresee their full unfoldment. But if past history is a guide we may say that each previous segment will be integrated into the new component, and the unfolding of each new aspect will further demonstrate the reach of man's mind and the extent of his dominion over nature. The gestalt we envision is at present seen through a glass darkly, but it is the coming science of man of the next century, when all these branches of humanistic psychology will be welded together in a *structure d'ensemble* greater than interest in giftedness, greater than interest in creativity, greater, in fact, than anything except mankind's unlimited potential. For the present powers of genius are the mere earnest of greater powers to be unfolded. But all this was known long ago, and *Popol Vuh*, the Mayan Bible, says it best:

> Let there be light!
> Let the dawn rise over heavens and earth!
> There can be no glory, no splendor
> Until the humanistic being exists,
> The fully developed man.

References

Arieti, S. *Creativity: The Magic Synthesis.* New York: Basic Books, 1976.

Aschner, M. J., and Bish, C. B. (Eds.). *Productive Thinking in Education.* Rev. ed. Washington, D.C.: National Education Association, 1968.

Bailey, S. K. "Education and the Pursuit of Happiness." Speech at Los Angeles, April 28, 1971, as reported in *UCLA Educator* 14:1 (Fall 1971).

Biondi, A., and Parnes, S. *Assessing Creative Growth.* Vols. 1 and 2. Great Neck, N.Y.: Creative Synergetic Association, 1976.

Bucke, R. M. *Cosmic Consciousness.* New York: E. P. Dutton, 1901.

Burt, C. "Parapsychology and Its Implications." *Psychological Abstracts* 41 (1967):3603.

Einstein, A. *New York Times,* March 29, 1972, p. 24, col. 6.

Erikson, E. *Childhood and Society.* New York: Norton Press, 1950.

Getzels, J. W., and Jackson, P. W. *Creativity and Intelligence.* New York: Wiley, 1962.

Ghiselin, B. (Ed.). *The Creative Process.* Berkeley: University of California Press, 1952.

Gowan, J. C. *Development of the Creative Individual.* San Diego, Cal.: W. Knapp, 1972.

Gowan, J. C. *Development of the Psychedelic Individual.* Buffalo, N.Y.: Creative Education Foundation, 1974.

Gowan, J. C. *Trance, Art, and Creativity.* Buffalo, N.Y.: Creative Education Foundation, 1975.

Gowan, J. C. "Background and History of the Gifted Child Movement." In J. C. Stanley, and others (Eds.), *The Gifted and Creative: A Fifty Year Perspective.* Baltimore: Johns Hopkins University Press, 1977.

Gowan, J. C., Demos, G. D., and Torrance, E. P. *Creativity: Its Educational Implications.* New York: Wiley, 1967.

Guilford, J. P. *Way Beyond the IQ.* Buffalo, N.Y.: Creative Education Foundation, 1977.

Hall, G. S. *Life and Confessions of a Psychologist.* New York: Appleton, 1923.

Hallman, R. J. "The Necessary and Sufficient Conditions for Creativity." *Journal of Humanistic Psychology* 3:1 (1963).

James, W. *The Varieties of Religious Experience.* New York: New American Library, 1958. Originally published, 1902.

Kohlberg, L., and Mayer, R. "Development as the Aim of Education." *Harvard Educational Review* 42 (1972):449–96.

Maslow, A. *Motivation and Personality.* New York: Harpers, 1954.

Parnes, S., Noller, R., and Biondi, A. *Guide to Creative Action.* Rev. ed. New York: Scribner's, 1977.

Piaget, J. *Play, Dreams and Imitation in Childhood.* New York: Norton, 1962.

Prince, W. F. *Noted Witnesses for Psychic Occurrences.* Hyde Park, N.Y., 1963.

Rothenberg, A., and Hausman, C. R. (Eds.). *The Creativity Question.* Durham, N.C.: Duke University Press, 1976.

Shields, S. "Ms. Pilgrim's Progress ... " *American Psychologist* 30:(1975):852–57.

Simpson, E. J. *The Classification of Educational Objectives: Psychomotor Domain,* Urbana: University of Illinois Press, 1966.

Sullivan, H. S. *The Interpersonal Theory of Psychiatry.* New York: Norton, 1953.

Terman, L. M., and others. *Genetic Studies of Genius.* Stanford, Cal.: Stanford University Press. Vol. I, 1926; Vol. III, 1930; Vol. IV, 1947; Vol. V, 1959.

Wallas, G. *The Art of Thought.* London: C. Watts, 1926.

Wechsler, D. *The Collected Papers of David Wechsler.* New York: Academic Press, 1974.

2 The Academically Talented Project: Gateway to the Present

CHARLES E. BISH

If we would know where are are, we must understand whence we have come and how; this story is a recital of that journey. It is hard to convey to this generation the peaceful and quiet atmosphere of the Fifties. Eisenhower was president—a universal father figure who was trusted by all. Most people were in the process of raising large families; they were concerned with the present, not the future, with a happy life, not public service, and complacency was the order of the day. It was back to normalcy after World War II. True, there were some voices raised to suggest that educational matters needed modernization: Admiral Rickover's was one, but it took something big to wake up America from its apathy. That event occurred on October 4, 1957. It was the launching of the Russian Sputnik I.

Not long after the blast-off of Sputnik I, it became clear that the beep-beep of this 184-pound ball in space had caught the attention of more Americans than the blast of the H-bomb and had also stung their national pride. Curiously enough, instead of blaming the government, Americans blamed the educational system. The reaction

From *The Gifted Child Quarterly* 19:4 (1975). Used by permission.

was to do something at once about an educational system that would allow this to happen. And there was just enough which was plausible in the total mix to lend credence to the complainers whose theme was that mathematics and science had been downgraded in the schools and not enough attention had been paid to upgrading scholarship of the abler students.

Before discussing the major reaction to Sputnik of the National Education Association, it is necessary to notice that there were some early efforts in the direction of curriculum change for the gifted and talented. Among these had been Terman (1926), Hollingworth (1926), and, in the early Fifties, the writers Witty (1951), Brandwein (1955), Brown and Johnson (1952), Birch (1954), Bayley (1955), and Gowan (1955) were among those who had written thoughtfully about some aspect of gifted child education. Perhaps the most important author of the decade was Guilford who, after his famous APA Presidential address of 1950 predicting the existence of Structure of Intellect factors of Intelligence, went out and measured these factors including a slab which he called "divergent production" (but which is more popularly stereotyped as "creativity"). Although in those days the confluence of creativity and giftedness had not occurred, other early laborers in the creativity area were Calvin Taylor who held the first creativity conferences in Utah in 1955–57, and Alex Osborn who wrote "Applied Imagination" in 1954 and founded the Buffalo Problem-Solving Workshop shortly after. But perhaps the most important example was that of the Physical Science Study Committee headed by MIT professor J. R. Zacharias which published a bulletin of curriculum reform in 1957. Finally should be mentioned the Congressional *National Defense and Education Act*, the governmental reaction to Sputnik which became law about this time.

One should also mention as contributing factors the School Mathematics Study Group directed by E. G. Begle of Stanford and influenced significantly by the work of Max Beberman, Gertrude Hendrix, David Page, and Patrick Suppes. These areas of curriculum modification in science and mathematics had a significant effect in "hardening" up the curriculum for gifted students.

The major attack on education came from Admiral Rickover in an article in the *Atlantic Monthly* for February, 1958. This article, which pointed emphatically to weaknesses in education in mathematics and science in the public schools, named this factor as the chief culprit in the failure of America to match the Russians in space. At the same time, the Council for Basic Education also launched an attack on the language arts curriculum.

Into this somewhat charged atmosphere stepped Dr. John Gardner (now head of Common Cause), and at that time president of the Carnegie Corporation of New York, and author of the book *Excel-*

lence. In conjunction with Dr. William G. Carr, the executive secretary of the National Education Association, and with the aid of a Carnegie grant, the NEA Invitational Conference on the Academically Talented Pupil was convened in Washington on February 6–8, 1958. James Conant, former president of Harvard, was the chairman, and Dr. N. Bryan, the conference director. This conference was the first time that most writers and leaders in the area of the gifted had ever met each other; in addition it attracted the attention of an important cross-section of the educational community.

Dr. Conant himself offered several important suggestions. It was he who defined the gifted as the upper 2 percent of the school population and the talented as those over one standard deviation above the mean (roughly the top 15 percent in a typical high school). For these people, Conant said, we need to examine the curriculum to be sure it is challenging enough.

The NEA sold out of 8,000 copies of the conference report within three months. Because of this evidence of national interest the Carnegie Corporation agreed to provide a grant to the NEA which would finance a project to implement the suggestions made at the Conference for a three-year period. In September of 1958, the writer was appointed to the position of Director of the Academically Talented Project.

Three basic decisions were made quickly: (1) because of limited funds the personnel was limited to the Director and a secretary, (2) the program for assisting schools in strengthening curriculum for the academically talented was to be announced through the NEA journals, and (3) requests would be mailed to schools asking information about existing programs for the gifted and talented, including materials, so that the project could establish a clearing house for information. Another idea which came early was cooperation with the various professional curriculum disciplines in mathematics, science, and other areas to develop joint effort. As a result of these overtures it became evident that even large conferences would not reach more than a handful of the target audience, and that it was therefore necessary to (1) develop publications which would be acceptable to subject teachers in the several areas of curriculum, (2) find a way to distribute in substantial numbers these publications with the endorsements of the professional associations involved, (3) personally to appear before as many teacher groups as possible to promote the philosophy of an emphasis on programs for the academically talented and the use of the publications to modify the curriculum for them, and finally (4) to serve as a consultant to state affiliates or school systems which wished help in planning programs concerned with the objectives of the project.

During the latter part of 1958 and early 1959, the wind was blowing in our favor. The Project office was almost inundated with material for the clearing house—about thirty state departments had sent in materials and some large cities, among them Cleveland, Chicago, and Los Angeles, New York, St. Louis, Houston, and Miami, and a much larger number of smaller districts. Requests to speak at meetings of school personnel and PTAs were far more than could possibly be accepted.

In order to develop rapidly curriculum publications, it was decided to utilize the rich resources within the NEA in the shape of its curriculum affiliates. Accordingly, twelve of the Executive Secretaries of these affiliates became involved in the project to prepare a booklet. Each started by naming a committee of about twenty-five who would be invited as guests to Washington for three days and address themselves to the subject of what should be done in their area to help the academically talented. After each conference, the deliberations were assembled into a first draft of a publication of about 100 pages, then put into final form and mailed to each member of the affiliate group involved. Dr. Lyle Ashby arranged for the NEA to handle sales and return net proceeds over cost to the Project budget. Thus were born the famous "little green booklets," of which over 300,000 were eventually distributed. These started with subject titles such as research and administration, and went through the entire curriculum subject by subject, ending in 1961 with a bibliography of writings in the area. There were also booklets on guidance and the elementary curriculum.

The "little green booklets" achieved very wide distribution. Because they had been given to affiliate members and sponsored by the NEA affiliate they did not have the usual onus of most material for the gifted, as they came from inside and not outside the professional organization. Thus the [distribution of these] booklets had a great deal of influence on curriculum development in the nation's schools, as it came from the subject area and was not something imposed from the administration.

During 1959 it was decided to plow back into the Project funds received from honoraria and publication sales. This pleased the Carnegie Corporation, as it doubled the effectiveness of the grant, and was a large factor in its several renewals. Another idea was to develop a newsletter containing summary statements of Conference Reports for easy reading and publicity. Mailings to school and college personnel were then made. At the end of 1961, a quarter million of the little green booklets had been distributed and sales were exceeding expectation requiring reprinting. Still another effort resulted in a film developed by the help of Dr. Ned Bryan, and distributed through the NEA. As a result of these and other favorable factors, the Carnegie grant was renewed for an additional three years.

A questionnaire circulated to over 2,000 school systems showed that the effectiveness of the Project was greatest in rural and small independent districts, least in large cities. Accordingly an assistant director, Dr. Russ Cox, was named to work with the writer and visit in as many large city systems as possible. Entree was gained in many instances through introductions by Dr. Lawrence Derthick, formerly the U.S. Commissioner on Education (and a well-known figure to many big-city superintendents), who joined the NEA staff in 1961.

While the curriculum subject conferences had been proceeding on schedule in 1961 as a result of the counsel of such figures as Gallagher, Gowan, Passow, and Suchman, it was determined that a need existed to bring together research leaders for an exchange of views on the subject of creativity and giftedness. Readers with long memories will recall that it was at this time that the work of Getzels and Jackson and of Paul Torrance had linked the two together. The conference of about twenty-five invited researchers convened in April, 1961. While no chairman was designated, the acknowledged leader was J. P. Guilford of Structure of Intellect fame. Also present were professors Getzels, Gallagher, Newland, Aschner, Goldberg, Suchman, Wilson, Taylor, Torrance, Ward, Fliegler, Gowan, Hendricks and Passow, representing most of the active workers in the joint areas. The conference was in many respects the highlight of the Project to date. A second conference on Productive Thinking with most of the same leaders, with the addition of a few others, was convened in 1963. Doctors Goldberg and Aschner summarized the conference, and from their efforts and interpretation a significant document emerged. Out of it came the first Project book, the Aschner and Bish edited compilation of readings called *Productive Thinking in Education*. This book, which came out in 1963, sold out of print and was revised and reprinted in 1968 with additional material by Williams. This book sold out of a print order of 10,000 in 1970, and a Japanese translation was authorized.

Because of the general reception by the nation, the Carnegie Corporation was willing to provide yet another extension of the grant. This time the direction of thrust was to develop a newsletter "Accent on Talent," which, through the NEA address computer, was sent free to the 88,000 schoolhouses in the USA. The twelve issues of this newsletter which came out in three years proved to be collectors' items, since they contained capsule material of practical import written by nearly every leader in the field. They were very readable and immensely popular with teachers.

Changes, however, were occurring. Dr. John Gardner had left Carnegie for the Cabinet; the U.S. caught and passed the Russians in Space. The New Frontier turned to the Great Society, and emphasis on the gifted and talented changed to emphasis on the education of disadvantaged students. The violence of the Sixties and civil strife succeeded the peaceful and halcyon days of the Fifties. Time was running out. The Project director still made many trips to the nation's schools to fulfill speaking commitments, and one to Russia on a survey educational mission. He was also a continual consultant at the summer workshops on improving the creativity of gifted children held under the direction of J. C. Gowan at San Fernando Valley State College, where he helped not only in the creative curriculum interventions for 350 gifted children per summer but in the start of a whole new generation of researchers in the area of the gifted, with the training of staff which produced Professors Kay Bruch, Juliana Gensley, Norma Jean Groth, Joyce Sonntag-Hagen, Linda Silverman, Martin Levine, Sandra Kaplan, Charlotte Malone, and USOE internist James Curry. Thus the Project had direct input into the training of a new generation of leaders.

In summary, during the eleven years of the Carnegie–NEA Project for the Academically Talented Student, the following were accomplished:

1. Nearly fifteen conferences brought together (often for the first face-to-face situation) most of the leaders in the area both in curriculum, administration, and guidance, thus enormously facilitating communications in a developing discipline.
2. Fifteen different "little green books" were produced in as many differentiated areas, and a total of nearly 350,000 distributed.
3. A book of readings, *Productive Thinking in Education,* sold out of two editions of 20,000 copies.
4. A newsletter in 1960–61 distributed eight issues for a total of 24,000 copies.
5. *Accent on Talent* was developed and distributed in twelve issues in 1966–69, with cameo articles by all major writers in the area of giftedness and creativity. Three quarters of a million were mailed to approximately 87,500 elementary and secondary schools.
6. The Director and his assistant participated in 413 conferences, programs, consultations, and presentations. The total air miles traveled was 436,000.
7. Through six years of consultantship with the San Fernando Valley Creativity Workshops, the Project had direct input in the training of an entire cadre of younger scholars, researchers, and professors in the area of the gifted.

It is not for us to attempt to prejudge the verdict history will bring in concerning the lasting worth of the Project. But at least it bridged a gap between the apathy of the post-war Fifties and the demands of the Seventies. In the Fifties, talent was something we could waste; in the Seventies it is something we must conserve. In the Fifties, creativity was comparatively unknown; in the Seventies it has become the means of salvaging civilization from the many challenges which confront it. In the Fifties we were blind to the potential talents in the poor, in minority groups, and in women; performance was a privilege for middle and upper class WASP males; in the Seventies creativity and the actualization of the talents of all groups is a necessity if we are to survive.

During this important transitional period, the Project maintained vital communication between scholars, the public, and each other. Those of us who have manned the communication lines between these two sets of opposites, situated in the same culture only twenty years apart, have played a humble part in the educational and intellectual progress of the nation, but it may prove to have been a vital one in those days which will someday be remembered as BFAC (before federal aid to creativity). We are now about to enter that period, to which the past is but prologue, but perhaps a necessary one.

Bibliography

Bayley, Nancy. "On the Growth of Intelligence." *American Psychologist* 10:805–18, 1955. See *Journal of Genetic Psychology* 75:169 ff., 1949; *Journal of Gerontology* 10:91–107, 1955.

Birch, J. W. "Early School Admission for Mentally Advanced Children." *Exceptional Children* 21:84–7, 1954.

Brandwein, P. F. *The Gifted Child as a Future Scientist.* New York: Harcourt-Brace, 1955.

Brown, E. K., and Johnson, P. G. *Education for the Talented in Mathematics and Science.* Washington, D.C.: Department of Health, Education, and Welfare, 1952.

Conant, J. B. (chairman). *The Identification and Education of the Academically Talented in the American Secondary School.* Conference report. Washington, D.C.: National Education Association, 1958. See also *NEA Journal* 47:218–19, 1958; *School and Society* 86:225–27, 1958; *English Journal* 47:368–71, 1958.

Gowan, J. C. "The Gifted Underachiever—A Problem for Everyone." *Exceptional Children* 21:247–49, 1955. See also "The Gifted Child: An Annotated Bibliography," *California Journal of Educational Research* 16:72–94, 1955.

Hollingworth, Leta. *Gifted Children.* New York: MacMillan, 1926.

Osborn, Alex. *Applied Imagination.* New York: Scribners, 1954.

Rickover, H. G. *Education of Our Talented Children.* New York: University Press, 1957. See also *Atlantic Monthly*, February, 1958.

Taylor, C. W. (Ed.). (*First, Second, Third*) *Research Conference on the Identification of Creative Scientific Talent.* Salt Lake City: University of Utah Press, 1955, 1957, 1959.

Terman, L. M. (and others). *Genetic Studies of Genius.* Five vols. Stanford, Cal.: Stanford University Press, 1926–59.

Witty, Paul (Ed.). *The Gifted Child.* Boston: D.C. Heath, 1951.

3 Intellect and the Gifted

J. P. GUILFORD

Introduction

When I faced the imminent need to prepare this paper, a quick excursion into the writings on the gifted child revealed that volumes had already been said. I was particularly impressed with the contributions in the book *Educating the Gifted,* edited, and written in large part, by Gowan and Torrance (1971).

It is good to know that many enlightened things are already being done in locating talents and in nurturing them toward their highest potentialities, although I gather that the number of places in which this occurs is still smaller than it should be. In education today, there is, indeed, quite a contrast to the situation some 15 to 20 years ago, when the goal often seemed to be to force all children into the same mold or pattern, intellectually and emotionally. In general, it appears that there is now a greater recognition of individuality. This is a long step toward genuine democracy, which, above all, involves respect for the individual, tolerance for his idiosyncracies, so long as they are harmless, and opportunities for all children to "actualize" themselves, to use Maslow's expression.

It seems to be agreed that the primary instigating source of interest in the gifted in recent years was the flight of the first Russian Sputnik. Our nation's position in the competition for world leadership was suddenly threatened. One solution, contributed by education, was to produce more creative and inventive scientists and engineers, and this focused attention upon gifted youth, from which source those

Note: Based upon an address given to the National Association for Gifted Children and the California Association for Gifted Children, Long Beach, Calif., February 24, 1972.
From *The Gifted Child Quarterly* 16:2 (1972). Used by permission.

high-level saviors were to come. We rose to the occasion. We helped put men on the moon for all to see, and they brought back some moon rocks and moon dust. Thus, among the side effects or secondary gains from the space program has been a new focus on individual differences in education, which is not confined to children in the upper tails of the curve, but applies along the scale.

When Dr. Gowan first asked me to appear on this program, he suggested some alternative titles, all of which emphasized creativity. As you know, the subject of creativity has been in the educational atmosphere during the past two decades, apart from the need for inventive scientists and engineers. It has naturally been considered in connection with educating the gifted, and much has been written about this aspect of the subject. But I like to look at things more broadly, and the title that Gowan put in the program for me gives the scope that I wanted. Intelligence is broader than creativity but, in my view, includes creativity.

If I could do nothing else, I should like to leave you with an increased acceptance of the idea that in education we must take a multivariate view of intelligence. The fact that intelligence is not a single, all-purpose variable but a "coat of many colors," to use a bad metaphor, has not been sufficiently realized, and not enough has been done about it. And if you have already accepted the multivariate principle, I should like to sell you on the idea of the structure of intellect (SI) as the frame of reference for use in thinking about learning and teaching problems. I think it can be said that the role of the SI model has been increasing in education, but in only a few places has anything approaching its full potential been utilized (Figure 3.1).

I shall review with you only a few of the SI model's general features, hoping that most of you already have at least some acquaintance with it. I shall point out some of the advantages of the model, with some reference to other taxonomies. I shall mention some of the points of relevance for the model in education and make some suggestions for future operations that should help to raise the quality of education, including the training of teachers.

If the number of projected intellectual abilities in the model is overwhelming, let me say first that of the 120 cells involved, 98 have been investigated by factor analysis, and 98 cells have known abilities. It should be considerable relief to realize that all you really need to know are the 15 categories of abilities—the five kinds of operation, the four kinds of content, and the six kinds of product—and how they go together.

The question often arises as to whether the 120 abilities are all mutually independent; whether, after all, there is some broad variable even underlying *all* of them, like Spearman's *g*. My answer to that

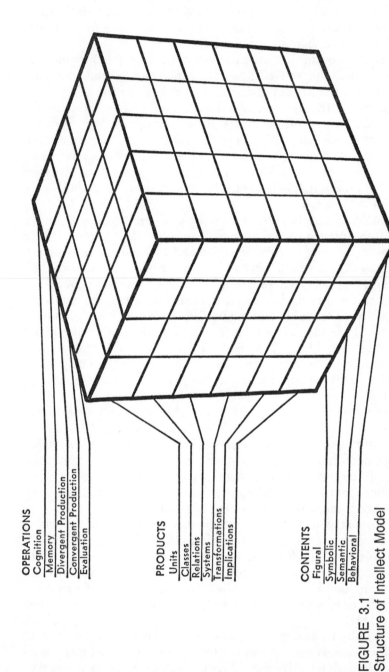

OPERATIONS
Cognition
Memory
Divergent Production
Convergent Production
Evaluation

PRODUCTS
Units
Classes
Relations
Systems
Transformations
Implications

CONTENTS
Figural
Symbolic
Semantic
Behavioral

FIGURE 3.1
Structure of Intellect Model

The structure of intellect model, within which each little cube represents a unique combination of one kind of operation, one kind of content, and one kind of product, hence a distinctly different intellectual ability or function.

question is that the evidence is decidedly against the idea of a g factor, in the nonpathological population. There are just too many zero correlations among pairs of tests of the abilities. In our research over 20 years at USC, among more than 48,000 coefficients of correlation between pairs of tests, as many as 18 percent were below +.10 and could be regarded as zero.

There are some signs, however, that there exists a number of somewhat broad underlying abilities which are in line with at least some of the 15 categories. Examples would be a general memory ability, a general semantic ability, or a general transformation ability. Abilities of lesser generality might be in the areas such as visual memory, behavioral divergent production, or symbolic cognition.

I am not set against the idea that the higher-order intellectual factors do exist, but I do not accept present orthodox factor-analytic procedures for demonstrating them. I often suspect that when it appears that two basic factors are correlated, because they have some tests in common, we have possibly failed to put needed experimental controls in the tests so as to exclude all except one SI ability per test.

It is sometimes remarked that the SI model is merely a systematic way of classifying tests. This is a curious statement, in view of the fact that we infer the nature of an ability from the class of tests that are loaded on it. We try to see what psychological requirement the tests impose in common upon individuals, and from that information we define the ability. I regard the model as descriptive of both tests and abilities.

A New Point of View in Psychology

I have made a great deal of the point that the SI abilities refer to different functions that are differentiated within each individual. Each ability means that the individual processes certain kinds of information in certain ways. This reasoning has led to the proposal of an operational-informational (O–I) psychology. In the history of psychology there was considerable debate whether psychology should describe mental events in terms of acts or in terms of content. The "content" was consciousness, not to be confused with the "content" of SI theory, which is information. No system of psychology has included both act and content in any comprehensive way.

My operational-informational view does bring in both act and content, which are like two sides of a coin. I have often felt that traditional psychology has failed to give education the sound scientific basis that it needs. Only here and there has it offered some useful principles. Operational-informational psychology that is based upon the structure of intellect offers a much greater range of useful principles so far as intellectual functioning goes; a kind of grammar for all thinking. It does not, of course, take care of the important aspects of motivation and emotion, except as they enter into the behavioral-content category of the SI model. We very much need a good taxonomy of motives, emotions, and feelings. Those phenomena may yet be brought into an operational-informational point of view in terms of self-generated information.

Evidence for Multiple Variables

From General Observation

Even apart from the SI model, there is considerable evidence for accepting a multivariate view of intelligence. Two items of general information may be cited. Those who have dealt with the teaching of gifted children readily observe that strong talents may lie in special directions. The abilities are not all concerned with getting high grades in the general run of courses. Closer observation should reveal other special talents, and also some deficiencies.

It is also frequently mentioned that many children from disadvantaged homes have special talents, in spite of moderate test IQs. From reports on observations of the disadvantaged gifted, we find some consensus that they are relatively high in visual-figural abilities, and some of them possibly in auditory- or in kinesthetic-figural abilities, about which we know next to nothing, as yet. They may also be high in figural-divergent-production abilities, as well as cognition and memory abilities in the same content areas. At the lower end of the IQ scale, we even find an occasional idiot-savant, who, although low in educability, has some special ability, perhaps in numerical skills, memory for numbers, or musical talent of a kind. All these diverse talents come within my comprehensive conception of intelligence.

SI Abilities in School Learning

More refined evidence comes from relating scores on tests of various SI abilities to measures of achievement in different school subjects. Obtaining information through reading is, of course, the most common activity of school learners, and reading comprehension depends most upon the SI ability CMU (cognition of semantic units), or the traditional factor of verbal comprehension. Incidentally, we can see how, beginning with Binet, the IQ tests came to emphasize this ability overwhelmingly.

But in *beginning* to learn to read, other abilities are now known to be important. They are figural abilities, both visual and auditory, they pertain to units, and they involve not only cognition but also memory and evaluation. The new reader must process words as visual units and words as auditory units accurately, he must remember them, and he must check to make sure of their identities. Still other figural abilities may yet be found important, for example, those pertaining to implications, for the new reader must learn connections of that kind, formerly known as associations.

Other memory abilities (for symbolic and semantic transformations) are related to reading achievement at later elementary stages. And at the high-school level, our research at USC found that reading to obtain information is related to a number of transformation abilities, some of them outside the memory category. Reading is, indeed, a very complex affair psychologically, and it depends upon different SI abilities at different stages of learning and probably in reading for different purposes.

In an extensive experiment on the learning of concepts, where the concepts were principles to be acquired by induction, we found quite a number of the SI abilities to be involved. The most important ones were concerned with classes as the kind of product, and memory as the kind of operation. Curiously enough, no test in the more common IQ scales appears to be concerned with abilities to handle classes. I shall point out another reason for the seriousness of this oversight later.

We have evidence that in mathematics, from arithmetic to advanced calculus, and with students from junior high school to the graduate school, different combinations of SI abilities are relevant. The study of involvements of SI abilities in different school subjects has only just begun.

SI Abilities in Different Populations

One indication of the validity of the SI abilities is that they have been demonstrated in quite varied populations. Some of them have been found differentiated in different parts of the world, including students from China, the Philippines, and East Africa. They have been demonstrated at different ages of childhood and adolescence as well as in adults in the USA. As many as 30 SI abilities have been reported to be differentiated by the age of six, and many earlier than that. In our own experience, we found that at the ninth-grade level, certain abilities were as well differentiated for children of near-average IQ as for those of high IQ.

This direct kind of evidence is definitely against the Garrett hypothesis, which has held that factorial abilities develop in the child by successive differentiation from a general ability that prevails in infancy. From the best information that we have, the SI abilities are differentiated as early as we can test for them, and this depends upon the child's spheres of experiences. The child's first experiences are very much limited to figural and behavioral content, but he soon gains information of semantic content, and later some of symbolic content. Appearance of evidence for SI abilities must await the appropriate experiences. The physiological mechanisms underlying them and that will be called into play when those experiences arrive probably preexist the experience. I shall not enter the nature-nurture conflict here.

In the context of education, the taxonomy that aims to cover the intellectual functioning of the learner and has the more direct parallels with the structure of intellect is that designed by Bloom and his associates. Bloom's taxonomy puts the emphasis on the operation aspect, with little or no attention to contents and products of information, as such. In this respect, it is very incomplete. The categories of the model were generated from the armchair, and to my knowledge they have not been empirically tested by factor analysis, which is the natural experimental route to taxonomies. The categories therefore have the status of untested hypotheses.

Bloom's operation categories do implicitly include the five SI operation categories, but only that of evaluation corresponds on a one-to-one basis. Even then, the conceptions of what evaluation means or includes differ somewhat. Three of Bloom's categories are redundant in that they could all be included under the SI concept of cognition. These are his categories of "knowledge," "analysis," and "comprehension." Possibly his "knowledge" category should be equated to the memory store of individuals, which is not an operation and not an SI category. Memory as an operation *is* an SI category, and it is concerned with putting information *into* storage.

Bloom's "application" seems to cut across the two SI operations of cognition and one of the production categories, or both. His "synthesis" category clearly pertains to productive thinking. Incidentally, in our first analysis of creative-thinking abilities at USC, we expected to find both analysis and synthesis as factorial abilities, and we included a liberal number of tests designed to measure both expected abilities. They failed completely to appear, their intended tests going in different directions. There is this empirical test of two of the Bloom hypotheses.

Some educators look to Piaget for their source of concepts. Although his writings are full of concepts pertaining to intellectual functioning, and they were derived from systematic observations, they also lack the empirical tests that would show whether or not they refer to unitary features of mental life. Piaget has lacked a systematic taxonomy, having instead a collection of concepts that are only incidentally interrelated. For one thing, he has been more concerned with the development in the child of semantic concepts, such as those of "conservation" and "reciprocity." He recognizes an important distinction between concrete and abstract operations, which, in SI terminology, are regarded as kinds of content—figural and semantic. His concept of synthesizing may be said to imply production. That of hypothesizing suggests the SI product category of implication. He also has much to say about two other kinds of products—classes and relations. Thus, all three dimensions of the SI model are implicitly recognized, but they are not distinguished as such.

A Dynamic Principle

So much for the structure of intellect as a model and frame of reference, and for setting some matters straight as I see them. Going now beyond intelligence, I will propose a very general principle that I am sure many of you find acceptable. It has been expressed in different ways from time to time. It is to the effect that an individual who is high on an ability has also an urge to use it. This may be an instance of a more basic biological principle that a bodily structure designed to function in a certain way has a built-in drive to use that structure. As E. L. Thorndike one time asserted, to use a structure normally is rewarding. Not to be able to use it may be frustrating. From more modern knowledge regarding frustration, we expect a consequence to be aggression and violence, or resignation and perhaps ill health. Failure to use a function means lack of further development and even atrophy.

A principle of relation of abilities to motivational traits has been pointed out in psychoanalytic theory. I cannot accept the view that the possession of special motivation comes first and is the cause of the ability, however. One could say that this is a hen-and-egg problem. Of one thing we can feel more sure. As the individual discovers that he can do a certain kind of thing very well, he is thus rewarded, he repeats the exercise of the ability, and it grows. A kind of circularity is involved. I think that in numerous instances, the child just accidentally discovers that he has a certain talent. The moral of this is that we should arrange experiences so as to make such discoveries possible.

Good empirical evidence is lacking for the validity of the principle that I proposed, but this is largely because we have lacked the taxonomies of both abilities and interests that are needed for a test of it. Needed are sets of parallel abilities and interests. There is some evidence suggesting that in testing it, we should not correlate abilities and interests across individuals, but rather we should correlate profiles of the two kinds within individuals.

The dynamic principle does account for the very commonly observed fact of intrinsic motivation in performance of self-selected tasks. This suggests that, more than has been common practice, there should be opportunities for children to engage in self-initiated tasks. Of course, if a learning regime for a child were to include only self-selected tasks, he would tend to become an overspecialized individual. A helpful counteractive motivational influence is the child's capacity for boredom for the overexercise of a hobby. With ingenuity, we can also make the child feel that tasks that we actually select for him seem self-selected to him. There may also be a related source of motivation in the fact that the child is rewarded from seeing substantial *gains* in competence.

Are there motivational parallels to SI abilities? Perhaps not to particular abilities so much as to categories of abilities. At least in high school and college, it is fairly obvious that broad interests tend to vary along the lines of the four content categories of the SI model. Interests in visual-figural information is exhibited in liking for concrete subjects, in mechanics, the arts, and engineering. Interest in the semantic area would direct individuals toward literature, writing, the humanities, and the sciences. Mathematics is largely a symbolic area. And many students take to politics, with high interest in people and their behavior, and in influencing or managing them.

As to special interests along the lines of operation categories, I think of only one clear example. In some of our Project research we found a bit of evidence in the form of two factors that could be interpreted as interest in divergent production and convergent production. Incidentally, it may not surprise some of you to know that the correlation we found between scores for these two variables was a negative .30.

There is no good evidence regarding interests along the lines of products of information, but I might suggest that one or more of the so-called cognitive-style factors may be such motivational variables. One factor is said to be a preference for broad classes over narrow classes. Classes are one kind of SI product. There is other evidence for a preference for complexity. One SI product is obviously concerned with complexity—that of systems. Liking for complexity may go with strong systems abilities. And then, those who like puns, riddles, and puzzles, in general, may be reflecting an interest in transformation, coupled with strong transformation abilities.

Applications of SI in Education

What do some of these things mean for education? As I see it, from a distance, to be sure, there appear to be a number of needs. Certain things might be done, or, if already done, might be done more extensively, to the advantage of learners.

Insofar as education has the objective of increasing the intellectual powers of individuals, we now have much clearer goals, with a basic taxonomy that points more directly at subgoals and also implies procedures by which we may achieve them. You probably know that where common classroom instruction has been observed systematically in order to determine to what extent the different SI operations were employed, it has been found that production abilities were slighted, and also evaluation, to some extent. It often seems to be assumed that between kindergarten and the graduate school, the learner is merely a consumer of knowledge. It is also assumed that if we give him the information, he will be able to use it. We know now that both assumptions are incorrect, and that following them has tended to make school experiences often unattractive, unrewarding, and even frustrating.

It cannot be said that all SI abilities are equally important for all individuals, and value judgments will need to be made as to where the emphases should lie. Needs for divergent-production abilities, because of their demonstrated relation to creative production and problem solving, are being recognized. And where steps are being taken to cultivate those abilities, many benefits have been reported. In addition to the intrinsic rewards that students experience, there are general increases in self-esteem and self-confidence, and even some behavior problems are solved.

Development of Abilities

There are numerous ways in which SI functions can be exercised. Probably the best general approach is to teach subject matter in various courses in ways that stimulate productive thinking, when abilities in that area are to be emphasized. I hasten to add that examinations should also call for productive thinking, for students prepare for the kind of examinations they expect to have. Another general approach is to give special mental-calisthenic exercises. These can be designed by analogy to the tests that are known to measure the abilities in question. We know that first-rate musical performers or golf players, for example, do not reach peak form and award-winning performance without engaging in hours of special exercises. The same is probably true of the SI functions.

A third way of improving performance in the use of SI functions would be to teach children and youth, as early as they can understand, the nature of their intellectual resources. I recall that Torrance reported that children improved in performance in divergent-production tests after only a short period of instruction on the nature of the relevant abilities. A teacher has just told me that he teaches the SI model to his minority-group children in grades four to six, and how to apply the concepts to arithmetic and other school subjects. It has been found that administrative personnel become more innovative in their daily work after instruction on divergent-production abilities, more so than others who have had only exercises.

Transfer of Learning

The SI functions are important sources of the phenomenon of transfer of learning: transfer to something that we all hope to achieve in education. Without it, teaching efforts would be interminable, and at best, very inefficient. Each SI ability represents a *class* of tasks or activities, such that exercise in one of them generalizes to other members of the class. Such transfers can probably be broadened to extend beyond a particular function, by pointing out to learners the parallels between abilities. Thus, having had exercises with seeing relations in visual-figural information, if the learner realizes what he is doing, and acquires a tactic or strategy of a particular kind, he should be more ready to see relations between words, in a parallel kind of task.

Individualized Instruction

It is commonly agreed that where children are permitted and are stimulated to learn as individuals, each according to his own needs and interests and at his own rate, the experiences are generally beneficial. The recognition of unevenness of intellectual abilities and interests within persons as well as between persons makes freedom for individual development all the more relevant. I recognize that where a teacher has a roomful of 35 children, such an approach seems in the category of wishful thinking. But ways are being found for treating the individual learner, and still other ways will be found by the creative educator.

Some writers suggest that, in the extreme, each learner might have his own curriculum. We have to remember, of course, that our society has its own legitimate curricula. If there are to be individualized curricula, ways can undoubtedly be found to mesh them with those of the society of which the child is a part. We can also take advantage of what I think is another principle. If a child is given opportunities to satisfy his own goals, he is more ready to accept society's goals.

Needs for Testing

The conceptions and procedures that I have mentioned imply much more extensive testing, for the general purpose of keeping our fingers on the pulse of the developing child, with respect to both intellectual growth and achievement of curricular goals. From such information we should be ready to prescribe treatment in the form of the next educational steps. Continued health and development would thus be assured. In spite of recent pressures to eliminate intelligence tests, but in answer to them, it would be desirable to institute periodic testing of relevant SI abilities, the tests for which still need to be developed, for the most part.

In regard to achievement testing, although I do not subscribe to the general views of B. F. Skinner, I do urge a much more general application of the principle of reinforcement that he has promoted. This means that achievement testing should be very frequent and it should be aimed at quite specific objectives. The child should be given much feedback information. He needs to know when he has made errors and the nature of those errors, and to have this information very promptly. My theory of reinforcement in learning is that it is largely a matter of feedback information that confirms or disconfirms the learner's responses. It thus carries its own reward or lack of reward. These principles point clearly to the need for tutoring—human tutors if possible, gadget tutors, if not.

It goes without saying that information from psychological tests should be utilized. But the information should be used by those who know how to interpret test results and to apply them wisely. In places where tests of intelligence have been discontinued, under public pressure, I suspect that it was not because the tests did not furnish useful information but because the information was misinterpreted or misused. Incidentally, in the selection of gifted children, the use of tests should not be prescribed by legislators but left to the experts.

Instruction on Traits

Earlier, I urged that the child be given information regarding his intellectual resources as soon as he can comprehend and make use of it. I would extend this suggestion to include other traits of personality —temperament traits, and traits of motivation, including needs, interests, and attitudes. Such information should also help the child to achieve a better conception of his own personal identity. This might

forestall the need for complaints such as we have heard during the
past ten years from young people to the effect that they do not know
who they are.

There need be no formal course in psychology, but some of its
principles, particularly as they are concerned with personality,
which I equate to individuality, could be worked in, in different
connections. This instruction should also aim at the growth of tolerance for individual differences, which is so badly needed today, as
diverse people are thrown together. Odious comparisons should, of
course, be frowned upon.

Growth of Social Intelligence

Education should give more explicit attention to social intelligence, or behavioral abilities or functions. Of the 30 behavioral abilities forecast by the SI model, 12 have been investigated and
demonstrated by factor analysis, those in the operation categories of
cognition and divergent production. These findings lend encouragement for expecting to find the remaining 18 behavioral abilities. The
potential importance of all these abilities should be found wherever
it is important for persons to understand one another and to influence
one another's behavior.

I note that some educators who have been concerned with development of social skills in the gifted have made it a point to select
some leaders among their special groups. Effective leaders should be
high in at least some of the behavioral abilities. They should communicate more fully with other people and should develop skills in
managing them. One of my graduate students who worked with
juveniles on probation told me that he came to the conviction that
delinquents could almost be classified in two groups. Either they are
low in behavioral comprehension, hence make social mistakes, or are
easily led to do so, or they are high in behavioral cognition and
divergent production. Members of the latter group become
manipulators and are sometimes gang leaders. They even manipulate
their parents and teachers. One implication of this is that along with
social training, we must also develop personal and social responsibility. We should not aim to develop exploiters of people.

There are several ways in which schools can develop social or
behavioral abilities. The playground and the classroom can be
laboratories. The teacher of literature can contribute in teaching
literature. There are opportunities in drama and in role-playing exercises. I have noted in a recent news item that the U.S. Office of
Education is launching a new program that may feature "sensitivity

training." Without necessarily endorsing the use of this device with children, I should say that it is in the area of training for behavioral cognition. It should, of course, be used with discretion.

Education for Creativity

Much has been said and done regarding training the gifted for creativity, especially by Gowan and Torrance. Among those selected as gifted by reason of high IQ, we should expect to find a higher proportion of children who are already superior in divergent-production abilities. But many high–IQ children are low on divergent production, and in that sense may be called creative underachievers. Development of creative skills in the gifted group promises the greatest payoff for individuals and for society.

Training for creativity is usually aimed at improving divergent-production abilities, and that is the kind of outcome achieved. But I should like to emphasize the point that there is another important aspect of creative talent, found in the product category of transformation. When we interviewed quite a number of creative scientists, engineers, and others, and asked them to rate the importance of various SI abilities to them in their work, they tended to rate the transformation abilities higher than the divergent-production abilities. It is true that four of the transformation abilities are also concerned with divergent production, but most of the 20 transformation abilities are outside the divergent-production category.

Whereas divergent-production abilities make us more fluent, or able to produce quantities of ideas, transformation abilities make us more flexible, which leads to unusual or novel ideas, for which a quality index is more important. Some children, and others who are recognized among the creative gifted, show their flexibility by their flair for appreciating and producing wit and humor. Transformations provide one of the important bases for wit and humor, for example, in the form of puns. A riddle illustrates this point. The riddle goes, "What is a common name for an abortion in Czechoslovakia?" The answer is that in Czechoslovakia, an abortion is called a "cancelled Czech."

Understanding a pun is cognition of a semantic transformation, which is a shift in meaning. Now some of those who understand puns readily may not be able to remember them, as we found in our research. It is sometimes said that the English are somewhat slow in this respect, so you hear jokes like the following. One Englishman, having heard the Czechoslovakian riddle, tried to tell it to another. He said "I heard a smashing joke yesterday. What do they call an abortion in Czechoslovakia? Give up? It's a check that has been cashed." He remembered something of the fact, which is a unit of information, but not the transformation.

If we wanted to see how well a person could *produce* such a transformation divergently, we might give him the task: List a number of different ways that you could use to refer to an abortion in Poland. He might say "an early liquidation," or "the end of a Pole," for example.

It seems to me that in this rapidly changing world, one of the best things we could teach children is how to be flexible where necessary. Adjustment to life depends more and more upon it. There was never a greater need for creative problem solving, and this often depends upon transformation abilities. Transformations are by no means confined to puns.

I would just mention a couple of other suggestions on educating for creativity. One is that besides giving exercises in productive thinking and transformations, and giving information regarding those facts of mental life, there is a need for teaching self-criticism; hence evaluation abilities or functions come into the picture. We are told that the creative person is more independent and less attentive to criticism of his productions offered by others. It is therefore important that he learn to evaluate his own output. But, as in the techniques of brainstorming, he should separate the two activities in time. That is, he should produce first, without self-criticism, for self-criticism puts a damper on productivity, and he should evaluate later.

The other suggestion is that in training for fluency and flexibility we do not neglect the child's memory store. Highly creative people who have expressed themselves on what makes them creatively productive agree that it is essential to have in memory storage a good supply of information of the kind they are going to use. Although this objective has evidently been overplayed relatively in the past, it should not be discarded for the future. Problems cannot be solved without having the information needed to solve them. Interpretations of the problems and suggested solutions must come largely from the memory store. But a critical condition for storing information so that it can be easily retrieved for use is that it be well organized. Organization depends upon the manner in which the information is learned and stored, upon how it is classified and labeled. This puts the focus on the manner in which information is learned.

Labels on information prepare it for ready retrieval when the appropriate cue arrives. This is illustrated by one of our common divergent-production tests, for the ability of ideational fluency. One task asks examinees to list all objects they can think of that are both white and edible. The cues here are class specifications—things white and edible. As you will find in your own efforts to recall something, you utilize class ideas as cues. The role of classes in retrieval is another reason for having respect for the class abilities, which I urged earlier in connection with the learning of concepts. Other cues for retrieval can be relations, systems, and implications, three other products that need attention in systematic learning.

On Teacher Training

The suggestions that I have made imply some changes in teacher training. My emphasis upon the multivariate view of all personality traits, including intellectual abilities, calls for more instruction on individual differences of all kinds. This would be aimed not only toward a basis for the better understanding of learners and knowing what the educational task involves but also a preparation for teaching self-understanding on the part of learners.

There should be more attention on social intelligence in teacher training. Selection of students for teacher training might give some attention to the status of applicants in this respect. Trainees and teachers should be encouraged to improve their skills in understanding others and in dealing with them creatively. Teachers need to be keen observers of those whom they teach, in order to take advantage of feedback information provided by cues from the behavior of the learners. Although based on science, teaching is an art rather than a science. Programming of the teaching session may be well-planned, but there is no escape from the need for extemporaneous programming as events unfold. This requires social intelligence.

Teacher training should extend beyond the preparation of professional teachers. As I note the writings on educating the gifted, I am impressed with the frequent reference to the need for involving the parents of the child. It is important, of course, that there should be as little hiatus as possible between the goals and the values of home and school. Where the child is in a special program, there is all the more reason for the parent's understanding the purposes and even the treatments of that program. There is a parallel in child psychotherapy, where it is found that substantial progress cannot be made without some enlistment of aid from the family.

From the way in which things have gone in our society in recent years, it would appear that, in general terms, we have not prepared young people well enough for parenthood. Part of such training should prepare parents to play the role of teacher. Recent research has fairly well demonstrated that intellectual development is most rapid and much of it has occurred before the child enters kindergarten. The most critical period, when environmental influences can have their greatest effects, seems to be near the age of two. At that age, ordinarily, the parent is the one who has the most significant contacts with the child.

Although training for parenthood should begin in high school, there is still time to prepare parents to meet problems of childhood and adolescence while in college or in adult education. An excellent opportunity for preparents as future teachers should be to have older children in school tutor younger ones, a practice that is already known in places.

All of these things will, of course, take money; lots of it. And we are in a period when financial support for education is uncertain and unstable. While education of the gifted can be readily defended as an exceptionally good investment for society to make, it may too often be regarded by those who do not understand as one of those so-called "frills" that we could get along without if we have to. A nation that can spend $30 billion for shots at the moon and Mars and other far-off places can surely find money for improvements in education. I say that the exploration of inner space, with the benefits that should follow, should have at least as high priority as the exploration of outer space. In fact, future explorations of outer space will depend upon explorations of inner space. What is more, even our survival also depends upon them and on their findings about that cantankerous thing called human nature.

References

Gowan, J. C., and Torrance, E. P. (Eds.). *Educating the Ablest.* Itasca, Ill.: F. E. Peacock, 1971.

Guilford, J. P. *The Nature of Human Intelligence.* New York: McGraw-Hill, 1967.

Guilford, J. P. *Intelligence, Creativity, and Their Educational Implications.* San Diego, Calif.: Robert Knapp, 1969.

Guilford, J. P. Roles of structure-of-intellect abilities in education. *Journal of Research and Development in Education,* 1971, 4, 3–13.

Guilford, J. P., and Hoepfner, R. *The Analysis of Intelligence.* New York: McGraw-Hill, 1971.

Chapter Two

Developmental Characteristics

Introduction

A gifted child may be defined as one whose rate of development on any significant intellectual variable is significantly greater than that of the generality (Gowan & Demos, 1964, p. 33). Besides simplifying the definition of giftedness, the developmental variable allows us to look for ways of developing creativity in children. Longitudinal studies are one way to research this problem; we need more of the type of research done by Lewis Terman in the *Genetic Studies of Genius* (Terman & Oden, 1959).[1] Fortunately, J. C. Flanagan's Project TALENT (1960) will help carry on this tradition, as will the research that Julian Stanley (1976; see Reading 7 in Chapter III) is conducting on precocious mathematical talent. E. P. Torrance (1972; see Reading 4) has reported some follow-up research connecting childhood measurement of creativity with adult performance, but it is a great pity that longitudinal research like Terman's, but with creativity added, is not presently ongoing. This lack will hamper future progress, and the need for having started such research in the present will become obvious.

Characteristics of gifted children are usually discussed in terms of age, sex, and socioeconomic status (SES) differences. The importance of the latter variable is well illustrated in the famous study of Bonsall and Stefflre (1955) which showed that when gifted and average children are compared without controlling this variable, the gifted area is always significantly higher in SES, and when the SES variable is controlled almost all the personality differences between gifted children and the average disappear.[2]

Case studies of gifted children have fallen into disuse, although the inquisitive reader will find a number in *The Gifted Child Quarterly*, 11:25–27, and in the book *The Gifted Child: Case Studies* (Hauck &

---

[1]For recent material on Terman and the gifted, see Seagoe (1975) and Stanley, George, and Solano (1977).
[2]See also Khatena (1978 C), chap. 7.

Freehill, 1972). Excellent case studies of creative geniuses by Kathleen Montour have recently begun to appear (1976, 1978). The modern counterpart of the case study is the sociological investigation of "the creativogenic society" (a term coined by Arieti, 1976, p. 313 ff.), using statistical techniques. D. K. Simonton (1975, 1977, 1978) especially has shown the relationship of cultural variables to the maximization of various kinds of creative performance. Such research is very important, because finding out the causes of the accidental renaissances of the past could provide a blueprint for a planned, permanent renaissance of the future.

Traits commonly attributed to gifted children include curiosity, initiative, originality, expression, perceptually open imagination, superior judgment, good elaboration, rapid learning, visualizing relationships, superior vocabulary, inquisitiveness, and wide knowledge and information. However, many of these traits are characteristics of creative children as well, rather than just gifted children.

Ann Duncan (1969), in a NAGC Monograph on developmental behavior rates of gifted children contrasted with average children, concluded that the gifted were significantly quicker in their reactions and that this speed increased with grade levels. All the correlations were positive and significant, indicating the presence of a second-order factor, "g." Rate of performance and rate of development are evidently related in gifted children. It takes them less time to perform and to develop.

The senior editor, J. C. Gowan, has explored escalation into some of the higher cognitive stages of development in his books *The Development of the Creative Individual* (1972) and *The Development of the Psychedelic Individual* (1974). A quote from the former work identifies the developmental characteristics of superior individuals as follows:

> This is certainly the time for some thoughtful reader to ask why it is necessary to talk about superior individuals at all if one is discussing a developmental problem. This question deserves a careful answer.
>
> 1. By superior individual we mean an individual of superior intelligence which would place him in the top two stanines or the upper 11 percent. (It is indeed possible that the future will go to an operational definition of giftedness which is that a "gifted" child is one that has the potentiality to become creative. If this is true, the definition of giftedness on the IQ scale will need to be dropped to about 120, or top 10 to 11 percent.) The basis of experience indicates that these individuals are more likely to become self-actualized than others. Maslow (1954, pp. 202–03), in his famous study, picked no historical

figures who were not in this category; indeed, it would be difficult to describe a self-actualized cretin. Let the reader pick his own candidate for self-actualization and then discover if he is not of this level of intelligence.

2. Such individuals appear to have a longer mental growth span than others. They appear to continue growing in mental age even into their seniority (whereas others decline) according to the Terman study (1954) followup, which found mental age still increasing at age 50.

3. Superior individuals seem to have a "higher ceiling," permitting them access into higher developmental stages which ordinary people seldom attain. This is like "overdrive" on an expensive car.

4. Superior individuals accomplish cognitive tasks more quickly and hence go through stages more thoroughly. They, therefore, develop more fully during their life span than do others.[3]

The vocational development of gifted children was investigated by Gowan and Norma Jean Groth (1968). They found that gifted boys had cleared the fantasy stage of vocational choice by age 11, but girls had more complex vocational problems which were still further obscured by the special functions of womanhood. The creative development of gifted women, a subject which has seen much recent research, has necessitated a new chapter in this edition (Chapter XI). Another change has been a shift in emphasis from static personality characteristics to the developmental process.

As developmental concepts permeate further the educational literature, we may expect considerable research into the differential rates of completion of various developmental tasks, of which vocational adjustment is only one. Eventually, light may be shed upon the higher adult tasks (such as ego-integrity and self-actualization) of superior adults.

---

[3]J. C. Gowan, *The Development of the Creative Individual* (San Diego, Calif.: R. Knapp, 1972), p. 73.

4 Career Patterns and Peak Creative Achievements of Creative High School Students Twelve Years Later

E. PAUL TORRANCE

As a rather clear profile of the characteristics of the creative child unfolded during the 1960s, there arose widespread skepticism and opposition to concerns about the more humane treatment of creative children and about a more creative kind of education in general. The skeptics expressed doubt that the children we have identified as creative will produce useful creative achievements as adults. The opponents contended that creative children such as those identified in our research are a menace to society.

Only long-range predictive validity studies and longitudinal developmental studies can answer the serious charges of these critics. My associates and I recognized this need when we initiated a program of creativity research in 1958. It is still too early to obtain follow-up data on the elementary school children identified as creative in 1958 and 1959. I do have the results of the 12-year follow-up of the high school students tested in 1959 and I shall try to summarize the highlights concerning their career patterns and peak creative achievements. First, let me describe the basic study. Then I shall present data concerning the following questions:

1. Do young people identified as creative during their high school years become productive, creative adults?
2. Is seven years after high school graduation or twelve years after high school graduation a better time to obtain predictive validity data?
3. Do the unusual occupational choices of creative high school students persist and become realities?
4. What are the most common career routes of creatively gifted young people?
5. In what fields do students identified as creative on the basis

From *The Gifted Child Quarterly* 16:2 (1972). Used by permission.

of a general test of creative thinking ability achieve creatively as adults?

6. How does the nature of the peak creative achievements of the more creative students differ from that of their less creative peers twelve years later?

The Basic Study

The basic study was initiated in September, 1959. The total enrollment of the University of Minnesota High School (grades 7–12) were administered the *Torrance Tests of Creative Thinking* (1966). A majority of the 392 subjects were sons and daughters of professional and business people. At this time, however, the enrollment also included a large block of students from a less affluent neighborhood lacking a school building. The mean intelligence quotient of the total group of students as assessed by the Lorge-Thorndike test was 118, and the mean percentile rank of the *Iowa Tests of Educational Development* was 84 on national norms.

The test battery consisted of the following tasks: Ask Questions, Guess Causes, Guess Consequences, Product Improvement, Unusual Uses of a Tin Can, and Circles. The creativity tests were scored in 1959 according to the scoring guides then in use for the following variables: fluency (number of relevant responses), flexibility (variety of categories of responses), inventive level (following the criteria of the United States Patent Office), elaboration (amount of detail used to describe how ideas would be executed). In 1961, all tests were rescored for originality according to a guide developed at that time. The interscorer reliability of each of the scorers in all cases was in excess of .90 for all variables.

Near the end of the senior year, the subjects were administered a five-item peer nominations or sociometric questionnaire. Subjects were asked to make three nominations on the basis of each of the following criteria:

1. Who in your class come up with the most ideas?
2. Who have the most original or unusual ideas?
3. If the situation changed or if a solution to a problem wouldn't work, who would be the first ones to find a new way of meeting the problem?
4. Who do the most inventing and developing of new ideas, gadgets, and the like?
5. Who are best at thinking of all the details involved in working out a new idea and thinking of all the consequences?

Seven-Year Follow-Up

The first follow-up of this study was with the class of 1960 and was executed in 1966, using a questionnaire designed by Erickson (1966) and Torrance (1969a, 1969b). The instrument requested information concerning the subject's marital status, number of children, occupation, spouse's occupation, highest level of education attained, undergraduate and graduate colleges attended, honors, employment experiences, post–high school creative achievements, a description of peak or most creative achievement, and a statement of aspirations.

Data were received from 46 of the original 69 subjects. An index of Quantity of Creative Achievements was developed from the subjects' self-reports of the following categories of recognized and acknowledged creative achievements:

Poems, stories, songs written
Poems, stories, songs published
Books written
Books published
Radio and television scripts or performances
Music compositions published
Original research designs developed
Philosophy of life changed
In-service training for co-workers created
Original changes in work situation suggested
Research grants received
Scientific papers published in professional journals
Business enterprises initiated
Patentable devices invented
Awards or prizes received for creative writing, musical composition, art, etc.

An index of quality of creative achievement was obtained by having five judges (all advanced students of creativity) rate on a ten-point scale the originality of the most creative achievements. An index of quantity of creative behavior was obtained by assigning a weight of one for each achievement attained once or twice and a weight of two for each achievement attained three or more times and then adding the weights. The five judges also rated the degree of originality necessary to realize each subject's vocational aspiration.

By combining the Fluency, Flexibility, Originality, and Elaboration scores through stepwise regression, multiple correlation coefficients of .50 (with Highest Creative Achievement), .46 (with Quantity of Creative Achievements), and .51 (with Creativeness of Aspirations) were obtained.

Twelve-Year Follow-Up

Procedure

A 12-year follow-up of the 1959 University (Minnesota) High School population ($N = 392$) was conducted in 1971. At the time the data reported here were analyzed, completed questionnaires had been obtained from 251 of the subjects. The questionnaire was similar to the one used in 1966 but in addition requested descriptions of the subject's three most creative or peak post–high school achievements. Generally, subjects supplied rather complete data, rich in information about what has been happening to young people now between the ages of 25 and 31.

A measure of quantity of creative achievements was obtained by adding the number of creative achievements checked and/or listed by each subject. The measure of quality of highest creative achievements was based on the ratings of five expert judges of the descriptions of the three most creative achievements reported by each subject. The judges were instructed to rate these data on a ten-point scale in terms of the levels of creativity reflected in the three achievements described. The level of creativeness of aspirations was based on similar ratings of the statements of each subject concerning what he would most like to do in the future, assuming the necessary talent, training, and opportunity. The mean reliability coefficient of the five judges was .91.

Results

Combining the scores on the creativity test battery to predict the combined creativity criteria, a canonical correlation of .51 was obtained for the full sample. A canonical correlation of .59 was obtained for men alone and one of .46, for women alone. While the predictive validity of the tests is significant at better than the one percent level for both women and men, the finding gives some credence to the belief that the creative achievements of women are somewhat less predictable than those of men.

Time and Predictability of Creative Achievement

At the time my associates and I analyzed the data from the 1966 follow-up of the class of 1960, there was much to suggest that the

TABLE 4.1
Product-Moment Coefficients of Correlation Between
Creativity Predictors Established in 1959 and
Criterion Variables Established in 1966 and in 1971

| | Criterion Variables | | | | | |
| | Quality | | Quantity | | Motivation | |
Predictors	1966	1971	1966	1971	1966	1971
Intelligence test	.37*	.45*	.22	.46*	.32	.41*
High school achievement	.20	.47*	.09	.38*	.15	.46*
Peer nominations on creativity criteria	.13	.34*	.13	.39*	.18	.38*
Fluency (TTCT)	.39*	.53*	.44*	.54*	.34	.49*
Flexibility (TTCT)	.48*	.59*	.44*	.58*	.46*	.54*
Originality (TTCT)	.43*	.49*	.40*	.54*	.42*	.51*
Elaboration (TTCT)	.32	.40*	.37*	.43*	.25	.41*

*Coefficient of correlation is significant at the .01 level

differences between the high and low creatives would in time be increased rather than decreased. Follow-up data from 46 members of this class were obtained in 1966 and from 52 in 1971. Table 4.1 presents the product-moment coefficients of correlation between the summary predictors and the criterion measures for both studies. It will be noted that there is a completely consistent trend for the validity coefficients to increase, as predicted. The most startling increase is noted for the sociometric or peer nomination predictors. The coefficients increased from .13, .13, and .18 to .34, .39, and .38, or from insignificant relationships to relationships significant at the .01 level. Intelligence Quotient and achievement scores also show better prediction. However, the creativity measures of fluency, flexibility, and originality still have a slight edge over Intelligence Quotient and achievement.

Unusual Occupational Choices

Numerous critics of the Getzels and Jackson (1962) study have deplored the finding that highly creative high school students tend to choose unusual occupations. Counselors have pointed out that such choices are unrealistic and that such goals can lead only to failure and disillusionment. To determine whether or not highly creative high school students actually find fulfillment in unusual occupations, the responses of the 251 subjects of this study were analyzed according to the same criteria used by Getzels and Jackson.

The following occupations were classified as conventional: lawyer, doctor, teacher, professor, engineer, housewife, psychologist, carpenter, salesman, draftsman, nurse, copy editor, news reporter, stockbroker, heavy equipment operator, farmer, and the like.

The following occupations were classified as unconventional: adventurer, inventor, writer, entertainer, artist, dancer, film maker, product designer, pot maker, plastic surgeon, dog trainer, (woman) Justice of the Supreme Court, President of the United States, centerfielder of the St. Louis Cardinals, and the like.

Following the criteria of Getzels and Jackson, unusual combinations of occupations were also classified as unconventional. The following are a few examples of these:

> One person is teaching American Public Policy and Constitutional Law with a master's degree from the London School of Economics, an apprenticeship as a Mississippi "Freedom Rider," experience as a teacher in a "Freedom" school, law training at Yale and the University of Minnesota, and a Ph.D. in history at Stanford University.

> One person is "a general practitioner of medicine who is at the same time involved in system design research and teaching in a rural community."

> One plans to "write science fiction, children's fantasy, detective stories (not poetry—there is no conceivable way of getting money out of it, except occasional grants late in one's career. I write poetry because I have to and I 'work at' it but I don't consider it work). I don't seriously expect to earn my living writing but I do expect to supplement what I will earn as a teacher."

Both the present and projected occupations were classified according to these criteria. The high and low creativity groups were determined by a median split by sex within each grade on the basis of composite scores on the battery of creative thinking tests administered in 1959. Results are available for 113 of the high creatives and 138 of the low creatives.

It was found that 62 (or 55 percent) of the high creatives and 13 (or 9 percent) of the low creatives are currently in unconventional occupations. The difference in proportions yields a chi square of 66.48, significant at better than the .001 level.

When future aspirations or projected occupations were classified, 80 (or 71 percent) of the high creatives and 44 (or 32 percent) of the low creatives expressed aspirations for unusual occupations. This difference in proportions yields a chi square of 37.63 significant at better than the .001 level.

Common Career Routes

The following six common career routes were identified among the subjects of the study:

Direct route to career without delays

Delays in career attainment due to military service

Delays or interruption in career attainment by marriage and family

Delays for related educational experiences

Delays for related work experience

Delays for irrelevant work experiences.

In some cases, careers were delayed by more than one force. In such cases, an effort was made to determine the major source of the delay. For example, one of the women was married soon after dropping out of high school. Her marriage, however, did not really delay her attainment of a successful career as an artist. It was working for a year as a taxi driver and other experiences which at least seem irrelevant to her becoming an artist.

TABLE 4.2
Course of Career and Creative Achievement and Aspiration:
Means and F-Values

Course of Career	Means		
	Quantity	Quality	Aspiration
Delayed by related educational experience	26.0	39.1	38.1
Delayed by related work experience	25.4	35.6	34.8
Delayed by irrelevant work experience	18.5	29.9	29.4
Delayed by military service	9.7	21.5	25.1
Direct route to career	8.9	23.8	25.1
Delayed by family and/or marriage	6.7	24.5	24.4

Note: F (Quantity)   = 16.888; *df.* = 5.138; *p.* < .001
      F (Quality)   = 21.815; *df.* = 5.138; *p.* < .001
      F (Aspiration) = 16.261; *df.* = 5.138; *p.* < .001

The means for subjects classified in each of these six categories are shown in Table 4.2 for the criterion variables along with the F-values. It will be noted that the analyses of variance yield F-values significant at better than the .001 level for each of the three criteria. The highest attainments are reported by those whose careers were delayed by related experience and those delayed by relevant work experiences. The lowest attainments were reported by those whose careers were delayed by family and marriage, those who took a direct route to their careers, and those delayed by military service. A mid-position was held by those whose careers were delayed by work experiences that appear to be irrelevant to the attainment of career goals.

TABLE 4.3
Course of Career Pattern and Creativity Predictors:
Means and F-Values

	Rela. Work Exp.	Rela. Educ. Exp.	Marr. and Family	Irrel. Work Exp.	Mili. Ser.	No Detour	F
Verbal fluency	69.8	64.8	61.1	58.5	47.8	46.8	7.094*
Verbal flexibility	40.2	39.6	38.3	36.4	31.1	29.9	6.510*
Verbal originality	71.7	70.0	52.2	58.0	39.2	38.8	7.373*
Verbal inventiveness	48.5	44.7	40.3	36.1	28.2	30.8	7.421*
Figural fluency	23.9	22.1	23.7	19.5	17.9	17.1	5.489*
Figural flexibility	16.3	16.5	16.7	14.7	12.8	12.3	5.495*
Figural originality	22.2	22.5	21.9	19.5	15.7	15.3	4.138
Figural elaboration	40.3	41.5	34.6	44.9	33.2	32.8	2.885
Intelligence Quotient	123.8	118.7	116.6	126.2	112.4	117.8	1.049
Achievement (ITED)	87.7	86.3	78.9	91.9	67.6	78.1	3.259

*Significant at .05 level

Table 4.3 presents similar data for the summary predictor variables. Significant F-values are obtained for all of the verbal measures, figural fluency, and figural flexibility. Both Intelligence Quotient and educational achievement as measured by the Iowa Tests of Educational Development failed to produce significant differences.

Again, there is a rather general tendency for those whose careers were delayed by relevant work or educational experiences to have the highest creativity scores. The third position, however, was held by those whose careers were delayed by marriage and family in most instances. Those whose careers were delayed by military service and those who entered their careers without detours tended to have the lowest scores on the creativity predictors. It is interesting to note that the group having the highest mean Intelligence Quotient and the highest rating on the Iowa Tests of Educational Development consisted of those whose careers were delayed by irrelevant work experiences. It will also be noted that this group had the highest mean elaboration score.

Foreign Study or Work Experience

For fifty-two of the subjects of this study, foreign study or work experience was mentioned as a part of their career preparation or development. In most cases, the foreign study was in Germany, Austria, France, Italy, England, Holland, Norway, or Sweden. A few, however, reported experiences in Japan; these were primarily in the visual arts such as printmaking, pot making, and the like.

Thirty-three (or 29 percent) of the high creatives and 19 (or 14 percent) of the low creatives reported foreign educational and/or work experiences. The resulting difference in proportions yielded a chi square of 9.011, significant at the .005 level.

Fields of Creative Achievement

The *Torrance Tests of Creative Thinking* are designed to be tests of general creativity, and the choice of test tasks represents a deliberate attempt to include an optimum sample of ways of thinking creatively.

To explore the role of the predictors in creative careers in specific fields, each subject was given a rating in each of the following areas: visual art, music, creative writing, science-medicine, business-industry, and leadership. A rating of one was given subjects reporting no creative achievements in the area in question; a rating of two was given if the subject reported one or two creative achievements in an area or a larger number of moderate achievements in the area; a rating of three was given if the subject reported a large number of high-quality achievements in the area. These ratings and the number of areas in which each subject reported creative achievements were correlated with each of the predictor variables.

These analyses are too complex for detailed presentation, but a number of gross trends can be noted. Table 4.4 presents the significant product-moment coefficients of correlation for the class of 1960. Creative achievements in writing were most easily predicted, followed by creative achievements in science and medicine and in leadership. Only figural fluency, figural elaboration, consequences flexibility, and product improvement flexibility yielded a significant positive relationship in visual arts. Only sociometric originality, unusual uses of tin cans fluency, and flexibility yielded significant correlations with music achievement. For achievement in business and industry there were three significant negative predictors (inventiveness, ask questions originality, and guess causes originality) and three significant positive ones (sociometric elaboration, unusual toy dog uses fluency, and unusual toy dog uses flexibility).

Twenty-seven of the 33 creativity predictors yielded statistically significant correlations with the number of different areas in which subjects reported creative achievements.

As might be expected, the predictors work differently for men and

TABLE 4.4
Statistically Significant Coefficients of Correlation
in Predicting Adult Creative Achievement in
Specific Areas for the Class of 1960 (N = 52)

Predictors	Visual Arts	Music	Creat. Writ.	Sci. Med.	Bus. Ind.	Ldr.	No Areas
Intelligence quotient			.38	.24			.29
Achievement (ITED)			.36				.29
Verbal fluency			.52				.53
Verbal flexibility			.57				.58
Verbal originality			.58				.48
Verbal inventiveness			.60		−.33		.43
Figural fluency	.24		.25				.38
Figural flexibility				.31			.30
Figural originality				.35			.26
Figural elaboration	.22		.34				.45
Sociometric fluency			.27			.31	.26
Sociometric flexibility						.40	
Sociometric originality	.28	.32	.46				
Sociometric inventiveness			.36			.40	.28
Sociometric elaboration					.24	.38	
Sociometric total			.38			.21	.29
Ask fluency			.36				.29
Ask flexibility			.32				.31
Ask originality			.45		−.35		
Causes fluency			.48				.34
Causes flexibility			.36				
Causes originality			.55		−.23		.40
Consequences fluency			.39				.48
Consequences flexibility	.22		.62			.27	.64
Consequences originality			.55	.21			.48
Product impr. fluency			.47				.45
Product impr. flexibility	.21		.34				.37
Product impr. originality			.31				.37
Uses toy dog fluency			.36		.25		.58
Uses toy dog flexibility			.39	.33	.24		.53
Uses toy dog originality			.35	.23			.42
Uses tin cans fluency		.29	.45				.49
Uses tin cans flexibility		.27	.31				.39
Uses tin cans originality			.46	.22			.42
Syntheses of circles			.36	.20			.42
Usual visual perspective			.34	.30			.35

women. In the field of creative writing, figural originality predicts for
men but not for women and figural elaboration predicts for women
but not for men. The same is true for sociometric elaboration. In
science and medicine, only the sociometric predictors work for
women. None of the sociometric predictors work for the men in this
area; however, 24 of the creative thinking ability variables yield
significant correlations for creative achievements in science and
medicine for men. In the field of creative leadership, the sociometric
variables work quite well among the men but not among the women.
Intelligence Quotient and achievement as measured by the Iowa
Tests work quite well among the women but not among the men. The
measures derived from the Ask-and-Guess Activities work rather well

among the men but not among the women; the reverse, however, is true of the measures derived from the unusual uses activities. In visual art, figural originality works positively for men but negatively for women. Figural elaboration, however, works positively among the women but not among the men. In the music area, sociometric originality and sociometric total worked quite well among the men but not among the women.

Peak Creative Achievements

At the grossest level, we may ask whether the young adults identified as highly creative in 1959 report more peak creative achievements than the low creatives. Table 4.5 presents the number and percentage of the highs and lows reporting none, one, two, and three peak or "most creative" achievements. The chi square of 27.37 is significant at the .001 level. Almost twice as many of the high creatives described three peak achievements as did the low creatives. Similarly, three times as many of the low creatives as the high creatives described no peak achievements.

TABLE 4.5

Chi Square Analysis of Number of Peak Experiences Described by Students Identified as High and Low Creatives in 1959

Number Peak	Highs		Lows	
Exp. Described	Number	Percent	Number	Percent
None	12	10.6	48	34.8
1	10	8.9	22	15.9
2	14	12.4	17	12.3
3	77	68.1	51	37.0

Note: Chi square $= 27.36$; $df, = 7$; $p, < .001$

These differences become even more impressive when the nature of the peak creative achievements of the two groups are examined. Many of the achievements described by the low creatives might be described as "cop-out" experiences. For example, one of the men in this group ranked his creative achievements as follows:

1. Dodging the draft.
2. Dropping out of college.
3. Taking LSD.

Some of the high creatives also cited withdrawal kinds of experiences, but they were of a different quality from those typical of the low creatives. The following are examples:

TABLE 4.6
Nature of Most Creative Achievements Reported by Total
Sample by Sex and Creativity Level

Area of Most Creative Achievements	Males		Females		Total	
	Hi.Cr. (N=60)	Lo.Cr. (N=75)	Hi.Cr. (N=53)	Lo.Cr. (N=63)	Hi.Cr. (N=113)	Lo.Cr. (N=138)
Family, children, marriage	5	10	10	23	15	33
Writing (poetry, novels, drama, children's books)	8	3	18	4	26*	7
Educational innovations, materials	6	8	11	3	17	11
Style of teaching, performance of students, etc.	4	1	13	9	17*	10
Visual arts, including crafts	9	9	15	14	24	22
Creative photography, filmmaking	8	6	2	3	10	9
Dissertation, research paper, etc.	10	3	12	2	22*	5
Research publication, new theory, new instrument	7	7	6	3	13	10
Writing (editorial, advertising, etc.)	1	4	8	6	9	10
Music, composition and performance	9	6	6	1	15*	7
Self-discovery, lifestyle, realization of own humanity	3	4	4	7	7	11
Fashion and costume design, etc.	0	0	9	9	9	9
Human relations, organization, leadership	12	4	7	8	19*	12
Construction and arch. design	4	7	3	0	7	7
Medical, surg. disc.	14	1	0	0	14*	1
Civic projects	3	1	5	4	8	5

*Differences significant at .05 level

One of the high creative women "quit working for Merrill, Lynch, Pierce, Fenner & Smith, Inc., not because they were bad but because they were very silly." She is now in Spain, has written three novels, compiled a volume of poetry, and has written and performed songs for the guitar.

Another of the women ranks her most creative achievement as "Helping my husband design and build a home on an inaccessible piece of mountain property." In addition to the three experiences requested, she added, "learning that you can do more things and in a more satisfying manner by breaking with U.S. customs. To travel is to hitchhike with tent and sleeping

bag, home is where you are, and food is not just in small packages and cans."

One of the younger highly creative men ranks as his second
most creative achievement the "planning and construction of
my cabin in northern Minnesota." His top achievement, however, was in the area of his work, "research in enzymology of
human lactate dehydrogenase and development of an electro-
phoretic assay system for quantification from serum." His third
ranked achievement was in the sphere of his hobby, oil painting.

A rather common note in the accounts of the high creative group
is the desire to escape for renewal temporarily from society's "rat
race," but to continue contributing to society in some unique, creative way.

Table 4.6 presents for the high and low creative groups by sex the
frequencies of the more common categories of peak creative achievements. The most striking and statistically significant differences are
for: writing such as poetry, novels, dramas, short stories, etc. (chi
square = 17.50, $df. = 1$, $p. < .01$); medical and surgical discovery (chi
square = 15.04, $df. = 1$; $p. < .01$); dissertation research (chi square
= 16.24; $df. = 1$; $p. < .01$); musical composition (chi square = 5.22;
$df. = 1$; $p. < .05$); human relations and organization (chi square =
3.78; $df. = 1$; $p. < .05$).

Conclusions

From the results that I have cited, it can be concluded that:

1. Young people identified as creative during the high school
    years do tend to become productive, creative adults.
2. At least twelve years after high school graduation appears to
    be a more advantageous time than seven years for a follow-up
    of adult creative achievements.
3. The unusual occupations pressed as choices by highly creative
    high school students tend to become realities.
4. Highly creative high school students tend to develop careers
    which involve detours for relevant but unusual combinations of
    training and/or experience. More of them include study or
    work in a foreign country as a part of their career development
    than do their less creative peers.
5. Creative achievements in writing, science, medicine, and
    leadership are more easily predicted by creativity tests admin-

istered in high school than are creative achievement in music, the visual arts, business, and industry.

6. Young adults identified as highly creative in high school more frequently than their less creative peers attain their peak creative achievements in writing, medical and surgical discovery, dissertation research, musical composition, style of teaching, and human relations and organization. The low creatives tend to report as peak achievements "cop-out" or "drop-out" experiences unaccompanied by constructive action, while many of their more creative peers reported withdrawal experiences either for periods of renewal or for creating a new and more humane life style.

In interpreting the results of this study, it must be remembered that most of these young people have had reasonably good opportunities to achieve their potentialities. It would be unreasonable to expect such positive findings from a disadvantaged population with limited opportunities. However, creative talent among all levels of populations and in other cultures should be studied.

References

Erickson, G. The Predictive Validity of a Battery of Creative Thinking Tests and Peer Nominations among University of Minnesota High School Seniors Seven Years Later. Master's research paper, University of Minnesota, 1966.

Getzels, J. W., and Jackson, P. W. *Creativity and Intelligence.* New York: John Wiley and Sons, 1962.

Torrance, E. P. *Torrance Tests of Creative Thinking: Norms-Technical Manual.* Research ed. Princeton, N.J.: Personnel Press, 1966.

Torrance, E. P. Prediction of Adult Creative Achievement among High School Seniors, *Gifted Child Quarterly, 13,* 71–81, 1969. (a)

Torrance, E. P. Will Creatively Gifted High School Seniors Behave Creatively Seven Years Later? *TAG Gifted Children Newsletter, 12(1),* 24–31, 1969. (b)

Torrance, E. P. Identity: The Gifted Child's Major Problem. *Gifted Child Quarterly, 15,* 147–155, 1971. (a)

Torrance, E. P. Is Bias Against Job Changing Bias Against Giftedness? *Gifted Child Quarterly, 15,* 244–248, 1971. (b)

5   The Development of the Creative Individual

J. C. GOWAN

Considering the individual differences among one's fellows with regard to most aspects of physique or personality, one is immediately struck with the fact that (a) the variance is real and (b) its magnitude is ordinarily measured in percentages. Henry may be 20 percent taller than Edward, 30 percent heavier than Jack, and 25 percent brighter than Clyde; but he is unlikely to be twice as tall, as heavy, or as bright as anyone else.

Surprisingly enough this situation does not hold in regard to creativity. On any kind of creative scale used (and creative production of adults is as reliable as any), some individuals are found whose creative production exceeds that of their fellows, not by percentages, or even simple magnitudes; but it is more likely ten, fifty, or a hundred times as great. Obviously these fortunately creative persons are not that much different. Something has happened to turn them on. Creativity is a "threshold" variable. The nature of what that "something" is—the analysis of that threshold—is the task of this paper.

Development as a Parameter With Discrete Levels

We have been accustomed to thinking of development as if it behaved like growth—a smooth progression on an old-fashioned S-curve. But newer research suggests that this is not so; that instead, development is like a Fourier series, or a flight of locks, namely a staircase-like parameter of hierarchical nature with discrete levels. Now a parameter is a variable which takes on only a relatively small number of values, roughly spaced equally apart. Let us see how this model fits developmental process.

Stated in other words, our task is to determine the nature and direction of developmental change. But this change involves more than mere growth, for development is to growth as quality is to quantity. The apple enlarges, but it also ripens. We see this transformation clearly in the changes wrought by sexual maturation, but there are several other examples of development change, each important in forming the adult individual.

Lewin left our discipline a valuable tradition in borrowing so freely

---

From *The Gifted Child Quarterly* 15:3 (1971). Used by permission.
Paper presented at 18th Annual Meetings of the National Association for Gifted Children, May 3–5, 1971, Regency Hyatt House, Chicago.

from the models of physical science. In understanding the principles of energy transformations, it may be useful to follow his lead and to consider an analogous situation from physics involving latent heat. Assume that we have one gram of water at $-100°$ C. We add 100 calories and heat it to $0°$ C, but it does not unfreeze from its icy form. To change it to water will take 80 more calories, which is known as the latent heat of fusion. The 80 calories are applied and we now have water at $0°$ C. One hundred more calories are applied, and the water now heats to $100°$ C, but it does not become steam. To effect that, 540 more calories must be applied to change water from the liquid to the gaseous state. We apply 540 more calories and our water now vaporizes. In raising the ice from $-100°$ C to steam at $100°$ C, we have applied 200 calories to change temperature and 620 calories to change the state or form of the material, an amount over three times as large.

Why has three times as much energy been required to change state as to make an obvious change in temperature? The answer must lie in the added properties of the liquid and gaseous forms as contrasted with the solid. The binding of this energy results in a more complex formation and, hence, in such emergent properties of water as surface tension and solvency and kinetic energy in steam.

Our analogy suggests that developmental stages similarly bind energy which results in emergent properties. They are not mere vague areas on a smooth growth curve which shade into one another; they are as well defined and discrete as different levels of water in a flight of locks. Energy has been transformed and bound to escalate the developmental process from one level to another—just as energy is necessary to lift a canal boat in a lock—and this bound energy permits the more complex expressions, formations and emergent properties of the new stage. In short, older stages have been reorganized and reintegrated into the new form which has new emphasis and new characteristics. Their basic patterns have been superseded with new organization; it is not so much that their old order has been lost as that a new order has been emphasized. The same situation prevails in music when a theme originally played on a single orchestral instrument is *developed* so that it is now heard on a choir of different instruments in a more complex form. The theme is not lost, but it is changed through elaboration and varying emphases and sequences.

But why should there be developmental stages at all? Why cannot development, like growth, be one smooth accretion? The answer seems to lie in the critical aspect of energy transformations, within the individual, at least in the opinion of several noted theorists. According to Erikson (Evans, 1967, p. 13), Freud's original formulation of sexual developmental stages was based on "the imagery of a transformation of energy." Sullivan (1953) based his theory of self-group interaction of "dynamisms" which he defined as "the relatively enduring patterns of energy transformations, which recurrently characterize interpersonal relations." And Arieti (1967, p. 334) notes that the primary process is not so much regression in the service of the ego but "an energy accessibility and availability."

The transformation and focusing of energy is the essence of both the developmental and the creative process. It is first necessary to focus energy through attention because the amount of energy available to the individual is not enough unless it is collected and not allowed to diffuse. Through the attention of the mind, this energy is focused so that it may be transformed and induce a change of state. The areas on which attention is focused are respectively first one then another of the tripartite modes of "the world," "I" and "thou." Otherwise the available energy would be weakened and diffused if expended upon all at the same time. The analog of an automobile battery supplying a high voltage spark to the different pistons in succession comes at once to mind. This sequential aspect of focusing suggests itself at once as the reason for periodicity in developmental stage theory.

Periodic Aspects of the Theory of Developmental Stages

It is surprising how few researchers or theorists have considered periodicity as a function of human development, despite the ample opportunity for its observation both in the natural elements (the Mendeleev periodic table) and in human biology (the menstrual cycle in women). Periodicity occurs when the same pattern of events is seen to run through a higher development as has been contained in a corresponding pattern from a lower sequence. Mathematically, $1 - n$ isomorphisms are discovered due to the influence of two overriding independent variables. In the periodic table of the elements, these are the numbers of electrons in the shells and the number of protons in the nucleus. Awareness of these variables helps us to fill spaces in such a model and hence to make predictions and draw conclusions and extrapolations. This must be done with caution because, while nature is generally orderly, it may provide some surprises since the world of experience is often more complex than man's anthropomorphic view of it. Even the periodic table reveals this in its divagations among the rare earths. While being aware of the possibility of periodicity in human development, which would point to underlying variables, attempts should not be made to fit the theory of developmental process into a Procrustean bed. Thus it is possible to speculate that since Freud's five affective developmental stages fit rather neatly the chronological ages of Piaget's five cognitive stages, and since Erikson has built four more stages out of the last Freudian (genital) stage, some future theorist may find four associated cognitive stages in adulthood—it is possible, but we should not be unhappy if it does not quite match.

The goodness of fit of the Freudian (sexual libido), Eriksonian (ego-strength) and Piaget (cognitive development) theories to developmental stages is remarkable, however. When these various views are brought together synoptically, one begins to sense periodic rhythms which reveal that the whole conceptualization of developmental stage theory is more significant than has been heretofore realized. Indeed, these stages may be divided into a tripartite grouping depending upon the direction of the attention of the psyche, whether outward toward the world, inward toward the self, or with love toward another person.

Figure 5.1 clearly shows the periodic nature of developmental stages, consisting of triads of stages of infancy, youth, and adulthood. The horizontal triads consist in reality of three categories: the world, the ego, and the other, with the third personal pronoun (it, they) characteristic of the first stage, the first personal pronoun (I) characteristic of the second, and the second personal pronoun (thou) of the third. We have dubbed the columns "latency," "identity" and "creativity," respectively, and indicated the Eriksonian and Piagetian names for the stages—taking the liberty of filling in some guesses for the cognitive aspects of the latter three stages. Thus the diagram becomes an open-ended periodic table of developmental stages which may be used as a model for testing and hypothesis making in regard to developmental process.

Each stage has a special relationship and affinity for another three stages removed from it. Stages one, four, and seven (trust, industry, and generativity) are noticeable for a peculiarly thing-oriented, sexually latent aspect dealing with the relationship of the individual with his world of experience. In stage one it is the world of percepts; in stage four, the size, shape, form, and color of things and what one can make out of them; in stage seven, the world of significant others (such as children) who are not love objects in a libidinal sense. This may also broaden to the world of ideas, formulas, productions, art creations, and other "mental children." Freud, by naming the fourth stage, "latency," intuitively grasped the thing-oriented, nonaffectively valent nature of this stage and its columnar family. The drop in sexual interest as the child "cools" it through the oedipal resolution entering stage four is particularly noticeable. He literally stops trying to "make people" in favor of making things. Not so easily spotted— because often adults have difficulty in entering the generativity period—is the sexual abatement in favor or nurturance of children or

ATTENTIONAL MODES → DEVELOPMENTAL LEVELS ↓		LATENCY 3. it, they THE WORLD	IDENTITY 1. I, me THE EGO	CREATIVITY 2. thou THE OTHER	
INFANT	ERIKSON (Affective)	TRUST vs. MISTRUST ①	AUTONOMY vs. SHAME & DOUBT ②	INITIATIVE vs. GUILT ③	
	PIAGET (Cognitive)	SENSORIMOTOR vs. CHAOS	PREOPERATIONAL vs. AUTISM	INTUITIVE vs. IMMOBILIZATION	
YOUTH	ERIKSON (Affective)	INDUSTRY vs. INFERIORITY ④	IDENTITY vs. ROLE DIFFUSION ⑤	INTIMACY vs. ISOLATION ⑥	
	PIAGET-GOWAN (Cognitive)	CONCRETE OPERATIONS vs. NONCONSERVATION	FORMAL OPERATIONS vs. DEMENTIA PRAECOX	CREATIVITY vs. AUTHORITARIANISM	
ADULT	ERIKSON (Affective)	GENERATIVITY vs. STAGNATION ⑦	EGO-INTEGRITY vs. DESPAIR ⑧		
	GOWAN (Cognitive)	PSYCHEDELIA vs. CONVENTIONALISM	ILLUMINATION vs. SENILE DEPRESSION		

FIGURE 5.1
The Erikson-Piaget-Gowan Periodic Developmental Stage Chart

sublimation to create some innovative production which occurs with parenthood or mastery of some medium. It is as if the "name of the game" changes so that the primary attention is focused off libidinal drives to other more thing-oriented objects.

A second common aspect of the first, fourth, and seventh stages is the immersion in the world of the senses. It is a practical time when things get done and changes occur. In combination with this regard for the external world, there is a certain calmness or coolness of the ego which results in a lack of self-consciousness. The infant, the boy, and the parent are so busy with their activities, so completely absorbed in experiencing, that they have little time to assess their feelings or to search for their identity. After the tasks of this stage are completed, they will return to a new identity search on more advanced levels, fortified with their accomplishments in the real world.

By contrast with the previous, the second, fifth, and eighth stages are ego bound, ego oriented, and ego circumscribed. They are all about "me" (my identity, my existence and interpersonal relationships, and my salvation). They are times of searching introspection, of withdrawal rather than return, of defiance of authority, rather than obedience to it, and of "marching to the music of a different drum." In each of these periods man tries to come to terms with himself. In stage two he finds his identity or ego, in stage five he redefines it in terms of what he can do as a young adult, and in stage eight he again redefines it in terms of the meaning of his life and death in the cosmos.

Parents and society often find those involved in this set of stages rather difficult to live with. Whether it is the infant's negativism, the adolescent's clamor for independence, or the budding saint's march to the sea to make salt, the attitude and action of the individual is frequently anathema to authority figures, be it active resistance or passive disdain.

For the individual in these times of withdrawal, it is very easy to believe that no one understands us, that we are somehow different, unique, and incongruent with the rest of humanity. We often spend too many hours in self-examination, either in reproach or adulation with "the world forgotten and by the world forgot." If the world is "too much with us" in stages one, four and seven, it is too little with us ofttimes in stages two, five, and eight, for we are busy examining our own navels. One consequence of this overemphasis on introspection is a kind of moodiness which results from the discrepancy between what the ego wants itself to be and what it finds it can be and do.

Stages three and six (initiative and intimacy) deal with the love relationship and its expansion from narcissistic self-love through oedipal love of parents, to generalized heterosexual love, to fixation on some individual person. (For all we know there may exist stage nine, where agape love, in the manner of a Buddha or Messiah, embraces all mankind.) Since love is requisite for creation on a mental as well as a physical plane, it is not surprising that stages three and six have special interest for us as students of creativity. Creativity first develops in the initiative stage from the control over the environment experienced through the affectional approach of the opposite-sexed ˙parent. A similar feeling occurs in the sixth stage (intimacy), when adolescent creativity is normally enhanced through the inspiration of the opposite-sexed beloved figure. In the latter instance, however, biological consummation can in some cases reduce the high energy potential aroused so that it is more often when this consummation is delayed, or prevented at least in part, that we get great art, music, and literature. Obviously this kind of situation differs with different individuals, some of whom (like Elizabeth Barrett Browning) find fulfillment in love and block in the frustration of it.

To Become More Creative, More Love Is Needed

In consequence of the connection between love in our lives and creativity, if we want to become creative, we should put more love into our lives. Most of us live on a starvation diet so far as love is concerned. What man could not create if he were universally admired, valued, and inspired? This principle is not to imply that sexual freedom or promiscuity is a prerequisite for creative action, but it does suggest that more openness and demonstrativeness in love and affection in all our social relationships, more awareness of our feeling aspects and less inhibition of them, might open up doors now closed by custom.

Barron (1963) reports that creative persons find other ways to deal with impulse than suppressing it. Who has not found inspiration in the unexpected valuing of himself by another? Indeed, this phenomenon and the power release that accompanies it is one of the great sources of energy in group therapy sessions or in Rogerian basic encounter groups.

In saying that stages three and six are those in which the I-thou relationships and creativity are particularly emphasized, we do not mean to imply that creativity is completely absent at other stages of development. It is just that the developmental process naturally emphasizes these factors at these times. Love and hence creativity may enter our lives environmentally at any time, and to the degree that one is found in abundance the other is likely to be present. In these instances, something personal has occurred—some vivid experience or significant relationship not predicated in the developmental sequence—and it is this personal good fortune, rather than the developmental syndrome, which has released creative power.

If latency stages one, four, and seven may be described as "cool" and the identity stages of two, five, and eight are introspective, then stages three and six may best be characterized as loving, spontaneous, and joyful. Here affectional impulses are at their height; here one gives the identity one has just discovered to another; here the world and the self become fused in the wonder of the beloved—the up phase when all goes well and one is comfortable and sure of one's beloved results in great happiness. But when one is alone, and things are scary, without one's beloved (who may be paying too much attention to a younger sibling or a rival lover), then one is consumed with jealousy and lives in the depths of despair.

The key question of both the third and sixth stages is, "Am I in control of my environment through the aegis of my beloved or is my environment in control of me?" Developmental tasks of different periods have a different flavor, however, even if they refer to the same basic issue. The possessive jealous oedipal love of a son for his mother in the third stage is different from the heterosexual genital intimacy of a young man in the sixth stage. Both of these stages give creativity an extra impetus, but the two kinds of creativity have different flavors and characteristics. This fact has led many researchers to note that the child's creativity is not the same as the creative production of young adults. The creativity of the third (initiative) stage is exhibitionistic, dramatic, often repetitive, and generally fragmentary. The creativity of a young adult is characterized by more unity, coherence, daring, and brilliance. It is truly novel, and often displays scope, mastery, and vigor. Whether the one develops into the other depends, of course, on environmental conditions. A good start helps the growing child to a more open style of life. Environmental deprivation, however, may force him to become destructive or hostile or fall by the wayside. Even too much success in the initiative period may give his creativity a "kooky" turn which does not allow him to integrate it into future development or come to grips with the disciplinary skills of the industry period.

Another youth may blossom in late adolescence without the benefits of narcissistic creativity because, having learned his basic skills and formal operations well, he has somehow been able to break through into the creative ground. Longitudinal research may eventually show that form prevails in general and that a good start in the third stage is the best assurance of another successful round in the sixth stage. Incidentally, this kind of longitudinal follow-up is badly needed research. One becomes creative as a by-product of the inspiration of the beloved. One strives to please, and in pleasing the loved one, pulls things out of the preconscious that one hardly knew were there. Or alternatively, because one's mental health is improved, one finds the preconscious teeming with treasure to share with the beloved, and these goodies often bubble forth without conscious effort.

Whatever has potential for creativity has potential for destructivity also. Vishnu and Shiva are but different aspects of Brahma. We do not find it surprising that the young child creates and destroys practically in the same breath. For some reason, however, we are surprised that university students, deep in the intimacy period, who are denied their creative outlets through stereotyped teaching of obsolete curriculum and authoritarianism, turn to destructiveness in trying to express themselves. Our Puritan ethic of inhibition is also offended when the same youth demonstrate the more undiscriminating and public forms of love and affection. Perhaps we would be better to ask if there is a message for us in this unacceptable behavior and to consider what we might do to make higher education more innovative and more humane.

Oedipal Origins: Magic Nightmare or Creative Fantasy

While the individual of enough mental health should be creative at all ages and stages, we find in reality that creativity is expressed in stage spurts. The genesis of creativity lies in the third stage (initiative-intuitive period) when the child is drawn oedipally to the parent of the opposite sex. He may be plunged into a creative fantasy conceptualization of his world, through which with parental help and love he gains some control over the new forces in his environment, or he may experience a magic nightmare without parental help when the environment controls him, and he is powerless.

The creative fantasy is apparent when an able and healthy child in the third stage receives the full affectional approach of the opposite sexed parent. Creative individuals, hence, tend to have oedipal and electral complexes. Boys who are affectionally close to their mothers and girls who are unusually close to their fathers during the years from four to seven tend to become more creative than others of similar ability. The child in this period responds to the warm affection of the opposite sexed parent by freely enlarging the bridge between his fantasy life and his real world. The affectionate adult who values the child's ideas stimulates and encourages the child to produce ideas and show off intellectually. The emotional support encourages the child to draw freely from past experiences, and to retrieve half-forgotten ideas from the preconscious. Thus he becomes able to dip further into this area and come up with more creative ideas than another child whose efforts in this direction might be inhibited by his parent's disapproval or negative judgments.

The child's successes in winning the affection from the opposite sexed parent gives some semblance of reality to the oedipal fantasies of this period. The bridge between fantasy and reality becomes strengthened while at the same time the child feels "in control," and he grows in the power to discriminate between what is and what is longed for. This control is perhaps what Kris meant by "regression in the service of the ego." This kind of creativity is exhibitionistic, with intrusive, phallic qualities characteristic of the stage. Because more boys are close to their mothers during this period than there are girls close to their fathers, may be one explanation why there later are more creative men than women in the world of adults.

At this time the child discovers his individuality in a world of powerful and forbidding adults. He recognizes his wants and impulses, and senses the strength of his will which can be satisfied either through action or fantasy. Each may lead to pleasure or pain, to joy or guilt, and to growing power and success or to helpless immobilization. For the child this period can be a creative fantasy or a magic nightmare, on the one hand a full expression of the Sullivanian "good-me" and on the other a frightening experience of the "not-me," depending upon the degree of control he can exert as compared with the controls exerted upon him by the significant adults in his life.

Some of the best-loved and most enduring fairy tales in the world center around this theme of a child imprisoned in a magic kingdom, surrounded by powerful good and evil personifications, who later prove to be impotent. In *Alice in Wonderland, Through the Looking Glass,* and *The Wizard of Oz* a powerful like-sexed figure (The Queen of Hearts, The Red Queen, and the Wicked Witch of the West) attempts the immobilization of the child protagonist. After a series of scary adventures aided by weak, male, nonhuman models (The White Rabbit, The White Knight, and Dorothy's three companions) the child triumphs over and reveals the actual impotence of the magical figure. Alice says: "You're nothing but a pack of cards" and herself becomes a queen; Dorothy discovers that even the kindly wizard of Oz is a fake and gets back to Kansas on her own. This discovery that adults do not actually have the magic powers ascribed to them by the child signals the transformation from the magic nightmare of the third stage to the work-a-day world of the industry stage.

Stabilizing the Creative Function

During the third developmental stage (initiative period) some very significant processes occur within the developing child, as he is confronted with the following tasks:

1. The child learns whether to cope or defend (Bruner).
2. The child learns the symbolic representation of experience (Bruner).
3. The child moves along the (Rank) continuum from adapted to creative.
4. The child "establishes his preconscious" (Kubie) and learns to operate the creativity cycle.

Let us discuss these in turn.

The Child Learns Whether to Cope or Defend

If you were a knight in a country where there were fire-breathing dragons you would have two choices. One would be to remain within your castle walls, and defend against the dragons by making the moat deeper and the battlements higher. You could imagine worse and worse dragons until one finally came to get you. On the other hand you might decide to face the danger and go down fighting. Then you would practice up on jousting, get the best horse, sword, and coat of mail (and asbestos) you could find, and one fine morning ride across the moat prepared to do battle.

And if you survived you would probably find out that the dragons were not as bad as they had been rumored to be. This is coping.

The writer once talked with a gifted boy about seven who said he had 35 ways of going home from school so he would not be beaten up by other little boys. When asked how many times he had been beaten up he said, "Never," but that was because he had 35 different ways of going home from school. Here was a child so busy defending against imaginary dangers he had little time to cope with the real world.

He Learns the Symbolic Representation of Experience

Bruner (1966) tells us that at about stage three children are going through the enactive, iconic, and eventually symbolic representation of experience. Through reaching symbolic representation a child can make his experience intellectually negotiable, that is, he can describe and communicate it. With this comes the satisfaction of what Sullivan calls "consensual validation": one can have the relief of finding out that one's experience is not unique and uncanny (part of Sullivan's "not-me") but common to others, and hence may be incorporated without fear into the "me." This reassurance enables the child to continue learning because he feels enough ego-strength to cope with and reach out for new experience, rather than to withdraw with fear and defend against imaginary dangers.

The symbolic representation of experience is a big feat for any child, since it frees him from much of the "nightmare" trauma which precedes consensual validation, but it is even a more important achievement for the gifted child, since it involves him in creative fantasy. More exactly, the early mastery of this task while he is still in the third stage (initiative-intuitive period) exposes him to the creative possibilities of his preconscious while he has gained the ability to communicate them verbally.

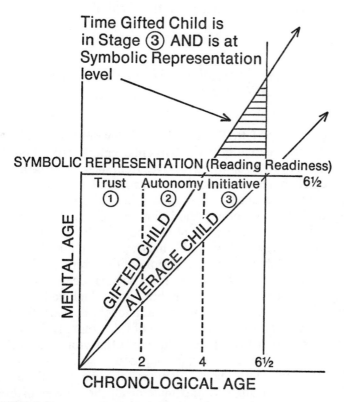

FIGURE 5.2
Diagram Showing Why Gifted Child Is
More Likely to be Verbally Creative

Our argument is better represented graphically than otherwise. In the accompanying diagram (Figure 5.2), let the lower horizontal line represent chronological age, and the left vertical mental age. The first three stages are marked off vertically, and the upper horizontal

represents the mental level of symbolic representation, roughly reading readiness, reached for the average child at six and a half years of
age approximately. The lower diagonal line represents the growth of
the average child which intersects at six and a half MA and CA. The
upper diagonal represents the growth of the superior child, progress-
ing at a sharper slope and reaching the level of symbolic representation for a considerable space while still in the initiative period. Thus
this child is able to produce and communicate verbal concepts at a
time when he is still highly influenced by fantasy, which gives its
special enhancement to his developing verbal creativity. Since IQ is
a rough measure of the slope of the diagonal, the minimum slope to
get much of this benefit is about 1.2, which may be the reason why
verbal creativity seems to demand a threshold of about 120 IQ (1.2
$\times$ 100).

The Child Moves Somewhere Along the Continuum From Adapted to Creative

The psychoanalyst Otto Rank held useful views regarding adapted,
conflicted, and creative growth. The child enters stage three (the
initiative period) with some ego reserves from stage two (the autonomy period). He has learned that he is not part of his mother and that
he can on occasion successfully oppose her. The will, primitively
developed in the autonomy period, flowers fully in the next stage
when the child becomes master of his body and finds it a source of
never-ending energy. This period brings a thrusting initiative which
carries the child into multiple dimensions of discovery. In the previous stage, his occasional failures to meet societal demands (such as
toileting) was a vice, for it was something over which he had little if
any control. Doubt and shame were bad enough. But now the child
discovers that in this wonderful Garden of Eden there is the serpent
of sin, engendered by his will when he makes the wrong choice. This
discovery invests choice making (as opposed to strict obedience to
parental demands) with special dangers—the danger of fear and
guilt, the danger of anxiety, and most of all the danger of being
immobilized and not being cherished—the Sullivanian "bad-me."
    The joy and sheer delight which the child finds in all kinds of new
and creative discoveries is now balanced by the remorse, guilt, and
anxiety which is brought home to him by punishment for some of
these forbidden efforts. ("You must not touch or take this; you must
not say that; you must not do the other thing.") Thus the development
of initiative brings joy and satisfaction on one side and guilt and
immobilization on the other.

The child who is too thoroughly frightened by his mistakes and by parental prohibitions at this stage will give up; he may decide it is best to be completely docile and not risk any painful consequences. In time he will learn to conform automatically, not even for expedience, and this guilt-induced immobilization or conformity will later be extended from judgmental parents to a prescriptive school, to a religious creed and an authoritarian society. In later life this man, conscientious but pathetic, will write poignantly in his memoirs, as did the late George Apley, "You can't escape Boston."

Many children are stronger than this and persist in reaching out to find values and experiences other than those sanctioned by parents. Those who fight alone or with minimum adult support feel very "conflicted," to use Rank's phrase. Eternally obsessed with guilt feelings, they develop neurotic tendencies always to fight or flee. And while the neurosis is positive in that it shows the fight is still going on, it is fatal or nearly so for the creative impulse. For the energy which should go into productivity goes instead into waging the war within or fighting "The Inner Conflict," and this is indeed what Kubie (1958) means by *The Neurotic Distortion of the Creative Process*.

Finally there is the lucky creative child who somehow wins through neurotic involvement to find most of his creative potential intact. This may be due to the affectional support of the opposite sexed parent, whose warmth puts a higher valence on creative activities, and enables the child to uncover and make available his preconscious areas within the ego's reach. The close relationship also blunts the threat of parental prohibition and convinces the child that fewer things are denied and that more things are possible and permitted.

The fantasy of this period which seems to remain in the preconscious of the average child is brought more to reality by the bright child. Whereas through fear and repression of the experience as a magic nightmare, many children seem to have almost aborted this stage of development, the creative child seems able to bring more of this experience from the "not-me" area to the "good-me" area. He almost seems to have overstayed his leave in this kingdom, and its door to fantasy is always left slightly ajar. The loving parent has provided a wide and safe platform for consensual validation. When the child reports having seen a fire-breathing dragon, for instance, the mother does not scold him for telling a lie, but asks playfully "What color was it?" As with the trauma of birth, very few children come through these stages completely unscathed. And so the creative youngster is apt to retain a superabundance of joy, activity, and discovery, only to pay for this outburst of energy by a cyclic slack time characterized by guilt, resentment, or immobilization. Thus parental reactions during the third stage of initiative have helped mold

the child into one of the types described by Rank as adapted, conflicted, or creative.

He Establishes the Preconscious and Learns to Operate the Creativity Cycle

The mechanism of growth toward new conceptualization or of any
creative reorganization involves the release of the present conceptualization followed by a fluid state, out of which arises a new and
higher organization. An old concept that is too restricted to accommodate new experiences must be adjusted much as one would slip
out of a tight pair of shoes, wander around in the grass for awhile in
one's bare feet, and then get into a new and larger pair. Psychologically, relaxation of the cognitive structure apparatus occurs through
the procedure of free play which somehow disengages the too tightly
bound concept and hands the whole business to the preconscious.
The preconscious in some manner reorganizes the construct and
enlarges it, and under suitable conditions leaks the salient aspects of
the reorganization back to the conscious mind. The psychotherapy
slogan "Unfreeze, change, and refreeze" applies here. Free play
unfreezes the concept and makes it fluid. The preconscious changes
it, and the new concept is again refrozen into the cognitive structure.
Let us investigate this critical process in some detail.

Piaget (1951:147-50) states "The underlying structure of play is
constituted by a certain reorientation of the ego to reality." Sadler
(1969), in advocating play as a pathway to personal freedom and
creativity, equates play with creative perception. He notes that Piaget sees play primarily as a function of assimilation. Kubie (1958:56)
remarks on the application of free association to creativity:

> In psychological affairs, free associations are our Gallup poll
> —they sample what is going on in the mind. Consequently
> creativity itself depends upon the process of free association
> which makes possible preconscious analogic processes yet at
> the same time exposes them to deformation under the influence
> of concurrent unconscious processes.

Sadler (1969), in investigating playful perception, notes the relationship of focal attention to the development of a healthy creative personality. He says:

> It is also a perceptual mode that pertains to play. The creative
> edge of perception whereby we remain open and sensitive to
> new meanings and increasing awareness of life possibilities
> originates in and is sustained through play....

Play reveals itself as a basic existential form to keep one's world open not defensively but creatively.

Getzels and Jackson (1962:99) refer to this sense of playfulness in their subjects as follows:

It is almost as if the creative adolescents experience a special delight in playful intellectual activity for its own sake. They involve themselves in the game-like task ... seemingly because of the intrinsic pleasure that accompanies their use of fantasy.

The importance of play as an avenue to the preconscious is seen in that Koestler (1964) devotes a whole chapter to "Playing and Pretending" in *The Act of Creation*. Kubie (1958:39) tells us that the free play of preconscious process simultaneously accomplishes two goals:

1. It supplies an endless stream of old data rearranged into new combinations of wholes and fragments on grounds of analogue elements.
2. It exercises a continuous selective influence not only on free associations, but also on the minutiae of every thinking, walking, talking, dreaming and indeed every movement of life.

Lieberman (1967:395) even notes that there are two kinds of play:

The young child's playfulness, and the playfulness outside the play situation shown by the adolescent ....
Both the kindergartner and the adolescent represent important age points for the identification and encouragement of divergent thinking. In the preschool years one might say that spontaneity flows uncensored by the logical operations that mature after eleven.

Lieberman feels that the necessity to toy with ideas and relationships may be one factor separating the two kinds of play. It is remarkable how Lieberman's opinions confirm what has earlier been asserted here about the emphasis on creativity in stages three and six, with two kinds of creative production consequent. Her thesis connects this difference with the difference in play, whereas ours is a somewhat wider view, but it is obvious that play and free association form one concomitant of the "I-thou" relationship out of which the creative process emerges. Lieberman connects playfulness with a sense of humor, a personality correlate often noted in creative persons.

Harold Greenwald (Otto & Mann, 1968:16) explains it well: "Play on the other hand is by its very nature creative. One of the few really outstanding teachers I once had defined art as "concentrated play." In the same article Greenwald quotes Otto as distinguishing seven kinds of play: (1) the spontaneous play of a child, (2) adult play with children, (3) play with animals, (4) play with nature (such as rolling in the grass), (5) primitive play (making mudpies), (6) thrill play (speeding, skiing, or flying), and (7) mastery play (sports). To which we would add (8) sexual play, (9) fantasy play (reveries, day dreams, etc.), (10) mimetic play (in which the same process is repeated or rehearsed), (11) hobbies (stamp collecting), and (12) unconscious play (rubbing coins together in one's pocket as an unconscious outlet for tension).

The common elements here are (1) the exhibition of nonutilitarian energy, (2) in a relaxed or regressed mode, (3) de-emphasizing the cognitive and controlling aspects, and (4) inviting preconscious and unconscious flux. It is not surprising that among the outcomes of play are a restoration of joy and satisfaction, a realigned conceptual stance which has resulted from the freeing and flow of previously anchored concepts, and a residual seepage of reorganized and hence creative ideas from the preconscious into the conscious mind.

This process of regression to the preconscious through free play and daydreaming fantasy apparently gets its start during the third (initiative stage) when the child with an oedipal or electral attachment to the parent of the opposite sex develops this ability to dip into the preconscious to bring back creative ideas. The key factors in this process are first the courage to explore this "nightmare" area with its uncanny "not-me" aspects, and the second the attentional shift through fantasy and free play to garner peripheral concepts from the preconscious. Kubie (1958), in his masterpiece *The Neurotic Distortion of the Creative Process*, first stressed the importance of this preconscious function in creative production. He states that preconscious processes are attacked by both superego and ego prohibitions and by unconscious drives. Somehow the preconscious has to grow healthy enough to ward off these attacks and still fulfill its capacity to select and rearrange the data of experience into creative and innovative forms. Kubie believes that the preconscious part of the psyche is the major source of man's creative abilities.

By "establishing the preconscious" we mean the practice of making preconscious experience easily available to the reach of the ego, and of bolstering the preconscious (through use) against the attacks of the other aspects of the psyche. The child through exercising his fantasy to please his mother learns implicitly the rules of relaxation, free association, and play which are requisite for him to gain access into his shadowed area.

With much repression the psyche involves a weak preconscious, barricaded from assaults from either side, and a large area of unconscious motivation, unavailable to conscious use. Little of past experience is available in adaptive behavior. With freedom from threat and supportive parental relations, the preconscious is enlarged at the expense of the unconscious; consequently much more of past experience becomes available for ego use.

Various writers have described the tripartite compartments of the psyche similarly. Freud used three terms: unconscious, preconscious, and conscious, and others used similar tripolar divisions. Thus Sullivan (1963:161) describes similar functions as "bad-me," "not-me" and "good-me." "Bad-me" is more conscious than Freud's construct, but organized as a process variable around increasing anxiety; whereas "not-me" designates frightening, uncanny experiences such as those encountered in dreams, nightmares, and dissociated behavior. "Good-me" is of course a part of conscious positive self-concept.

Such a view immediately suggests that the preconscious is the source of man's creativity, particularly when it is strengthened, protected, and enlarged through regular use and through increasing mental health. The "establishment" of the preconscious is evidence that the individual is not at war with himself, not alienated from experience, not a split personality. He can be creative because almost all his past experiences, in chewed up and digested form, ready to be reattached to new concepts, are available to his preconscious collator. It has at its disposal a vast assortment of biological impulses, tabooed acts, rejected compromises, affective pains and pleasures, remembered facts, personal feelings, horrifying nightmares, and a host of other material, none of which has been suppressed, but all of which can be reused (much like old newspapers) to print a new edition. What is in the new edition depends on how much freedom the editor (preconscious) has from the incursions of the conscious and unconscious.

The essence of process both towards greater mental health and greater creativity lies in the strengthening and developing of the preconscious so that it enlarges to assume a bigger and more important share in the tripartite membership of the individual psyche. This aggrandizement signals improved mental health and progress toward self-actualization, of which creative performance is an early indication. McLuhan and the Existentialists both emphasize a better balance between rational and pararational aspects of the psyche, and perhaps in this insistence they are merely restating the thesis which has just been illustrated here.

A good deal of space has been devoted to a full explanation of the function of play and oedipal retrieval through free association and fantasy to "establish the preconscious" as a healthy, working, viable member of the psyche, able to protect its boundary, and more easily available to the use of the ego. But it now must be emphasized that this is the beginning, not the end, of a developing creative life style which will escalate in future stages and gain new repertoires and techniques. The child will learn, for example, implicitly to honor the Wallas stages of preparation, incubation, illumination, and verification, and not to abort them or hurry them. He will also discover that the process of creative production is a cycle in which the positive amplitude is creativity, and the nonproductive part of the cycle need not result in negative or destructive reactions to self or others, but should be used for rest and relaxation. But the beginnings in "establishing the preconscious" are crucial. Kubie (1958:143) sums it up: "Creativity is a product of preconscious activity. This is the challenge which confronts educators of the future."

Creativity as Evolutionary Development: Throwbacks and Throw-Forwardings

Creativity is a characteristic not only of individual human behavior, but also of the species in general. What is true of the development of the superior individual is also true of the developing aspects of man generically. The emergence of creative abilities is not only a triumph of individual development but, as Bucke (1923) points out, the harbinger of evolutionary progress for all mankind. Astronaut Armstrong echoed these ideas when he first stepped onto the moon: "This is a small step for man; a giant step for mankind."

In the grand progression of evolutionary life, each man has a small degree of freedom, for he can choose within limits to ride in the van or to bring up the rear. The atavist in society is a throwback to former days, a reconceptualization of the past. The creative man, by contrast, is an earnest of the future, a throw-forward to a better humanity. He constitutes an implicit and intuitive statement of powers yet to be fully apprehended by the race. That his clutch on these powers is sometimes weak and spasmodic should not bother us, for it was Browning who said: "A man's reach should exceed his grasp, else what's a heaven for?"

The sense of destiny, of being caught up in process towards the future, a quality exhibited by many creative or self-actualized people, is part of an existential act of becoming in which one is thrown forward into the living actualization of one's potentialities. One becomes in flux like the electron in orbit, having energy and momentum, but not position or fixity.

The guilt-immobilized, uncreative, reactive individual is transparent and easily recognized. His dress, manner, and attitude betray stress, fixity, and stasis. He is role-typed, not versatile, tense not relaxed, uneasy not confident, superstitious not flexible, bound not free, phlegmatic not buoyant, static not dynamic, stolid not energetic, dull not scintillating, dowdy not chic, inhibited not spontaneous, inert not active, self-conscious not selfless, discouraged not happy, and an object of sympathy rather than personally appealing.

Life is more than mere intervals between trips to the toilet; it can be intervals between trips to the stars. Is it more meaningful to regard man as a reactive being or as a creative mind? If man is a reactive being, a mere brute creature imprisoned in a universe for which he has no responsibility, he is much like the steer that grazes the plain, and like the steer he will end up butchered. But if man is a creative mind, he has a part in the noumenon of that creation, and in the alteration of that open-ended universe, and can intervene constructively in his own future and in the future of his species.

Creativity is the process of transforming the horrors and fears of the Sullivanian "not-me" into a productive fantasy in the preconscious mind. There is a magic aura to this transformation in which the critical question is whether the ego is to be controlled and immobilized by this frightening environment (as one is in nightmares), or whether the ego through the help of a powerful parental figure is able to organize this apparent chaos, control these magic elements, and transform them into a creative fantasy, replacing horror with harmony.

Shakespeare illustrates both the process and the product of this metamorphosis in Ariel's song:

> Full fathom five thy father lies
> Of his bones are coral made;
> Those are pearls that were his eyes;
> Nothing of him that doth fade
> But doth suffer a sea change
> Into something rich and strange;
> Sea nymphs hourly ring his knell;
> Hark, I hear them; Ding-Dong, Bell.
>
> —*The Tempest* 1:2

Here Ariel represents the ego, aided by the parental figure of Prospero, the good magician. Out of the substance of a drowned cadaver (surely a most horrible object), there is nothing "but doth suffer a sea change/into something rich and strange." The horror, dread and uncanniness of the "not-me" become muted and transformed into value, approbation, and beauty, and the end result is creative fantasy in its ultimate form.

Conclusion

Piaget once stated that the course of human development is away from egocentricity toward freedom. Every aspect of life shows this upward escalation. For as all life strives upward, each individual life tries, however briefly, to become a god before it becomes an ape. For if man is the foetalization of the ape, differential psychology would point out that the ablest among men represent even more youthful stretchout of the plastic periods. This allows for the full eight stages (and perhaps more) to be included in our life span.

We start by trying to perfect in our developing brain an imperfect isomorphism between the external world and our concepts. If we progress to the end, keeping up environmental stimulation after the biological development has left off, we can become saint-like both cognitively and affectively. The mind first becomes capable of full representation of the external world, then merges with it in experience, finally to become part of the noumenon of that experience and so capable of influencing external events.

These are brave words, but man is a brave species. We may come from dust, but our destiny is in the stars. Thoreau, that rustic seer, closed *Walden* on a similar optimistic note, for speaking of the future of mankind he prophesied: "That day is yet to dawn, for the sun is only a morning star." And old Socrates told us the same thing long ago:

> For if man had this power to contemplate beauty absolute, unfettered and untarnished by all the colors and vanities of human life, dwelling in that blissful realm alone, he would bring forth not images of beauty, but beauty itself, and so would become immortal and become the friend of the Gods.

Bibliography

Arieti, S. *The Intrapsychic Self.* New York: Basic Books, 1967.

Barron, F. *Creativity and Mental Health.* New York: Van Nostrand, 1963.

Bruner, J. *Towards a Theory of Instruction.* Cambridge: Harvard University Press, 1966.

Bucke, R. M. *Cosmic Consciousness.* New York: E. P. Dutton, 1923. (Originally published, 1901.)

Evans, R. I. *Dialog with Erik Erikson.* New York: Harper and Row, 1967.

Getzels, J. W., and Jackson, P. W. *Creativity and Intelligence.* New York: J. Wiley and Sons, 1962.

Koestler, A. *The Act of Creation.* London: Hutchinson, 1964.

Kubie, L. *The Neurotic Distortion of the Creative Process.* Lawrence: University of Kansas Press, 1958.

Lieberman, J. N. "A Developmental Analysis of Playfulness as a Clue to Cognitive Style." *Journal of Creative Behavior* 1:391–397, 1967.

Otto, H. A., and Mann, J. (Eds.). *Ways of Growth: Approaches to Expanding Awareness.* New York: Viking Press, 1968.

Piaget, J. *Play, Dreams and Imitation in Children.* London: Routledge and Kegan Paul, 1951.

Rank, Otto. *Art and the Artist.* New York: Tudor Publishing Co., 1932.

Sadler, W. A. "Creative Existence: Play as a Pathway to Personal Freedom." *Humanitas* 5:57–90, Spring, 1969.

Sullivan, H. S. *The Interpersonal Theory of Psychiatry.* New York: W. W. Norton Co., 1953.

6   The Eminent Genius In History: The Critical Role of Creative Development

DEAN KEITH SIMONTON

Why is it that some periods in history are veritable Golden Ages replete with great creative giants, whereas other historical periods yield a dearth of first-rate minds? Concretely put, what are the historical circumstances responsible for the emergence of a Shakespeare, Michelangelo, Beethoven, or Aristotle? Although a number of classical and recent studies have attempted to address this question (e.g., Gray, 1958, 1966; Kroeber, 1944; Naroll, Benjamin, Fohl, Fried, Hildreth & Schaefer, 1971; Schaefer, Babu, & Rao, Note 1; Sorokin, 1937–1941), these investigations ignore what I consider to be a very critical distinction between two phases of a creator's life. On the one hand, sociocultural events may influence the productive period of a creator's life. For example, warfare may have an adverse impact on a person's creative output at a particular point in his or her career. On the other hand, sociocultural events may affect the developmental period of a creator's life, a possibility having more rich implications for understanding the foundation of creativity. Perhaps a special set of political, cultural, and social conditions is most conducive to the development of creative potential in a youthful genius. In

From *The Gifted Child Quarterly* 22:2 (1978). Used by permission.

adulthood, that creative potential then becomes fully actualized in the form of prolific and significant creative productivity. Thus, it is quite conceivable that the creative genius is either made or broken during childhood, adolescence, and early adulthood. So complete knowledge of the historical forces behind a creative genius requires that productive and developmental period influences be carefully segregated.

In a series of recent investigations I have attempted to discern the consequences of this distinction. One of the most significant findings is that developmental period influences are far more important than productive period influences. In other words, the development of creative potential is often critically affected by external events, whereas creative productivity is virtually immune from such influences. To support this generalization, let me first mention the few productive period influences which have been found, and then turn to the numerous and significant developmental period influences.

Adulthood creativity fails to be affected by a diverse array of possible influences, including personal problems or life changes (Simonton, 1977a), social honors and rewards (Simonton, 1977a), contemporary revolts or rebellions (Simonton, 1975c, 1977a), and cultural persecution (Simonton, 1975c). Moreover, of the three variables which do operate during the productive period, two are not all that surprising. Thus it is hardly astonishing that creative productivity is adversely affected by physical illness (Simonton, 1977a), nor is it utterly novel to show that creative productivity is a curvilinear inverted backwards-J function of the creator's age (Simonton, 1975a; 1977b). The remaining causal factor is war. Although a series of earlier inquiries found no relationship between war and creativity (Naroll et al., 1971; Simonton, 1975c, 1976b, 1976d, 1976e, 1977b), these studies failed to distinguish several kinds of war. When such a distinction is implemented, as I have done very recently, a curious result obtains: Although balance-of-power wars fought close to the creative individual tend to discourage productivity, balance-of-power wars fought far away tend to encourage productivity (Simonton, Note 2). Whatever the substantive interpretation of this difference, the fact remains that war is the only sociocultural event which affects creativity during the productive period.

Influences on Creative Development

Nonetheless, when we survey the relationship between external events and creative development, a diversified list of influences has been found. The following seven are probably the most important:

1. *Formal Education.* In a multivariate analysis of the 301 emi-

nent geniuses studied by Cox (1926), I found that achieved eminence
is partly a function of the amount of formal education (Simonton,
1976a). Significantly, the precise form of this function depends on
whether eminence was achieved as a creator (scientist, philosopher,
writer, artist, or musician) or as a leader (soldier, statesman, revolutionary, or religious leader). For creators, eminence is a curvilinear
inverted-U function of formal education. Thus formal education
tends to increase creativity up to a certain point, after which it has
a negative effect. Clearly some formal education greatly aids the
development of creative potential, but excessive amounts may inhibit creative development by enforcing an overcommitment to traditional perspectives. This finding fits nicely with some previous
research on creative development in contemporary children (e.g.,
Torrance, 1962). Curiously, for leadership the functional relation
between eminence and formal education is strictly negative: The
ultimate achievement of politicians, soldiers, and religious leaders is
inhibited by the kind of training offered by colleges and universities.
Incidentally, it is worth pointing out that the positive correlation
which Cox (1926) found between IQ and eminence is spurious. Even
though her 301 geniuses are much brighter than average—more than
four standard deviations above the mean—the correlation between
IQ and eminence within the sample vanishes when a timewise sampling bias is controlled (see Simonton, 1976a). Naturally, this finding
fits in better with contemporary research suggesting that above an
IQ of around 120, intelligence bears little relationship with creativity.

   2. *Role-Model Availability.* Recent studies have shown that the
number of eminent creators in one generation is largely a function of
the number of eminent creators in the previous generation (Simonton, 1974, 1975c). In other words, the more creative individuals
available for emulation when a genius is in his or her developmental
period, the greater the increase in creative potential. Subsequent
research has indicated that the availability of role models increases
creativity largely through a single intervening variable, namely, creative precociousness (Simonton, 1977b). The greater the number of
adult creators around for possible imitation, the sooner the youthful
genius begins producing creative works. This creative precociousness then leads to enhanced creative productivity and creative longevity, which in turn raise the eventual level of achieved eminence.
Although role-model availability tends to increase creative eminence, two additional research findings indicate the complexity of its
impact. In the first place, and most obviously, the effectiveness of
role models depends on the discipline. Certainly a precocious musical genius is going to be more influenced by those geniuses in the
preceding generation whose achievements are also musical rather

than scientific or literary. Interestingly, when creativity in one discipline does influence creative development in another discipline, the impact is not always beneficial. For instance, there is evidence that the number of religious leaders in one generation has a negative effect on the number of philosophers to emerge in the next generation (Simonton, Note 3). Thus religious activity is not conductive to creative development in philosophy, probably because religious leaders provide "negative role models" of philosophical thinking (cf. Simonton, 1975b, 1976d). The second complication in the relation between role-model availability and creativity is that the former variable can have certain adverse effects as well. For example, even though philosophical creativity is increased if a genius has many philosophers as role models during his or her developmental phase, attainment of the highest ranks as a thinker may be hindered by an excess of role models (Simonton, 1976e). What seems to happen is that a potential genius may make a premature commitment to a particular school of thought, that is, the youth may become a disciple rather than break completely new ground (also see Simonton, 1977b). Hence, even though role-model availability has a generally positive effect on creative development, its impact can be reversed when we consider those creators in the highest of all ranks.

3. *Zeitgeist.* In one study I attempted to determine the relationship between the fame of a given thinker and the prevailing zeitgeist (Simonton, 1976e). Is it the case that the major minds in the history of ideas tend to be ahead of their time? Or is it the case that the major figures in intellectual history tend to be highly representative of their contemporary zeitgeist? A multivariate analysis of 2,012 famous thinkers in Western history revealed a surprising result: The answer to both of these questions is "no"! Rather than epitomize the prevailing beliefs and mores of their generation, and rather than be precursors of the subsequent generation's zeitgeist, the most eminent philosophers tend to be *behind* their times. Unlike the lesser thinker, the major thinker seems to be most influenced by the zeitgeist which dominated the intellectual scene during his or her developmental period. What seems to be happening is that the most famous thinkers are synthesizers who take the accomplishments of the preceding generation and consolidate them into a single, unified philosophical system. Because the most eminent intellects are thus preoccupied with elaborating the ideas to which they were exposed during their developmental period, these thinkers tend to be least representative of their contemporary zeitgeist and of future intellectual trends.

4. *Political Fragmentation.* In a pioneer cross-historical investigation, Naroll et al. (1971) tried to discover what political and economic circumstances are most favorable to creativity in four

civilizations. The one variable found to have a consistent effect was political fragmentation, or the number of independent states into which a civilization is divided in any given century. Unfortunately, Naroll et al. used rather large timewise units, and therefore they could not determine whether political fragmentation acts on creative productivity or on creative development. Nonetheless, I have argued that political fragmentation indicates a large amount of cultural diversity and that cultural diversity tends to nurture the development of creativity (Simonton, 1974, 1975c). Such cultural diversity tends to encourage the capacity for divergent thinking, remote association, breadth of perspective, and related cognitive attributes required for a fully developed creative potential. Although the evidence is not unambiguous (Simonton, 1976c, 1976e), one transhistorical study of 5,000 creators from Western civilization has shown that political fragmentation may indeed more significantly affect creative development than creative productivity (Simonton, 1975c): If the number of sovereign political units increases, the number of eminent creators tends to increase after about a 20-year lag. But political fragmentation apparently does a lot more than encourage creative development, since the philosophical beliefs of eminent thinkers may be influenced by the amount of political fragmentation prevailing in their youth. In a cross-lagged correlation analysis I found that thinkers who grow up in times of political fragmentation are more likely, as adult creators, to espouse empiricism, skepticism, materialism, temporalism (e.g., evolutionary change), nominalism, singularism (viz., individualism), and the ethics of happiness (e.g., hedonism or utilitarianism) (Simonton, 1976f). So not only does political fragmentation tend to heighten creative development, but additionally it tends to shape the content of the creator's intellectual base.

5. *War.* The ideology of the mature thinker is also influenced by the occurrence of warfare during the stage of creative development. In fact, the impact of war on the youthful genius is virtually the opposite from that of political fragmentation. Thinkers whose early years were characterized by constant warfare tend to be *less* likely to advocate empiricism, skepticism, materialism, temporalism, nominalism, singularism, and the ethics of happiness (Simonton, 1976f). Thus while political fragmentation tends to encourage the development of a mind open to experience, change, individualism, and material welfare, war tends to discourage such intellectual qualities.

6. *Civil Disturbances.* Yet a third political variable tends to affect the ideology of the adult creator by influencing the course of creative development. Thinkers whose youth was surrounded by popular revolts, rebellions, and revolutions tend to adopt highly polarized philosophical positions as adults (Simonton, 1976f). On the

one hand, some thinkers exposed to civil turmoil may become extremely committed to the ideas of empiricism, skepticism, materialism, temporalism, nominalism, singularism, determinism, and the ethics of happiness. On the other hand, some thinkers exposed to the same events may become strongly devoted to the ideas of rationalism or mysticism, idealism, eternalism (i.e., unchanging reality), realism (in the medieval sense), universalism (e.g., collectivism or socialism), indeterminism (viz., free will), and the ethics of principles. Even though civil disturbances thus polarize the forthcoming generation in quite contrary directions, the intriguing fact remains that such political events have a truly potent effect on creative development. The exposure to political conflict seems to instill the need to take extreme stances on philosophical issues as well. Given this finding, it is perhaps not surprising that civil disorder also encourages general creative development, as one empirical study has shown (Simonton, 1975c). That is, eminent creators in Western history tend to be most likely to grow up in times of revolts, rebellions, and revolutions, especially those directed against large empire states. Such disturbances seem to heighten cultural diversity in a given civilization (Simonton, 1975c; cf. Simonton, 1976c).

7. *Political Instability.*   So far we have not mentioned any political events which might hinder the development of creative potential in the youthful genius. But imagine, if you will, a political milieu where violent conflict among the ruling elite is the natural order of things, where a coup d'etat by some military figure is commonplace, where political assassinations are the norm, or where strife among rival claimants to the throne is chronic. Such political instability might well prove detrimental to the development of creative potential. And two recent studies have actually shown that political instability, while having no appreciable impact on creative productivity, does damage the prospects for creativity in the forthcoming generation. The first study examined 5,000 eminent creators in Western civilization and discovered that such creators were less likely to grow up in times of political instability (Simonton, 1975c). The second study focused on 2,012 thinkers and revealed that the most famous intellects in Western history tend not to grow up in times of political instability (Simonton, 1976e). Thus, coups d'etat, military revolts, dynastic conflicts, political assassinations, and like internecine struggles among the powers-that-be tend to decrease both the number of creators and the quality of those creators who survive the adverse circumstances. Why? It seems that to be creative requires the belief that the world is somewhat predictable and controllable, and accordingly that personal efforts will eventually prove fruitful, even if only in the long run. In terms of Rotter's (1966) External-Internal dimen-

sion, creative individuals probably must feel they have internal locus of control. When a young genius is exposed to political anarchy, this internalistic disposition may fail to develop. Hence, the ultimate impact of political instability is to destroy the development of creative potential, and thereby undermine the prospects for achievement in adulthood.

Conclusion

It must be stressed that research on the sociocultural context of creative development is a relatively recent enterprise. So future research may add many more influences, including economic and demographic factors. Still, the evidence gathered to date allows us to conclude that sociocultural conditions play a significant part in the development of creative potential in the youthful genius. The following three social-psychological processes are especially central to creative development:

1. The potential genius must have access to numerous role models very early in life. Without such models, the genius may have a lower probability of being precocious, and such precociousness is apparently essential to creative productivity and longevity in adulthood.

2. Exposure to cultural diversity also seems to nourish the precocious youth. Thus, on the one hand, political fragmentation and civil disturbances tend to increase creative potential by injecting an awareness of diverse perspectives, whereas excessive formal education can harm creative potential by placing too much emphasis on a restricted range of solutions to creative problems.

3. The young genius adapts to the political environment by generating a set of philosophical beliefs. Should the genius grow up to become a thinker, these intellectual adaptations will influence his or her philosophical leanings. Even more importantly, certain political events may produce an ideological disposition which proves antithetical to adulthood creativity. This latter possibility may be illustrated by the manner in which political instability inhibits creative development by producing a fatalistic Weltanschauung in the would-be genius.

So, to offer a partial response to the question posed at this paper's outset, the Golden Ages of history may have given the young genius the necessary role models, the cultural diversity, and the philosophical commitment essential to the development of creative potential. This potential was then merely actualized in adulthood without much hindrance or help from external events.

Reference Notes

1. Schaefer, J. M., Babu, M. C., & Rao, N. S. *Sociopolitical causes of creativity in India 500 BC–1800 AD: A regional time-lagged study.* Paper presented at the meeting of the International Studies Association, St. Louis, March 1977.
2. Simonton, D. K. *Techno-scientific activity and war: A yearly time-series analysis.* Manuscript submitted for publication, 1977.
3. Simonton, D. K. *Intergenerational networks among creative disciplines: A cross-lagged correlation analysis.* Unpublished manuscript, University of Arkansas, November 1974.

References

Cox, C. *The early mental traits of three hundred geniuses.* Stanford, Calif.: Stanford University Press, 1926.

Gray, C. E. An analysis of Graeco-Roman development: The epicyclical evolution of Graeco-Roman civilization. *American Anthropologist*, 1958, *60*, 13–31.

Gray, C. E. A measurement of creativity in Western civilization. *American Anthropologist*, 1966, *68*, 1384–1417.

Kroeber, A. L. *Configurations of culture growth.* Berkeley: University of California Press, 1944.

Naroll, R., Benjamin, E. C., Fohl, F. K., Fried, M. J., Hildreth, R. E., & Schaefer, J. M. Creativity: A cross-historical pilot survey. *Journal of Cross-Cultural Psychology*, 1971, *2*, 181–188.

Rotter, J. B. Generalized expectancies for internal versus external control of reinforcement. *Psychological Monographs*, 1966, *80*, (1, Whole No. 609).

Simonton, D. K. *The social psychology of creativity: An archival data analysis.* Unpublished doctoral dissertation, Harvard University, 1974.

Simonton, D. K. Age and literary creativity: A cross-cultural and transhistorical survey. *Journal of Cross-Cultural Psychology*, 1975, *6*, 259–277. (a)

Simonton, D. K. Interdisciplinary creativity over historical time: A correlational analysis of generational fluctuations. *Social Behavior and Personality*, 1975, *3*, 181–188. (b)

Simonton, D. K. Sociocultural context of individual creativity: A transhistorical time-series analysis. *Journal of Personality and Social Psychology*, 1975, *32*, 1119–1133. (c)

Simonton, D. K. Biographical determinants of achieved eminence: A multivariate approach to the Cox data. *Journal of Personality and Social Psychology*, 1976, *33*, 218–226. (a)

Simonton, D. K. The causal relation between war and scientific discovery: An exploratory cross-national analysis. *Journal of Cross-Cultural Psychology*, 1976, *7*, 133–144. (b)

Simonton, D. K. Ideological diversity and creativity: A re-evaluation of a hypothesis. *Social Behavior and Personality,* 1976, *4,* 203–207. (c)

Simonton, D. K. Interdisciplinary and military determinants of scientific productivity: A cross-lagged correlation analysis. *Journal of Vocational Behavior,* 1976, *9,* 53–62. (d)

Simonton, D. K. Philosophical eminence, beliefs, and zeitgeist: An individual-generational analysis. *Journal of Personality and Social Psychology,* 1976, *34,* 630–640. (e)

Simonton, D. K. The sociopolitical context of philosophical beliefs: A transhistorical causal analysis. *Social Forces,* 1976, *54,* 513–523. (f)

Simonton, D. K. Creative productivity, age, and stress: A biographical time-series of 10 classical composers. *Journal of Personality and Social Psychology,* 1977, *35,* 791–804. (a)

Simonton, D. K. Eminence, creativity, and geographic marginality: A recursive structural equation model. *Journal of Personality and Social Psychology,* 1977, *35,* 805–816. (b)

Sorokin, P. A. *Social and cultural dynamics* (4 vols.). New York: American Book, 1937–1941.

Torrance, E. P. *Guiding creative talent.* Englewood Cliffs, N.J.: Prentice-Hall, 1962.

Chapter Three

Program

Introduction

Time was when any chapter such as this would have been given over to a discussion of the relative merits or demerits of acceleration, grouping, and enrichment. After a lot of heated discussion, we found out that acceleration is an easy way research universally favors at any level, but it runs counter to the prejudices of many parents and educators. Grouping may be necessary, but it is not a sufficient procedure; it is what happens in class, not how the class is grouped, that counts. The most effective types of grouping appear to be those based on clearly differentiated levels in a specific skill, such as reading groups. Enrichment is a nice word for a nonexistent practice.

Rather than these shibboleths, it is the innovation in the total program that counts, and this innovation is closely related to costs and funding. The readings to follow have been selected as examples of this approach; here we would like to discuss how such programs can be introduced into the public schools. The key is state legislation, which involves proper funding, a program of teacher training, a state staff of knowledgeable individuals, and demonstration, experimentation, and research centers.

While several states, notably Illinois and California, have pioneered in funding programs for the gifted in public schools, it is Connecticut which has the model legislation, and we acknowledge indebtedness to William Vassar, Connecticut State Consultant for the Gifted, in this description. The Connecticut legislation does not make the error of tying the reimbursement program to a given IQ level; rather it specifies about 3 percent of the most intellectually talented, having extraordinary learning ability in the creative arts, and an additional 3 percent of those talented in other ways, as eligible. The method used to identify may be developed by the school district but must be approved by the state consultant. The legislation is permissive, not mandatory, and reimburses two thirds of the excess cost per pupil without limit. While the program requires prior approval, it does not have to be resubmitted each year. Professional personnel must spend at least one third of their time with the gifted to have their salaries prorated as reimbursable expense, which covers personnel, material, transportation, and consultants. The consultants need not be certified.

No program for the gifted, however, gets far without planning and a budget. The expense connected with a gifted child program varies considerably from district to district where such programs are in operation. Additional financial costs are not necessarily implied. Sometimes additional costs can be absorbed into the regular budget, in such ways as the time of the counselor, the extra use of library or laboratory equipment, or more consumption of supplies. Some provisions, such as enrichment, grouping, or acceleration in certain forms, may not result in any extra cost.

If a program, however, continues beyond the experimental stage and is realistically geared to the special needs of able pupils, special costs are bound to arise. Even enrichment in the heterogeneous classroom leads to released time for teacher preparation; as a matter of fact, when carried out properly, this is one of the more expensive ways of taking care of the gifted, since it involves so much individual attention. By contrast, grouping is a much more efficient way of dealing with gifted children so far as overall cost is concerned. The only method which actually has possibilities of lowering the cost of education is acceleration, because a given child is in school less time. In view of this fact, it is somewhat surprising that acceleration is not more often employed, especially in small districts where cost factors may be critical.

The major costs of a program for gifted children can be broken down into the following categories:

1. Identification, including testing, counseling, etc.
2. Curriculum adjustment, including staffing and materials.
3. Social services, including guidance, administration, transportation, capital outlay, secretarial help, evaluation, reporting, public relations, and the like.

Cost of identification can be high. Some districts have been able to reduce this item in the following way:

1. The regular testing program should be employed as a screen to select children who will be considered further. At least twice as many should be located by the screen as will later be used in the program.
2. Further testing will be required for those pupils who to all appearances should be in the program, but who fail to qualify. Teacher referrals should have weight here.
3. Only in cases of doubt or conflict between methods will the

selectors resort to individual testing, which is expensive and takes considerable time.

4.   Between those who are obviously "in" and those who are certainly "not," there will be a "twilight zone" where multidimensional factors which seem of value to the selectors will operate.

It may be possible to cut corners and save costs in identification, but it is otherwise in providing curriculum adjustments. For it is in this area that the cost of outlay bears the closest relationship to the desired result. Special staffing, equipment, and materials are vital if gifted children are to receive proper enrichment. Though an occasional talented and devoted teacher can sometimes accomplish the next-to-impossible, it is unrealistic to expect that the average classroom teacher can, without extra help or training, successfully enrich curriculum content for the occasional gifted child in a heterogeneous class. Released time and in-service training cost money, as do special coordinators, teacher-consultants, secretaries, psychologists, suppliers, books, and equipment, but it is here that expenditures must be made if results on any scale are expected. The district has to make a value judgment of whether it wants its abler students dependent upon the largess of an occasional intellectual philanthropist, or whether it wishes to secure results for which it is willing to pay.

The special services connected with the program for the gifted are less often spelled out, and in many cases either neglected or else incorporated into the general budget. They are, however, important, and need to be recognized and provided for.

There are a number of factors in individual districts which have important bearing on costs of a program for the gifted. Selectivity of the program comes first. A district selecting 1 percent of its children for such a program will have a more intensive process, involving higher per capita costs, but lower total costs than a district involving 10 percent of its children. Second comes district size. It is generally easier to cut per capita costs in a large district than in a small one. This is especially true when the number of gifted children in the district permits group rather than individual methods to be utilized. Other factors involve the grade level at which curriculum adjustments are conducted, the type of adjustment, teaching personnel, space requirements, use of extra material, and the like. While costs will differ considerably in different parts of the country, and at different times, it is suggested that only a minimum program would set costs as low as $100 per child per year, and that more satisfactory levels of support would be found at the $200–$500 range. These supports were found in a survey of California districts in the late 1950s (Gowan & Winward, 1960). In more general terms, cost per gifted child should be about half to three quarters the cost of educating an exceptional child in the same district.

One aspect of the increased cost of a program for gifted children which needs to be emphasized is the hidden benefits that such costs provide in terms of increased scholastic atmosphere for all children. Better books in the library, better trained and more stimulating teachers, renewed interest in art and science cannot be confined to a small group, but radiate outwards to all members of the school in some measure. Teachers who come to assess more clearly individual differences among gifted children soon begin to assess individual differences among all children, and special talents and aptitudes perhaps less than gifted but still worthy of cultivation may be unearthed. Library and laboratory materials of the latest manufacture have a way of attracting many more than just the highly verbal members of the class. For this reason, bringing enrichment materials into every school and classroom can be a rewarding educational experience for everyone. A substantial budget allowance should therefore be made to cover for each school the costs of the latest books and encyclopedias, including upper level texts, reference works, and special instructional and display materials. These supplemental needs will be directly related to library and laboratory facilities and instructional material already available in the district. It is especially important to bring the library and the laboratory to the elementary school child.

While financial support from foundations and philanthropic organizations is helpful in initiating programs for the gifted child, it is difficult to maintain programs on this basis. If the value of the program is once established, if the child can profit by the time and effort spent, then the financing of the program on either a local or state level, or a combination basis, is desirable. Society cannot expect to receive more than it is willing to pay for.

In summary, financial investment in a gifted child program can be justified for the following reasons:

1. Investment in the instruction of the able pupil will undoubtedly benefit society more than similar amounts of money invested in the instruction of other students.

2. Most school districts have generally accepted the philosophy that the instructional program should be so designed that it will meet the unique needs of every student. If this is so, then extra support for all types of special students is justified.

3. If the spending of extra money for mentally retarded children can be justified on the basis of their special needs, then comparable expense is justified for the child at the other end of the scale. This naturally leads to the conclusion that financial support from the state, in addition to the local district, is needed.

In operating a program for gifted children, one must realize that large sums of money expended on the program do not necessarily ensure a highly successful result. Interest and ability on the part of the teachers are vital factors. A good program for the gifted is the outcome of good morale and guidance practices rather than the cause of them. It is conceivable that little or no expense in one district might produce a program far superior to a costly one in another district. In general, however, if such a program is to meet the needs of these children, a substantial budget allotment will need to be made. The public can be expected to advocate and support these extra budget items once it is convinced of their necessity and importance. With educational leadership this is not a difficult task in an age where science is not only the touchstone of prosperity, but the key to survival.

7 The Case for Extreme Educational Acceleration of Intellectually Brilliant Youths

JULIAN C. STANLEY

My thesis is that the overly glamorously entitled supplemental educational procedures known as "enrichment" are, even at best, potentially dangerous if not accompanied or followed by acceleration of placement in subject matter and/or grade. Stated more simply, for highly precocious youngsters acceleration seems to me vastly preferable to most types of enrichment. This appears to be especially true where mathematics and mathematics-related subjects are concerned.

But what do I mean by "enrichment" and "acceleration"? Unless we agree on the differences between such processes, my points may be obscured in the minds of those who consider enrichment to be a form of acceleration and acceleration as being enriching. To me, "enrichment" is any educational procedure beyond the usual ones for the subject or grade or age that does not accelerate or retard the student's placement in the subject or grade. Admittedly, some ambiguity remains after this definition, because it does not tell what is usual for the subject, grade, or age. Illustrations of four types of enrichment may produce more agreement among us.

One of these forms of enrichments—unfortunately, quite commonly used—is what might be termed "busy work." It consists of more of the same, greater in quantity than is required of the average student in the class but not different in level. One of our most mathematically precocious boys, an eighth grader with an IQ of 187 who had already skipped a grade, was requested by his Algebra I teacher to work every problem in each chapter, rather than just the odd-numbered ones. He could have completed the whole course with distinction in a very few hours without needing to work many problems, but his teacher was trying to hold him for 180 50-minute peri-

From *The Gifted Child Quarterly* 20:1, (1976). Used by permission.

Updated version of a speech originally presented at the Pacific Northwest Research and Evaluation Conference, Seattle, Washington, May 22, 1975. Presented at the annual meeting of the National Association for Gifted Children in Chicago on October 24, 1975.

ods. It is a pity that at the beginning of the school year he was not allowed to take a standardized algebra test, learn the few points he did not already know, and move on to Algebra II within a few days. At the end of the seventh grade a boy less able than he scored above the 99.8th percentile on a standardized algebra test (missing only two items out of 40) without ever having had the course called "algebra." Another, more brilliant boy scored 40 out of 40 when still a seventh grader. These are not typical youngsters, of course, but in three years of math talent searching in Maryland we have found more than 200 others rather like them.

There is a happy ending to the story of the boy oppressed by busy work in his beginning algebra course. After the eighth grade he studied all of his mathematics part time at the college level, for credit. This took him through college algebra and trigonometry, calculus, advanced calculus, and linear algebra with an initial B and subsequent A's. He also completed an introduction to computer science course in the Johns Hopkins day school with a grade of A at age 12. Furthermore, he completed college chemistry through two semesters of organic chemistry with A's. At age 15 years, 2 months he became a full-time student at Johns Hopkins, having sophomore status because of his 39 credits already earned and living happily in a dormitory. As an electrical engineering major he completed the first college year with eight A's and only one B. It seems likely that he will be elected to membership in the Phi Beta Kappa Society and initiated while still 16 years old!

Though this boy did manage to turn the usually stultifying effects of busy work into great motivation to detour further such obstacles and forge ahead, it would seem quite difficult to make any general positive case for this type of "enrichment."

A second type often used is what I shall term "irrelevant academic enrichment." It consists of setting up a special subject or activity that is meant to enrich the educational lives of some group of intellectually talented students. It pays no attention to the specific nature of their talents. If the activity is, for example, a special class in social studies, it may be meant for all high-IQ youths. The math whiz may enjoy it as a temporary relief from the general boredom of school, but it will not ameliorate his situation in the slow-paced math class. It may be essentially irrelevant to his main academic interests.

My third type of enrichment, "cultural," might also be considered irrelevant to the direct academic needs of intellectually gifted students, but it seems much more worthwhile. The special social studies class already used as an illustration of irrelevant academic enrichment merely introduces earlier what should, in a good school, be available at a later grade level. Cultural enrichment means supplying aspects of the performing arts such as music, art, drama, dance, and creative writing that are usually slighted in public schools. This will serve the unmet needs of most students, however, not just of those with high IQ's or special intellectual talents such as great mathematical reasoning ability or mechanical comprehension. If supplied specifically for those students talented in one or more of the performing arts, however, cultural enrichment becomes merely a type of "relevant enrichment," which I describe next.

If a student is given advanced material or higher-level treatment of in-grade topics in areas of his or her special aptitudes, the enrichment might be said to be "relevant" to those abilities. For example, mathematically able youths might have a unified integrated modern-mathematics curriculum from kindergarten through, say, grade 7, in lieu of the usual mathematics sequence for those eight grades. This could be splendid, but imagine the boredom that would surely result if as eighth graders such students were dumped into a regular Algebra I class.

If the special mathematics curriculum extended from kindergarten through the twelfth grade, it would be crucial that students completing it well should not begin in college with the standard introductory mathematics courses there. The same considerations could be adduced for splendid English, science, or social science curricula. The more relevant and excellent the enrichment is, the more it calls for acceleration of subject-matter or grade placement later. Otherwise, it just puts off the boredom awhile and virtually guarantees that eventually it will be severer than ever.

Thus in my taxonomy there are four main types of enrichment: busy work, irrelevant academic enrichment, cultural enrichment, and relevant academic enrichment. All of these except cultural enrichment may be viewed as horizontal, because they are usually tied closely to a particular grade or narrow age range and are not meant to affect the age-in-grade status of the participating students.

By contrast, academic acceleration is vertical, because it means moving the student up into the higher school level of a subject in which he or she excels, or into a higher grade than the chronological age of the student would ordinarily warrant. If a seventh grader is allowed to take algebra, usually at least an eighth-grade subject, that is subject-matter acceleration. If a student is allowed to skip a grade, that is grade acceleration.

Often these two types of acceleration should go together. For example, if a high-school student scores well enough on Level BC of the calculus test of the national Advanced Placement Program, he will earn quite a few credits that can be used at many colleges. At Johns Hopkins he would enter ready to take advanced calculus and also with 27 percent of the credits needed to complete the freshman year. Passing three or four Advanced Placement courses will give him sophomore status at a number of colleges such as Harvard.

Entering college before completing high school is another example of grade-skipping. We have helped an·11½-year-old boy to become a full-time college student, quite successfully, at the end of the sixth grade. He skipped grades 7 through 12. Two 13-year-old boys entered Johns Hopkins right out of the eighth grade. A 14-year-old came at the end of the ninth grade. Another 14-year-old enrolled as a college sophomore after skipping grades 7, 9, 10, 12, and 13. It will be illuminating to see in some detail how he accomplished this remarkable speed-up.

We first heard of this boy, whom I call Sean, in the fall of 1971. As a sixth grader whose twelfth birthday came that December 4, he was rather old-in-grade. According to local rules he could have been a seventh grader, but his parents had moved to Baltimore from another section of the country that had more restrictive entering regulations. Sean had greatly impressed the teachers in the elementary school he attended, so during the summer following the fifth grade he participated in a special computer-science project conducted by the Maryland Academy of Science. Through local newspaper publicity the Academy heard of our new programs for mathematically and scientifically precocious youths. It recommended Sean to us, thereby making him the first participant in our five-year study that the Spencer Foundation had recently funded, although before it we had enrolled the two 13-year-olds as regular freshmen at Johns Hopkins.

Sean proved to be exceptionally able, both quantitatively and verbally, but especially with respect to mathematical reasoning ability. He had not yet learned much mathematics, however. For example, he did not know the rule for dividing one common fraction by another (that is, invert the second fraction and then multiply), but learned the rule and its proof quickly—as Professor Higgins said in "My Fair Lady", "with the speed of summer lightning."

Sean was not in a high enough grade that year to enter our first mathematics competition, which was restricted to seventh and eighth and underage ninth graders. It was not until we formed our first fast-mathematics class in June of 1972 that he, now 12½ years old, began to get special educational facilitation from us. The story of that class is told in Chapter 6 of our *Mathematical Talent* book, which appeared in 1974 and covered the background and first year of the study. The class continued until August of 1973, and Sean was one of its two stars. He completed four and one-half years of precalculus mathematics well in 60 two-hour Saturday mornings, compared with the 810 45- or 50-minute periods usually required for Algebra I through III, plane geometry, trigonometry, and analytic geometry.

Sean skipped the seventh grade, which in Baltimore County is the first year of junior high school, and in the eighth grade took no mathematics other than the Saturday morning class. Also, during the second semester of the eighth grade he was given released time to take the introduction to computer science course at Johns Hopkins. He found this fascinating and at age 13 easily made a final grade of A.

While still 13 years old Sean skipped the ninth and tenth grades and became an eleventh grader at a large suburban public high school. There he took calculus with twelfth graders, won a letter on the wrestling team, was the science and math whiz on the school's television academic quiz team, tutored a brilliant seventh grader through two and one-half years of algebra and a year of plane geometry in eight months, played a good game of golf, and took some college courses on the side (set theory, economics, and political science). He even successfully managed the campaign of his 14-year-old friend for the presidency of the student council. This left time to prepare for the Advanced Placement Program in calculus and, entirely by studying on his own, also in physics. He won 14 college credits via those two exams.

During the summer after completing the eleventh grade, Sean took a year of college chemistry at Johns Hopkins, as usual earning good grades. That enabled him to enter Johns Hopkins in the fall of 1974 with 34 credits and therefore sophomore status. He lived at home and commuted to the campus with his mother, who took a position at Johns Hopkins in order to make this easier (14-year-olds aren't permitted to drive automobiles, no matter how far along in college they are!). During the first semester he took *advanced* calculus, number theory, *sophomore* physics, and American government, making A's on the two math courses and B's on the other two courses. Also he began to get involved in campus politics. He got along well socially and emotionally. As he told an Associated Press reporter who asked about this, "Either social considerations take a poor second to intellectual ones, or there are no negative social effects ... The most significant aspect of my life is having skipped grades."

Let us recapitulate here. Sean began by being "enriched" in the Academy of Science summer program for brilliant elementary-school pupils. That served as a good background for the college course in computer science, which was intended to be both enriching and accelerative. The fast-mathematics class provided a radical acceleration, because it telescoped into one year of Saturday mornings four and one-half years of precalculus mathematics. Skipping grades 7, 9, 10, and 12 was also highly accelerative, as were the college courses taken and the Advanced Placement exams passed.

Sean is unusually bright, of course, and extremely well motivated, but he is by no means the ablest youth we have found. He had done the most different accelerative things, though. By contrast, another mathematically and verbally brilliant boy simply took a college course each semester or summer term from age 12 to age 15. Besides that, he skipped the second, eleventh, and twelfth grades. This combination of college courses and grade skipping enabled him to enter Johns Hopkins at age 15 years 2 months with 39 college credits, that is, 30% of the way through the sophomore year. Another boy skipped grades 8, 11, and 12, took 17 credits of college courses, and earned 8 college credits in calculus via the Advanced Placement exam. In the fall of 1974 he entered Johns Hopkins at barely 15 years of age with 83% of the freshman year completed.

Many students in the study, including some girls, are *eager* to move ahead faster than the usual age-in-grade lockstep. They do so with ease and pleasure. We find that the combination of great ability and personal eagerness to accelerate educationally virtually guarantees success. Nearly all of our 23 early entrants to college thus far have done splendidly in their studies and social and emotional development. Only one has performed poorly. He was a brilliant but headstrong 14-year-old who signed up for a heavy load of extremely difficult courses and then would not study enough. Compared with the academic and personal record of the typical Johns Hopkins student, the early entrants have been truly outstanding.

Perhaps our most interestingly different course has been college calculus for two hours on Saturday mornings to supplement highschool calculus so that students can do well on the higher level of the Advanced Placement calculus exam. With a class composed mainly of well-above-average tenth graders, but with one student only 11 years old, this went along so well from September until the first of February that by then everyone in the group knew more calculus than most college students learn in two semesters. By early May only 9 college students in 1,000 scored higher than the lowest-scoring one of the 13 students in this class—and that wasn't the 11-year-old! All of these special students scored excellently on the higher level of the national Advanced Placement Program examination in calculus in May of 1975 and earned a year of college calculus credit. Nine of them earned the highest score reported—that is, 5 on a 5-point scale, meaning "extremely well qualified to enter college Calculus III." A new class with 24 students began in the fall of 1975. All of them are eleventh or twelfth graders, some as young as 15 years old.

Recently we had an extreme example of what powerful predictors of achievement their scores on difficult tests can be for intellectually gifted youths. The mathematics department at Johns Hopkins conducted a test competition for eleventh graders. We heard about it only a week before the test date and got permission to tell some of our participants about it. We hastily located the names and addresses of 19 persons who as eighth graders three years earlier had scored high on the SAT–M in our first talent search. These were not our very best, because most of those had moved along beyond the eleventh grade; several were already in college. Of these 19, 10 came for the test. Seven of them had not been identified by their high-school mathematics teachers, and one of the three so identified was a member of our calculus class whose father teaches mathematics at Johns Hopkins.

Fifty-one students entered the contest, and their scores ranged from 140 down to 2. One of our group, not nominated by his teachers, was far ahead of anyone else, with 140 points. The math professor's son ranked second with 112 points. Another of our group ranked third with 91 points. The highest scorer not in our group ranked fourth, with 82 points. The other seven nominated by us ranked only down to 23.5 out of the 51. Isn't it a bit frightening that a single score from a test administered three years earlier identified high math achievers much better than did teachers who have known their students for at least seven months?

This is congruent, however, with Terman's finding long ago that teachers could not identify students with extremely high IQ's well. Apparently, the math classes simply do not tap the best abilities of mathematically brilliant students, whereas the difficult test does. There's a moral in this for those who lean too heavily on teachers' recommendations where intellectually gifted children are concerned. In selecting early entrants in our study we pay far more attention to scores on advanced tests and other evidence of marked precocity than we do to school grades, or recommendations, because most of the high-school courses are not at an appropriate level of difficulty and challenge for such students.

It should be no surprise that educational acceleration works well when highly able, splendidly motivated students are given a variety of ways to accomplish it. From Terman's monumental *Genetic Studies of Genius* and Pressey's definitive 1949 monograph on *Educational Acceleration,* through the experiences of the University of Chicago, Shimer College, the Ford Foundation's large early-entrance study of the 1950's, Worcester's and Hobson's work, and Simon's Rock College, up to the radical accelerative techniques we are developing, it is clear that acceleration can work much better than so-called academic enrichment for those students who really want it. Counterexamples are rare and likely to be atypical. For every William Sidis who renounces intellectual pursuits because of extreme, and apparently quite unwise, parental pressures, there are many persons such as Norbert Wiener and Sean who benefit greatly from the time saved, frustration avoided, and stimulation gained.

We believe that concentrating efforts on preparing "teachers of the gifted" to enrich curricula is, while far better than nothing, a relatively ineffective and costly way to help the ablest. At least, such teachers should help provide the smorgasbord of accelerative opportunities and counseling in their use that many such students need.

The procedures that we propose are not expensive. Most of them actually save the school system time and money. One does not need a large appropriation in order to encourage grade skipping, identify students ready to move through mathematics courses at a faster-than-usual rate, encourage early graduation from high school, help certain students enroll for courses in nearby colleges or by correspondence study, promote advanced-placement exams, or even set up special fast-math courses. More than money, they take zeal and a distinctive point of view.

Persons who hear about our study usually ask, "But what about the social and emotional development of the students who become accelerated?" We often counter with "What about the intellectual and emotional development and future success of students who yearn for acceleration but are denied it?" For more than six years we have been studying the social and emotional development of youths accelerated in a variety of ways. If the acceleration is by their own choice, they look good indeed. Part of the problem is in the minds of those skeptics who automatically assume that one's social and emotional peers are one's agemates. Performance of gifted youngsters, including ours, on such personality measures as the California Psychological Inventory shows that emotionally they are more like bright persons several years older than themselves than they are like their own agemates. There is considerable variability, of course, but on the average they are better matched socially and emotionally with able students who are older. Thus, just as their intellectual peers are not their agemates, their social and emotional peers aren't, either. For clarity of discourse it would seem wise not to use the word "peer" in this type of argument without prefacing it with one or more adjectival modifiers.

Another question often asked us is, "Why do you start with 12- and 13-year-olds who reason superbly mathematically? That is awfully narrow. Why not be broader?" Well, neither mathematics as a field nor our various procedures are "narrow." Mathematics undergirds much of man's highest endeavors. In a sense, it is probably the most generally useful subject (although, of course, some philosophers would argue about that statement). We try to approach talent in mathematics comprehensively, but we deliberately chose to specialize in this area where great precocity often occurs because one can be splendid in mathematics without yet having had many of the usual life experiences of an adolescent or adult. Also, because of this precocity, many students in school are horribly bored. Imagine having to serve time in first-year algebra for 180 50-minute periods when one knows the subject well the first day of class! That is by no means an uncommon occurrence, and it may partially explain the lack of interest in mathematics among many bright persons.

My own motivation to help accelerate the mathematical progress of fine mathematical reasoners grew out of my early background: graduated from college at age 19 years 1 month; was a high-school teacher of science and mathematics from age 19 to 23; specialized in educational and psychological measurement and statistics as a doctoral student; did post-doctoral work in mathematics at the University of Michigan and mathematical statistics at the University of Chicago; am a Fellow of the American Statistical Association; and have had great interest in mental measurement since 1938. It seems sensible to specialize in what one knows and likes best. Many educational researchers do not like mathematics *per se*. Of course, they should concentrate elsewhere.

With more than 2,000 mathematically able boys and girls already identified, we do not have time and facilities to look for latent talent or potential achievers, worthy though that pursuit surely is. We leave that to the many persons who prefer to specialize in identification and facilitation of underachievers, "late bloomers," and the "disadvantaged gifted." Aside from some concern about sex differences in mathematical precocity, we have not tried to screen in a set percent of any group. From socioeconomic and ethnic standpoints, however, the high scorers have been a varied lot.

A well-known quotation from Thomas Gray's famous elegy sums up the case for seeking talent and nurturing it:

> Full many a gem of purest ray serene
> The dark unfathomed caves of ocean bear;
> Full many a flower is born to blush unseen,
> And waste its sweetness on the desert air.

Another poet tells us that "A man's reach should exceed his grasp, or what's a heaven for?"

It is our responsibility and opportunity to help prevent the potential Miltons, Einsteins, and Wieners from coming to the "mute inglorious" ends that Gray viewed in that country churchyard long ago. The problem has changed little, but the prospects are much better now. Surely we can greatly extend both the reach and the grasp of our brilliant youths, or what's an educational system for?

References

Keating, Daniel P. (Ed.). *Intellectual talent: Research and development.* Baltimore, Md.: Johns Hopkins University Press, 1975.

Oden, Melita H. The fulfillment of promise: 40-year follow-up of the Terman gifted group. *Genetic Psychology Monographs,* 1968, 77, 3–93.

Pressey, Sidney L. Educational acceleration: Appraisal and basic problems. *Bureau of Educational Research Monographs,* Ohio State University, No. 31. Columbus: Ohio State University Press, 1949.

Stanley, Julian C.; Keating, Daniel P.; and Fox, Lynn H. (Eds.). *Mathematical talent: Discovery, description, and development.* Baltimore, Md.: Johns Hopkins University Press, 1974.

8   The Role of Instructional Material in Teaching Creative Thinking

JOHN F. FELDHUSEN AND DONALD J. TREFFINGER

In 1974 we received a grant from the National Institute of Education to conduct a dissemination project on the teaching of creative thinking and problem solving. Specifically the purposes of the project were as follows:

1. Conduct a field study of teachers' perceptions of their problems and needs in teaching creativity and problem solving.
2. Review the published material for teaching creativity and problem solving.
3. Review the research on teaching creativity and problem solving.
4. Prepare a report for teachers offering guidance and directions in this area.
5. Design, conduct and evaluate a workshop for teachers on creativity and problem solving.

Our efforts were to focus on the needs of teachers in schools which enrolled large numbers of minority students and students from economically disadvantaged families.

As an approach to the first purpose we interviewed and gave questionnaires to 408 elementary teachers in five cities: Indianapolis, Atlanta, Kansas City, Los Angeles, and Lafayette, Indiana. The results were reported in an article in *Psychological Reports* (1975).

From *The Gifted Child Quarterly* 21:4 (1977). Used by permission.

Briefly they showed that teachers know very little about special methods or materials for teaching creative thinking and problem solving; that they would be willing to devote more teaching time to this area; and that they would prefer to do the teaching of creative thinking or problem solving in connection with regular instruction in language arts, social studies, math, or science. They were quite divided in their opinions concerning the question, "Do minority and disadvantaged students need special methods and materials?"

For the second purpose we sifted through countless journals, bibliographic sources and catalogs to identify the published material which might have some value in teaching creativity and problem solving. Then we ordered sets of all hopeful material and examined them carefully, using these guidelines:

1. There should be a defensible theoretical rationale for the material in relation to the goal of teaching creativity and/or problem solving.
2. Research or evaluation evidence for its effectiveness would be desirable.
3. Good teaching strategies should be suggested.
4. The material should be attractive and motivating for children.
5. It should be conveniently usable in the typical classroom. Out of the vast collection of materials we received, we succeeded in identifying a basic set of about sixty very fine sets of published material.

We conducted a review of published research and ERIC reports in fulfillment of the third purpose. This was a relatively discouraging activity from one point of view, but encouraging from another. Very few of the published materials have undergone any systematic research or evaluation. A few, however, have been extensively researched, such as the *Productive Thinking Program* (Covington, Crutchfield, Davies, & Olton, 1972), the *Purdue Creative Thinking Program* (Feldhusen, Treffinger, & Bahlke, 1970), or *Thinking Creatively* (Davis, 1973). The results of research with these and a few other published and unpublished sets were highly positive. Thus it seemed safe to conclude that, even without extensive formal research or evaluation, reasonably well-designed materials which were based on a sound rationale should be effective in teaching creative thinking and problem solving.

The fourth purpose was to prepare a report for teachers offering guidance and direction in teaching creativity and problem solving. That has been accomplished in the form of a book which will be published by Kendall-Hunt Publishing Company (Feldhusen & Treffinger, 1977). The book includes chapters on the special needs of minority and disadvantaged students, methods for encouraging creativity and problem solving, reviews of published material, and suggestions for initiating a classroom project. Preliminary evaluations of the materials in workshops and university courses have been favorable.

The fifth purpose of the project was to design, conduct and evaluate a workshop program for teachers on creative thinking and problem solving. Our workshop provides a flexible plan which can be presented in as little as two hours or expanded to a day or even a week. It features a set of slides which introduces key concepts and methods for teaching creativity and problem solving, teacher participation throughout the workshop, a slide show review of published materials, and a "shopping tour," with our book in hand, through an extensive display of the actual published materials. The workshop has been conducted in a number of cities throughout the United States. Formal evaluations have indicated that the teacher-participants learn a great deal from the program and find it stimulating and enjoyable. A recent article in the *Journal of Creative Behavior* (Feldhusen & Treffinger, 1976) described the workshop and reported the evaluation results.

Using Instructional Packages and Individualizing Instruction in Creativity and Problem Solving

Instruction in creative thinking and problem solving has long been characterized by group or total class activities in which the teacher leads, talks, or displays her creative abilities while most students remain passive or even inattentive to the instruction. Only in individualized, carefully planned, participatory activities are students able to exercise their own creative and problem solving abilities. High quality instructional materials always involve a *small* amount of exposition, directions, or didactic instruction and a *large* amount of carefully planned practice and reinforceable activity.

Some teachers are very actively involved in developing individualized or self-instructional learning packages for their students. These packages may utilize books, films, filmstrips, activities, or worksheets from a variety of published sources, or they may depend upon teacher-created materials. These projects are named in a variety of ways: Learning Centers, Learning Stations, modules or mini-courses, Learning Packages, and many others. While they are quite useful in teaching basic subject matter, it is also important to recognize that they can be used to teach creativity and problem solving.

The teacher can do this in several ways. First of all, published material for teaching creativity and problem solving can be incorporated into packages which are being used. Second, if the package utilizes material previously developed by the teacher, or other published material specifically concerned only with the subject matter, a variety of specific methods and techniques can be used to develop supplementary creativity and problem solving activities and exercises for the students. Finally, the teacher can develop her own instructional package to teach creativity and problem solving.

Guidelines for Teacher-Planned Projects

We have developed several general guidelines to assist teachers who plan to develop their own instructional packages.

The first major guideline is to know the basic components of an instructional package.

Two models for the design of instruction are presented. These models of instruction deal primarily with the organization and planning involved in the production of instructional material packages.

The first model we offer is the basic model of instruction pioneered by Glaser (1962). There are four aspects to this model: planning instructional objectives, assessing entering behavior, planning and implementing teaching activities, and assessing how much has been learned. We use this model as a general guide or orienter, recognizing its somewhat offensive technological orientation.

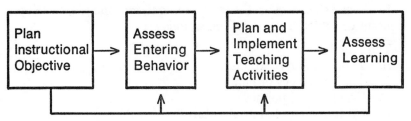

Basic Model of Instruction

Once these basic parts of an instructional model are understood, the actual structure of instructional materials can be examined. One widely used form is the Learning Activity Package (LAP). A LAP is a totally individualized mode of instruction. It provides for students' individual and differential rates and styles of learning, and for the different ability levels of the students. A LAP provides a working outline that tells the student what he is expected to accomplish, presents materials and activities that will help meet objectives, and provides for self-testing and evaluation of achievement. These are the basic components of a Learning Activity Package:

1.   An introductory overview to orient and motivate students.

2. Objectives stated informally and at students' levels.
3. Self-Tests or inventories. For creativity objectives these may often take the form of self-ratings, checklists, etc.
4. Learning materials and activities. These may be in many and varied forms. Listed below are just a few examples of kinds of materials and activities that may be used.

   a) Optional or taped lectures.
   b) Information sheets.
   c) Resources and guidance in using resources.
   d) Experimentation.
   e) Media (filmstrips, video-tape, films and film loops, slides and transparencies).
   f) Discussion sessions, simulated activities, and other small group activities.

5. Evaluation of student learning.

The second major guideline is to develop goals or objectives.

Many advocates of behavioral objectives insist that teachers begin work in developing a unit of instruction by writing the objectives. A better way to begin is by preparing a subject matter or content outline. The outline will not be used as a lecture guide, but will be used to develop objectives which focus on specific abilities to be taught through the topics in the content outline.

In a social studies class, the teacher might, for example, develop a content or subject matter outline as follows:

The Family:
A. Types of family structure.
B. The economics of family life.
C. Families and politics.
D. Evolution and family structure.
E. Current trends in family life.

Under each of these headings the teacher would also be likely to identify subtopics to be taught.

After the general content outline has been prepared, the creative thinking and problem solving skills to be developed should be identified. This can be accomplished with a charting procedure which we have developed for writing objectives (Feldhusen & Treffinger, 1971; Treffinger, Hohn, Feldhusen, Bleakeley, & Huber, 1976).

You begin the process by drawing a chart on a large sheet of paper. Enter the content outline at the left side of the page, from top to bottom leaving two inches or so at the top for column headings. Next, horizontally across the top of the page, enter the thinking skill or processes to be included. As a suggestion, consider these categories for the levels of thinking skills: (1) information-comprehension, (2) creative thinking, (3) synthesis skills, and (4) problem solving. Level 1 is probably self-explanatory. Level 2 includes the divergent thinking operations of fluency, flexibility, originality, and elaboration. Level 3 refers to synthesis projects in which students research a topic and prepare a report or product. Level 4 refers to all types of problem sensing and solving activities.

For each box in the chart, we ask, "Will this instructional package attempt to teach the learner this part of the content, using this thinking skill?" Not every topic in the content outline will necessarily have to be included under *every* thinking skill, of course. We make a small check in each box we plan to incorporate into the package. Our decision is based on a judgment of the potential of developing a particular thinking skill through that topic.

Next, we must examine each of the boxes which have been checked, one at a time. If a box is checked, the package should include some activity for the student to learn using that particular thinking process or skill. Thus, for each such box, there should be one or more instructional objectives.

For example, for the first topic, the information-comprehension box might be checked. That means that the student will use this package to learn some basic ideas about types of families. Here is an illustrative objective: To be able to identify and describe several different basic types of families. For the topic "Families and politics" creativity was checked. Here is an illustrative objective: Think of several unusual ways families might become involved in politics. For the topic "Evolution of the family" synthesis skills was checked. Here is an illustrative objective: Prepare a report, using library resources, concerning the structure of families in several primitive cultures. For the topic "Economics of the family," problem solving was checked. An illustrative objective: Using maps and library resources, try to determine why Eskimo villages are located as they are. Many more objectives would probably be written for this unit. The first level, information-comprehension, is usually checked for each topic, and thus there is an objective at that level for each topic.

The result of this analysis will be a set of objectives in which the content *and* the thinking skills are planned. Note that this is merely a planning device; it does not impose any sequence in which the student will study the material, but merely maps out in a systematic way the content and thinking skills that will be developed in the package.

The third major guideline is to search for and select creativity instructional materials, methods, and tasks to achieve the objectives.

In developing an instructional packet, it is not necessary that every part of the packet be originally prepared for that purpose. Existing published resources can be used very effectively. Thus, it is desirable to search for useful resources *before* actually beginning planning procedures and specific student learning activities. Books, articles, worksheets, problem sets, and exercises can all be used or adapted to relate to the planned objectives. There may also be published self-instructional programs, tapes, films, slides, filmstrips, models, demonstration kits, and other supplementary material that will be useful and save the time and expense of developing new materials. Some of these resources may be incorporated into the packet with only minimum change; others may require modifications, excerpting, and the development of study guides to tell students how to use them.

Another step that is useful to take before actually beginning to design specific learning activities for a package is to review methods and techniques for teaching creativity and problem solving. These techniques should provide useful ideas for designing learning activities for individuals, small groups, or large groups. Another source of good ideas to review before starting to plan learning activities are tasks that have been used frequently in creativity research and training studies to foster students' creative thinking abilities.

The fourth guideline, then, is to assemble the learning activity package and evaluate it.

Careful thought should be given to the actual procedures for using the package in the classroom. What materials will each student receive? How will they be distributed or made available in learning centers, files, or student folders? What kinds of products will be called for, and how will the student be expected to demonstrate completion of the activities for any of the objectives?

In general, as we develop the package, we should try to include a variety of activities, so that students may use different skills during a unit of study and complete several different kinds of products. Providing a variety of experiences, along with a blend of individual and group work, will help sustain the students' curiosity and interest. When testing is necessary, we can often arrange for it to be done individually.

The plan for learning activities should be checked very carefully, to determine the amount of time various activities may require, the adequacy of resources and supplies, and to plan any sequence that will be important for the student to observe.

Time requirements for any activity may vary considerably among students, of course. However, we can make a general assessment of the total amount of instructional time that may be required, on the average. Then we consider how long it will take the fastest and slowest students to complete various activities, using best estimates on the basis of their previous efforts. Some thought should be given as to how to accommodate students' differing time requirements. Should some activities be required of every student, regardless of how long they will take? Are there some activities that might be omitted for slower students or added for faster ones? Are there some objectives (and corresponding activities) that may be reserved as "optional work" for students who progress more rapidly? Are there alternative packages or assignments (or opportunities for free reading, recreation, or relaxation) that should be planned in relation to individual pacing of the learning experiences? (Feldhusen, Rand & Crowe, 1975.)

The plans for resources should also be checked carefully. If equipment is needed, will it be available when needed? Will individual students be able to obtain it? Will they know how to use it? If books, articles, or other material are incorporated into the packet, will there be sufficient copies available for the number of students who may need it at the same time?

If the Package seems to be successful, the next step might be to have other teachers examine it and try it in their classrooms. Will it work when the teacher's biases, enthusiasm, and guidance are removed and neutral teachers give it to new groups of students? Packages which survive this level of evaluation can become useful instructional materials in the school for a number of years.

Conclusions

Developing an instructional package is a valuable experience for the teacher. In addition to having some new instructional material to use in the classroom, the teacher will learn much about students' learning processes. Of course, the kind of planning activities described in these steps, and the amount of time required to complete them may seem to place a great demand on the teacher's energy. However, we have found that teachers who have learned to employ a systematic approach to instructional planning have found it to be a valuable tool. Often teachers will find that time spent in planning instruction pays its dividends later, in increased classroom efficiency and greater satisfaction.

We are also optimistic that with the wealth of excellent published material for teaching creativity and problem solving which is now on the market and with guidance, teachers can develop greatly improved instruction in this area for all students. However, we are also of the opinion that these materials and methods can be unusually valuable in meeting the needs of gifted and highly creative students.

In two publications we have inventoried the characteristics of gifted students (Feldhusen, 1963; Feldhusen, Treffinger, & Elias, 1969) and have especially argued that they can profit more than other students from self instructional materials and procedures. Now, after conducting our review, we are also convinced that these gifted and creative students can profit immeasurably from the power of these methods and materials to develop thinking abilities and problem solving skills. Above all else, gifted and creative students have tremendous potential for intellectual and artistic development and these methods and materials can help them reach that potential.

References

Covington, M. J., Crutchfield, R. S., Davies, L. B., & Olton, R. M. *The Productive Thinking Program.* Columbus, Ohio: Charles E. Merrill, 1972.

Davis, G. A. *Psychology of Problem Solving,* New York: Basic Books, 1973, pages 133–49.

Feldhusen, J. F. "Programming and The Talented Pupil." *The Clearing House,* 1963, *38,* 151–54.

Feldhusen, J. F., Rand, D. R. & Crowe, M. B. "Designing Open and Individualized Instruction at The Elementary Level." *Educational Technology,* 1975, *15,* 17–21.

Feldhusen, J. F., & Treffinger, D. J. "Psychological Background and Rationale for Instructional Design." *Educational Technology,* 1971, *11,* 21–24.

Feldhusen, J. F., & Treffinger, D. J. "Teachers' Attitudes and Practices in Teaching Creativity and Problem Solving to Economically Disadvantaged and Minority Children." *Psychological Reports,* 1975, *37,* 1161–1162.

Feldhusen, J. F., & Treffinger, D. J. "Design and Evaluation of a Workshop on Creativity and Problem Solving for Teachers." *Journal of Creative Behavior,* 1976, *10,* 12–14.

Feldhusen, J. F., & Treffinger, D. J. *Teaching Creative Thinking and Problem Solving.* Dubuque: Kendall/Hunt, 1977.

Feldhusen, J. F., Treffinger, D. J., & Bahlke, S. J. "Developing Creative Thinking." *Journal of Creative Behavior,* 1970, *4,* 85–90.

Feldhusen, J. F., Treffinger, D. J. & Elias, R. M. "The Right Kind of Programmed Instruction for The Gifted." *Journal of The National Society for Performance and Instruction,* 1969, *8,* 6–11.

Glaser, R. "Psychology and Instructional Technology." In R. Glaser (Ed.) *Training Research and Education.* Pittsburgh: University of Pittsburgh Press, 1962, pages 1–30.

Treffinger, D. J., Hohn, R. L., Feldhusen, J. F., Bleakley, J., & Huber, J. *Handbook for Individualized Instructional Design.* Lawrence, Kansas: Unpublished technical report, October, 1976.

9 The Enrichment Triad Model: A Guide for Developing Defensible Programs for the Gifted and Talented

JOSEPH S. RENZULLI

Introduction

The purpose of this article is threefold. First, I would like to register some concerns about the appropriateness of many activities that parade under the banner of gifted education, activities that may be intrinsically valuable in and of themselves, but essentially indefensible as the mainstay of programs that serve gifted and talented students. The second purpose will be to present an enrichment model that can be used as a guide in the development of qualitatively different programs in this area of special education, and by so doing try to provide defensible answers to questions such as:

What is (or should be) different about the types of learning experiences that are advocated for gifted students?

Isn't what you are doing for the gifted also good for nearly all youngsters?

Unless we can provide satisfactory answers to these questions, programs that serve superior students will be extremely vulnerable to both the critics of gifted education and to persons who may be sympathetic with this area, but who also feel that special services for gifted and talented youngsters are essentially a luxury item that schools can easily get by without. But more importantly, answers are necessary for persons within the field, the true believers in special education for the gifted who occasionally experience pangs of conscience because they can defend programs philosophically but not programmatically or in terms of the day-to-day experiences that are provided for gifted youngsters. Another aspect of my concern about defensibility deals with the magic word, individualization, which is being offered by many people as a panacea for meeting the needs of gifted and talented students. Although individualized learning is an important goal for all youngsters, many educators have misinterpreted both the meaning and process of individualization to the point where this very valuable concept has become nothing less than an-

---

From *The Gifted Child Quarterly* 20:3 and 21:2 (1976–7). Used by permission.

other piece of educational hocus-pocus. It is not uncommon, for example, to find students in well-publicized individualization programs working at their own rate of speed, but on the *same* worksheets and activities. This approach obviously respects certain characteristics of learners; however, individualization of rate or pace without additional differentiation in areas such as content, learning style, and teaching strategies fails to respect the total set of characteristics that bring gifted and talented youngsters to our attention.

What We Can't Defend

My first concern about present-day practices in gifted education grew out of a variety of experiences, the most notable being a long-standing involvement in the evaluation of programs that serve youngsters of unusually superior ability.

An almost universal finding in my evaluation work has been that gifted students enjoy taking part in special programs! In trying to discover the reasons for such enjoyment I find that two types of responses almost always lead the list. The first is simply that they enjoy the freedom of choice regarding the activities in which they engage in special programs and the second is that they like freedom from the usual pressures often associated with getting assignments in on time, taking tests, and having to complete work in a very restricted environment—an environment with inflexible time allocations, prescribed textbooks and other resources, and limited choices in the ways in which they go about carrying out their work. I am very much in favor of these reasons for student satisfaction. At the same time, however, it has occurred to me that students frequently like their special program for the same reason that they like recess! It is difficult to pursue this topic without sounding like some kind of ogre who is against freedom of choice and a free and open learning environment, so let me emphasize that I believe these two things should be absolute essentials in any program for the gifted. In fact, it is precisely these things that I always recommend as the first program objective for guiding the education of gifted and talented students.

Program Objective No. 1:

> For the majority of time spent in the gifted programs, students will have complete freedom to pursue topics of their own choosing to whatever depth and extent they so desire; and they will be allowed to pursue these topics in a manner that is consistent with their own preferred style of learning.

In conducting evaluative studies, however, I have witnessed far too many programs for the gifted that are essentially collections of fun-and-games activities; such activities lack continuity and show little evidence of developing in a systematic fashion the mental processes that led these children to be identified as gifted. On many occasions I have observed children walking into a resource room for the gifted, taking a game off the shelf (sometimes a very challenging and exciting game), playing the game until their class period is over, and returning the next day to engage in some similar type of activity. In questioning teachers about the purpose or objectives of such activities, the standard reply is almost always that it is "challenging" and that the children are "really enjoying" what they are doing.

The feedback from the students in situations such as this is almost always superlative, but I think that you can see why I have compared this situation to recess or some other type of recreational activity. Although I firmly believe that gifted students should have a generous opportunity to participate in a wide variety of exploratory experiences and activities that might be described as recreational thinking, I also believe that an important part of all programs for the gifted should focus on *systematic* development. I simply mean that we as professional educators in a specialized area should know and be able to defend the types of processes that are being developed through the activities that gifted children pursue in special programs. I firmly believe in freedom of choice so far as topic and learning style are concerned, but I also believe that once a youngster has decided upon an area that he or she would like to pursue, it becomes the teacher's responsibility to assist that youngster in developing the skills of inquiry that will make him or her a "first-hand inquirer" in the particular area in which he or she chooses to work.

Another aspect of my evaluation work has frequently led to a somewhat disappointing finding. In questioning gifted youngsters about projects on which they have worked in their special programs, I often have discovered that with the exception of freedom of choice in topic selection and a greater amount of flexibility in the ways that they can pursue their topics, there has been very little difference between regular and special programs so far as the level or quality of inquiry was concerned. I frequently asked youngsters, "What was the most interesting or creative thing that you did this year in your special program?" After asking the youngsters to tell me a little about their projects or products, I then raised questions about the ways that they pursued their goal. "What types of references did you use? What did you learn from this project? What was the purpose of the study? If you were doing this same project in your regular classroom what would you do or have done differently?"

Frequently the answers come back in a somewhat less than

imaginative fashion. The references consisted of the same encyclopedias or library books to which they would have access in the regular school program. Responses to questions about what they learned often were expressed in terms of knowledge or facts; and answers to questions about differences between the regular school program and the special program were almost always answered in terms of freedom of choice, lack of pressure, and the absence of grading. Sometimes the only difference was that they did their work on a rug on the floor rather than seated at a desk or at a library table! I must reiterate that I am in favor of freedom of choice, lack of pressure, and even rugs on which children can work more comfortably, but once in a while, I would like to have some of my questions answered in terms of *qualitative differences in the instructional process.*

Evaluative findings such as these have caused me to raise serious questions about the defensibleness of special programs for the gifted and talented. Are we really doing anything different with these children aside from providing them with a freer atmosphere in which they can take a break from the boredom and routine of the regular classroom and perhaps play games that are interesting but largely irrelevant to their overall development?

The extent to which *all* students can pursue knowledge as a first-hand inquirer or turned-on professional is not yet known. As far as gifted students are concerned, however, the history of human achievement (and indeed, the history of many programs for the gifted) is filled with examples of bright young people who not only emulated the methods of professionals, but who were in fact professionals themselves. Gifted kids *can* unquestionably function in the manner of true inquirers **and** it is for this reason that I believe the second general objective of programs for the gifted should be to develop in each youngster the skills necessary for advanced levels of inquiring in his or her areas of interest.

Program Objective No. 2

The primary role of each teacher in the program for gifted and talented students will be to provide each student with assistance in (1) identifying and structuring realistic solvable problems that are consistent with the student's interests, and (2) acquiring the necessary methodological resources and investigative skills that are necessary for solving these particular problems.

I first became interested in the second program objective of gifted education when I began to examine the assumption that programs for the gifted should be concerned with the higher mental processes and the logical implication that follows—education for average and slow students should focus on the lower mental processes. This assumption is patently ridiculous. I believe that *all* students should develop their powers of creativity, critical thinking, analysis, evaluation, etc. I believe that sensitivity to social issues, a concern for human values, and the development of a healthy self-awareness should be important educational goals for all people, regardless of whether or not they have been classified as gifted. Furthermore I believe that gifted students must put in some "quality time" on the so-called lower mental processes—plain old knowing and understanding. Contrary to what some of the oracles would have us believe, knowledge *is* important, and comprehension *is* necessary, not as ends in and of themselves, but as stepping stones to the more creative and productive endeavors that we typically associate with persons in the gifted or genius category.

In his book *The Nature of Human Intelligence,* J. P. Guilford points out that one way in which a genius excels ordinary persons is that he or she possesses a wealth of stored products of information (p. 319). According to Guilford, there is considerable recall of information and transformational activity whenever the creative/productive person is engaged in the development of a new product, idea, or type of information.

Before I go any further, let me hasten to assure you that I am definitely not advocating a return to the content-centered curriculum or the type of teaching that dealt largely with the accumulation and regurgitation of facts. Those were the "bad old days" that emphasized knowledge for the sake of knowledge. Such an approach unquestionably resulted in the vast amount of criticism that has been justifiably leveled at the educational establishment, and this is precisely the type of learning that we are against in gifted education. But at the same time I *am* interested in the role that knowledge and information processing play in the education of gifted persons, and I feel that one of the easiest ways that we can escalate the level of the gifted person's learning environment is to escalate the ways in which he or she goes about selectively retrieving, managing, and using various types of information in the process of first-hand discovery and creativity.

The Enrichment Triad Model

This section will describe and attempt to show the relationships that exist between the three different types of enrichment. The first two types, General Exploratory Activities and Group Training Activities, are considered to be appropriate for all learners; however, they are also important in the overall enrichment of gifted and talented students, for at least two reasons..First, they deal with strategies for expanding student interests and developing the thinking and feeling processes, and for this reason they are viewed as necessary ingredients in any enrichment program. Second, and perhaps more importantly, these two types of enrichment represent logical input and support systems for Type III Enrichment, which is considered to be the only type that is appropriate mainly for gifted students.

Type III Enrichment, entitled Individual Investigations of Real Problems, is the major focus of this model, and approximately one-half of the time that gifted students spend in enrichment activities should be devoted to these types of experiences. Because of the importance of Type III Enrichment in the present model, Type III experiences will be described in the final subsection and a rationale will be developed to support the assertion that investigations of real problems should be the mainstay of programs for the gifted and talented. Suggestions will be offered in an effort to provide some practical guidance for implementing Type III experiences. Although some practical suggestions regarding Types I and II are discussed in this section, these two types of enrichment have received a great deal of attention in contemporary educational literature and therefore will be discussed here only as they interrelate with Type III.

Before getting into a description of the three types of enrichment, however, I would like to point out a few assumptions underlying the model. The first assumption relates to the way in which I will define the entire concept of "enrichment." By enrichment I simply mean experiences or activities that are above and beyond the so-called "regular curriculum." Since I am defining enrichment in relation to other aspects of the regular school experience, I would like to discuss briefly a few concerns about the regular curriculum and how it relates to the concept of enrichment.

This leads me to the second assumption underlying this enrichment model. The learner has two other dimensions that must be respected in an enrichment situation, and even an advanced course may fail to take account of (1) the student's specific content interests and (2) his or her preferred style(s) of learning. An almost universal finding in the evaluation work that I have done in numerous programs for the gifted has been that the greatest source of student satisfaction almost always resulted from the students' freedom to pursue topics of their own choosing in a manner with which they themselves felt most comfortable. Thus, the second underlying assumption is that enrichment activities (with the possible exception of some Type II activities) must show complete respect for the learner's interests and learning styles, and that the point of entry for all enrichment must be an honest and sincere desire on the part of the student to pursue a particular topic or activity of his or her own choosing. Piaget has pointed out many times that all learning should emanate from the spontaneous interests and activities of students. Although there may be some disagreement with this statement so far as certain basic or required skills are concerned, I believe that student interests should be the cornerstone of all enrichment activities. This approach almost always guarantees a highly motivated learner, but it also means that we must offer students many options, including the option to give up on a project if their interests change.

The third and final assumption underlying the model has to do with when and where enrichment opportunities are offered. Since the model deals with basic aspects of learning, I have no predetermined notions about the physical circumstances under which enrichment experiences should take place. It could be in the regular classroom as an extension of the regular curriculum or it might be in a special resource room or independent study carrel in the library. It might take place in the community (indeed, Socrates did it in the marketplace in Athens), in a college classroom or laboratory, or even through a correspondence course in which the student never comes face to face with his or her instructor. It might involve one child or many children, and it does not necessarily require that only gifted children be involved in certain group projects which hold enrichment opportunities. The unique feature is, however, that if a particular student has a superior potential for performance in a particular area of sincere interest, then he or she must be allowed the opportunity to pursue topics therein to unlimited levels of inquiry.

Type I Enrichment: General Exploratory Activities

Type I Enrichment consists of those experiences and activities that are designed to bring the learner into touch with the kinds of topics or areas of study in which he or she may have a sincere interest. A good Type I Enrichment situation should involve very little structure, and at the same time, students and teachers should be aware that these situations have very purposeful objectives. By providing students with a wide variety of opportunities to become exposed to different areas of potential interest, youngsters can begin to make their own decisions about the topics that they might like to explore at greater depths and higher levels of involvement. Thus, one of the major objectives of Type I Enrichment is to give both students and teachers some hints about what might be a bona fide Type III Enrichment activity for a single youngster or small group of students who have a common interest. A second objective of Type I Enrichment situations is to assist teachers in making decisions about the kinds of Type II Enrichment activities that should be selected for particular groups of students.

At least three general guidelines are suggested to help achieve the objectives of Type I Enrichment. First, although a great deal of exploratory freedom must be permitted, students should be made aware from the very beginning that they are expected to pursue exploration activities purposefully; and that after a given period of time has elapsed, each youngster will be responsible for analyzing his or her own experiences and coming up with some alternative suggestions for further study. The amount of time required for exploratory activities will, of course, vary with each student and experience has shown that many students will know from the very beginning which areas or topics hold special fascination and thus warrant further investigation along the lines that will be proposed in the section of this model dealing with Type III Enrichment. Long-standing interests that have grown out of the regular curriculum or the environment in general are "naturals" for Type II Enrichment and should usually be given priority consideration in the design of in-depth investigations. There may, however, be times when it will be wise to encourage certain students to broaden the scope of their interests by exploring areas with which they have had no previous experience. A youngster who, for example, has a singular and deep-seated interest in geology should not be discouraged from pursuing this area of study, but at the same time, he or she should at least be systematically exposed to other fields of potential interest and encouraged to broaden his or her horizon.

The second guideline for achieving the objectives of Type I Enrichment deals with strategies for exposing students to a wide variety of topics or areas of study from which they might like to select problems for in-depth investigations. Developing categorical interest centers in the classroom or resource room, and stocking these centers with materials that are *broadly* representative of selected themes or fields of knowledge will help to expand students' perspectives on particular areas of study. The selection of appropriate materials for the interest centers is especially crucial because *our objective here is not simply informational,* but we are attempting to provoke curiosity about the dynamic nature of a field and an interest in doing further research. Thus, it is recommended that the materials in each center include descriptive information *about* particular fields of knowledge in a given field. For example, a center on historiography (rather than history!) should include books that capture the excitement and joy of discovery that a historian experiences when he or she uncovers an overlooked document, an unpublished letter, or an old newspaper that sheds new light on an important problem. Descriptions of the work of historians and the contributions that they have made by imaginatively reconstructing the events of the past are much more relevant to the objectives of Type I Enrichment than the usual references that we typically associate with the study of history or the history section of the school library. Books (or other materials) that deal with information about subjects should answer questions such as:

Why do we study history?

What does history do for mankind?

What kinds of questions does the historian ask and of whom?

Where does the historian look for evidence?

What are some of the great discoveries of historians?

What are the different types of historians, and in what ways is history categorized?

What qualifies as a historical document?

How does the historian move from raw data to conclusions and generalizations?

Perhaps the following books will serve as further examples of what is meant by information *about* a field of knowledge rather than collections of accumulated information in the field itself:

Carr, Edward H. *What Is History?* Alfred A. Knopf, Inc., New York, 1962. A very good volume on the nature of history. The author stresses the need for historical objectivity and presents the notion that history is an ongoing dialogue between the past, the present, and the future.

Collingwood, R. G. *The Idea of History.* Oxford University Press, Fair Lawn, N.J., 1946. Two-thirds of this book trace the development of historiography in the Western world. The last part develops the author's own particular notions of history as the recreation of human thought in its historical context.

Gottschalk, Louis (Ed.). *Generalization in the Writing of History.* The University of Chicago Press, Chicago, 1963. A symposium by eminent historians on the role of generalization in history. While many divergent points of view are presented, there is agreement that no historical accounts of events or periods can avoid making generalizations.

Hughes, H. Stuart. *History as Art and as Science.* Harper and Row, Publishers, Incorporated, New York, 1964. The author views history as a discipline which draws ideas and methods from the behavioral and social sciences and from the humanities. Chapter 3 presents the contact points between history and psychoanalysis in explaining human motives.

Potter, David M. *People of Plenty.* The University of Chicago Press, Chicago, 1954. A severe indictment of historians in their study of national character. Advocates that historians should increasingly use the methods of the behavioral and social sciences and proceeds to illustrate how this can be done on the topic of American national character. (See Massialas and Cox, 1966, pp. 57–58.)

Winks, Robin W. *The Historian as Detective.* Harper and Row, Publishers, New York, 1968. This lively collection of essays focuses on the theme that historians must collect, interpret, and explain evidence using many of the same techniques employed by detectives conducting criminal investigations. Parallels can also be seen between the work of historians and present-day "investigative journalism."

Note that in the case of each of the above books, we are dealing with descriptions about the subject of history and the work of historians rather than the facts and findings of persons who have worked in this field. Although materials of this type should be the major focus of interest centers, other types of high-interest material should also be included. For example, local or state history books might provoke in some youngsters the idea that they also can do investigation in their hometown. Or books that deal with particular aspects of history (e.g., military, diplomatic, ecclesiastical) may serve as examples of how historians in the real world specialize on very limited segments of this vast field of knowledge. Other materials that might spark ideas in the minds of budding young historians include copies of old newspapers, photocopies of sample town documents, old maps, railroad timetables, or advertisements, and perhaps some sample records from businesses that have served the community for many years. If your town has a local historical society perhaps it might loan various materials for display in the interest center. Additional materials can probably be obtained from the state historical society or director of archives, and college, state, or local librarians may be able to provide you with copies of any and all books that deal with the history of your area. Interest centers might also contain some materials that describe career opportunities in various fields and information such as brochures, newsletters, and journals that are published by professional societies and organizations. Local or state department of education specialists in career education can provide valuable assistance in locating these types of materials.

The development of a successful interest center can be a very creative endeavor on the part of the teacher. Although some informal guidelines have been offered here, the teacher's own experience and imagination should be exercised to the fullest in making the interest center come alive with thought-provoking materials. Students who have completed investigations in particular areas may want to contribute their products to the centers and also recommend items that they think will be highly stimulating to other youngsters. If other young people from throughout the nation (or world) have done outstanding work in a certain area of knowledge, descriptions or samples of these materials should be included in order to help students realize that age is not a limiting factor in making contributions to various fields of art and knowledge.

The development of interest centers is obviously a task that cannot be accomplished overnight; however, a continuous effort on the part of all persons working in the gifted program can result in a wide variety of exploratory alternatives. In order to provide options that will meet the diversified interests of all students it is recommended that a long-range goal be established to provide interest centers in the following areas:

1. The social sciences. Broadly conceived to include areas not ordinarily covered in the regular curriculum, such as anthropology, economics, political science, psychology, sociology, demography, and the judicial and legal sciences.
2. The physical and life sciences.
3. Mathematics and logic.
4. Music, the visual arts, and the arts of movement and dramatic production. Including puppetry, film making, set design, improvisation, interviewing, public speaking, choreography, play production, clothing design, interior and landscape architecture, and all types of crafts.
5. All aspects of writing. Including advertising, literary criticism, journalism, and technical writing as well as the more common areas of written expression such as poetry, play writing, short stories, autobiography, etc.
6. Philosophy, ethics, and social issues. Including critical contemporary problems that are controversial because they involve judgments based on morals or values (e.g. welfare, due process, civil rights, political corruption, etc.)

Another strategy for promoting Type I Enrichment consists of inviting resource persons to make presentations to groups of gifted students; however, the same logic that holds true for field trips should be applied here. Resource persons should be carefully selected in an effort to involve individuals who are actively engaged in contributing to the advancement of art or knowledge in their respective areas of endeavor. Local historians, poets, dancers, architects or photographers who are "turned-on professionals," who feel that they are creatively reconstructing the fields in which they work or to which they devote some of their leisure time—these are the types of persons who are especially appropriate as human resources for gifted and talented youngsters. Indeed, one of the reasons that we have selected particular students for participation in special programs is because we believe that they have a superior potential to develop their capacity for creative production. Thus, it seems only logical to escalate the entire concept of using community resources by bringing these students into contact with persons who are themselves creative producers.

Interest centers, field trips, and exposure to community resource persons are, of course, organized approaches to Type I Enrichment; however, students should also be given opportunities to look into any and all types of topics that are available. Simply browsing in libraries or bookstores or participating in unstructured group discussions may yield favorable results. These discussions might be based on an "interest-focusing question" (e.g., What would you like to be said about you at a testimonial dinner given at the time of your retirement?) or an interest questionnaire. It is important, however, for students to constantly and conscientiously keep the goal of general exploratory activity in mind. Although exploration should be enjoyable and have personal growth value in and of itself, each student should keep in mind that exploratory activities are a rare opportunity to identify his or her own personal curriculum, an opportunity that seldom presents itself in the regular school program. It is also an opportunity for students to get in touch with their own interests and concerns, and thus has value as a self-actualization experience.

The third and final guideline for helping to achieve the objectives of Type I Enrichment deals with the direction that exploratory activities should give to teachers in selecting Type II Enrichment activities. As will be pointed out in the following section, a vast array of process-oriented materials is available for individual and small group activity; however, some rhyme or reason should exist for deciding which materials should be used with particular youngsters. The teacher must be a sensitive observer of the spontaneous activities of his or her students so that if one group of youngsters shows an interest in politics, for example, the teacher may then decide to use a simulation game which deals with various processes of political decision making (e.g. Political Party Nominating Game, Politics in Benin, Domino, or POLIS—Political Institutions Simulation). Another group, however, may be extremely interested in rocks and minerals, thus leading the teacher to decide that some exercises in the process of classification (using science materials) might be of value. Still another group might express an interest in producing a play, and thus some group training in creative dramatics may be warranted. Although group exercises should be open to all who would like to participate, they should nevertheless always emanate from the interests of at least some youngsters. This rationale for selecting Type II activities will help to respect the first objective of programs for the gifted, which places major emphasis on the interests of students.

Type II Enrichment: Group Training Activities

Type II Enrichment consists of methods, materials, and instructional techniques that are mainly concerned with the development of thinking and feeling processes. An important concept to keep in mind as we discuss this section of the model is that Type II Enrichment activities consist almost entirely of *training exercises,* and we should view them in a fashion analogous to the way that we view the physical exercises of an athlete in training. A good way to understand the nature of these types of activities is to compare them with content-oriented learning situations in which the major objective is to increase the learner's storehouse of knowledge or information in a particular segment of the curriculum. The information may take many forms, but the important characteristic of content-oriented learning is that major emphasis is placed on the assimilation of conclusions, whether they be facts, principles, or higher order generalizations. By way of contrast, the objective of Type II Enrichment is to develop in the learner the processes or operations (the "powers of mind") that enable him or her to deal more effectively with content. Over the years a variety of terms have been used to describe the thinking and feeling processes that are being categorized in this model under the general heading of Type II Enrichment. These terms have included critical thinking, problem solving, reflective thinking, inquiry training, divergent thinking, sensitivity training, awareness development, and creative or productive thinking. In addition to these general descriptions of the thinking and feeling process, specific behaviors such as the following have frequently been used to define various types of cognitive and affective processes:

Brainstorming	Fluency
Observation	Flexibility
Classification	Originality
Interpretation	Elaboration
Analysis	Hypothesizing
Evaluation	Awareness
Comparison	Appreciation
Categorization	Value Clarification
Synthesis	Commitment

Perhaps the best way to describe what is meant by mental processes or operations is to point out two well-known models that deal with the organization of psychological factors that are instrumental in human learning. *The Taxonomies of Educational Objectives* (Bloom, 1956; Krathwohl, 1964) and Guilford's *Structure of the Intellect Model* (1967) provide us with carefully developed systems for defining and classifying the cognitive and affective behaviors of which the human mind is capable.

In recent years an increasingly large number of process-oriented curriculum packages have been developed and it is recommended that persons in gifted programs devote some time to familiarizing themselves with these materials. Excellent compendiums of creativity training materials and simulation and learning games are available in the professional literature (see, for example, Treffinger and Gowan, 1971; Feldhusen, 1975; Zuckerman and Horn, 1973; Gibbs, 1974) and many new curriculum materials are now emphasizing process objectives rather than (or in addition to) content objectives. A broad and categorical knowledge of the various types of process-oriented activities (and teaching strategies) will enable the teacher purposefully to select materials that are in keeping with students' topical or subject-matter preferences. It should be emphasized that content relevancy is not always possible and there may be times when certain process activities are appropriate, with little or no regard for the type of content on which they focus.

As was pointed out in an earlier section of this article, many programs for the gifted have had a preoccupation with process activities. In fact, the relationship between the gifted education movement and the area of creativity training has grown so strong in recent years that many people are using the words "gifted" and "creative" synonymously. One of the major characteristics of most creativity training materials is that they allow for essentially open-ended responses, thus enabling brighter or more informed persons to ascend to higher levels of fluency, flexibility, and originality in the process of divergent problem solving. Similarly, the gifted education movement has fondly embraced the simulation and learning games approach to instruction because the open-ended nature of many activities provides opportunities for "on-your-feet thinking" rather than the mere regurgitation of facts, principles, or other predetermined conclusions. For these reasons, Type II Enrichment is considered to be a necessary ingredient in the total enrichment model; however, programs which focus exclusively on process training without further extension into Type III activities are likely to be both lopsided and indefensible. By lopsided I simply mean that students will spend all of their time practicing processes rather than actually using them in real inquiry situations. This approach would be analogous to a basketball team or dramatic group that spends all of its time practicing but never engaging in a real game or presenting a play before a real audience. Even the most exciting process training activities are, in the final analysis, still "exercises," and if they represent the total focus of a program, they then become the ends of education rather than the means.

Programs which focus completely on process training also place gifted education in an extremely indefensible position. There is virtually no area of training in the thinking and feeling processes that can be defended as being exclusively appropriate for gifted and talented students; and persons in general education would protest bitterly (and validly) if we claimed that gifted students should be the sole recipients of such "good things" as creativity training, critical thinking, or human awareness experiences. And yet, carefully selected Type II Enrichment activities can be defended for at least three reasons. Such activities, if appropriately selected, provide for a range of response options (i.e., they must be open-ended) so that youngsters with superior potential will have an opportunity to escalate their thinking and feeling processes to whatever levels their own natural abilities allow. We must keep in mind that giftedness and creativity are in the student's response (not the stimulus materials), and it is what the youngster brings to the learning situation that makes him or her gifted. Thus a major concern in selecting Type II activities is to focus on materials and learning experiences that have the power to "bring out" advanced levels of thinking on the parts of students.

By way of summary, Type II experiences are considered to be an essential component of a total enrichment model; however, one important consideration should serve as a guide in the use of these materials and teaching strategies. The experiences should be carefully selected so that they represent a logical outgrowth of student interests and concerns rather than mere random involvement in whatever happens to be available or whatever the teacher might have a fancy for. Purposefully selected Type II activities can help "tie together" the other two components of the enrichment model and thus provide a very defensible rationale for their use. But more importantly, by simply viewing Type II Enrichment as one aspect of a total enrichment model, we can help to avoid the danger of making process-oriented activities the be-all and end-all of a program for the gifted.

Type III Enrichment: Individual Projects

In Type III activities, students use real-word methods of inquiry to become "first-hand investigators" in the particular area in which they choose to work. A rationale, based upon research on gifted and talented persons in the adult world, was developed to support the appropriateness of Type III Enrichment for gifted youngsters.

The last section of the model is organized around the teacher's three main responsibilities in carrying out Type III Enrichment. These responsibilities are to provide each student with assistance in (1) identifying and focusing on solvable problems, (2) acquiring methodological resources and investigative skills, and (3) finding appropriate outlets for products.

Strategies for Identifying and Focusing on Solvable Problems. The first major responsibility of the teacher is to assist students in analyzing their own areas of interest. There are at least two approaches that the teacher can use to achieve this goal. The first approach is to organize a variety of "new exposure" experiences. These experiences should enable youngsters to learn about the full range of investigative opportunities and areas of creative expression that are open to them. This can be accomplished by inviting involved, "turned-on" professionals into the classroom; by consulting the literature on career education, hobbies, and recreational activities; or by asking parents and other community resource persons to share their interests.

The second strategy for helping youngsters to examine their interests is through the use of an instrument entitled *The Interest Analyzer.* This instrument contains a number of hypothetical situations that are structured to elicit general patterns of interest (e.g., performing arts, mathematical, business and historical, etc.) When using this instrument, students should be given maximum freedom of choice in deciding how and with whom they would like to discuss their responses.

Providing Students With Methodological Assistance. Once areas of interest are identified, the teacher needs to provide students with the tools of inquiry appropriate for the field of investigation being pursued. In order to do this, it is recommended that teachers learn how to teach some general exercises in inquiry training. It is also suggested that teachers familiarize themselves with the existence, nature, and function of the full range of reference materials that are available for in-depth study in most fields. In some instances, these materials will involve nonprint as well as print media.

The third and most important thing that must be learned in order to promote Type III Enrichment is how to identify and locate how-to-do-it books. Almost every field of study has such guides, and some are written at relatively elementary levels. It is important to secure and to analyze these resources in terms of an individual youngster's reading and conceptual level and to serve as a translator whenever a concept is beyond the child's level of comprehension.

Finding Appropriate Outlets for Student Products. The final responsibility of the teacher is to help students communicate the results of their investigative work in a realistic and meaningful manner. For assistance in finding appropriate outlets for students' products, teachers can consult with creative/productive professionals and with persons from various interest groups. Local organizations, such as historical societies, science clubs, dramatic groups, etc., might allow or even encourage students to present their work at monthly meetings or have articles published in their newsletter, journal, or annual publication. Teachers should also consider submitting students' products to children's magazines that routinely include the work of young people (e.g., *Highlights for Children, Kid's Magazine*).

These are only some of the many possible outlets that should be explored for the purpose of helping to make student products real. Unless teachers take the time to perform this function in an energetic and creative manner, there is little likelihood that Type III Enrichment will achieve a truly qualitative difference from the usual project activities that are popular in most programs for the gifted.

References

Bloom, B. S. (Ed.). *Taxonomy of Educational Objectives: Handbook I: Cognitive Domain.* New York: Longmans-Green, 1956.

Feldhusen, J. F., and others. *Teaching Children to Think: Synthesis, Interpretation and Evaluation of Research and Development in Creative Problem Solving.* West Lafayette, Ind.: Purdue University, 1975.

Gibbs, G. I. *Handbook of Games and Simulation Exercises.* Beverly Hills, Cal.: Sage Publications, 1974.

Guilford, J. P. *The Nature of Human Intelligence.* New York: McGraw-Hill, 1967.

Krathwohl, D. R., and others, *Taxonomy of Educational Objectives: Handbook II: Affective Domain.* New York: David McKay, 1964.

Massialas, B. G., and Cox, C. B. *Inquiry in the Social Studies.* New York: McGraw-Hill, 1966.

Treffinger, D. J., and Gowan, J. C. "An Updated Representative List of Methods and Educational Programs for Stimulating Creativity." *The Journal of Creative Behavior* 5:127–139, 1971.

Zuckerman, D. W., and Horn, R. C. (Eds.). *The Guide to Simulations —Games for Education and Training.* Lexington, Mass.: Information Resources, 1973.

* * * * *

Editor's note: This article, first printed in *The Gifted Child Quarterly* has been expanded into a monograph by Dr. Renzulli; *The Enrichment Triad Model* was published by the Creative Learning Press, 530 Silas Deane Hy., Wethersfield, CT, 06109 in 1977.

Chapter Four

Curriculum

Introduction

"What am I doing in this class for gifted students that couldn't be done equally well by an outstanding teacher in a heterogeneous class?" This is the prime curriculum question which should be asked by every teacher of the gifted in every classroom period. Unless the teacher is doing something which is *qualitatively* different, then the program is not viable, and the segregation of the gifted has been in vain. Thus the *sine qua non* of planning a curriculum for gifted students is a differentiated program.

Such a qualitative difference in a gifted child curriculum involves several aspects:

1. *Deeper study than an average class could handle.* Examples would be, in language arts, study of phonetics, elementary philology, etymology, word cognates in different languages, and so on, and in elementary mathematics, study of higher arithmetic, binary and octal notations, numerical permutations and combinations, numerical trigonometry and logs, series, mathematical induction, or statistics. Similar more profound probings could be undertaken in history and in science. Such work always goes beyond the standard texts and requires teachers who have majored in the subjects and know them very well. Earlier departmentalization will be required. The aim should be not accelerated material, which the student would get ordinarily later on, but material which is of such qualitative complexity that it cannot be handled by the average student. Such complexity might include the expectation of hypothesis formation at the formal operations level at a time when the gifted child is at the concrete operations level chronologically.

2. *A change in the teacher's function, from director of learning to facilitator.* The wise teacher will realize that he or she cannot hope to be an expert in all aspects of gifted child education and will instead attempt to facilitate children's learning as an independent researcher. The use of libraries and laboratories is a first effort in this

direction which allows the children to work on projects on their own. A second is the use of mentors and other paraprofessionals who have a special expertise that the teacher does not share. The development of independence and research skills allows the children finally to operate on their own in what J. S. Renzulli (1976) calls a Type III enrichment situation, in which the child works on a practical problem whose solution may be socially useful.

3. *A greater amount of curriculum material.* Gifted children operating at their maximums can consume up to four or five times as much curriculum material as is used in an ordinary classroom. Hence the teacher needs to find curriculum material which is suitable, which will be used later in regular classrooms, and the addition of which will not be seen by the child as a penalty. For example, doubling the number of homework exercises to be done by a gifted class over that assigned to the average class will ordinarily be seen as a penalty for being gifted.

One of the real possibilities of freeing the gifted child for more individualized instruction lies in the use of computer terminals on shared time or with other programmed learning devices, such as IPI, which will allow individual instruction to take place for the uncommon student. The peculiar potential of this means of teaching bright children has been noted by Feldhusen (1963; 1969), Hanson and Komoski (1965), and Renzulli (1970).

4. *Greater processing of curriculum material.* Essentially, this means that the structure of intellect (SOI) operations on the material should be much more than cognition and memory; they should extend to divergent thinking and evaluation with consequent decision making from alternatives. Such a purpose may be handled through the use of curriculum games or simulations, or the production of some creative outcome such as a poem, painting, or other art form. The area of values in the affective domain should also be stressed: What value outcomes are there for society or for individual development?

5. *The intentional use of curriculum materials to develop creative thinking.* This final point should never be lost sight of. Since our aim is determining how to make the gifted child creative, we constantly need to teach creative techniques. Every unit should be checked for opportunities of this nature. The three readings following this introduction have been chosen with this concept in mind. The first involves training in research skills; the second contains probably the most easily learned method of producing creative learning situations out of the SOI concept, and the third looks at a utopian curriculum for the gifted.

While no journal can by itself provide the spate of curriculum material necessary for teachers of the gifted, the editor of *The Gifted*

Child Quarterly (aided greatly by dedicated guest editors), has provided special issues on the following topics:

Creativity. 19:3 (Fall 1975), 21:4 (Winter 1977), 23:4 (Winter 1979).
Language Arts. 20:1 (Spring 1976).
Mathematics. 20:3 (Fall 1976).
Science. 21:1 (Spring 1977).
Art. 20:4 (Winter 1976).
Teacher Training. 21:2 (Summer 1977).
Guidance. 21:3 (Fall 1977).
Minority Gifted. 22:2 (Fall 1978).
Gifted Females. 22:4 (Winter 1978).
Family of Gifted. 22:3 (Summer 1978).
Curriculum Games. 23:2 (Summer 1979).
Incubation. 23:1 (Spring 1979).
Demonstration and Project Centers. 23:3 (Fall 1979).

10 Teaching Gifted Elementary Pupils Research Concepts And Skills

E. PAUL TORRANCE AND R. E. MYERS

The teaching of research concepts and skills has usually been reserved for the graduate-school period. Discussions on teaching elementary pupils how to do research are usually limited to procedures for "looking something up in the library" and almost never touch upon the concepts and methods of creative scientific research. Textbooks on methods of teaching in high school and in the undergraduate college are seldom much better. Yet, important discoveries have been made by elementary pupils, high school students, and undergraduates. Louis Braille at the age of 10 conceived of his idea for an alphabet for the blind and by 15 had worked out the details. Many of the world's most outstanding medical discoveries were made by undergraduate students or were begun during the discoverer's undergraduate days (Gibson, 1958).

The senior author has for some time believed that most research concepts and many research skills could be taught to elementary pupils, especially gifted ones. It was his belief that if gifted children could be taught these concepts and skills at an early age, they would have available some powerful tools to aid them in their thinking. This should make learning more exciting and the search for "truth" more rewarding. For the past three years, he and his staff have had the opportunity to test this idea in part through a five-day course taught to the High Achievers Class at the Riverside Elementary School of Bloomington, Minnesota.

Each year, the course has been varied. In many ways, the 1961–62 course was a better balanced one than previous courses and will be described briefly. It may suggest quite different ideas among some workers. Some may want to expand the program as the authors developed it or select from it.

The 1961–62 class consisted of 46 pupils selected on the basis of

From E. Paul Torrance and R. E. Myers, "Teaching Gifted Elementary Pupils Research Concepts and Skills," *The Gifted Child Quarterly*, Vol. 6 (1962), pp. 1–6. Reprinted by permission of E. Paul Torrance and *The Gifted Child Quarterly*.

achievement and intelligence (minimum Stanford-Binet IQ, 135). Each morning these pupils functioned as two separate groups under different teachers. (Gilbertson, 1960). During this period, they followed essentially the same curriculum as other sixth-grade classes, with the exception that they had lessons in French. This left the afternoons free for other ventures. On alternate weeks they worked on their "strengths and weaknesses" under the direction of their teachers. During other weeks, both groups studied for a week with "Alter Teachers" who were expert in some special field such as: chemistry, journalism, dentistry, music, psychology, architecture, law, and the like. The course on Educational Research was conducted as a part of the alter-teacher program jointly by the authors and in cooperation with the principal, Mr. Joseph Buzzelli, and the teachers, Mr. Darrell Miller and Miss JoAnn Johnson.

Objectives

The major objectives of the course on Educational Research were:

1. To familiarize gifted elementary pupils with some of the most powerful concepts of research in the behavioral sciences, in order that these concepts might become tools in the learning and thinking early in their school careers.
2. To communicate to gifted pupils the excitement of doing original research, exploring the unknown and pushing forward knowledge.
3. To provide experiences in participating in educational research and in conducting experiments with real consequences.
4. To develop in gifted elementary pupils some skills in formulating hypotheses, testing them, and in reporting the results.

What Is the Research Process?

On the first day, the children learned that there are many things which teachers and other educators do not know about how to help boys and girls to learn most effectively. They learned that one of the ways of finding out about these unknowns is through research. The youngsters offered their own ideas about research—ways of digging into things, looking things up, experimenting, etc. They learned that research involves a more or less formal, systematic, intensive process of carrying on the scientific method.

In quick order, the sixth-grade pupils experienced some of the research process through the "What's in the Box" game.[1] The two classes which comprised the High Achievers at Riverside School were separated, one group working under each of the authors. In each case the group was told that the object in the box was round. The group then made some wild guesses of round things which might be in the box. They then wanted to experiment—lifting, shaking, smelling, and otherwise examining. One group found that the object made no sound and immediately eliminated all objects which would make a sound, which were rather heavy, and the like. The other group found that the object in its box made a sound, was light, and was apparently quite small. This group then eliminated soft objects, heavy objects, and large objects. Both groups at this point made some more guesses and started asking questions which could be answered by "yes" or "no." One by one, they eliminated the guesses they had made and finally guessed the correct identity of the object—in one case, a powder puff; in the other, a Sucret (cough drop). This was then verified.

The person who identified the object then described the process of *synthesis* by which he arrived at the correct answer. From this, the class identified the following steps in the process:

1. Recognizing that you don't know something.
2. Making wild guesses on the basis of available facts.
3. Experimenting, testing, eliminating guesses.
4. Making better guesses.
5. Asking questions to test hypotheses (guesses).
6. Eliminating bad guesses on the basis of additional information.
7. Making better guesses, synthesizing facts obtained.
8. Verifying the final answer.

Three Kinds of Research

The High Achievers then learned that there are three major kinds of research and that the concepts learned in the "What's in the Box?" game are applied to each of them. They grasped easily the essential characteristics of historical, descriptive, and experimental research and learned that they would explore each firsthand during the week.

---

[1]The authors are indebted to Lawrence Conray, School of Education, University of Michigan for the "What's in the Box?" idea for teaching multiple hypothesis-making and related concepts.

Historical Research

Historiography and the process of doing historical research were introduced first. Right in class, the pupils were given the first of two "How Did You Grow?" exercises which required them to plot the trends in their own development from first through six grade in shoe size, height, curiosity, reading speed, imagination, spelling ability, independence in thinking, and arithmetic computation.

The first day ended with a real challenge to the youngsters—they were invited to engage in some actual historical research. The High Achievers were given a set of the same charts they had just filled out and were told to collect all of the data they could to test the trends which they had already hypothesized.

On the next day the class reported dozens of sources they had used: parents, teachers, brothers and sisters, other relatives, photograph albums, report cards, old clothing and shoes, baby diaries, and the like. They agreed that these could be classified either as records or witnesses. The children found that they had been introduced firsthand to the problem of *bias* and of *evaluating evidence* and reaching a *conclusion*. They found that even their parents perceived their development in vastly different ways and guessed why.

Descriptive Research

In order to give some experience with a descriptive study, the High Achievers were administered the Ask-and-Guess Test, using the picture of Old Mother Hubbard. First, they asked as many questions as they could about the picture and the events occurring in it. Then they spent five minutes making guesses about causes and another five minutes guessing consequences. After they had counted the number of questions and recorded them on the blackboard, they decided that one way of using these data to describe the group would be to find the average or mean. They noted that the girls had a larger mean (12.17) than the boys (9.43) but could not tell whether or not such a difference was just an accident—a matter of chance. They were introduced to the concept of levels of confidence and the *t* test. It was found that this difference could be accepted at about the 2 percent level of confidence; that is, it would fail to occur in only about two cases in one hundred.

In a similar manner, the concepts of the median, the mode, variance, and the like were developed.

Experimental Research

On the third day, the High Achievers served as subjects of an experiment on the effects of differential rewards upon creative thinking. To teach the concepts of randomization, experimental treatments, and the like, the two classes were divided randomly into Groups A and B. This was done by means of drawing assignment cards which had been carefully shuffled. Torrance and Myers tossed a coin to see who would have Group A and who would have which treatment. A prize of two dollars was offered to the pupil in Group A who could think of the largest number of ideas, regardless of quality; and a prize of twenty-five cents was offered to the pupil who could think of the largest number of original ideas. The treatment for Group B was just the reverse—the pupil with the most original ideas was offered a prize of two dollars, while the one with the largest number of ideas, regardless of quality, was offered twenty-five cents. The task was to think of ideas for making a toy dog more fun to play with. Ten minutes were allowed for the task. A response was scored as original if it had been given by fewer than 5 percent of the subjects in the norm population for the Minnesota Tests of Creativity. Responses were also scored for fluency and flexibility.

The results of the experiment were reported the following day. The mean number of acceptable ideas by Group A was 23 and by Group B, 20.4. The mean originality score for A was 6.2 and for B, 12.2. The mean flexibility score for each group was 8.5. It was found that the difference for fluency could be accepted at about the 25 percent level; the difference in originality could be accepted at the 0.1 percent level; and, of course, there was no difference in flexibility. This gave the High Achievers understandable examples of differences in the degree of confidence which can be expected in some experimental studies. It also illustrated the principle that thinking is likely to be more original if originality is rewarded.

Concepts of Measurement and Quantification

The homework assignment for the second day of the course was to write an imaginative story on their choice of ten titles involving persons or animals with divergent characteristics, such as:

The Duck That Won't Quack
The Flying Monkey
The Boy Who Wants to Be a Nurse
The Girl Who Wants to Be an Engineer

The stories were used as the basis for developing concepts of measurement and quantification. It was seen rather quickly that the number of words, number of sentences, and the like could be counted and the numbers used to describe the stories. They computed the percentage who wrote on each topic. They also noted that the number of different kinds of words, different kinds of sentences, different kinds of errors, and the like might also be used to describe the stories. They were then asked how they could quantify such qualities as originality and interest. As a result of the ensuing discussion, they named almost all of the criteria for assessing originality and interest developed in Minnesota in 1961 when the Torrance Tests were first brought out.

An Experiment of Their Own

At the end of the third session, instructions were given for conducting an experiment of their own. First, there was a pilot study in which the High Achievers served as subjects. They were given the Horse-Trading Problem (Maier & Solem, 1952), which is as follows:

You bought a horse for $60 and sold it for $70. You then decided that you wanted the horse back. You had to pay $80 for it this time, but you sold it again for $90. How did you come out in all this trading? Did you make or lose any money? How much did you gain or lose, if any?

Nineteen of the children said thay they would make $10; 14 said that they would break even; 6 said that they would make $20. None said there would be a $30 profit, until the experimenter asked those who had not held up their hands if they had gotten $30—then some of those who had reported other numbers shifted to $30.

They were then given instructions for carrying out their own experiment on the following day. The class was divided into research teams of four or five members each. Each team was to conduct an experiment in a specified classroom in the third, fourth, and fifth grades. On the last day of the course the teams were to present their findings in research reports.

The experiment which the young researchers carried out involved presenting the Horse-Trading Problem to ten of the third, fourth, and fifth grade classes of the school and introducing an experimental variable which could be measured. In order to find out how their schoolmates might be influenced in arriving at their answers, each team collected cards upon which the subjects had written their answers and then "accidentally" dropped a slip of paper which had "30" written on it as they left the room. Later on, when the High Achievers returned to the rooms, they gave the subjects a chance to change their answers before the correct answer was revealed. The subjects were given a dittoed sheet which afforded them an opportunity to change their answers and also asked them if they had discussed the problem with anyone and who had influenced them if they had changed their answers.

When the teams came together they converted some of their findings into percentages and were taught how to use a nomograph to determine whether or not the differences in percentages were significant. The symbols for level of confidence bothered them because they had not been prepared for this, but with this out of the way they were able to determine level of confidence in their own experiments between percentage correct on the first trial and percentage correct on the second trial.

On the last day, the reports came in. In reporting, the High Achievers followed this outline:

1. *Purpose of the Study.*   Why did you perform the experiment? What was it that you didn't know? What were you trying to find out?

2. *Procedure.*   What was done? Who performed the experiment? What materials did they use? Who were the subjects? How many were there? What did the experimenter do and what did the subjects do? These things should be described in such a way that someone else could perform the experiment and obtain the same results.

3. *Results.*   What happened? What did you find out? This should include a presentation of your data in tables, charts, or the like.

4. *Discussion.*   What does it mean? Try to explain results and their meaning.

5. *Conclusions.*   What does it all add up to? What can you be reasonably certain about? How certain can you be?

Many of the reports were well organized and were written in good form. A number showed real ingenuity.

A Review and a Test

Following a brief review in which an attempt was made to consolidate the gains in knowledge which had taken place during the week, the pupils took a test which dealt with the basic ideas of the course. Judging from their responses, the High Achievers attained a good grasp of the fundamental concepts of educational research.

Some By-Products

One important by-product from teaching gifted elementary pupils research concepts and skills is the contribution which experiments conducted in such a setting make to the development and testing of new hypotheses, about the education both of gifted children and of others. The historical research project has provided the authors with a number of ideas which had never before occurred to them concerning the development of children and the ways in which parents perceive this development. The experiment conducted by the children helped us to plot in a new way the increase in peer influence and the decline in adult influence in searching for solutions to problems. These and other findings and leads will be presented in other reports.

References

Gibson, W. C. *Young Endeavour.* Springfield, Ill.: Charles C Thomas, Publisher, 1958.
Gilbertson, S. *The Second Report on the High Achievers Room.* Bloomington, Minn., Bloomington Public Schools, 1960.
Maier, N. R. F. and Solem, A. R. "The Contribution of a Discussion Leader to the Quality of Group Thinking: The Effective Use of Minority Opinion," *Human Relations,* Vol. 5 (1952), pp. 277–88.

11   Models for Encouraging Creativity in the Classroom

FRANK E. WILLIAMS

Recognizing and meeting the intellectual as well as emotional needs of children, which both lead toward uncovering their creative potential, have become respectable goals or purposes of education. As Dr. Donald W. MacKinnon (1969) reports, the characteristics of the creative process and person are distinguished, most generally, by two fundamental sets of traits, one intellective and the other attitudinal or motivational. This article will discuss a theoretical rationale for several cognitive-affective models from which a new model has been designed for use by the classroom teacher concerned about encouraging creativity through thinking and feeling behaviors among young children.

From Frank E. Williams, "Models for Encouraging Creativity in the Classroom," *Educational Technology Magazine,* 456 Sylvan Ave., Englewood Cliffs, N.J. 07632, December 1969. Reprinted by permission of the magazine.

Cognitive Domain

The first set of traits, but certainly not first in importance for being or becoming creative, requires a breadth and depth of knowledge and a set of thinking skills for recording, retaining, and processing one's cognized information. Such skills or multidimensional talents commonly go under the name of the cognitive domain and consist of a pupil's logical and rational concerns with what is—algorithmic truths. These are in almost every school's statements of behavioral objectives. Within this set of broad purposes or goals of education, classroom teaching emphasizes academic excellence, subject-matter mastery, and the learning of someone else's information. These are played for real with a great deal of time and effort spent on them by the classroom teacher and regarded as fair game in measuring and assessing a child's intellectual growth.

Most models of the cognitive domain are in the form of a taxonomy consisting of a sequential classification of from low- to high-order thinking processes. However, those mental processes such as hypothesizing, synthesizing, inventing, associating, transforming, relating, designing, translating, or combining have been used synonymously by many to define the creative process; yet they are only found within the higher stages or levels of these taxonomy models.

Formal Operations Stage
    Abstract-conceptual thinking
    Reasoning generalized
    Evaluation
    Hypothesizing
    Imagining
    Synthesizing
Concrete Operations Stage
    Analyzing
    Conscious of dynamic variables
    Measures
    Classifies things in groups or series
Pre-Operational Stage
    Symbols and representations
    Actions on perceptive impulses
    Self-centered
    Static-irreversible thinking
Sensory-Motor Stage
    Mute—no use of verbal symbols
    Learns to perceive—discriminate and identify objects

FIGURE 11.1
Piaget's Stage Theory of Intellectual Development

For example, Piaget's (Flavell, 1963) stage theory of intellectual development (see Figure 11.1) places those mental abilities (italicized terms) which define and describe the creative process in the formal operations stage, as can be seen appearing at the top level of this taxonomy. Even in Bloom's *Taxonomy of Educational Objectives* (1956) (see Figure 11.2), the processes of synthesis are the most predominant ingredients of creativity and likewise appear as higher level thought processes at the fifth step of this model.

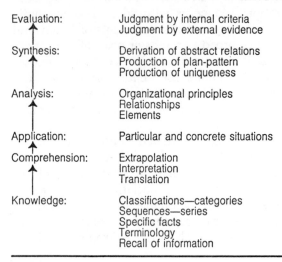

FIGURE 11.2
Bloom's Taxonomy of the Cognitive Domain

Those who have developed taxonomy models advocate that later operations are built upon earlier ones, and that intellectual development follows an ordered sequence. They say a child is incapable of learning these higher level thought processes before earlier ones are mastered. Here is where we get into trouble when teachers want to encourage a young child's creative potential, because these models indicate that creative thinking consists of higher mental processes which may not develop much before middle childhood. Yet, all primary grade teachers are aware of how free and open every young child is to be imaginative, inventive, flexible and perceptive *at his or her own intellectual level.* That is to say, surely the young child may not be able to break new boundaries, at least in any sophisticated degree, by creating new concepts in the physical sciences; but he or she may be highly original and imaginative in dealing with their own discoveries and uses of already existing scientific concepts. Hence, there are some questions raised by classroom teachers when they attempt to apply taxonomical models of cognition for curriculum development or for planning learning experiences which encourage those thinking processes associated with a child's creative potential.

Affective Domain

Another set of traits equally important for being or becoming creative is that broad area of aesthetic concerns for feeling, beauty, and form. These make up another important area of educational objectives which deal with attitudes, values, dispositions, and motivations of the pupil *to want to* do something with information, data, and knowledge which has been cognized. Such feeling processes include a pupil's inward openness to his own hunches, nudges, guesses, emotions, and intuitive feelings about facts which he has become sensitive to and is curious about. These personal-motivational factors may be most crucial and make the real difference for the pupil to be willing to appreciate either their own or others' creative productions. These are processes which cause the pupil to operate as much by feeling as by logic because he is able and willing to deal with fantasy, imagination, and emotion in terms of things that might be—heuristics. This is the insightful person who has the courage to be a bold risk-taker by venturing past the edges of the familiar; who is curious about other possibilities and alternatives rather than dealing with absolutes and permanencies; who uses his imagination to reach beyond artificial or limited boundaries; and who is willing to delve into the complexities of intricate problems, situations, or ideas just to see where they will take him. Here we are talking about experiences within an educational program that legitimize feelings, offered by teachers who have empathy for intuition and guessing rather than always expecting the child to know. The affective domain has likewise been presented by Krathwohl (Krathwohl et al., 1964) as a taxonomical model (see Figure 11.3).

Most teachers would agree that thinking processes really cannot

---

Internalizing (automatically characterizes a way of life)

↑

Conceptualizing (organizing a value system)

↑

Valuing (appreciation and commitment)

↑

Responding (willingness and satisfaction)

↑

Receiving (sensitive and aware)

FIGURE 11.3
Krathwohl's Taxonomy of the Affective Domain

operate without feeling processes. Even as Krathwohl states, "nearly all cognitive behaviors have an affective component." One involves the other, and they cannot be separated. It is possible to attain feeling goals by cognitive means; and also to attain thinking goals by affective behaviors. The better the pupil feels about some fact or piece of data the more curious he becomes, at the conscious level, to want to dig in and learn more about it. And vice versa, the more he knows about a subject or area of knowledge, the better he appreciates and values it. Closely related to a pupil's need for knowledge and information is his preference for an internal set of values and personality dispositions which are nonintellective and comprise the affective domain. I would argue very strongly that a combination of both domains, cognitive and affective, is what makes for *effective* human development and the fully-functioning, creative individual.

Piaget (1967) writes,

> There is a close parallel between the development of affectivity and that of the intellectual functions, since these are two indissociable aspects of every action. In all behavior the motives and energizing dynamisms reveal affectivity, while the techniques and adjustment of the means employed constitute the cognitive sensorimotor or rational aspect. There is never a purely intellectual action, and numerous emotions, interests, values, impressions of harmony, etc. intervene, for example, in the solving of a mathematical problem. Likewise, there is never a purely affective act, e.g., love presupposes comprehension. Always and everywhere, in object-related behavior as well as in interpersonal behavior, both elements are involved because the one presupposes the other.

Even though professional educators have for a long time talked about motivating the pupil and building positive self-concepts, attitudes and values, classroom practices for dealing systematically with the promotion of affective behaviors are usually infrequent, and if they do occur many teachers really cannot explain what happened or evaluate affective behavioral changes within pupils. There is a new trend for programs which humanize education, but when measurement or assessment is called for the usual cognitive instruments are used; i.e., convergent thinking such as IQ, achievement, or subject-matter recall tests. And it should be pointed out that so-called creativity tests, even though their instructions ask the pupil to use his imagination and be curious, are scored solely on four divergent production factors which are cognitive. These are fluent thinking, flexible thinking, elaborative thinking, and original thinking, all identified and operationally defined by Guilford's work and his

Structure of Intellect Model (1967). There are no direct measures of affective processes derived from current creative thinking tests which have been used predominantly by researchers and teachers to assess children's creative potential.

Relationship Between the Cognitive and Affective Domains

Attempts to bridge cognitive thinking with affective feeling pupil behaviors or processes have so far been relatively sparse. Michaelis' (Michaelis, Grossman, & Scott, 1967) book for elementary school teachers discusses evaluating pupil progress in the substantive areas of the curriculum by taxonomical categories across both cognitive and affective domains according to level of increasing complexity. This book attempts to blend the various stages of the cognitive domain to comparable stages in the affective domain by subject area.

Albert Eiss and Mary Harbeck (1969) have published a book which discusses scientific behavioral objectives in the affective domain. Within this book Dr. Eiss presents and discusses an instructional systems model consisting of a closed, feedback loop which relates psychomotor-affective-cognitive domains together. Williams' (1968) Model for Implementing Cognitive-Affective Behaviors in the Classroom attempts to bridge four specific intellective traits with four attitudinal or temperament traits among elementary school pupils.

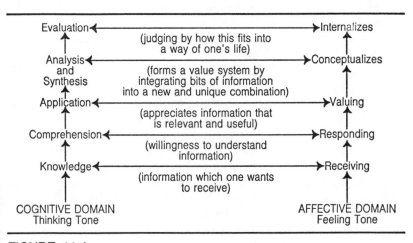

FIGURE 11.4

Figure 11.4 indicates a hierarchical order, interrelated schema between cognitive and affective domain models. Even though this

schema is one attempt to bridge the two domains, it still lacks definitive application when early grade teachers want to foster creativity
because both models are taxonomies with placement of those processes which comprise this human phenomena at higher levels.
There are some differing viewpoints among cognitive theorists concerning such categories arranged according to level of increasing
complexity, with each category dependent on the preceding ones.
Bruner (1960), for instance, has for some time stressed the importance of guiding students to discover how knowledge at any level is
related, and indicates that *appropriate method or strategy* to bring
this about may be most important. Piaget (Ginsberg & Opper, 1969)
likewise indicates that it is possible to accelerate some types of learning by suitable environmental stimuli, and suitable methods may
expedite processes of intellectual development. There are some who
claim creative processes may only appear later in the life of the child
because before this time he lacks an appropriate cognitive structure
in order to make new associations which are novel or unique. Others
say that by appropriate teaching strategies, learning conditions, and
a multitude of different opportunities in a lush environment, any
normal child can be creative at his own particular level of creativeness. Thus, different theories about how cognitive and affective processes develop among young children do exist.

What may be one method of alleviating these discrepant viewpoints is a different kind of system or model other than a taxonomy.
Such a system has been utilized by Dr. J. P. Guilford for his Structure
of Intellect Model of cognitive abilities (Figure 11.5). By means of a
three-dimensional, cubical model, he adopted a morphological approach to conceptualize intellectual abilities.

A morphology is a way of considering form and structure as an
interrelated whole, and differs from taxonomy in that there is no
hierarchical order implied. One very simple example of a morphology is that of forming a chemical compound. When you put two or
more chemical elements together, i.e., sodium and chlorine, the relationship of both form a new chemical compound—salt. According to
Guilford's model, up to five mental operations may be performed
upon four types of content to produce six kinds of products resulting
in 120 ($5 \times 4 \times 6$) possible kinds of intellectual acts.

As Mary Meeker (1969) in her new book states, "The order [of
abilities] is strictly conventional; that is, no priority—logical or psychological, developmental or hierarchical—is intended either within
or between the categories of classification." The model, then, implies
an interrelated classification of human abilities, many of which contribute to intellectual creativity.

But since Guilford's Structure of Intellect Model was never intended to be used for curriculum planning or for classroom teachers, and

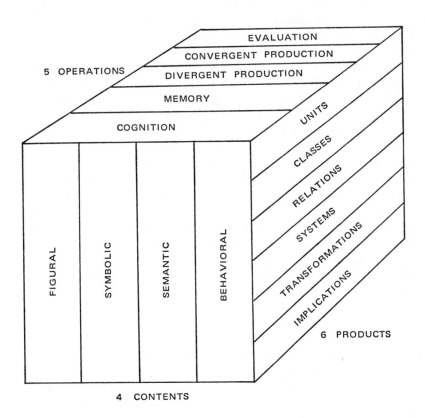

FIGURE 11.5
Guilford's Structure of Intellect Model

it does not include any affective factors, another model or adaptation of existing models was needed. Such a model or morphological structure has been designed by Williams (1966a; 1968) as a modification of Guilford's model for the purpose of implementing certain thinking and feeling processes directly related to creativity in the classroom. Figure 11.6 shows this three-dimensional cube, much the same as Guilford's cubical model, with each dimension made relevant to an ongoing elementary school program. The structure characterizes an interrelationship between one or more strategies employed by the teacher (Dimension 2), across the various subject-matter areas of the curriculum (Dimension 1) in order to elicit a set of four cognitive and four affective pupil behaviors (Dimension 3). What the teacher does or the media she or he uses is strategy, but how the pupil thinks or feels is process; and both are related to subject-matter content.

Dimension 1 lists subject-matter areas of a conventional elementary school curriculum. However, it is felt it may be possible to substitute subjects from any other grade level, including high school and college, in this dimension.

Dimension 2 initially listed twenty-three styles or strategies in a prototype model which teachers can employ in their classroom teaching. Upon extensive field testing of the model this list of strategies had been reduced to eighteen, which avoided a great deal of overlap between some strategies.

These have been devised empirically from studies of how all good teachers operate implicitly in the classroom. Teaching styles or strategies become a means, through subject-matter content, toward an end for fostering eight thinking and feeling pupil behaviors. As one considers these eighteen teaching strategies which can be appropriately applied across all subject-matter areas a vast number of combinations for learning become apparent.

Dimension 3 consists of eight processes deduced from theoretical studies of how children think and feel divergently. These divergent production factors are certainly most crucial when encouraging a child's creative potential but have received less attention or have been commonly ignored in the traditional curriculum and classroom. Hence, this dimension of the model is intended to focus upon those cognitive and affective processes that undoubtedly are most vital yet have been seriously neglected or at most treated randomly in school classrooms. These pupil behaviors become goals or objectives within themselves, and are regarded as ends to be achieved in classroom teaching.

The model is an applied yet complex structure, based upon theoretical constructs, interrelating a repertoire of eighteen ways for a teacher to cause pupils to think and feel creatively across the substantive areas of the curriculum. Assuming that the teacher is able to install it across the six subject-matter areas shown, the model indicates there are 864 ($8 \times 6 \times 18$) possible interrelated combinations for classroom teaching!

It has been used as a working structure for curriculum planning and as an instructional system to improve teacher competencies through in-service training at project schools across the country. An accompanying training program integrated across the model has been designed to show teachers how it is possible to encourage the eight creative processes directly through subject matter content rather than indirectly or in isolation of the regular school program.

Use of the model has likewise been focused upon classifying instructional media, such as books and films and teachers' developed and field tested lesson ideas designed for use in primary and elementary education (see Williams, 1968; 1970). It is currently being used

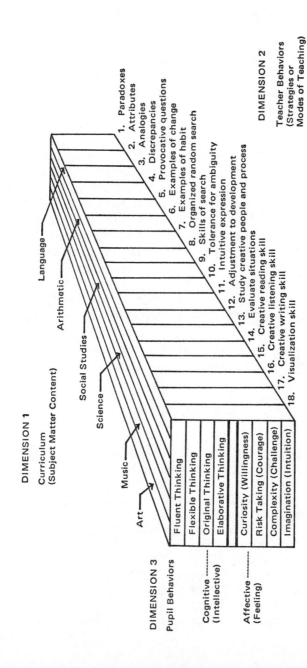

FIGURE 11.6
A Model for Implementing Cognitive-Affective Behaviors
in the Classroom

as a classification system for some of the more recent kits and instructional programs which have concentrated upon a process approach to learning, particularly those relevant to promoting divergent production behaviors in young children. Some of these include the Science Improvement Curriculum Study, the AAAS—Science, a Process Approach Program, the EDC—Man, a Course of Study, the Reading 360 Program, the Peabody Language Development Kits, the Taba Social Studies Program, and several of the Inquiry Approach Programs. The model is also being adopted by one state department of education program for gifted and talented youth by changing the content dimension, since such children are in need and capable of handling different subject areas other than the regularly established curriculum.

This model, unlike the others discussed herein, is essentially directed toward and has utility for both pre-service and in-service education programs. It can be used to develop more competent teachers, requiring no radical change in curriculum materials or content. Teachers can be trained to adapt their normal curriculum to the promotion of these important cognitive-affective behaviors among pupils. The model itself specifies terminal behaviors or competencies for which both the pupil and the teacher may aspire. As an interaction model, it specifies performance objectives for both teacher and pupil related to the subject-matter curriculum. In spite of recent emphasis on the necessity for integrating cognitive with affective processes, the gap between what is known about the nature and development of thinking-feeling processes and how this is translated into instructional practices is still enormously wide. This model may serve to somewhat narrow this gap, at least within the area of divergent production.

References

Bloom, Benjamin S. (Ed.). *Taxonomy of Educational Objectives, Handbook I: Cognitive Domain.* New York: David McKay Co., Inc., 1956.

Bruner, Jerome S. *The Process of Education.* Cambridge, Mass.: Harvard University Press, 1960.

Eiss, Albert F., and Harbeck, Mary Blatt. *Behavioral Objectives in the Affective Domain.* Washington, D.C.: National Science Supervisors Association, 1969.

Flavell, John H. *The Developmental Psychology of Jean Piaget.* Princeton, N.J.: D. Van Nostrand Co., Inc., 1963.

Ginsberg, Herbert, and Opper, Sylvia. *Piaget's Theory of Intellectual Development.* Englewood Cliffs, N.J.: Prentice-Hall, Inc., 1969.

Guilford, J. P. *The Nature of Human Intelligence.* New York: McGraw-Hill Book Co., 1967.

Krathwohl, David R.; Bloom, Benjamin S.; and Masia, Bertram B. *Taxonomy of Educational Objectives, Handbook II: Affective Domain.* New York: David McKay Co., Inc., 1964.

MacKinnon, Donald W. "The Courage to Be: Realizing Creative Potential." In Louis J. Rubin (Ed.), *Life Skills in School and Society,* A.S.C.D. Yearbook. Washington, D.C.: National Education Association, Association for Supervision and Curriculum Development, 1969.

Meeker, Mary Nacol. *The Structure of Intellect.* Columbus, Ohio: Charles E. Merrill Books, Inc., 1969.

Michaelis, John U.; Grossman, Ruth H.; and Scott, Lloyd F. *New Designs for the Elementary School Curriculum.* New York: McGraw-Hill Book Co., 1967.

Piaget, Jean. *Six Psychological Studies.* New York: Random House, Inc., 1967.

Williams, Frank E. (Ed.). *Seminar on Productive Thinking in Education.* Creativity Project, Macalester College, St. Paul, Minn., 1966(a).

Williams, Frank E. "Creativity in the Substantive Fields." Revised paper from a chapter in "Perspective of a Model for Developing Productive Creative Behaviors in the Classroom," in Frank E. Williams (Ed.), *Seminar on Productive Thinking in Education.* Creativity Project, Macalester College, St. Paul, Minn., 1966(b).

Williams, Frank E. *Classroom Ideas for Encouraging Thinking and Feeling.* Buffalo, N.Y.: D. O. K. Publishers, Inc., 771 E. Delavan Ave., Buffalo, 14215, 1970.

Williams, Frank E. "Creativity—An Innovation in the Classroom." In Mary Jane Aschner and Charles E. Bish (Eds.), *Productive Thinking in Education.* Washington, D.C.: The National Education Association, 1968.

12 Education of the Gifted in Utopia

J. C. GOWAN

I've decided to scrap the speech I had originally prepared for this occasion in favor of telling you about a curious experience which recently occurred to me. I suppose the inciting episode was listening to a brilliant and futuristic presentation by Paul Torrance at the APA

From *The Gifted Child Quarterly* 22:1 (1978). Used by permission.
Originally presented at the NAGC convention, San Diego, Calif., 1977.

meetings in San Francisco last August. By chance at the same time I was rereading *Island* by Aldous Huxley (1962). If you know about Huxley's last novel, you know it was a vision of a future island utopia. Apparently, the combination worked on my dream imagery one night, for I found myself visiting a school for gifted children in the year 2000.

As you know, many things which you take for granted in a dream are not quite clear afterwards, so I cannot tell you where the school was, at what grade level the classes were, whether the curriculum I observed applied only to the gifted or to a larger group, nor even how the gifted were defined. I cannot be specific as to the length of these "minicourses," though obviously they were shorter than the Carnegie unit; likewise, I don't know anything about the departmentalization or administration which produced this program. What I do know is that I saw scenes from classrooms used to develop talent and creativity, and that these words were understood in much wider context than we now consider them. I am sorry not to be more specific about this dream of the future, but in such visions we look through a glass darkly and should not be surprised that all corners are not equally illuminated.

The dream, with its many scenes of classroom operation, produced a profound impression on me which caused me to remember many key phrases. In some cases I do not recall exactly what they meant, though it seemed clear enough at the time. To help elicit these memories from the preconscious, I have not hesitated to break into the dream narrative with quotations from eminent writers which appear to my conscious mind to bear on the same or a similar subject. I hope it is understood that these efforts at scholarship are interpolations made in an attempt to clarify ideas, concepts, or phrases which may not be completely clear otherwise. Finally, I would point out, in answer to possible criticism from curriculum experts, that such material is better adapted to college level than to secondary or elementary children. The history of education is a history of the "trickling down" of curriculum from higher to lower levels, which, indeed must take place if children are to catch up with the increasing amount of material to be learned each generation.

I have also divided the class scenes up by sections, due probably to the way I operate analytically. This division, however, was not apparent in the dream, where one thing seemed to flow into another, and everything seemed connected to everything else. I have, therefore, for purposes of clarity, divided up the scenes into eight categories, but this may be artificial and arbitrary.

I should perhaps also add in postscript to this introduction that, while I do not remember any of the usual classroom material being taught, this may be because I only remember the unusual and novel aspects. I do not wish to imply that in such a school there would be no basics.

I. Genotypics and Biologetics

A great deal of emphasis was devoted to an understanding of the development of the individual in all aspects—cognitive, affective, and psychomotor. The basis was the Piaget-Erikson developmental stage theory, with its five aspects of escalation: succession, discontinuity, emergence, differentiation, and integration. This was regarded as the carrying over of the quantum principles to behavioral science, and it was believed that students should study every aspect of their own development, including the physical. A great deal of attention was paid to physical and mental health, including endocrine intervention to make bodies more healthy and beautiful, and to maintenance group counseling to monitor mental health. A candid and explicit course in human sexuality and marriage was carried on in a very scientific manner, so that people knew all about themselves. But the thrust of these efforts was not toward sex or aggression, as with us, but more in the direction of the full flowering of the individual and his enhanced options and powers.

Says Huxley (1963:206):

> What are boys and girls for in America? Answer: For mass consumption, mass communications, mass advertising, mass opiates ... Whereas in Russia boys and girls are for strengthening the state ... What are [our] boys and girls for? ... For actualizing; for being turned into full-blown human beings ... To become what you really are ...

This impetus toward self-actualization was seen in several ways:

1. An emphasis upon a transition from formal operations (convergent thinking) to creativity (divergent production) in the secondary school years.
2. An emphasis on ego development and self-esteem in adolescents, but an equal emphasis on the fact that such personal development also involved ego-dispersal in the later stages, first in love of another, then in nurturance of children, finally in altruism to society.

Genotypics also included biographics, a selective study of the biographies of geniuses and creative persons, but with a different sort of emphasis than would be given today. Outstanding lives were analyzed in accordance with critical stages and the environmental pressures or advantages which occurred at those periods. The Land (1972) theories of accretive, replicative, and mutualistic growth, as well as developmental stage theory, were used to measure the success of development toward self-actualization in the individual, of which creativity was an unfailing earnest. The analysis of the struggles of genius, especially in the early years, and particularly the obstacles placed by the status quo in the path of advanced thinkers helped the students to identify with these protagonists, and so with their problems, which were soon to become their own.

Shot through this entire study of individual development was the concept of consciousness, which was considered to be a major variable, though admittedly undefined. Nevertheless, it was in constant evidence, in discussion, in reference, and in thought, so that major or minor changes in consciousness and different states of consciousness were issues of the first importance. I detected three emphases here that were different from those I was familiar with. First, consciousness was spoken of as a singular which did not seem to have a plural; second, there was attention to and study of various altered states of consciousness; and third, the singularity of each stage of consciousness was seen as justified by the fact that there appeared to be a set of common percepts for each state which were dependent on that state, the percepts of the normal state being that of our ordinary physical universe.

II. Phenotypics and Ecologetics

As the first area, genotypics, referred to the development of the individual, phenotypics and ecologetics referred to the development of the species. As with the former area, the emphasis here was on flow and development rather than on a static view of mankind. Here, mankind was seen in the process of change, an existentialist view of being and becoming, if you will. Among minicourses, there were offerings in energetics (the use of life energies, including some we do not now understand), ecology (a better appreciation of Spaceship Earth and the conservation of its resources), utopias (from Plato to Huxley), futuristics (the study of and planning for the future), and species evolution (and the directions to which a few present geniuses pointed). There were also courses in social policy (especially a study of which subgroup each culture systematically persecuted and how this could be avoided), historics from a dynamic point of view (à la Toynbee and Spengler), and finally something which the students called "the glass bead game" after the book of the same title by Herman Hesse (1969).

I looked up the reference in *The Glass Bead Game* in an effort to gain a better understanding of the game, and abstracted the following explanation from pages 31–40:

> The game was first nothing more than a witty method for developing memory and ingenuity among students and musicians ... though it has long ceased to have anything to do with glass beads. The inventor, ... an eccentric ... but humane musicologist, used glass beads instead of letters, numerals, notes and other ... symbols .... One player would call out ... motifs or initial bars ... whereupon the other had to respond with a continuation ... a contrasting theme ... it was an exercise in memory and improvisation ....
>
> Two or three decades later the game ... was taken over by mathematicians .... The mathematicians brought the game to a high degree of flexibility, so that it began to acquire something approaching a consciousness of itself .... It was now so far developed that it was capable of expressing mathematical processes by special symbols and abbreviations .... At various times the Game was taken up and imitated by nearly all the scientific and scholarly disciplines, ... classical philology and logic ... the visual arts ... architecture .... Thereafter more and more new relations, analogies and correspondences were discovered among the abstract formulas obtained .... The astronomers, the classicists, the scholastics, the music students all played the Game according to their ingenious rules .... It was at this point that [an innovator] applied himself to this problem [of diversity] .... He invented for the Glass Bead Game the principles of a new language, a language of symbols and formulas in which mathematics and music played an equal part ... so that the game evolved into the quintessence of intellectuality and art ... the mystic unity of all separate members of the universe of letters ....

Another aspect of phenotypics was a thorough discussion of the creativogenic society—the society in which creativity maximally flourishes. Present initial research by Kroeber (1944), Gray (1966), Arieti (1976), and Simonton (1975), had been expanded in the intervening years, so that there was complete knowledge about what kind of society and social institutions were maximally capable of producing each kind or category of creative talent. Particularly useful (and presently nonexistent) research had been done on the specific social sanctions which prevent or dull creativity in women. All this was presented and studied factually, so that adolescents might be forewarned. Peer group support through special seminars and extensive guidance, especially for gifted girls, helped to ameliorate the often severe social and group pressures against adolescent creativity or divergence.

III. Creativity

I was pleased to see that creativity at last had a solid part in the curriculum, being taught directly and not as an adjunct to another course. Among the familiar methods taught were those of Guilford (the SOI), Parnes (the Creative Education Foundation) and Torrance, as were synectics and brainstorming. Further advances on the SOI applications by Williams and Meeker had been made, and autogenic training was offered, though this bridged into the right hemisphere area. There was a great deal of practice in workbooks, which bespoke further revisions of the *Actionbook*. Tests by Torrance, Khatena, Treffinger, and others here present were used to measure creativity. Among the persons presently neglected but utilized in this curriculum was Upton (1963), especially on analogy. The development of thinking from categorization to analogy and finally to isomorphics (a study of the equivalence in analogies) was emphasized. Bertalanffy (1968:81 ff.), the founder of general systems theory, notes that it depends on isomorphisms, which in turn rest on cognition and organization. He points out analogy (superficial similarity), homologies (identical basic laws in different disciplines), and the explanation of specific laws as special cases. He concludes that these general notions "acquire exact expression ... only in mathematical language."

While there was a great deal more follow-through elaboration on these courses than any we have, I realized that of all the areas I dreamed about, this was the one where the rationale and paradigms were mainly in place, and where the major impetus for the future lay in development and production.

IV. Somatics

The area of somatics is perhaps nearest to our physical education, though with a profound difference. Where ours is on group skills which often lead to aggression and team rivalries, theirs seemed to be on individual bodily exercises which reduced stress and contributed to health. While our physical education exalts youth, theirs was a preparation for lifelong body exercises which produced vigor in maturity and old age. The Hindu asanas, daily bodily exercises of hatha yoga, had been modified for Western adolescents and were much in evidence. *Tai chi* (rhythmic body movement which seems to promote meditation in movement) was also featured. But perhaps the most important innovation I saw was Reichian breathing and other unstressing devices, such as chanting, rolfing, and re-evaluation counseling, which were used for getting out anger and other negative emotions. These "hostillectomy" sessions were daily and even constant rituals for the purpose of immediately dissipating anger in the circumstance where it arose, for stress was not allowed to accumulate.

As usual, Huxley (1962:212) had anticipated it:

> An angry or frustrated child has worked up enough power for a burst of crying, or bad language, or a fight. If the power generated is sufficient for any of these things, it's sufficient for running or dancing, more than sufficient for five deep breaths .... An irritated person who takes five deep breaths releases a lot of tension, and so makes it easier for himself to behave rationally. So we teach our children all kinds of breathing games, to be played whenever they're angry or upset. Some of the games are competitive ....

A kind of Orff *Schulewerk*, a chanting, stamping, noisy dance was also employed to reduce tension, exercise muscles, and establish learning through rhythms. Somatics of most kinds seemed to involve music. And I should add that there was much evidence of music and art in the schoolrooms, but I took this for granted in such a place.

V.　Phenomena of the Normal State of Consciousness

The area of phenomena of the normal state of consciousness included what we should call science and mathematics, but with the subtle difference that the name implies: namely, all physical phenomena were junior to the ordinary state of consciousness. There were minicourses in astrophysics, particle physics, and astronomy, so set up that they could be understood by nonscience majors. There seemed to be more emphasis on nuclear, subnuclear, and astronomical aspects of physics than we have. Mathematics consisted of more emphasis on exponential functions, binary notations and logs, statistics, group and set theory, and computer and artificial languages. Their interest in science seemed more open-ended than ours, more willing to consider the observer as interacting with the experiment and more able to accept the nontangible nature of subparticle reality. There were also references to matters which I did not understand but which were understood by the students without explanation, as though there had been a great deal of breakthrough discoveries in science since the present.

One new scientific study which impressed me was "synchrony," which, as near as I can explain, was a study of co-incidence in time, space, and magnitude. (I have used the hyphen to indicate that it was more than coincidence, although something like it.) It was also more than Jungian syncronicity, though, again, something like it. It had a lot to do with resonance on the same frequency, and the phenomena of sidebands and beats when the frequency or other magnitudes were almost but not quite equal. It was obvious that there had been a scientific breakthrough in the intervening years which directed more emphasis to this whole concept and in a different way than I was able to understand. Scientific ethics was also a part of this unit.

In the area of scientific theory, I was especially interested in another shift in emphasis. Whereas I had been taught science as if the theory were true, these young people were exploring science to find out which of several alternate theories was most heuristic, that is, to see which theory gave them the most practical mileage in understanding and predicting the widest range of events. There appeared to be no thought or consideration given to the fact that one theory was "true" and the others "false," or that one theory was "truer" than another. This kind of freedom encouraged the development of independent hypotheses of which no one was ashamed if they didn't work very well. It also, for reasons which escaped me, encouraged mathematical but nonphysical models such as those of simple finite groups of three and four (which had much earlier been envisaged for quark models). There was also more emphasis on the probability function attached to the "truth" value of theories. This was apparently a newly invented statistic which enabled one to qualify a theory or hypothesis with the confidence level of credibility one should attach to it.

A final point that I keenly remember from the dream was that history had also been changed in emphasis from a history of politics, government, war, and battles to a history of science and art. It was evidently felt that the historical progression of ideas liberating man was more important than the historical progression of laws liberating mankind.

When I asked why there was no advanced laboratory work in biologic manipulation of DNA and RNA cells, I was told that recombinant and other advanced techniques were forbidden on the secondary level, as they were considered too dangerous.

VI. Communication

Instead of language arts in this dream of the future, there was something called communication. It started with communication theory, a completely different way of looking at the process in the manner of MacLuhan or Chomsky. This was then divided into verbal and nonverbal methods. On the verbal side, it led to a study of phonetics, then comparative philology, including both foreign and artificial languages which some students tried their hand in constructing. Also stressed was the importance of meaning, the concept of a single semantic for each word, and the extensional and intensional use of words. The restricting aspect of language, as seen in tensed verbs which divide time into arbitrary parts, was discussed. On the nonverbal side, it led to a study of gesture, expression in the body, dancing, empathy, intuition, archetypes, images, dreams, ritual, and art—all forms of interpersonal communication in the nonverbal mode.

A directive, intensive journal method of creative writing was universally employed, so that every student had a personal journal in which he wrote every day, often after a reverie or incubation period. The journal was divided into different parts (à la Progoff, 1975), namely daily log, stepping stones, twilight imagery, time-life dimension, dialog with persons, events, dream log, and inner wisdom dialog. Students became facile in self-examination and expression. Also, the journal served as an outlet and a confessional for those who needed it. Its contents were private and need not be divulged, but they could be read to the teacher, counselor, or class if desired, and many fine pieces of poetry and other creative writing resulted.

The development of the ego and its dispersal in genotypics had a parallel in the categorization of meaning and then its extension to several meanings in a further study called "meta-symbolic calculus," in which symbols acquired several meanings and one constructed running prose, punning on the double or triple meanings. This seemed so clear in my dream but is now so difficult to explain. It is a little like saying: "If you don't go to other people's funerals, they won't come to yours," which is ludicrous at one level but true at another. There seems now little difference between this study and that of the glass bead game, but they seemed distinct at the time. To paraphrase Guilford, when one is dealing with divergent production of semantic transformations and implications, it is difficult to separate the general from the particular.

Some of this had already been predicted by our best minds. Says Upton (1963:228), in summarizing a brilliant analysis of semantics:

> The law of essential ambiguity . . . is an expression of the idea that if language is to function as the servo-mechanism of a community of free minds, some of its symbols must be conveniently polysemantic, and most of them must be free to become so.

The idea that a symbol can act not only as a constant but also as a variable, moving in meaning from one value of a parameter to another with change in development or social custom, is a powerful but necessary advantage of language. The 21st-century education took fuller advantage of this, thereby discovering generalizations such as "Bad exchanges drive out good exchanges," which is true whether the medium of exchange is currency, barter, or common courtesy. Such flexibility in thinking was developed by the "meta-symbolic calculus" that students were always able to see the forest rather than the trees and could deal with symbolic transformations with ease.

VII.   Incubation and Imagery

Perhaps nowhere did the curriculum of this dream school depart more from present standards than in the emphasis on using incubation to develop imagery. The paradigm employed here is that when through various incubation techniques the dominance of the left cerebral hemisphere is broken, imagery occurs in the right hemisphere (similar to that on a TV screen), and such images can be transferred to verbal creative output by the left hemisphere, or directly to artistic output by the right hemisphere.

Incubation (as its discoverer, Wallas, 1926, noted) involves techniques of relaxation, so that the hold of the cognitive left hemisphere on consciousness can be allayed. Fantasy, reverie, and dreams are common names for the spontaneous appearance of this faculty, though future educators were not willing to wait for that to happen by itself but had developed methods for stimulating it in the classroom. As a matter of fact, I was told: "When the study of creativity was new, people tried to stimulate it through facilitating preparation, which is a necessary but not a sufficient condition for it. We, having done that, try also to stimulate it through incubation—and this is the major advance."

Incubation started with laboratory work in guided imagery. In a quiet and shuttered classroom, musical records with various provocative sounds similar to those produced by Torrance and Khatena were played, and a few simple suggestions from the teacher sufficed to start creative imagination flowing. Some product, a drawing, a piece of writing, or a solution to a problem usually came out of these sessions.

Next came training in something called "withdrawal," although the nearest synonym we have for what was done would perhaps be meditation. It was recognized that withdrawal from the tyranny of the percepts was the final step in the liberation of the consciousness begun by Piagetian "decentering" and by the freeing which subjunctive contingency gives to the formal operations stage over the tyranny of the present indicative in the concrete operations stage. Objectivity, according to their views, could only be found by total disengagement from the object, at least for a time. It was realized that different temperaments needed different methods so a number were taught, including Eastern and Western meditation, psychosynthesis, autogenic training, something called BEST, Nichirin Shosho chanting, and several others. Students were encouraged in the private, daily use of whichever one they liked the best.

A final and most surprising aspect of this unusual area of curriculum was work in time distortion. (Again checking Huxley, 1962:210, I read "And it is only in very deep trance that a person can be taught to distort time.") Not all students could learn this, but for those who could the advantages were obvious—very rapid learning, which was equivalent to quasi-artificial genius. In disbelief, I again read in Huxley, 1962:210:

> Short cuts to memorizing ... short cuts to calculating and thinking and problem solving .... You listen to the teacher's suggestions and you sit there for a long, long time .... When you've been brought back, you look at your watch. Your experience of two hours was telescoped into exactly four minutes of clock time .... Result: I was capable to cover far more ground than I could possibly have covered ... in the ordinary way. You can imagine what happens when somebody with a genius IQ is also capable of time distortion.

Although I was much interested in this spectacular method of enhancement of intelligence I was not given much further information about it; it was probable that even they did not fully understand it. When I asked about this, they replied with a question, "Does the fact that you don't understand what electricity is keep you from using it?" I was told, however, that in a few precocious individuals such powers could be extended into telepathy and precognition, although psychologists were concerned about possible harmful effects of developmental forcing in this sensitive area.

VIII. Philosophics and Theoretics

The experiences involved in philosophics and theoretics were a sort of capstone, combining many other aspects under a common head. Again it is necessary to explain that students "played" with theory rather than espousing belief. Consequently there was not the personal investment in letting go an old concept and trying out a new one.

First there was a review of communications theory and of major world religions, but again in a very detached way, from the point of view of developing a repertoire of theories rather than as articles of belief. Then there was a study of general systems which saw all thought as unified in process under a diversity of forms and applications. Each science and discipline was isomorphic to every other science, except that it had special variables and constants. Bertalanffy (1968:38) states the purposes and aims of general systems theory as:

> A tendency toward integration, centered in a general theory of systems, aiming at exact theory in nonphysical fields, which develops universal principles toward a goal of unity in science which can lead to integration in scientific education.

In this logic and mathematics played a leading part.

General systems were followed by a study of major paradigms and homologues which synthesized and summarized earlier isomorphic relationships in the creativity studies. Among those which were familiar to me were the complementarity principle in physics, the quantum theory of discontinuity, the Pribram hologram model, the right hemisphere analogue to a radio receiver, and several others. Some which had been discovered in the intervening years were quite beyond me.

Finally, there was an introductory study of noetics, the analysis of mind and consciousness. Much of this was beyond me, but some equivalence seemed to be made between the inner world of the mind and the outer world of events and things, as if each were the inverse of the other. It was obvious that a great deal of progress had been made in this area.

Two writers, Carl Jung and Teilhard de Chardin, especially figured in this area. The former was remembered for his concepts of archetypes and the "collective unconscious," both of which were seen as generating entities or motifs in noetics. The latter was remembered for his concept of the "noosphere," which was his term for consciousness. Describing it Chardin said (1961:180):

> The biological change of state terminating in the awakening of thought does not merely represent a critical point that the individual or the species must pass through. Vaster than that, it affects life itself in its organic totality, and consequently it marks a transformation affecting the state of the entire planet.

The Wild Rose Analogy

I wish I could remember a more satisfactory conclusion to this dream, which left many questions unanswered. But as suddenly as it had come, it vanished, and I was walking through an enormous field of wild red roses. "How many roses are there here?" said a voice. "Oh, at least a million," I answered. "Are there any sports among them?" the voice queried. "Yes, here is one," said I, appropriately sighting one which had flecks of white on its petals. "And how many such sports do you think there are here?" asked the voice. "Oh, probably a thousand, if one assumes that once every thousand roses there is some mutant variation." "And could these mutants be developed into distinctive colors and patterns?" inquired the voice. "Of course, for that is the way our domestic varieties originated," I replied. "Ah," said the voice, "but you had to have a gardener who believed in the possibility of such development and then set about to accomplish it." "That is true," I agreed.

There are many more children than roses, and they are much more important. Do some of them have talents and potential in exotic abilities which we do not even understand, and so cannot begin to stimulate? The gardener has produced a domesticated rose much bigger and more beautiful than the wild variety; could we do the same with children? But who will be the gardener for humanity? What are the talents of man? Are we sure we know them all? What, if any, are the boundaries of his abilities? Or are they as evanescent as was the limit of the four-minute mile? What might we accomplish if we truly educated our children for the maximization of all the talents they possess?

A century ago lightning calculators were exhibited as sideshow freaks. Since my dream I am haunted by the nagging possibility that some children possess similar exotic talents, which, because they are not appreciated by society, are not cultivated or stimulated. We are therefore back looking at the wild rose mutation, rather than visualizing what it might become with husbandry. What are some of the possible powers of mankind?

Could empathy, for example, extend to telepathy? Could spatial visualization extend to nonspatial visualization? Could intellectual accretion and learning become telescoped into instantaneous knowledge and understanding? Some otherwise saintly and truthful mystics have told us that this is so. And it might not be amiss to check out this possibility.

Hunt and Draper (1964:20) tell us of the powers of the electrical wizard Nicola Tesla: "He was conscious of certain phenomena before his eyes which others could not see. He envisioned objects and hypotheses with such reality and clarity that he was uncertain whether they did nor did not exist." Before we regard Tesla's powers as miraculous or his biographers as liars, let us remember that when a picture of the scene is chromokeyed behind a newscaster as he describes a news event, we do not react in disbelief, nor do we when we see a virtual image in a holographic display. Science has sanctified these miracles, so we believe them though most of us cannot explain their technology. If geniuses like Tesla are forerunners, then it might be useful to recognize the possibility of such unusual talents and begin to study how to develop them in others.

In conclusion, let me go back to the speech of Huxley's (1963:208) minister of education on the child and his potentialities:

> How does he do his thinking, perceiving and remembering? Is he a visualizer or a non-visualizer? Does his mind work with image or with words, with both at once, or with neither? How close to the surface is his storytelling faculty? Does he see the world as Wordsworth and Traherne saw it when they were children? And if so, what can be done to prevent the glory and the freshness from fading into the light of common day? Or in more general terms, how can we educate children on the conceptual level without killing their capacity for intense nonverbal experience? How can we reconcile analysis with vision?

Here are the problems of education consequent upon the differential functions of the right and left hemispheres, posed clearly a decade before psychology discovered the difference. As Dr. Parnes has clearly told us, problem finding is the necessary precursor of problem solving. Today we have found that El Dorado exists; we also have a map for getting there, and we have less than a quarter of a century left to make the immense journey.

References

Arieti, S. *Creativity: The Magic Synthesis.* New York: Basic Books, 1976.

Bertalanffy, L. V. *General Systems Theory.* New York: George Braziller, Inc., 1968.

Casteneda, C. *Tales of Power.* New York: Simon & Schuster, 1974.

Chardin, Teilhard de. *The Phenomenon of Man.* New York: Harper, 1959.

Course in Miracles. Foundation for Inner Peace, 1 W. 81st St. No. 8D, New York 10024, 1976.

Gowan, J. C. *Development of the Psychedelic Individual.* Buffalo, N.Y.: Creative Education Foundation, 1974.

Gowan, J. C. *Trance, Art and Creativity.* Buffalo, N.Y.: Creative Education Foundation, 1975.

Gray, C. E. "A Measurement of Creativity in Western Civilization." *American Anthropologist,* 60:13–31, 1966.

Hesse, H. *The Glass Bead Game.* New York: Holt, Rinehart & Winston, 1969.

Hunt, I., and Draper, W. W. *Lightning in His Hand.* Hawthorne, Calif.: Omni Publications, 1964.

Huxley, A. *Island.* New York: Harper & Row, 1962.

Kroeber, A. *Configurations of Culture Growth.* Berkeley: University of Calif. Press, 1944.

Land, G. L. *Grow or Die.* New York: Random House, 1972.

Parnes, S.; Noller, R.; and Biondi, A. *A Guide to Creative Action.* Rev. ed.; *Creative Actionbook.* Rev. ed. New York: Charles Scribner's Sons, 1977.

Progoff, Ira. *At a Journal Workshop.* Dialog House, 45 W. 10th St., New York 10011, 1975.

Simonton, D. K. "Sociocultural Context of Individual Creativity." *Journal of Personality and Social Psychology* 32:119–1133, 1975.

Upton, A. *Design for Thinking.* Palo Alto, Cal.; Pacific Book Publishers, 1963.

Wallas, G. *The Art of Thought.* London: Watts, 1926.

Chapter Five

Guidance

Introduction.

Perhaps nowhere else in this book will the observant reader note as much of a break with the past as in this chapter. Formerly a chapter on guidance would have been almost exclusively devoted to identification and to underachievement. In this book identification is in a separate chapter, and underachievement is not treated at all. An explanation is in order.

Studies of underachievement have not produced very fruitful results, and attempts to handle underachievement through guidance techniques have generally been unsuccessful. The senior editor was one of the first writers to open up this field (Gowan, 1955; 1957; 1960 a). Since then, there has been a spate of writing in this area, the general consensus of which is that underachievement has a variety of causes, and efforts to cure it have not been very successful. One of the problems in the literature has been that researchers have been unwilling to define underachievement in precise terms. A definition recommended more than 20 years ago that underachievement is the performance of one or more standard deviations below capacity has yet to be widely adopted for research purposes. The statistical problem inherent in definitions such as one grade level below placement are so serious as nearly to destroy any possibility of producing effective criterion groups for study or treatment.

Studies of the causes of underachievement have been somewhat more successful. Papers by Patterson (1962) and Roth and Meyersburg (1963) definitively review causes. These papers, as well as J. C. Gowan's three articles cited above, will be found in Gowan and Demos (1965). Another compendium is that of Kornrich (1966). The general thrust of this material is that where underachievement can be traced to personal causes, it has roots in hostility, alienation, emotional disturbance, lack of elementary skills such as reading, and a generalized asocial pattern which prevents normal development. Guidance seems most effective in the elementary years, and recovery appears to involve (1) early identification and guidance, (2) a supportive teacher or counselor, and (3) remedial skills training in a sympathetic atmosphere.

The biggest objection to the studies on underachievement is that most authors fail to distinguish guidance for the gifted from ordinary guidance procedures. The theme of the articles which have been selected for this chapter is that gifted and creative children present special problems to counselors, and guidance services must take account of these. This specialization of guidance services for special children is a very important departure from the past.

Major counseling problems presented by the highly creative student are likely to center around his isolation and estrangement from his peers and teachers, what appear to be "unrealistic" career choices, divergent values and attitudes, and the like. Counselors can do much by working with teachers to help them understand the creativity in talented students and show them how to use procedures which will implement the greater development of creative thinking in all students.

Counselors need to understand the special blockages to the development of creative thinking. Among those which appear most prominent and obvious are the following: premature attempts on the part of parents and teachers to eliminate fantasy, restrictions on manipulativeness and curiosity, overemphasis on prevention, overemphasis on sex roles, fear and timidity, emphasis in education on verbal skills, and limitations of resources for working out ideas.

The counselor should also recognize that the values and attitudes of highly creative students are likely to be different from those of other students. The very facts that they are capable of divergent thinking, have unusual ideas, and are independent in their thinking are likely to make their values and attitudes different from the norms of their group. Some of these differences are highlighted in a study by Getzels and Jackson (1962). They found that for the high IQ group, the rank-order correlation between the qualities they would like for themselves and the qualities making for adult success was .81; for the high creativity group it was .10. Among the highly intelligent, the correlation between the qualities they desire and the qualities they believe teachers favor was .67; for the highly creative group, it was minus .25. In other words, the highly creative student desires personal qualities which have little relationship to those he believes make for adult success and which are in some ways the opposite of those he believes his teachers favor. Thus, counselors should recognize that the desire to emulate the teacher is absent or weak among creative students.

Getzels and Jackson also found a certain mocking attitude on the part of the creatives toward what they call the "all-American boy"—a theme almost totally lacking in the stories of the highly intelligent group. Again, this highlights the counselor's problem in helping the highly creative student to learn to be independent without being obnoxious.

In summary, counselors and guidance workers should be concerned about understanding creativity in talented students. Such an understanding is important from the standpoint of personality development and mental health, the acquisition of knowledge and understanding, vocational success, and social welfare. A variety of materials are being developed and tested for identifying creative thinking at all educational levels and guiding its fuller development. New directions have been toward the development of procedures for identifying creative talent at an early age and for understanding its development during the important early school years. The direction has been toward materials which can be manipulated and which yield such measures as Inventivlevel, Spontaneous Flexibility, and Constructiveness; materials which permit exploration through "asking" and "guessing" (formulating hypotheses) concerning the causes and consequences of behavior, and the like.[1]

Those who wish a more detailed discussion of guidance for the gifted should consult J. C. Gowan and C. B. Bruch, *The Academically Talented Student and Guidance* (Boston: Houghton Mifflin Co., 1971), the special issue (Fall 1977) of *The Gifted Child Quarterly*, or Gowan (1968).

---

[1]E. P. Torrance, "Counseling Problems of Highly Creative Individuals," in J. C. Gowan and G. D. Demos (eds.), *The Guidance of Exceptional Children* (New York: David McKay Co., Inc., 1966), pp. 86–91. By permission of D. McKay Co., copyright owners.

13 Counseling With Gifted and Talented Students

RONALD T. ZAFFRANN & NICK COLANGELO

Differentiated guidance for the gifted, based on the obvious acceleration in their developmental task schedule, is an outgrowth of the work of three men and their students: John Rothney, John Flanagan, and John Gowan. These three have more in common than their first names; they were all students during the early thirties of John Brewer and Truman Kelley at the Harvard Graduate School of Education. Brewer, who wrote the first book on educational guidance, was a colleague of Frank Parsons; and Kelley, who did the first doctoral dissertation on educational guidance, was the statistician for Lewis M. Terman. So all three came by their dual interest in guidance and in gifted children as a legacy from their teachers.

Rothney went to Wisconsin where he founded the unique Guidance Laboratory for Gifted Students, a model of such practice. The laboratory was carried on with great success by Rothney and eventually turned over to his pupil Marshal Sanborn, who in turn turned it over to C. J. Pulvino, and then to Nick Colangelo. Flanagan, who was more interested in the measurement area (he wrote one of the first factor analytic theses), founded and became president of the American Research Institute, and developed Project Talent, a longitudinal study of the top 5% of high school students. Gowan became a guidance trainer interested in the gifted and has produced a long list of books and articles on the guidance of the gifted, as well as editing *The Gifted Child Quarterly*. Most of what we know about guidance of the gifted has come from these men and their students.

Two practicum-demonstration theaters where the theories of these men have been implemented have been the Research and Guidance Laboratory at the University of Wisconsin and the Summer Gifted Child Creativity Classes at San Fernando Valley State College (now California State University—Northridge) during the 1960's. The former is the subject of a published article (Colangelo & Pfleger, 1977), and the latter has been discussed in the literature (Gowan, 1972a,

---

From *The Gifted Child Quarterly* 21:3 (1977). Used by permission.

Gowan & Bruch, 1971, Gowan & others, 1969). Both involved training counselors to work specifically and differentially with gifted children. One of the specific discoveries made in the latter workshop was
that for gifted children to become mentally healthy enough to be
creative they needed far more than the usually expected amount of
guidance—they were able to absorb the full-time services of a counselor in *each* classroom of 25 (Gowan, 1968a, 1968b; Gowan &
others, 1969). Among other graduates of the training of this workshop
are Kay Bruch, Juliana Gensley, Charlotte Malone, Norma J. Groth,
Joyce Hagen, and James Curry.

In the remainder of this article we shall look at three aspects of
dealing with the gifted and talented which involve ideas and issues
which evolved from such experience. These points may be subsumed
under three headings:

1. Developmental guidance program.
2. Differentiated counseling.
3. Mental health and the affective domain.

Developmental Program

Counseling with gifted and talented students should take place
within a *developmental program* organized and maintained for these
youngsters. That is, it is organized and run according to the ever-
changing needs of growing youngsters. Such a program takes these
needs into account and is structured around them. A developmental
guidance program for gifted and talented youth must be based on the
unique needs and concerns of these students.

The concepts of developmental guidance were perhaps first best
enunciated by Blocher in his book *Developmental Guidance* (1966).
Taking a hint from Maslow (1954), he sees guidance as assisting in
bridging the discontinuities which are experienced by every growing individual. There are, as Shakespeare tells us, various stages in
life, and the full escalation of development does not occur without
the kind of strong mental health which guidance for maintenance
(rather than for crisis) provides. These stages have been foreshad-
owed in Havighurst's developmental tasks of adolescence (1964) and
in Ginsberg's fantasy, tentative, and realistic stages of vocational
choice (1951). They have also been implied cognitively by Piaget
(Gowan, 1967a), and affectively by Erikson (1963), and by Sullivan
(1953). Hershenson (1968) explicated a life-stage developmental system paralleling Eriksonian stages. Gowan (1971b, 1972b) combined
the cognitive and affective aspects into a unified developmental
stage theory. We quote from Gowan (1971b):

We may state the new principles in a series of theorems:

1. Developmental process is best understood through a periodic table of developmental stages, consisting of triads:

Latency	*Identity*	*Creativity*
1. Trust	2. Autonomy	3. Initiative
4. Industry	5. Identity	6. Intimacy
7. Generativity	8. Ego-Integrity	

2. Each stage has a special affinity for another three removed from it. Stages 1, 4, and 7 are noticeable for a thing-oriented, sexually latent aspect, dealing with the world of experience. Stages, 2, 5, 8 are ego-bound, ego-oriented, and ego-circumscribed. Stages 3 and 6 are times of love for self and others and of creativity.

3. Within each stage development occurs through cycles of integration and differentiation (Chickering, 1969:293).

4. The effect of environmental experience or stimulation on an individual depends upon that individual's characteristics and readiness for development (Chickering, 1969:293).

5. Continual environmental stimulation is required for escalation into the self-actualizing levels.

6. There is danger that either too much success or failure at any stage will cause arrest in that stage.

7. Meta guidance is the most useful means for assuring that moral and mental development will continue into the self-actualizing levels after physical development has ceased.

To quote again from Gowan (1968a):

Let us look at some key concepts in the developmental field. The notion of development differs from that of mere growth in that it involves a change of quality, whereas growth involves only a change in quantity, therefore, involves escalation over time. The process is not merely progression, but the unfoldment of a new idea or motif. Development may also be considered as a quantum phenomenon with identifiable levels and stages instead of the myth of a smooth curve of progression. Moreover, each stage contains characteristics appropriate for its full efflorescence, and also embraces the germinal matter for the proper development of the next stage. Thus each stage is the necessary, but not the sufficient precursor of the next.

If a developmentalist theory such as Erikson's "Eight Stages of Man" (1963) truly reflects the onward course of personality expansion, maturation, and humanization from infant trust to senior integrity, then it ought to be possible to order the aspects of counseling cases in terms of a graduated series of arrests of such development at various levels. Furthermore, each arrested state should have its own psychological and social characteristics and symptoms and each should be measurable on a different personality scale.

In addition, the social penalties for arrested development should decrease in magnitude as the stops occur at higher levels; and the morality used by society to control behavior in such an arrested individual should decrease in severity. Out of such a taxonomy of developmental psychopathology one could expect clear diagnosis of cases, and subsequent emergence of specific modes of treatment.

Differentiated Counseling

A wise man once said: "Nothing is more unequal than the equal treatment of children with unequal needs and talents." If guidance is the individualizing of education, it follows that it needs to be differential. There are some special guidance problems which gifted children face, which need specialized attention from counselors who themselves have received specialized training. Here are some of them from Gowan (1960):

1. They may be faced with an embarrassment of riches in trying to make wise occupational and educational choices.
2. There may be problems attendant upon upward social mobility.
3. They may become aware of developmental tasks before they have the physical resources to solve them.
4. They may have more need than usual to develop the specialized interests which go with certain professional occupations.
5. There may also be problems connected with the lack of adult model figures.

One of the problems which many gifted youngsters face in connection with guidance has been expressed with some humor by a gifted student as the perennial question of "How far out beyond the safety railing can I lean without going over the cliff?" Gifted students are bright enough to know that they deviate in characteristics considerably from the norms and to see that, in consequence, many generalizations that apply to the average student do not apply to themselves. The problem for them is to discriminate between those situations which apply equally to all persons, regardless of ability, and those which apply to them with diminished force. For example, the gifted student frequently finds that he can take one or two courses in excess of the requirements and that he does not need this or that prerequisite. It takes a wise counselor to help him discriminate between those experiences he can safely telescope and those that he should undertake in as full measure as the next student.

Very often the physical education coach does a better job in this area than the counselor. First, the coach teaches and practices what Paul Brandwein (1953) called "the predisposing factor" and what Joe Renzulli (1976) refers to as "task commitment." It involves the development of strong and wholehearted will to excel at the task so that most of one's attention and waking hours are devoted to it. This involvement gives idealistic youth what William James called "the moral equivalent of war" and is necessary to preserve creativity and avoid alienation.

Secondly, the coach also knows that one cannot get superior performance out of youth without group solidarity, and he uses group cohesiveness constantly in the segregation of his charges, for practice, games, and sometimes even meals and lodging. Yet most counselors oppose the grouping of gifted adolescents, seemingly unconscious of the well-known fact that the herd instinct at this period is so strong that peer sanctions will prevent most boys from creativity, and most girls from even showing their superior intelligence.

Areas of Concern

The concerns of gifted and talented youngsters are divided and discussed here according to the following groups: personal/social and educational concerns, career and vocational concerns, gifted women, and developmental arrests.

Social and Educational Concerns. One of the most prevalent myths about gifted students is the belief that no special considerations are needed in their personal and social development. Some educators feel that gifted possess all the innate qualities to propel them to healthy, productive development. The research on gifted abounds with references to the unique personal and social needs of gifted that require the counselor's attention (Goldberg, 1965; Gowan & Demos, 1964; Keating, 1976; Newland, 1976; Sanborn, 1974).

Peerness is essentially a term that refers to mental age rather than chronological age (Newland, 1976). However, students are usually grouped by chronological age. Definitions of gifted include the concept that "gifted is a removal from the norm." Given this, it is not surprising that problems of isolation, boredom, and nonconformity are associated with gifted. The gifted is often in a situation (class/grade) that does not meet his or her social, emotional, and intellectual needs.

A lack of peers contributes to a lack of communication. People need to communicate to others who have similar needs, interests, and abilities. Gifted would have fewer opportunities for "equal" communication since there would be few (if any) peers in their immediate surroundings. Lack of communication is a basis for social "maladjustment" (Newland, 1976).

1. *Group Work.* Since gifted students are in the minority, efforts can be made by counselors to bring them together in groups. Gifted students in a group can benefit from the knowledge that they are not "alone" and share their feelings and perceptions with their "peers." Group members could offer support to each other since they are experiencing and perceiving similar problems. Such a group would offer the counselor a wealth of information and insight into the personal/social perceptions of gifted students. This information could be used by counselors to enlighten parents and teachers on the characteristics of these students.

2. *Personal Writing.* An activity used with success at the Research and Guidance Laboratory of the University of Wisconsin-Madison has been personal essay writings with gifted students (Pulvino, Colangelo, & Zaffrann, 1976). Gifted students are usually very skilled in writing and can express their personal/social concerns in writing. Whereas it is sometimes difficult to talk about "personal concerns," writing offers a more comfortable means of expression. Personal essays can be used by counselors as stimulants for further personal interviews as well as sources of unique information. Gifted adolescents should be encouraged to keep a personal journal.

3. *Study Skills.* It is often the case that gifted and talented students are handicapped by not knowing how to study or how to learn. One activity for school counselors to focus on is study skills—for example, units on note-taking, summarizing, studying for exams, reviewing, memorizing, reading for fun, test-taking. In this way these students can learn the skills by which they not only begin to take responsibility for their own education, but also help teach other students these same skills.

4. *Reading.* Gifted students may also need assistance in reading. It may be that they get good grades and do well on tests, yet cannot read very well. Reading at grade level, for example, may represent a remedial reading problem for a gifted child. Since postsecondary education is likely for most of these youngsters, counselors need to examine this area. For example, counselors could easily keep a record from each student regarding a number of key areas (Sanborn et. al., 1971):

1. How much time do you spend each week reading things you do not have to read as part of your school assignments?
2. What have the members of the school staff done to encourage your reading beyond required class work?
3. What encouragement have you received in your home?
4. List the magazines and newspapers you read most regularly.
5. What reading did you do during the past summer?
6. List the titles of the books you have read in the last two months.
7. What do you like to read best? Be specific about the nonfiction and fiction areas you read.

Such information—gathered from all gifted students—not only keeps counselors abreast of students' reading habits but can serve as a jumping-off point for counseling sessions regarding educational concerns.

5. *Testing.* Another area of educational concern is testing. Since most gifted students are often "tested to death" for a variety of reasons (selection and screening for a gifted program; college entrance; scholarships; research and program development), it might be helpful to offer questions here which counselors might ask themselves regarding the testing program in their school.

1. Why do you give these tests to gifted students? What kinds of information do you want? Do these tests really give you that information? Is there a better way to get that information other than from testing?
2. What is done with the information from tests? Is it used as feedback to students? Parents? Is it used for program development regarding the needs of students?

Perhaps a few general cautions on testing might be appropriate regarding gifted programs and testing (Rothney, Danielson, & Heimann, 1958):

1. *Don't* confuse testing the performance of pupils with *inventorying* feelings, attitudes, interests, and what are often called personality traits. Although inventories look like tests they are not *tests*.

2. *Don't* try to set up some mythical level of ability from a test score and expect a pupil to work up to that level at all times in all areas of study.

3. *Don't* compare pupils' scores with norms unless there is reason to believe that cultural circumstances are similar.

4. *Don't* give so many tests that no one has time to interpret them individually to children, their parents, and their teachers.

5. *Don't* be misled by test titles. Study the items.

6. *Don't* expect too much from tests. They do not measure all of

the school's objectives. And they provide only a small sample of what they do measure.

7.   *Don't* use a test simply because others do. Don't use one unless it serves one of· *your* purposes.

8.   *Don't* be "taken in" by the term reliability. It has a special meaning in testing and measurement that is more limited than the dictionary meaning of reliability.

9.   *Do* use carefully selected tests cautiously. They *may* help in understanding the individual pupil and suggest the next steps in his education.

Career and Vocational Concerns.   Another area of concern for some gifted and talented students is the career and vocational area. Counselors need to focus on the unique needs of gifted youngsters regarding careers and vocations. A variety of career guidance models has been presented and discussed elsewhere (Ginsberg, 1951; Walz et al., 1974; Perrone, 1976). For the purposes of this article, specific *issues* relating to career guidance of gifted will be addressed.

Sanborn (1974) discussed critical factors of career guidance with gifted and talented students. They are briefly discussed here.

Multipotentiality.   Gifted students are often proficient in a number of academic and career areas. It is often difficult to choose only one or two areas from among several available diverse career choices. School counselors need to invest more time and energy with individual gifted youngsters because of the number of realistic career choices available to them. Aptitude and interest tests are often needed here.

Expectations.   Most youngsters must face the issue that significant others—parents, relatives, teachers—have expectations for them regarding careers. But the problem of gifted students in this area is special. On one hand, many parents—knowing that their children have superior ability—expect them to accomplish great things: to enroll in the most prestigious colleges and universities, to get the best grades, to win awards, to consistently do well on exams, to enter "status" careers. This may bring about frustration and pressure for students—pressures which they cannot and should not have to handle. In addition some gifted students simply do not want to attend the most prestigious schools or do advanced work or enter high-profile, status professions.

On the other hand, many parents ignore or disbelieve the unique characteristics and abilities of their gifted children. For example, some rural families expect their children to continue working on the farm after high school graduation, to enter the father's business, to carry on the family name. However, individual students—aware of their unique abilities, interests, gifts—may aspire to professional positions which require specialized training and advanced college work.

These instances illustrate how expectations of others can bring about career dilemmas for gifted youngsters—dilemmas which school counselors need to recognize and focus on in the counseling program. These areas include both school and family.

Most gifted and talented youngsters enter college; many continue for advanced degrees or specialized training programs. This requires an unusual investment in terms of money, time, energy, and self. Yet many gifted students are not equipped or prepared to devote this kind of personal and economical investment when they are required to do so—usually while they are still in high school. It is the job of the school counselor and guidance personnel to help gifted students explore potential careers to make the wisest and most fulfilling career choices for themselves and their futures. As Torrance (1976) points out, new careers created by scientific progress are especially likely for bright creative youth.

Gifted Women Like most young women, gifted and talented girls must face the issue of choosing between a career and a family— or arranging for both simultaneously. Some young women may want to begin a career yet feel pressure and expectations from others (parents, friends, even future mates!) to get married and begin a family. Conversely some girls indicate a desire to start a family first and to consider a career later in life—yet they feel other expectations for a career, due to their proficiencies. Counselors need to sensitively apply a family approach to assist gifted women in making career decisions.

After research on the vocational problems of gifted girls, Gowan and Groth (1972) declared:

> It is evident that girls need better model figures for occupa-
> tional choice than they now have. They also need help in mak-
> ing wise choices, particularly in that there is very likely to be
> a career for them after motherhood. Our society is greatly in
> need of the unused brainpower that is represented by bright
> girls. We can no longer allow them to take menial and marginal
> part-time jobs as they get into their forties.

Unseem (1960), along the same lines, poses to the counselor three basic questions:

> 1.   How can the needs of our society be translated into per-
> sonal aspirations for our bright young women?
> 2.   How can counselors rethink the timing of their activities
> so that the bright young girl will get a realistic view of and
> consequent planning for her two lives of motherhood and a
> career?
> 3.   How can counselors help girls view their lives as wholes

and not segments so that the care (*cum* motherhood) will embrace bright women who are fully functioning?

Developmental Arrests, Dysplasias, and Malfunctioning. Gifted children who do not become creative are usually suffering from some form of development arrest, a split between the level (stage) of development in the cognitive and affective area (a dysplasia), (Gowan, 1974:ch. 5), or other malfunctioning of development which consumes the free energy otherwise manifested as creativity. Obviously the prevention and therapy for such dislocations are a guidance and counseling problem. Failure to escalate cognitively from the concrete operations to the formal operations stage is a problem every counselor is familiar with in the high school student who cannot handle the "if-then" contingency and hypothesis-making of science and plane geometry. Similarly most underachievement in the gifted can be traced to failure to escalate from preoperational to concrete operations in grade school. There is not space here to develop these ideas further, but literature on them may be found elsewhere.

Such considerations naturally lead us to the next topic.

Mental Health and the Affective Domain

The affective domain is the natural curriculum of the counselor, as the cognitive domain is of the teacher. Both Erikson and Kohlberg have pointed clearly to this conclusion, yet it is surprising how few counselors understand it. Receiving, Responding, Valuing, Conceptualization, and Values Complex (Krathwohl & others, 1964) are of course useful in promoting the mental health and hence the development of all children, but in the case of gifted children they are vital in ensuring creativity.

Group guidance is one way of developing and maintaining a value system in gifted children (Gowan & others, 1970), although this may also be handled through special affective domain units in the curriculum (see Massialas & Zevin, 1967; Gensley, 1975; for an excellent listing of affective materials and techniques, see Treffinger, 1976). Because this subject is not well understood or treated by most counselors, we again quote from Gowan and Demos (1967) on the subject of promoting creativity through increasing mental health and better attitudes:

> Creativity in gifted children is a cycle which must be stabilized if it is to function. The down phase of the wave often consists of hostility, resentment or other destructive tendencies, which if persistent will dampen out the creativity cycle. It is

here that gifted children need support—large quantities of it, not for the eradication of emotional problems, but for the positive mental health which one must have to be creative at all.

The authors then note some typical problems encountered with gifted children:

1.   The parents frequently have ambivalent relationships with them. They are proud of the child but tend to denigrate his unusualness.

2.   It is difficult for the young gifted child to find true peers, and the lack of these means he does not learn to socialize.

3.   Many bright children never have an opportunity to realize their true capabilities in doing truly outstanding work, because their teachers never provide them with some challenges.

4.   Our actions as well as our words must confirm the child's talents.

5.   Gifted children may become upset and need help when they find material which they can't immediately handle.

6.   We need to ease bright children into social leadership. Bright children need to learn the ropes of leading in such a way that they are respected and followed, not isolated.

Conclusion

In summary, a good counseling program for gifted students involves developmental guidance, differentiated guidance, and the facilitation of mental health and creativity through the affective domain.

The counseling program implies that what is offered has been organized and tested, with the result being a systematic program consisting of goals, objectives, rationale, a variety of counseling methodologies to meet those objectives, and a systematic means of evaluating what has or has not been accomplished.

A counseling program for gifted students is not simply a set of services offered sporadically and unorganized to gifted youngsters—for example, testing, occasional counseling sessions, placement, referral. The program is not an addition to the guidance department in terms of staff, resources, funding, space or time allotment. The program is also not simply a temporary, short-term, stopgap measure which is likely to end as soon as temporary funds ran out.

The leadership of such a program can be organized in a variety of ways. The school counselor is in a particularly advantageous position to serve as leader or program director. Such a counseling program is also a part of the regular school budget, not relying totally on external funding for its existence. Such a program can play a very significant part in the creative development of the gifted individual.

In an era of increasing crises and challenges facing mankind it becomes a matter of survival to seek to maximize the development of the most productive human resources. For this reason a more concentrated approach to the gifted is imperative. Yet, due to an erroneous belief that a talented person will succeed against all odds, the educational and developmental needs of the gifted continue to be neglected. It has been demonstrated that this group is the most educationally deprived of all groups of students in the United States (U.S. Commissioner of Education, 1972). These students are placed in schools and programs where they work often at a minimum of their capacity, much to the detriment of their talent and a consequent loss to our nation.

There is an abundance of information on the gifted (U.S. Commissioner of Education, 1972; Getzels & Jackson, 1962; Gowan & Demos, 1967; Goldberg, 1965; Sanborn et al., 1971; Wing & Wallach, 1971; Gowan & Torrance, 1971) produced in research, educational, and enrichment experiments. Yet, this information does not reach most schools and parents. It is not implemented where it is most needed.

School counselors can provide this information link. To do this, they must first become involved in working with gifted and talented students (Abraham, 1976; Gowan & Bruch, 1971). This involvement may occur through a variety of roles: as a guidance specialist with gifted students; as a consultant to teachers, administrators, and parents; as a researcher in terms of program development, program evaluation, and action research. In this way counseling can fully implement its responsibility to help gifted children become creative adults.

References

Abraham, W. "Counseling the Gifted." *Focus on Guidance,* 9:1:1–11, 1976.

Blocher, D. *Developmental Guidance.* New York: Ronald Press, 1966.

Brandwein, Paul. *The Gifted Child as a Future Scientist.* New York: Harcourt Brace, 1953.

Chickering, A. W. *Education and Identity.* San Francisco: Jossey-Bass, 1969.

Colangelo, N., and Pfleger, L. R. "A Model Counseling Program for the Gifted at Wisconsin University." *Gifted Child Quarterly* 21:3:321; 25, Fall, 1977.

Erikson, E. "Eight Stages of Man." In *Childhood and Society.* New York: Norton Press, 1963.

Gensley, J. "The Gifted Child in the Affective Domain." *Gifted Child Quarterly* 19:307–9, 1975.

Getzels, J. W., and Jackson, P. W. *Creativity and Intelligence: Explorations with Gifted Students.* New York: Wiley, 1962.

Ginsberg, E., and others. *Occupational Choice: An Approach to a General Theory.* New York: Columbia University Press, 1951.

Goldberg, M. L. *Research on the Talented.* New York: Bureau of Publications, Teachers College, Columbia University, 1965.

Gowan, J. C. "The Organization of Guidance for the Able." *Personnel and Guidance Journal* 39:4:275–79, December 1960.

Gowan, J. C. "Issues in the Guidance of Gifted and Creative Children." *Gifted Child Quarterly* 11:140–43, 1967.

Gowan, J. C. "Developmental Process and Guidance Implications." *California Personnel and Guidance Journal* 1:2:18–22, 1968. (a)

Gowan, J. C. "The Guidance of Creative Children." *Journal of Women Deans & Counselors* 31:153–61, 1968. (b)

Gowan, J. C. "The Development of the Creative Individual." *Gifted Child Quarterly* 15:3:156–74, 1971. (a)

Gowan, J. C. "The Development of Meta-Guidance." *California Personnel and Guidance Journal* 4:1:17–19, 1971. (b)

Gowan, J. C. *The Guidance and Measurement of Intelligence Development and Creativity.* Northridge: J. C. Gowan, 1972. (a)

Gowan, J. C. *The Development of the Creative Individual.* San Diego: R. Knapp, 1972. (b)

Gowan, J. C. *The Development of the Psychedelic Individual.* Buffalo: The Creative Education Foundation, 1974.

Gowan, J. C., and Bruch, C. *The Academically Talented Student and Guidance.* Boston: Houghton Mifflin, 1971.

Gowan, J. C., Coole, D., and McDonald, P. "The Impact of Piaget on Guidance." *Journal of Educational Psychology* 1:3:203–17, June 1967. (a)

Gowan, J. C., and Demos, G. D. *The Education and Guidance of the Ablest.* Springfield, Ill: Charles C Thomas, 1964.

Gowan, J. C., and Demos, G. D. "Managing the Post Partum-Depression in Creative Persons." *Gifted Child Quarterly* 11:90–92, 1967.

Gowan, J. C., and Groth, N. J. "The Development of Vocational Choice in Gifted Children." In Gowan, *Guidance and Measurement of Intelligence Development and Creativity.* Northridge: J. C. Gowan, 1972.

Gowan, J. C., and Torrance, E. P. *Educating the Ablest.* Itasca, Ill: F. E. Peacock Publishers, 1971.

Gowan, J. C., and others. "New Aspects in Guiding the Gifted." *Gifted Child Quarterly* 13:103–12, Summer 1969.

Gowan, J. C., and others. "Group Counseling in the Development of Self Concept." *California Personnel and Guidance Journal* 3:4:16–21, 1970.

Havighurst, R. J. "Youth in Exploration and Man Emergent." In H. Borow, *Man in a World of Work.* Boston: Houghton Mifflin, 1964.

Hershenson,D. B. "Life Stage Vocational Development Theory." *Counseling Psychology* 15:23–31, January 1968.

Keating, D. P. (Ed.). *Intellectual Talent: Research and Development.* Baltimore: Johns Hopkins University Press, 1976.

Krathwohl, D. T., Bloom, B. S., and Masia, B. B. *Taxonomy of Educational Objectives, Handbook II: Affective Domain.* New York: David McKay, 1964.

Maslow, A. *Motivation and Personality.* New York: Harper Bros., 1954.

Massialas, B. G., and Zevin, J. *Creative Encounters in the Classroom.* New York: Wiley, 1967.

Newland, T. E. *The Gifted in Socio-Educational Perspective.* Englewood Cliffs, N.J.: Prentice-Hall, 1976.

Perrone, P. *Career Development Model.* Unpublished manuscript, University of Wisconsin-Madison, 1976.

Pulvino, C., Colangelo, N., and Zaffrann, R. T. *Laboratory Counseling Programs: Counseling and Program Development for Gifted.* Madison, Wis.: Research and Guidance Laboratory, 1976.

Renzulli, J. "The Enrichment Triad Model," Part I, *The Gifted Child Quarterly* 20:3:303–27, Fall 1976; Part II, *The Gifted Child Quarterly* 21:1 Spring, 1977.

Rothney, J. W. M., Danielson, P. J., and Heimann, R. A. *Measurement for Guidance.* Harper and Brothers, 1958.

Rothney, J. W. M., and Sanborn, M. P. "Wisconsin's Program for Superior Students." *Personnel and Guidance Journal* 44:694–99, 1966.

Sanborn, M. P. "Career Development Problems of Gifted and Talented Students." In *Career Education for Gifted and Talented Students,* K. B. Hoyt and J. R. Hebeler (Eds.). Salt Lake City, Utah: Olympus Publishing Co., 1974.

Sanborn, M. P., Pulvino, C. J., and Wunderlin, R. F. *Research Reports: Superior Students in Wisconsin High Schools.* Research and Guidance Laboratory for Superior Students, University of Wisconsin-Madison, 1971.

Sullivan, H. S. *Interpersonal Theory of Psychiatry.* New York: Norton, 1953.

Torrance, E. P. "Future Careers for Gifted and Talented Students." *Gifted Child Quarterly* 20:142 ff., 1976.

Treffinger, D., and others. "Encouraging Affective Development." *Gifted Child Quarterly* 20:47 ff., 1976.

Unseem, Ruth. "Changing Cultural Concepts in Women's Lives." *Journal of the National Association of Women Deans & Counselors* 24:29–34, 1960.

U.S. Commissioner of Education. *Education of the Gifted and Talented.* Report to the Congress of the United States. Washington, D.C.: U.S. Government Printing Office, 1972.

Walz, G. R., Smith, R. L., and Benjamin, L. *A Comprehensive View of Career Development.* Washington, D.C.: APGA Press, 1974.

Wing, C. W., and Wallach, M. A. *College Admissions and the Psychology of Talent.* New York: Holt, Rinehart and Winston, 1971.

14   New Directions in the Guidance of the Gifted and Talented

PHILIP A. PERRONE AND CHARLES J. PULVINO

Introduction

While efforts to identify gifted children have been made since the start of the century (Baker, 1907; Whipple, 1924; Terman & others, 1925, etc.; Bentley, 1937; Sumpton, Norris, & Terman, 1950; Witty, 1951; and Terman, 1954), efforts to guide them did not originate until the fifties (Strang, 1952; Barbe, 1954; Barbour, 1954; Buchwald, 1954; Gowan, 1955; Neuber, 1957; Conant, 1958; Gowan, 1960; NEA, 1961).

Despite these attempts it was not until 1958, when Congress reacted to "Sputnik" with passage of the National Defense Education Act, that federal emphasis was directed toward this population of students. Legislation was provided to prepare counselors who could better identify and guide gifted and talented high school students. Schools were funded to develop programs which could effectively channel gifted and talented youth into the sciences and engineering. History shows that to a large degree the program was successful. The United States put the first man on the moon, took close-up pictures of Mars, and successfully completed interplanetary soil sampling.

Although the program was successful it does not appear that defining gifted and talented as high-achieving science and mathematics students resulted in either a comprehensive definition of gifted and talented or in a comprehensive program for identifying, educating, and guiding the gifted and talented students. The educational pendulum apparently is taking shorter swings, because the needs of gifted and talented pupils are coming to the fore once again—and the concern is broader than in 1958. It appears today the concern is for the individual as well as society. Moreover much of the present sup-

From *The Gifted Child Quarterly* 21:3 (1977). Used by permission.

port comes from parties directly involved with gifted students, their parents and school personnel.

The Research and Guidance Laboratory at the University of Wisconsin has been studying and guiding and following the development of superior high school students since the Sputnik era in 1958. Although we have been interested in individual high school students and their later accomplishments, at this time we want to broaden our scope and thus find it necessary to develop a comprehensive definition of gifted and talented and differentiated guidance for them. In this regard it seems useful to utilize the Office of Education's definitions of talented and gifted. A talented student is defined in terms of performing in the highest 15% among a peer population in both measures of cognitive development and measures of performance or achievement. A gifted student is defined in terms of performing in the highest 3% among a peer population in measures of cognitive development and measures of performance or achievement (U.S. Senate Subcommittee Report, 1972).

Rationale

In developing the present framework we have been attracted by the writings of many people. Gowan (1974) has described a developmental stage theory associating Erikson's life stages (affective component) with Piaget's cognitive developmental stages. Gowan links affective and cognitive components to three attentional modes (the world, the self, and interpersonal relations) in infancy-childhood, adolescence, and adulthood. Table 14.1 represents this linkage.

Information in Table 14.1 fails to represent adequately the complexity and interrelatedness of the various components. It is our belief that the affective dimension provides the necessary conditions for cognitive development and that at higher levels of cognitive development all previous affective conditions must be present. If this hypothesis is correct, educational emphasis would have to be on establishing and maintaining a positive affective environment, without which cognitive development would not occur. It is our contention that further research is needed to investigate the relationship between the affective and cognitive domains. Also, research regarding the latter stages of affective and cognitive development is sparse compared to the research generated regarding the first five stages. It appears that understanding the creative process is linked to knowing more about these latter stages of Piaget's and Samples' hierarchies.

Table 14.2, adapted from Samples (1975), indicates the hierarch-

TABLE 14.1
Erikson-Piaget-Gowan Developmental Stages

	Infancy-Childhood Affective–Cognitive	*Youth-Adolescence Affective–Cognitive*	*Adult Affective–Cognitive*
The World	Trust–Sensorimotor (Perception emerges)	Industry–Concrete Operations	Generativity–Psychedelia
The Self	Autonomy–Preoperational (Child can decenter from immediate precept)	Identity–Formal Operations (Child can formulate hypotheses and think logically) -----------*	Ego Integrity–Illumination
Relating to Others	Initiative–Intuitive (Child can imagine incomplete connection between precept and conceptualization)	Intimacy–Creativity (Child is able to create concepts)	

*At this transition point we hypothesize that the individual has achieved field independence.

ical functions of the left hemisphere as described by Piaget and proposed metaphorical functions of the right hemisphere posited by Samples.

TABLE 14.2
Functions of the Right and Left Hemispheres

Left Hemisphere Function
Rational Mind
(Piaget)

Formal Operations Stage:
12 years of age. Ability to think in ways that result in problems being solved without direct experience with the qualities involved. Its hallmark is abstract deduction.

Concrete Operations:
7 to 12 years of age. Beginning to translate experience preferentially into generalizations that can be approached mentally without experience.

Pre-Operational Stage:
18 months to 7 years. Cannot translate experience into abstract representation or symbolism. Discriminates between modes of sensory input but shows little preferences toward abstraction.

Sensory-Motor Stage:
Birth to 18 months. Treats all experience without preference of input. So involved with senses and sensory experience that abstractions are of little importance.

Right Hemisphere Function
Metaphoric Mind
(Samples)

Inventive Mode:
The mind uses existing knowledge to create objects and processes that have never existed. There is a total synergic combination of external and/or internal qualities with no link to precedent. *All metaphoric and rational modes may contribute.*

Integrative Mode:
Personal analogy, becoming something. Total immersion; e.g., becoming a ball—feeling, sensing the way a ball rolls, bounces, etc.

Comparative Mode:
Direct analogy such as "a city is like a heart, one pulse beat in the morning when corpuscles (traffic) flow in and another pulse beat at night when corpuscles (traffic) flow out."

Symbolic Mode:
Substitution of symbols for natural realities, e.g., I-90 for a four-lane road running from Chicago to Minneapolis.

Ornstein (1972) sheds additional light on the hemispheric function of the brain. He suggests that "although each hemisphere shares the potential for many functions, and both sides participate in most activities, in the normal person the two hemispheres tend to specialize" (p. 51). Ornstein's statement can be pictorially represented by a Venn diagram in which the logical (left) hemisphere circle overlaps the metamorphic (right) hemisphere circle. This overlap portion indicates the potential for generalized function, and the nonoverlapped, the potential for specialization.

In this conceptualization the left hemisphere is involved with analytic, logical thinking and the right hemisphere is holistic in nature and is primarily responsible for intuition, feelings, space orientation, and diffuse processing of information. Whereas the left hemisphere processes information linearly, the right processes information holistically. The two "halves" have the specialized potential for approaching problems from two quite different perspectives. It is in this potential that they are functionally complementary.

Another perspective regarding the rational mind and metaphoric mind is suggested by Rollo May (1977). May describes two types of learning humans experience. One type is determinism, where one acquires new facts, new data, new habits, and new behavior patterns which can be viewed as having a logical or left hemispheric origin. The second type is freedom, which is based upon assumption of transference, resistance and other functions of the unconscious and is metaphoric or right hemispheric based.

Field Dependence–Field Independence

Thinking in terms of the brain's specialized halves has led us to examine other human behaviors frequently characterized as dichotomous. The work of Witkin (1977) has been most enlightening and has led to a variety of suggestions, including:

1.   Field-independent persons are more likely to be aware of their own needs, feelings, and attributes which they experience as distinct from those of others. This distinction in effect provides an internal frame of reference to which the person may adhere in dealing with others.

2.   Field-independent persons show significantly more nonverbal behaviors (such as arm crossing, leg crossing, absence of forward leaning) . . . interpreted as reflecting a need to gain psychological distance from others.

3.   Field-dependent persons are likely to be attentive to and make use of prevailing social frames of reference.

4.   Field-dependent persons . . . take greater account of external

social referents in defining their attitudes and feelings ... particularly under conditions of ambiguity.

5. A relatively field-independent person is likely to overcome the organization of the field, or to restructure it, when presented with a field having a dominant organization, whereas the relatively field-dependent person tends to adhere to the organization of the field as given.

6. Field-independent people attempt to use an hypothesis-testing approach and field-dependent persons a spectator approach to concept attainment.

Our questions at this point are whether field dependence-independence is a direct function of hemispheric specialization. If it is, can we assess field dependence-independence by measuring hemispheric functioning? What are the educational implications if this relationship exists?

Convergent–Divergent Thought

Investigation of convergent-divergent thought processes follows closely on the examination of hemispheric specialization and field dependence–field independence theory. Combining these two lines of inquiry leads us to the following:

Convergent thinking is illustrative of rational thinking in that there are formed (learned) associations between external stimuli (ES) and responses (R). Learning-appropriate generalizations and discriminations are essential in being judged logical. The correctness and appropriateness of responses are determined (externally) by others.

Within social parameters the individual should learn to become less dependent, less externally evaluated, and more independent and self-evaluative. We make the same differentiatiation Samples (1975) makes regarding the meaning of stimulation and motivation. Stimulation is external or extrinsic and is provided by the culture. Motivation is intrinsic, born inside, calling itself to action. You cannot determine whether behavior is stimulated or motivated without knowing the individual's thought processes, including the reasons for his/her behavior. An appropriate learning environment provides the individual stimulation, support, and reinforcement which in turn should produce a relatively secure, intellectually curious individual who eventually can be motivated, self-reinforcing, and self-evaluating.

At the highest levels of divergent thinking the individual should be able to respond to external stimuli with appropriate learned responses or respond with a newly created response. Individuals can also create stimuli (internally created stimuli) to which they can respond. Responses may be evaluated externally and internally and these evaluations may frequently be in conflict. It is being suggested that convergent thinking capability is necessary but not sufficient for higher levels of divergent thought and that the highest levels of divergent thought *encompass the highest levels of convergent thought and high levels of metaphoric thought.* In effect this corresponds with the Inventive Mode listed at the top of Samples' hierarchy. This hypothesis is consistent with the research of Getzels and Jackson (1962), DeBono (1971), Johnson (1972), Olson (1977) and Crockenberg (1972)

The work of Getzels and Jackson (1962), Torrance (1962), and more recently Wallach and Kogan (1965) makes a strong case for focusing on the attributes/characteristics of convergent and divergent thinking as the key to enhancing the ultimate development of gifted and talented persons. Research and analysis of research on the relationship of divergent and convergent thinking by Wallach and Kogan provides a convincing argument that although convergent and divergent thinking are related at lower levels, they appear to be unrelated at higher levels.

Educational Considerations

Our present system of characterizing gifted or talented persons as being *either* high convergent *or* high divergent thinkers may reflect more upon the nature of learning environments (home, school, and community) and their impact (reinforcements) on individual personality development than be indicative of fundamental differences among persons.

May (1977) sheds some light on this issue in his discussion of anxiety that accompanies freedom or creativity. He suggests that there is no insight without some anxiety and that anxiety is a primary reason people reject freedom. Anxiety occurs because insight consists of two possibilities—of failure or of success. The sense of failure can explain why people block off most original ideas before they reach consciousness, repressing ideas that are counter to views of esteemed others. May concludes that courage is necessary to accept constructive anxiety and that individuals in a supportive environment need less courage to be creative. Positive reinforcers in home, school, and community may allow an individual to be creative by effectively reducing fear of failure.

To more adequately determine the impact of home, school, and community, to better understand creative anxiety, and, ultimately, to be able to understand differences between individuals we must assess how individual students incode and decode stimuli. To help us we have turned to the work of Grinder and Bandler (1975, 1976), whose research indicates that the language individuals use is indicative of how they process data from their world. They hypothesize that of the data processed through the five sensory input channels, the three major input channels are vision, audition, and kinesthetic, and the remaining two channels—smell and taste—are apparently of little use as ways of gaining information about the world.

Grinder and Bandler believe that individuals gain meaning from their experiences and store them for future use by creating a map or model of their experiences which are called *representational systems*. Individuals store their experiences directly in a representational system most closely associated with sensory input channels. For each individual, there are more or less highly developed, or preferred, representational systems which parallel the visionary, auditory, and kinesthetic input channels.

In addition, an individual may have preferred short- and long-term storage systems and preferred retrieval systems which correspond to their primary mode for obtaining data. Little is know about how these systems operate, either individually or collectively. What may shed light on the underlying organizational structure of these systems, however, is the theoretical work being accomplished with split-brain research. Samples' (1975) work described earlier suggests development of visual metaphoric, symbolic thinking (a right hemisphere function) occurs readily in some cultures and that individuals from those cultures are frequently able to create extensive "maps" of their world which are extremely rich in detail, informationally accurate, and readily retrievable. Individuals in the Anglo-American culture, by contrast, apparently have difficulty in utilizing visual metaphoric, symbolic processes and experience greater success in sharing their representation of the world with symbolic images such as the written word, a left hemispheric function.

Conclusion

What is suggested by the research of Samples (1975), Ornstein (1972), and Sperry (1974) is that different cultures educate their youth in a differential manner, some focusing on left hemispheric functioning, others on right hemispheric functioning. Given this belief it is important to assess educational influences of majority and minority cultures to determine which activities, customs, beliefs, influences, etc., lead to development of one hemisphere or the other. Secondly, it is our assumption that development of diverse potential in both hemispheres of the brain is preferable to development of one hemisphere only. Therefore, it is important to assess an individual's cognitive style, representational systems, and consequent learning preferences so that educational offerings can be designed and implemented which will enhance the person's strength while ameliorating his/her weaknesses. More productivity from both hemispheres is the desired outcome. May (1977) emphasizes this point with his statement that without determinism (convergent thinking), and the predictability that goes with it, we have *anarchy*. Without freedom (divergent thinking), and the exuberance that goes with it, we have *apathy* (p. 9).

Another desired outcome of educating gifted and talented pupils is creativeness. Creativity has traditionally been viewed as a process which is determined to exist by its products. You cannot equate product and process. It appears to us to be more fruitful to research the necessary conditions for creativeness which are represented by field-independent and high convergent and divergent intelligence which we believe are produced by affective support and cognitive stimulation.

As more becomes known through our research and the research of others, we will modify assumptions presented in this paper. Educational procedures that result should lead to better educated gifted and talented youth, a society that better utilizes the talents of all its citizens, and an end to crisis programming such as that which was ushered in by Sputnik.

References

Baker, J. H. *American Problems.* New York: Longmans, Green & Co., 1907.

Barbe, W. B. "Differentiated Guidance for the Gifted." *Education* 74:306–11, January 1954.

Barbour, E. "Counseling Gifted H.S. Students." *California Journal of Secondary Education* 29:476–79, December 1954.

Bentley, J. E. *Superior Children.* New York: W. W. Norton & Co., Inc., 1937.

Buchwald, Leona. "The Counselor's Role in Identifying and Guiding the Superior Child." *Baltimore Bulletin of Education* 31:16–17, June 1954.

Conant, J. B. "The Identification and Education of the Academically Talented." *NEA Conference Report,* Washington, D.C., 1958.

Crockenberg, S. B. "Creativity Tests: A Boon or Boondoggle for Education?" *Review of Educational Research* 42:1:27–45, 1972.

DeBono, E. *The Use of Lateral Thinking.* Toronto: Holt Publishing Co., 1971.

Garrett, S. V. "Putting Our Whole Brain to Use: A Fresh Look at the Creative Process." *Journal of Creative Behavior* 10:239–49, 1976.

Getzels, J. W., and Jackson, P. W. *Creativity and Intelligence.* New York: John Wiley & Sons, Inc., 1962.

Gowan, J. C. "The Gifted Underachiever—A Problem for Everyone." *Exceptional Children* 21:7:247–49, 1955.

Gowan, J. C. "The Organization of Guidance for the Able." *Personnel and Guidance Journal* 39:4:275–79. December 1960.

Gowan, J. C. *Development of the Psychedelic Individual.* Buffalo, N.Y.: Creative Education Foundation, S.U.C., 1974.

Grinder, J. and Bandler, R. *The Structure of Magic.* Vols. 1 and 2. Palo Alto, Calif.: Science and Behavior Books, Inc., 1975, 1976.

Johnson, D. M. *Systematic Introduction to the Psychology of Thinking.* New York: Harper, 1972.

May, R. "Freedom, Determinism, and the Future." *Psychology* (trial issue), April 1977, 6–9.

National Education Association. *Guidance for the Academically Talented.* Washington, D.C., 1961.

Neuber, M. A. "When a Child Has High Potential." *School Executive* 76:70–1, April 1957.

Olson, M. "Right or Left Hemisphere Processing in the Gifted." *The Gifted Child Quarterly* 21:116–21, 1977.

Ornstein, R. *The Psychology of Consciousness.* New York: W. H. Freeman & Co., 1972.

Piaget, J. *Play, Dreams, and Imitation in Childhood.* New York: W. W. Norton Co., Inc., 1962.

Samples, B. "Learning with the Whole Brain." *Human Behavior,* February 1975, 17–23.

Sperry, R. W. "Messages from the Laboratory." *Engineering and Science,* January 1974.

Strang, R. "Guidance of the Gifted." *Personnel and Guidance Journal* 31:26–30, 1952.

Sumpton, M. R., Norris, D., and Terman, L. M. *The Education of Exceptional Children.* 49th Yearbook, NSSE. Chicago: University of Chicago Press, 1950.

Terman, L. M. "The Discovery and Encouragement of Exceptional Talent." *American Psychologist* 9:221–30, June 1954.

Terman, L. M., and others. *Mental and Physical Traits of 1,000 Gifted Children.* Stanford, Cal.: Stanford University Press, 1925. (See also *The Promise of Youth,* 1930; *The Gifted Child Grows Up,* 1947; and *The Gifted Group at Midlife,* 1959.)

Torrance, E. P. *Guiding Creative Talent.* Englewood Cliffs, N.J.: Prentice-Hall, 1962.

U.S. Senate Subcommittee on Education. Report, Committee of Labor and Public Welfare, Education of the Gifted and Talented, March 1972.

Wadsworth, B. J. *Piaget's Theory of Cognitive Development.* New York: David McKay Co., Inc., 1975.

Wallach, M. A. and Kogan, N. *Modes of Thinking in Young Children.* New York: Holt, Rinehart & Winston, 1965.

Whipple, G. M. (Ed.). Yearbook of NSSE, Chicago: University of
    Chicago Press, 1924.
Witkin, H. A., et al., "Educational Implications of Cognitive Style."
    Review of Educational Research 47:1:1–64, 1977.
Witty, P. A. (Ed.). *The Gifted Child.* Boston: D. C. Heath, 1951.

15   Differentiated Guidance for the Gifted: A Developmental View

J. C. GOWAN

The full implementation of the rights inherent in the Constitution
and the Declaration of Independence has been described as the
major task of the 20th century. If all men are equal politically, but
differ in talents, then they have inalienable rights to equal educational opportunity to mature these individual potentials. The past
decade has seen a remarkable awakening to the validity of these
rights for the exceptional human beings in our society. One evidence
of this awareness has been an increased concern for the special needs
and individual differences of all types of exceptional children including the gifted. But this process of individualizing the curriculum to
the needs and abilities of the student is known as guidance.

Two centuries ago, Pope told us: "The proper study of mankind is
man." Man's development involves escalation into life-stages having
different characteristics, as Piaget, Erikson, and the writer have elsewhere pointed out. This continued escalation into the higher stages
is most clearly seen in the gifted and talented, because their intellectual energy means they are more likely to continue to develop mentally after they have stopped growing physically. The task of
guidance is to assist in this escalation over developmental discontinuities, by removing personal and environmental stress from the
individual. Hence guidance is not just for the crisis removal of psychopathology, but for the maintenance of continual development
progress without which creativity, ego-integrity, and self-actualization cannot become fully manifesting.

Concern for the qualities of exceptional human beings arises out of
an exceptional concern for the qualities of all human beings. Thus a
good guidance program for the gifted is an outgrowth of a good

From *The Gifted Child Quarterly* 21:3 (1977). Used by permission.

general guidance program, just as the latter is in turn an outcome of an intelligent and democratically oriented school administration.

But concern without knowledge of procedure can be sentimental at best, and dangerous at worst; what is needed is the carrying over of the principles and objectives of guidance to fit the special cases involved in the education of the gifted. If we postulate that school guidance seeks to help children solve their developmental tasks on schedule, it remains only to assess how this principle needs to be modified in the guidance of the gifted. Obviously the gifted need differential guidance, just as they need a differentiated curriculum; equally obviously this guidance must be concerned with their developmental acceleration.

We have noted that guidance for the gifted depends upon a high degree of empathy for the individual and idiosyncratic characteristics of the gifted. Certainly these young people have just as much right to guidance in developing to the fullest their multipotentiality as any other child. But many counselors who champion the rights of the general student to such help feel threatened or put off by the gifted student with his uncommon differences. Guidance for the gifted is very much like Christianity—it really hasn't been tried on an effective basis by people who are prepared to practice it.

As the early pioneers in guidance, less than a generation removed from the founders of the movement, we are still in the panacea phase of treating symptoms instead of developing structural content to deal with specifics. We decry individual diagnosis in favor of a general positive regard. We have confused our discipline with that of psychotherapy, which is concerned with the normal development of adults, whereas we are (or should be) concerned with the normal developmental problems of growing children. As a result we know very little that is specific about the genesis of the guidance problems of the gifted child.

We can best discharge our job as guidance workers in schools by understanding better the developmental process and its guidance implication as they apply to all children, and then modify our treatment in terms of the individual differences we find in a particular group. For example, whereas a psychotherapist is attempting to remove stress from his patient, we are more interested in getting the child to accommodate to a reasonable amount of stress, modified to fit his individual tolerance level.

I think it is important to point out that a vocation is a calling and not necessarily a job. Making a life, as Thoreau has reminded us, is more important than making a living. And often the gifted student marches to the music of a distant drum. We may not be able to adjust him to society, for he may perceive much in society that should itself be adjusted.

In the case of guidance for gifted adolescents, the counselor's job is less to adjust the student to society than it is to help him with the Havighurst adolescent developmental tasks, so that he may become creative. These tasks, as you remember, are (1) the breakaway from home, (2) social adjustment, (3) sexual adjustment, (4) vocational adjustment, and (5) intellectual/moral adjustment. In this large endeavor the counselor's curriculum is the Krathwohl taxonomy of the affective domain: receiving, responding, valuing, conceptualization, and value complex—in other words by cultivation of mature emotional attitudes and moral integrity. By and large counselors do a miserable job in this, and that is one reason why there are so many alienated gifted adolescents. If the counselor does the job right, the end product is a creative youth—if he does it wrong, the end product is a delinquent or maladaptive one.

At the San Fernando State College Workshops for the Gifted Children we invested very large amounts of guidance, not for the curing of psychopathology, but in order to help children become creative. If we are to ask children to step off the dime of psychological safety which they have built for themselves, and risk status in creative effort, we need to give them supportive approbation, and to help them gain the ego strength and self-confidence to hold in tension longer the stress occasioned by complexity and disorder out of which creative innovation is born. Our guidance program differed from that in a good modern school in several ways:

1.   There is a grade counselor for every class of 25 children, plus two head counselors.

2.   The counselor and the teacher are a unified team; the counselor frees the teacher of all classroom activities except the development of curriculum and direction of learning.

3.   Since the counselor is in class with the children, she sees behavior (it is not just reported to her); moreover when abnormal behavior occurs, she has a baseline of previous observations with which to observe it.

4.   The counselor concentrates on improving the mental health of the children, not just on treating symptoms in crisis situations. She has time and opportunity to treat directly with children, to know all of them and their parents on an intimate basis, and to establish friendship with them.

5.   The counselor is taught to recognize the two prime tasks of guidance:

    a)   helping the normal developmental tasks of the child.
    b)   helping with the special problems occasioned by the giftedness of the child.

6. Since there are several counselors in adjacent classrooms, there is much opportunity for professional consultation, discussion, and support. The almost instant availability of the head counselor is also helpful in this regard. Such back-up helps the counselor's own mental health and is reflected in the classroom atmosphere.

7. The counselor is accessible before class begins in the morning. Many children come to her and relieve tensions by talking briefly. Some get a little extra attention and love; others get desired valuing on a creative thought, a new poem, or a new possession. This all just naturally happens if the counselor is around—ready to receive, respond, and value. Such psychological "grooming" helps the child channel his thoughts and energies onto the class curriculum. Obviously children could get by without this, but they are the more creative for having it.

8. The counselor is in an ideal situation to use both individual and selected group counseling toward accomplishing an objective in whatever manner is most appropriate. Individual and group dynamics can be used to reinforce each other.

9. There is opportunity to contact parents on a positive note, just to let them know that all is going well. Many parents report they have never before been contacted by a counselor except for negative information. Students quietly singled out and praised have the same surprised reaction.

Vocational choice for able youth is complicated by the many alternatives from which they often must select, plus the fact that high-level youth may feel that because others are making their occupational choices, they must now make theirs too. Here the young person needs help if he is undecided. While many gifted youngsters make choices early, some do not. The able youth who is high on persuasive, literary, and social service interests should often almost complete a liberal arts course of study before deciding on law, education, the ministry, or some other professional or business career. These conscientious youngsters need reassurance that there is nothing tragic in not being able to make up their minds at this time.

Another matter which the counselor could impress upon the young people in his charge, by group counseling if necessary, is that one learns more quickly what one *does not* want to do, than what one does want to do. Useful progress can be made by uncommitted youth who can say of certain areas, "I definitely don't want to do that." Indeed, one of the chief values of summer jobs or job experience is that one learns which areas to avoid. These rejects provide useful clues for the counselor.

Another area in which the counselor can help is in matching aptitudes and interests. These two generally uncorrelated aspects of personality sometimes agree and sometimes do not. Where aptitudes and interests are both high in an area, the counselor could point this out and suggest further explorations along these lines. Where interests are strong and aptitudes weak, he may warn against it; and this may be a useful form of elimination. Where aptitudes are strong and interest weak, he had better keep silent, for fear of prejudicing the client against the particular area. Finally, where both aptitudes and interests are weak, he can generally get the youth to agree that this area is not appropriate.

Of course for those in the medical, scientific, or engineering areas whose vocational plans seem to formulate early, the counselor, if aptitude and interest profiles coincide, can simply support them; or he can, if he notes certain weaknesses, gently steer them to that aspect of a general area where the weakness will be less felt. A student with scientific interests, for example, but with less strength in mathematics, might be guided into the biological rather than the physical science areas. The counselor should also be alert for hidden secondary interests which in later life may be satisfied by a hobby or may open new vistas in a direction which the student does not yet realize. A future engineer with strong persuasive interests might consider engineering administration or patent law. One who has high literary interests might consider technical writing or teaching of science. One who is skilled in mathematics perhaps would be wise to stay in production, while one with artistic interests may consider drafting or architectural design. It is assumed, of course, that all these students are gifted with high-level aptitudes. These students will profit by professional internships.

The vocational counseling of those individuals who are especially talented in art and music, or who show high interests therein, poses difficult problems in our society. The problem is not so much one of guidance as it is of a culture which does not offer enough outlets for these interests and aptitudes. Consequently, if there is any doubt, the person might be guided into a secondary interest area for a vocation and into the art or music area for an avocation. Very high levels of both competency and interest should be required for positive direction into these fields and job possibilities probably should not be encouraged unless the student will have an independent income. The "generally gifted" should probably use their talents for avocational outlets and seek their primary vocation in more financially secure areas. Most experienced counselors know that interest in these two areas often coincides with a personality which doesn't mature vocationally as quickly as some others, and these "anti-philistines" actively resist this developmental task, some to the exasperating degree of the "beatnik" attitudes. While no rejoinder is very satisfactory to this kind of attitude and the underachievement which often goes with it, perhaps the best device is guidance into an unspecialized general education or liberal arts college course of study, and then possibly to go into the field of teaching or writing.

Regarding vocational education, counselors should not force gifted students (such as those previously described who have clear-cut occupational goals already established) into vocational education. After all, guidance is dedicated to the welfare of the individual and not to the aggrandizement of a particular program. The loss of an extra solid needed for preparation in science, engineering, or medicine may be serious. For the gifted youth who has no clear occupational goals and no strong motivation, vocational education may be very helpful in at least providing him with experience in, and knowledge about some of the vocational choices he does not want. This is important since youth learns to make good vocational choice only by avoiding poor ones. Such education may also keep him from dropping out of school by providing a class or workshop of extreme interest to him. One would hope, however, that when gifted youth are placed in vocational courses, it should not be in lockstep, but in some program which offers progress at an individual rate. For example, all gifted children need typing. Few of them need a semester of it. In short, outside of professional apprenticeship, vocational education appears to be indicated for some but not all gifted youth. Finally we should realize that vocational education for the gifted should be based on the realization that the successful bright student will probably enjoy a long succession of increasingly important jobs in his career development, representing different facets of a single vocational cluster, in accordance with the Ginzberg principle of becoming more and more specialized.

There is one further guidance problem best handled by counseling which is most often found with the able and which does not fit any of the previous pigeonholes. It is the constellation of problems attendant upon the youth who is highly upwardly mobile from a lower socioeconomic background. There is probably no more poignant plight that meets the counselor's variegated experience than this.

In the first place, cutting across social gradients always makes it appear to the individual that he is in the wrong, and the reaction formation built up here may result in a generally offensive social aggressiveness which will later prove a handicap. Frequently, the youth is not fully aware of his situation, and just listening to him with some attempt made at easing his worry may be useful. When one is climbing the ladder of socioeconomic status one sees others at odd angles and perspectives, and so it is not surprising that the youth may get a "worm's-eye view" of what he is approaching, and an ambivalent picture of what he is leaving.

Besides listening, the counselor can, on occasion, offer an explanation of some of the problems of "climbing the ladder." He can also try to occupy his client's time in the company of the group toward which the youth is heading, whether in cultural, social, or work activities. The young person may well need his manners formed, and will usually profit from an introduction to cultural activities, including music and the arts, as well as to successful adults. A scholarship away to college is, of course, an excellent idea. The youth cannot be expected to understand family frictions and it may be best to get him away from them.

Oftentimes helping him find a part-time job to take care of pressing financial needs is imperative, for very often these youngsters go out on their own and show a pattern of family rejection from the outset. One of the places where some ties can be formed with the counselor's help, however, is in the matter of adult model figures. Such a youth needs a superior adult man and a superior adult woman for his "spiritual" mother and father. He has probably had a great deal of difficulty already because of the psychological rejection of his parents. Perhaps the counselor himself can provide one of these figures, but a great effort should be made to provide the youth with others, such as professional persons in the community, or men and women of breadth and culture. The upwardly mobile youth feels the rebelliousness of the disinherited and disenfranchised person, and because of his youth, spirit, and ability, this tendency can make him potentially dangerous. He needs to be someone's protege, to know the giving without expectation of return from some parental hand that he can respect. Only then can he blunt the predatory force which he has needed to break through the social barrier by his later emulation of this example of the ability to help and nurture others.

Needless to say, this kind of activity on the counselor's part takes time and energy. It is, however, one of the most rewarding experiences that the adult can have. The counselor can enlarge his usefulness by acting sometimes as a financial aids worker, so that lay persons of affluence and influence in the community who are predisposed to good works can have the pleasure of actively contributing to the background of an outstanding individual.

One of the most important reasons for good articulation between high school and college is that guidance problems are continuous and developmental and do not suddenly stop at the time of commencement. Indeed there should be a steady escalation in career jobs. If there is enough rapport so that the high school counselor can pass onto his college colleagues information about particular students, a great deal of lost motion can be avoided. For example, some youths are well determined vocationally by the end of high school, while others will need careful guidance as late as their junior year in college. Such youths should be encouraged in high school to seek counseling later while in college and the high school counselor should have confidence that it will be provided at that time.

This discussion should not be conducted without a word about the special problems of gifted girls. It is a sad commentary on American social beliefs that in the country that has pioneered most of the reforms which have restored the rights of women we are still so backward in regard to stereotyping occupational outlets for women. In some respects, women constitute our largest minority group—a group which is actually a majority in numbers, but which continues to be stereotyped and discriminated against both in training opportunities and in career positions. It once used to be felt that women were not fitted physically for some of the professional fields. There is some evidence to believe, however, that genetically women may be superior to men because of the composition of a more complete chromosome structure.

Effective counseling and guidance can plan a particularly important role in providing girls with the information and help they need in order to complete college and secure a career in a particular field. Occupational information outlining the advantages and attractions of various careers for women needs to be widely circulated, but more important is the individual counseling by trained counselors, from elementary to graduate school, who can not only help girls with promising potential to continue to emphasize academic achievement but also help every girl to prepare for some type of career commensurate with her particular aptitudes, interests, and personality characteristics.

When one thinks of how many jobs existing in the 1970's were not even thought of in the 1930's, it becomes obvious that it is futile to try to give gifted youth specific occupational training for the 21st century. What we need to do instead of fitting youth to a procrustean bed is to try to stimulate and develop any and all talents which exist in any individual to an exceptional degree. While careful clinical diagnosis of individual aptitudes and interests is not popular with counselors nowadays, the youth who has many talents needs special help in choosing and developing that particular one which may benefit him most in the future by allowing him to use it to benefit society. Interestingly enough, this reward for the individual is also a vicarious reward for a counselor, just as it is for a successful coach. To see undeveloped talent in youth, to nurture and stimulate it, to encourage the interest and discipline to exploit it fully is a task from which the counselor, the student, and society will all benefit. May we all devel-

op the insight to see the potential in gifted students and to help them
actualize it.

Bibliography of the Writings of J. C. Gowan on Guidance for Gifted

"The Gifted Underachiever." *Exceptional Children* 21:7:247–49,
1955. See also *Exceptional Children* 24:3:98–101, 1957; *Journal
of Counseling Psychology* 7:91–95, 1960.

"The Organization of Guidance for the Able." *Personnel and Guidance Journal* 39:4:275–79, December 1960.

With George Demos. *Education and Guidance of the Ablest.* Springfield, Ill.: Charles C Thomas, 1964.

Guidance of Exceptional Children. New York: David McKay Co.,
1965. Rev. ed., 1972.

With George Demos and Paul Torrance. *Creativity: Its Educational
Implications.* New York: John Wiley & Sons, 1967.

"Ways to Help Gifted Children Become More Creative." *Gifted
Child Quarterly* 9:1:3–9, Spring 1965.

"Issues in the Guidance of Gifted and Creative Children." *Gifted
Child Quarterly* 11:140–43, Autumn 1967.

"Managing the Post-partum Depression in Creative Persons." *Gifted
Child Quarterly* 11:2:290–92, Summer 1967.

With Norma Jean Groth. "The Development of Vocational Choice in
Gifted Children." *CERA Summaries,* 1968. Also in Gowan,
*Guidance and Measurement of Intelligence Development and
Creativity.* Northridge: J. C. Gowan, 1972.

With Doris Coole and Peggy McDonald. "The Impact of Piaget on
Guidance." *Journal of Educational Psychology* 1:3:208–17, June
1967.

"The Guidance of Creative Children." *Journal of Women Deans and
Counselors* 31:154–61, Summer 1968.

With four others. "New Aspects in Guiding Gifted." *Gifted Child
Quarterly* 13:103–12, Summer 1969.

With Kay Bruch. *The Academically Talented and Guidance.* Boston:
Houghton Mifflin Co., 1971.

With Paul Torrance. *Educating the Ablest.* Itasca, Ill.: F. E. Peacock
Publishers, 1971. 2nd ed., with Joe Khatena and E. Paul Torrance, 1979.

"Why Some Gifted Children Become Creative." *Gifted Child Quarterly* 15:1:13–19, 1971.

"The Development of the Creative Individual." *Gifted Child Quarterly* 15:3:156–74, 1971.

"Relation between Creativity and Giftedness." *Gifted Child Quarterly* 15:4:239–43, 1971.

*The Guidance and Measurement of Intelligence, Development and
Creativity.* Northridge: J. C. Gowan, 1972.

The Development of the Creative Individual. San Diego: Robert Knapp, 1972.

The Development of the Psychedelic Individual. Buffalo: Creative Education Foundation, 1974. (Ch. 2 contains development stage theory)

Trance, Art, and Creativity. Buffalo: Creative Education Foundation, 1975. (Ch. 4 contains views on development of creativity)

Chapter Six

Identification and Evaluation

Introduction

Perhaps the most significant development concerning the education of gifted children since Lewis Terman's 1954 paper is the emergence of an expanded concept of giftedness. Educational psychologists have invented and developed an increasing variety of procedures for identifying a greater number of different kinds of intellectually gifted children.

Although most programs for gifted children still use the traditional measures of intelligence and/or achievement as the bases for identification, here and there programs have experimented with other kinds of measures. In Illinois there have been a number of programs with emphases on the creatively gifted. There have also been such programs in Oregon, Nebraska, Connecticut, and elsewhere which have used measures of creative thinking in the identification process. Both measures of IQ and measures of creativity appear to be essential in identifying giftedness. In spite of large differences in mean IQ (23 to 26 IQ points), elementary and secondary school pupils high on creativity but not high on IQ achieve as well as those high on IQ but not on creativity, as measured by standardized achievement tests. Children high on measures of creativity appear to become alienated from peers and teachers and manifest behaviors which elicit pressures from their peers.

When gifted children were defined as those with Stanford-Binet IQ's over 130, identification was a relatively easy process. Under the expanded definition, identification becomes a considerably more complex problem. (Some means of simplification may be found in Reading 17 in this chapter.) The essential problem is how to identify all or nearly all of the gifted children without having to administer individual tests to all the school population. This means that nontest methods of identification or committee procedures have had wide acceptance.

E. P. Torrance (1965) indicated the following as guideline descriptions of the student:

1. Reacts positively to new, strange, or mysterious elements in his environment.
2. Persists in examining and exploring stimuli to know more about them.
3. Is curious, investigative, asks penetrating questions.
4. Has original approach to problem solving and unusual solutions.
5. Is independent, individualistic, self-sufficient.
6. Is imaginative, fantasy creating, a story teller.
7. Sees relationships.
8. Is full of ideas, verbal; has conversational fluency.
9. Prefers complex ideas, irritated or bored by routine.
10. Can occupy time usefully without being stimulated by the teacher.

Two other examples of personality aspects often identifying creative children are a strong and persistent sense of humor, and dominance and self-sufficiency, which may appear as stubbornness.

To help identify gifted children, teachers can use self-identification techniques, such as asking about hobbies and out-of-school activities, or crisis experience descriptions, such as asking a child to write his obituary.

The use of tests to identify gifted children involves first the use of a "screen" and then the use of an individual test follow-up. But all screens let in some flies and keep out some sun. The techniques involved in screening are described in the following extract from J. C. Gowan and G. D. Demos, *The Education and Guidance of the Ablest*:

In more technical language a screen on a particular variable will incorrectly keep out a certain percentage who actually should be admitted (false negatives), and admit a certain percentage of those who should be kept out (false positives). The weight of the social sanctions on these two areas varies. For example, in keeping carbon monoxide gas out of tunnels, stringent controls are on controlling the false positive side; that is, in rejecting anything that has characteristics like the poison gas. Whereas, in screening the earth for diamonds, it is important to cut down on the false negatives; that is, on the rejections of stones which are really diamonds. In our case, the sanctions (while not extreme) are more clearly toward the latter example than the former; that is, we look for screens which have low error in overlooking children and are not so much concerned with their efficiency in picking up all they screen.

Defining *effectiveness* as the percentage of the able which any one method locates, we want one with high effectiveness. Defining *efficiency* as the percent of the gifted in the whole group tested by the procedure, we would like moderate efficiency. We are also interested in methods, whatever their effectiveness or efficiency, which will pick up potentially able children overlooked by other methods. We shall define this latter variable by its negative aspect of *communality* and shall therefore seek methods which leave *low communality*.

Such procedures assume that there is a true criterion, just as there is a "true" intelligence quotient, and then sets up the Binet as the best estimate of this true criterion. While some may wonder if the Binet is effective in locating high potential in leadership, motivation, creativity, etc., the answer is *no*, but it is one of the best measures that we have to date.

Pegnato and Birch (1959) measured the effectiveness and efficiency of other instruments using it as a criterion. They noted the following means of identification at the junior high level: (1) teachers' judgments, (2) honor roll listing, (3) creative ability, (4) student council membership, (5) superiority in mathematics, (6) intelligence test results, and (7) achievement test results.

Method	Effective %	Efficiency %
Teachers' judgments	45	27
Honor roll	72	18
Creativity	10	11
Student council	14	16
Mathematics	56	2
Otis Beta cutting at		
115 IQ	92	19
120 IQ	71	27
125 IQ	44	38
130 IQ	22	53
Achievement test results	80	22

These results indicate that a cut score of 115 IQ on the Otis locates 92 percent of the gifted for the most effective single screen, but it picks up five times as many children as can be uitlized in the program. Higher IQ cuts drop this effectiveness score alarmingly. While other group tests may be more effective than the Otis, we do not have information on them at present. Hence one suggestion would be that the group test used to locate able children be cut at a point yielding five times as many as will ultimately be in the program.

The authors concluded that group intelligence tests cannot be relied on as the sole method at this level. The combination, however, of a group intelligence test and an achievement test located 97 percent of the gifted. This is one of the best extant studies arguing for multidimensioned identification methods.

Pegnato and Birch also reported that achievement test results had the second highest effectiveness percentage of 80 percent and that the combination of the two located 97 percent of the gifted eventually picked up on the Binet. It is the writers' feeling that this represents the minimum effectiveness level which should be demanded from the combination of screens used.

A replication and elaboration of the Pegnato procedure was reported by Blosser (1963). Using ninth grade students he attempted to determine the efficiency and effectiveness of the Otis, the Henmon-Nelson, the DAT Verbal, Numerical, and total battery, against the Stanford-Binet as the criterion. For the screening of gifted children at 136 or higher on the Stanford-Binet (similar to the Pegnato and Birch data) he obtained the following results:

	Cut-off	% Efficiency	% Effectiveness
Otis	120 IQ	36	81
	115 IQ	24	100
Henmon-Nelson	125 IQ	58	94
	119 IQ	25	100
DAT V+N	55 raw	40	94
	47 raw	24	100
DAT verbal	33 raw	38	94
	26 raw	19	100
DAT num.	22 raw	26	93
	21 raw	22	100

Thus the table gives the minimum cut score which located all the gifted. It will be seen that usually the test efficiency was about one-quarter, that is, it located four times as many students as later proved gifted. Similar data for Stanford-Binet IQ 129 were also provided. No one test proved superior to the others in either efficiency or effectiveness. It would be interesting to read further research on such a procedure using combined measures involving creativity assessments in combination with group mental tests. Such research would be most useful in providing a safe method of reducing the burdensome task of giving individual tests.[1]

Evaluation of gifted child programs has had a long but difficult history, primarily because the continuance of such programs depends not on research findings but on a value judgment by the community and society. Evaluation studies may be divided into those which examine outcomes and those which examine the presence or absence of structure presumed necessary to produce the outcomes. Naturally, the first method is the better, but it is also much more difficult, since outcome variables are not usually available until many years later. Admittedly the best outcome of a gifted child program is adult creativity and self-actualization, so that proximate variables which measure process in this direction may be accepted. This chapter includes an evaluative scorecard which measures structure (Reading 17); but really effective evaluation of function awaits longitudinal studies using the creativity variable.

---

[1]Reprinted from J. C. Gowan and G. D. Demos, *The Education and Guidance of the Ablest* (Springfield, Ill.: Charles C Thomas, Publisher, 1964). Courtesy of Charles C Thomas, the copyright owners, Springfield, Illinois. For an update on this issue, see Gear (1978).

16 Identifying Gifted Students for a Program

J. C. GOWAN

The following is suggested as a special identification program to be modified in specific particulars by local requirements.

1. Select beforehand an approximate percentage of the students for the program, depending upon local wishes and value judgments. It is suggested that this percentage should not be less than 1% and not more than 10%, except in exceedingly atypical schools. Let the percentage target by represented by $P\%$.
2. Use a group test screen, and cut at a point which will give $5P\%$. Take the top tenth of this group and put them into the program without more ado. Put the rest of the group into the "reservoir."
3. Circulate to each classroom teacher a paper in which he or she is asked to nominate the:

   a) Best student.
   b) Child with the biggest vocabulary.
   c) Most creative and original.
   d) Child with the most leadership.
   e) Most scientifically oriented child.
   f) Child who does the best critical thinking.
   g) Able child who is the biggest nuisance.
   h) Best motivated child.
   i) Child the other children like best.
   j) Child who is most ahead on grade placement.
   k) Brightest minority group child in the class in case there are more than five, and one has not been named heretofore.
   l) Child whose parents are most concerned about increasing the enrichment of his educational progress.

4. Use an achievement battery and cut at a point which will yield

---

From John Curtis Gowan, "Identifying Gifted Students for a Program," *Accent on Talent,* Vol. 2 (1967), p. 1. Reprinted by permission of the author and *Accent on Talent.*

$3P\%$. Make a list of all students who are in the top tenth in numerical skills; add both of these lists to the "reservoir."

5. Together with the principal, curriculum staff and guidance staff, plus a few teachers, go over and make a list of children who:

    a)   Have held leadership positions.
    b)   Achieved outstandingly in any special skill (such as arithmetic).
    c)   Are the best representative of minority groups.
    d)   Have influential parents.
    e)   Are examples of reading difficulties but believed bright.
    f)   Are believed bright but may be emotionally disturbed.
    g)   About whom any single individual feels he might be in the program. Put these in the "reservoir."

All pupils in the "reservoir" should now be ranked as to the number of times they have been mentioned.

All children having three or more mentions should be automatically included in the program.

All children having two citations should be sent to Binet Testing.

The Binet equivalent for the $P\%$ cut should be determined and any child above this cut placed in the program. If it is feasible, children with one mention should be Bineted with the same results. The remainder of the children are in the "hands of the committee." Each case should come up individually, and some of them should be placed in the program despite a Binet below the cut score. Special consideration should be given to (1) minority group children, (2) emotionally disturbed children, (3) children with reading difficulties, and (4) children with marked leadership or creative talents.

The committee should not be afraid to include children in the program because of social considerations, but each child who comes up before committee consideration should have an individual test.

It is believed that such an identification program:

1. Is reasonably effective in finding most of the able children.
2. Is reasonably efficient in cutting costs of individual testing to the bone and in conserving valuable committee time, which needs not be spent on consideration of children who obviously go into such a program.
3. Provides the multiple criteria which are so important in locating all of the able.
4. Is flexible enough to provide for special cases.

If such a program is adopted, it will be found that the size of P will tend to grow. This should not be a source of worry. The best answer to "where do we stop" is not to stop until at least one member of the screening committee thinks the committee has gone too far in letting students into the program. At any time in the program there ought to be children answering to the following descriptions that somebody thinks don't belong there: (1) a minority group child, (2) a slow reader for his ability, (3) a "nuisance," (4) an emotionally disturbed child, (5) somebody's relative, (6) an original creative child, or (7) a school leader. If the program doesn't do anything for any one of these children, they can always be taken out with a minimum of educational damage. If it does do something for them, the guidance committee has the satisfaction of knowing either that (1) it has made a good guess, or (2) that it has acquired an important friend.

17 The California Criterion Scorecard for Evaluation of Gifted Child Programs

J. C. GOWAN

Directions for Using This Scorecard

Below are 25 items, 20 of which apply to both elementary and secondary schools, and the last five of which apply only to secondary schools. Each item has four parts; each part can be answered "yes" or "no." For each part answered "yes" one point is added: each item hence has a potential value of zero to four. It is suggested that 2 is the average per item, that 4 represents progress a standard deviation or more above the average, and that 0 represents the opposite, with intermediate scores in proportion. Or the totals may be added and compared to a perfect score of 100 for secondary and 80 for elementary schools.

1. *Public and Professional Interest*

_____1. Public interest has been shown by a lay committee which has been in existence for a year and made a report to the Board of Education.

_____2. There has been cooperation between lay and pro-

From John Curtis Gowan, "The California Criterion Scorecard for Evaluation of Gifted Child Programs," *The Gifted Child Quarterly*, Vol. 9 (1965), pp. 156–58, 160. Reprinted by permission of the author and *The Gifted Child Quarterly*.

fessional staff as shown by (a) public meetings with professional staff participation, (b) a continuing joint lay-professional committee.

_____3. Marked public support of the program is indicated by (a) letters to and articles in the local press, (b) the involvement of a service club, (c) other specific evidence of public interest.

_____4. Professional community members have offered their services in cooperation with any phase of the program.

2. *Action of the Board of Education*

_____1. Have devoted meeting time to subject, and promoted public interest.

_____2. Have voted funds for an experimental program.

_____3. Have voted funds to an amount equaling 1% of total school budget of $100 per child.

_____4. Have increased the appropriation for the program.

3. *Administrators*

_____1. Have been permissive in allowing interested staff to experiment.

_____2. Have taken lead in bringing in speakers and consultants.

_____3. Have provided in-service training.

_____4. Have spoken publicly in favor of a strong program.

4. *Community Relations*

_____1. There is a program of public information as represented by a pamphlet, bulletin, or other document for public release.

_____2. A supervisory leader is directly involved at least half time in the program, and makes public statements.

_____3. Articles about the program appear in the local press.

_____4. Expert consultant help from outside the district has been used.

5. *The Staff and Teaching Personnel*

_____1. Are involved and show interest and ingenuity in adapting the program.

_____2. Have produced a handbook, pamphlet, or mimeographed material.

_____3. Have in a majority of cases had in-service training.

_____4. Include at least one person who has written an article for a professional journal about the program or reported it at a convention.

6. *Staff Allotment*

_____1. At least one person in the central office is there because of the program.

_____2. There is at least one extra reserve teacher, teacher-consultant, or the time of one teaching position allotted to teach the program.

_____3. Additional psychometrist or counselor time has been allotted.

_____4. A definite earmarked budget exists for supplies, material, books.

7. *Curricular Adaptations Include*

_____1. Acceleration.

_____2. Grouping in special classes.

_____3. Special enrichment work for the highly gifted.

_____4. A comprehensive program from kindergarten through grade 12.

8. *Teachers*

_____1. There is at least one extra teacher per hundred gifted students.

_____2. There has been at least one year of special in-service training for a majority of teachers in the program.

_____3. The average special class has less than 25 children in it.

_____4. Teachers are carefully selected for program on a basis of competence, interest, and training, not as a result of school politics or status.

9. *Administration of the Program*

_____1. One trained individual has overall responsibility for the program.

_____2. This person is actively advised by a volunteer committee of teachers and central office representatives.

_____3. The program is comprehensive in extending through all grades, using many methods, and having broad objectives.

_____4. There is an advisory lay committee.

10. *Guidance Services*

_____1. Is headed by a person especially credentialed, or with a master's degree in guidance, or both.

_____2. At the secondary level includes a specialist in college placement and scholarships; at the elementary level includes at least a half-time guidance counselor in every elementary school.

_____3. Involves a ratio of counselor to students of not more than 1/300 in secondary schools, 1/500 in junior high schools, and 1/900 in elementary schools.

_____4. Has space for interview privacy, and each gifted child receives at least one private interview per year.

11. *Identification*

_____1. Ability **and** achievement testing is given at least every other year.

_____2. Multidimensional criteria, including teachers' recommendations, are used in the selection process, but final judgment is in the hands of the committee.

_____3. Time and personnel for individual testing are available.

_____4. Provision is made for locating the gifted child who may be hidden by reason of lack of reading skill or by minority group status.

12. *Regarding the Library*

_____1. There is opportunity during lunch hour for students to read in a library.

_____2. Students, under certain circumstances, may go to the library during class periods and before or after school.

_____3. Positive action, including visitation, is taken to acquaint students with library facilities both in the school and in the community.

_____4. Research is encouraged by librarians who are interested in the able; they promote a friendly library atmosphere, waive restrictions regarding types and numbers of books which can be withdrawn, and give instruction in library methods.

13. *Program*

_____1. There is a summer program for the able.

_____2. There is an advanced placement program in high

school and an acceleration program in elementary school which accelerates 1% of the total school population by the time they enter junior high school.

_____3. There are remedial skills programs in reading and mathematics for which gifted children are eligible.

_____4. There is scheduling flexibility as seen in the secondary school by seven or more periods per day, or in the elementary school by released time provisions for gifted students to have out-of-class experiences.

14. *Program Specifics*

At Secondary level:

_____1. 7 years of math and science.

_____2. 4 years of English and 3 of social studies.

_____3. At least 6 compositions per semester in English.

_____4. 17 solids in high school.

At Elementary level:

_____1. Algebra before the ninth grade.

_____2. Phonics and grammar.

_____3. Mathematics enrichment involving higher arithmetic, number theory.

_____4. Science enrichment.

15. *Program Specifics*

_____1. Laboratories open for student work in both high school and junior high school, science demonstrations with lab equipment in elementary school.

_____2. Club and interest activities are sponsored and encouraged.

_____3. Three years of foreign language in secondary school, some language experience below the ninth grade in elementary school.

_____4. Prestige is accorded for activities other than athletic, especially those involving creativity.

16. *General School Atmosphere*

_____1. There is a tradition of scholarship, fostered by the faculty.

_____2. There is an effective guidance service.

_____3. There is good faculty morale and cooperation.

_____4. There is a democratically oriented administration.

17. *Reactions of the Gifted*

_____1. The reactions of the gifted students to the program have been preserved on paper.

_____2. A majority of them like and approve of the program.

_____3. Their suggestions have resulted in some changes.

_____4. Parents have been acquainted with the program and their views have also been collected.

18. *Reactions of Teachers*

_____1. There has been a record of teacher reactions to the program.

_____2. The majority of those involved are in favor.

_____3. Their suggestions have resulted in changes.

_____4. Teachers do not feel overburdened as a result of the program.

19. *Follow-Up*

_____1. There is a follow-up service which has resulted in a report during the last two years.

_____2. Time to perform follow-up has been provided.

_____3. Other methods of evaluation have been used.

_____4. Reactions of parents and the public have been recorded.

20. *Behavior Deviations*

During the last two years there has not been *more than one* instance of any of the following:

_____1. Able youngster getting into serious difficulties involving suspension, dismissal, or criminal activities.

_____2. Marked dissatisfaction on the part of parents of a gifted child.

_____3. The withdrawal of the able child from school by parents and his placement in another system or private school on account of dissatisfaction with the program.

_____4. Serious failure on the part of a student to accept the responsibilities of school citizenship not covered in part 1 (such as psychotic withdrawal, gross negligence resulting in serious damage to property or injury, social maladjustment, serious emotional disturbance, or the like.)

(Items from here on apply only to secondary schools)

21. What percent of the able students are underachievers? (Un-

derachievement is defined as class work standing one standard deviation or more below the ability level.)
(0) over 25%. (1) 18–24%. (2) 13–17%. (3) 10–12%. (4) less than 10%.

22. What is the percent of dropouts among the able in grades 9–13?
(0) over 10%. (1) 7–10%. (2) 4–6%. (3) 1–3%. (4) less than 1%.
23. What percent of the able go on to college?
(0) 50%. (1) 70%. (2) 84%. (3) 90%. (4) 98%.
24. What percent of the able take more than 16 solids in four years?
(0) 30%. (1) 50%. (2) 70%. (3) 84%. (4) 90%.
25. What percent of the able receive scholarships to college?

(0) 16%. (1) 30%. (2) 50%. (3) 70%. (4) 84%.

18 Educating the Gifted Child: Challenge and Response in the USA

JOE KHATENA

The overwhelming advances in so many significant facets of our lives in the Twentieth Century, especially over the past 50 years, brought into sharp focus the recognition that these outcomes were made possible by people who were exceptionally gifted and talented —people who comprise our richest natural resource. We have also become convinced through observation and research that we can not only tell, with reasonable expectancy of accuracy, who among us have the potential of becoming contributors to progress but also that we can to a large extent arrange circumstances in our environment to help realize this more fully and speedily. Of course with experience we have come to understand that we are not in complete control of events, though we can to a great extent do something about it if we designed our strategies well, and by so doing allow, wth the

From *The Gifted Child Quarterly* 20:1, 1976. Used by permission.

Paper prepared for a panel discussion entitled "Educating the Gifted and Talented, Retrospect and Prospect," presented at the World Conference on Gifted and Talented held in London, England, September, 9, 1975.

For a further update, also see J. Khatena, "Some Advances in Thought on the Gifted," *Gifted Child Quarterly* (1978).

least chance of error, the operation of arranged circumstances to bring about the successful achievement of our goals.

This presentation will consider some of the major contributions in the United States that have been made by way of identifying giftedness, providing special educational opportunity for the gifted, recognizing some of their special problems, legislation and its implications for special educational opportunities for the gifted and talented, and other private and public supportive efforts for the advancement of the gifted and talented.

Identifying Giftedness

The subject of identifying giftedness has not been altogether settled: on the one hand we have the problem of deciding what qualities of human beings can be categorized as gifted and on the other hand we have the problem of deciding the extent to which they are measurable. Prior to 1950 the attempt at identification had as its theoretical base intelligence and its correlates in achievement; and measures that were used ranged from verbal and performance IQ or a composite of both, as instanced by measures like the individually administered Stanford-Binet or the Wechsler scales, or the generally group administered California Test of Mental Maturity, the Raven's Progressive Matrices, and the Goodenough-Harris Draw-a-Man test, to tests that subscribed to the measurement of many intellectual abilities, as for example the Primary Mental Abilities, Differential Aptitude Tests, and the Multiple Aptitude Tests. Among the standardized achievement measures used in the United States for the purpose of screening gifted children have been the Stanford Achievement Test, California Achievement Test, and the Metropolitan Achievement Test. Of course sometimes reliance was also placed upon teacher observation and school grades. All in all, however, the emphasis of identification was on high IQ indices and school achievement.

From the investigations of geniuses and other categories of highly gifted people came clues about their unique characteristics which indicated that the gifted were generally physically and psychologically healthier people, certainly more mature and intellectually ahead of their age-mates, excelling in most human and educational activity.

After 1950 thoughts about the gifted expanded to include not only conceptions of the intellect as a multifaceted potential but also the idea that giftedness could manifest itself in many different ways apart from academics, to include talent in highly specialized areas of achievement. Relative to the expanded concept of intelligence was the Structure of Intellect Model (Guilford, 1967), which focused attention not only on the many ways a person could be intelligent but also suggested that there were qualitative differences in intellectual functioning which included divergent (and the less precise but more inclusive term, creative) thinking. The ramifications of this fresh conceptualization of intellectual function were great: it has significantly influenced measurement of intellectual abilities in the United States, providing the much needed framework for the development of all kinds of educational opportunities for children in general and gifted children in particular, and it has stimulated an overwhelming abundance of research in areas related to identification, nurture, and concomitant problems.

The characteristics of the gifted child now included the component of creativity; and to the earlier concepts of gifted people could now be added elements of behavior that were creative, spontaneous, and nonconforming, that involved a more sensitive apprehension and interaction with the external environment, that identified more intense emotional involvement and commitment, that involved creative leadership and adjustment adeptness far above the ordinary.

Of the many definitions of creativity the two which have been most productive of instrument development are Guilford's divergent thinking and redefinition abilities as components of the Structure of Intellect Model, and Torrance's definition of creativity as a process of becoming sensitive to problems, deficiencies, gaps in knowledge, missing elements, disharmony, and so on; identifying the difficulty; searching for solutions, making guesses, or formulating hypotheses about the deficiencies; testing and retesting these hypotheses and possibly modifying and retesting them; finally communicating the results (Torrance, 1974a). To these may be added for instance the definitions as given by Wallach and Kogan (1965) as the ability to generate or produce within some criterion of relevance many cognitive associates and many that are unique, or my definition of originality as the power of the imagination to break away from perceptual set so as to restructure anew ideas, thoughts, and feelings into novel and meaningful associative bonds (Khatena & Torrance, 1973).

Among the foremost psychologists in the field of creativity measurement are Guilford and Torrance. Generally, their measures give major roles to abilities known as fluency (the number of responses that are produced), flexibility (shifts in thinking from one category of thought to another), originality (statistical infrequency of responses or unusualness, remote association and cleverness), and elaboration (the adding of details to the basic idea or thought expressed), though their approaches to the problem of measurement differ. While Torrance (1966, 1974a) attempts to measure these abilities through the presentation of several complex tasks designed to trigger the expression of these several abilities at one and the same time, Guilford

(1967) attempts to measure divergent thinking by using a test format which generally requires the subject to respond to many stimuli, each setting out to measure a specific component of the Structure of Intellect Model.

The various measures of creativity produced by Guilford and his associates relate to Divergent Production Abilities of the Structure of Intellect Model and have in the main been used with adult and adolescent populations, although some work with them has involved younger children (Guilford, 1967, 1975). Measures relevant to 18 of the 24 Divergent Production Abilities are described in *The Nature of Human Intelligence* (Guilford, 1967) and do not include Divergent Figural Relations and Divergent Symbolic Transformations with measures of the Behavioral components of Divergent Production Abilities included in a paper by Guilford, Hendricks, and Hoepfner (1968).

The Torrance Tests of Creative Thinking batteries (1966, 1974) present either verbal or figural material in the visual modality, while *Thinking Creatively with Sounds and Words* (Torrance, Khatena, & Cunnington, 1973) presents visual or sound material in the auditory modality, with both sets of creative measures calling upon subjects to use their imagination to produce relevant and unique responses, and with both developed for use by children and adults.

Other measures available are by Wallach and Kogan (1975), Schaefer (1970, 1975) Starkweather (1971), and the like. The 1975 Summer issue of *The Gifted Child Quarterly* has devoted itself to some up-to-date developments in the area of creativity measurement, and the contributions of Guilford (Creativity Tests for Children), Feldhusen and Houtz (Purdue Elementary Problem Solving Inventory), Torrance (Ideal Pupil Checklist), Schaefer (Similes Test), Khatena (Imagination Imagery and Onomatopoeia and Images), Malone and Moonan (Behavioral Identification of Giftedness Questionnaire), and Bruch (Assessment of Creativity in Culturally Different Children) should be noted.

Much of measurement research in terms of validity, reliability, and normative studies has followed the construction of instruments relative to creative thinking abilities and has been reported in the respective norms-technical manuals or in numerous papers. Associated with this is the greater awareness and sensitivity to attendant problems, and many studies over the past decade or so have concerned themselves with the problematic issues of measuring creativity which have pivoted around such issues as definition, dimensionality, item sampling, scoring, reliability, validity, conditions of test administration, usability, culture fairness and relevance, and norms (e.g., Anastasi & Schaefer, 1971; Guilford, 1971; Khatena, 1971; Mackler & Shontz, 1965; Treffinger & Poggio, 1972; Yamamoto, 1966).

The issue of dimensionality refers in particular to IQ and creativity relative to the constructed measures. It has received some special attention, at first by the well-known Getzels and Jackson study (1962) and later in the eight partially replicated studies by Torrance (1962) which basically indicated that some fundamental differences existed between children identified as highly intelligent and those identified as highly creative, such that taking the upper 20 percent of a given population on an intelligence test alone would miss 70 percent of those who would be identified as gifted by a test of creative thinking (Torrance, 1970). MacKinnon's paper (1964) emphasized that a certain amount of intelligence is required for creativity but beyond that point, being more or less intelligent did not determine creativity; and Wallach and Wing's study (1969) on the creativity-intelligence distinction suggested that since a wide range of talented accomplishments that society may wish to sustain and nourish are lost to view by a too heavy reliance on intelligence screening measures, we ought to depend upon identification of ideational ability (a concept quite extraneous to intelligence) that is supportive of talented accomplishment as well.

The evidence suggests that these differences appear to be more a function of the measures used rather than qualitative differences in intellect on the one hand, and style of intellectual functioning that has called for the operation of creative thinking abilities and their emotive correlates more or less often on the other hand.

While all this seems to have added to our difficulties, we do have measures that can aid us to make quite appropriate identification of gifted children. Whether we use the deviation IQ index or the Creative Thinking Abilities indices, the highly intellectually creatively gifted can be identified as those people whose scores are two standard deviations and more above the mean relative to the ability or abilities measured. We are generally talking about the upper 5 percent of a population who are gifted, though some variation does exist about whether we should lower or raise this cut-off point in the selection of gifted children for special educational opportunities. Generally, there is an increased tendency today to screen for both intelligence and creativity. It must be noted that the term "gifted" as used today refers to more than general intellectual and creative thinking abilities; it also refers to high leadership ability, visual and performing arts abilities, and psychomotor ability (Marland, 1972), though bias for intellectual ability still exists in the selection process.

Nurture of the Gifted and Talented

Developmental acceleration of creative mental functioning

through planned environmental enrichment has been claimed and generally substantiated by the research in "Compendium of Research on Creative Imagination," I and II (Creative Education Foundation, 1958, 1960), the works of Osborn (1963), Khatena (1973a, 1975), Meeker (1969), Meeker, Sexton, and Richardson (1970), Parnes (1967a, 1967b), Parnes and Noller (1973), Renzulli (1973), Treffinger (1975), Torrance (1965a, 1972), Williams (1971), and others.

In the main, enrichment of the learning environment has taken the forms of enriched curriculum materials and physical surroundings; more effective methodological approaches; psychological climates conducive to optimum learning; enrichment of learning in regular classrooms; provisions of correspondence courses and tutoring; placement in advanced grades or classes; attendance of college classes by high school students; special counseling or instruction outside classrooms; sensitivity training; individualized instruction through such means as team teaching, nongraded plans, independent study; special classes for the highly gifted with specially trained teachers, supervisors, and consultants; special groups; curriculum improvement through programs which emphasize higher level thought processes, creativity, divergent thinking; and special attention to the emotional and social adjustment of gifted pupils and the like (Marland, 1972; ERIC/CEC, 1975).

Children have been taught to learn creatively in many different programs, and the approaches reported by 142 studies have been recently abstracted and summarized (Torrance, 1972) as training programs emphasizing the Osborn-Parnes Creative Problem-Solving procedures; programs involving packages of materials such as the Purdue Creative Program; the creative arts as vehicles for teaching and practicing creative thinking; media and reading programs designed to teach and give practice in creative thinking; curricular and administrative arrangements designed to create favorable conditions for learning and practicing creative thinking; teacher-classroom variables, indirect and direct control, classroom climate, and the like; motivation, reward, competition, and the like; and testing conditions designed to facilitate a higher level of creative functioning or more valid and reliable test performance. To these must be added the recent applications by Torrance (1974) of creative thinking operations and creative problem-solving techniques to train people to think ahead and anticipate problems that they will need to solve in the future in creative ways. Description of much of these and other relevant information can be found in an updated list of methods and educational programs for stimulating creativity prepared by Treffinger and Gowan (1971).

Some Problems of the Highly Gifted

Along with the attention given to measurement and nurture came an awareness of the special problems highly intelligent and creative children experience as they grow up. The research on the *Genetic Studies of Genius* by Terman (1959) and Oden (1968) reported in two follow-up investigations (over 35 and 40 years, respectively) that the geniuses studied had grown to be gifted adults who maintained their intellectual ability, had lower mortality rates, good physical and mental health, manifested minimal crime, ranked high in education and vocational achievements, were active in community affairs, and held moderate political and social views, and with two-thirds of them feeling that they had realized their potential. Another study (Cox, 1969) concludes that geniuses are characterized in childhood not only by superior IQ but also by traits of interest, energy, will, and character that foreshadow later performance. However, Oden (1968), in attempting to assess correlates of vocational achievement and genius, compared 100 most and least successful male geniuses and found that the most successful men came from families having higher socioeconomic status and giving more encouragement to succeed; ranked higher as adolescents in volitional, intellectual, moral, and social traits; and had more self-confidence, perseverance, and integration toward goals. In addition, although scholastic achievement had been similar in grade school, half as many of the least successful men had graduated from college. They were also found to be more prone to emotional and social difficulties. Kenmare (1972) found that geniuses are also characterized as being typically schizophrenic because of the difficulty in synthesizing their personal life and their existence as impersonal creative process, and that erotic love typified their lives.

Torrance (1962, 1965b) has given considerable attention to the problems that gifted children face as a result of their conflicting interaction with the environment: the creative energizing forces that dominate the life of the highly creative child set him up in a position of independence and nonconformity in relation to the group of which he is a member, often leading to confrontations of one kind or another which require that he either learn to cope with arising tensions, with consequent productive behavior and mental health, or that he repress his creative needs, with consequent personality disturbances and breakdown. Coping strategies are suggested by Torrance in two of his books, *Guiding Creative Talent* (1962) and *Mental Health and Constructive Behavior* (1965b).

The concern that most of these problems are culture bound and arise from the negative attitudes of our society toward creatively gifted individuals has been expressed by many prominent thinkers (e.g., Barron, 1963; Getzels & Jackson, 1962; Gowan & Bruch, 1971; Kubie, 1958; Gallagher, 1964; Khatena, 1973b; Krippner, 1967; Torrance, 1970). As this applies to the gifted disadvantaged, the gifted underachiever and dropout, the physically handicapped gifted, and the emotionally disturbed gifted, a good summary can be found in a book by Gowan and Bruch (1971) and in a recent ERIC/CEC selective bibliography (1975).

Support for Special Educational Opportunities

Although our knowledge of the gifted and talented and what we can do for them has increased over the years, it has not been without considerable frustration over the obstructionism of a public education system that is essentially geared to a philosophy of egalitarianism. The first really significant step to counteract this problem, however, took the form of an Act of Congress that included in the Elementary Amendments of 1969 (Section 806) provisions relating to gifted and talented children. This was signed into law on April 13, 1970 (Marland, 1972). It required the Commissioner of Education to determine the extent to which special educational assistance programs were necessary or useful to meet the needs of gifted and talented children, to evaluate how existing federal educational assistance programs can be more effectively used to meet these needs, and to recommend new programs, if any, needed to meet these needs; further, the Commissioner was to report his findings, together with recommendations, not later than one year after the enactment of this act (Section 806c of Public Law 91–230).

This led Commissioner Marland to indicate the immediate steps the Office of Education could take in 1972 to launch the federal program for the gifted and talented, with no need for new legislation, while providing for long-range planning at the federal, state, and local levels, by both the public and private sectors, to systematically ameliorate the problems identified by the study. These efforts would take the form of a planning report on the federal role in education of gifted and talented children; assignment of program responsibility and establishment of a Gifted and Talented Program Group comprised of a nucleus staff augmented by working relations with staff from programs throughout the Department which would have significant potential to benefit gifted and talented children; a nationwide inventory and assessment of current programs for the gifted and talented; the strengthening of state educational agencies toward more effective provision of educational programs for the gifted and talented; leadership development and training of representatives from the states at institutes whose program would aim at the development of a strategic plan for the education of gifted and talented; career education models in line with the existing ones developed by the National Center for Educational Research and Development; experimental schools devoted to the individualization of programs to benefit gifted and talented students as a comprehensive design to effect education reform; supplementary plans and centers relative to encouragement of Title III ESEA in cooperation with the Office of Education Gifted and Talented Program Group to support still further the efforts of agencies within the state to provide special programs for the gifted and talented; ten regional offices with a part-time staff member identified as responsible for gifted and talented education who would act as liaison with the Office of Education National Office, provide developmental assistance to state agencies, effect continuous dissemination of information, and give management assistance to specialized regional activities as they arise; and higher educational opportunities for the gifted and talented to be determined and implemented by the Office of Educational Gifted and Talented Program Group.

Three years after their formulation these objectives have found realization in the establishment of the Office of Education for the Gifted and Talented, Office of Education Regional Part-time Directors, the Educational Resource Information Center Clearinghouse on the Gifted and Talented, the National Leadership Training Institutes, Internships to the Office of Education for the Gifted and Talented, Cooperative Interstate Projects supported by the Title V (Section 505) funds, a Gifted Students Symposium, and many state projects on the gifted and talented.

Hal Lyon's letter of February 19, 1975, to friends of the gifted and talented noted that the passage of the Education Amendments of 1974 (Section 404) has given to the Office of Education for the Gifted and Talented statutory authority to administer programs for gifted and talented children and youth which are administered by the Office of Education, for which purpose $2.56 million has been appropriated. He also indicated that a call for proposals would be shortly forthcoming and outlined allocation of funds for different categories of expected projects, namely, state comprehensive programs, a consortium of academic institutions and internships that will award graduate credit and degrees to potential leaders, a technical assistance project, exemplary projects relative to special groups of gifted and talented youth, and an analysis of requirements for the gifted and talented and dissemination of the information to practitioners project.

Support has also come from state, county, and local agencies and in many states in the US this has become imperative through state law. In addition, support has come in the form of volunteer community mentor projects, and from foundations like Robert Sterling Clark Foundation and the Explorers Club. Directions have also come from expert professionals working as individuals or in teams at universities or colleges (e.g., University of Connecticut, University of Georgia, University of South Florida) and other educational organizations (e.g., Western Behavioral Sciences, Creative Educational Foundation) in providing training for teachers and other personnel needed to facilitate the education of the gifted and talented, and in providing consultation services to agencies engaged in programs for the gifted and talented. To these must be added the efforts of private schools like the Mirman School for the Gifted in California.

Further significant contributions are also being made by national organizations dedicated to serve the interests of the gifted and talented, such as the National Association for Gifted Children, The Association of the Gifted, The American Association for the Gifted, and the Creative Education Foundation, three of which disseminate nationally and internationally up-to-date knowledge in the areas of the gifted and talented through their journals, namely, *The Gifted Child Quarterly*, the *Journal of Creative Behavior*, the *Exceptional Child*, and *Talented and Gifted Newsletter*.

Last but not least let us not forget the concerned, viable, and dedicated support of parents, working either in groups or as individuals, cutting across all boundaries of educational, political, and legislative agencies to plead eloquently and cajole energetically the cause of the gifted and talented.

Implications and Future Directions

The wheels have been set in motion and there is no turning back. The forward thrusts will gather momentum and the next few years will see not only special educational opportunities for the gifted and talented provided everywhere in the country but also the beneficial effects on different segments of the school population who will be educated in productive ways.

The need for facilitators and leaders of the gifted and talented will require many more colleges and universities to offer training programs leading to certification and granting of degrees at the masters' and doctoral levels. Related to this will be the establishment of consortiums of academic institutions that will bring together the best talent in common effort to prepare leaders for effective management and advancement of gifted and talented education.

Research will receive fresh impetus and new directions from these developments, leading to greater refinements in more precise identification operations with the aid of computer technology, more deliberate and effective educational programming leveled at needs specific to individuals, more sensitive approaches to the handling of emotional and deprivation problems of the gifted and talented directed toward greater productivity, and the flexible use of reward and reinforcement systems to direct and enhance the development and acceleration of the gifted and talented at times when they most need the help, with effective shifting from extrinsic to intrinsic motivational controls.

The establishment of several technical assistance centers, possibly like Gallagher's proposed model but with a system of linkups among these centers for competent handling of national as well as local needs and goals, is likely.

Also likely is the use of sounder evaluation models having roots in good design and measurement procedures, not only aimed at appraising the progress of various programs and projects but also aimed at providing directions for program refinement and growth to ensure both their internal validity as well as generalizability.

Regional offices of education aimed at promoting and assisting the educational opportunities of the gifted and talented at the interstate levels will have considerable positive effects at the local levels as well.

More efficient and accurate storage of data on the gifted and talented will take place with the help of the ERIC/CEC system as it expands its abstracting and dissemination services not only to individuals but also to institutions and government agencies committed to plans for more effective educational intervention for the gifted and talented.

The establishment of closer working relations among the several national organizations for the gifted and talented has already begun, and some further ties with world organizations like the NAGC of London will be the expected outcome, possibly leading not only to international conferences but also to exchange of expert professional and technical assistance, and exposing gifted and talented children to the best the world community can offer.

In effectively meeting the challenge of our times we need people who are not only extremely bright but have capabilities of adapting themselves to the dynamics of ever changing circumstance. The raw materials are ours, expertise is with use, and the time is ripe: We will be architects to the brilliant and productive people of the future.

References

Anastasi, A., & Schaeffer, C. E. Note on the concepts of creativity and intelligence. *Journal of Creative Behavior,* 1971, 5(2), 113–116.

Barron, F. *Creativity and psychological health.* Princeton, N.J.: Van Nostrand, 1963.

Cox, C. M. *Genetic studies of genius;* Vol. II, *The early mental traits of three hundred geniuses.* Stanford, Calif.: Stanford University Press, 1969. (ERIC Abstract 31649)

Creative Education Foundation. Compendium of research on creative imagination (1958 & 1960). In S. J. Parnes & H. F. Harding (Eds.), *A source book of creative thinking,* pp. 343–368. New York: Scribner's, 1962.

Educational Resource Information Center/CEC. *Gifted and talented research: A selective bibliography.* Exceptional Child Bibliography Series, no. 639. Reston, Va.: ERIC/CEC, 1975.

Educational Resource Information Center/CEC. *Gifted—handicapped, disadvantaged, and underachievers.* Exceptional Child Bibliography Series, no. 660. Reston, Va.: ERIC/CEC, 1975.

Gallagher, J. J. *Teaching the gifted child.* Boston: Allyn & Bacon, 1964.

Getzels, H. W., & Jackson, P. W. *Creativity and intelligence: Explorations with gifted children.* New York: John Wiley, 1962.

Gowan, J. C. & Bruch, C. B. *The academically talented student and guidance.* Boston: Houghton Mifflin, 1971.

Guilford, J. P. *The nature of human intelligence.* New York: MGraw-Hill, 1967.

Guilford, J. P. Some misconceptions regarding measurement of creative talents. *Journal of Creative Behavior,* 1971, 5(2), 77–87.

Guilford, J. P. Varieties of creative giftedness: Their measurement and development. *Gifted Child Quarterly,* 1975, 19(2), 107–121.

Guilford, J. P., Hendricks, M., & Hoepfner, R. Solving social problems creatively. *Journal of Creative Behavior,* 1968, 2(2), 155–164.

Kenmare, D. *The nature of genius.* Westport, Conn.: Greenwood Press, 1972. (ERIC Document Reproduction Service No. EC 05 1317)

Khatena, J. Some problems in the measurement of creative behavior. *Journal of Research and Development in Education,* 1971, 4(3), 74–82.

Khatena, J. Imagination and production of original verbal images. *Art Psychotherapy,* 1973, 1, 113–120. (a)

Khatena, J. Problems of the highly creative child and the school psychologist. Paper presented to the Southeastern Region of the National Association of School Psychologists at White Sulphur Springs, W. Va., on November 16, 1973. (b)

Khatena, J. Creative imagination imagery and analogy. *Gifted Child Quarterly*, 1975, 19(2), 149–160.

Khatena, J., & Torrance, E. P. *Thinking creatively with sounds and words: Norms-technical manual.* Research ed. Lexington, Mass.: Personnel Press, 1973.

Krippner, S. The ten commandments that block creativity. *Gifted Child Quarterly*, 1967, 11(3), 144–156.

Kubie, L. W. *Neurotic distortion of the creative process.* New York: Noonday Press, 1958.

MacKinnon, D. W. *Identification and development of creative abilities.* Berkeley: University of California, Institute of Personality Assessment and Research, 1964. (ERIC Document Reproduction Service No. ED 027 965)

Mackler, B., & Shontz, F. C. Creativity: Theoretical and methodological considerations. *Psychological Record*, 1965, 15, 217–238.

Marland, S. P., Jr. *Education of the gifted and talented: Report to the Congress of the United States.* Vols. I and II. Washington D.C.: U.S. Government Printing Office, 1972.

Meeker, M. N. *The structure of intellect: Its interpretation and uses.* Columbus, O.: Charles Merrill, 1969.

Meeker, M. N., Sexton, K., & Richardson, M. O. *SOI abilities workbook.* Los Angeles: Loyola-Marymount University, 1970.

Oden, M. H. *The fulfillment of promise: 40-year follow-up of the Terman gifted group.* Stanford, Calif.: Stanford University, Department of Psychology, 1968. (ERIC Document Reproduction Service No. EC 02 1688)

Osborn, A. F. *Applied imagination.* 3rd ed., New York: Scribner's, 1963.

Parnes, S. J. *Creative behavior guidebook.* New York: Scribner's, 1967. (a)

Parnes, S. J. *Creative behavior workbook.* New York: Scribner's, 1967. (b)

Parnes, S. J., & Noller, R. B. *Toward supersanity: Channeled freedom.* Buffalo, N.Y.: D.O.K., 1973.

Renzulli, J. S. *New directions in creativity.* New York: Harper & Row, 1973.

Schaefer, C. E. *Biographical inventory: Creativity.* San Diego, Calif.: Educational and Industrial Testing Service, 1970.

Schaefer, C. E. The importance of measuring metaphorical thinking in children. *Gifted Child Quarterly*, 1975, 19(2), 140–148.

Starkweather, E. K. Creativity research instruments designed for use with preschool children. *Journal of Creative Behavior*, 1971, 5(4), 245–255.

Terman, L. M. *The gifted group at mid-life: Thirty-five years' follow-up of the superior child. Genetic Studies of Genius*, Vol. 5. Stanford, Calif.: Stanford University Press, 1959. (ERIC Document Reproduction Service No. ED 022 298.)

Torrance, E. P. *Guiding creative talent.* Englewood Cliffs, N.J.: Prentice-Hall, 1962.

Torrance, E. P. *Rewarding creative behavior.* Englewood Cliffs, N.J.: Prentice-Hall, 1965. (a)

Torrance, E. P. *Mental health and constructive behavior.* Belmont, Calif.: Wadsworth, 1965. (b)

Torrance, E. P. *Torrance Tests of Creative Thinking: Norms-technical manual.* Research ed. Princeton, N.J.: Personnel Press, 1966, 1974.

Torrance, E. P. Broadening concepts of giftedness in the 70's. *Gifted Child Quarterly,* 1970, 14(4), 199–208.

Torrance, E. P. Can we teach children to think creatively? *Journal of Creative Behavior,* 1972, 6(2), 114–143.

Torrance, E. P. *Torrance Tests of Creative Thinking: Norms-technical manual.* Lexington, Mass.: Personnel Press, 1974. (a)

Torrance, E. P. Preliminary notes on sociodrama as a creative problem-solving approach to studying the future. Georgia Studies of Creative Behavior, University of Georgia, Athens, Georgia, 1974.

Torrance, E. P., Khatena, J., & Cunnington, B. F. *Thinking creatively with sounds and words* (children's and adults' versions). Lexington, Mass.: Personnel Press, 1973.

Treffinger, D. J. Teaching for self-directed learning: A priority for the talented and gifted. *Gifted Child Quarterly,* 1975, 19(1), 46–59.

Treffinger, D. J., & Gowan, J. C. An updated representative list of methods and educational programs for stimulating creativity. *Journal of Creative Behavior,* 1971, 5(2), 127–139.

Treffinger, D. J., & Poggio, J. P. Needed research on the measurement of creativity. *Journal of Creative Behavior,* 1972, 6(4), 253–267.

Wallach, M. A., & Kogan, N. *Modes of thinking in young children.* New York: Holt, Rinehart & Winston, 1965.

Wallach, M. A., & Wing, C. W., Jr. *The talented student: A validation of the creativity-intelligence distinction.* New York: Holt, Rinehart & Winston, 1969.

Williams, F. E. *Total creativity program for individualizing and humanizing the learning process.* Englewood Cliffs, N.J.: Educational Technology Publications, 1971.

Yamamoto, K. Do creativity tests really measure creativity? *Theory into Practice,* 1966, 5, 194–197.

Chapter Seven

Teachers and Teacher Training

Introduction

Despite a vast amount of research, too little is still known about the qualifications and characteristics of effective teachers in general, let alone those of the gifted. For a general summary of the problem, see Gage's *Handbook of Research on Teaching* (1963), or Gowan (1960b). Ryans (1961) identified three factors: democratic, responsible, and original. Gowan and Demos (1964, p. 391) identified the teacher of the gifted as more responsible and organized; with better background; more vigorous, stimulating, resourceful, and original; less threatened by students; and more able to delegate tasks than to give orders.

Administrators selecting teachers for such roles might look for those with vitality, energy, stimulating personality, strong intellectual backgrounds, and rigorous demands for learning. They go early to school and often stay late; they have close contacts with books, libraries, laboratories; they give evidence of professional and scholarly eminence, producing things outside of school; they volunteer for work with the gifted; they have original ideas and try to carry them out; and their rooms are more stimulating than neat.

While it helps for teachers of the gifted to be gifted, it is not necessary, especially if they are not threatened by children who are brighter than they, or who sometimes know more about a certain subject. Administrators should be aware of the need to departmentalize earlier for gifted children in the elementary school; the background in mathematics and science of teachers working with the gifted is especially important if they are the only teachers with whom gifted children will come in contact.

What kind of teacher helps most to activate the creativity of bright students? Both Walker (1966) and Bruch (1965) investigated this problem in doctoral theses and found that the relations are not simple. Walker found relationships among aspiration level, intellectual climate, student morale on the part of a given high school, and stu-

227

dent creativity. Bruch found that more effectively creative teachers tended to make their students more visible creatively. There was considerable interaction in both studies, indicating that the relationship between either school press or teacher personality and student creativity is not easy. Spaulding (1963) in another excellent doctoral study entitled the "Affective Dimensions of the Creative Process," investigated the effect of teacher attitudes and classroom behavior on gifted children. Most related to increases in pupil self-esteem was the teacher's behavior: "Calm acceptant transactions, in general, with private individualized instruction and a concern for divergency, attention to task, and the use of task appropriate procedures and resources." Spaulding also noted that the acceptant climate, while necessary, did not appear to be significant, but that some structuring is also necessary. The creative student wants a higher degree of autonomy and responsibility in working out learning problems within clearly defined limits.

R. J. Hallman notes that

The creative teacher provides for self-initiated learning; (1) he sets up nonauthoritarian learning situations, (2) he encourages children to overlearn, that is, to saturate themselves with information out of which new ideas spring, (3) he encourages creative thought processes, (4) he defers judgment, (5) he promotes intellectual flexibility, (6) he encourages self-evaluation, (7) he helps students become more sensitive, (8) he knows how to make use of a question, (9) he provides opportunities for students to manipulate materials, ideas, concepts, tools and structures, (10) he assists the students in coping with frustration and failure, and (11) he urges people to consider problems as whole.[1]

The problem of training teachers for work with the gifted has not been faced on many university campuses. One exception is the program at the University of Georgia under the direction of E. P. Torrance. Here there is a specialized program leading either to a master's or doctor's degree for those who are to specialize in the education of gifted children. The curriculum consists of 10 different courses in the area of gifted which, with electives, make up 100 graduate quarter hours. These courses include characteristics, learning abilities, practicum, seminars, identification and assessment, internship and supervision, and guidance.

It is regrettable that so little attention is paid to the training of

---

[1] R. J. Hallman, "Techniques of Creative Teaching," *Journal of Creative Behavior*, Vol. 1 (September 1966).

teachers of gifted children. Outside of the University of Georgia only a few other places in the country are prepared to undertake this training, in the sense of having professors who have researched and published on the subject. These include Johns Hopkins, the University of Connecticut, the University of Kansas, and Purdue. These, of course, may change as the key professors move or retire. In this connection, the University of South Florida had a good program under Dorothy Sisk, and will again, presumably, if she returns there from her USOE directorship of the Office of the Gifted and Talented. Another place to watch is Mississippi State University, where Joe Khatena has taken over as chairman of the Education Psychology Department.[2] We should also mention Columbia University, which has the federal fellows grant. A further listing of such institutions will be found in *The Gifted Child Quarterly* 21:2 (Summer 1977), which features training.

During the ten years he directed the San Fernando Valley State College Summer Workshops, J. C. Gowan learned a lot about training teachers of the gifted, some 500 of whom went through the program. One can train teachers for the gifted in a classroom and out of a textbook, but it is better when the experience is an integrated one. Some notes garnered from those days follow:

1. *Integrated experience.* The operation works best when it's an integrated experience which involves demonstration, teachers, teacher trainees, counselor trainees, aides, parents, and, of course, gifted children. This means that experience in the classroom for teacher and counselor trainees and aides is vital, as supplementing lectures and theory. A parental support group is a necessary part. In such an operation, the selection and development of a high-level, mentally healthy, creative, and open training staff of demonstration teachers is crucial. The operation cannot be mounted during the school year without outside funding, but it can be put on in the summer time as a self-supporting procedure.

2. *Cognitive models.* To avoid gimmickry, new cognitive models must be introduced during the lectures. These should include as a minimum:

   a) The Guilford Structure of Intellect (Guilford, 1967).
   b) The Taxonomy of Educational Objectives in the Cognitive Domain (Bloom, 1956) and the Affective Domain (Krathwohl & Bloom, 1966).
   c) Piaget's cognitive developmental stages (Flavell, 1963).

---

[2]For his suggestions to teachers, see Khatena (1977).

d) Erikson's "Eight Stages of Man" (Erikson, 1950).
e) Developmental Stage Theory (Gowan, 1972).
f) Bruner's views (Bruner, 1966).
g) Buffalo Creative Education Foundation (Parnes, Noller, & Biondi, 1977).

3. *Affective growth and cognitive development of staff and trainees.* We cannot instruct gifted children competently and effectively unless we continue to develop ourselves. Remaining a lifelong student is only the cognitive tip of the problem. We need to enhance our own creativity and mental health, and this service needs to be performed for and by both staff and trainees. It is of vital necessity that the demonstration teachers be good models of this self-actualizing process. Administration must devise affective and recreational means to enhance staff and trainee morale and cohesiveness. Guidance, feedback, and continual evaluation should be a part of this process. It is impossible adequately to care for the needs of gifted children without high staff morale.

4. *Guidance.* Guidance is essential if we are to help gifted children become creative—much larger amounts of it than it might be supposed that "health" gifted children need. A counselor trainee in every classroom should be the goal. Developmental guidance stemming from developmental stage theory is the key to operation (Gowan, 1972). The special guidance needs of gifted children should be made known to the counselor trainees, and the affective curriculum developed. Brandwein's "predisposing factor" should also be utilized (Brandwein, 1956).

5. *Paraprofessional support.* The university professor or administrator who tries to develop such an enterprise will quickly find that he has not the energy to run it properly without massive parental support, which can only be accomplished by the sponsorship of a large and well-run local association for gifted children. Among aspects which such an organization can handle include selection and registration of gifted pupils (not trainees), transportation, supplies, clerical help, parent representatives on site, publicity, legal and insurance matters, first aid, security, A-V equipment, field trips, and evaluation. Such useful aid will leave the administrator free to concern himself with the actual training of teacher and counselor trainees, the supervision of demonstration teachers, and the planning of lectures and theoretical instruction.

6. *Notes.* Such a program is easier to operate in the summer than at any other time. It is best operated in the morning only, to avoid food problems and costs. We have never found day

school summer operations for those above the ninth grade to work out well; the optimum range seems to be grades 3–9. The volunteer nature of such a program for children is necessary; any discipline problems should be removed from class and school. Departmentalization in grade 5 is good practice. We found four to six weeks of operation is about right. Each trainee should be in a gifted child classroom for as much time as possible, working under supervision with the children; we held lectures at 8 a.m. and the children were in school from 9 to noon.

Since our primary effort is to increase and unlock the creativity of both the trainees and the children, it may be useful to state some of our beliefs about this process. The procedure is synergistic; it requires an integration of cognitive models, affective growth, guidance, mental health, high morale, and personal support for faltering egos. When this mix is brought together with high-level demonstration teachers and the right director, an escalation of an emergent kind takes place—something like an atomic explosion resulting from the coming together of a critical mass of uranium. Levels of creativity and accomplishment never before equalled become possible in such an environment; these breakthroughs engender higher levels of mental health which in turn feeds back to more understanding. The result is a kind of a nondrug high, which, under suitable conditions, stays with and inspires those who have had such an experience.

19 What Makes a Creative Person a Creative Teacher?

J. C. GOWAN AND CATHERINE BRUCH

There has been a good deal of speculation about what can be done in the classroom to make children more creative. One of the stock answers to this question is "creative teachers." This answer leads to the next question: "How do you tell that the teachers are, in fact, creative?" and if they are not, "How do you make them more creative?" Some lines of reasoning have led to a more or less loosely enunciated hypothesis which looks something like the following:

A. You can identify creative persons by some test or rating of behavior in teacher training.

B. You put this person in the classroom and he will emit creative classroom behaviors which you can measure.

C. The teacher's creative classroom behaviors will result in increased creativity on the part of the students which you can also measure.

The hypothesis expressed simply says: "A causes B which in turn causes C." The trouble with the hypothesis is that attempts to validate it have generally been unsuccessful. The relationship between A, B, and C, if any, is evidently not a simple cause-and-effect one. One can assume, of course, that there are threshold levels between each of the steps, but it seems even more sophisticated to assume that there may be some missing ingredients along the way. Perhaps it takes more than just a creative person to make a teacher who is effectively creative. Perhaps it takes more than just an effectively creative teacher to ensure that children will become more creative. Perhaps these are necessary, but not sufficient conditions. This paper reports research attempting to get at the missing ingredients.

The locale of the experiment was a creativity workshop conducted

From John Curtis Gowan and Catherine Bruch, "What Makes a Creative Person a Creative Teacher?" *The Gifted Child Quarterly*, Vol. 11 (1967), pp. 157–59. Reprinted by permission of the senior author and *The Gifted Child Quarterly*.

at San Fernando Valley State College in the summer of 1966, of which the senior author was director and the junior author assistant director. The workshop involved 350 gifted children, in 13 classes, 13 demonstration teachers especially selected for their creative ability, 13 counselors, one for each class, and 66 teacher trainees. The Gough Adjective Check List was used. We asked our demonstration teachers to describe themselves; we asked our consultants (who included some nationally prominent individuals) to describe the creative teacher. From this criterion group we got an N of 22. We divided the workshop trainees into three groups of 22 and asked them to describe themselves. (The use of three control groups instead of one was a rough method of controlling the variance within the groups.) We then required that each of the 300 adjectives on the check list discriminate between the criterion group and each control group at the 10% level of significance, and between the average of the control groups at the 5% level of significance. We thus obtained a positive and a negative set of adjectives; the positive being used more and the negative adjectives being used less of the criterion group than any of the control groups. In the case of the negative adjectives most of them were never used to describe the criterion group. The reader should notice that our adjectives are not merely those used to describe effectively creative teachers (for there were many describing such teachers which did not meet our criteria). They must be more significantly used to describe effectively creative teachers than when applied to teacher trainees, interested in creativity but presumably not yet proficient in inculcating it in pupils. In this way, we hoped to pick up the missing ingredient.

The rationale for our experiment then obliged us to sort the culled adjectives into a rough factor analysis of dimensions, and then try to see what else besides creativity was involved. Results are given in Table 19.1.

Before describing the factors in Table 19.1, let us first note that they are not in order of size of variance as in a factor analysis. Cluster I is clearly energy versus apathy, and we have labeled it: "Energetic enterprise versus deliberate quiet." Cluster II has a masculine-feminine feeling. (We removed the two negative adjectives "effeminate" and "feminine" because we had not sufficiently controlled sex.) It sounds like Yang and Yin. We have labeled the cluster: "Self-confident daring versus dependent timidity." Cluster III has appeared in many teacher effectiveness studies (Ryans) as "warm-democratic teacher affect." It is exceptionally clearly delineated by several negative brush dimensions involving various kinds of negative selfish behavior, most of it showing immaturity, or neurotic tendencies. It is these negative adjectives particularly that were never used to describe creatively effective teachers. We have labeled this cluster

TABLE 19.1
Empirical Distribution of Gough Check List Adjectives Describing
Effectively Creative Teachers More Significantly Than Controls

I	II	III	IV	V
active	adventurous	outgoing	clever	imaginative
energetic	courageous	praising	ingenious	original
enterprising	daring	relaxed	insightful	spontaneous
initiative	self-confident		intelligent	suggestible
			inventive	uninhibited
			resourceful	unconventional
				zany
deliberate	cautious	aloof	careless	commonplace
lazy	conservative	arrogant	hasty	conventional
meek	dependent	autocratic	impatient	formal
peaceable	submissive	confused	reckless	inhibited
quiet	timid	complaining		practical
		cynical		reserved
		defensive		thrifty
		fault-finding		
		fearful		
		forgetful		
		headstrong		
		immature		
		irritable		
		moody		
		pleasure-seeking		
		preoccupied		
		sarcastic		
		self-centered		
		shy		
		stern		
		stubborn		
		suspicious		
		temperamental		
		tense		
		touchy		
		withdrawn		
		worrying		
Energetic	Self-confident	Outgoing	Focused	Original
enterprise	daring	euphoria	wisdom	intraceptivity
versus	versus	versus	versus	versus
deliberate	dependent	immature	scattered	authoritarian
quiet	timidity	negativism	energy	conventionality

"Outgoing euphoria versus immature negativism." Cluster IV is straightforward enough on the positive side, but it has an interesting negative pole. The anonyms of the positive pole are obviously not ever going to be used as self-descriptive of teaching candidates, but it appears that scattered nervous energy is more characteristic of the trainee than the expert. The emphasis here is on control. We have therefore labeled the cluster "Focused wisdom versus scattered energy." The final cluster highlights an artistic radicalism versus a philistine conventionality. The authoritarian dimension and the anal character are much in evidence. We have called it "Original intraceptivity versus authoritarian conventionality." There was only one adjective we couldn't fit in somewhere. It was (negative) "flirtatious." We ascribe it to statistical error.

We can now ask our question: "What makes a teacher effectively creative?" Obviously a lot more than just being a creative person. The teacher needs a great deal of energy, self-confident daring, a warm outgoing nature especially free of a host of immature negativisms, and besides being intelligent and original the teacher must be free of hasty, impatient behavior on the one hand and of anal authoritarianism on the other. With such an order it is not surprising we have so much trouble in getting creative behavior in students.

20   Instructional Management Systems: A Model for Organizing and Developing In-Service Training Workshops

Applications for Trainers of Teachers of the Gifted and Talented

JOSEPH S. RENZULLI

As its name implies, this model is designed to provide a system for developing in-service training modules that can be used by persons who will have the responsibility for training teachers. These persons might be college faculty members, educational consultants, or classroom teachers who are assuming leadership roles in staff development. This version of the model was developed with particular reference to trainers of teachers of the gifted and talented. The model grew out of a concern about the questionable effectiveness of short-term workshops and the limited impact that these one-afternoon or one-day experiences usually have on teachers who are attempting to acquire new skills in relatively short periods of time. Although short-term workshops have a great potential for bringing about educational improvement, this potential will not be realized unless we avoid haphazard approaches that do not provide for the *continuous* development of workshop participants. The one-shot "dog and pony show" type of workshop conducted by a charismatic

From *The Gifted Child Quarterly* 21:2 (1977). Used by permission.

visiting "expert" might provide us with the inspiration needed to get started, but a more organized approach is required if there are going to be any follow-through and long-term benefits.

In the area of education for the gifted and talented, we are faced with somewhat of a dilemma. On one hand, there is an almost urgent need to prepare qualified teachers for the rapidly growing number of school programs that serve this segment of the student population. At the same time, there is a limited number of undergraduate and graduate training programs, many teachers are unable to participate in full-time study, and limited human and financial resources prohibit the implementation of comprehensive (long-term) training programs. Thus, the short-term workshop represents one of the few viable alternatives for meeting the training needs in this area of special education.

The Instructional Management System (IMS) approach for organizing in-service training is intended to assist trainers in the design, development, and dissemination of information about teaching strategies and instructional materials. One of the major objectives of an IMS is to compress a large amount of highly relevant information into a relatively short training period. A second objective is to provide a "structure of knowledge" about the topic or teaching strategy that is being presented in the IMS. Such a structure will enable trainees to continue their study of a particular topic in a systematic and organized fashion. By carefully structuring the topic and providing a wealth of back-up information and materials, the in-service trainer can extend the potential impact of a workshop far beyond the one or two hours that are actually spent in face-to-face relationships with trainees.

A third objective of the IMS approach is to provide a series of "packaged" workshops that can be easily used by other trainers. A great deal of time and effort is required for the development of a comprehensive IMS, but once the material has been collected and organized, *other* trainers can benefit from the work of persons who have actually developed the systems. Quite obviously, the developer of an IMS will have certain levels of understanding that may not be achieved by other trainers who follow in his or her footsteps, but at the same time, each user of an IMS will bring to it his or her own knowledge, experience, and dynamic qualities (i. e., "personality"). Thus, each user of an IMS has the opportunity to make creative adaptations and additions to the system.

An Instructional Management System for training teachers of the gifted and talented is basically a coordinated body of information that is designed to accomplish the objectives discussed above. This information usually consists of four general types, each of which will be described in the following sections.

I. Rationale

The first part of an IMS should consist of a brief rationale that points out *why* a particular approach to learning is appropriate and challenging for gifted students. One of the major criticisms of programs for the gifted is that they frequently consist of activities that are essentially appropriate for all learners. For this reason, it is important to explain to workshop participants the unique extensions, modifications, and adaptations that are possible when working with highly able youngsters.

An abbreviated example of such a rationale may help to clarify this point. The area of creativity training is almost universally recommended as a major approach to working with gifted and talented children. Although such training is good for all youngsters, there are at least two major reasons why it is a defensible practice for gifted youngsters. First, creativity training focuses on the development of a thinking process (rather than content mastery). The development of such processes is particularly important for persons who have the potential to be the leaders and problem solvers of the future. Youngsters with extremely advanced abilities should be provided with equally advanced levels of creativity training so that they can bring this process to bear on the problems that they will attack, both now and in their future lives.

The second part of the rationale that supports the use of creativity training with the gifted and talented is perhaps even more compelling than the first. One of the key features of a good creativity training exercise is that it is open-ended—that is, there are no predetermined (correct) responses. For this reason, the respondent can "go as far" as his or her intelligence, background, and motivation (to solve the problem) allow. In other words, *giftedness and creativity are in the response,* not the problem or training exercise.

Consider the following creativity training exercise: "What would happen if the world's energy supply were suddenly reduced by 50 percent?" This exercise could be used with young children, with college students, and even with the president's advisors on energy policy. Quite obviously, older, brighter, and more knowledgeable persons will provide more sophisticated responses, but nevertheless, the problem is open-ended enough to be a challenge to a wide variety of persons. In a regular classroom, all youngsters could respond to this problem; however, the gifted child's greater knowledge, abstract reasoning ability, and understanding might result in more creative suggestions.

The rationale for an IMS need not be long and elaborate, but it should point out the essence of a particular approach to learning so far as the gifted and talented are concerned. An important item that should be included in all rationales is the ways in which we are attempting to *extend* or *escalate* learning experiences beyond the level that is appropriate for all learners. Basically, the rationale should provide the workshop participant with a ready-made answer to the question: Why is (this particular learning activity) especially appropriate for gifted and talented students?

II. Workshop Activities and Materials

A. *Theoretical Information.*

This information usually consists of books and articles that provide a theoretical basis for the topic being covered in the IMS. For example, in the area of creativity training, information about *basic* principles, models, and theories might be covered by making reference to the work of E. Paul Torrance or J. P. Guilford. It is important to keep in mind that most teachers will *not* be interested in "too much theory," and therefore this part of the training should simply attempt to answer the following two questions:

1. What are the basic principles underlying this particular learning activity?
2. What are the major reference works in this area of involvement?

The second question is intended to serve those persons who would like to do some further study in a particular area. The best way to assist these persons is by providing a short but carefully selected bibliography of basic reference materials. It is at this point that the developer of an IMS can use his or her knowledge and time effectively, and thereby save time for workshop participants. It is better to provide participants with three or four key references (that strike right at the heart of the problem) than a long but unselected bibliography.

B. *Demonstration Activities*

Activities that demonstrate teaching strategies or the appropriate use of certain materials should be the central focus of a workshop. These activities should be demonstrated with children or workshop participants and every effort should be made to encourage the actual involvement of teachers. One of the major criticisms of most workshops is that participants spend too much time "sitting and listen-

provide participants with some guidance for this activity. Therefore, one of the responsibilities of an IMS developer should be to construct an evaluation form that calls attention to important characteristics of materials in the area upon which the IMS focuses. In view of the widely varying degrees of quality that exist among commercially available materials, it is important for in-service trainers to provide some direction in separating well-developed materials from the "junk" that has inundated the education market. Once again the developer's advanced knowledge of a particular area will save participants a great deal of time so far as developing evaluative criteria is concerned.

III. Student Materials

A. *No-Fail Introductory Activities*

The effectiveness of many new activities is often dependent upon the initial success that both teachers and students have with the new materials. Thus, it is important to provide teachers with an introductory activity that will work well under almost any circumstances. The developer of an IMS should take great care to search out or construct a few "no-fail" introductory activities. These activities should be demonstrated in the workshop, and participants should practice using the activities until they feel completely confident about their ability to use them with their own students. Many teachers have difficulty "getting started" on new teaching strategies, and therefore a major responsibility of the in-service trainer should be to provide no-fail entry activities that will bridge the gap between the workshop and the classroom.

B. *Student Information About the IMS*

One of the things that we often neglect to do in our teaching is to inform students about the educational objectives of learning activities. Professional educators who work in the area of the gifted spend a great deal of time talking about the "higher mental processes," but, all too often, children still believe that the major goal of learning is to acquire information. If one of our goals is to be more process oriented (rather than content oriented), then we should spend a small amount of time actually teaching youngsters about the meanings of various processes. The developer of an IMS in the area of simulation and learning games, for example, should prepare a sample list of postgame discussion questions that will enable students to analyze a simulation experience in terms of their personal and social growth or the development of their logical thinking abilities.

In other words, we can help students to analyze the process-goals of simulation by providing workshop participants with some examples and guidelines relating to this activity. This often-neglected but very important step in the overall learning process will help gifted students gain a greater appreciation for differentiated experiences.

C. Guidelines for Productivity in the IMS

One of the goals of a good program for the gifted should be to provide advanced opportunities for creative and productive involvement for students who are particularly motivated in a certain area of study.[2] The developer of an IMS can help to achieve this goal by supplying workshop participants with some carefully selected references or guidelines for productivity in a particular area.

Perhaps an example will help to clarify this dimension of an IMS. Let us assume that as a result of one or more teacher-directed activities in simulation and learning games, a certain youngster decides that she would like to try her hand at developing a game. At this point, the teacher should be aware of resources such as the following:

> Glazier, Ray. *How to Design Educational Games*. Cambridge, Mass.: ABT Associates, 1969.
> McConville, Robert. *The History of Board Games*. Palo Alto, Calif.: Creative Publications, Inc., 1974.

Both of these books are excellent how-to-do-it references. The developer of an IMS should continually be collecting such materials and passing them along to teachers. This type of reference material will provide excellent guidance for extending or escalating the creative/productive abilities of gifted students.

D. Advanced Training Opportunities and Resources

Students with extremely advanced potentials may need access to training that is above and beyond that which can ordinarily be provided in a regular school setting. Such opportunities might consist of music camps, writers' workshops, summer stock theater groups, college or internship programs. They might also consist of community

---

[2]A more detailed discussion of this objective and strategies for achieving it can be found in J. S. Renzulli, *The Enrichment Triad Model: A Guide for Developing Defensible Programs for the Gifted and Talented*. Wethersfield, Conn.: Creative Learning Press, 1977.

persons with special talents or abilities. Once again, the developer of an IMS can provide invaluable assistance to workshop participants by (1) supplying them with a list of such resources, and (2) providing guidelines that will enable teachers to compile their own lists of local and regional advanced-level opportunities.

IV. Program Evaluation

The final type of information that should be provided in workshops based on the IMS approach consists of methods by which the teacher can obtain evaluative information about instructional effectiveness. The developer of an IMS should collect and disseminate to workshop participants questionnaires, tests, behavioral observation checklists, and interview schedules that will enable teachers to gather and analyze student feedback. An IMS on creativity training, for example, should include a brief listing and description of the major creativity tests and rating scales that are available in this area of development. Similarly, an IMS on independent study should provide participants with a copy (or reference) to *The Student Attitude toward Independent Study Questionnaire* (SATIS-Q).[3] Evaluative information obtained through the use of feedback mechanisms can serve the twofold purpose of helping teachers to improve their instructional approaches and providing empirical support for programs that serve gifted and talented youth.

Summary

The system for in-service training presented above is, obviously, much more complicated than the "one-to-one workshops" that are currently popular in many areas of education. (In a one-to-one workshop, teachers learn a particular skill which they, in turn, teach to their children.) The IMS approach also places a rather large and time-consuming responsibility on persons who develop a system because it requires the scholarly and comprehensive treatment of a particular topic. But it is precisely this investment of the developer's time, coupled with the IMS organizational pattern, that will allow for maximum coverage of a topic in a relatively short period of time and will encourage teachers to pursue a topic beyond the one or two hours spent in the workshops. If we are going to advance the level of in-service training in the preparation of teachers for the gifted,

---

[3]See J. S. Renzulli and R. K. Gable, "A Factorial Study of the Attitudes of Gifted Students toward Independent Study," *Gifted Child Quarterly*, 1976, 22:91–99.

then it is important to go beyond workshops that are merely informative or entertaining.

One of our goals in teaching gifted children is to provide them with the tools for continuous learning and involvement—learning that will extend *beyond* the single lesson or activity. Shouldn't we provide similar learning experiences for teachers of the gifted?

21 Meeting the Needs of Gifted Children and Teachers in a University Course

JOHN FELDHUSEN

A number of children in the typical elementary classroom have far-above-average talents and creative abilities or are substantially advanced in their basic skills. Strong demands upon the teacher's time and efforts come from the large group of average, the small group of below-average, and the occasional learning disabled children in the classroom. Thus, there is often little time left for the gifted, creative, and talented children and those who are substantially advanced in basic skills.

We conducted a survey among the teachers and pupils of an area school and found that teachers and students agree that there is a need for special attention for gifted, creative, talented, and academically advanced children which teachers currently find difficult to provide. We have also been conducting a special educational program for these children in area schools and have found that parents recognize this need and are anxious to help their children get into such programs.

The problem requires an innovative program because of the special needs and conditions of gifted, creative, and talented children. Just giving them more of the typical classroom offering will not meet their extra needs. Renzulli (1976) and Gowan (1976) have both argued recently that our major goal must be to develop the creative thinking and problem-solving abilities of these children so that they can become more independent and self-sustaining as learners and so that they can eventually become greater contributors to the development of our society.

From *The Gifted Child Quarterly* 21:2 (1977). Used by permission.

The purpose of this article is to describe a continuing, cooperative program between Purdue University faculty, staff, and students and the administration of three public schools. The program (1) provides university graduate students with structured, practical experience with gifted and talented children' and adolescents, and (2) provides some worthwhile educational experiences for the children.

The major vehicle for this program is a course of instruction with the title, "Gifted, Creative and Talented Children." It is open to graduate and undergraduate students. Since it is taught evenings during regular semesters, many area teachers enroll in it. During the summer it is taught as a four-week workshop. The course is limited to 35 students each time it is offered. Most of the enrollees are elementary teachers or teacher education students in elementary education.

The course is divided into six units. We use Self-Instructional Guides (SIG) to direct student work in each unit. The SIGs do the following:

1. Introduce a new unit.
2. State objectives.
3. Prescribe some readings.
4. State the written assignment.

We are mastery oriented in this course. On all papers and assignments students can improve their performance to the grade level they are working for. If a paper or assignment is not satisfactory, they can do it over and thereby hope to improve their grade.

Class sessions are devoted to active learning. There are some short lectures and a number of demonstrations. Some of the time students work in small groups on instructional design problems, simulations, and games. They also have time to work on plans for the field experiences.

All basic readings are drawn from the following assigned texts:

Gallagher, S. J. *Teaching The Gifted Child.* 2nd ed. Boston: Allyn & Bacon, 1975.

Torrance, E. P., & Myers, R. E. *Creative Learning and Teaching.* New York: Dodd, Mead, 1970.

David, G. A. *Psychology of Problem Solving.* New York: Basic Books, 1973.

Taylor, I. A., & Getzels, J. W. (Eds.). *Perspectives in Creativity.* Chicago: Aldine, 1975.

Feldhusen, J. F., & Treffinger, D. J. *Teaching Creative Thinking and Problem Solving.* Dubuque: Kendall/Hunt, 1977.

The field experiences are conducted in nearby schools. All students in the course are required to participate. However, teachers on the job, about half the enrollees, may carry out the activity in their own classrooms.

Children are selected for participation in the program from area schools by teachers from kindergarten through grade ten. Teachers complete Renzulli's "Scale for Rating Behavioral Characteristics of Superior Children" (1971) and follow other guidelines which we supply. IQs are not used in the identification but standardized achievement test data are utilized. Children who are advanced a year or more in reading, mathematics, or language skills are likely candidates for the program. After the children are identified, parent permission is secured.

The cognitive objectives of the program are to develop students' ability to:

1. Produce multiple ideas for various cognitive tasks (fluency).
2. Think of a wide range of ideas for differing tasks (flexibility).
3. Be original and create relatively unique or innovative ideas (originality).
4. Develop basic ideas and fill in interesting and relevant details (elaboration).
5. Ask questions which clarify puzzling and ambiguous situations.
6. Use effective techniques in solving closed (single solution) and open (multiple solutions) problems.
7. Synthesize ideas in creative project activities.
8. Evaluate alternative ideas or solutions in problem situations.
9. Sense and clarify problems in a variety of situations.
10. Exercise self-motivation, direction, and independence in learning and project activities.
11. Carry out an independent program of free reading at a challenging level appropriate to the level of reading skill.
12. Use language effectively in speaking and writing.

The affective and social objectives of the program are to develop students' capacity to:

1. Work with other students of similar ability in project activities.
2. View themselves as competent and effective learners.
3. Respond positively to various types of cognitive activities (favorable attitudes toward creative thinking, problem solving and cognitive project activities).
4. Clarify their own values systems.
5. View themselves as competent creative thinkers, problem solvers, and independent learners.

The program of activities is carried on during the school day in one large school and after school in two others. The children are organized into grade-level groups of 8 to 12 children, and each such group is led by one Purdue student. Sometimes children are combined across grade levels. If the program is conducted during the school day there is close coordination with the regular teacher to find a suitable time and to coordinate the program with regular classroom activities.

The Purdue students meet with their groups once a week for 1½ to 2 hours. Groups meeting after school begin immediately after school is dismissed. Generally an effort is made to meet the requirements suggested by Gowan (1976) for a gifted child program:

1. Creativity is the objective.
2. Verbal activity is emphasized.
3. The student leader is a facilitator.
4. A peer group is organized.
5. Affective curriculum is provided.
6. There is an atmosphere of excellence.

Instructional materials and procedures are provided for the students, but they must plan the specific ways they will use them. We have recently been guided in planning activities by Renzulli's Triad Model (1976), which provides an excellent progression from simpler to more complex activities. Renzulli's *New Directions in Creativity* (1973) has also been an excellent source of instructional materials and activity. Our own book *Teaching Creative Thinking and Problem Solving* (Feldhusen & Treffinger, 1977) is also a useful reference to published materials. We have secured copies of all the material and allow students to use it in their work with children.

During the summer session these practicum activities are carried out in the same schools two afternoons a week. During the summer special efforts are made to promote reading activities among the children in the program, although there is some stress on supplementary reading during the regular semester too. The school librarians assist the students in finding books and material for the children.

Many children are regular enrollees in our program over a period of years. Parents are very supportive and helpful. They must provide transportation for their children if they are in the after-school program, since these are rural schools and buses leave immediately after school. We meet with the parents twice each semester and summer session and are pleased to have their continuing support and encouragement. We also make continuing efforts to provide guidance to the parents on how they can best help their children develop all their talents and abilities. At our regular meetings with parents we give short lectures and provide handouts which they can read to learn more about how to work with the children.

This program seems to provide effective learning experiences for the students enrolled in the course on Gifted, Creative, and Talented

Children. We have evaluated their efforts by direct observation of their work with children, by assessment of the amount they have learned as reflected in tests and assignments, and by inventorying their attitudes toward the course and practicum activities. All the evidence is highly positive. We have also secured attitudinal evaluation from the children, parents, regular teachers, and school administrators, and they too are highly positive in their regard for the program. We seem to be meeting important needs of the Purdue students and the gifted children in this program.

References

Feldhusen, J. F., & Treffinger, D. J. *Teaching Creative Thinking and Problem Solving.* Dubuque: Kendall/Hunt, 1977.

Gowan, J. C. (Ed.). From the classroom. *Gifted Child Quarterly,* 1976, 20, 357–360. (Department Staff: Dorothy Sisk)

Renzulli, J. S. Scale for rating behavioral characteristics of superior students. *Exceptional Children,* 1971, 38, 243–248.

Renzulli, J. S. *New Directions in Creativity.* New York: Harper & Row, 1973.

Renzulli, J. S. The enrichment triad model: A guide for developing defensible programs for the gifted and talented. *Gifted Child Quarterly,* 1976, 20, 303–326.

Chapter Eight

Parents

Introduction

This chapter is concerned with the two ways that parents can help their gifted children; that is, through group associations and through their individual efforts. Since the readings mostly center on individual efforts within the family, we will briefly explore here some aspects of local parental associations for gifted children. Such associations are necessary to monitor, protect, and supplement a gifted child program in the schools. In addition to these functions, they can press for legislation, enlighten the community pressure groups, hold out-of-school classes such as Saturday sessions in special subjects, engage in and sponsor teacher education and in-service training, and perform many other useful functions. A tie-in with the National Association for Gifted Children is helpful.

Some rather unorthodox rules of operation have been found helpful by the San Fernando Valley Association for Gifted Children, the largest such association in the world, numbering over 1,500 members. These suggestions are as follows:

Rule 1. Identify yourselves as an organization *for* gifted children, not an organization *of* parents of gifted children. Anyone who is interested in helping gifted children is eligible to join.

Rule 2. Keep professional educators out; they only cause trouble. Professional educators in a community should be put on the Advisory Board and consulted when necessary; they should not function as officers or members of the organization.

Rule 3. Keep men out; they only cause trouble. Women are more practical in getting things done with a minimum of fuss, argument, red tape and oratory. Men will devote their time to legalistic aspects, constitutions, by-laws, incorporation and the like. Men should be consulted, when advisable, and should, of course, be invited to the evening public meetings, but executive meetings of the Board should be held during the day and involve mothers in a coffee-klatch in someone's kitchen.

Rule 4. Don't beg. Never ask for money. People who give money own part of the action. Give service instead, and when your organization has satisfied customers tell them how much it will cost to put that piece of service on a paying basis. Organizations that spend their time and energies looking for funds have too little energy to do much good for children.

Rule 5. No matter how meritorious the cause or the candidate, unless it is integrally tied to the cause of gifted children, avoid it. Don't get the organization involved in any other cause or activity. You have enough to do with promoting this one.

Rule 6. You can get further with the local educators by a carrot rather than by a stick. Invite the superintendent to the executive board meeting on some occasion. Get local service clubs to put gentle pressure on recalcitrant school officials.

Rule 7. Remember that the goal of your organization is to transfer the parents' selfish interest in their own gifted child to an altruistic interest in the community's gifted children. The focus of the club ought to be in the community and in community service. Members pay dues because they get service. One service that members can get is a reduced tuition for private lessons for their children sponsored by the organization.

Rule 8. Develop a Newsletter to keep communication channels functioning.

Rule 9. Constantly seek to indoctrinate the new members, and bring their knowledge and attitudes up to par with those who have been in the organization longer.

Rule 10. Give as many club members as possible "a piece of the action." Have many committees actively engaged in operation, library, hospitality, research, teacher education, child enrichment, legislation, lectures, parent orientation, and the like.

Ways Parents Can Help Their Gifted Children Become More Creative

A. *Providing a Fostering Attitude*

1. Do not set up unconscious unfavorable evaluation. Upgrade rather than belittle the child's concept of his ability to create, while remaining relatively realistic about valuing products. Be sympathetic to the first abortive efforts of creativity in young children.

2.   Provide a warm and safe psychological base from which to explore and to which children may return when frightened by their own discoveries. Psychological safety is necessary before we can risk ourselves creatively.

3.   Be tolerant yourself of new ideas. Be respectful of children's curiosity, questioning, and ideas. Seek to answer their questions. If questions or ideas are too wild, help children to rephrase them in somewhat sharper or more realistic terms. Instead of saying: "That's silly or impossible," say "It would be easier to answer that question if you took this fact into consideration."

4.   Provide stimulating experiences of a cultural, social, or motor nature to direct children's attention to new and challenging facts. When children have digested these experiences and are ready to process them, be receptive as well as stimulating.

5.   Help children name and classify things. Give them a sense of order and meaning. In helping children value their ideas, attach meaning, worth, and value to as many ideas and life experiences as possible.

6.   Creative children are self-starters, with high energy, humor, independence, and initiative. These can be hindered by too much supervision. Let the child be alone as he wishes and carry things out on his own.

7.   Heighten sensory awareness of children by helping them to value and enjoy sensory percepts and experiences without guilt. Point out the beauty of the simple, the joy of observing nature closely, the delight in craftsmanship and mastery of a discipline, and so on. Teach them to half close their eyes to see a landscape anew or the beauty of a snowflake. We need guides in strange territory.

8.   Mothers should seek to reward the efforts of their young sons and fathers those of their young daughters.

9.   Think what people do to stamp out creativity, then do the opposite. Think of various authoritarian attitudes: conventionalism, aggression, submission, anti-intraception, stereotyping, projectivity; then try to behave oppositely.

10.   Respect individual differences. Don't just merely tolerate them. Be glad people are different; don't just put up with the fact. Be flexible enough to accept children as worthwhile whatever talents they may have.

B.   Facilitating the Child's Own Mental Health

1.   Help the child to *value*. A child needs to be valued and to have his ideas valued before he can value others or their ideas. Valu-

ing is an objective of the affective learning domain. Parents must seek to help children build their own value systems, not the parents.' The values a creative child builds may be divergent ones, hence he may not wish to emulate his teacher or parent. This may annoy parents, but they should concentrate on the child building *some* set of values, not necessarily *theirs.*

2.   Parents have to take care of children's needs in the Maslow hierarchy before they are ready for the luxury of cognitive actualization. Body needs, safety, love, social-ego needs cannot be paramount in a child who is ready to risk ego-capital on creative efforts. If a child is thinking about what others think about him, if his place with them is insecure enough to be of great concern to him, he cannot be creative.

3.   Parents must help children handle disappointment and doubt when they stand alone in some creative act which their fellows do not understand. The child must be able to reward his ego internally in place of the social applause he would like but does not get. He must give up the childish feeling of wanting to be either first or last and learn to be satisfied with a respectable "batting average" of payoffs for his wild ideas. He must realize that though a creative person stands alone he is not an unloved pariah. Instead he must learn to become a divergent but constructive member of society, able to reward himself when social approval is slow to come.

4.   Children also have to become more comfortable with ambiguity. There are areas in life where there is more than one answer to a question, and others where because the question is not well asked, there are no answers at all. The child has to learn to live with this kind of intellectual tension without aborting the ideas which produce it.

5.   The adult's handling of a number of socially disapproved kinds of behavior also seems to have a great deal to do with the child's concept of himself as a valuable creative person. Parents should help the young child distinguish between lying and fanciful tales, the older child to discriminate between means and ends, the adolescent to discriminate between emotions and body-feelings.

6.   Creative children, in their long march to cultural achievement, pass through many cultural discontinuities. Guidance help is needed here. The child needs to see himself as someone who can and who does perform. He too can write, paint, create, or experiment.

7.   Parents should give early rewards for creative behavior. They should make sure that every child's efforts (no matter how poorly executed) bring him enough satisfaction to want to try again. In this connection parents should keep alive the zest for creative activity in young children by halting an activity before they run out of steam.

8. Creativity is involved with easy access to the preconscious, hence with making impermissible impulses permissible; that is, with the social transformation of the libido. Children need help in learning how to lean far enough into themselves to capture these floating ideas, and sympathy, not disapproval, in early and crude attempts to make these ideas socially acceptable.

9. Creation walks a tender line; children cannot create when they are fearful or worried. Adults can help by praising nascent creative efforts and by not scotching initial creativity, however crude, by criticism. An air of sympathetic expectancy for the creative function on the part of all is important, as is a general attitude of warmth and affection. All of us (children especially) tend to create things for those we love.

C. Facilitating the Creative Child's Social Relationships

1. Parents should help the creative child become a "reasonable adventurer" by establishing risk-taking in a cognitive sense as a desirable and useful strategy. This is particularly so when risk-taking is a function of the individual in a particular situation and not a matter of chance only. (That is, when it is a realistic bet.) Children also need help in refining their risk-taking by learning to concentrate on finer degrees of categories rather than being satisfied to predict rougher degrees. (It's harder to diagnose the 1 condition out of 10 than 1 out of 2.) The end product is a person who is willing to take reasonable cognitive risks (or intuitive leaps) because he realizes the payoff value in hitting a real discovery or breakthrough.

2. Parents should help gifted children maintain the essentials of their creativity, at the same time helping them to avoid public disapproval, to reduce socially caused tensions, and to cope with peer sanctions.

3. Whenever a child is proving to be nonconstructively creative (being naughty, for example) parents can help him turn around to the constructive side by giving him more responsibility.

4. Parents should help creative children to become constructive rather than nonconstructive nonconformists. The difference is situational in the first instance versus compulsive in the second. Remember that a child's mind is a twin volcano of creativeness and destructiveness, and the more we open the creative fountain the more we tend to close the destructive one. The child who is denied constructive cognitive creative outlets may become creatively devious.

D. Facilitating the Child's Own Cognitive Development, from Simple to Complex

1.   Parents should help children learn that their minds are more than memory banks and that they should not be satisfied with just spewing out data from memory, as they have often been taught to do by teachers who value this.

2.   Parents should help children mediate process. When they pour data in they should help children process this data by asking and valuing results which require its transformation into decision, action, and application.

3.   Parents should provide change of pace in learning so that they consciously alternate active and quiet times, being with others and being alone, introspection and extroversion, intake and response, humor and seriousness, controlled tension in learning and controlled relaxation when learning is complete. This systolic and diastolic, withdrawal and return aspect of learning is also an aspect of the creative function.

4.   Parents should attempt to indicate standards in mass media such as TV, films, and magazines and help children evaluate their judgments. Evaluation periods and creative periods should be kept separate and distinct. (A "B" movie differs from an "A" movie in that you know what is coming next.)

5.   Parents should not shirk from giving complicated explanations when they are called for, or from portraying nature as complex instead of oversimplifying it. They should also help children to refine their questioning so that they ask questions to which there are answers.

6.   Parents should discriminate carefully between periods of learning which are to be evaluated and those which are not. A good athletic coach has practice. Some teachers act as though the child is always in a game for keeps. Creative action cannot come about under conditions of heavy evaluation. One of the principles of brainstorming is that evaluation is temporarily suspended. Hence parents need to make it clear that students are not making mistakes when they are practicing. They are learning different ways of not getting the answer, but they are narrowing down the remaining possibilities.

E. Facilitating Peer Friendships

Gifted children, especially young ones, often have difficulty in making friends. The average child starts to make friends (psychologists say he gets into the peer state) at about the age of seven. At this time there is a marked withdrawal from the family, and the child finds someone just like himself, same age, same sex, same clothes, same breakfast food, same TV shows with whom to identify. Parents often think the child has fallen under the evil influence of the neighbor's child, and the neighbor thinks the same thing. Despite parental anguish the child is learning a most important lesson—how to identify with others. It is terribly important to be able to get along with and be liked by other members of your own sex, and this is the time when boys and girls alike learn to be "regular fellers."

But a gifted boy, for example, one in a hundred, has to know 100 other children to find one like himself, and half the time the hundredth child is a girl, and he's sunk. It does no good to tell a boy at this stage that the world is made up of all kinds of people, and he must like them all. He starts in by identifying with someone like himself. Many gifted children develop imaginary playmates to fill the void left by not having any true peers. Educators should allow for cluster grouping in the elementary grades, and parents should bus children around after school to find others they can play with. A gifted child with a chronological age of 8 and a mental age of 11 can't be expected to play with average children of either age—he won't get along with his age peers, and average children aged 11 won't admit him to their games. He needs to find another child who is 8 but thinks like 11. This may take some parental doing but it's much better than letting the child develop lonely antisocial habits because no one else seems to be like him. When a child becomes so absorbed in his own activities that he doesn't have friends, it's because he hasn't had a chance to make the right kind.

F. Helping the Gifted Child Become Creative through Reading

There are at least three steps parents can take to encourage creativity through reading. The first is: Read aloud to your child frequently. Poetry is extremely good for this purpose. Stevenson's *A Child's Garden of Verses* is an example, but there are many others. Showing picture books to the younger child and singing together with children around the piano are other good activities. For the older child, reading an excerpt and then telling the child to read the rest may be a good introductory device. Reading up to a half-hour per day with children is a very useful way to get interaction with them.

The second step, which follows naturally from the first, is to make the child see that you enjoy the activity, and that your mind is engaged in it as well as his. "What do you suppose happened next?" encourages the child to tell a story. "Why do you suppose Piglet felt like that?" gets him to think about feelings. Parents can throw in questions which make children think as they read to them. The fun and interest of reading should be emphasized by example. Parents might also improvise on well-known nursery rhymes to make jingles of their own and encourage children to imitate them; this gets the children started on the first step to their own creations.

The third step is to pick books which have intraceptive content—that is, those that cause the child to make creative responses. E. P. Torrance, in an article entitled "Ten Ways of Helping Young Children Gifted in Creative Writing and Speech" (1962c) describes some books which do this well. One is Bruno Munari's *Who's There? Open the Door* (World Publishing Company, 1957) in which children have to guess which animal is at the door. Another Munari book is *The Elephant's Wish*, in which the child has to guess what the elephant wants to become. In *Let's Imagine Thinking Up Things*, by Janet Wolff (E. P. Dutton, 1961), the child has to come up with divergent ideas about what a circle could be used for. The monthly publication *Highlights for Children* (Homesdale, Pa.) has a lot of this material. Cole and Colmore's *The Poetry-Drawing Book* (Simon & Schuster, 1960) suggests other ways for children to express their creativity as a result of verbal stimulation. These materials and others like them provide opportunities to develop the child's imagination.

Another recommendation by Torrance is to use mythology and drama, including fables, fairy tales, and the like to enrich imagery. Greek and Roman mythology is helpful to the child in other ways, and these stories should be read to children. Children like to play with words, and a book like A. Reids' *Ounce, Dice, Trice* (Little Brown, 1958) will set them off. Others such as Babcock's *Did You Ever Read a Clock Upside Down?* (Reeves Soundcraft Corp, 1962) help them to take a different look. Lenore Klein's *What Would You Do If . . . ?* (W. R. Scott, 1961) helps children think divergently. All these books stimulate children's response in some direction.

A final point parents might think about is that having stimulated children to think, they should be encouraged to record and preserve their thoughts. These may be in verse or prose or illustrated, but each child should have a journal in which to record his ideas and either show them to others or keep them private as he feels best. We help children to become verbally creative by making the process of change easy for them.

These are some of the steps in the creative process which the parent can actively encourage.

Twenty-five Suggestions for Parents of Able Children[1]

1. They are still children. They need love but controls; attention but discipline; parental involvement, yet training in self-dependence and responsibility.
2. Consonance of parental value systems is important for their optimum development. This means that there should not be wide disagreements over values between parents.
3. Parental involvement in early task demands, such as training children to perform tasks themselves, to count, tell time, use correct vocabulary and pronunciation, locate themselves and get around their neighborhood, do errands and be responsible, are all important.
4. Emphasis on early verbal expression, reading, discussing ideas in the presence of children, poetry, and music are all valuable. Parents should read to children. There should be an emphasis by parents on doing well in school.
5. The lack of disruption of family life through divorce or separation, and the maintenance of a happy, healthy home are important in raising able children, as well as other children.
6. Since able children often have vague awareness of adult problems such as sex, death, sickness, finances, war, etc. which their lack of experience makes them unable to solve, they may need reassurance in these areas.
7. Parents can see to it that the gifted child age six or above has a playmate who is as able, even if he has to be "imported" from some distance.
8. The role of good books, magazines and other aids to home learning, such as encyclopedias, charts, collections, etc. is important.
9. Parents should take the initiative in taking able children to museums, art galleries, educational institutions, and other historical places where collections of various sorts may enhance background learning.
10. Parents should be especially careful not to "shut up" the gifted child who asks questions. In particular, he should not be scolded for asking, nor should it be inferred that this is an improper or forbidden subject. The parent may, however, insist that questions not be asked at inappropriate times, and may require the child to sharpen or rephrase questions so as to clarify them. Sometimes questions should not be answered completely, but the reply should itself be a question which sends the child into some larger direction. When the

[1]From J. C. Gowan, "Twenty-five Suggestions for Parents of Able Children," Vol. 8 (1964), pp. 192–93. Reprinted by permission of the author and *The Gifted Child Quarterly*. For Khatena's suggestions on this topic, see Khatena (1978c).

parent cannot answer the questions, the child should be directed to a resource which can. Sometimes questions call for clarification of concepts, as with the young child who asked, "Why aren't all these rockets liable to shoot down God?"

11.   There's a difference between pushing and intellectual stimulation. Parents should avoid "pushing" a child into reading, "exhibiting" him before others, or courting undue publicity about him. On the other hand, parents should seek in every way to stimulate and widen the child's mind, through suitable experiences in books, recreation, travel, and the arts.

12.   The gifted child usually has a wide and versatile range of interests but may be somewhat less able to concentrate on one area for a long time. Parents should encourage children who have hobbies to follow through on them, to plan and strive for creditable performance and for real mastery, rather than "going through" a lot of hobbies or collections in a short time.

13.   Parents should avoid direct, indirect, or unspoken attitudes that fantasy, originality, unusual questions, imaginary playmates, or out-of-ordinary mental processes on the part of the child are bad, "different," or to be discouraged. Instead of laughing at the children laugh with them and seek to develop their sense of humor.

14.   Parents can avoid overstructuring children's lives so that they have no free time. Sometimes parents are concerned that gifted children spend some time in watching TV or reading comic books. While they should not spend all their time in doing so, they cannot be expected to perform at top capacity at all times.

15.   Respect the child and his knowledge, which at times may be better than your own and impatient of authority. Assume that he means to do right, and that deviations are not intentional. Do not presume on your authority as a parent except in crises. Allow much liberty on unimportant issues. Try to give him general instructions to carry out in his way rather then specific commands to carry out in yours.

16.   Gifted children are sometimes impatient of conventions. Have a frank talk with your child about the importance of conventions, such as driving on the right-hand side, where he can see the social advantages, and then point out that other conventions of politeness, manners, courtesy, and regard for others have similar bases in experience.

17.   Whenever possible talk things out with him where there has been a disciplinary lapse. He is much more amenable to rational argument than are many children and usually has a well-developed sense of duty.

18.   Give him the stimulation of private lessons in some skill in

which he excels. See that he has social membership in worthy groups. Foster special experiences outside the home by letting the child travel alone or visit friends overnight. Try to facilitate his chance to talk alone with an adult authority in some line that interests him.

19. Try to improve his sense of taste in mass media, TV, radio, cinema, newspapers, comics, reading, art, etc. Discuss the basis for taste and give him some experience with new forms of expression in the arts.

20. Take time to be with him, to listen to what he has to say, to discuss ideas with him.

21. Be a good example yourself, and try to find worthy adult model figures of both sexes outside his family for him to know.

22. Support school efforts to plan for able children. Help to interest the PTA in the problem. Support study groups on gifted children. Form with other parents into cooperative endeavors.

23. Investigate scholarship programs of your community for other gifted children and help provide them.

24. Work to provide better community understanding of, and appreciation for, the role of the able child in society and the importance of community planning.

25. Support community action for able children, including bonds and school taxes for extra educational advantages. Advocate more guidance and special education for the gifted.

Bibliography for Parents of Gifted Children

What to do with a gifted child in the home:

Harrison-Ross, P., and Wyden, B. *The Black Child: A Parents' Handbook,* New York: Peter H. Wyden, 1973.
This book does not have much on gifted children specifically, but it is one of the few good books for black parents.

Kaufmann, F. *Your Gifted Child and You.* Reston, Va.: Council on Exceptional Children, 1976.
This deals specifically with gifted children and has a good list of resources for parents of such children.

Khatena, J. *The Creatively Gifted Child: Suggestions for Parents and Teachers.* New York: Vantage Press, 1977.

Mangum, G. L.; Gale, G. D.; Olsen, M. L.; Peterson, E.; and Thorum, A. R. *Your Child's Career: A Guide to Home-Based Career Education.* Salt Lake City: Olympus Publishing Co., 1977.
This is about the only book there is for parents on career education of their children. It does not say much about gifted children specifically, but much of its content deals with the career problems of gifted children.

Directory of gifted child programs in schools:

Axford, L. B. *A Directory of Educational Programs for the Gifted.* The Scarecrow Press, 52 Liberty St., Metuchen, N.J. 08840. 1971.

Case studies of gifted children:

Hauck, Barbara, and Freehill, M. G. *The Gifted: Case Studies.* Dubuque, Iowa: W. C. Brown Co., 1972.

How to start a gifted child association:

Write to San Fernando Valley Association for Gifted Children, 17915 Ventura Blvd., Encino, Calif. 91316, for their brochure on starting a club.

See *The Gifted Child Quarterly*, 19:3 (Fall 1975), pp. 249–60. National Association for Gifted Children.

22 Parent Perspective: Only The Learner Can Learn

JULIANA GENSLEY

Gifted children come in all sizes, shapes, and denominations. By the same token, their parents bring diversified talents to the task of giving them care and nurture. Some day in the remote future a formula may be devised for producing a gifted adult. But in 1969, parenthood is still an art.

During the summer of 1968, a group of mothers of gifted children were brainstorming in a lecture hall at San Fernando Valley State College. As the discussion progressed, they discovered that they had all instinctively practiced one technique. Each mother agreed that she had, from their first meeting in the hospital, talked to her infant as a person.

It would have been interesting to discover if each mother had also *listened* to her child with understanding and insight.

Communication must be a two-way process. No matter how many schools of learning theory have existed, the end product is evaluated in terms of what the learner can communicate about what he learns. No matter how much a parent tries to help his child, with books and trips and enriching experiences, he cannot regulate the child's assimilation. The parent may learn a great deal through these shared experiences. In this case the parent becomes the learner. But he cannot learn for his child.

Yet children, on their own, are learning all the time. Listen to their conversation. Watch what activities they select for themselves. Observe their role playing. Encourage their brainstorming.

In one of Piaget's studies children were given some information and were asked to explain it to a second child of the same age. The second child then explained it to the adult experimenter. Piaget interpreted these responses in terms of communication skills. There is a deeper significance. The child's concepts are revealed. How

From Juliana Gensley, "Parent Perspective: Only the Learner Can Learn," *The Gifted Child Quarterly*, Vol. 13 (1969), pp. 49–50. Reprinted by permission of the author and *The Gifted Child Quarterly*.

much did he learn from the experimenter's information? The child's interpretation had to be made in terms of his own background.

Parents of gifted children frequently ask advice about what they should do to develop their children's potential. They are greatly concerned with input. They are eager to do what is right, to provide the necessary opportunities.

Among these opportunities should be:

A chance to select some of his own learning activities.

A chance to talk to an interested adult.

A chance to role-play.

A chance to experiment.

A chance to explain to other children.

A chance to be enthusiastic and to receive an enthusiastic response.

A parent cannot give his child everything, no matter how extensive his resources might be. But he can give his child a chance to learn in his own way. In the process, the parent may become a learner, also. What a delightful prospect!

23   Education for Parents of the Gifted

CHARLOTTE E. MALONE

In 1970, while teaching an adult education class for parents of gifted children in Los Angeles, I made a survey of parent observations and attitudes toward their gifted children. The results of the survey support a convincing argument in favor of parent education and guidance as a necessary component of education for gifted children.

The adult education class was open to all adults, and a number of teachers found it worth their while to attend. Fifty-five parents were enrolled in one class, with a total of seventy-seven gifted children represented by them. The parent group included a subgroup of eleven, 20 percent, who were born outside the United States, some who were still learning English. About half of these were from European countries, with the other half immigrating from Asian countries. Another fourteen were first-generation citizens with remaining ties to

---

From *The Gifted Child Quarterly* 19:3 (1975). Used by permission.

their mother countries. The socioeconomic status of the parents ranged from professionals to day laborers. All were sufficiently motivated to devote one evening a week to attend the parent education class.

The first survey questionnaire was designed to identify pertinent characteristics of the parents and children represented by the group. The results were as follows:

1. 10 parents knew their own IQ, and it fell into the range above 130.
2. 15 felt that by comparing themselves with contemporaries, they could say that they were probably gifted.
3. 18 felt that by comparing their spouses to those of their contemporaries, they could say that their spouses were gifted.
4. 12 felt that neither they nor their spouses were gifted.
5. 41 children had been formally identified as gifted by their respective schools.
6. 19 had been placed in special advanced classes or groupings but with no parent counseling to explain the placement.
7. 9 children were preschool and were judged gifted by their parents.
8. 8 were older and out of public school.
9. 6 were thought to be underachieving to a significant degree (four boys and two girls).

A second questionnaire was related to the reaction of parents to IQ tests, behavior of their gifted children, and parent perception of the state of happiness of their gifted children. When asked whether IQ tests indicated the true ability of their children, half of the parents believed they did, with the other half being dissatisfied with test results.

Dissatisfied parents agreed that abilities could only be partially tested—they specified personality and inquisitiveness as not being testable. A number of parents stated that they didn't have enough understanding of the tests to know if they showed true abilities of their children. Four parents reported that their children were just learning to speak English and noted that the language problem would have necessarily affected the test results.

Of the parents who agreed that IQ tests did reflect their child's abilities, three reported that the child's strong points matched the strong areas shown in the testing. Four parents were quite surprised to learn that their children had IQs as high as the test showed. Others stated that their children's behavior substantiated the test scores.

When asked to respond to a question comparing the happiness of their own gifted children to that of average children, parents replied: not as happy (14); as happy (25); happier than the average child (25).

Qualifying statements on this question centered around answers marked "not as happy." Two children were judged as too serious—overly concerned with world problems. Two other children were described as being lonely, and two children were called impatient. Qualifiers for the "as happy" answer indicated that it is not uncommon for gifted children to seem happy at home but to report that they are unhappy at school.

Parents were asked to describe ways in which their gifted children behaved as they expected gifted children to behave at home, in school, and with friends and then to describe ways in which the children did not behave as parents would expect gifted children to behave in these same areas. From these responses an adjective checklist was prepared.

Adjectives were placed in one column with antonyms placed in a second column to check for consistency. Thus, a parent marking a given child as "confident ... *almost never*," and "unsure ... *nearly always*" would show consistency. The checklist was tested twice as it was being prepared to eliminate the most disconcerting semantic problems. Where there were several gifted children in a family, parents were asked to mark the checklist in reference to the one who behaved most like a gifted child, in their opinion. Results of this questionnaire showed that, of the behaviors explored, characteristics most often observed were: (1) inquisitiveness, (2) sensitivity, (3) communicativeness, (4) persistence, and (5) confidence. It is gratifying to note that some exemplary gifted programs are now incorporating these characteristics into their curricular planning.

Expressed needs of the parents were more counseling and a knowledge of teaching methods. Counseling was being requested in the areas of discipline, developing strengths, guiding sensitivity, and determining the rights of parents. Teaching methodology was requested so that parents could fill areas in which they felt the schools were not succeeding. The parents recognized that children have different kinds of learning styles and hoped to provide facilities and a proper atmosphere in their homes so that their children could develop individual styles of learning.

In summary, parents are requesting help in the guidance of their atypical, gifted children. They do not have the standard societal models to direct their interaction with their children, and they are aware that the potential for productivity is greater in their children than in most. In addition, adult education for parents of gifted is needed to interpret school placement and programs.

Parents of gifted children, or gifted parents—as often they are—can be the greatest source of support or the biggest headache for school districts, depending on how well they understand what is happening to their children. What is more, parents of gifted children, when they have been treated as mature adults, have the capacity to become involved in the needs of children other than their own. A small investment in time and money in this area reaps a lot of mileage, support that is dearly needed by most school districts today. Education for parents of gifted can only result in positive change!

24 Parents and the Creatively Gifted

JOE KHATENA

You and I have mutual interest in children—that one phenomenon which gives meaning to life while continuously challenging the incompleteness of our understanding of it. When my third child arrived my wife and I thought that the experience we had with the first two children should make it easier to raise the third: thirteen years later, we are still trying to validate the observation without success.

It is my intention to talk about my observation of the gifted child and what we as parents can try to do for him so that he may take his place as a productive member of society. But before I do, I would like to preface it with a few thoughts Joseph Bledsoe recently expressed in a talk (1973) to parents and teachers of gifted and superior students at Cullowhee, North Carolina. He spoke of something quite easily overlooked by many of us interested in the gifted, and that is that the gifted child is first a child with the same basic needs as other children, and that we as parents need to love him not for his achievement but for what he is, that we need to assist him to incorporate in his value system his greater responsibility to serve society because of his greater abilities, and that we should temper our attempts to stimulate him artistically and intellectually by encouraging him to initiate the activities.

Recently a parent wrote to *The Gifted Child Quarterly* expressing her concern about her child who she knew was gifted and the impact this would have on others in her community if she were to talk about it:

If I were to say that I had a retarded or physically handicapped child, people would believe me. No one would resent me, and most reactions would be sympathetic. Having a gifted

---

From *The Gifted Child Quarterly* 18:3 (1974). Used by permission.

child, however, I know I do better keeping quiet. People wouldn't believe me, and they would resent me. "Another bragging mother," I would be called. .... In a small town, especially, it is wiser not to mention it.

This mother is not alone in her perception of the complications of having her gifted child recognized in her community. Instead of finding increased joy in sharing what really is a community resource she feels she had better hide it from others for fear of being scorned, envied, and even hurt—a failing for which she is not necessarily responsible since she, like so many others, is the product of cultural processing.

It seems proper at this juncture to suggest the hypothesis that the parent of the gifted child is the single most significant person in the child's life, and by far the most potent lead to the child's attempts to realize his full potential. That is why it is of primary importance for parents to possess the appropriate orientations and attitudes toward the gifted child. Recall, for instance, the true story reported about two years ago on the Today show of an Irish novelist who as a child wrote a novel of great strength using his toe (taking twelve years to complete the work, since the rest of him was paralyzed), partly because his mother showed him love and understanding, made him feel significant, gave meaning to his life, and showed great appreciation for his talent. She had done for this boy at home what Plato had advocated the state do for the young when he stated that "What is honored in one's own country is what will be cultivated." That is what I am sure most of us would like to do for our gifted children if we could.

At one time we thought that children who did well on tests of intelligence were gifted, and even the man in the street seemed to know all about IQ or intelligence quotient. We also knew that when a child on the Stanford-Binet or Wechsler Intelligence Scale for Children had an IQ of 130 and over he was exceptionally bright. Today, while this may still be the case, we are not so sure if it tells us the whole story, and more and more are we becoming convinced that a child can show how bright he is in many different ways. And those of us who are familiar with Guilford's structure of intellect model (1956) have begun to realize how complex human mental functioning is and that a person may have the potential of at least 120 intellectual abilities.

What we have to recognize is the shift that has taken place over the past 20 or 25 years in our thinking regarding the concept of giftedness. Exceptional ability is no longer thought of in terms of IQ but extended to include many mental abilities. Guilford would have us recognize that of the five thinking operations that may be used in almost any intellectual act—knowing and understanding (cognition), recalling and retrieving (memory), thinking in a way that fetches one right answer or solution (convergent thinking), thinking in a way that produces many possible answers or solutions (divergent thinking), and making judgments (evaluation)—divergent (or creative) thinking is the most neglected both in schools and in intellectual measures.

Of course since 1950 much has been done to correct both these deficiencies, and now we do have much more creative teaching done in schools and a number of sound instruments to assist in the identification of creative thinking abilities for their more appropriate direction and nurture (e.g., Guilford, 1967; Torrance, 1966; Khatena & Torrance, 1973). While these helps are available to teachers and psychologists, they are not to parents.

I think that it would be a significant contribution to the cause of the gifted if parents can be provided with information on identification procedures that they can use to gain valuable clues about their children's abilities for direction toward nurturant strategies that would encourage productive behavior. My prime concern will be to make you familiar with a few approaches you can take to identify your children as creatively gifted and to share with you some of the strategies that have been successfully tried, especially in the learning situation, to facilitate the expression of creative talent.

Parent Identification of the Creatively Gifted Child

The creatively gifted child is a child who on traditional IQ measures will appear to be quite bright, though at times such measures may pick him out as exceptional. As a result, far too many of our very bright children pass unnoticed by the education system that often relies on such measures to help select children for special programs where such programs exist. But such measures do not allow creatively gifted children to show the full extent of their abilities. Creatively gifted children are no different from children with high IQ except that they use creative thinking strategies and the imagination more often as they interact with the world around them. It is increasingly recognized today that we need to use a composite of several measures if we intend to adequately screen children for their intellectual potency. There are quite a number of good measures commercially available to do this, but use of these measures requires skill and training, and they usually are not available to schoolteachers or parents. However, this does not mean that the teacher or parent can do nothing in the way of identifying creatively gifted children. Observation has been the chief technique we have used over the years, and it is about observation as a method of measurement that I am going to talk to you. The kind of observation we have and still use generally is informal observation, by which we obtain gross clues about the subject of our attention. I am suggesting that we need to use a more systematic method of observation if we are to more adequately identify the creative child.

Recently Lewis E. Walkup (1971) suggested some practical approaches to the detection of creativity, several of which I think can be adopted for use by parents to advantage. For instance, you may be watchful of his activities and observe how much of what he does is of a productive nature, or if he exhibits a creative habit of mind by the way he recalls the beautiful aspects of his study and work, or his love for intellectual activity and a preference for problem solving over rote learning. The extent to which he visualizes when he thinks of a problem or the strategies (convergent or divergent thinking operations) he uses when given a relatively simple problem in his own area of interest to solve can also be observed, or get him to interact with another child known to be highly creative and notice the kind of thinking they do.

One way I have approached the identification of the creative individual is by structured observation. The creativity checklist I constructed a few years ago entitled *Something About Myself* (Khatena, 1971a, 1972a) is based on three major ways creative individuals may reveal themselves—through personality traits, thinking operations, and products. Joseph Bledsoe and I have found through factor analysis (1973) that creative people tend to show themselves as environmentally sensitive having initiative, intellectuality, individuality, and artistry. What you need to do is to observe your children for such qualities that would fall in one or several of these six categories:

If your child is *environmentally sensitive* you will find him relating his ideas to what can be seen, touched, or heard, showing interest in beautiful and humorous aspects of experiences, and having sensitivity to meaningful relations.

If he has *initiative* you may find him producing and/or playing leads in dramatic and musical productions, producing new formulas or new products, and bringing about changes in procedures or organization.

If he possesses *self-strength* he will exhibit self-confidence in matching his talents against others, resourcefulness, versatility, willingness to take risks, desire to excel, and organizational ability.

If he has *intellectuality* he will show intellectual curiosity, enjoyment in meeting challenging tasks, imagination, preference for adventure over routine, liking for reconstruction of things and ideas to form something different, and dislike for doing things in a prescribed and routine way.

If he shows *individuality* traits you will find him having preferences for working by himself rather than in a group, seeing himself as a self-starter and somewhat eccentric, critical of others, thinking for himself, and working for long periods without getting tired.

If he exhibits *artistry* he is one who is involved in the production of objects, models, paintings, and carvings, he has received prizes or has had his products exhibited or has written stories, plays, poems, and other literary pieces.

Observation of these qualities will give you clues as to whether your children are creatively gifted and in what ways. This will suggest the need for more formal screening services, possibly with the purpose of having your child referred for participation in programs for the gifted where these exist in your state, county, town, or school, and where these do not, for tutorial or special instruction in your child's talent area. More than this, you will yourself know the strengths and weaknesses in the gift patterns of your child so that you may encourage and enhance his talents, provide him with home opportunities for expression of productivity, and even reward him for creative expressions.

Some Approaches to Encourage the Creatively Gifted Child to Produce

Knowing more about your child and his gifts will certainly help you determine what can be done for him. It is not too difficult to help him to be productive, and besides it can be tremendously exciting to both of you and would certainly add to the meaningful relationship you already have with him. Theory and practice in this area of knowledge have given us many clues as to how to set about encouraging creative behavior, except that what has been written about these approaches has not been primarily for parents. So you will have to adapt for home use what has been written for teachers and others directly concerned with the child's schooling.

For instance, Sidney J. Parnes is very well known for his contribution to and management of creativity workshops at Buffalo, and in a recent conference he suggested a two-dimensional model for parents' use in developing the preschool child's creative potential, with fluency (the ability to produce many ideas), flexibility (the ability to produce many ideas showing shifts in thinking), originality (the ability to produce unusual and infrequent ideas), elaboration (the ability to add details to the basic idea), and sensitivity (the ability for keen awareness of possible implications) as creativity traits to be encouraged in activities such as story-telling after dinner, play with parents and siblings, and mealtime conversations. For instance he suggests that the parent could stop several times and ask the child what he thinks might happen next; or after finishing the story he could ask the child how else it might have ended; or he could urge the child to think of several different endings (and in this way encourage the production of many and many different kinds of responses—fluency and flexibility), or to think of the strangest or funniest ending he could imagine (originality), or to think of many specific ways he could make the ending of the story more interesting (elaboration), or to think of all the things that might happen if certain of these or other changes were made in the story (sensitivity) (1968, p. 246). To help parents effectively apply this model in the home, Parnes would have them become familiar with the theoretical background for the nurture of creative behavior in young children so that they may work individually and in groups to derive a wide variety of specific ideas as to how to strengthen the above-mentioned creativity traits of their children. This you can do in part by reading his widely used text entitled *Guiding Creative Behavior* (1967) published by Charles Scribner's, or preferably attend one of his workshops during the Annual Institute at State University College in Buffalo, New York.

Paul Torrance's delightful little book entitled *Creativity* (1969) gives special focus to the young child in the preschool and early elementary school years. The book is highlighted by a chapter on what parents can do to help. In this chapter he lists eight ways parents can help their children learn creatively, as follows: by respecting the curiosity needs of children; by encouraging exploration, experimentation, fantasy, testing and developing creative talent; by preparing them for new experiences; by transforming their destructive energy into productive behavior; by emphasizing growth rather than punishment; by using creative ways for solving conflicts; by providing opportunities to make contributions; and by supplementing and reinforcing school efforts. Torrance gives many illustrations, but let me quote just two of them:

> Parents are sometimes irritated by the constant demands children make upon their time for attention. Children can be awfully impatient.... There are countless ways that can be devised to make waiting easier and more useful for creative development. In one family, the two daughters acted like they were being put through a great ordeal if they had to sit in the car for two minutes to wait for someone. The mother improvised a *touch and tell box* that is now standard car equipment. Into a small box she put an earring, a nail, a roller, a rubber band, a

scrap of wool cloth, and some other items. The children love trying to identify these with their eyes closed. As the mother changes the contents of the box from time to time, she noted that the children are developing a discriminating sense of touch. Irritating moments have become moments of learning. (pp. 61–62)

Karen, a nine-year-old, complained that she had nothing to write about. Her teacher's best efforts to encourage her failed, yet Karen's speech was very fluent. One day Karen's mother decided to write down Karen's conversation just as she expressed herself. At the end of the day, the mother read Karen's conversation back to her. Karen couldn't believe that what she had heard were all of her own ideas. The mother continued to do this for a while and collected the recorded conversations into a book entitled Karen's Compositions. Karen decided then that *writing is just like talking.* From then on she began to write with great ease and pleasure. (p. 62)

My own experimental work (e.g., Khatena, 1971a, 1973a; Khatena & Dickerson, 1973) on helping children to think in creative ways by using several creative thinking strategies, namely breaking away from the commonplace and finding unusual ways of thinking; restructuring, or pulling apart components of an idea, thought, or experience and rearranging the parts into fresh combinations; and synthesis, or the putting together of hitherto separate entities in productive arrangements, suggests yet another approach.[1] For instance, we could use the principle of *restructuring* by showing children a picture of, say, the three wise men of Gotham and encourage them to ask questions which cannot be answered merely by looking at the picture, then ask them to guess causes and consequences about the characters and their actions as warm-up activities, and follow this up by getting them to restructure three elements of the picture, namely, the three wise men, the bowl, and the sea, into an unusual and interesting story. An example of *synthesis* using verbal material could begin by showing children the picture of the nursery rhyme "Dr. Foster went to Gloucester" and get them to tell something about it. A second picture which shows Tommy Tucker singing for his supper could then be introduced with similar warm-up activities. Children could then be asked to tell a story using a combination of the characters and situations on both pictures, with encouragement to make their story as unusual and interesting as they can.

---

[1] For further details, see Reading 36 in Chapter XII.

The same can be done with nonverbal materials. To use Torrance's touch and tell box, children can be encouraged, for instance, to guess what, say, three or four items in the box are with their eyes closed and then after several such exercises as warm-up activities they can be asked to select three or four of the most interesting guesses they have made to put together as elements or characters of a story which they can make up. Once again they can be encouraged to use their imagination.

To these creative thinking strategies may be added the use of *analogy* by which children can understand and manipulate their environment in productive ways. Last year I had suggested (Khatena, 1972b) that we use words, with their objective meanings and emotional connotations, to convey to others our ideas, feelings, and perceptions about the world. However, should we find ourselves trying to communicate thoughts, feelings, or experiences that do not lend themselves to easy expression, we search for some familiar object or situation to which our thought-feeling complex can be related, as for instance the occasion when Art Linkletter asked a little boy on one of his television shows, "What does happiness mean to you?" and the reply he received was, "Seeing my ma and pa kiss." In a more recent study with children (Khatena, 1973b) I reported some examples of children's imagination at work producing analogies, given verbal stimuli. Let me give you a few examples of these analogies with the onomatopoeic word relative to their evocation in parentheses: "a bird landing heavily on her nest" (crackle); "fly-catching plant closing pores" (buzz); "a tree growing out of its bark" (moan); "a handful of fingernails scratching on a blackboard" (growl); "violin on a dog's nerves" (ouch); "eraser tearing paper by mistake" (groan); "a barber cutting a man's hair fast" (jingle); "a frightened lizard" (zoom); "a witch melting" (fizzy).

You may find many leads in the various commercially available programs and texts on the subject as well; these include the *Imagi-Craft Series* by B. F. Cunnington and E. P. Torrance, or the *Idea Books* by R. E. Myers and E. P. Torrance, both published by Ginn, or materials by J. S. Renzulli entitled *New Directions in Creativity: A Creative Training Program for the Language Arts* published by Harper and Row, or the *Total Creativity Program for Elementary School Teachers* produced by F. E. Williams and published by Educational Technological Publications.

To sum up, then, I have attempted in this presentation to make you realize that as parents you can actively get yourselves involved in the identification of your creatively gifted children, that you can do much towards channeling them for special programs where these exist or provide tutorial or other relevant services for the development of their special abilities and talents, and that you yourselves can become part of the excitement of developing and guiding their creative expression, self-actualization, and mental health.

All in all, your task as parent is never an easy one and often does not seem to fetch anticipated rewards. But think how exhilarating it must be to unlock the creative potential of your child to its optimum realization, and like the good Socratic-type teacher "kindle a fire of intellectual enthusiasm and develop within him the knowledge of what he can become."

References

Bledsoe, J. C. The gifted child in the family and the importance of self-esteem. Paper presented to Parents of Gifted and Superior Students and Teachers at Western Carolina University, North Carolina, 26th July, 1973. (University of Georgia, Athens, Ga.)

Bledsoe, J. C., and Khatena, J. Factor analytic study of Something About Myself. *Psychological Reports,* 1973, 32, 1176–1178.

Gowan, J. C., and Torrance, E. P. (Eds.). *Educating the ablest: A book of readings on the education of gifted children.* Itasca, Ill.: F. E. Peacock, 1971.

Guilford, J. P. Structure of intellect. *Psychological Bulletin,* 1956, 14, 469–479.

Guilford, J. P. *The nature of human intelligence.* New York: McGraw-Hill, 1967.

Khatena, J. Something About Myself: A brief screening device for identifying creatively gifted children and adults. *Gifted Child Quarterly,* 1971, 15(4), 262–266. (a)

Khatena, J. Teaching disadvantaged preschool children to think creatively with pictures. *Journal of Educational Psychology,* 1971, 62(5), 384–386. (b)

Khatena, J. Attitude patterns as providing validity evidence of Something About Myself. *Perceptual and Motor Skills,* 1972, 34, 563–564. (a)

Khatena, J. The use of analogy in the production of original verbal images. *Journal of Creative Behavior,* 1972, 6(3), 209–213. (b)

Khatena, J. Developmental patterns in training children between the ages of 5 and 11 to think creatively with pictures. *Educational Trends,* 1973. (a)

Khatena, J. Imagination imagery of children and the production of analogy. *Gifted Child Quarterly,* 1973, 17(2), 98–102. (b)

Khatena, J., and Dickerson, E. G. Training sixth grade children to think creatively with words. *Psychological Reports,* 1973, 32, 841–842.

Khatena, J., and Torrance, E. P. *Thinking Creatively with Sounds and Words: Norms-technical manual.* Research ed. Lexington, Mass.: Personnel Press, 1973.

Parnes, S. J. A suggested model for parents' use in developing the child's creative potential. In F. E. Williams (Ed.), *Creativity at home and in school.* St. Paul, Minn.: Macalester Creativity Project, 1968, pp. 245–249.

Torrance, E. P. *Torrance Tests of Creative Thinking: Norms-technical manual.* Research ed. Princeton, N.J.: Personnel Press, 1966.

Torrance, E. P. *Creativity.* San Rafael, Calif.: Dimensions, 1969.

Walkup, L. E. Detecting creativity: Some practical approaches. *Journal of Creative Behavior,* 1971, 5(2), 89–93.

Chapter Nine

Creativity

Introduction

Creativity and giftedness are different rooms in the mansion of intellect; this finding is one of the major contributions of the Guilford Structure of Intellect which constitutes the base for most of the interest in creativity during the past 30 years. The Getzels and Jackson (1962) study cited in the introduction to Chapter V showed that of the top fifth in creativity, only 30 percent were among the top fifth in giftedness, but that the creative group achieved as well as the gifted group. Since some gifted children are creative and some are not, two very important questions immediately arise: What causes the difference? What can education do about it?

Views about creativity range from a hardheaded rationalism which avers that it can be taught like any other subject, to a mystical, psychedelic attitude which holds that it borders on the supernormal. Osgood, Parnes, and the Buffalo school are examples of the former; while Huxley, Barron, Koestler, and Krippner have some measure of the latter. Creativity as applied to education is just a minor aspect of creativity research, as witnessed by the Buffalo, Utah, and IPAR groups, all of whom have been interested in scientific, defense, business, and industrial aspects, as well as the problem of helping children become more creative.

There are three major theories as to why some gifted children are more creative than others. The first is the "structure of intellect theory," namely, that these children have abilities in the "divergent productions slab." The second is the Maslowian "mental health theory," namely, that creativity is an outcome of good mental health and progress toward self-actualization. The third is the "anti-authoritarian theory," namely, that democratic backgrounds and styles of life produce less rigid and more original persons who are, therefore, more creative. To these we might add a fourth, the "Oedipal theory," namely, that creativity is the product of the child's response to the close affectional approach of the opposite-sexed parent during the initiative period from four to seven (Gowan, Demos, Torrance, 1967, pp. 9–13). Even more recent views (Gowan, 1972) hold that creativity is an emergent characteristic of the escalation of developmental process when the requisite degrees of mental health, mental ability, and environmental stimulation are present. It is accentuated particularly in the third and sixth Eriksonian stages (initiative period from four to seven, and intimacy period from the late teens through the early twenties). Through good mental health, the expression of creativity is related to the growth, strength, and availability of the preconscious area, via play and daydreams, to the demands of the conscious mind. Thus creativity in able youth is an indication of good mental health and continued developmental process which would mark it as a way station toward later self-actualization.

Very recent research on imagery, in which Joe Khatena has been a leader, indicates the close relationship between imagery, creativity, and the right hemisphere, imagery being the vehicle through which incubation produces creativity in the right hemisphere of the brain. These important developments have necessitated a new chapter on this subject in this edition (Chapter XII).

Since the original edition of this book, E. P. Torrance (1972) has closed a research gap by showing that high youthful creativity test measures do in fact correlate well with later creative performance in young adulthood. This longitudinal study has helped verify the stability of the creative entity.

All three editors, J. C. Gowan as well as Khatena and Torrance, have been constant in their attention to research and writing in this area. Of Torrance's many books on the subject, the following in particular deserve attention: Guiding Creative Talent (1962a), Rewarding Creative Behavior (1965), Creative Learning and Teaching (with R. E. Myers, 1970), and Discovery and Nurturance of Giftedness in the Culturally Different (1977). Gowan's books include Creativity: Its Educational Implications (with George Demos and E. P. Torrance, 1967), The Development of the Creative Individual (1972), The Development of the Psychedelic Individual (1974), and Trance, Art, and Creativity (1975). Khatena's book The Creatively Gifted Child: Some Suggestions for Parents and Teachers (1978c) has many practical implications for educational creativity. Moreover, each editor has produced a large number of articles on creativity, many of which may be found in The Gifted Child Quarterly. A special issue on creativity (Fall 1975) was edited by Khatena, and another one (Winter 1977) was edited by Don Treffinger.

Tests of creativity by the editors include Khatena and Torrance (1973, 1976), Torrance (1974), Torrance and Myers (1970). See also Gowan (1975). For personality correlates of creativity, see Stanley, George, and Solano (1978).

Outside the writings of the editors, the following represents a recent recommended bibliography on creativity: Arieti (1976), Biondi and Parnes (1976), Feldhusen and Treffinger (1976), Gallagher (1975), Guilford (1967, 1977), Keating (1976), Parnes, Noller, and Biondi (1977), Renzulli (1977), Rothenberg and Hausman (1976), Stanley, Keating, and Fox (1974), and Stanley, George, and Solano (1977).

25 In Search of Creativity: Some Current Literature

MARVIN L. DICE, JR.

The Quest for an Educationally Valued Conception of Creativity

Recognition of the major concerns within the current literature regarding the nature of creativity has caused some authors to investigate conceptions of creativity (Cochrane, 1975; Lake & Houghton, 1975; Kantor, 1975; Tasse, 1975; Trachtman, 1975). In a philosophical analysis, Cochrane (1975) has attempted to enlighten the reader by questioning the wisdom of fashionable educational theory. A further objective of the analysis considered a number of different conceptualizations of creativity. Conceptualizations of creativity described were: Imitation, Novelty, Iconoclasm, Recapitulation of Creativity, Central Paradigms of Creativity, and Creativity Consistent with Aesthetic Standards. In the same study Cochrane argued further that simple logic would most often lead to the rejection of a creative methodology in teaching, since by definition standard methodology should be methodology which is successful.

In an investigation of the literature regarding the French view of creativity, Tasse (1975) described most of the French literature in terms of characteristics of creativity which have been categorized as either the phenomenon of invention or creativity. The author reported that the invention category contained documents found under the headings of inventions, discovery, scientist, and genius, while on the contrary the creativity category was most often associated with literary and artistic enterprise. Among several items contributed by Tasse regarding the French view of creativity was the finding that the French hold both a charismatic and laborious conception of the creative individual. The author reported further that this difference of perspective had led some writers to overemphasize insight, whereas others were so reductionistic that insight was minimized to the point of careful work. Tasse concluded that the problem with conception

From *The Gifted Child Quarterly* 20:2 (1976). Used by permission.

of the creative individual is a misinterpretation of the role of insight in creativity.

A review of the literature related to the community which fosters the creative act indicated that historical periods have served as springboards for creative yield (Trachtman, 1975). The author cited instances of qualitative difference between winners of the Pulitzer Prize in poetry, music, and drama in the '20s, '30s, and '40s and winners in the '60s and '70s. The author concluded that the climate for great creation is probably prerequisite to creation.

In an investigation of curriculum documents in English, Kantor (1975) reported that similarities exist between arguments for creativity expressed in the present literature and arguments set forth in the early writings of this century. The author reported in particular that the pendulum of thought appears to swing back and forth between a conservative traditional perspective and a liberal progressive point of view. The author reported further that two issues appear repeatedly in English curriculum documents. The first issue is a controversy between intrinsic satisfaction and utilitarian purpose, and the second issue concerns questions regarding the possession of creative ability.

Lake and Houghton (1975) reported that creation is more likely the result of an evolutionary process rather than a process in which the final nature of the creation is understood immediately. Data for the study were gathered by tracing the developments in the invention of Christopher Cockerell's Hovercraft. These authors reported further that the "Hover principle" initially "consisted of a complex confusion of ideas, percepts and engineering know-how" (Lake & Houghton, 1975, p. 21).

Conceptual Models of Creativity

In an attempt to present a model of creativity, Gowan (1975) proposed a model of the relationship between the conscious mind and numinous element. In particular, the model was based on Harry Stack Sullivan's terms, prototaxic, parataxic and syntaxic. Gowan described the relationship between Sullivan's three terms and three proposed modes of experience. A further objective of the investigation presented properties of syntaxic procedures which are capable of playing a part in the process of creation.

The problem of investigating creativity assumes new dimensions in view of a conceptual model of creative visual intelligence. Edmonston (1975) described behaviors of creative artists and analyzed written testimonials concerning artistic processes. The data of these analyses were presented as an outline of the components of creative visual intelligence. It was hoped that this model would prove useful in attempts to improve the future of teaching.

Matrices Restrictive of Creativity

The literature indicated that the acquisition of verbal knowledge and its structure may inhibit creativity (Jensen, 1975; Poulson, 1975). Poulson (1975) argued that although language is useful, the more language and logical thought are employed, the more likely it is that the user becomes a victim of confinement in language and logical thought. The author cautioned further that imprisonment in language may be isolating the individual from visual mental activity, instinctive and nonverbal behavior, intuitive thinking, and the direct perception of reality (Poulson, 1975). Poulson argued further that confinement in language was the result of the societal use of language as a vehicle to communicate heritage, history, and humanity.

Jensen (1975) contributed further to this work when he presented an outline of metaphorical constructs used in the problem-solving process. The author pointed out that metaphors have channeled our world perspective and have provided us with insight into the nature of our problems and their solutions. The metaphors described were: (a) Metaphors of Restoration, (b) The Horney Metaphor, (c) Unification Metaphors, (d) Creational Metaphors, and (e) Metaphors Drawn from Nature.

Requirements of Creativity

The problem of investigating creativity assumes new dimensions in view of the requirements of creativity (Frey, 1975; Getzels, 1975; Miller, 1975). In an investigation of how problems are found in the investigation of solutions, Getzels (1975) argued that the initial question in the earlier stages of problem solution is often of greater import than what occurs in the later stages of problem solution. The author illustrated the point by asking the reader to consider a situation whereby two automobile travelers on a deserted country road develop a flat tire. Getzels reported that one traveler "defines the dilemma by posing the problem: 'Where can we get a jack?' " (p. 15), while the more imaginative traveler "defines the dilemma by posing the problem: 'How can we raise the automobile?' " (p. 15). Needless to say, the better problem finder makes use of a nearby pulley and is back on the road before his friend who is unable to ask the correct question. The author concluded by leaving the reader with the mental picture of the inadequate problem finder trudging wearily toward a distant service station.

Frey (1975) contributed further to this work when he cautioned that technology was insufficient in the formation of accurate counselor judgments. The author advised that counselors devote more time, as everyone should, to isolating metatheoretical principles needed to develop their own experience-based processes. The author cautioned further that we are often trapped "by the stereotype of the scientist who refuses to deal adequately with nonverbal imagery and irrational unconsciousness" (Frey, 1975, p. 25). Frey concluded by reminding the reader that many of the great scientists and artists of the past were unafraid of valuing the primary process.

In an attempt to present an account of the dimensions of creative prose, Miller (1975) argued that writing and speaking are made effective by an attitude of mind. Among several items of information contributed by the author regarding the dimensions of creative prose was the conviction that the attitude is actualized by a concern for our common language and a sincere desire to utilize its potential in the most productive way possible.

The Measurement of Creativity

A review of the literature related to the measurement of creativity indicated that presently the major objective of measurement is to devise an easily administered and scored instrument which will predict creative behavior (Davis, 1975; Payne, Halpin, Ellett & Dale, 1975; McCormack, 1975; Wallbrown & Huelsman, 1975; Ward, 1975). In an investigation of instruments which purport to predict creative behavior, Davis (1975) argued that the most productive approach lies in the use of personality and biographical information. The author reported further that the Davis *How Do You Think* Creativity Inventory was internally consistent and predicted creativeness.

Payne, Halpin, Ellett, and Dale (1975) contributed further to this work when they investigated the relationship between selected personality factors and Torrance and Khatena's concept of creative personality. Payne et al. found that the highly creative academically talented reported personality characteristics of experimenting, assertive, less intelligent, shrewd, and reserved, while on the contrary the highly creative artistically talented reported personality characteristics of experimenting, assertive, self-sufficient, tender-minded and expedient. These authors concluded further that highly creative gifted groups reported personality characteristics of the academically talented.

McCormack (1975) investigated the use of figural forms in the Torrance Test of Creativity as an inherent verbal bias against very young or verbally underdeveloped children. The work of Torrance (1968) had shown that the examiner should "avoid giving examples of illustrations of 'model responses.' This tends to reduce the originality and in some cases it even reduces the number of responses produced" (Torrance, 1968). This study (McCormack, 1975), however, did not support Torrance's contention. The author found that nonverbal protocols tended to be related to experimental subjects' high scores.

In an investigation of the intercorrelation between Mednick's *Remote Associates Test* of creativity and Wallach and Kogan measures of creativity, Ward (1975) found that both measures shared little variance, and that the former measures were strongly correlated to IQ and achievement. The author reported that these data challenge Mednick's theoretical rationale of *Remote Associates Test* performance. Ward found that in children, *Remote Associates Test* performance is dependent upon characteristics different from the number of associative responses within the behavioral repertoire.

Wallbrown and Huelsman (1975) contributed further to the support of the validity of Wallach-Kogan measures of creativity when they investigated creativity operations for inner-city children. The authors reported that creativity products in two areas of visual art were collected from each child and rated by judges on originality and effectiveness of expressions. The authors found that a positive relationship was obtained between judges' ratings and creativity measures. These authors reported further that the subject sample of their investigation was different from that of the subject sample of the original Wallach-Kogan study.

The Teaching of Creativity

A review of the literature related to the teaching of creativity indicated an interest in fostering the teaching of creativity (Egan, 1975; McCormack, 1975; Park & Heisler, 1975; Parnes, 1975). In an investigation of questions that promote high-level thinking, Egan (1975) argued that most educationally valuable kinds of questions are those which give breadth and depth to understanding. Egan contributed further to this work when he developed the Structural Communication technique for the purpose of encouraging superior intellectual processes. The technique is based on a response medium from which students compose answers. The response medium takes the shape of a matrix which is comprised of answers to divergent questions on topical areas of the presented material. Egan (1975) argued that the response medium was sufficient to cover most questions asked of the material for educational purposes.

McCormack (1975) described a five-year study to investigate the inclusion of training in creative thinking in general education science courses. The author reported that the project included five experimental and five control groups of university students. Lectures for both experimental and control groups were identical, but laboratory and related take-home activities were changed. Among several items contributed by the change to the experimental group was the inclusion of instruction in the use of brainstorming. The author reported that the data derived from the administration of the Torrance Tests of Creative Thinking indicated improved fluency, flexibility and originality. Data for this same study on a science achievement test, however, were not significant.

Parnes (1975) described the development of the Creative Education Foundation's Annual Creative Problem-Solving Institute. The author reported that the foundation was able to actualize imagination expansion in the various stages of the problem-solving process. The author noted that emphasis was currently directed toward the evaluation and implementation components of problem solving.

Park and Heisler (1975) described a physical education program which emphasizes convergent and divergent thinking phases. The authors reported that the program was based on a movement and discovery method of learning, of which design was generally applicable to other subject matter.

In the investigation of the relationship between creative dramatics instruction and creativity in children, Schmidt, Goforth, and Drew (1975) randomly assigned 78 second semester kindergarten students to experimental and control groups. These authors reported that instruction consisted of half-hour sessions in creative dramatics which were held twice a week for a period of eight weeks. The authors reported that data for this study were obtained from several creativity measures adapted by Rotter, Langland, and Berger (1975) from measures by Wallach and Kogan (1965). The authors reported further that these data indicated that creative dramatics instruction produces significant differences in creativity.

Conclusion

The present study reviewed the current literature regarding the nature of creativity and presented major concerns appearing in the literature. These concerns appear to be initial steps toward a more comprehensive understanding of creativity. Further research and study will be required.

References

Cochrane, D. Teaching and creativity: A philosophical analysis. *Educational Theory*, 1975, 25, 65–73.

Davis, G. In frumious pursuit of the creative person. *Journal of Creative Behavior*, 1975, 9, 75–87.

Edmonston, P. A conceptual model of visual intelligence. *Journal of Creative Behavior*, 1975, 9, 51–60.

Egan, K. How to ask questions that promote high-level thinking. *Peabody Journal of Education*, 1975, 52, 228–234.

Frey, D. The anatomy of an idea: Creativity in counseling. *The Personnel and Guidance Journal*, 1975, 54, 23–27.

Getzels, J. Problem finding and the inventiveness of solutions. *Journal of Creative Behavior*, 1975, 9, 12–18.

Gowan, J. Trance, art, and creativity. *Journal of Creative Behavior*, 1975, 9, 1–11.

Jensen, V. Metaphorical constructs for the problem-solving process. *Journal of Creative Behavior*, 1975, 9, 113–124.

Kantor, K. Creative expression in the English curriculum: A historical perspective. *Research in the Teaching of English*, 1975, 9, 5–29.

Lake, G., and Houghton, J. Levels of creativity: An illustrative example. *Journal of Creative Behavior*, 1975, 9, 19–22.

McCormack, A. Training creative thinking in general education science. *Journal of College Science Teaching*, 1974, 4, 10–15.

McCormack, A. Nonverbal administration protocols for figural tasks of the Torrance tests of creative thinking. *Journal of Creative Behavior*, 1975, 9, 88–96.

Miller, M. The dimensions of creative prose. *Journal of Creative Behavior*, 1975, 9, 61–67.

Park, R., and Heisler, B. School programs can foster creativity through physical education. *Education*, 1975, 95, 225–228.

Parnes, S. A program for balanced growth. *Journal of Creative Behavior*, 1975, 9, 23–28.

Payne, D., Halpin, G., Ellett, C., and Dale, J. General personality correlates of creative personality in academically and artistically gifted youth. *Journal of Special Education*, 1975, 9, 105–108.

Poulson, M. Anarchy is a learning environment. *Journal of Creative Behavior*, 1975, 9, 131–136.

Rotter, L., Langland, L., and Berger, D. The validity of tests of creative thinking in seven-year-old children. *The Gifted Child Quarterly*, 1975, 15, 273–278. Cited in T. Schmidt, E. Goforth, and K. Drew, Creative dramatics and creativity: An experimental study, *Educational Theatre Journal*, 1975, 27, 111–114.

Schmidt, T., Goforth, E., and Drew, K. Creative dramatics and creativity: An experimental study. *Educational Theatre Journal*, 1975, 27, 111–114.

Tasse, C. Insight, the trouble maker: The French writers of the 20th century before creativity. *Journal of Creative Behavior,* 1975, 9, 137–146.

Torrance, E. *Directions manual and score guide: Figural test booklet B.* Princeton: Personnel Press, 1968. Cited in A. McCormack, Nonverbal administration protocols for figural tasks of the Torrance tests of creative thinking. *Journal of Creative Behavior,* 1975, 9, 88–96.

Trachtman, L. Creative people, creative times. *Journal of Creative Behavior,* 1975, 9, 35–50.

Wallach, M., and Kogan, N. Modes of thinking in young children: A study of the creativity-intelligence distinction. Cited in T. Schmidt, E. Goforth, and K. Drew, Creative dramatics and creativity: An experimental study. *Educational Theatre Journal,* 1975, 27, 111–114.

Wallbrown, F., and Huelsman, C. The validity of the Wallach-Kogan creativity operations for inner-city children in two areas of visual art. *Journal of Personality,* 1975, 43, 109–126.

Ward, W. Convergent and divergent measurement of creativity in children. *Educational and Psychological Measurement,* 1975, 35, 87–95.

26 Varieties of Creative Giftedness, Their Measurement and Development

J. P. GUILFORD

Never in its history has the human family encountered so many serious problems of so many kinds, whether in the pursuit of fulfilling the basic needs for food, shelter, and security, or in its search for better living. All genuine problem solving requires at least a minimum of creative thinking. The problem solver must take one or more novel steps in his mental functioning, and novelty is the sine qua non of creativity.

Of all the children who become the responsibility of educators, the "gifted" ones have the most probable potential for becoming effective problem solvers. The general picture, unfortunately, is that only a few of them actually fulfill such promise, either for lack of immediate need, motivation, or development of skills in creative thinking. We can educate those children either with or without the cultivation

From *The Gifted Child Quarterly* 19:2 (1975). Used by permission.

of such talents; they will ordinarily not blossom to full extent on their own.

These generalizations are supported by consistent findings of low correlations between scores from tests of creative-thinking abilities and IQ. We have the further information that although creative-thinking talent is commonly greatest among children with high IQs, high IQs *are not sufficient.* Many children with high IQs are low, even very low, in creative aptitudes (Guilford & Hoepfner, 1966; Guilford & Christensen, 1973). On the other hand, it has been abundantly shown that creative-thinking skills can be substantially increased by means of proper treatments (Parnes & Noller, 1973; Torrance, 1972).

It is a truism that if we wish to manage something we must know something about it, and the better informed we are, the more control we can achieve. The same is true of the fostering of creative problem solvers. The first thing to realize is that creative thinking is not just one mental function; it comprises quite a variety of things. If we are to know what operational steps to take in order to facilitate their development, we must take an analytical view of the problem; we must regard creative talent as a multivariate affair.

Following our early efforts to understand creative thinking in the Aptitudes Research Project at the University of Southern California in the 1950s (Wilson, Guilford, Christensen, & Lewin, 1954), we suggested applying four concepts: fluency, flexibility, originality, and elaboration. These concepts have gained a certain amount of attention in connection with investigations in psychology and education. But in the course of further research, it became apparent that there are several kinds of fluency and of the other three traits. There are different abilities of functions involved, all of which come under those broader concepts. When the structure-of-intellect model became fully developed in the late 50s, more meaningful distinctions were made among these various functions. One of the objectives of this article is to point out the distinctions among different kinds of fluency, and so on. This can best be done by making references to the structure-of-intellect (SI) model. For the benefit of some readers, it will be necessary first to say something about that model.

Intellectual Abilities in General

The geometric representation of the SI model as a cubelike figure has been shown in many places (e.g., Guilford, 1967). It represents three aspects of mental functioning, each by means of a dimension of the model. Each intellectual ability or function is distinguished from all others by having a unique combination of a certain kind of mental operation, a certain kind of informational content, and a certain kind of informational form or product. Intelligence itself is defined as a systematic collection of abilities or functions for processing different kinds of information in different ways, information differing both with respect to content (substance) and to product (mental construct). This definition has a place for creative-thinking abilities within the realm of intelligence. There is no need to contrast these two concepts, as is sometimes stated or implied.

The kinds of operations and of information now included within the SI model are given in the following lists:

Operation:
    Cognition, Memory, Divergent Production, Convergent Production, Evaluation.
Content:
    Visual-figural, Auditory-figural, Symbolic, Semantic, Behavioral.
Product:
    Unit, Class, Relation, System, Transformation, Implication.

Kinds of Intellectual Operations

The concepts in these lists will be very briefly characterized. Cognition is simply knowing, as its Greek root suggests. In terms of an information-processing psychology, it is a matter of coding or constructing items of information. The brain does this for us. The operation of memory, in this context, is merely the step of putting information into storage, of fixing it in the brain; nothing more.

The two production operations are alike in that both are very dependent upon the retrieval of information from storage. The "production" part of the terms should be emphasized. It simply means that when you are given a certain item, or items, of information you come up with other items as a consequence. Unlike the operation of cognition, which merely involves the construction of items of information, production is reaction to the cognized information. Contrary to what some writers seem to think, divergent and convergent production are not complete opposites. The significant difference is that in divergent production, the situation is more or less open. A number of different, alternative productions are logically possible and may occur. In convergent production, the given information is so restrictive that only one response is fully acceptable. Some writers have taken their cue from my early characterization, which stated that convergent production means giving "the one right answer," forgetting the productive aspect of the concept. Actually, tests of cognition, memory, and evaluation also ask for "one right answer" to each item, so this specification alone does not distinguish convergent production.

Evaluation involves comparisons and judgments. Two items of information may be compared with respect to certain criteria. We can say that they are identical, they are merely similar, or they are neither. We may say that the two are logically consistent or inconsistent, compatible or incompatible. A problem that is understood calls for a solution that has certain specifications. Thus, there is involvement with criteria of judgment, set up by those specifications. This is all a part of our general need for checking on our own behavior, which goes on all the time.

Major Kinds of Information: Content

Information comes in the five recognized codes given in the list of contents above. Other codes may be added to the list eventually, such as kinesthetic or tactual. No investigations have been made in those areas as yet in terms of distinguished abilities. Each code is a different language, in which the products are its parts of speech and particular items of its kind of information are its vocabulary. We use all of them, and we make translations from one to another constantly, insofar as vocabularies are parallel. We are intellectually multilinguals! It takes separate abilities to deal with each language.

The nature of the visual and auditory codes should be very familiar to the reader. The other codes are also actually familiar, but their labels may not be. Symbolic information is composed of signs that, in use, commonly stand for something else. Letters, words, and numbers are the most obvious examples. Semantic items of information are thoughts, when those items are not images. Images are in the figural categories. Behavioral items are psychological events that we perceive in others and in ourselves; in others indirectly by means of expressive behavior ("body language"); in ourselves directly. There is a separate, but parallel, set of abilities for each kind of content. About a hundred SI abilities have already been demonstrated by factor analysis, representing all operation and content categories, except that investigations in the auditory-figural area have been limited.

The Structures of Information: Products

It was said before that the brain structures the various products. It does this from sensory input and with the help from the memory store. So far as we know, there are only six general kinds of products. A consideration of the basic nature of each of the six kinds is interesting psychology, but that subject is beyond the space available here. I shall only briefly characterize them.

Units are things taken as wholes, without analysis. They are basic, in that all other kinds of products depend upon them, in the way of combinations, for example. Pairs of units are involved in implications and in relations. An *implication* exists in any associated pair, in which member A implies member B, as when 2 + 2 implies 4, clouds imply rain, and a smile implies friendliness. The concept of "implication" means something more than that of "association," for it involves a logical tie between two things. Two *related* things are also associated, or one implies the other, but there is a meaningful connecting link between the two, as when we know that 5 is greater than 2, that "hot" is the opposite of "cold," and Judy loves Tom.

Products usually involving three or more units are classes or systems. The "class" in this context is really a class idea. A number of things belong to the same class because they have one or more attributes in common—triangles, hats, prohibitions, etc. Cognition of classes involves abstraction and generalization. The abstracted idea is the *class*, in the context of the SI model. A *system* is an organized set of units in certain relations to one another. Most sentences are semantic systems; they are organized thoughts. Sequences of three or more things are also systems; a list of numbers or words, or a series of events. Two things only in sequence would have only the relation of before or after.

Quite different from all the others is the product of *transformation*, which is a change of some sort. Visual figures and melodies can be modified. Puns are shifts in meaning and are therefore semantic transformations. When you reinterpret the behavior of another person, you are cognizing a behavioral transformation.

Incidentally, I have been reminded that the same six kinds of products apply to all nature in general. Everything that exists is in the form of one of such products. This is only natural, when we remember that our mental experience is intended to represent the world about us. It is thus represented in the same form as it exists.

Creative Abilities in the Structure of Intellect

What has the SI model to offer toward understanding creative thinking and creative talent? It is easy to point out how the different kinds of informational content relate to spheres of creative endeavor in daily life. It is easy to show where the different kinds of operations contribute to creative problem solving, some of them more crucially than others. The provisional constructs of fluency, flexibility, originality, and elaboration can be given much more definite and useful meanings, primarily in terms of SI products.

Creative performances in human society seem to occur along the lines of the SI content categories. Those who are high in the region of visual-figural functions are likely to show preference for and superior achievement in activities and professions that stress concrete things of a visual nature—visual artists, inventors, architects, engineers, and the like. Those high in auditory abilities should have their greatest chances of success in creative output in music—composing, arranging, and stylistic performance. Productive mathematicians and developers of mathematical theory in science should be expected to excel in the symbolic abilities. Semantic abilities offer potentialities in the fields of writing, science, teaching, and planning. Creative performances of salesmen, politicians, statesmen, policemen, jurists, and teachers should reflect high behavioral abilities. These alignments do not preclude the same person excelling in more than one content field, but such geniuses as Leonardo da Vinci are rare indeed.

All the kinds of operations can make their contributions to problem solving, but some of them, the productive functions, are more critical. Although it seems to be generally recognized that divergent production (DP) contributes most to creative thinking, the value of convergent production should not be overlooked, by any means. Scientists have told us, in effect, that in their own experiences convergent production is of prime importance. This is natural, when we remember that scientists are looking for "right answers." Cognition and memory collect needed information and store it. The productive functions retrieve it and use it. Evaluation tells us whether we have interpreted the problem correctly and also whether the solution satisfies the requirements.

It is among the kinds of products of information that we find the most enlightenment concerning fluency, flexibility, originality, and elaboration. All of these constructs have been more or less tied up with the operation of divergent production, but that is not always the case. At any rate, to say that they are forms of divergent production does not help us enough in understanding them. They must be better differentiated. We do that next by means of examples from some psychological tests.

Measurement of Some Divergent-Production Abilities

The examples are taken from the author's battery of *Creativity Tests for Children* (Guilford, 1973). Most of the tests are essentially revised adult test forms that had been based upon series of factor analyses. The major changes were in rewriting instructions for the benefit of younger readers. The tests were aimed at grades four to six, but they should be usable even with adults, for no mention is made of "children" except in the examiner's manuals.

The tests are for DP abilities but are restricted to the two content areas of visual-figural and semantic, which are regarded as being of most common importance in the educational process. For the Form A battery, five of the six DP abilities are covered in each content category. In Form B, a sixth semantic test was added. The very brief descriptions of tests that follow should add meaning to what has already been said about some SI concepts, as well as providing a basis for distinguishing among the four broader constructs. The three-letter code label for each ability (in parentheses) begins with a D (for divergent production) in all cases. The second letter is F (for visual-figural) and M (for semantic content) in the two sets of tests, respectively. The third letter in each case stands for the product, and it is the initial letter of the product name. The nature of the task in each test will be stated.

Among the visual tests are:

Make Something Out of It (DFU). Given a very simple figure, such as an ellipse, name objects that could be made out of it by adding other lines.

Different Letter Groups (DFC). Given a set of eight selected capital letters, classify three of them at a time in different ways.

Making Objects (DFS). Using five given simple geometric forms, construct several different stated objects by combining those forms as needed.

Hidden Letters (DFT). Given a somewhat complex, geometriclike figure in 50 replications, use lines selected in it to form letters.

Adding Decorations (DFI). Given outline drawings of familiar objects, such as of furniture or dress, add inner lines by way of decorations.

Among the semantic tests are:

Names for Stories (DMU). Given a short outline of a story plot, suggest different appropriate titles for the story.

What To Do With It (DMC). Given the name of a common object, such as a shoe, and its common uses, list other, uncommon uses for it.

Similar Meanings (DMR). Given a familiar word, give a number of synonyms for it.

Writing Sentences (DMS). Given a set of five familiar nouns, write different sentences, each containing three of those words.

Kinds of People (DMI). Given a picture of a common object, such as a glove, name different kinds of work or occupations that it might suggest.

Picture Writing (DMT).   Given a word that has several different
meanings, or aspects, sketch roughly different figures or designs
that might represent those meanings, e.g., for the word "heavy."

For further bits of information regarding the tests it can be said
that each test is composed of two separately timed parts. Each part
contains one to four problems. The average test takes about ten
minutes to administer. Scoring is facilitated by means of detailed
scoring guides. No test is scored for more than one SI ability. The
intercorrelations are thus kept very low (averaging about .25), which
means a relatively low degree of redundancy and a high degree of
information regarding intraindividual differences.

Kinds of Fluency, Flexibility, Originality, and Elaboration

To come back to interpretations of the provisional constructs in
terms of SI products, the varieties can now be explained. In a broad
sense, all DP tests are essentially measures of fluency abilities, the
facility with which ideas are produced, the ideas being of all six kinds
of products. But, traditionally, three particular forms of fluency were
recognized, all in the semantic category. There are, of course, parallel
abilities within the figural and other content areas. The three traditional types of fluency were: ideational fluency, which was later
identified as DMU; associational fluency, which became DMR; and
expressional fluency, to become DMS. Reference to the tests just
described for those abilities will show how these ideas work out in
practice. Giving different titles for a story (Names for Stories) means
producing alternative units of semantic information, each title being
a unitary idea. In the DMR test, Similar Meanings, the relation does
not remain constant (it is that of similarity); the response relations are
varied. Giving different sentences containing repeated words, in the
Writing Sentences test, means constructing alternative semantic systems.

Two abilities for flexibility were recognized very early, but they
differed not only with respect to product but also as to kind of
content. What was called "spontaneous flexibility" had to do with
changes in direction of thinking when one is not instructed to do so,
or need not do so. This title was suggested particularly by performances in the Brick Uses test, which simply tells the examinee to list
all the uses he can think of for a common brick. The score for flexibility is the number of times that he shifts from one category of uses to
another. Now a category is a class, and when later the product of class
became recognized, it was natural to identify the ability more precisely as DMC—DP of semantic classes. A better test provides similar

tasks for a number of objects, as seen in Alternate Uses of the adult form, or What To Do With It in the children's form. In the latter cases, the common use of each object is stated, so unusual uses must be given, which means that every additional response means essentially a shift to a new class.

The other type of flexibility was labeled "adaptive" because it involved changes in direction in thinking in order to solve problems. This is characteristic of match-problem tests, in which the examinee must take away a specified number of matches, leaving a specified number of complete squares or triangles, and he must do this in a number of different ways to obtain a good score. It was later recognized that the examinee is actually producing alternative transformations in configurations of lines, and the ability is really DFT of the SI model. The children's Hidden Letters test involves taking lines given in one use or configuration and converting them to other uses or configurations, which is figural transformation.

When parallels between visual-figural and semantic abilities became recognized, it was then seen that a semantic ability that had been known as "originality" is actually the parallel ability DMT—DP of semantic transformations. In the history of this "originality" factor, it was found that one of the most faithful indicators of individual differences in it was a Plot Titles test, when it was scored for the number of clever titles listed. Responses in this test are clever in most instances because they involve transformations. The story is reinterpreted, a new emphasis is given, or a pun is involved. It had been intended that a plot-titles test would be similarly used for children, but it was found that children in grades 4–6, at least, give so few clever responses (many none at all) that its use was precluded. The test Picture Writing proved to be satisfactory for children, as a similar, Alternate Signs, test had been for adults. This test seems to require transformations of a less drastic sort.

The idea for an elaboration function came about in a general study of abilities thought to be relevant in planning. One of the tests in the study was called "Planning Elaboration," in which, given the bare outline for an organized activity, such as putting on a play for paid admissions, the examinee is to list all the detailed steps that are needed. Along with other tests, it helped to determine a factor that was called simply "elaboration." In placing this ability in the SI model later, it was realized that what the examinee is doing is to produce a variety of semantic implications. The detailed steps that he gives are all suggested by the general plan. A better test, with more control of the examinee's work and more clearly satisfying the requirements of a DMI test, is the adult form of Possible Jobs or the children's form of Kinds of People. In either case, in doing the test, the kind of work is suggested (implied) by the pictorial symbol. The test is semantic in spite of the pictorial items because the produced items are semantic.

Importance of Transformations

The unique importance of DP functions for creative thinking has been generally emphasized, but perhaps equally important is the category of transformation abilities. Not all the transformation abilities reside in the DP category. They are to be found in all the operation categories, and, of course, in all the content categories. While there are 30 DP abilities in the SI model as described earlier (six products times five operations), there are almost as many (25) in the transformation category (five operations times five contents).

Cognitions are flexible, enabling us to revise our understandings and conceptions. Without this flexibility we should often be condemned to trying to solve the wrong problem because we have conceived it incorrectly. Known transformations are put into memory storages, so we can use them again, applying them in new situations. Incidentally, it has been demonstrated that remembered transformations are of significant help even in acquiring new information from reading (Hoepfner, Guilford, & Bradley, 1970). We have already seen examples of tests of divergent production of visual and semantic transformations. But transformations can also occur in convergent production as well, as seen in mathematical and scientific thinking. And they can be evaluated, as when scoring a plot-titles test, in deciding whether titles are clever or not clever.

SI Abilities in Education

The best single source of evidence that the various SI abilities are involved in education for creative problem solving, and also that they may be enhanced by special educational procedures, comes from the report of a most significant and comprehensive experiment in higher education. Parnes and Noller (1972, 1973) established a curriculum of four semester courses in the field of "creative studies," for freshmen and sophomores at New York State University College at Buffalo. An experimental group of students (E) who took the course were matched with a control group (C) that did not; both had applied for it. About 150 in each group started in the experiment, randomly assigned to the two groups.

The special educational procedures involved instruction regarding the nature of problem solving and exercises in solving various kinds of problems. Special techniques of brainstorming, checklists, synectics, etc. were employed. Tests for nearly 40 SI abilities were administered to both groups at the ends of various semesters. As to informational content, semantic and behavioral tests were emphasized because instruction was also emphasized in those directions. As to operations, the categories of cognition, divergent production, and convergent production were strongly emphasized, since little or no improvement was expected in memory or evaluation functions.

The results showed that whereas the E and C groups were essentially on a par in initial testing, numerous gains appeared in the E group. Differences favored the E group in 23 or 24 of the semantic abilities, 16 being significant. The E group also led in 8 of 9 behavioral tests, 4 differences being significant. In none of the visual-figural tests were there significant differences, where none was expected. In 3 of 7 symbolic tests there were apparent gains, but none was significant. Thus, the predictions of probable real gains were correctly located in semantic and behavioral content areas. The E group led in 10 of 10 tests of cognition, 7 differences being significant. The same group led in 13 of 14 divergent-production tests, 9 differences being significant. Differences were in the same direction in 7 of 8 convergent-production tests, 4 being significant. Only 3 evaluation tests were given and 1 memory test, in which no differences were found. It must be admitted that those two operation categories were not well explored. There should be reason to expect some gains in evaluation, since instruction in problem solving did give some attention to this question.

The report of the Parnes-Noller experiment did not mention effects of instruction with respect to different kinds of products. There is good reason to expect gains in some of them, transformations most of all. It should be added that these investigators used other evidence outside of test behaviors to demonstrate gains from their special instruction.

It can also be added that Torrance (1972) has assembled from numerous sources evidence that special instruction in creative thinking is effective in various age groups. There is also much scattered evidence that tests of DP abilities can help materially to predict achievement in ordinary academic courses and therefore have relevance beyond efforts aimed at improved problem solving.

A Few Implications for Educational Practices

What do all these indications mean with respect to education of the gifted child? A few general suggestions can be made in connection with selection of the gifted, their guidance, and their instruction. There are others that could be made.

It is probably safe to say that the single most commonly employed basis for selection of gifted children is a high IQ on the Stanford-Binet. If what is wanted is in the form of high grade-getters, this criterion is very likely the best basis. We can now evaluate this criterion in the light of SI categories. As to operations, the S–B scale overemphasizes cognition and memory, just as traditional education has tended to do. It underplays the productive abilities and evaluation. As to contents, it is very heavy with respect to semantic information, with little attention to visual-figural information, and none to auditory-figural or behavioral information. As to kinds of products, units and systems are clearly overemphasized, and the product of classes has no attention to speak of at all. It is not very obvious, but classes are of great importance in retrieval of information from storage, and hence in the production abilities in general. The Wechsler scales, and others, take small steps toward redressing some of these imbalances, in their inclusions of more nonverbal tests, but they all fall short of covering some of the more important aspects of potential for problem solving.

Thus, IQ scales may well be regarded as insufficient, with needs for supplementation with tests of other kinds. It could even be suggested that IQ tests could be replaced by semantic-divergent-production tests in the selection of the gifted, because of the one-way relation between the two kinds of measurement (Guilford, 1973). That is, we find that individuals who are very high on DP tests are almost sure to be high also in IQ, whereas those who are high in IQ are not sure to be high in DP abilities; indeed, they may be low. The nature of the supplementation of IQ scales would have to be decided with respect to the kinds of gifted that are wanted. Knowledge of SI abilities should offer a systematic guide. Unfortunately, there are as yet a limited number of standardized and published tests of SI abilities. For SI abilities that happen to be represented in IQ scales, Meeker (1969) has suggested ways of assessment of those abilities from the Stanford-Binet and Wechsler scales.

Guidance of the gifted child would depend in part upon knowledge of his profile on tests of SI abilities. His progress in development in various directions could become known through periodic testing on those abilities. The abilities are basic, so that information regarding development on any one of them should suggest a degree of progress in a whole class of mental performances.

As for implications of SI for instruction, certain things could be suggested as to procedures for teaching the gifted and nongifted alike. I have done so elsewhere (Guilford, 1968). They would take too much space here. Points at which knowledge of SI functions can be usefully applied can be readily found in curriculum construction, in making lesson plans, and in classroom activities. This is not to forget examinations, which should be used liberally extensively to provide feedback information for the student so that he may evaluate his own learning and correct his mistakes. Special attention to teaching the nature of problem solving, as well as special exercises in thinking, should have a place. Workbooks that provide material for such exercises have been prepared for adults by Parnes (1967) and for children by Meeker, Sexton, and Richardson (1970), for example. In this connection, I have advocated, and I still do, that the student be taught about the nature of his own intellectual resources, so that he may gain more control over them.

Summary

This article has emphasized the importance of conceiving creative giftedness in an analytical manner. Detailed conceptions enlarge considerably our possibilities of enhancing creative problem solving, in a world that badly needs it. This view finds systematic places for creative-thinking abilities or functions within the realm of intelligence. The traditional constructs of fluency, flexibility, originality, and elaboration were broken down in terms of structure-of-intellect abilities, which were illustrated by reference to a new battery of creativity tests for children. Some implications were suggested for selecting and educating gifted children.

References

Guilford, J. P. *The Nature of Human Intelligence.* New York: McGraw-Hill, 1967.

Guilford, J. P. *Intelligence, Creativity, and Their Educational Implications.* San Diego: Knapp, 1968.

Guilford, J. P. *Creativity Tests for Children.* Orange, Cal.: Sheridan Psychological Services, 1973.

Guilford, J. P., and Christensen, P. R. The one-way relation between creative potential and IQ. *Journal of Creative Behavior,* 1973, 7, 247–252.

Guilford, J. P., and Hoepfner, R. Creative potential as related to measures of IQ and verbal comprehension. *Indian Journal of Psychology,* 1966, 41, 7–16.

Hoepfner, R., Guilford, J. P., and Bradley, P. A. Transformation of information in learning. *Journal of Educational Psychology,* 1970, 61, 316–323.

Meeker, M. N. *The Structure of Intellect: Its Interpretation and Uses.* Columbus, Ohio: Charles E. Merrill Publishing Co., 1969.

Meeker, M. N., Sexton, K., and Richardson, M. O. *SOI abilities workbook.* Los Angeles: Loyola-Marymount University, 1970.

Parnes, S. J. *Creative Behavior Workbook*. New York: Scribners' Sons, 1967.

Parnes, S. J. and Noller, R. B. Applied creativity: The creative studies project. Part II: Results of the two-year program. *Journal of Creative Behavior*, 1972, 6, 164–186.

Parnes, S. J., and Noller, R. B. *Toward Supersanity: Channeled Freedom*. Buffalo: D.O.K., 1973.

Torrance, E. P. Can we teach children to think creatively? *Journal of Creative Behavior*, 1972, 6, 114–143.

Wilson, R. C., Guilford, J. P., Christensen, P. R., and Lewin, D. J. A factor-analytic study of creative-thinking abilities. *Psychometrika*, 1954, 19, 297–311.

27 Creativity and its Educational Implications for the Gifted

E. PAUL TORRANCE

After studying, experimenting, exploring, talking, and writing for over ten years about the educational implications of creativity for the gifted, it would seem that I should be able to set forth these implications clearly and neatly. In fact, I have been looking forward to doing this.

Now, I find the task an impossible one. As I sat down to look back at the work of the past ten years, no such encompassing synthesis would come. Instead, new and incomplete but exciting and absorbing ideas possessed me. I kept trying to fight them off and started to list the implications of one of my earliest findings concerning the identification of the creatively gifted (Torrance, 1962): if one uses only an intelligence test and thereby identifies the upper twenty percent as gifted, he would miss seventy percent of those who would be identified as falling in the top twenty percent on tests of creative thinking ability. In spite of many attempts by high status authorities in several fields to explain this fact away, it remains virtually unchanged. The seventy percent figure is surprisingly constant in hun-

From E. Paul Torrance, "Creativity and Its Educational Implications for the Gifted," *The Gifted Child Quarterly*, Vol. 12 (1968), pp. 67–78. Reprinted by permission of the author and *The Gifted Child Quarterly*.

dreds of studies, at different age levels, in different subcultures, using different tests of intelligence, and with different measures of creative thinking ability. Educators have not yet dared to dream of even the most obvious implications of this single finding. In fact, I found my own mind blocked and unwilling to continue my listing of implications.

Suddenly, I realized that my predicament was a very predictable one. Creativity is something infinite, and its possibilities can never be exhausted! Finally, I relaxed and allowed five of the most persistent and urgent of the implications that kept fighting for expression to take possession of me. Then, I became afraid.

I know that these implications will not be widely accepted. At best, I can formulate them only incompletely. I have been toying with these five ideas for several years, however, and they will not let me alone. Therefore, I give them to you incomplete, only partially tested, and controversial.

Necessary to Look to the Creatively Gifted Disadvantaged

I am especially hesitant to express the most persistent and urgent of the implications that have possessed me. For some time, I have been experiencing a dawning realization that in the future we shall have to depend upon creatively gifted members of disadvantaged and minority cultures for most of our creative achievements. In a way, this may have been true all along. To be a part of the advantaged, dominant culture, a person frequently has to sacrifice too much of his perception of reality and his search for the truth to make much of a creative contribution. Our creative achievers will be those who accept only those parts of the dominant culture which are true and who hold on to their individuality and their minority or disadvantaged culture. It will be they who possess the "different" element, the "divine discontent," and the clearness of vision to see that "the king wears no clothes."

I could cite famous examples from history to show how creative breakthroughs have come from disadvantaged groups. Critics would say immediately that this could never occur in our modern, technological, space age culture. Almost daily, however, dramatic examples quietly find their way into the news. Let me review three recent ones.

The March 25, 1968, *National Observer* reports an interesting item from Birmingham, Alabama, that seems to have been ignored by newspapers in the South. The bold experiments of a 17-year-old Negro boy, Bracie Watson, had stirred cautious excitement among scientists of the University of Alabama Medical Center. Bracie is confident that an animal ovum can be fertilized, and develop as an embryo outside the mother animal's womb.

Bracie Watson is the son of a mechanic and a schoolteacher. He first attracted attention in Birmingham as a ninth grader when he won a science contest with a successful skin graft involving chickens. He could not enter the regional contest then because Negroes were barred from competition. Later, by telephone and personal calls, he sought laboratory space at the University Medical Center to transplant a kidney from one dog to another. Members of the Center staff recognized Bracie's unusual creative scientific potential and approved his request. His kidney-transplant experiments eventually succeeded, and one dog with a transplanted kidney has since had puppies.

In the eleventh grade Bracie went to work on developing an artificial womb. He had read of the problem some mothers have in bringing their babies to full term. He speculated that in some instances a baby's chances would be improved if it could be moved to an artificial womb.

The embryologist with whom Bracie worked pronounced the whole approach as brazenly naive. This did not stop Bracie, however. He kept rat embryos alive as long as 14 hours in an artificial womb. They normally would have died within minutes after removal from the mother's womb. "He's unusual," said Dr. Ed Weller, the embryologist. When he is graduated from high school, Bracie plans to accept a full four-year scholarship to the University of Alabama and to pursue a doctorate in biochemistry.

The March 17, 1968, issue of the *Los Angeles Times,* in one of its articles on the "Brown Beret" or "Brown Power" movement in the high schools, tells some of the story of Dr. Julian Nava, the only Mexican-American on the Los Angeles Board of Education. One of the major complaints of the"Brown Beret" leaders was that Mexican-Americans and Negroes in the Los Angeles schools have been and still are being shunted by counselors and administrators into industrial arts classes and not permitted to enroll in college preparatory classes.

When asked if there is any validity to these complaints, Dr. Nava replied, "I was graduated from Roosevelt High in 1945. I was told to take auto shop. And I did. I did as I was told. Then I went into the Navy—and I wasn't a Mexican anymore, I was just Julian. It opened my eyes."

Dr. Nava continued, "But then in the Navy I was an auto mechanic —so I can't say that the advice was all bad. A lot of those decisions were based on what the high school counselors considered a 'realistic assessment of the chances of success.' They realized the chances, then, of a Mexican-American getting through college. I'm just worried for fear they're still making those 'realistic assessments.' I just wonder how many other Julians have ended up in auto shop, somewhere, and stayed there."

Dr. Nava, now 40, attained his Ph.D. in history at Harvard.*

The members of the "Brown Beret" are asking that they be given a chance to know their history and their culture. They are asking for compulsory bilingual and bicultural education and for teachers who know something of the Mexican cultural heritage and recognize their cultural traditions. They are asking for textbooks that show Mexican contributions to society, show the injustices they have experienced, and concentrate on Mexican folklore. They are asking for more effective testing procedures to identify potentialities for purposes of grouping and guidance. They are asking for more library materials in Spanish and that all school facilities be made more fully available to them for educational purposes.

The April 7, 1968, issue of the *Atlanta Constitution* reported a story about a Georgia native, Negro singer James Brown. Only a few years ago, James Brown had been a shoeshine boy in Augusta, Georgia. During the rioting following the death of Martin Luther King, Jr., Brown had gone on television and radio in the nation's capital to appeal for an end to looting and rioting. He pled, "Don't burn, give the kids a chance to learn. Don't terrorize—organize."

He continued, "I used to shine shoes on the steps of station WRDW in Augusta. I think we started at three cents, then five cents and six cents, never did get a dime. But today I own that station. That is Black Power. I didn't get a chance to finish the seventh grade, but I made it. I made it because you were with me and because I had honesty, and dignity, and pride."

There are many problems involved in implementing implications concerning creatively disadvantaged children. There are many problems of identification. The facts are that we do not do a very good job of identifying the gifted among disadvantaged groups of all kinds —Negroes, Mexican-American, Navajos, Zunis, Chippewas, Cherokees, hillbillies, the deaf, and the blind. Even the *Torrance Tests of Creative Thinking* (Torrance, 1966) are sensitive enough to make one aware of otherwise unnoticed potentialities among them. For example, I believe that populations of deaf children harbor many unusually creative persons. It took that wild and discredited "science" of phrenology to conquer the superstitious belief that deaf-mutes were utterly beyond the reach of human aid (Bakan, 1968). A phrenological analysis of Laura Bridgman's skull "proved" that she had an active, intelligent brain and as a consequence she became the first deaf-mute to be systematically educated. It is my hope that another

---

*[*Editor's update:* Dr. Nava (1978) is now professor at California State University (Northridge), and a member of the Los Angeles School Board.]

set of discredited techniques, the *Torrance Tests of Creative Thinking*, may play a role in showing that deaf-mutes can think creatively and can make useful creative contributions. I believe a start has been made. Dr. Rawley Silver has administered the figural tests of creative thinking to some of his deaf art students, and I would describe many of their performances as being phenomenal. Silver, however, has been unable to obtain much cooperation from rehabilitation authorities in helping these gifted youngsters receive training. Their scores on verbally oriented intelligence and achievement tests are so low that they are regarded as uneducable.

Not only are there difficulties in identifying creatively gifted children among disadvantaged groups, there are still more serious difficulties in providing them with professional help that will make more frequent the happy accidents of the Bracie Watsons, the James Browns, and the Julian Navas. In fact, there have been almost no sustained, systematic professional attempts to do this. One such pioneering effort is Dr. George Witt's LEAP, or Life Enrichment Activity Program for creatively gifted, disadvantaged Negro children. Now, Witt says that it was nothing but a miracle that any of the original 16 children in the program remained (Golden, 1967). He observed, "We had nothing but trouble at first. The kids teased and berated each other." He described how one of the little girls came in the first day and looked at her reflection in the mirror and said, "You're nothin and nobody, and you're always gonna be nothin and nobody." They could not believe it when someone selected them because they were special and that they are somebodies. These children have made amazing strides in learning and in creative achievement. Critics maintain that any child, given as much attention as Witt's youngsters have been given, would develop their creative talents. To this criticism, Witt replied, "They say of course that it can be done but no one has ever done it. I'm interested in proving that it can be done." For his attention, Witt chose creatively gifted, disadvantaged children. At the University of Georgia, Dr. Catherine Bruch, the coordinator of our programs in the area of the gifted, has chosen the gifted disadvantaged as an area of emphasis.

Creatively Handicapped and Special Education

As my second implication, I am suggesting that the "creatively handicapped" be adopted as a new category in the field of Special Education of Exceptional Children. I know that it will impress even this sympathetic audience as a wild idea. Actually, the logic for this implication is rather clear. There are many children whose behavior problems stem from the differences their abilities create between them and other children and between them and their teachers. Their learning difficulties arise from the incompatibility between their abilities and learning preferences on one hand and the teaching methods and system of rewards of the school on the other. If brought together with other creatively gifted youngsters, they would no longer be misfits. If taught in ways compatible with their abilities and interests their achievement might soar.

Those of us who have been interested in special provisions for gifted children have frequently been told that it is hopeless to expect support for improved programs of education for them. Critics have said that the plight of the mentally retarded, the blind, the deaf, and the crippled arouses sympathy. They argue that the gifted are well endowed and can take care of themselves. Apparently they have been blinded to the countless tragedies of gifted children who are powerless to help themselves and are the object of hate and agression. The letters I receive from creatively gifted young people and parents of creatively gifted children tell me that they are wrong.

Recently, Robert E. Samples (1967) in *Saturday Review* gave us the tremendously sensitive and disturbing story of Kari, whose handicap was her creativity. Samples wrote that Kari appears strange to the conformity-cloistered society around her. He said that she creates a guilt in the cliché-makers which they transform to resentment. They pressure her in the direction of the norm and her resistance is interpreted as immaturity and stubbornness that must be overcome. Kari was the one student in her class who defended the heroine in Hawthorne's *The Scarlet Letter* for having the courage to be apart from the society and at the same time damned her for being dishonest to herself. In the ensuing argument, she contended that virtue was in doing what had to be done, rather than "obeying like a starved rat the corridors of a maze somebody else built." The frightened teacher gave her a "D" for her participation. Samples concluded that "We need the Karis, all of them, but how can they be saved? The simplicity of the answer is as frightening as it is demanding: We must be more like Kari" (Samples, 1967; p. 74).

My response to Samples' solution is that it is too idealistic. It will be too long before we can develop any large number of teachers who can become like Kari, teachers who can be truly empathetic with creatively handicapped children. In programs of special education, I believe that it is reasonable to expect that we can develop enough teachers for special programs for creatively handicapped-gifted children who are serious misfits in regular classrooms and school programs.

Although the logic of this idea is quite reasonable to me, I realize that most educators will place it in the category of science fiction. In fact, a recent issue of *Analog Science Fiction* (Foray, 1968) gives us an excellent idea of how a school for creatively handicapped-gifted children might be established and implemented. The children in Thorley School of the *Analog* story were ESP gifted. The teachers were also gifted and trained in ESP. This was not known to the public, however, and the school was privately endowed. Public school psychologists and counselors referred to Thorling the children they could not get through to, especially the kindergarteners they did not even wish to try to get through to. Thorling School accepted some of these and rejected others. When asked to explain the school's criteria for acceptance, the principal explained, "We take the children we can help." The children they could help, of course, were the ESP gifted. Their behavior problems usually came from the differences their ESP abilities created between them and other children. There were, of course, problems with accreditation, and the *Analog* story revolves about a visit from the accrediting board. All of the children cooperated to conceal the fact that Thorling was a school for the ESP gifted and used their ESP abilities to do so. Their conclusion, however, was that people lacking this sensitivity were so unaware of the ESP abilities of others that no efforts are required to hide such abilities.

Need for a "Time-Out" of School

At a time when there is national concern about reducing school dropouts, it is perhaps dangerous to suggest that any group of children or adolescents be encouraged or permitted to drop out, even temporarily. Therefore, I shall use the term "time-out" and suggest that we institutionalize it in such a way that such children would still be in school, just outside of the curriculum.

A number of people who have studied the school experiences of people who have made historically important creative achievements have noted that many of these eminent people had had time-outs. These time-outs are periods when the normal activities of school were suspended and the boy or girl had a free period in which to think, plan, read unrestrainedly, or meet a new group of people under new circumstances. Goertzel and Goertzel (1962) estimated that at least ten percent of the 400 notables in their study described a "time-out" period which significantly influenced their later development. They specifically cited Winston Churchill, John F. Kennedy, H. G. Wells, Charles Evans Hughes, William Randolph Hearst, Richard Byrd, Edna St. Vincent Millay, Louis Brandeis, Marie Curie, and others. Among present-day notables, Edwin Land is one who dropped out of school and came up with a number of inventions, including Polaroid.

I have long been impressed with the high incidence of time-outs in the lives of the world's notables, and I can even claim a time-out of my own of about six months to recover from the aftermath of a ruptured appendix at age ten. I have known many creatively gifted children and adolescents in trouble for whom I would like to have prescribed a time-out. As a consequence, I have wondered how such time-outs could be institutionalized in such a way that chances of success would not be ruined for the child or adolescent involved.

I must admit that I was too fainthearted to suggest such a procedure until I learned about Elizabeth Drews' (1968) experience with Fernwood in Oregon. In the Colton (Oregon) Consolidated School, 24 students were randomly selected from grades 7, 8 and 9. Two very capable teacher-counselors told these young people as they sat in their bare classroom that they could make theirs the kind of school they wanted. "They could find out what was important to them and then work on what was important." The arrangement of the room and what it was to contain was up to them. Since the experiment began in September, the out-of-school environment proved to be irresistible. When the students realized that they were really free to choose, they reveled in it. Only one or two of the students would sit through even the most dynamic lecture prepared by the teachers. In the free environment of Fernwood, they sought out personal refuges, sometimes in groups, but often singly.

The most confirmed low achiever and general misfit, according to Drews, was a boy of 16—a nonreader with a tested IQ that placed him in the moron category. He was generally belligerent and was mean to younger students. He had been thrown out of school repeatedly and had come back more resistant to learning each time. He had been an habitual truant but his attendance at Fernwood was perfect. At first he spent all of his time outdoors. Gradually he gained enough peace of mind to overcome his aversion to school and to enter the classroom. Then, as Drews wrote, "By dint of alchemy or miracle (and perhaps with the aid of a stack of 200 plus or minus comic books) he learned to read. Next he began to become social. He learned to play chess, occasionally beating his teachers. By the time the experiment was abandoned in December because of cancellation of funds, he had become an excellent conversationalist who could talk about war and peace as well as the vagaries of the weather. A year after the program ended, he was spending half of each day helping mentally retarded children in a special room, and he is known for his gentleness and loving ways."

At Fernwood, there was time to listen to music, build things, plan trips and go on them, read books and talk about them, and form natural and meaningful interpersonal relationships. At home, these youngsters had usually been engaged in endless chores. At school, relentless bells had dictated when the mind was to be turned on and off and what words their eyes were to focus upon. The curriculum was text-centered and fact-oriented. Talk, except in recitations, was regarded as idle chatter, discouraged in the classrooms, and forbidden in the halls. At Fernwood, there was freedom to dream and envision what one might be and become. The warmth and trust of the teachers finally won over the more reluctant students.

Many exciting things occurred during Fernwood's four-month existence. A nonreader began to read without the pressure of applied methods and scheduled class periods. Those who had habitually failed English discovered that they could speak fluently and well when they could talk about something of interest. A boy who had been indifferent to mathematics did four months of work in three days and ended up six weeks ahead of his former classmates. They became aware of changes in themselves and near the end of the term commented that they had not destroyed property at Fernwood—not even those who had been the most hardened marauders. One of them said, "I was not closed in at Fernwood. I wasn't in a cage or cell, so I didn't need to destroy." These students did not "lose ground" by being out of the regular school program for four months. All except two of them did better work and received higher grades upon return to school than they had done prior to the free experience.

Free to learn in their own ways about things that they wanted to know, the students made almost all of the suggestions of things to do. Some of them became so addicted to reading that parents complained. Four girls decided to go to England to widen their horizon and searched diligently and in vain for jobs for 14-year-olds. They decided to become columnists and began writing a teen-age column which they sold to the local paper. Later a publisher of teen-ager paper "discovered" their talent and one of them was asked to become his editor. Only history will reveal what else is yet to come from this rather bold experiment.

I am sure that not all students—or even all creatively gifted students—need time-outs. I suspect, however, that many of them do and would profit thereby. Neither am I saying that it must be set up as Elizabeth Drews described in the Oregon experiment. Time-outs can be provided in many ways. For Fannie Hurst (1967), it was provided by her assistant principal. She was frequently "sent up to his office" for many minor misdemeanors such as prompting other students, reading extraneous books during study hours, and writing essays for classmates in exchange for geometry homework. The assistant principal showed little interest in her violations but, as she described, "he diagnosed and articulated for her much of the groping confusion that must have been responsible for her itchy malaise" (Hurst, 1967; p. 26). He talked with her about her major interest, writing, and gave her guidance in her reading. He read the "literary efforts" she produced in his office as disciplinary measures and encouraged her to follow her inclinations to write. She continued to devise misdemeanors so that she would be "sent up to his office." These experiences gave her a kind of time-out.

Sponsors and Patrons Outside the School

Almost always wherever independence and creativity occur and result in outstanding creative achievement, there has been some other individual who played the role of "sponsor or patron." This role is played by someone who is not a member of the peer group, but who possesses prestige and power in the same social system. He does several things. Regardless of his own views, the sponsor encourages and supports the creative young person in expressing and testing his ideas and in thinking through things for himself. He protects the individual from the reactions of his peers and of authorities long enough for him to try out some of his ideas and become productive.

In the past, I have suggested to school psychologists, school counselors, and principals that they were in positions to play the role of sponsor or patron to creatively gifted children. After much thought and over twelve years of experience trying to play this role as major adviser to certain graduate students, I have developed doubts that professional personnel within the school can really play this role very successfully. Graduate advisers and other school and university personnel may occasionally have to go to bat for a creatively gifted student. Many times they may succeed. I doubt, however, that the sponsor role can be sustained successfully by professional personnel within a school without damage to the school and the child. What I believe would be more productive would be for professional personnel to help creatively gifted children find sponsors or patrons in the community.

Dr. George Witt, in his project with creatively gifted disadvantaged children, has demonstrated the feasibility of this idea. In his first summer program, Witt found community sponsors for each of his creatively gifted, disadvantaged children (Torrance & Witt, 1966). One boy worked with an architect at his office once a week. One girl met three hours a week with a creative clothing designer to design and make her own clothes. One boy met once a week with the head of an audiovisual center; another visited a professor of zoology once a week to learn how to write a poem. One girl visited a newspaper reporter and identified herself as a "woman of the press." One boy met weekly with an attorney to discuss some of his interesting cases.

In Witt's continuing programs, arrangements have been made for a creative family to sponsor each child. These families invited the creative disadvantaged children to do creative things with them during week-ends. This program has now been expanded and many exciting and worthwhile outcomes have resulted. I believe that such experiences can be integrated into school programs. If not, perhaps the provision of sponsors for highly creative children might become a challenging task for local chapters of the National Association for Gifted Children!

Using the Built-In Motivation of Creative Learning

Now that many American schools have seriously assumed the task of educating all children, we are suddenly aware that there is a "motivation gap." There is a gap between what children want to learn and what the schools want to teach them. This motivation gap is perhaps especially acute for many creative youngsters. What they need most of all, of course, is the built-in motivation of creative ways of learning. The education of all children could be vastly improved, in my opinion, by making much greater use than there now is of the built-in motivation power of creative ways of learning. For creative children, it is essential.

We can usually improve almost any kind of human functioning, increase learning rates, or change undesirable behavior to more desirable behavior in most persons by increasing or decreasing motivation in the form of external pressures (rewards and punishments). Most educators think of motivation only in this sense. With unmotivated learners and low achievers, especially the highly creative ones, it has been my observation that external pressures, whether in the form of reward or punishment, rarely promote desirable behavior. In fact, we can seldom "make" a creative student learn, achieve, or work harder, if he chooses not to do so. With some children and adults, the more we reward them the worse they behave and the less they learn, and likewise the more we punish them the worse they behave. I am convinced that this is frequently true of highly creative children.

Even when reward and/or punishment succeed temporarily, they do not supply the inner motivation necessary for continued achievement. Such motivation is short-lived and requires continuous reapplication. The inner stimulation from creative ways of learning makes the reapplication of rewards and punishments unnecessary. Although rewards are less erratic as motivators than punishment, they are still quite erratic in motivating learning.

Man is an inquisitive, exploring kind of being, who cannot keep his restless mind inactive even when there are no problems to be solved.

He seems to be unable to keep from digging into things, turning ideas over in his mind, trying out new combinations, searching for new relationships and struggling for new insights. Man's search for beauty —the aesthetic—is almost as relentless. A particular individual may not search for beauty in a painting or in a sonata. Maslow (1954) learned from a young athlete that a perfect tackle could be as aesthetic a product as a sonnet and could be approached in the same spirit of creativity and achievement. From a housewife, he says that he learned that a first-rate soup is more aesthetic and represents a higher level of achievement than a second-rate painting. From a psychiatrist, he learned of the aesthetic delight in his everyday job of helping people create themselves.

I have tried to identify the most essential characteristics of educational methods that provide the self-motivating influences of creative ways of learning. Perhaps the most essential of these is incompleteness or openness. Many outstanding creative people have commented upon the power of incompleteness in motivating achievement. Ben Shahn (1959), in discussing his creativity in painting, described how he traps images like some inventors trap ideas. He explained that these images are not complete, saying, "If I had a complete image I think I would lose interest in it." To him, the most rewarding thing about painting is the exploration and discovery that he finds. Compton (1953), in his case studies of Nobel prize winners in science, concluded that it is not the love of knowledge but the love of adding to knowledge that is important in motivation for achievement.

A pupil may encounter incompleteness outside of school and this may motivate his achievement, or he may encounter incompleteness in the classroom. The incompleteness may be encountered in pictures, stories, objects of instruction, the behavioral settings of the classroom, or in structured sequences of learning activities. In my current work with five-year-olds, I encourage children to see all knowledge as incomplete. I show them a picture or read them a story and then I ask them to think about all of the things that the picture or the story does not tell about the events described and then to ask questions about these things. In answering their questions, information is frequently given as incomplete. The incompleteness and changing nature of the objects presented are emphasized.

Perhaps my own favorite strategy of building in motivation in a learning activity through creative processes is to have the learner produce something—a drawing, a story, a papier-maché animal, etc. —and then to do something with what they have produced. This is a central feature in the ideabooks for elementary and junior high school pupils created by Myers and me (1965a, 1965b, 1965c, 1965d, 1966) and the Imagi/Craft materials created by Cunnington and me

(1965). This is also a central feature of the *Just Supposing* exercises I am developing now for use with preprimary children.

Educational and psychological literature is filled with successful experiences in which creative writing has motivated still other kinds of learning. Maya Pines (1967), after surveying the leading programs for teaching preprimary children to read, concluded that all of the most successful ones had one thing in common. They all elicit the child's creativity by letting him make up his own words and stories almost from the beginning.

Just why educational methods in which children produce something that leads to doing other things are so powerful in motivating additional learning and creative achievement is not altogether clear. Some people maintain that the power of such methods comes from the fact that human life is meaningless without creativity and that consequently creativity excites creativity. Truly creative poetry can stimulate the scientist and the creative insight of the scientist can stimulate the poet. Others (Flanagan, 1959) have explained that the more creative acts we experience, whether they are our own or those of others, the more we live, and anything that makes a person more fully alive is likely to facilitate creative achievement. Some creative products, however, are far more powerful than others in motivating achievement. Mary O'Neill's (1961) *Hailstones and Halibut Bones,* for example, seems almost always to impel children to write poems about color, experiment with color, and find out things about color. The creative productions of one child also seem to impel others to similar efforts. Perhaps this is because they present a challenge that is within attainment. It may be that their very imperfections motivate achievement.

A third kind of built-in motivation is to be found in the questions children ask. The child's "wanting to know" is reflected in the number and kinds of questions he asks.

By the time a child enters school for the first time he is on his way to learning the skills of finding out by asking questions. When he enters school, however, the teacher begins asking all the questions and the child has little chance to ask questions. Furthermore, the teacher's questions are rarely asked to gain information. The teacher almost always knows the answer. Real questions for information are rare. Questions asked in the classroom are usually to find out whether the child knows something that the teacher knows.

Just imagine how stimulating it would be if teachers really asked children for information! If teachers did this, children would ask questions far more freely and with greater skill and excitement. Pupils and teachers would be kept busy finding out what they want to know.

Even if motivation for learning and achievement is intense and sustained, there is still a need for guidance. Unless there is some guidance and direction from the teacher, most children will cease to develop after a certain stage and will become discouraged. Creative ways of learning, in fact, call for the most sensitive kind of guidance and direction possible. They call for intense listening and observing and giving the kind of guidance that will make all honest efforts to learn and achieve rewarding enough to sustain motivation. The teacher must deal with the disparagement, ridicule, and criticism of the other children.

Perhaps the most important thing for the teacher or parent of a creative child to remember, however, is that once learning and achievement have been motivated, it is dangerous to stop them. The teacher's aim should be to seek out the child's own best motivations and possibilities and guide these to the most fruitful development. Halting strongly motivated learning is like caging a bird in the act of migration. It is useless to offer him crumbs and berries. He will leave them untouched and beat his wings against the bars of the cage until he is given the free air and sky. Rewarding desirable behavior and punishing undesirable behavior in creative children are to no avail!

References

Atlanta Journal Washington Bureau. "Georgia Soul Singer Pleads for Race Peace." *Atlanta Journal—Constitution,* April 7, 1968.

Bakan, D. "Is Phrenology Foolish?" *Psychology Today,* Vol. 1, No. 2 (1968), pp. 44–51.

Compton, A. H. "Case Histories: Creativity in Science." In E. P. Torrance, *The Nature of Creative Thinking.* New York: Industrial Relations Institute, 1953.

Cunnington, B. F., and Torrance, E. P. *Imagi/Craft Series.* Boston: Ginn and Company, 1965.

Drews, Elizabeth M. "Fernwood: A Free School" (mimeographed). Portland: Portland State College, 1968.

Flanagan, D. "Creativity in Science." In P. Smith (Ed.), *Creativity,* pp. 103–9. New York: Hastings House, Publishers, Inc., 1959.

Foray, V. "Practice!" *Analog Science Fiction,* February 1968, pp. 139–60.

Goertzel, V., and Goertzel, Mildred G. *Cradles of Eminence.* Boston: Little, Brown and Co., 1962.

Golden, T. "LEAP: An Experiment in Creativity for Gradeschoolers." *Sunday Pictorial, New Haven (Conn.) Register,* February 19, 1967, pp. 6–9.

Hurst, Fannie. "The Melody Lingers On." In M. L. Ernst (Ed.), *The Teacher,* pp. 23–28. Englewood Cliffs, N.J.: Prentice-Hall, Inc., 1967.

McFadden, J. M. "Bracie's Science Project Startles the Professionals." *The National Observer,* March 25, 1968.

Maslow, A. H. *Motivation and Personality.* New York: Harper & Row, Publishers, 1954.

Myers, R. E., and Torrance, E. P. *Can You Imagine?* Boston: Ginn and Company, 1965. (a)

Myers, R. E., and Torrance, E. P. *Invitations to Thinking and Doing.* Boston: Ginn and Company, 1965. (b)

Myers, R. E., and Torrance, E. P. *Invitations to Speaking and Writing Creatively.* Boston: Ginn and Company, 1965. (c)

Myers, R. E., and Torrance, E. P. *For Those Who Wonder.* Boston: Ginn and Company, 1965. (d)

Myers, R. E., and Torrance, E. P. *Plots, Puzzles, and Ploys.* Boston: Ginn and Company, 1966.

O'Neill, Mary. *Hailstones and Halibut Bones.* Garden City, N. Y.: Doubleday & Co., Inc., 1961.

Pines, Maya. *Revolution in Learning.* New York: Harper & Row, Publishers, 1967.

Samples, R. E. "Kari's Handicap—The Impediment of Creativity." *Saturday Review,* July 15, 1967, pp. 56–57, 74.

Shahn, B. "On Painting." In *The Creative Mind and Method,* pp. 20–21. Cambridge, Mass.: WGBH—FM, 1959.

Torgerson, D. "Start of a Revolution? 'Brown Power' Unity Seen behind School Disorders." *Los Angeles Times,* March 17, 1968, section C, pp. 1–5.

Torrance, E. P. *Guiding Creative Talent.* Englewood Cliffs, N.J.: Prentice-Hall, Inc., 1962.

Torrance, E. P. *Torrance Tests of Creative Thinking: Norms-Technical Manual.* Research ed. Princeton, N.J.: Personnel Press, Inc., 1966.

Torrance, E. P., and Witt, G. P. "Experimental Grouping on the Basis of Creative Abilities and Motivations." *The Gifted Child Quarterly,* Vol. 10 (1966), pp. 9–14.

Witt, G. P. *The Life Enrichment Activity Program: A Community Children's Culture Center.* Hamden, Conn.: George P. Witt, 1965.

28   Major Directions in Creativity Research

JOE KHATENA

The 1950s seem to be the cut of years differentiating the meager from the prolific investigatory activities in the area of creativity.

From *The Gifted Child Quarterly* 20:3 (1976). Used by permission.

Although creativity was of research interest before the 1950s and empirical investigations concerning creative genius may have sprung from Galton's study of hereditary genius, the exploration tended to pivot on philosophical speculation and anecdotal reports of creative mental functioning like Wallas' four-step creative problem-solving model (preparation, incubation, illumination, and revision), Grippen's study of the creative artistic imagination of children between the ages of 3 and 7, Rossman's studies of inventors, and Lehman's study dealing with problems of age and productivity.

Little had been done to measure the creative thinking abilities of children, adolescents, and adults except in terms of ingenuity and originality (see Guilford, 1967; Torrance, 1962). It seems as if the lack of a scientific model for the study of creativity hindered the development of this discipline. Although the spirit of the times had its own share in energizing such study, Guilford's Presidential Address to the American Psychological Association in 1950 on the Structure of Intellect Model, with attention given to the hitherto neglected divergent thinking abilities within that model, appears to have lit the fuse for the explosion of knowledge and research in the area of creativity.

The development of creativity research has progressively accelerated over the years, despite criticism from some quarters (e.g., McNemar, 1964; Thorndike, 1963; Wallach, 1968, 1973). This research has primarily been concerned with theory and definition of creativity relative to its identification and measurement with attendant problems, population differences, cross-cultural patterns, and a few other directions of research.

Theory of Creativity

The complexity of the concept of creativity has been recognized by many in the field (e.g., Gowan, 1972; Roweton, 1973; Torrance, 1974) and has been the source of apprehension and misgivings especially in terms of its measurement correlates. There is considerable lack of agreement over the definition of the term (Torda, 1970), since the word "creativity" has, through usage, become associated with many aspects of creative behavior and mental functioning that range along a cognitive-emotive continuum. The problem of definition is compounded by variant descriptions of the energy source of creativity, each dependent on the several existing theoretical models of human functioning.

In addition, each person who takes an interest in creativity naturally gets interested in a particular way; that is, he or she enters the continuum at a particular point according to interest, need, obvious viewpoint, compulsion, or for some other reason. Decisions to do particular pieces of research are thus subject to the very conditions often being researched, the interactive relationships between the cognitive and the emotive. This unholy welter has prompted Torrance to warn that creativity studies might not be popular for a while yet. But I do not believe we should be deterred. The more that is said and written about creativity, the more attention will have to be paid to it. We are going to make mistakes in identifying it and in interpreting it, but our whole human existence is based on mistakes and their correction. The fact that so many people have so many ideas about creativity means we have a richer field to plow, and that is a cause for rejoicing.

Gowan's Theoretical Classification

Gowan (1972) has classified creativity along a continuum which ranges from rational to psychedelic. His breakdown is as follows:

1. *Creativity as Cognitive, Rational, and Semantic.* This classification places creativity within the realm of problem solving and hearkens back to the studies of leaders such as Parnes and Guilford and others who have been interested in creativity as a component of intellect.

2. *Creativity as Personal and Environmental Relative to Child-rearing Practices.* Here the concern is more heavily weighted toward personality correlates that hinge upon originality, energy, and, in particular, self-concept.

3. *Creativity as a High Degree of Mental Health.* Studies with this orientation have been produced by figures such as Maslow and his school and emphasize openness to experience and antiauthoritarian influences.

4. *Creativity as Freudian.* Freud spoke of creativity as the sublimation of the sexual urge, which is a source of artistic activity and the main source of cultural energy, compensation, or the collective unconscious. From this base has sprung the candid neo-Freudian view —that the Oedipal crisis which occurs during the narcissistic stage is the genesis of creative functioning. A variation of this theme views creative accomplishments as sublimations of aggressive, phallic, or incestuous desires and hence as refinements of basic drives and primary processes. The preconscious is viewed as the source of man's creativity and its development is considered central.

Much of what Gowan said about creativity and the way we draw upon it is related to opening up the preconscious and bringing that material to the conscious level. He intimated that this activity is both governable and ungovernable, that there is both an "open sesame" which can be called on at will and a latent creative force which bubbles to the surface of its own volition.

5. *Creativity as Psychedelic.* Here Gowan traces the connections between creativity and hypnotism, extrasensory perception, and other paranormal aspects such as precognition.

Gowan's classification is a comprehensive attempt at definition and a complex one. He has pooled together a complex body of literature and provided a useful framework for understanding it.

Roweton's Theoretical Classification

Roweton's efforts (1973) suggested six theoretical approaches to the interpretation of creative behavior: definitional, behavioristic, dispositional, humanistic, psychoanalytic, and operational. The psychoanalytic, humanistic, and operational approaches are quite similar to Gowan's Freudian, mental health, and cognitive classifications, respectively, with the dispositional approach similar to Gowan's cognitive and mental health categories as described above.

According to Roweton, the definitional approach attempts to conceptualize what creativity is, and though not easily subjected to empirical verification, it often provides a rich source of testable hypotheses to experimental psychologists. The behavioristic approach to creativity leans heavily on association and reinforcement theories, with some attention being given to the effects of incubation and transfer. While my own approach to creativity is not a behavioral one, I believe it is important to point out the values of this perspective, which lends itself to a more parsimonious expression of what we mean by creativity because it is based on observed behaviors and performances. While inferences are not always easy to draw or deductions easy to make, the data are, at least, concrete.

Definition of Creativity and Instrumentation

Since the understanding of the term, creativity, is dependent on its theoretical source, its definition has to be thought of in an appropriate context. Lack of agreement concerning definition of this term can be traced not only to the many different ways people can be creative, but also to the fact that explanations of these behaviors derive meaning in part from the referential theoretical models. Hence, there is need to describe and define operationally the particular credentials and/or abilities which people possess. From that point we need to press further toward the construction of instruments which measure the qualities described and defined, sometimes called the theoretical construct validities of the instrument.

Two definitions of creativity have been most productive of instrument development: (1) Guilford's divergent thinking and redefinition abilities as components of the Structure of Intellect Model, and (2) Torrance's definition of creativity as a process that involves sensing gaps or disturbing missing elements, forming hypotheses, communicating the results, and possibly modifying and retesting these hypotheses. To these may be added such definitions as the ability to generate or produce within some criterion of relevance many cognitive associates and many that are unique (Wallach & Kogan, 1965), and the power of the imagination to break away from perceptual set so as to restructure ideas, thoughts, and feelings into novel and meaningful associative bonds (Khatena & Torrance, 1973).

Research on Instrumentation

Much of the measurement research on validity, reliability, and norms has resulted from the construction of the instruments themselves. This research is available to readers in test manuals and numerous published articles.

With the construction of measures of creativity, a greater awareness and sensitivity to attendant problems has arisen. Many studies over the past decade or so have been concerned with the problematic issues of measuring creativity which have pivoted around such concerns as definition, dimensionality, item sampling, scoring reliability, validity, conditions of test administration, usability, culture fairness and relevance, and norms (e.g., Anastasi & Schaefer, 1971; Guilford, 1971; Khatena, 1971c; Mackler & Shontz, 1965; Treffinger & Poggio, 1972; Yamamoto, 1966).

While often hypertechnical in nature, this literature is necessary as a kind of anchoring device. Unfortunately, much of this information is still widely scattered. The ERIC abstracts available through computer searches contain large gaps. *Psychological Abstracts* is enormously useful but not thoroughly comprehensive. *Dissertation Abstracts* helps fill some of the lacunae, but what is needed is a more centralized information servicing and disseminating operation which would combine what have heretofore been isolated systems.

Research on Nurturing Creativity

Interest in the nurturing of creativity has been considerable. This has resulted in numerous studies on the effects of various training programs that have attempted to increase productive performance under different environmental conditions of children, adolescents, and adults.

A comprehensive summary of the results of 142 studies that used the Torrance Tests of Creative Thinking as one of the criterion measures was reported by Torrance (1972a). Ways of teaching children to think creatively were classified as follows:

1. Training programs emphasizing the Osborn-Parnes problem-solving procedures or some modification of them.
2. Other disciplined approaches such as training in general semantics or creativity research.
3. Complex programs involving packages of materials such as the Purdue Creativity Program, the Covington, Crutchfield, and Davies Productive Thinking Program, and the Myers and Torrance Ideabooks.
4. Programs using the creative arts as vehicles for teaching and practicing creative thinking.
5. Media and reading programs designed to teach and give practice in creative thinking.
6. Curricular and administrative arrangements designed to create favorable conditions for learning and practicing creative thinking.
7. Variables related to teachers and classrooms, indirect and direct control, and classroom climate.
8. Testing conditions designed to facilitate a higher level of creative functioning or more valid and reliable test performance.

Torrance's paper also contained a comprehensive and useful bibliography which will serve researchers and practitioners in the field to good effect.

Research on the Disabled, Disturbed, and Disadvantaged

Another viable area of research on creativity attempts to extend knowledge of the creative mental functioning of retarded children, blind and deaf children, emotionally disturbed children, and disadvantaged children and to determine what can be done to facilitate their growth and productivity (e.g., Bruch, 1975; Cooper, 1973; Halpin, Halpin & Torrance, 1973; Johnson, 1974; Kaltsounis, 1969; Khatena, 1971d; Peters & Torrance, 1972; Turner, 1972).

Cross-Cultural Research

There has also been a growing interest in cross-cultural research which can largely be associated with the initial and comprehensive research of Torrance. In a paper summarizing creativity research at the University of Georgia during the period 1966 to 1973, Torrance (1973) reported on cross-cultural research with subjects in grades 1 through 6 drawn from schools in Western Samoa, Norway, India, West Germany, and the segregated black culture of the United States. He commented on continuity and discontinuity features in creative mental functioning and development relative to various cultural groups.

Other cross-cultural creativity research done by Torrance's students at the University of Georgia includes studies on bilingualism as it affects the creative thinking abilities of Mexican youth (Carringer, 1972); sex differences in creative development (Coone, 1968); conception of situational causality in India, Western Samoa, Mexico, and the United States (Langgulang, 1971); development of causal thinking of Mexican and United States children (Langgulang & Torrance, 1972); originality of the Thais and Chinese (Rungsinan, 1972); and creative and causal thinking skills relative to Mexican student-faculty perception of situational causality (Walker, Torrance & Walker, 1971).

Research on Creative Imagination Imagery

Relatively little research has been done on imagery, especially as it relates to the creative imagination. One of the major causes for this can be traced to its rejection by Watson and the ascendency of behaviorism in the 1920s. The readmission of imagery as an appropriate subject of study in psychology after 30 years of ostracism followed renewed interest by American psychologists in cognitive processes in the early 1950s (Holt, 1964; Richardson, 1969). The renewal of interest in imagery may be due to the view that images are indirect reactivations of earlier sensory or perceptual activity rather than mental mechanisms (Bugelski, 1970). However, this resurgence of interest in imagery tended to confine itself to the study of after imagery, eidetic imagery, and memory imagery (Pavio, 1971; Richardson, 1969). Studies on imagination imagery have related to the following:

1. *Hypnagogic imagery.* Imagery which comes in the semidream state between sleep and wakefulness.
2. *Perceptual isolation imagery.* Imagery which occurs when ex-

ternal stimuli are radically reduced under controlled conditions.

3. *Hallucinogenic drug imagery.* Chemically induced images from such drugs as LSD, peyote, and mescaline.
4. *Photic stimulation.* Any relatively slow, rhythmic visual stimulation that induces a trancelike state or drowsiness that may, in turn, facilitate image formation.
5. *Pulse current imagery.* Imagery induced by electrical impulses externally applied to the temples to stimulate the appearance of imagery.
6. *Non-drug-induced hallucination.* Imagery such as that experienced by schizophrenics, mystics, and shamans.

Common to all these studies is the reduction of external stimuli operating on an individual to a level that frees him or her to attend to an inner world of stimulus events and allows the subject to experience imagination imagery (Richardson, 1969). However, the need to study types of creative imagination imagery hitherto neglected has been stressed by both Richardson (1969) and Pavio (1971). Richardson cited only two studies done on the creative correlates of imagination imagery, one on perceptual isolation and its positive consequences on Guilford's measures of creativity (Kubzanski, 1961) and the other on the facilitatory effects of LSD on creative problem solving (Harman, McKim, Mogar, Fadiman, & Stolaroff, 1966).

Since then, several other studies on imagination imagery as it relates to creativity have been done. For instance, MacKinnon (1971) investigated imagery production under the effects of hypnosis; Krippner, Dreistadt, and Hubbard (1972) summarized and discussed a group of studies that attempted to relate the right or nondominant hemisphere of the brain to the creative person's experience of nonordinary reality through hypnosis, visual imaging processes, psychedelic drugs, dreams, extrasensory perception, and self-actualization. On the subject of hypnosis, creativity, and the imagination, two comprehensive reviews have documented the area: one by Bowers and Bowers (1970) and the other by Sheehan (1972).

Leonard and Lindauer (1973) explored the relationship of aesthetic activities, imagery arousal, and creativity correlates. Torrance (1972b) studied the tendency of adolescents and young adults to produce images of unusual visual perspective on the repeated figures activity of the Torrance tests as a predictor of creative achievement. In addition, a few other papers have attempted to find relationships between creative talents in music and the ability to produce original verbal images (Torrance & Khatena, 1969), and between personality characteristics, activities, and attitudinal patterns and the production of original verbal images (Khatena & Torrance, 1971, 1973).

Two papers which have added to the growing interest in the area of creative imagination relate to source material in discovery by analogy (Gordon, 1974) and metaphorical thinking and the production of similes (Schaefer, 1975). Studies have also dealt with the creative imagination and imagery-analogy correlates (Khatena, 1975) and the production of original verbal images by deaf and hearing children.

Measuring Creative Imagination Imagery

A major problem in studying the function of imagination and imagery has been the lack of objective measures. Although the need for appropriate instrumentation has not ceased, it has been relieved in part by the construction and development of instruments that attempt to measure creative abilities (e.g., Guilford, 1967; Torrance, 1974). Although Guilford and Torrance did not directly attempt to measure the creative imagination in terms of its imagery correlates, the measures they produced did suggest that the study of imagination imagery might begin with the study of creative abilities. Measures of creative components of intellectual functioning now exist, and these have prepared the way for the study of creative imagination imagery. Of particular value to the study of creative imagination imagery have been two measures of verbal originality, Onomatopoeia and Images and Sounds and Images, now available as a test battery entitled *Thinking Creatively with Sounds and Words* (Torrance, Khatena, & Cunnington, 1973).

Verbal Imagery

Studies on the creative imagination and its imagery correlates have been approached in a number of ways. Several experimental studies examined the effects of teaching college adults to think more creatively upon their production of original verbal images, scored for originality by the principle of statistical infrequency and relevance (Khatena, 1970a, 1970b, 1973c; Khatena & Barbour, 1972; Khatena & Parnes, 1974). Results have generally been favorable. Two of these studies explored the effects of creative levels upon training adults to produce original verbal images and analogies as well, and found that both creative and less creative people benefit from training to think in creative ways (Khatena, 1973a).

Several other experimental studies investigated the differential effects on production of original verbal images produced by presenting onomatopoeic stimuli to adults, adolescents, and children at fixed and variable time intervals (Khatena, 1970a, 1971a, 1972b, 1973d, 1973e). The results of these five studies indicate that when the time interval is fixed, the imaginations of adult subjects function effectively to produce original verbal images, given sufficient warm-up, and that the imaginations of children and adolescents are sensitized more rapidly to produce original verbal images. Further, when the time interval is varied and subjects are identified as high, moderate, and low creatives, the imaginations of high-creative adults and children operate best in producing original verbal images when given moderate time deadlines, whereas the imaginations of high-creative adolescents function best when given as much time as needed.

To these studies may be added two cross-sectional developmental studies relative to the production of original verbal images by children between the ages of 8 and 19 (Khatena, 1971b) and between the ages of 9 and 19 (Khatena, 1972a). Results from these studies indicate that drops do occur in the development of the imagination and its original verbal image correlates between grades 3 and 12 or between ages 8 and 19. The period that seems to stand out is the upper elementary grades—grades 4 to 6, or between the ages of 9 and 11. A longitudinal study was also done with the same children producing original verbal images over a four-year period beginning at the age of 8 years (Khatena & Fisher, 1974). The findings provided support to the earlier observation that some loss in verbal image production appears to occur in children at the ages of 9 and 10 years and a gain occurs at 11 years.

Analogy and Image Structure

Two studies were concerned with the production of personal, direct, symbolic, and fantasy analogies with simple and complex image structures by high-original college adults and children (Khatena, 1972c, 1973b). The results of the adult study showed that highly original men and women significantly preferred to use the direct analogy form and simple rather than complex image structure. The study with children showed that highly original boys and girls at all age levels significantly preferred to use the simple image, direct analogy form as well, with boys producing complex images somewhat more frequently than girls. Further, it was found that as original children grew older, the number of direct simple image analogies produced decreased, with a corresponding increase in the number of complex images produced. Peak productivity in terms of the simple image with corresponding reversal of the complex image occurred at the age of 12 years for boys and 13 years for girls.

Some Research Directions on Creative Imagination Imagery

Creative imagination imagery offers many research openings for better understanding of the process of mental functioning which may lead to favorable consequences relative to diagnosis, counseling, remedial treatment, and educational intervention. Studies may be undertaken to explore various personality structures such as rigidity versus flexibility, open versus closed mindedness, and external versus internal locus of control as they relate to creative imagination imagery.

Moreover, investigations need to be done on the relationship of creative mental functioning and vividness of imagery in the several sense modalities on the one hand, and of controlled versus autonomous imagery on the other. Imagination imagery as produced by children, adolescents, and adults along continua of intellectual potency, mental health, and emotional stability offers yet other approaches. Exploration of cultural and subcultural variations in the production of imagination imagery along a continuum of sufficiency and deprivation may also be done. It is important to realize that research in the area of imagination imagery hitherto difficult to investigate may now be attempted under conditions that are scientifically appropriate and with a much better chance of producing valid conclusions.

References

Anastasi, A., & Schaefer, C. E. Note on the concepts of creativity and intelligence. *Journal of Creative Behavior,* 1971, 5(2), 113–116.

Bowers, K. S., & Bowers, P. G. *Hypnosis and creativity: A theoretical and empirical rapprochement.* Research Report No. 11. Unpublished manuscript, University of Waterloo, 1970.

Bruch, C. B. Assessment of creativity in culturally different children. *Gifted Child Quarterly,* 1975, 19, 164–174.

Bugelski, B. R. Words and things and images. *American Psychologist,* 1970, 25, 1002–1012.

Carringer, D. C. *The relationship of bilingualism to the creative thinking abilities of Mexican youth.* Unpublished doctoral dissertation, University of Georgia, 1972.

Coone, J. G. *A cross-cultural study of sex differences in creative development.* Unpublished doctoral dissertation, University of Georgia, 1968.

Cooper, J. B. *The relationship between creativity and intelligence in the educable mentally retarded child.* Unpublished doctoral dissertation, University of Georgia, 1973.

Gordon, W. J. J. Some source material in discovery-by-analogy. *Journal of Creative Behavior*, 1974, 8(4), 239–257.

Gowan, J. C. *Development of the creative individual*. San Diego, Cal.: Robert R. Knapp, 1972.

Guilford, J. P. *The nature of human intelligence*. New York: McGraw-Hill, 1967.

Guilford, J. P. Some misconceptions regarding measurement of creative talents. *Journal of Creative Behavior*, 1971, 5(2), 77–87.

Halpin, G. M., Halpin, W. G., & Torrance, E. P. Effects of blindness on creative thinking abilities of children. *Developmental Psychology*, 1973, 9, 269–274.

Harman, W. W., McKim, R. H., Mogar, R. E., Fadiman, J., & Stolaroff M. J. Psychedelic agents in creative problem solving: A pilot study. *Psychological Reports*, 1966, 19, 211–227.

Holt, R. R. Imagery: The return of the ostracized. *American Psychologist*, 1964, 19, 254–264.

Johnson, R. A. Differential effects of reward versus no-reward instructions on the creative thinking of two economic levels of elementary school children. *Journal of Educational Psychology*, 1974, 66(4), 530–533.

Kaltsounis, B. Impact of instruction on development of deaf children's originality of thinking. *Perceptual and Motor Skills*, 1969, 29, 298.

Khatena, J. Repeated presentation of stimuli and production of original responses. *Perceptual and Motor Skills*, 1970, 30, 91–94. (a)

Khatena, J. Training college adults to think creatively with words. *Psychological Reports*, 1970, 27, 279–281. (b)

Khatena, J. Adolescents and the meeting of time deadlines in the production of original verbal images. *Gifted Child Quarterly*, 1971, 15, 201–204. (a)

Khatena, J. Production of original verbal images by children between the ages of 8 and 19 as measured by the alternate forms of onomatopoeia and images. In *Proceedings of the 79th Annual Convention of the American Psychological Association*, 1971, 187–188. (b)

Khatena, J. Some problems in the measurement of creative behavior. *Journal of Research and Development in Education*, 1971, 4(3), 74–82. (c)

Khatena, J. Teaching disadvantaged preschool children to think creatively with pictures. *Journal of Educational Psychology*, 1971, 62(5), 384–386. (d)

Khatena, J. Development patterns in production by children aged 9 to 19 of original images as measured by sounds and images. *Psychological Reports*, 1972, 30, 649–650. (a)

Khatena, J. Original verbal images of children as a function of time. *Psychological Reports*, 1972, 31, 565–566. (b)

Khatena, J. The use of analogy in the production of original verbal images. *Journal of Creative Behavior*, 1972, 6(3), 209–213. (c)

Khatena, J. Creative level and its effects on training college adults to think creatively with words. *Psychological Reports*, 1973, 32, 336. (a)

Khatena, J. Imagination imagery by children and the production of analogy. *Gifted Child Quarterly*, 1973, 17, 98–102. (b)

Khatena, J. Imagination imagery and original verbal images. *Art Psychotherapy*, 1973, 1, 113–120. (c)

Khatena, J. Production of original verbal images by college adults to variable time intervals. *Perceptual and Motor Skills*, 1973, 36, 1285–1286. (d)

Khatena, J. Repeated presentation of stimuli and production of original responses by children. *Perceptual and Motor Skills*, 1973, 36, 173–174. (e)

Khatena, J. Creative imagination imagery. *Gifted Child Quarterly*, 1975, 19,149–160.

Khatena, J., & Barbour, R. L. Training music majors in college to think creatively with sounds and words. *Psychological Reports*, 1972, 30, 105–106.

Khatena, J., & Fisher, S. A four-year study of children's responses to onomatopoeic stimuli. *Perceptual and Motor Skills*, 1974, 39, 1062.

Khatena, J., & Parnes, S. J. Applied imagination and the production of original verbal images. *Perceptual and Motor Skills*, 1974, 38, 130.

Khatena, J., & Torrance, E. P. Attitude patterns and the production of original verbal images: A study in construct validity. *Gifted Child Quarterly*, 1971, 15, 117–122.

Khatena, J., & Torrance, E. P. *Thinking Creatively with Sounds and Words: Norms—Technical Manual.* Rev. ed. Lexington, Mass.: Personnel Press, 1973.

Krippner, S., Dreistadt, R., & Hubbard, C. C. The creative person and nonordinary reality. *Gifted Child Quarterly*, 1972, 16, 203–228; 234.

Kubzanski, P. E. Creativity, imagery and sensory deprivation. *Acta Psychologia*, 1961, 19, 507–508.

Langgulang, H. *A cross cultural study of the child's conception of situational causality in India, Western Samoa, Mexico, and the United States.* Doctoral dissertation, University of Georgia, 1971.

Langgulang, H., & Torrance, E. P. The development of causal thinking of children in Mexico and the United States. *Journal of Cross-Cultural Psychology*, 1972, 3, 315–320.

Leonard, G., & Lindauer, M. S. Aesthetic participation and imagery arousal. *Perceptual and Motor Skills*, 1973, 36, 977–978.

Mackler, B., & Shontz, F. C. Creativity: Theoretical and methodological considerations. *Psychological Record*, 1965, 15, 217–238.

MacKinnon, D. W. Creativity and transliminal experience. *Journal of Creative Behavior*, 1971, 5(4), 227–241.

McNemar, Q. Lost: Our intelligence? Why? *American Psychologist*, 1964, 18, 871–882.

Pavio, A. *Imagery and verbal processes*. New York: Holt, Rinehart & Winston, 1971.

Peters, R. W., & Torrance, E. P. Effects of triadic interaction on performance of five year old disadvantaged children. *Psychological Reports*, 1972, 30, 747–750.

Richardson, A. *Mental imagery*. New York: Springer, 1969.

Roweton, W. E. *Creativity: A review of theory and research*. Occasional Paper No. 7. Buffalo, N.Y.: The Creative Education Foundation, 1973.

Rungsinan, W. *A study of the scoring of originality of creative thinking on Thai and Chinese cultures*. Unpublished master's thesis, University of Georgia, 1972.

Schaefer, C. E. The importance of measuring metaphorical thinking in children. *Gifted Child Quarterly*, 1975, 19, 140–148.

Sheehan, P. W. Hypnosis and the manifestation of imagination. In E. Fromm & R. E. Shor (Eds.), *Hypnosis: Research developments and perspectives*. Chicago: Aldine Atherton, 1972.

Thorndike, R. L. The measurement of creativity. *Teachers College Record*, 1963, 44, 422–424.

Torda, C. Some observations on the creative process. *Perceptual and Motor Skills*, 1970, 31, 107–126.

Torrance, E. P. *Guiding creative talent*. Englewood Cliffs, N.J.: Prentice-Hall, 1962.

Torrance, E. P. Can we teach children to think creatively? *Journal of Creative Behavior*, 1972, 6(2), 114–143. (a)

Torrance, E. P. Tendency to produce unusual visual perspective as a predictor of creative achievement. *Perceptual and Motor Skills*, 1972, 34, 911–915. (b)

Torrance, E. P. Cross-cultural studies of creative development in seven selected societies. *The Educational Trends*, 1973, 8(1–4), 28–38.

Torrance, E. P. *Torrance Test of Creative Thinking: Norms—Technical Manual*. Lexington, Mass.: Personnel Press, 1974.

Torrance, E. P., & Khatena, J. Originality of imagery in identifying creative talent in music. *Gifted Child Quarterly*, 1969, 13, 3–8.

Torrance, E. P., Khatena, J., & Cunnington, B. F. *Thinking Creatively with Sounds and Words* (child & adult versions). Lexington, Mass.: Personnel Press, 1973.

Treffinger, D. J., & Poggio, J. P. Needed research on the measurement of creativity. *Journal of Creative Behavior*, 1972, 6(4), 253–267.

Turner, S. M. *The effects of frustration, sex, mode of behavior, and organicity on nonverbal creative thinking of emotionally disturbed children*. Unpublished doctoral dissertation, University of Georgia, 1972.

Walker, P. C., Torrance, E. P., & Walker, T. S. A cross-cultural study of the perception of situational causality. *Journal of Cross-Cultural Psychology*, 1971, 2, 401–404.

Wallach, M. A. Review of the Torrance Tests of Creative Thinking. *American Educational Research Journal,* 1968, 5, 272–281.

Wallach, M. A. Ideology, evidence and creativity research. *Contemporary Psychology,* 1973, 18, 162–164.

Wallach, M. A., & Kogan, N. *Modes of thinking in young children.* New York: Holt, Rinehart & Winston, 1965.

Yamamoto, K. Do creativity tests really measure creativity? *Theory into Practice,* 1966, 5, 194–197.

Chapter Ten

Disadvantaged Gifted Youth

Introduction

Under the impetus of the Economic Opportunities Act, talent hunts supported by the Ford Foundation, and other developments, serious attention is now being devoted to the search for giftedness among economically and culturally disadvantaged children. One of the kinds of talent searches which might be most fruitful would be for the creatively gifted.*

In recent years, a number of graduate students have administered tests of creative thinking to such economically and culturally disadvantaged groups as Negroes in segregated schools in the South, Negroes in large cities in the North, Indians in New Mexico and Oklahoma, Mexican migrant children in Texas and California, and delinquent youths in large cities.

In all instances the investigators have found outstandingly gifted youngsters on these measures—youngsters whose IQs would place them in the average or below-average capacity. Already there are apparently a number of difficulties in seeing creative potentialities in these disadvantaged children and in motivating them to achieve these potentialities.

Common Misperceptions

A few common misperceptions have made it difficult in the past to envision creative potentialities in economically and culturally disadvantaged children.

---

*This introduction has been abstracted from E. Paul Torrance, "Identifying the Creatively Gifted among Economically and Culturally Disadvantaged Children," *Gifted Child Quarterly*, 8:171 ff., 1964. Dr. Torrance has had published a new book on the subject: *Discovery and Nurturance of Giftedness in the Culturally Different* (Reston, Va.: Council for Exceptional Children, 1977). See also his chapter on the disadvantaged in Stanley and others (1978).

One of these misperceptions is represented in the common assertion that anyone who possesses a spark of creativity will somehow contrive to show this potentiality in spite of neglect, punishment, and coercive pressures. It is agreed that creative persons worth anything have always met with apathy, opposition, ridicule, and scorn and that they always will. Thus, no matter how great one's creative possibilities, this giftedness is of no social importance unless the person is able to prevail against these forces.

My own observations, the lessons of history, and findings from recent research convince me that these are dangerous fallacies that threaten national health and welfare. In our longitudinal studies we see children in the process of sacrificing needlessly, it seems to me, what promised to be an outstanding creative potential. It is true that some of them will sacrifice their creativity only for a time and will regain it, when they learn how to cope more constructively with coercive pressures. For some children, however, these pressures are intense and/or prolonged and I fear that they shall never recover. Instead, I fear that they will choose the path of delinquency, crime, and mental illness—or, at best, a life of mediocrity, conformity, and unrealized possibilities. I suspect that those who will be working with the Disadvantaged Youth Opportunity Centers will find many such young people.

A second common misperception that blinds us to creative potentialities among disadvantaged children is caused by emotional reactions to certain kinds of socially disapproved behavior, particularly behavior disapproved by the middle-class society of the United States. Creatively gifted youngsters from disadvantaged backgrounds are bound to appear to middle-class teachers and counselors as hopelessly crude and unsophisticated, quiet, strongly emotional, critical of others, stubborn, perhaps even negativistic, unwilling to accept things on the teacher or counselor's say-so, timid, and perhaps even fearful. They will find that these very same youngsters have reputations for disturbing the established procedures of the classroom, playground, or other group to which they belong. Some of these youngsters may even seem haughty and self-satisfied, even though unsophisticated and timid. All of these are characteristics that are strongly disapproved by teachers and counselors in the United States. They are also characteristics that make it difficult for teachers and counselors to offer helping relationships and to reward socially desirable kinds of achievement when they appear. Yet these same characteristics are found among some of the most highly effective, productive, and creative people who have made truly outstanding contributions to our society.

29 The Education of Disadvantaged Gifted Youth

J. C. GOWAN

Interest in the education of disadvantaged gifted youth runs high these days, more from social considerations of conscience than from cognitive research. It would therefore be easy to prepare a paper cut to the popular fancy indicating that disadvantaged gifted youth need help, that many disadvantaged children are gifted even though they don't test that way, and issuing some general platitudes while avoiding the specifics of curriculum adaptation. Such an approach might leave the cursory reader happy, whether or not he is a Jensenite or a Behaviorite. But that is not what the reader should expect, for if we want answers to difficult questions, it is necessary to ask and answer simpler specifics first.

To start with definition and assumption: *giftedness* is defined as placement in the top half of the ninth stanine, or the top two percent, or an IQ of over 130. The Stanford-Binet Intelligence test does not plumb an innate quality of the cognitive soul; it fallibly measures the criterion of future academic performance. The word *disadvantaged* ostensibly refers to poverty and low socioeconomic status in the family. Note there is a difference between the youth's own potential socioeconomic status and that of his family background. The nature and extent of this difference (seen only in a land of opportunity like ours) is one of the most interesting and important psychological variables for the educator.

The scion of a Jewish or Oriental immigrant family may not be culturally disadvantaged even though his parents are poor. The alien cultural tradition may actually give advantage in terms of rich cultural background, and the rapid rise of many sons of immigrants to managerial and professional positions attests to the advantages of their heritage. It is customarily felt that Mexican-American families are culturally disadvantaged, but consider recent Cuban emigrés.

From John Curtis Gowan, "The Education of Disadvantaged Gifted Youth," *California Journal for Instructional Improvement*, December 1969, pp. 239–51.

With the same language handicap, surely no group has made faster adjustment to American life. It is the same adjustment which the Anglo-Saxon Kentucky hillbillies have failed to make for three centuries. The problem is not so much an ethnic difficulty as one of socioeconomic class status. *We will therefore define disadvantaged as being reared by poor, lower-class, native parents out of the cultural mainstream.*

So we have now refined the issue to a discussion of upwardly mobile youth from a culture of lower class poverty out of the cultural mainstream, who nevertheless have test capacities for high future academic performance. This is a somewhat anomalous situation, because one of the variables most closely associated with academic performance is socioeconomic status. Whether one believes in Sheldon's t (Sheldon, 1) or merely feels that the tests are biased in favor of status (which they are), the effect is very obvious. What we become interested in then are cases where there is marked discrepancy between the youth's potential status and the actual status of his parents. Those who feel that this is an elitist view should remember that high talent is always confined to a small percentage of the population; we cannot make everyone gifted anymore than we can guarantee happiness for all; what we can do is to see that those who have potential are not debarred because of status.

There is also evidence connecting upper socioeconomic class status (SES) with creativity, and with many of the personality differences seen between gifted and average children. One of the first of these results came from a paper by Bonsall and Stefflre (2) which showed that when gifted and average children are compared, the gifted are of higher SES. When this bias is removed, almost all the differences between gifted and average children disappear. Other researchers, including Bond (3), Frierson (4), Cicirelli (5), Dentler and Mackler (6), Smith (7), and Torrance (8) are unanimous in pointing out that creativity is more often found in upper SES than in lower SES children.

We stress the importance of transferring the issue from an ethnic to a SES area because of the consequent reduction of the SES variable. While nothing may be done to change a child's ethnic background, a great deal may be done to improve his potential SES. Indeed, some of us think that this has been the main business of the American school in actualizing the American dream.

This move allows us to brush aside questions on three areas, often associated with, but, in our view, not integral parts of this article, namely: (1) controversies (such as the Jensen material) regarding racial differences in intelligence; (2) advocacy of Head Start and other early stimulation as a method of drastic improvement of IQ in creating large numbers of gifted children in minority groups; and (3) reappearance of the Watson theory of behaviorism that intelligence is entirely environmental.

There are other human influences of good teachers that cannot be duplicated by electronic devices. We must learn how machines and human beings can live together, and what things human beings can do better than machines. We may be sure that there will always be moral, social, and educational values which never can be developed through the use of machines, but which from now to eternity must be achieved solely through association of human beings with other human beings.

It is in the human relations area that the future teacher of reading has a supreme role to play. There are the human relationships between teacher and child for which no automatic device can substitute: the growing together in understanding of teacher and pupil; the encouragement and sympathy of a warm, friendly teacher; the satisfaction of a smile or nod of approval; the soft touch of a hand on the shoulder when one successfully completes a difficult learning task; the personal stimulation of a teacher who believes in you and expects you to do your best. These personal relationships are far more potent in a learning situation, more lasting in memory than skills or subject matter. Such interactive relationships of a human teacher with a living pupil must always supplement inhuman, impersonal automatons in teaching.

Characteristics of the Gifted Disadvantaged

What are disadvantaged gifted children like? There is not much concrete evidence here. From what we have just said, one can see that there is already a powerful factor acting against the identification of high intelligence—low socioeconomic status. The factor which sustains talent against the adverse effects of environment is almost always creative potential. Hence, most disadvantaged children have very high creative potential. Another way of saying the same thing is that creativity tests offer another route for identifying disadvantaged talent besides the usual verbal IQ.

It will be worthwhile, therefore, to look at some of the personality factors of the highly creative individual. A study by Gowan and Bruch (9) located the following personal factors among highly creative teachers: (1) energy, (2) courage, (3) mental health and absence of neurotic traits, (4) adaptive intelligence, and (5) originality and nonconformity as opposed to authoritarian tendency. These can easily fit the disadvantaged gifted child.

Cultural disadvantage operates on the bright child very much as does emotional disturbance. It tends to flatten out his peak performance and to make it inconsistent, keeping it below test potential. Motivational, nutritional, developmental, social, and cultural factors are probably all involved. Gifted disadvantaged children tend to have their effectiveness destroyed by alienation (Gowan, 10). This can take many forms. It is often an exaggeration of the alienation seen in advantaged gifted children with emotional problems. One of the most common of these is so much hostility or resentment toward authority that creative performance is blocked.

A good discussion of the characteristics of disadvantaged gifted may be found in Tannenbaum (11). Here Gallagher reviews Frierson's doctoral thesis which found significant differences between upper and lower SES students in the Cleveland Major Work Program (Frierson, 4). Gallagher credits Riessman (12) as summarizing differences in learning style of the disadvantaged child as physical, not aural; content centered, not form centered; externally oriented, not introspective; problem centered, not abstract centered; inductive, not deductive; spatial, not temporal, slow and patient, not quick and facile. Bruch (13) credits Torrance with the following list of strengths of the creative disadvantaged: high nonverbal fluency and originality; high creative productivity in small groups; adept at visual art expression (also noted by Rogers, 14); highly creative in movement, dance, and physical activity; highly motivated by games, music, sports, humor, concrete objects, and language rich in imagery. Bruch sees disadvantaged students as having differential strengths in certain areas of the Guilford Structure of Intellect, particularly in areas of figural strength (visual, auditory, and kinesthetic), in behavioral content areas (social intelligence), in divergent operations (creativity), and in product transformation. This would indicate that the divergent production of figural and behavioral transformations would be two ability cells in which the disadvantaged gifted may excel. Unfortunately, the behavioral and figural areas are not well researched, which results in few tests being available for them. Bruch points out that the disadvantaged youth has often been characterized as ingenious and resourceful in coping with the difficulties of slum life and in sizing up social situations of danger or opportunity quickly.

Research on Educational Efforts

Before turning to adaptations for the disadvantaged gifted, it may be useful to mention two attempts at formulation of the issues. Paul Torrance (8) discusses three issues pertaining to college admissions for disadvantaged gifted students:

1. Should we seek to identify talents valued by the Establishment or those valued by the subculture?

2. What are the talents exhibited by disadvantaged gifted students?
3. How early should attempts be made to identify and encourage disadvantaged gifted children?

Elsewhere (Gowan, 15), we have identified six issues in the education of the disadvantaged gifted youth:

1. How do we tell if the child is really gifted?
2. How do these children differ from advantaged gifted, and what is the significance of the difference?
3. What is the age at which intervention must alter background to prevent irremedial difficulty, and what should be the form and extent of remediation?
4. Can intervention remedy defects in socioeconomic status, achievement, and creativity?
5. How does intervention combat "clan effect"?
6. How do we make guidance effective with disadvantaged gifted?

Research on educational efforts for disadvantaged gifted youth is mainly concentrated in the following four areas: (1) general, including administrative and curriculum adaptations, (2) the effects of resi dential programs, (3) the identification, stimulation and encouragement of exotic factors of intellect, and (4) the effects of large amounts or unusual kinds of guidance.

General

General articles describing educational procedures for dealing with disadvantaged gifted students have been presented by a number of writers. High (16) discussed programs for bright children in slum schools. Karnes and others (17) discussed the educational implications of the characteristics of disadvantaged gifted. Lloyd (18) reported on developing the creativity of culturally deprived children. McCabe (19) made a progress report of the New York efforts on behalf of bright slum children. Torrance (20) offered suggestions for motivating the disadvantaged gifted child.

The most extensive paper on curriculum for slum children of talent was prepared by Passow (21) for a Columbia University conference. As the director of the Horace Mann–Lincoln School, he has had experience in finding curriculum adaptations for both types of children. He points out in this paper that the Guilford Structure of Intellect model implies a choice of curriculum which will provide a particular goal of encouraging or stimulating each particular factor of intellect possessed by the child. Thus the concern with creativity has resulted in a more systematic analysis of curriculum content and methodology. In addition, changes resulting in greater depth and breadth, the introduction of interface subjects (such as mathematics of science, or the biology of space), the infusion into the elementary school of units from such college majors as anthropology, psychology, biophysics, sociology, etc., have special relevance for the able. Passow feels that what is required for curriculum development with bright disadvantaged children is an understanding of the patterns of abilities possessed by individual children, and then the provision of the proper match between the child's abilities and needs, and the curriculum activities. He points out that curriculum change, not administrative provision, is the focus of progress. Integrated programs which consider the range of individual differences and which produce relevant curriculum can spill over in benefits to general education as well as for able slum children.

Residential Programs

The effects of residential programs on disadvantaged children have been explored only slightly, but they appear to offer promising leads. The twenty-four-hour control on the environment of the bright child helps to break the "clan effect" which holds back so many disadvantaged gifted youth. The evident increase in guidance and in the availability of model figures is also helpful.

The precursor of this sort of thing was the summer program for gifted children developed by Killian at Cullowhee, N.C., which led to the establishment of the North Carolina Governor's School. A somewhat similar program at St. Paul's School, Concord, N.H., is more geared to disadvantaged gifted rural youth. Casebeer (22) has developed a very promising program, Project Prometheus, at Southern Oregon State College, Ashland, which concentrates on the development of objectives in the affective domain for bright children.

The program that has attracted the most attention as being constructed specifically for the disadvantaged gifted is the Lincoln-Governor's School at Lexington, Ky., reported by Tisdale (23) and Von Schlutter (24). Of a total school enrollment of 98, 51 are male, 42 are black, and 66 are from cities. When they come, these disadvantaged children do not have good self-concept; they do not know how to concentrate, how to organize, or how to study. Being oriented to short-term goals, they disregard the arts and are suspicious of authority. They need structure, and wish concrete rather than abstract experiences. They do not have stable interest patterns or positive life goals. The residential program is one of readjustment whereby the staff tries to turn the pupils on to the benefits of a good education.

Exotic Factors of Intellect

The identification, stimulation or exploitation of exotic factors of intellect, specifically not those usually identified in intelligence tests, has received considerable impetus from followers of Guilford. Meeker (25) devised ways of weighing Stanford-Binet items for creativity and other structure of intellect factors, and Bruch (26) reported a method of getting a "creativity quotient" from the famous test. Gallagher (27) characterizes the disadvantaged gifted child as a visual rather than an auditory learner, and notes his dependence on concrete rather than abstract experiences. Miller (28) reported a talent search in the Pittsburgh slum schools which found 2.6% of children in five black schools had IQ's over 116. Rogers (14), after a Bridgeport study, feels that the superiority he found for disadvantaged gifted students in visual arts skills represents an area which can be exploited. Torrance (29) lists a number of nontest indicators of talent for the disadvantaged. He cites evidence that children in the 110–125 IQ bracket may score high on creativity tests, and believes that even lower IQ scores may yield creatives among the disadvantaged. He also suggests that one can observe which children have the least need for guidance when planning an activity; one can determine how well they can anticipate a correct solution when reporting their inner feelings; one can pose complex issues, and see which students take a hopeful rather than a defeatist attitude; one can find out who comes up with the most ideas in a brainstorming session, who tends to lead, who has courage to stand alone on his ideas. As better and newer tests are developed for the exotic factors we shall have better methods of identification, and hopefully find more able disadvantaged children.

Guidance

The effects of large amounts or unusual kinds of guidance on disadvantaged gifted students have received some attention. One of the first studies was the JHS 43—Manhattan Guidance Project which escalated into Higher Horizons. Here, as described by Passow (21), Brickman (30), and Hillson and Myers (31), large amounts of guidance seemed to have remarkable effects in holding bright slum children in school and in sending them to college. These efforts improved motivation, reduced failure, and were generally very successful. Amran and Giese (32) used counseling and other procedures to produce large gains in self-concept and creativity among Upward Bound college freshmen. A smaller group guidance program using resource community members for vocational information was reported by Demaris (33) working with San Francisco slum children.

It is our belief that there are remarkable benefits both in large amounts or unusual kinds of guidance. We have elsewhere reported (10) that "normal" gifted children easily used the services of a full time counselor on a 25/1 ratio (12 times as much guidance as is recommended by most writers in the field). Apparently, even children "without problems" need guidance of this amount to feel supported enough to become creative. Disadvantaged gifted children will probably require even more. "Unusual kinds" of guidance is probably best illustrated by the "predisposing" attitude discussed by Brandwein (34) as induced in his students in science. It is the same kind of total interest developed by great coaches in their athletic charges. It suggests that the formation of an "academic varsity" in high school would be one method to combine guidance and curriculum in such an endeavor; practical methods for accomplishing this have been discussed elsewhere (Gowan & Demos, 35).

Perhaps no one has proliferated suggestions for the guidance of able children to the extent of Paul Torrance. His two books (36, 37) contain many hints for inducing creativity which will be applicable to the disadvantaged gifted youth. In a paper "Understanding Creativity in Talented Students" (in Gowan & Demos, 38) he noted the isolation and estrangement from others, the unrealistic career choices, the need for change in values and attitudes, all of which apply to the disadvantaged gifted. In six different articles in Gowan, Demos and Torrance (39) he pleads for more sympathetic understanding of the latent creativity of children. In yet another article "Motivating the Creatively Gifted among Disadvantaged Children" (Gowan & Demos, 40), he indicates that guidance is needed to clear up the blocking caused by irrelevant curriculum, lack of communication, too difficult or too easy intellectual tasks, no chance to use latent creative abilities, no chance to learn preferred ways, lack of rewards for certain kinds of excellence, and lack of purposefulness. Torrance brings keen sympathy with the plight of the disadvantaged gifted child, and gives many suggestions about things teachers and counselors can do to help him become more creative.

Turning nearer to home, we have elsewhere made various suggestions regarding various aspects of guidance, as follows: improving self-concept of disadvantaged children (Gowan & Demos, 40); correcting underachievement (Gowan & Demos, 38; Gowan & Demos, 35); guidance in improving the creativity of gifted children (Gowan, Demos, & Torrance, 39).

It is our opinion that the following procedures are necessary if intervention for the disadvantaged gifted is to be effective:

1. Individual guidance to change self-concept.
2. Group guidance for the maintenance of morale, with the introduction of suitable model figures.
3. Remedial skills taught under special learning conditions by sympathetic teachers.

We illustrate the combination of these methods in the counselor's handling of one of the most difficult guidance challenges—the constellation of problems consequent upon high upward mobility in a bright youth from a slum background. In the first place, cutting across social gradients always makes it appear to the individual that he is in the wrong; the reaction formation built up here may result in a generalized aggressiveness which will later prove a handicap. When one is climbing the ladder, one sees others at odd angles and perspectives. So it is not surprising that the youth gets a cynical view of what he is approaching, and an ambivalent picture of what he is leaving. When values are in flux, the model figure of the counselor is that much more necessary.

Besides listening and advising, the counselor can, on occasion, offer an explanation of "climbing the ladder." He can also occupy his client's time in the company of the group toward which he is heading, whether in cultural, work, or social activities. The youth will usually profit from an introduction to cultural activities, including arts and music, as well as to successful adult community models. Providing these model surrogates is very important. The upwardly mobile youth feels the rebelliousness of the disenfranchised person, and because of his youth, spirit, and ability, this tendency can make him potentially dangerous. He needs to be someone's protege, to know the giving, without expectation of return, from some parental hand that he can respect. Only this experience can blunt the predatory force which he has needed to break through the social barrier and ensure his later emulation of this example to help and nurture others when he reaches the top.

Conclusion

From the above analysis, the following conclusions and recommendations are made:

1. While much is known about the gifted child, and about the disadvantaged child, comparatively little is known about the disadvantaged gifted youth; much more research is necessary.

2. Research in these areas and in their interface may be expected to benefit general education, as well as special education, by uncovering new and salient aspects of both curriculum and guidance.

3. As Guilford says, we are moving toward education defined as the goal of stimulating whatever factors of intellect the student possesses. This implies choice of curriculum and invention of specific teaching methods for practice in improving specific abilities.

4. Administrative procedures (such as grouping) are less important than breakthroughs in the quality of curriculum and guidance which will interest and predispose the child to learn.

5. For these objectives to be successful there must be a program of (a) curriculum innovation, (b) individual guidance to improve self-concept, (c) group guidance with model figures to maintain morale, (d) remedial skills taught by a sympathetic teacher.

6. We know little about the effects of massive amounts of guidance on bright children, but some early probes are promising. Residential schools seem useful as experiments because they provide this.

7. The identification, stimulation, and exploitation of exotic factors of intellect in the case of disadvantaged gifted, particularly in the behavioral and figural areas, appear to have real promise; here is another example where curriculum and test modification needs to take place.

8. The use of modeling and model figures from the community is particularly helpful in group guidance activities with disadvantaged gifted children.

9. Unusual kinds of guidance, such as have been illustrated earlier, may be especially relevant in upgrading and preserving the creativity of disadvantaged gifted youth.

10. In general the remedy for the problems presented by disadvantaged gifted children is to start in early and involve them in as many types of guidance and curriculum, and with as many diverse adult models as possible, enlisting the cooperation of the home background whenever feasible.

Concern for the qualities of exceptional human beings arises out of an exceptional concern for the qualities of all human beings. As our regard for the potential development of all human beings rises, we become more conscious of the needs of the disadvantaged among us. Thus the idea of adapting education through curriculum and guidance changes to the special problems of the disadvantaged gifted youth is part and parcel of the central educational and social task of the Twentieth Century—to make "equality of opportunity" true in deed as well as in word.

Notes

1. Sheldon, W. T. *Varieties of Delinquent Youth.* New York: Harper, 1949.

2. Bonsall, Marcella, and Stefflre, B. "The Temperament of Gifted Children." *California Journal of Educational Research* 6:162–65 (September 1955).
3. Bond, H. M. "The Productivity of National Merit Scholars by Occupational Class." *School and Society* 85: 267–68, 1957.
4. Frierson, E. "Upper and Lower Status Children: A Study of Differences." *Exceptional Children* 32: 83–90 (October 1965).
5. Cicirelli, V. G. "Religious Affiliation, Socioeconomic Status, and Creativity." *Journal of Experimental Education* 35: 90–93, 1966.
6. Dentler, R. A., and Mackler, B. "Originality: Some Social and Personal Determinants." *Behavioral Science* 9: 1–7, 1964.
7. Smith, R. M. "The Relationship of Creativity to Social Class" (mimeo). Pittsburgh: School of Education, University of Pittsburgh, 1965.
8. Torrance, E. P. "Issues in the Identification and Encouragement of Gifted Disadvantaged Children." *The Association for the Gifted Newsletter* (CEC), 1969.
9. Gowan, J. C., and Bruch, Catherine. "What Makes a Creative Person a Creative Teacher?" *Gifted Child Quarterly* 11:2:157–59, 1967.
10. Gowan, J. C. "Alienation." *California Personnel and Guidance Association Journal* 1:1:4–7, 1968b.
11. Tannenbaum, A. J. (Ed.). *Special Education and Programs for Disadvantaged Children and Youth.* Washington, D.C.: NEA, CEC, 1968.
12. Riessman, F. *The Culturally Deprived Child.* New York: Harper-Row, 1962.
13. Bruch, Catherine. "A Proposed Rationale for the Identification and Development of the Gifted Disadvantaged" (mimeo). University of Georgia, 1969.
14. Rogers, D. A. "Visual Expression: A Creative Advantage of the Disadvantaged." *Gifted Child Quarterly* 12:110–14, 1968.
15. Gowan, J. C. "Issues in the Education of Disadvantaged Gifted Children." *Gifted Child Quarterly* 12: 115–19 (Summer 1968).
16. High, P. B. "Educating the Superior Student in the Deprived Area School." *The American Teacher Magazine* 48: 506 (December 1963).
17. Karnes, M. B., and others, "Culturally Disadvantaged Children of Higher Potential: Intellectual Functioning and Educational Implications" (mimeo). 200 pp. Champaign, Ill.: Community Unit 4 School District, September 1965. (cf. Ed. o18 505).
18. Lloyd, Jean. "Developing Creativity with the Culturally Deprived." *Instructor* 75:27, 108, 116 (February 1966).
19. McCabe, A. R. "Progress Report: The Intellectually Superior Child in a Deprived Social Area" (mimeo). New York: East Harlem Demonstration Center, 1965.
20. Torrance, E. P. "Motivating the Creatively Gifted among Disadvantaged Children." *Gifted Child Quarterly* 9:9–13, 1965.

21. Passow, A. H. "The Gifted and the Disadvantaged: Some Curriculum Insights." Paper prepared for conference, Teachers College, Columbia University, 1965.
22. Casebeer, Robert. "Project Prometheus." Paper read at APGA convention, Las Vegas, April 1969.
23. Tisdale, W. J. "The Lincoln School for Disadvantaged Able Students." Paper prepared for CEC convention, New York, April 1968.
24. Von Schlutter, C. E. "Exceptional Kentucky Youth Learns in Residence." *National Vocational Guidance Association, Gifted Student Interest Committee Newsletter* 9:3:2 (May 1969).
25. Meeker, Mary. *The Structure of Intellect: Its Use and Interpretation.* Columbus, Ohio: Charles Merrill, 1969.
26. Bruch, Catherine. "The Creative Binet." Paper read at CEC conference, New York, April 1968.
27. Gallagher, J. J. "The Disadvantaged Gifted Child." In A. J. Tannenbaum (Ed.), *Special Education and Programs for Disadvantaged Children and Youth,* pp. 42–58. Washington, D.C.: NEA, CEC, 1968.
28. Miller, T. M. "A Search for Talent in Economically Distressed Areas." *Gifted Child Quarterly* 8:179–80, 1964.
29. Torrance, E. P. "Identifying the Creatively Gifted among Economically and Culturally Disadvantaged Students." *Gifted Child Quarterly* 8:171–76, 1964.
30. Brickman, L. "Project ABLE: An Experiment in Guidance." *High Points,* 45:24–27 (April 1963).
31. Hillson, H. Y., and Myers, Florence. *The Demonstration Guidance Project, 1957–62.* New York: Board of Education, 1963.
32. Amran, F. M., and Giese, D. R. "Creativity Training: A Tool for Motivating Disadvantaged Students." *Research in Education* 3:9:98 (Eds. o18 210), 1968.
33. Demaris, R. W. "Planning Occupational Experiences for Culturally Disadvantaged Gifted Children." *Gifted Child Quarterly* 11:79–85, 1967.
34. Brandwein, P. F. *The Gifted Child as a Future Scientist.* New York: Harcourt Brace, 1955.
35. Gowan, J. C., and Demos, G. D. *The Education and Guidance of the Ablest.* Springfield, Ill.: C. C Thomas, 1964.
36. Torrance, E. P. *Guiding Creative Talent.* Englewood Cliffs, N.J.: Prentice-Hall, 1962.
37. Torrance, E. P. *Rewarding Creative Behavior.* Englewood Cliffs, N.J.: Prentice-Hall, 1964.
38. Gowan, J. C., and Demos, G. D. (Eds.). *The Guidance of Exceptional Children.* New York: David McKay Co., 1965.
39. Gowan, J. C., Demos, G. D., and Torrance, E. P. *Creativity: Its Educational Implications.* New York: John Wiley & Co., 1967.
40. Gowan, J. C., and Demos, G. D. (Eds.). *The Disadvantaged and Potential Dropout: Compensatory Educational Programs.* Springfield, Ill.: C. C Thomas, 1966.

41. Gowan, J. C. "Issues in the Guidance of Gifted and Creative Children." *Gifted Child Quarterly* 11:2:140–43, 1967.

30   Creative Positives of Disadvantaged Children and Youth

E. PAUL TORRANCE

How realistic is our dream of educating to the extent of their potentialities children who live in poverty?

Reading some of the recently published accounts of what happens in classrooms in big city ghettos and other disadvantaged areas gives one a feeling of hopelessness. Just try reading such accounts as Bel Kaufman's *Up the Down Staircase* (1964), Robert Kendall's *White Teacher in a Black School* (1964), Elizabeth M. Eddy's *Walk the White Line* (1965), James Herndon's *The Way It Spozed to Be* (1965), Margaret Anderson's *The Children of the South* (1966), Herbert Kohl's *36 Children* (1967), Jonathan Kozol's *Death at an Early Age* (1967), and Robert Coles' *Dead End School* (1968). Even though I fear that the picture presented by these accounts is fairly realistic insofar as the great bulk of the education of disadvantaged children is concerned, I do not believe that our dream is an impossible one or one that we should surrender easily. Certainly we get a glimmer of what might result from a more optimistic assessment of the potentialities of disadvantaged children from such work as E. R. Braithwaite's *To Sir, With Love* (1959), Robert Rosenthal and Lenore Jacobson's *Pygmalion in the Classroom* (1968), and Robert Glasser's *Schools Without Failure* (1969).

It is not possible to estimate accurately the amount of unawakened and unrecognized potential lost each year. Joseph H. Douglass (1969), Staff Director of the 1970 White House Conference on Children and Youth, recently estimated that some 80,000 of the youth who drop out each year have IQs within the top 25 percent of the population—that is, 110 or better. He also estimated that this potential will never be tapped and will be irretrievably lost. Douglass also reported that very few school systems throughout the country have

From E. Paul Torrance, "Creative Positives of Disadvantaged Children and Youth," *The Gifted Child Quarterly*, 13:71–81, 1969.

instituted programs for the identification of the talented and that there is no follow-through in the few programs that have been initiated. He reports further that programs for the retrieval of talent among the disadvantaged are practically nonexistent. Douglass further challenges that "no satisfactory method yet has been devised to discover or predict talent potential among individuals who, for economic and cultural reasons, are not in the mainstream of American life."

Issues Concerning Unrecognized Potential

I am optimistic about the possibilities of discovering talent potential among disadvantaged children and youth. In several sources, I (Torrance, 1963, 1968, 1969) have suggested possible approaches and given information about my own very limited work on this problem. I believe that George Witt's (1968) LEAP Project in New Haven, Connecticut, and Kay Bruch's (1969) work in Athens, Georgia, indicate that the possibilities are indeed exciting and that the idea of awakening and recognizing extraordinary potentialities among disadvantaged children is much more than "an impossible dream."

I must admit, however, that the dream is an impossible one as long as we insist on identifying and cultivating only those kinds of talent that the dominant, advantaged culture values. We must also look for and cultivate talents of the type that are valued in the various disadvantaged subcultures of our country. Can't we see that this is what the youth in disadvantaged subcultures have been trying to tell us during the past two or three years? Why do you suppose Mexican-American students strike to get more books written in Spanish in school libraries and to protest the tendency for high school counselors to insist that they concentrate on shop courses? Why do you suppose black students sit in at colleges and demand departments for the study of black culture and a hand in awarding scholarships? Why do you suppose young Indian leaders are calling for "Red Power" and demanding the right to develop a separate Indian way of life? Why do you suppose Puerto Ricans are joining with blacks to get control of neighborhood schools?

Obviously, all of these movements represent efforts by disadvantaged groups in our society to gain more power over their lives. They are trying to develop pride in themselves and their heritage. They are searching for more favorable and more realistic self-images. James Brown, the black soul singer, pleads, "Say It Loud, I'm Black and I'm Proud." I see underneath all these movements a plea that educators recognize and cultivate talents of the type that are highly valued in the various disadvantaged subcultures of our country.

My position (Torrance, (1969) is that not only should we identify and cultivate the talents valued by a particular subculture but that we shall be more successful if we do. Criticisms of our established talent assessment procedures when applied to disadvantaged children and youth are too well known to be enumerated. On the positive side, we can point with some degree of success to the identification and cultivation of talent among disadvantaged groups in instrumental and vocal music, dancing, dramatics, visual art, and athletics. Even here, there has been gross neglect of talent. There has always been far more of this kind of talent than we have been willing to recognize and use. These are kinds of talents that are valued among disadvantaged cultures in the United States, and I believe a survey would show that we could locate a higher proportion of high-level talent in these areas among disadvantaged than among advantaged groups.

I have offered two suggestions for finding hidden talent among disadvantaged children, and my colleague, Kay Bruch, has offered a third. It seems to me that a part of the difficulty, but only a part of it, lies in the nature of the talent tests whatever their nature. Most of them require that the child respond in terms of the experiences common in our dominant, advantaged culture. The disadvantaged child is not permitted to respond in terms of his own experiences, the experiences common in his culture or unique to himself. Most tests of creativity—and the *Torrance Tests of Creative Thinking* (Torrance, 1966) in particular—permit disadvantaged children to respond in terms of their own experiences. This increases the chances of obtaining responses and makes it possible to evaluate the responses in terms of the child's experiences, whatever they might be.

Other problems of talent identification lie almost completely outside the nature of the instruments used in the process. In order to obtain an indication of potentiality from a child, it is necessary to motivate him to display that potentiality and to feel psychologically safe in doing so. In my own work with disadvantaged black children, I have used the creativity workshop as a format for accomplishing this goal. In this format, I have found that tests of creative thinking ability take on more power than in typical situations (Torrance, 1968). Even in formal situations, disadvantaged children perform rather well on the figural tests of creative thinking ability (Torrance, 1967). Their performance on the verbal tests, however, is quite poor in the formal school testing situation. This is, of course, in line with numerous findings concerning the generally poor performance of disadvantaged children on almost all kinds of verbal tests and on speeded or timed tests.

In the creativity workshop, three procedures were used to elicit the hidden verbal abilities for which we were searching. No tests were given until there had been time for the creative processes of the children to become awakened. No time limits were imposed. The examiners offered to record the children's ideas. These procedures were generally quite effective. No one observing these activities or the resulting products could have said that these children were non-verbal.

Bruch (1969) has made another important point. She contends that for the disadvantaged the identification question cannot be whether they perform on tests of intelligence or achievement at a currently high level, but whether there are indices of probable development to higher levels than those at which they now function. She offers as an example a youth who had demonstrated exceptional talent in music, a culturally valued talent among the black disadvantaged. She argues that this youth may also be able to function more fully through latent abilities in academic areas. She suggests that through his specific culturally valued talent, music, a developmental program could be built for the needed abilities in vocabulary fluency and comprehension, mathematical symbolic thinking, and other thinking processes.

On the basis of studies of disadvantaged groups, I believe I have identified a set of creative positives that occur to a high degree among disadvantaged children and upon which I believe we can build successful educational programs for awakening many potentialities. The following is a list of these creative positives:

1. *High Nonverbal Fluency and Originality.* On the figural forms of the *Torrance Tests of Creative Thinking* (1966), disadvantaged groups almost always hold their own or even excel similar advantaged groups. This seems to hold true in a variety of localities throughout the United States and for Negroes, American Indians, Mexican-Americans, and Caucasians. Frequently, however, their figural flexibility and elaboration are less outstanding. I have also noticed high fluency and originality, and sometimes flexibility and elaboration as well, in creative movement or dance. It also comes out in games, problem-solving activities, and the like.

2. *High Creative Productivity in Small Groups.* In my experience, I have found disadvantaged children to be more highly productive in small groups than in individual or large group situations. They even become quite verbal in small group creative problem-solving situations and seem less inhibited than more advantaged children. Leaders emerge and are given support by the rest of the group.

3. *Adept in Visual Art Activities.* In every disadvantaged group with which I have worked there have been surprisingly large numbers of gifted artists. In some cases, they have persisted in being copyists rather than trusting their originality. This seems to be more

characteristic of the Negro than of the American Indian and Mexican-American groups on which we have data. Even the gifted Negro artists become more imaginative and inventive as they become involved in group activities such as puppetry, making giant murals, and the like.

4. *Highly Creative in Movement, Dance, and Other Physical Activities.*   Disadvantaged children seem to take naturally to work in creative movement, dance, and other physical activities. Many of them will work hard at these activities and develop considerable discipline. In our workshop last summer we gave some emphasis to hula hoop activities. Two of the girls in the workshop won district championships, and one of them later won the city championship and was second place winner in the state contest. None of the boys in our workshop showed the discipline to practice with hula hoops to attain championship form. If we had encouraged them to enter the Frisbee contest, they might have developed such discipline.

5. *Highly Motivated by Games, Music, Sports, Humor, and Concrete Objects.*   The warm-up effects of games, music, sports, humor, and the like seem to enable disadvantaged children to achieve a higher level of mental functioning than otherwise attained.

6. *Language Rich in Imagery.*   In telling stories, making up songs, and producing solutions to problems, their language is rich in imagery.

Although we must obtain data from other disadvantaged groups and complete additional analyses of the data we already have, the findings seem clear enough to warrant a few rather gross implications. First, if you are searching for gifted children among disadvantaged populations, you will be assured of greater success if you seek them in the areas I have identified than in traditional ways. Second, more serious consideration should be given to careers in the creative arts and sciences for disadvantaged youth than we have in the past. When asked about their aspirations, almost no disadvantaged children express choices in the creative fields (Torrance, 1967). Yet many disadvantaged persons who have attained success have done so in the creative fields, especially where talent has known no limits.

Awakening Unrecognized Potential

I know of no large-scale, deliberate attempts to identify and awaken creative talent among disadvantaged groups. Frank Standage in Project Talent Search in Eastern Kentucky has administered 10,000 Appalachian youngsters the *Torrance Tests of Creative Thinking* and has launched a program for recognizing and awakening the potentialities indicated by the results of this particular talent search. It is too early even to speculate about the outcomes of this project except to say that a wealth of outstanding talent is being found among these rather disadvantaged youths. The only sustained project of which I am aware in which creatively gifted disadvantaged children have been identified through tests, then recognized, and provided a program designed to awaken their potentialities is the Life Enrichment Activity Program or LEAP initiated and sustained by George Witt at New Haven, Connecticut.

Preliminary Results of the Life Enrichment Activity Program

George Witt (1968) initiated a program over three years ago for a group of 16 highly creative, lower-class Negro children in a ghetto setting. He believed that highly creative children are injured more in such settings than are their less creative peers. Witt selected his 16 highly creative children from the second through fourth grade of a ghetto school solely on the basis of tests of creative thinking (*The Torrance Tests of Creative Thinking* and one test task that Witt himself devised).

Twelve of the original 16 children have continued in the program for over three years and all of them have manifested high-level creative skills in such fields as music, art, science, and writing. Much work has been done with the families. In many instances, the high creative talents of siblings have been recognized and opportunities have been provided for them to have music, art, ballet, and other kinds of lessons from outstanding teachers. In a few instances, it has been possible to help parents of the children upgrade their job skills and acquire better jobs.

In fashioning a program for highly creative, inner-city children, Witt attempted to incorporate the following major characteristics:

1. Be clearly structured but flexible.
2. Provide for opportunities to be rewarded for solving problems.
3. Be viewed by one and all in a positive light.
4. Be tangible; and have many activities conducted in the homes.
5. Have enough competent adults in charge to minimize the need for the ubiquitous instant jeering and quarreling.
6. Continue controls indefinitely.
7. Involve exciting people from the inner and non-inner city.
8. Design all learning experiences so that exciting perceptual-

motor experiences precede, accompany, and follow cognitive growth.
9. Be intimately coordinated by a director expert in individual, group, and community dynamics.
10. Provide for the support, control, and involvement of the children's families, parents, and siblings.

Each year, Witt reports, new structural elements have been added to the program as the children, their families, and the programs have grown.

During the first part of the program the specialists who worked with the program began to doubt that the children who had been selected had any kind of creative potentialities. Witt encouraged them to keep working, however, and he continued working with the children and involving their families. Before the end of the first summer, all of the children had exhibited outstanding promise in at least one creative field, and many of them had shown unusual promise in two or more areas.

It would be hazardous to predict the adult futures of the twelve children who have continued in the program devised by Witt and called "LEAP" (Life Enrichment Activity Program). The present indications, however, are that these children are developing talents that are highly valued both in their own subcultures and in the dominant culture, that their families are supporting their development and in most cases developing along with them. There are indications that such talents can be identified at least as early as age eight and that there is a bountiful supply of such talent in almost all disadvantaged groups.

In my search for imaginative projects at the high school level, I came across a promising one (Howe, 1969) in which girls from Goucher College taught poetry in a vocational-technical high school in the inner-city area of Baltimore. This experience demonstrates how creativity development can awaken unrecognized potentialities under what would appear to be very improbable situations. The Goucher undergraduates had not been trained as teachers but they knew and loved poetry and they knew about "open questions" that provoke deep, creative thinking about poetry. The students were tenth-grade boys in the auto mechanics curriculum. The school faculty was quite skeptical about what would happen with untrained teachers. The teaching was in small groups of five or six students. The poems selected by the Goucher girls ranged from very brief "pop" poetry to a relatively long narrative poem by Robert Frost called "Out, Out." They taught the boys about open and closed questions and that they did not have to play the traditional game of closed, single-answer questions. As the boys discovered that they could actually determine curriculum, they become less shy about saying what they liked. They enjoyed solving the puzzles posed by some of the poems. They liked poems that were difficult but not too difficult. They thought that a poem had to have "something to say." There were serious discussions about the way the students lived, about such matters as race, policemen, drugs, war, religion, etc.

How can we evaluate such experiences? How do we know that such creative experience awakened unrecognized potentialities? The project participants had several discussions about how they could get an evaluation without testing the students. Finally, they decided to give the boys four poems that they had not previously seen. The boys were asked to write on one of the four poems that they particularly liked and to explain why they did and what the poem was saying. Most of them wrote freely, assured that their papers would not be corrected or graded. One of the school's regular teachers who had been skeptical all along conducted her own experiment. She gave the same writing assignment to the other classes in the school which had not had this kind of creative experience in poetry. She admitted that by any standards the boys taught by the Goucher students were superior to the others. This may sound like a miracle but it isn't. I do not think that this experience tells us that teachers do not need to learn methods. They do. I think the Goucher undergraduates had learned some good methods. They knew the methods of open-ended questions. They understood that poems communicate feelings and that the teacher's method must help students get to the poem's words by encouraging and permitting open response to feelings. Even when we do not share ideas or values, we share feelings. We also share the language of feeling—sadness, joy, suffering, anger, wonder. Perhaps this is a way into language for deprived children and young people who are labeled as nonverbal.

What Else Is Needed?

In stressing the importance of creativity development in awakening unrecognized potential, I must make it crystal clear that I do not see it as a panacea or cure-all. We all know that much else is necessary. Certainly we must see that basic physiological and psychological needs are satisfied. Unrecognized potential in children will not be awakened as long as they are hungry, cold, inadequately clothed and housed—as long as their lives are unsafe—as long as they feel that they do not belong—as long as their dignity is not respected—as long as they experience no love, respect, or self-esteem. If this unrecognized potential is to be awakened, children must be supplied with what Maslow (1968) calls B-values—love, truth, beauty, and justice.

Maslow points out the well-known fact that if you take away all love from children, it can kill them. Children need truth in the same way. The child deprived of truth becomes paranoid, mistrusting everybody, searching for hidden meanings. Deprivation of beauty also causes illness. Children become very depressed and uncomfortable in ugly surroundings. It affects their whole being—memory, thinking, creativity, judgment. Deprivation of justice also sickens, and history tells what happens to people deprived of justice for a long time.

For unrecognized potential to become awakened there must be a feeling of purpose—a feeling of destiny. The hippies in California told me that I am too achievement-oriented in my thinking about creativity. Perhaps I am, but I have always insisted upon the importance of the intrinsic motivation inherent in creative ways of learning and creative activities. Extrinsic motivations may be effective in many instances, but both rewards and punishment are quite erratic in their effects. Even when they are effective, they must be applied again and again to keep learning going. Maslow (1968) tells the amusing anecdote of a psychology class which played a prank on their professor by secretly conditioning him while he was delivering a lecture on conditioning. The professor, without realizing it, began nodding more and more. By the end of the lecture he was nodding continually. As soon as the class told the professor what he was doing, he stopped nodding. After that no amount of smiling on the part of the class could make him nod again. Truth had made the learning disappear. The very essence of creativity development is the search for the truth. Such learning is enduring, and there is built-in motivation that keeps the process going.

Another thing we all know is that we must be willing to pay the price of awakening unrecognized potential. It takes energy, imagination, hard work, and money. We are reminded of this on every hand. In reviewing Ronald Goldman's (1968) book, *Breakthrough,* which analyzes the life experiences of a number of eminent people who came up through poverty, Brian Jackson (1968) states the problem as follows:

> ... Every wretched primary school in the rundown centers of our big cities has as much latent talent in it as any Hampstead kindergarten. But we shall see little evidence of it, and that distorted, till we civilize our priorities, and begin by spending most money on those children who had least to start with.

References

Anderson, M. *The Children of the South.* New York: Farrar, Straus and Giroux, 1966.

Braithwaite, E. R. *To Sir, with Love.* Englewood Cliffs, N.J.: Prentice-Hall, Inc., 1959.

Bruch, C. "A Proposed Rationale for the Identification and Development of the Gifted Disadvantaged." Athens, Ga.: Department of Educational Psychology, University of Georgia, 1969.

Coles, R. *Dead End School.* Boston: Atlantic-Little, Brown, 1968.

Douglass, J. H. "Strategies for Maximizing the Development of Talent among the Urban Disadvantaged." Paper prepared for the 47th Annual Convention of the Council for Exceptional Children, April 9, 1969, Denver, Colorado.

Eddy, E. M. *Walk the White Line.* Garden City, N.Y.: Doubleday & Company, Inc., 1965.

Glasser, R. *Schools without Failure.* New York: Harper and Row, 1969.

Goldman, R. J. *Breakthrough.* London: Routledge & Kegan Paul, Ltd., 1968.

Herndon, J. *The Way It Spozed to Be.* New York: Simon and Schuster, 1965.

Howe, F. "Untaught Teachers and Improbable Poets." *Saturday Review* 52(11) (March 15, 1969), pp. 60–62, 79.

Jackson, B. "Going through the Mill." *The Guardian (Manchester)*, December 20, 1968.

Kaufman, B. *Up the Down Staircase.* Englewood Cliffs, N.J.: Prentice-Hall, Inc., 1964.

Kendall, R. *White Teacher in a Black School.* Chicago: Henry Regnery Company, 1964.

Kohl, H. *36 Children.* New York: New American Library, 1967.

Kozol, J. *Death at an Early Age.* Boston: Houghton Mifflin Company, 1967.

Maslow, A. H. "Goals of Humanistic Education" (tape recording). Esalen Institute, Big Sur, Calif., 1968.

Rosenthal, R., and Jacobson, L. *Pygmalion in the Classroom.* New York: Holt, Rinehart and Winston, Inc., 1968.

Torrance, E. P. *Education and the Creative Potential.* Minneapolis: University of Minnesota Press, 1963.

Torrance, E. P. *Rewarding Creative Behavior.* Englewood Cliffs, N.J.: Prentice-Hall Inc., 1965.

Torrance, E. P. *Torrance Tests of Creative Thinking: Norms—Technical Manual.* Research ed. Princeton, N.J.: Personnel Press, Inc., 1966.

Torrance, E. P. *Understanding the Fourth Grade Slump in Creativity.* Athens, Ga.: Georgia Studies of Creative Behavior, 1967.

Torrance, E. P. "Finding Hidden Talents among Disadvantaged Children." *Gifted Child Quarterly,* 1968, 12, 67–78.

Torrance, E. P. "Issues in the Identification and Encouragement of Disadvantaged Children." *TAG Gifted Children Newsletter* 11 (2) (March 1969), pp. 48–55.

Witt, G. *The Life Enrichment Activity Program: A Brief History.* New

Haven, Conn.: LEAP, Inc., 363 Dixwell Avenue, 1968 (mimeographed).

31 Assessment of Creativity in Culturally Different Children

CATHERINE B. BRUCH

Cultural Conditions

Two similar definitional groups, sometimes overlapping yet at other times distinctive as to the populations described, will be dealt with in this article. The term "disadvantaged" refers primarily to the populations who are restricted in access to mainstream cultural experiences due to economic disadvantagement. The term "culturally different" deals with those cultural or subcultural groups whose cultural environment differs from that of the mainstream or general culture.

Disadvantagement and cultural difference may both be present in the same group. Where both apply, developmental experiences in children would be least like those of the mainstream culture. A particular group's psychosocial distance from the mainstream should be considered in assessment. Since degrees of difference and specific variations occur for each subcultural or socioeconomic group, measurement efforts should be relevant to the qualities of the specific group under consideration.

Montagu (1974) notes complex societal changes needed if the highly developed majority population is to be effective in stimulating creativity in people from different cultural backgrounds. He views necessary conditions in every culture before latent potentialities for achievement can be expressed as: (1) a cultural background of respect for achievement in the child's family; (2) encouragement and rewards within the family and culture; and (3) societal conditions in which individual development has not physically hampered his ability to learn. He states that the necessary components for *basic opportunity* for achievement include freedom from a continuous pressure to survive, good health, and freedom from disease and malnutrition. He considers as another component that a child needs to grow within

---

From *The Gifted Child Quarterly* 19:2 (1975). Used by permission.

his own cultural background to foster the deeply rooted cultural meanings essential for stability in dealing with a broader, perhaps inhospitable, world. In the final component Montagu indicates that "for creativity and achievement, the encouragement and nurturing of high aspiration levels, the fueling and development of incentives, the promise and experience of rewards are necessary" (1974, p. 383).

The preceding necessary and sufficient conditions for the emergence of creativity in culturally different populations parallel, in a sense, the premises of Rogers (1962) and Maslow (1970). Rogers sets forth conditions fostering constructive creativity as psychological safety and psychological freedom. Maslow's position is that psychological and affective needs should be met before higher psychological attainments leading toward self-actualization and creativity can occur.

Implications of Cultural Conditions

It is obvious that the complex societal changes needed are major social concerns outside of the domain of this article. However, implications which emerge suggest that (1) psychological relevance in the measurement of creativity should be culturally based, and that (2) where "equal opportunity" for creative development is lacking, assessment procedures must be culturally fair.

Renz and Christoplos (1968) assume that "Areas or categories of giftedness are determined by the prevailing culture . . . . Each culture or sub-culture lays down, within the framework of its own value systems, those syndromes of behavior which are acceptable and/or those in which it will allow gifted behavior to be manifested" (p. 91).

Thus a subculture should assist in setting relevant criteria for measurement of creative abilities if we are to measure creativity within that group. And, in a group in which physiological or psychological disadvantagement is present, measurement should be in terms of the creativity syndromes within the group. In the sections which follow, general concerns in measurement of the disadvantaged and of the culturally different, and possible directions for measurement of creativity, will be discussed. Since the proposed cultural definition and cultural patterning of creativity has but little specification as yet, suggestions in the latter section must be considered as highly tentative.

General Measurement Concerns

Four main issues emerge from the literature on measurement and cultural differences. The predominant literature reported deals with the black subculture. Applicability to other subcultures, such as American Indians, Spanish-heritage Americans, white Appalachian groups, or similar populations, must be estimated in terms of the relative similarities of cultural conditions or values. Focus in the literature is upon measurement fallacies in IQ and achievement testing, but many of the problems deal also with issues of concern to measurement in general.

Issue I

An initial issue has to do with the middle-class, mainstream bases of measurement instruments. Many authors (Gallagher, 1974; Vontress, 1971; Adler, 1973; Voyat, 1969; Zach, 1972; Oakland, 1973; Gay & Abrahams, 1973; Jorgensen, 1973) agree that IQ tests were designed for middle-class populations, so that use of such tests for special programs limits selection to mainstream abilities (Gallagher, 1974).

A conflict of values between minority and majority cultures is evident in the mainstream culture's lack of recognition or underestimation of abilities in minorities (Gallagher, 1974; Gay & Abrahams, 1973). Since testing is based upon assumptions of middle-class opportunity, persons from the general culture overlook the fact that poor children often demonstrate inadequate test performance associated with neglect of physical and psychological needs. The culturally different and the disadvantaged frequently demonstrate low self-concept and motivation on mainstream tests.

"Cultural loadings" (Sullivan, 1973; Adler, 1973; and Zach, 1972) are present and information is biased in content (Jorgensen, 1973). Vontress (1971) indicates that tests require appropriate values and attitudes, and Jorgensen that subscales reflect social values. Vontress also points out that personality tests and interest inventories are irrelevant to culturally different children's experiences.

Williams (1974) and Oakland (1973) view use of culturally biased tests as maintaining racial bias and institutional practices. They reject "deficit" concepts reported by Jensen (1972), Shuey (1966), and others. Ginsburg (1972), one of those who oppose the "deficit" viewpoint, considers it a myth that IQ represents fundamental differences in intellect.

Alternatives to the "deficit" model are the "difference" and the "bicultural" models (Valentine, 1971). The difference model suggests a focus in measurement upon the characteristic experimental development of a particular culture. The bicultural model deals with the dual cultural experiences of ethnic or other cultural identity groups. In this model, compromise measurement procedures apply, combining relevant cultural and mainstream qualities. Vontress (1971) specifies that there is a need to determine the degree of assimilation to the general culture, and Bruch (1974a) has proposed that modifications of assessment for culturally different children be in terms of the extent of biculturation. That is, a child closest to his own cultural experiences should be measured with more cultural specificity; a child with a more acculturated background would be expected to need less cultural focus in measurement instruments or procedures.

Rejection of the deficit approach in favor of measurement concerned with cultural difference or with bicultural models is especially appropriate for assessment of creativity. Voyat (1969) notes that "The whole creative aspect of learning and teaching is completely lost in Jensen's point of view. The child is reduced to a ratio. The teaching act becomes a mechanical adjustment of narrowly identified capacities to severely limited learning goals" (p. 87).

Issue II

The second issue related to the neglect of known subcultural values, abilities, and specific knowledge in current assessment instruments and procedures (Jorgensen, 1973; Gerry, 1973). Jorgensen indicates that "No test developer has made a substantial study of the types of information valued in black culture, nor has any test developer established a frequency of usage table for black vocabulary, information which has been available for white populations since the early 1920s. Bruch (1974b) reiterates the need for modification of standardized instruments with consideration of word usage in various culturally different groups.

Vontress (1971) elaborates on the neglect of relevant language usage in that measurement criteria ignore the variations and subtleties of language of different cultural groups. Cultural values may dictate culturally-right but mainstream-wrong answers (Gallagher, 1974; Sullivan 1973; Gay & Abrahams, 1973; Jorgensen, 1973). Gallagher, reporting upon a conference on culturally different gifted children, found participants agreed that abilities such as those required for art, or personal attributes of persistence and initiative, were often excluded in selection of such gifted students.

The behavioral style required in testing does not utilize the personal style qualities of culturally different children (Vontress, 1971). Culturally relevant test materials are unavailable to motivate these children to perform test tasks (Jorgensen, 1973; Sullivan, 1973; Adler, 1973). In addition, peer pressures for cultural behavior may reduce their acting in a mainstream-approved fashion (Gallagher, 1974).

Koch, quoted by Ginsberg (1972), notes creativity as a quality which also has been misconstrued when he says: "The words deprived and disadvantaged may be thought to apply to (poor) children's imagination and their power to create things, and they do not. The tragedy ... is not that children lack imagination, but that it has been repressed and depressed ..." (p. vi).

Issue III

Further motivational negatives related to educators, test administrators, and test administration combine as a third issue. School staff are trained almost exclusively to use middle-class measurement instruments. Biases of educators who delimit their perceptions to the traditional IQ frame of reference are reinforced by the inability of some to accept cultural pluralism and measures of cultural pluralism (Gallagher, 1974). Teachers and administrators whose mainstream bias interferes with consideration of values from other cultures are unable to identify the cognitive or behavioral strengths of the culturally different (Gallagher, 1974; Oakland, 1973; Gay & Abrahams, 1973).

Test administrators' negative expectancies may affect the performance of those tested (Jorgensen, 1973; Gerry, 1973). Vontress (1971) points out a special problem for the child when a white examiner with a Southern accent is the administrator, for the child may then anticipate negative interaction. Black children may be more fearful of strangers, such as white examiners, according to Vontress, Gerry, and others (Adler, 1973; Gay & Abrahams, 1973). Vontress questions the white examiner's capability for rapport and emphasizes the special need for rapport during the dyadic relationships of individual testing. But, according to Gay and Abrahams, some black children may manipulate the tester.

Administration problems include the child's emotional resentment for a mainstream culture test (Jorgensen, 1973; Adler, 1973; Gerry, 1973). Sullivan (1973, citing Barnes, 1969) states that culturally loaded tests induce guessing and random responding behaviors. Low motivation leads also to less than full effort in responding. Tests which require reading (Vontress, 1971) and those requiring speed and fluency with words (Vontress, 1971; Adler, 1973) present difficulties in administration.

Adler and Jorgensen consider that examiners should attend to the impact of the social setting in order to maintain motivation and interest. Small group rather than large group administration is recommended. Vontress and Adler find culturally different children need special motivational preparation for testing. Jorgensen and Sullivan recommend a play atmosphere in the pretest setting for reliability and validity in the test administration. All authors cited in this section point out the grave importance of motivational factors for the adequacy of measurement findings with culturally different children.

Issue IV

The fourth general measurement concern has to do with fallacies of measurement in culturally different groups. In a conference report on culturally different gifted, Gallagher (1974) cites the conclusion of the conferees that a barrier to identification is the attitude that objective measurement is *the* way to measure, that nothing is worthwhile unless it is objectively measured. Another erroneous assumption is that culturally different children develop in the same manner as those from the mainstream, and that the IQ is therefore valid. Williams (1974) and Jorgensen (1973) seriously question the reliability and validity of IQ measures for different cultural groups. Others (Gallagher, 1974; Oakland, 1973) question the assumption that standardized tests predict adult achievement.

Ginsberg (1972) considers it a myth that these tests measure intellectual competence. He proposes as another myth the assumption that IQ tests measure innate ability relatively without the influence of experience. A further myth is that IQ tests measure unitary abilities. Ginsberg cites Binet in discussion of the complex acts of comprehension, perception, and memory required on the Stanford-Binet. Both Ginsberg and Gallagher confirm that IQ measurement represents a narrow definition of intellect, and a lack of a multiintellectual approach. Less easily measured variables are not tested though they may represent cultural abilities, while skills measured in school are infrequently emphasized in the child's cultural background.

Suggestions for Creativity Measurement in the Culturally Different

Task Construction and Content:

1. Items should relate to information and values relevant and acceptable to the specific subculture, and may contain mainstream tasks which are *equally appropriate for the main and the subculture.*
2. Consideration should be given to construction of instruments "culturally loaded" with tasks representing creative abilities within a given culture.
3. Verbal items and instructions should be so designed that vocabulary and syntax are readily comprehended by the sub-

cultural children at the developmental level for which the tasks are constructed. Pilot studies within the subculture should be made in order to eliminate overweighting of items on vocabulary rather than on creativity components such as divergent production (Guilford, 1967).

4. Measurement tasks should consist of additional creativity components (such as Guilford's transformations and implications products as well as divergent production) for diagnostic/teaching/learning applications. Differential strengths can be used to understand subcultural and individual creativity syndromes.

5. Test manuals should provide information about alternative types of valid responses, alternative response styles, and culturally relevant procedures for each cultural group. Use of nonstandard English, or other native language, should be acceptable. Examples of valid responses, etc., should be determined by measurement staff representative of the particular subculture.

Task Conditions and Methods:

1. Subcultural and/or bicultural identification of the children should be specified as an aid in interpretation of creativity within cultural or mainstream groups.

2. Motivational warm-up presessions should be included as part of the regular task administration. An atmosphere of play is recommended during warm-up and testing.

3. Regular, playful warm-up sessions are suggested prior to measurement in order to develop positive peer attitudes and adequate self-concepts regarding creativity testing.

4. Time limits, with "time-outs" between tasks, should be appropriate for the physical/mental energy levels of the children tested. Nutrition should be adequate prior to testing periods. Long task batteries may need several days of optimal administration conditions in order to maximize the creative energies of economically disadvantaged children, in particular.

5. Administration should be effected by examiners free from attitudes of mainstream bias and capable of rapport with subcultural children.

Personnel:

1. Training sessions should be held for personnel who administer creativity tasks to culturally different children.

2. Ideally, mainstream educators and psychologists should be

trained and evaluated by creativity-oriented staff from the subculture for building their skills in rapport.
3. When mainstream staff are lacking in understanding of cultural values and attitudes, training should also include awareness and development of such sensitivities.
4. Special administration problems detailed earlier under Issue III should be included in the training.
5. Personnel should be trained for attitudes of positive expectancies, such as "creative positives" (Torrance & Torrance, 1972), for the subculture.

Alternatives and New Directions:

1. Criterion-reference evaluation systems, with continuous measurement over time, could be utilized with concern for rate of progress (Drew, 1973). Creativity tasks, such as those specified by Bruch and Torrance (1972), could be the basis for design of criterion-reference continua.
2. Life experiences which relate to creative achievement could be evaluated in forms such as biographical inventories or tasks based upon evidences of creative behavior within the culture (Taylor, 1970; Torrance, 1971; Witt, 1971).
3. Situational tasks in which creative behaviors would be likely to emerge could be designed based upon culturally relevant experiences (Bruch, 1973).
4. Natural setting which provide motivation and opportunities for creative experiences could be utilized wherein careful and sensitive observation could occur (Torrance & Torrance, 1972).
5. Identification of creative abilities valued by a subculture could be systematically researched, with instrumentation and validation established by researchers from the subculture, as was done by Bernal and Reyna (1974).
6. Systematic environments could also be established wherein creative abilities could occur and be noticed by sensitive observers. Such real-life assessment could lead to instructional planning for experiences which were then assessed as to growth in creative abilities.
7. Peer nominations, self-reports, self-expression in creative media, and creative products could be assessed.
8. Creative style qualities, those personal variables generally characterizing creative persons (such as problem-solving, persistence, flexibility, risk-taking, playfulness, humor, etc.), could be observed and/or formulated into other appropriate measurement approaches or devices.
9. Especial attention could be paid to creative use of language:

wit and humor, cleverness in outdoing others in verbal games or "fancy talk," and elegantizing the language (Dillard, 1973).

Finally, creativity assessment, along with expanded and culturally relevant measurement of a broader range of abilities not found in the traditional measurement procedures, could be utilized as a means of improving upon prediction of success in life. Traditional methods, particularly those which present culturally different populations in a "deficit" manner, simply have not been predictive of real-life abilities to cope in spite of difficulties imposed by mainstream society, or to exceed expectations in unexplained ways. Assessment of creativity in culturally different and in disadvantaged children may provide a crucial key to planning learning and to predicting constructive potential for ultimate success.

References

Adler, S. Data gathering: The reliability and validity of test data from culturally different children. *Journal of Learning Disabilities,* 1973, 6(7), 430–434.

Bernal, E. M., & Reyna, J. *Analysis of giftedness in Mexican-American children and design of a prototype identification instrument.* Final report submitted to the Office of Gifted and Talented, USOE, and to NIE (Contract OEC–4–7–062113–307) General Laboratory, Austin, Texas, 1974.

Bruch, C. B. Modification of procedures for identification of the disadvantaged gifted. *Gifted Child Quarterly,* 1971, 15, 267–272.

Bruch, C. B. *Alternative measurement for culturally different gifted.* A paper presented at the North Carolina State Department of Education Conference on Culturally Different Gifted, Rougemont, N.C., December 13, 1973.

Bruch, C. B. *Identification of the strengths of the culturally different.* Paper presented at the annual convention of the National Association of School Psychologists, Las Vegas, Nevada, March 19, 1974. (a)

Bruch, C. B. *Issues in the testing of vocabulary in black children.* Paper presented at the Harcourt Brace Jovanovich Invitational Test Conference, Knoxville, Tenn., December 6, 1974. (b)

Bruch, C. B., & Torrance, E. P. Reaching the creatively gifted. *National Elementary Principal,* 1972, 51(5), 69–75.

Dillard, J. L. *Black English: Its history and usage in the United States.* New York: Vintage Books, 1973.

Drew, C. J. Criterion-referenced and norm-referenced assessment of minority group children. *Journal of School Psychology,* 1973, 11(4), 323–329.

Fishman, J. A., Deutsch, M., Kogan, L., North, R., & Whiteman, M. Guidelines for testing minority group children. In H. Passow, M. Goldberg, & A. J. Tannenbaum (Eds.), *Education of the Disadvantaged.* New York: Holt, Rinehart & Winston, 1967, pp. 155–169.

Gallagher, J. J. *Talent delayed—talent denied: A conference report.* Reston, Va.: Foundation for Exceptional Children, 1974.

Gay, G., & Abrahams, R. D. Does the pot melt, boil, or brew? Black children and white assessment procedures. *Journal of School Psychology.* 1973, 11(4), 330–340.

Gerry, M. H. Cultural myopia: The need for a corrective lens. *Journal of School Psychology,* 1973, 11(4), 307–312.

Ginsberg, H. *The myth of the deprived child: Poor children's intellect and education.* Englewood Cliffs, N.J.: Prentice-Hall, 1972.

Guilford, J. P. *The nature of human intelligence.* New York: Mc Graw-Hill, 1967.

Jensen, A. How much can we boost IQ and scholastic achievement? In A. Jensen (Ed.), *Genetics and education.* New York: Harper & Row, 1972, pp. 69–203.

Jorgensen, C. C. IQ tests and their educational supporters. *Journal of Social Issues,* 1973, 29(1), 33–40.

Maslow, A. H. *Motivation and personality.* Rev. ed. New York: Harper & Brothers, 1970.

Montagu, Ashley. *Culture and human development: Insights into growing human.* Englewood Cliffs, N.J.: Prentice-Hall, 1974.

Oakland, T. Assessing minority group children: Challenges for school psychologists. *Journal of School Psychology,* 1973, 11(4), 294–303.

Renz, P., & Christoplos, F. Toward an operational definition of giftedness. *Journal of Creative Behavior,* 1968, 2(2), 91–96.

Rogers, C. R. Toward a theory of creativity. In S. J. Parnes & H. F. Harding (Eds.), *A source book for creative thinking.* New York: Scribners, 1962.

Shuey, A. M. *The testing of Negro intelligence.* 2nd ed. New York: Social Science Press, 1966.

Sullivan, A. R. The identification of gifted and academically talented black students: A hidden exceptionality. *Journal of Special Education,* 1973, 7(4), 373–379.

Taylor, C. W. Most extreme cases of predicted percentile ranks from Alpha Biographical Inventory. Unpublished manuscript, Institute for Behavior Research in Creativity, Salt Lake City, 1970.

Torrance, E. P. Are the Torrance Tests of Creative Thinking biased against or in favor of "disadvantaged" groups? *Gifted Child Quarterly,* 1971, 15(2), 75–80.

Torrance, E. P., & Torrance, P. Combining creative problem-solving with creative expressive activities in the education of disadvantaged young people. *Journal of Creative Behavior,* 1972, 6(1), 1–10.

Valentine, C. A. Deficit, difference, and bicultural models of Afro-

American behavior. *Harvard Educational Review,* 1971, 41(2), 137–159.

Vontress, C. E. *Counseling Negroes.* New York: Houghton Mifflin, 1971.

Voyat, G. IQ: God-given or man-made? *Saturday Review,* May 17, 1969, 73–75.

Williams, R. L. The silent mugging of the black community. *Psychology Today,* 1974, 7(12), 32, 34, 37, 38, 41, 101.

Witt, G. The Life Enrichment Activity Program, Inc.: A continuing program for creative, disadvantaged children. *Journal of Research and Development in Education,* 1971, 4(3), 67–73.

Zach, L. The IQ debate. *Today's Education,* 1972, 61, 40–43, 65, 66, 68.

Chapter Eleven

Women

Introduction

In the original edition of this book there was no chapter on women. The fact that there is one in this revision recognizes the rapid cultural advance made in the interim regarding discrimination against gifted women and the consequent cultural waste of their potential creativity. This loss is probably the greatest reparable error which our society makes, and the recent attention given to the issue of developing the talents of gifted women testifies to its importance.

We shall not succeed at this task merely by invoking polemics against cultural discrimination. What we need is research to determine if there are other causes besides discrimination, and if there are specific ways in which discrimination acts. Then we can try to eradicate these factors. Everyone admits that women are at least as intelligent as men; but for some reason or reasons they are generally not as productively creative adults as men are. Let us brainstorm on some possible reasons why.

The routine of establishing the proposition can be performed in an armchair. Write down ten categories in which creativity has historically been measured—say, fine art, music, mathematics, science, governance, religion and sainthood, poetry, philosophy, literature, and medicine, for example. Now write down the first twenty names which occur to you of the greatest figures in each category. Now, look at the lists to see what percentage are women. If we attempt the (perhaps) even simpler task of picking the greatest geniuses the world has ever seen in these categories—say Leonardo, Beethoven, Gauss, Einstein, Lincoln, St. Francis, Tennyson, Spinoza, Shakespeare, and Pasteur, how many women are there in this group?

Let us also make quick stipulation on the other three ancillary variables, besides sex. Differences in creativity between the sexes are not due to differences in intelligence, to differences in age or socioeconomic status. There is, therefore, no interaction between these four variables on this factor. We have now cleared the decks for action with regard to the direct effects of sex on creativity.

Here are some possible hypotheses (none proved) as to why men are more creative than women:

1. Cultural discrimination.
2. Sexual dominance patterns established in mammals.
3. The fact that men make the rules about how creativity shall be measured.
4. The Gooch hypothesis (*Total Man*, Ballantine Books, 1974) that women represent a lower evolutionary type in which the cerebellum instead of the cerebrum is dominant.
5. Oedipal advantages males have (closeness to mothers during Narcissistic period).
6. A sex-linked gene such as the Y.
7. The fact that women have a physical outlet for creativity in the bearing of children.
8. The hypothesis that men incline to be rational and cognitive, while women are emotional and intuitive.
9. The testosterone levels, and the resultant tendency of males to explore and aggress.
10. Jungian differences between *animus* and *anima.*
11. The possibility that the pathway toward creativity in women may be fraught with more hazards to their mental health.
12. The possibility that meditation/healing and creativity are twin functions, and that women are more adept at the first and men at the second.
13. The possibility that in women creativity is a process whereas in men it is a product.
14. Natural selection causes in evolution, in that creative women do not leave as many descendants as noncreative women.

Let us immediately note that these possible causes are not mutually exclusive, so that we are not so much deciding between them as assigning possible variance to each. For example, it is perfectly obvious that *some* component of creativity differential in males/females is due to cultural discrimination. What is equally obvious to this writer (although not to many women), is that this is *not* the *only* reason. Perhaps it might be well to establish this fact at once. Fortunately, the means to do so requires only armchair thought.

Let us assume that cultural discrimination is the only reason (a favorite contention of some writers) and then see where this allegation gets us. If such blanket discrimination operates, it cannot operate differentially, that is it cannot operate in one area more effectively than in another. Let us now go back to our ten categories of creativity listed above. One finds immediately that there are four areas, governance, sainthood, poetry, and the novel, where there *are* significant numbers of creative women, Queen Elizabeth I, St. Teresa, Elizabeth Barrett Browning, and George Sand being notable examples in each class. Women are generally more fond of art and regarded as more aesthetic than men; why are there not percentage-wise as many great women artists as poets if discrimination operates upon all? There seems to be no answer to this question at present.

One of the most scholarly analyses of the differences between males and females was made by Maccoby and Jacklin (1974:110–114). They state: "It is well known that men are much more heavily represented than women in the ranks of outstanding creative artists, writers, and scientists." They believe "something in women's life situations" reduces their chance of creativity. In those instances where high-level production must at least partially result from training they note (p. 164) that such avenues "have been closed to women" under usual situations.

After having noted no sex differences in Piagetian logical reasoning tasks (1974:106, 109), their Table 3.13 cites 21 studies of divergent thinking or verbal creativity test results. On a sheer numerical count five favored males and ten favored females, indicating as they summarize "beyond the age of seven an advantage to girls." On nonverbal creativity (their Table 4.13), males have the advantage eight times and females eight times, for no advantage.

With regard to variables correlated with creativity, these authors report inconsistent results with regard to curiosity (p. 145), six studies favoring boys and four favoring girls. With regard to self-esteem (p. 152), six studies favored males and nine females out of an N of 39. With regard to confidence in task performance, men have a clear superiority, 11–0, in 14 studies (p. 155). With regard to internal locus of control (p. 156), the score is 4–3 out of 17 studies, no clear advantage. In self-concept (strength and potency, p. 158), the score is 7–0 out of eight studies. In social self-concept, however (p. 158), the score is 1–6 out of ten studies.

If we look at the women in the areas of governance, mysticism, and poetry for example, we are bound to admit that there is some truth to the matter of cultural discrimination. For it is at once obvious that in these three areas, there are reasons for the differential effects of diminished cultural discrimination. It is very hard (except under the Salic law) to discriminate against the female heir of a throne. Mysticism and poetry are two accomplishments which can be practiced in private and which require almost no training, and the avenues to which cannot be closed off to a denigrated group, as (for example) the specialized training in an art school or an institute of technology. One still wonders, however, if this fact fully explains why there are so few great women artists and musical composers.

A charge sometimes heard is that women spend their creativity in motherhood. If this be so, then a selection of men and women who lived childless and unmarried lives might be useful. If we look at the creative performance of these individuals, we again find that while the field has been much reduced, it is still the men who have the preponderance. Even in an occupation where virginity is a professional requirement, there have been more male than female saints.

Could it just be that men are more creative than women because men won't allow a creative woman to propagate herself? It's a case of biological adaptation through the generations. To simplify matters, let us suppose we start with a group of people in which men and women are equally creative, and suppose further, that each family has four children, one boy more creative one less, and two girls one more creative and one less. Now imagine these children to grow up and intermarry for say 20 generations. On the average the creative boy will develop into a more successful man than the noncreative boy, and hence he will tend to leave more descendants. But the noncreative girl will tend to leave more descendants than the creative girl because creativity in adult women is likely to interfere at least to some extent with marriage and family, and to some extent keep the woman less marriageable. True, there are some exceptions, but if this sort of natural selection goes on for a while, in a few dozen generations a stock will have selected itself whose men are more naturally creative and whose women less naturally so.

If this is true, then a great biological injustice has been done to women; and the only remedy is to remake societal mores so that men will not select noncreative girls for mates more often than creative ones.

32 Improving Predictions of the Adult Creative Achievement of Gifted Girls by Using Autobiographical Information

E. PAUL TORRANCE, CATHERINE B. BRUCH, AND JEAN A. MORSE

A long-range predictive validity study by the senior author (Torrance, 1972a, 1972b, 1972c) indicates that, using tests of creative abilities, it is more difficult to predict twelve years later the adult creative achievements of women than of men. The study reported herein is a further follow-up of this study to find out if the use of autobiographical information would improve prediction of the creative achievement of women.

While there has been much discussion in the literature about the relative merits of measures of creative thinking ability and biographical and personality data as predictors of creative achievement (Holland, 1961; MacKinnon, 1962; Taylor & Holland, 1964), it seems fairly obvious to the present authors that both types of measures are important. For creative achievement, a person must have not only the required abilities but the motivation and background experiences necessary to make use of these abilities.

The studies making claims for the superiority of personality and biographical data have generally been only with adults and not long range in nature.

Procedures

A long-range predictive validity study of the *Torrance Tests of Creative Thinking* was initiated in September 1959. These tests were administered to the total population of the University of Minnesota High School (grades 7 through 12). The mean intelligence quotient of the 392 students for which there were complete data was 118, and the mean percentile rank on the Iowa Tests of Educational Development was 84 on national norms.

From *The Gifted Child Quarterly* 17 (1973). Used by permission.

Follow-up data were obtained during the winter and spring of 1971 from 117 of the women and 119 of the men tested in 1959. The follow-up questionnaire requested information concerning their post–high school careers with special emphasis on their creative achievement, three most important achievements, and aspirations. Generally, subjects supplied rather complete data, rich in information about what has been happening to young people now between the ages of 25 and 31.

The creativity tests were scored in 1959 according to the scoring guides then in use for the following variables: fluency (number of relevant responses), flexibility (variety of categories of responses), inventive level (development of inventions which show a stride forward; creative strength; something unusual, remarkable, or surprising; novelty of implementation; prior failure and skepticism; etc.), and elaboration (amount of detail used to describe how ideas would be executed). In 1961, all tests were rescored for originality according to a guide developed at that time. The interscorer reliability of each of the scorers in all cases was in excess of .90 for all variables.

A measure of quantity of creative achievements was obtained by adding the number of creative achievements checked by each subject. The checklist called for reports of such achievements as the number of poems, stories, dramas, or novels published; musical compositions published; scientific and professional papers published; research grants obtained; patents and inventions; business or professional organizations created; awards in art, literature, music, or leadership; art exhibitions; and instructional materials created. The measure of quality of creative achievement was based on the ratings of five expert judges of the descriptions of the three most creative achievements reported by subjects. The measure of creative aspirations was based on similar ratings of the statements of the subjects concerning what they would most like to do in the future, assuming the necessary talent, training, and opportunity. The mean reliability coefficient of the five judges was .91.

When the senior author found that it was more difficult to predict the adult creative achievement of women in his long-range predictive validity study than the men, the other two authors joined with him to investigate this problem further. One aspect of this effort involved the administration of the *Alpha Biographical Inventory* (Institute for Behavioral Research in Creativity, 1968) to the 117 female subjects of the original study. This instrument is an outgrowth of the work of Calvin W. Taylor, R. L. Ellison, and their associates (Taylor & Ellison, 1967) and consists of 300 multiple-choice items involving life experiences and attitudes found to be associated with creative achievement. The young women in the original study were asked to respond as they would have in 1959.

Results

The subjects were asked not only to complete the 300-item *Alpha Biographical Inventory* and to try to recapture the feelings they had about their experiences over 12 years earlier, but also to complete additional instruments developed by the junior authors. Thus, it is not too surprising that complete Inventory responses were obtained from only 45 of the subjects. Most of these respondents expressed great interest in the study, and some of them wrote accompanying letters of several pages. Also, some of those who did not complete the Inventory wrote and expressed the difficulty they had experienced in trying to recapture the feelings they had in 1959.

In spite of these limitations, the authors believe that the data provide useful information concerning the issue under study. Furthermore, a comparison of the characteristics of the 45 respondents indicates that they are not significantly different from the total group of 117 women respondents and that the relationship between the predictor and criterion variables are about the same in both the responding group and the total group.

TABLE 32.1

Product-Moment Coefficients of Correlation Between Alpha Biographical Creativity Scale Scores and Other Predictors

Variable	Number	r	Level of Signif.
Fluency	45	.10	NS
Flexibility	45	.13	NS
Inventiveness	45	.18	NS
Total (1959 scoring)	45	.16	NS
Originality (1961 scoring)	45	.18	NS
Intelligence	45	.22	NS
Achievement (ITED total)	45	.21	NS

Table 32.1 presents the product-movement coefficients of correlation between *Alpha Biographical* Creativity Scale scores and the other predictors. As will be noted, none of these relationships is significant at the five percent level of confidence. Thus, the Creativity Scale of the *Alpha Biographical Inventory* appears to be assessing something essentially different from the other predictor variables.

Table 32.2 presents the product-moment coefficients of correlation between the predictors and each of the three criteria of adult creativity. It will be noted that both the *Alpha Biographical* Creativity Scale and the creative thinking ability scores are significantly related to the criteria of creative achievement. The best single predictor seems to be the inventiveness score of the *Torrance Tests of Creative Thinking*, followed in order by originality, total creativity score (1959 scoring), *Alpha Biographical* creativity, flexibility, fluency, intelligence quotient, and achievement as measured by the total score on the *Iowa Tests of Educational Development.*

TABLE 32.2
Product-Moment Coefficients of Correlation between Predictors and Criteria of Creative Achievement 12 Years Later

		r		
Predictor	*Number*	*Quantity*	*Quality*	*Aspirations*
Alpha Biographical	45	.38*	.39*	.37*
Fluency	45	.27	.31**	.26
Flexibility	45	.34**	.43*	.28**
Inventiveness	45	.48*	.60*	.49*
Total (1959 score)	45	.38*	.44*	.35**
Originality (1961)	45	.40*	.50*	.43*
Intelligence	45	.09	.37*	.32*
Achievement (ITED total)	45	.12	.35**	.23

*Significant at <.01 level
**Significant at <.05 level

It was decided to represent the creative thinking ability predictors by the total score obtained in 1959 and the originality score developed in 1961 in conducting the canonical correlation. Thus, the *Alpha Biographical Inventory* Creativity Scale score, the total creativity score, and the originality score were combined to predict the criterion consisting of quantity of creative achievements, quality of highest creative achievements, and creativeness of aspirations. A canonical correlation of .60, significant at the .01 level, was obtained. When this is compared with the canonical correlation of .43 for women in the original study, we obtain an index of the contribution of the Creativity Scale of the *Alpha Biographical Inventory.*

Discussion

Although the relatively small number of subjects and the "after the fact" nature of the *Alpha Biographical Inventory* data are limiting factors, the evidence presented herein argues strongly for the use of a combination of biographical information and creative thinking ability measures for predicting adult creative achievement of young women. Separately, these two kinds of measures predict the criteria only moderately, and their relationship to one another is not statistically significant. However, by combining them a canonical correlation of .60 is obtained, compared with one of .43 for the various ability measures combined. The importance of both types of predictors is illustrated dramatically in almost every case in which one or the other of the predictors failed to predict accurately. For example, women having high ability scores and low achievement tended to have low Creativity Scale scores on the *Alpha Biographical Inventory*, and those with higher achievement than would have been predicted by their ability scores tended to have exceptionally high scores on the Creativity Scale.

As in some of the earlier studies, the inventiveness score on the Torrance tests comes out surprisingly well with product-moment coefficients of correlation of .48, .60, and .49 with the criteria of creative achievement. It was with great reluctance that the senior author several years ago stopped using this score in work with the *Torrance Tests of Creative Thinking*. The scoring procedure was somewhat complex and was too time-consuming. Instead, the originality score has been developed and was applied in the canonical correlation conducted in the present study.

Of the predictors used in this study it is interesting to note that intelligence quotient and total achievement on the *Iowa Tests of Educational Development* are relatively less effective than both the Creativity Scale of the *Alpha Biographical Inventory* and the creative thinking ability scores. This is especially true in predicting the quantity index of creative achievements, the most objective of the criterion measures.

References

Holland, John L. "Creative and Academic Performance among Talented Adolescents." *Journal of Educational Psychology*, 1961, 52, 136–137.

Institute for Behavioral Research in Creativity. *Manual for Alpha Biographical Inventory*. Salt Lake City: Prediction Press, 1968.

MacKinnon, Donald W. (Ed.) *The Creative Person*. Berkeley, Calif.: General Extension, University of California, 1962.

Taylor, Calvin W., and Ellison, Robert L. "Biographical Predictors of Scientific Performance." *Science*, 1967, 155, 1075–1080.

Taylor, Calvin W., and Holland, John L. "Predictors of Creative Performance." In C. W. Taylor (Ed.), *Creativity: Progress and Potential*. New York: McGraw-Hill, 1964.

Torrance, E. P. "Creative Young Women in Today's World." *Exceptional Children*, 1972, 38, 597–603. (a)

Torrance, E. P. "Predictive Validity of the Torrance Tests of Crea-

tive Thinking." *Journal of Creative Behavior,* 1972, *6,* 236–252.
(b)
Torrance, E. P. "Career Patterns and Peak Creative Achievements
of Creative High School Students 12 Years Later." *Gifted Child
Quarterly,* 1972, *16,* 75–88. (c)

33 Developmental Process Theory as Applied to Mature Women

JULIA SIMPSON

The proper development of gifted women depends upon a better
understanding of developmental stages. In the study of such stages
one is impressed with the fact that different people, working at
different times and places, have come up with theories of development that fit together well. By understanding the levels to which a
fully liberated person might escalate, we are much better able to
diagnose barriers which prevent gifted women from reaching them.

The first two theories, Erikson's affective stages and Piaget's cognitive stages, have been combined by Gowan (1972a: 28, 1974:51).
We have added William Perry's stages, which we call conative stages,
and Lawrence Kohlberg's moral stages. The headings on the chart
(Figure 33.1) are Gowan's. The numbers 1, 2, and 3 across the top
refer to first, second and third person.

Erikson's eight stages deal with the affective areas of personality
expansion and ego-strength. Piaget, further expanded by Gowan,
deals with the cognitive or conceptual aspects of development. Perry
is concerned with the conative or "choice-making" aspects of intellectual and ethical development, and Kohlberg's theory concerns the
moral developmental stages.

It is interesting to look at these theories of development in relation
to each other and see how they all fall generally along the same lines
and how development in one area corresponds to another. All of the
placements on the chart are tentative, and each person who looks at
the chart will probably see areas where they would have placed some
things differently, but I think the main point is that they all seem to

From *The Gifted Child Quarterly* 21:3 (1977). Used by permission.
For more on the career and life satisfactions of gifted women, see Sears and Barbee,
pp. 28–66 in Stanley and others (1977).

		LATENCY
ATTENTIONAL MODES ⟶		3. it, they
DEVELOPMENTAL LEVELS ↓		THE WORLD
ERIKSON (Affective)	INFANT–CHILD	TRUST vs. MISTRUST Virtues: drive—hope
PIAGET (Cognitive)		SENSORIMOTOR vs. CHAOS Trust in percepts vs. unmeaningful chaos
PERRY (Conative)		BASIC DUALITY I Good vs. bad—right vs. wrong
KOHLBERG (Moral)		PREMORAL LEVEL Good is what is pleasurable; bad is what is painful or fearful
ERIKSON (Affective)	YOUTH	INDUSTRY vs. INFERIORITY Virtues: method—competence
PIAGET-GOWAN (Cognitive)		CONCRETE OPERATIONS vs. IV NONCONSERVATION Competence in "tool world" manipulation vs. magical thinking
PERRY (Conative)		MULTIPLICITY CORRELATE OR RELATIVISM SUBORDINATE Duality restructured in complex terms; "Everyone has a right to his opinion."
KOHLBERG (Moral)		CONVENTIONAL LEVEL (Stage 3) "Good-child" orientation; whatever pleases others and is approved by them; conforming
ERIKSON (Affective)	ADULT	GENERATIVITY vs. STAGNATION Virtues: production—care
GOWAN (Cognitive)		PSYCHEDELIA vs. CONVENTIONALISM Self-actualizing mind-expansion vs. authoritarian conventional conformity VII
PERRY (Conative)		INITIAL COMMITMENT First commitments or affirmations; acceptance of origins in self
KOHLBERG (Moral)		POSTCONVENTIONAL (Cont.) Universal principle orientation; right is defined in accord with self-chosen ethical principles; universality; respect for dignity of human beings as individuals

FIGURE 33.1

Developmental Stages as Applied to Women

Source: Erikson, Piaget, Gowan charts from Gowan (1972a:28; 1974:51.) Perry chart
from Perry (1970). Kohlberg stages from Kohlberg and Selman (1972:19–20).

IDENTITY	CREATIVITY
1. I, me	2. thou
THE EGO	THE OTHER

AUTONOMY vs. SHAME AND DOUBT Virtues: self-control—will power	INITIATIVE vs. GUILT Virtues: direction—purpose
PREOPERATIONALISM vs. AUTISM Identity development vs. psychotic block **II**	INTUITIVE vs. IMMOBILIZATION Creative fantasy vs. magic nightmare **III**
MULTIPLICITY-PRELEGITIMATE I am right; others are wrong or confused	MULTIPLICITY SUBORDINATE Trust in authority is not threatened, but multiplicity is perceived
PRECONVENTIONAL LEVEL (Stage 1) Obedience and punishment; physical consequences of action determine its "goodness" or "badness"	PRECONVENTIONAL LEVEL (Stage 2) HEDONISM; "right" is satisfying one's own needs

IDENTITY vs. ROLE DIFFUSION Virtues: devotion—fidelity	INTIMACY vs. ISOLATION Virtues: love—affiliation
FORMAL OPERATIONS vs. DEMENTIA PRAECOX **V** Logical thinking and hypothesis making vs. adolescent schizophrenia	CREATIVITY vs. AUTHORITARIANISM Creative functioning vs. "herd" behavior **VI**
RELATIVISM CORRELATE, COMPETING OR DIFFUSE Relativism perceived intrinsically is accepted generally, but without implication or commitment	COMMITMENT FORESEEN Relativism is accepted for all secular purposes, including binary judgment and action. Commitment seen as logical for action
CONVENTIONAL LEVEL (Stage 4) Law and order orientation; authority; doing one's duty; pulling one's weight	POSTCONVENTIONAL LEVEL— AUTONOMOUS General individual rights; standards agreed upon by society; majority rule.

EGO-INTEGRITY vs. DESPAIR Virtues: renunciation—wisdom	AGAPE-LOVE **IX**
ILLUMINATION vs. SENILE DEPRESSION Global brotherly compassion and altruism vs. depression and senile lack of reality orientation **VIII**	COSMIC KNOWLEDGE
ORIENTATION IN IMPLICATIONS OF COMMITMENT AND DEVELOPING COMMITMENTS Identity sensed in both content of commitments and in personal style of address to them. Membership with authority; commitments expended as growth	BECOME FUSED INTO UNITY EXPANDED IDENTITY
Continuation and expansion of last stage; reverence for life	MORAL { responsibility / ability / desire }

generally fit together and help to explain how the developmental processes take place.

Of course, the stages would not be as definite and clear-cut as shown on the chart. There would be overlapping and continuity from one stage to the next. I particularly see overlapping in Kohlberg's moral stages. Kohlberg's stages 1 and 2 would tend to merge in stage II, and his 2 and 3 would, I think, tend to merge in stage III. Perry's initial commitment would probably begin in stage VI rather than VII but would continue in VII along with developing commitments. Also, the basic duality of Perry's stage I would probably extend, to some extent, through all of the early stages.

Perry himself extrapolated the lower and higher positions in his stages for the general logic of the scheme. They didn't fit in with the age groups that he was studying. His developmental stages were used originally in showing how college students passed through different stages of ethical and intellectual development into maturity—a development from dualistic relativism to acceptance of generalized relativism and subsequent development in orienting oneself in a relativistic world through the activity of personal commitment. But we see this development as fitting into the whole developmental process.

Perry (1970:204–205) compares and contrasts his study to that of Piaget's developmental stages. He says that one way to look at his scheme is as adding an advanced "period" to Piaget's outline. This he would call the "period of responsibility." He feels that the first half of his chart reveals processes paralleling those of motoric, cognitive, and moral decentering, as portrayed in each of Piaget's periods. Perry feels that in the second half, the shift is away from spatial-cognitive, to more humanistic and philosophical concerns. This, I feel, is where the expansion of Piaget by Gowan fits in. I see the connection in the same sort of "outward" movement that Gowan talks about in his higher stages as Perry is discussing in his higher stages.

Kohlberg (in DeCecco, 1970:41–42) says that moral thought seems to behave like all other kinds of thought: "Progress through the moral levels and stages is characterized by increasing differentiations and increasing integration, and hence is the same kind of progress that scientific theory represents, and ... like scientific theory, moral thought expands to contain in a self-consistent way, a wider and wider experimental field." I see this as the same kind of "outward" focus as discussed in the higher stages of the other theories.

Kohlberg (1969:80) also compares his work with that of Piaget. He says that many of his stages coincide descriptively with Piaget's but differ in interpretation. He says that like Piaget (and we would add Perry, Erikson, and Gowan), he found age increases in notions of relativism of value, and in egalitarian denial of the moral superiority of authorities. So we can see in this the parallels of Kohlberg's stages to the others.

Some Aspects of Development

There are several basic ideas that we need to keep in mind when we talk about developmental stages. In *The Guidance and Measurement of Intelligence, Development, and Creativity,* Gowan (1972b:178) says that development differs from growth in that it involves a change in quality, whereas growth involves a change in quantity. He uses as an example an apple ripening, as well as enlarging. This example is particularly applicable in reference to adult developmental stages. Many people tend to think of developmental stages only as pertaining to children, but if we think in terms of quality of life, we can better understand the process of moving through the higher stages.

Another aspect of developmental stages that we must keep in mind is that development is not a smooth progression. Gowan (1972a:25) says, "Development is like a Fourier series, or a flight of locks, namely a staircase-like parameter of hierarchical nature with discrete levels." Development is escalation over periods of time.

There are five aspects of escalation that we need to keep in mind (Gowan 1972a:37–52). They are:

1. Succession—the fixed order or hierarchy of developmental processes.
2. Discontinuity—the input of energy to escalate development.
3. Emergence—each phase contains some of the last phase and the growth potential of the succeeding stages.
4. Differentiation—clarifies, fixates, and modifies the emphasis in developmental processes; the sudden switch in emphasis from one stage to the next.
5. Integration—synthesizes the others. "Puts it all together."

Kohlberg (Kohlberg & Meyer, 1972:458) states that "Attainment of a higher stage presupposes attainment of the prior stage, and represents a reorganization or transformation of it."

Perry (1970:46) says that we do not assume that development proceeds at a smooth rate, but in spurts or in stages. Stages refer to relatively stable forms, and the less stable forms which mediate between stages are transitions. He also states that the stages may vary considerably in duration from one person to another but will follow the same general pattern.

So we understand that each stage is successive—that growth from one stage to the next is sequential. But what we cannot assume is that growth or succession from one stage to the next is automatic. There are many reasons why individuals do not progress; why they get "stuck" in any particular stage and are unable to move on the next.

The reasons for, and the results of, the failures to move from one stage to the next are discussed in different terms by different authors. Gowan (1972b:179) lists seven ways in which a healthy person may be affected by environment at any particular developmental stage:

1. Lethally, that is, he may be killed.
2. Stunted, that is his further development may be stopped, so that he remains permanently at the present stage.
3. Blighted, that is while there may be further development, there will not be further escalation: the development sequence has been damaged.
4. Partially successful, that is the person will go on, but with some problems of arrested development, such as neurosis.
5. Successful, but only after strong effort and emotional expenditure, in which case the interests and attitudes will be haunted by an affective "ghost" organized around the continuing emotional aura required for the task. An example would be the adult "anal" personality.
6. Fully successful, without difficulty.
7. Overly successful; the person may come to enjoy the tasks and successes of this period so much, that they, and not the onward course of development, become the goal. This condition makes it difficult to incorporate and integrate the lessons of this stage into the succeeding ones.

Gowan (1974:48–49) also talks about developmental dysplasia. "Developmental stages are characterized by escalation which involves five separate, but interrelated aspects (which we discussed earlier), known as succession, discontinuity, emergence, differentiation, and integration; the concept of developmental dysplasia arises from a failure to escalate." It involves some aspect of developmental lag, arrest, or slowdown, which means that some part of the development of the individual is behind schedule.

This can be an absolute dysplasia, in which there is a disparity between the age of the individual, which should place him in one stage, and the different stage that he is actually in, or a relative dysplasia, in which there is a disparity between the cognitive stage and the affective stage. These are never more than two stages apart, however. The most common dysplasia in adult development is VII–V (parental–formal operations) in which the affective level reaches parental stage, but the cognitive level stays at formal operations.

Perry (1970:177–200), in discussing ways in which individuals get "stuck" at various levels, uses terms such as temporizing, retreat, and escape. He calls these alternatives to growth.

By "temporizing," Perry means a prolonged pause, but not entrenchment, in any of the stages. "He may pause for a year or more, often quite aware of the step that lies ahead of him, as if waiting or gathering his forces."

By "retreat," he means an active denial of the potential of a particular stage by a reaction of high anxiety or resentment, or by passive resistance, or by rebelling against being in that stage and retreating to an earlier one. He may have to retreat to an old position in order to assure himself that he is still his own person, and then having found that he is still free to choose, could reengage in the new stage.

Perry uses "escape" as a term meaning denying or rejecting the implications for growth in a particular developmental stage. In other words, the individual becomes encapsulated or limited to the particular stage that he is in. This can occur for many reasons, including one mentioned earlier of being *too* successful in a particular stage.

Kohlberg (in Kohlberg & Mayer, 1972:490) uses a term that we need to be familiar with, horizontal decalage. It is defined as the spread or generalization across the range of basic physical and social actions, concepts, and objects to which the stage potentially applies. Kohlberg feels that a focus upon horizontal decalage for "healthy" passage through stages is more important than acceleration to the next stage—that problems are presented by the premature development to a higher ego stage without a corresponding decalage throughout the stage. Acceleration without decalage makes the individual vulnerable to regression under stress later in life. This is similar to Gowan's idea of dysplasia.

One other aspect of development that we need to take note of is that affective tasks are not completed in the same stage that they are begun in. It is a continuing process that is begun in one stage, more fully developed and integrated in the next two succeeding stages, and finally is accomplished in the fourth stage ahead. This can be noted by a study of the different stages on the chart. Gowan (1974: 58) uses trust as an example of this continuing process. Trust is begun in stage I, integrates, and gives rise to autonomy in stage II, is fulfilled and enjoyed in a thrusting initiative in stage III, is reconfirmed as industry in stage IV, and is completed as the adolescent learns to trust his identity to his peers in stage V. In each of these changes there is escalation from level to level.

The same idea generally applies to all the developmental tasks. They are not necessarily completed in the same stage that they are begun in. Some aspects carry over from one stage to the next, and regression under stress is possible.

Development as Related to Women

Developmental stages, as pertaining particularly to women, is a field that has not been very fully explored but, I feel, is an area worthy of much attention, especially now, with the growing emphasis on the Women's Liberation Movement and the focus on women's roles. My own theory is that, for many women, more time will be spent in certain developmental stages, and that the progression through these stages may be quite uneven.

For reasons, whether inherent or cultural, that we do not fully understand, many women will need to spend more time fulfilling: the affiliation needs in stage VI, and the parental needs in stage VII, in the affective area; more time in stage V, formal operations, in the cognitive area, and in conventional level of moral commitment; and more time in stage VI, in conative development. (Perry defines commitment as "A conscious act or realization of identity and responsibility, a process of orientation of self in a relative world.")

These are the areas that I see the typical, traditional woman as spending most of her adult life in. I am not unbiased as to the "traditional woman's role," having spent most of my adult life as primarily wife, homemaker, and mother; but I am coming to realize, more and more, that this role is not for all women for all time, and that, as needs are filled in one stage, a woman or any individual, can be freed and stimulated to move on to the next—that a woman who is reaching toward self-actualizing, or ego-integrity, can fill different roles at different times of her life, perhaps even more so than a man.

In order to try to understand some of the reasoning behind this, we need to look at several theories. The first that I would like to examine is one that interprets some sex-linked differences, other than the obvious physical ones, as inherent.

Erik Erikson (1973) says that the existence of a productive inner bodily space, set in the center of female form and carriage, has a reality superior to that of the missing penis (to which Freud ascribed all of our problems). Erikson found in play therapy studies that girls emphasized inner space, and boys, outer space. He feels that if woman is actualized to the point that she can reflect, without apology, this "inner-space," she can bring her own unique talents and viewpoints to the leadership of the affairs of man. I see this as moving into stages of creative functioning and self-actualizing, ego-integrity, postconventional morality, and developing commitment.

Many women's liberation adherents reject this theory on the grounds that it is the same old idea of a man placing woman in a nurturing type of role, and they believe that is culturally influenced rather than inherent. But longitudinal studies of children have shown consistent sex differences, over a period of time, in activity, passivity, introversion, and extroversion. Females tend to be more passive, less active, more introverted, which would agree with Erikson's inner bodily space theory. Of course, there are cultural influences on these traits, and these too would be reflected in longitudinal studies, but studies of male and female monkeys have shown these sex-linked traits within a month after birth, so I don't think that we can dismiss the idea of inherent differences in these traits.

Another theory that I would like to discuss is that of Judith Bardwick. In *Psychology of Women* (1971), she talks about some of the sex-linked differences in the developmental processes that she has found in her work. One of these differences is that, for many reasons, the American girl rarely achieves an independent sense of self and self-esteem. She feels that boys' self-esteem is based mainly on achievement, and girls' mainly on acceptance. An independent sense of self, with a resulting sense of self-esteem, can only evolve when the individual alone sets out to attain goals and, with reasonable frequency, achieves them.

Because girls are more likely to continue in the dependent roles and are valued by significant adults because of this, they have less need to look within themselves for rewards or esteem. I see this as a failure to fully meet the identity needs of stage five. The achievement and identity needs of stage five are merged with the affiliation and intimacy needs of stage six. In other words, the achievement needs are not met independently but through another person.

Another interesting theory of Bardwick's (1971:138–39) is also in the area of identity. She says that identification is a developmental process and involves identification with both parents. The girl identifies with the personal qualities and the maternal role of the mother, but simultaneously identifies with the father when she loves and is loved by him. If a girl rejects the maternal role, or is rejected by the mother, or has an "achieving" mother or other female as role model, she may identify more with the father's role activity. In that way she may see herself as more capable of achieving success and self-esteem in more "masculine" activities. Gowan (1972a:17–18) refers to research done in this area in studying how creativity develops in a person. This research seems to show that children who relate more to the opposite sex parents were more likely to be creative.

It is interesting to note, in this context, that Eleanor Roosevelt, who is recognized by almost everyone as one of the most self-actualized women of our time, makes this point repeatedly in her book *You Learn by Living* (Roosevelt, 1960). She says that she had a close relationship with her father as a child and often felt rejected by her mother.

All of this indicates that development of a sense of self-esteem and achievement in stages IV and V, which are more difficult for a girl, would enable the individual to move on to creativity in stage VI. But, according to Bardwick, the majority of girls do not identify with achieving "masculine" roles. She says that most books on the subject of women are written by the achieving woman who is probably dissatisfied with the "feminine" role. Most of the studies on role satisfaction are done on female college students who have competed successfully enough to get into college and therefore are not really typical of the majority.

For most women, Bardwick feels that adult identity depends on affiliation. She feels that affiliative motives are dominant, that achievement motives are important, but secondary, until the affiliative needs have been met. Women perceive affiliation as the critical achievement for self-esteem only when they are secure in the nuclear family relationships and have feelings of self-esteem as females. Then they can permit the reemergence of achievement motivation.

This, of course, is not true for every woman, but for many women, I see this reemergence into achievement motivation as encompassing multiple roles. This is partly the motivation that I see in many mature women reentering school. When a woman can take her family and the affiliative relationship for granted, then she can extend herself in other directions and assume new roles and move into new developmental stages.

In discussing why women stay in this particular developmental stage so much longer than men, we can review some of the reasons that we discussed earlier as to why people get "stuck" at various stages. One of the most obvious in this case is that this may be the stage where most women are happiest and receiving the most rewards. There is safety and security in this role. They can be dependent and taken care of, and not have to take a lot of risks, and still feel that they are fulfilling a vital function, particularly as long as there are children in the home.

The "empty-nest" syndrome is familiar to most of us as the dilemma of the woman whose whole life has been built around her children, and then is no longer needed as mother, but has no other means of fulfillment.

We could also use Perry's term of escape here and speculate that woman's stay in the affiliative or generative stage is a form of escape, in that she is denying or rejecting the implications for growth in a particular developmental stage. This may partially explain why the Women's Liberation Movement is seen as extremely threatening to some very traditional women. It forces them to look at other possibilities that they are not ready to face.

Another explanation perhaps is the dysplasia theory. If her cognitive development is "stuck" in formal operations, and there can be no more than two stages' difference between cognitive and affective development, then she would not be able to move to, or probably even conceive of, a higher developmental stage.

Another possibility, of course, is that this is still the most culturally acceptable role for women. The affective areas of stages VI and VII, of love, affiliation, production, and care, are the roles that are accepted by most people in our society as the roles that women are "supposed" to fill. Also the conative and moral aspects of these stages seem best to fit the traditional role of women.

Conclusions

It can be a frightening and threatening experience to begin to feel the drive to move from one developmental stage to another—particularly so if the person has been very successful and secure in that stage. Perhaps, as suggested earlier, the more successful an individual is in a stage, the harder it will be to leave it. But women today, more and more, are attempting to find new roles for themselves, and I see this as attempts to move in development.

According to a recent article in *The New York Times* (Klemesrud, 1975), approximately 500,000 women all over the country have returned to school. Women are also entering or reentering the work force in increasing numbers. The woman who fuses achievement and affiliative needs will probably be motivated to return to the work force or to education for some meaningful volunteer activity) after 10–15 years of marriage (Bardwick, 1971). This indicates to me that the affiliative and generative needs have been met, or are being met, satisfactorily, and the achievement needs are reemerging in a search for paths to higher developmental stages.

I see the difference in the length of time that it takes many women to satisfy and feel secure in the intimacy and generative stages and the difference in development of achievement needs as major differences in the ways that men and women move through the later developmental stages. Whether these differences are due to innate, inborn differences, as suggested by Erikson's "inner-space" theory, or culturally acquired, I do not know. Many will argue that they are purely cultural differences in that women are "supposed" to stay home and care for the family, or go into purely nurturing professions, while men are "supposed" to meet achievement needs in the world of work and challenges.

But I see the developmental process as freeing both men and women, but particularly women, for multiple roles. I feel that further research and study are needed into how women can be helped to combine and enhance these multiple roles, either together, or at different stages in adult life.

Longitudinal studies are needed in the areas of developing achievement needs and fulfilling the needs of the intimacy and generativity stages of development of women. These studies will be particularly interesting in the next generation or so, in view of the influence of the women's movement.

Studies are needed concerning the need of many mature women to find a new role for themselves, whether this need is caused by an innate need to move to a higher developmental level, or culturally influenced, or as I suspect, a combination of both. I see a need for research to find out how she can best be helped in meeting these needs by the schools, counselors, employers, and society as a whole, and also to help herself, in rethinking and revaluing her life pattern, in her striving toward actualizing her full individual potential.

Bibliography

Bardwick, Judith. *Psychology of Women.* New York: Harper & Row, 1971.

Erikson, Erik H. "Inner and Outer Space: Reflections on Womanhood." In Stephen Berg (Ed.), *About Women.* Greenwich, Conn.: Fawcett Publications, 1973.

Gowan, J. C. *The Development of the Creative Individual.* San Diego: Robert Knapp, 1972. (a)

Gowan, J. C. *The Guidance and Measurement of Intelligence, Development, and Creativity.* Northridge, Calif.: J. C. Gowan, 1972. (b)

Gowan, J. C. *Development of the Psychedelic Individual.* Northridge, Calif.: J. C. Gowan, 1974.

Klemesrud, Judy. "When Husband and Home Aren't Enough." *New York Times,* February 2, 1975.

Kohlberg, Lawrence. In Richard C. Sprinthall, and Norman A. Sprinthall (Eds.), *Educational Psychology: Selected Readings,* pp. 75–87. New York: Van Nostrand Reinhold Co., 1969.

Kohlberg, Lawrence. In John P. DeCecco (Ed.), *Readings in Educational Psychology Today,* pp. 37–43. Del Mar, Calif.: Communications/Research/Machines, Inc., 1970.

Kohlberg, Lawrence, and Selman, Robert J. *Preparing School Personnel Relative to Values: A Look at Moral Education in the Schools.* Washington, D. C.: ERIC, 1972.

Kohlberg, Lawrence, and Mayer, Rochelle. "Development as the Aim of Education." *Harvard Educational Review,* Vol. 42 (November 1972), pp. 449–96.

Perry, William G., Jr. *Forms of Intellectual and Ethical Development in the College Years.* New York: Holt, Rinehart & Winston, 1970.

Roosevelt, Eleanor. *You Learn by Living.* New York: Harper & Brothers, 1960.

Sears, Pauline, and Barbee, Ann. "Career and Life Satisfactions among Terman's Gifted Women." In J. C. Stanley, W. C. George, and C. H. Solano (Eds.), *The Gifted and the Creative: A Fifty-Year Perspective.* Baltimore: The Johns Hopkins University Press, 1977.

34 Career Development of Gifted Women

JUDITH RODENSTEIN, L. R. PFLEGER, and NICK COLANGELO

Introduction

One of the most important tasks educators face is assisting in the career development of students. Perhaps the most recent evidence of the importance of career education is the approval by the House of Representatives of the Elementary and Secondary Career Education Act of 1977. This act provides for $275 million for kindergarten through 12th-grade career education activities over the next five fiscal years ("Career Education Bill," 1977).

An effective career development program should be predicated on the career development needs of the students it is designed to serve. Some problems of career development are common to nearly all young people. However, results of studies at the Research and Guidance Laboratory, University of Wisconsin–Madison over the past twenty years (Pulvino, Colangelo, & Zaffrann, 1976), together with practical experiences at the Laboratory have led to the discovery of unique career development problems of gifted and talented students. In addition, recent literature on the career development needs of gifted and talented students has rarely focused on the needs of gifted and talented females. The implicit assumption underlying this absence seems to be that society doesn't lose if women don't achieve their career aspirations. Career development for women has largely been incidental and irrelevant.

The purposes of this article are:

1. To report the unique career development needs of gifted and talented students.

From The *Gifted Child Quarterly* 21:3 (1977). Used by permission.

2. To emphasize the career development needs of gifted and talented females.
3. To present to educators suggestions for meeting these needs.

Career Development Needs of the Gifted

On the basis of research and experience with gifted and talented students in the Laboratory, and a review of literature on this topic, the following issues have emerged: multipotentiality, expectations, career as life-style, and career investment.

Multipotentiality

Career choice can be a difficult problem for young people who possess many interests and competencies (Parkyn, 1948; Strang, 1956; Sanborn & Wasson, 1966). The problem gifted students have is that they can be successful in so many areas. Thus they require special attention to narrow the choice. Their traits, interests, capacities, and alternatives present almost limitless possibilities for expression. In Terman's longitudinal study of men and women, for example, there are many instances of gifted who have been as productive in an avocation as in their chosen careers (U.S. Commissioner of Education, 1972). The multipotential student, as a result, needs to focus on more subtle and subjective aspects of career and life-style development than would be necessary for the general population in his/her age range.

Expectations

Gifted and talented students recognize and react to high expectations of parents, friends, teachers, and society in general (Hoyt & Hebeler, 1974). Gifted are encouraged to achieve high-status positions such as doctor, lawyer, professor, engineer, etc. These expectations tend to force limits on the kinds of career directions gifted can acceptably consider.

Within American society there appears to be a dynamic conflict of values (Bennis, 1970):

Achievement	vs.	Self-Realization/Actualization
Self-Control	vs.	Self-Expression
Independence	vs.	Interdependence
Full-Employment	vs.	Full Lives

The values on the left are considered *traditional* values and the right *emerging* values. Gifted students tend to be leaders in striving for and achieving emerging values.

In addition to these expectations, gifted women often find themselves in a position where they are expected to adopt dual roles which are conflicting. They are expected to behave one way because they are gifted and another way because they are women. Examples of conflicts which they must confront in their career development are:

1. A gifted student is expected to develop his/her own talent and be selfish in energy use *yet* a woman is expected to be selfless, nurturing, and giving.

2. A gifted student is expected to be active, exploring, and assertive in his/her demands *yet* a woman is expected to be passive and dependent.

3. A gifted student is expected to pursue a challenging career *yet* a woman is expected to run a household.

4. A gifted student is expected to develop his/her talents *yet* a woman is expected to put her career second to "her man's" career.

5. A gifted student is expected to succeed in the traditionally male-dominated careers such as science, medicine, math, and business *yet* a woman is expected to be feminine.

Career as Life-Style

It is not uncommon for gifted to regard their work as a major means of self-expression. Thus, for the gifted, occupational choice becomes a choice of life-style (rather than simply a job) with prime considerations being philosophical, social, and personal values and goals rather than economic and material ones (Hoyt & Hebeler, 1974).

The life-styles of gifted girls and women have been explained in terms of Maslovian needs (Groth, 1969). It was found that girls and women seem to be concerned with Maslow's level of "love and belongingness" until middle years. By the age of forty, however, their frustration mounts due to their lack of cognitive fulfillment—a need, particularly strong in gifted women, which has not been satiated in the family-oriented woman.

Career Investment

Most gifted students develop their talents through extended training and higher education, essentially society's channels to positions in the most sophisticated careers. This fact gives rise to several problems (Hoyt & Hebeler, 1974).

1. Commitments must be made relatively early and then pursued systematically.
2. A heavy investment in terms of time and financial resources is required.
3. It is difficult to change career directions once there has been considerable expenditure of time and resources.

Certain other forces seem to be at work with women regarding career development and investment:

1.   Attention to the development of one's special talents seems to be in conflict with the cultural expectations for the development of women.
2.   Females who conform to the expected sex-role of passivity and dependence may be less likely than their male counterparts to be identified as gifted and may capitalize less on opportunity.
3.   Females, including those who are gifted, have less credibility in academic and professional matters, and are often denied credit for individual contributions to group efforts (House, 1974).
4.   Historically, there has been less interest and investment in cultivating the academic and professional interests of women.
5.   The gifted female will be exposed to fewer same-sexed models than her male counterparts. This may be true in regard to live models in the school or community, as well as fictional models in literature and the media (Kaniuga, 1974).
6.   Overt discrimination in the form of reduced opportunities to receive fellowships and awards, participate in athletics and other organized activities, be admitted to graduate and professional schools all serve to limit the development of the potential of gifted women. (Title IX should work to alleviate the most overt acts of discrimination against women in the educational sphere.)
7.   The fear that successful achievement in traditionally male fields of endeavor may be perceived by others as a loss of femininity leads to what Matina Horner (1970) has labeled "the motive to avoid success." To the extent that the motive to avoid success is present in a gifted female's motivation system, she may be expected to perform below her potential.

Considerations for Meeting the Career Developmental Needs of the Gifted and Talented

The unique needs discussed above can provide the basis for planning specialized career education programs for the gifted and talented. Some considerations for program planning and implementation follow:

1.   In order to help gifted students develop their interests and skills in satisfying careers, the first step would be to assist students in recognizing their interests and skills. This would be an ongoing process from K-12, and could proceed into later life. Awareness, or discovery and understanding of one's interests and abilities, is the foundation of any systematic career development program.

2.   Gifted students need information about the avenues that are available in society for development of interests and talents. This information needs to be widely based so one is aware of the variety of choices rather than the limits. Information should come not only in objective (written material) form, but also in subjective (talking to people in the field, visiting a work site, etc.) form as well.

3.   Gifted students need the opportunity to test out some of their interests and skills. They need direct experiences—the opportunity to pursue their interests. Evidence from school systems in which the gifted have been given the opportunity to work with specialists of similar interests and to explore occupations first-hand indicates strongly that these experiences are of great value in allowing gifted students to assess career options and in motivating them to go to college. Some evidence exists that opportunities to work with community specialists increases the motivation and school performance of the gifted (Berger, 1963). Contributions of the gifted and talented made at other times in history came about through individual work affiliations and close tutorial relationships. Appropriate career education practices could contribute in similar fashion, and could be of particular significance for those with highly specialized talents.

4.   Gifted students need opportunities to think in terms of what it means for a multipotentialed individual to have a job, not just the process of getting a job. A multitude of interests and skills could be the cause of boredom or forms of job dissatisfaction not faced by other individuals.

5.   Gifted students need opportunities to explore and experience numerous life-styles and know models of people who are multipotentialed and yet lead successful and full lives.

Program Considerations for Gifted Women

Various strategies which can be implemented by schools to more adequately address the career development needs of gifted and talented women include:

1.   Teachers and counselors should reaffirm their belief in the uniqueness of all individuals and not let stereotypes, myths, or preju-

dices about either women or giftedness bias their perceptions and interactions with the gifted female student.

2.   Teachers and counselors should not be satisfied with irresponsible or lackadaisical career planning among gifted high school girls. At times an affirmative approach is called for in suggesting alternatives.

3.   Teachers, counselors and administrators can implement strategies to change the *opportunity* structure of school and community:

   a)   make affirmative efforts to begin identifying gifted and talented girls at an early age and make a commitment to continuing the identification process throughout the school years.

   b)   reduce overt barriers to pursuing opportunities for advanced work—allowing access to labs and other learning facilities, etc.

   c)   broaden the scope of counseling and guidance services to include such programs as achievement motivation training and assertive training.

4.   Teachers, counselors, and administrators can implement strategies to change the *reward* structure of the school and community:

   a)   assess types of rewards and recognition available to the gifted female student in the school and the community, and determine whether the reward structure is indeed operating to encourage independent action and whether rewards and recognition are tied to effort and achievement.

   b)   design new avenues of expression and recognition where lacking in the present reward structure.

5.   Teachers, counselors, and administrators can implement strategies to change the *support* structure of the school and community:

   a)   begin career guidance on a systematic basis as early as possible, even in the elementary school.

   b)   include in the career guidance program opportunities for gifted female students to integrate and synthesize career-relevant experiences.

   c)   design or program experiences for the gifted female student that would have a low probability of occurring spontaneously or naturally.

6.   Educators should make a concerted effort to identify female role models in the school and community. Encourage contact between these women and the gifted female student.

7.   Educators can encourage the formation of support groups made up of gifted female students. These support groups may be in the form of counseling groups or special interest groups.

8.   Appropriate school personnel can provide assertive training

and achievement motivation training for those girls who may need more self-confidence to develop their potential.

An example of a program in action is "Project Equality" in the Highline Public Schools in Seattle. The four areas of emphasis in the curricular programming are (1) expanding the role of women in the world of work, (2) identifying cultural stereotyping of goals into restricted roles, (3) revealing curricular stereotyping of materials and course content, and (4) recommending directions for change.

Summary

One of the important challenges to educators today is to provide for the career development needs of students. Effective programming must be predicated on the recognized career needs of youngsters. Gifted and talented students have career development needs which differ from other students. Some of these needs were discussed, as well as considerations for programming. Gifted and talented girls have career development needs different from gifted and talented boys. These needs have generally been neglected in the past. Some of the career development needs of gifted and talented females were discussed, along with suggestions for programming. The needs and considerations discussed in this article can provide the basis for effective career education programs for gifted and talented boys and girls.

Bibliography

Bennis, W. G. A funny thing happened to me on the way to the future. *American Psychologist*, 1970, *25*, 595–608.

Berger, R. Discovery of painting. New York: Viking Press, 1963.

Career education bill passes in House. *Guidepost*, APGA, Vol. 19, No. 15, April 14, 1977.

Groth, N. J. Vocational development for gifted girls—a comparison of Maslovian needs of gifted males and females between the ages of ten and seventy years. Paper presented at American Personnel and Guidance Association, 1969.

Horner, M. Femininity and successful achievement: A basic inconsistency. In Judith Bardwick, Elizabeth Douvan, Matine Horner, and David Guttman, *Feminine personality and conflict*, pp. 45–74. Brookline, Cal.: Brooks/Cole, 1970.

House, W. C. Actual and perceived differences in male and female expectancies and minimal goal levels as a function of competition. *Journal of Personality*, Vol. 42, No. 3, 1974, 493–509.

Hoyt, K., and Hebeler, J. *Career education for gifted and talented students.* Salt Lake City: Olympus Pub. Co., 1974.

Kaniuga, N. Working women portrayed in evening television programs. *Vocational Guidance Quarterly,* Vol. 23, No. 2, December 1974, 134–37.

Morse, J. A., & Bruch, C. Gifted women: More issues than answers. *Educational Horizons,* Fall 1970, pp. 25–32.

Parkyn, G. W. *Children of high intelligence: A New Zealand study.* New York: Oxford University Press, 1948.

Pulvino, C. J., Colangelo, N., & Zaffrann, R. *Laboratory counseling programs.* Madison: University of Wisconsin, Research and Guidance Laboratory, 1976.

Sanborn, M. P., & Wasson, R. Guidance of students with special characteristics. *Review of Educational Research,* April 1966, Vol. 36.

Strang, R. Gifted adolescent views of growing up. *Exceptional Children,* Vol. 23, October 1956, 10–15.

U.S. Commissioner of Education. *Education of the gifted and talented: Report to the Congress of the United States by the U.S. Commissioner of Education.* Washington, D.C.: U.S. Government Printing Office, 1972.

Chapter Twelve

Imagery and the Right Cerebral Hemisphere

Introduction

The magic and mystery of the imagination set in motion by creative energy have given articulation to our world, transforming reality to dreams and dreams to reality. William Blake saw it as "some source of spiritual energy" in whose exercise we experience in some way the activity of God. Samuel T. Coleridge regarded the imagination as an ability of first importance, since human beings involved in creative activities simulate in some way the creative act of God. More recently Bowra (1950) astutely observed the function of the imagination as a mysterious activity of the mind in the act of solving problems, since most of us "when we use our imagination are in the first place stirred by some alluring puzzle which calls for a solution, and in the second place enabled by our own creations in the mind to see much that was before dark or unintelligible."[1]

Not so long ago John Eccles (1958) presented his speculations on the function of the imagination and creativity, based, as he said, upon secure evidence as to the way information is conveyed to the cortex with a specificity that makes subsequent interpretation possible. In attempting to explain the characteristics of a brain exhibiting creative imagination he speculates that

> ... the creative brain must first of all possess an adequate number of neurons, having a wealth of synaptic connection between them. It must have, as it were, the structural basis for an immense range of patterns of activity. The synapes of the

---

[1]The first three paragraphs of this introduction are drawn from Joe Khatena, "Creative Imagination Imagery and Analogy," *The Gifted Child Quarterly* 19:2 (1975). For other writings by this editor, see Khatena (1971a, 1971b, 1971c, 1972, 1973a, b) and the references appended to the articles in this chapter.

brain should also have a sensitive tendency to increase their function with usage, so that they may readily form and maintain memory patterns. Such a brain will accumulate an immense wealth of engrams of highly specific character. In addition this brain possesses a peculiar potency for unresting activity; weaving the spatio-temporal patterns of its engrams in continually novel and interacting forms, the stage is set for the deliverance of a brain child that is sired, as we say, by creative imagination.[2]

Much of brain activity relative to the creative imagination has to do with imagery or the re-experiencing of images and its language correlates. Eccles (1958) goes on to suggest that by association, one image is evocative of other images, and when these images are of beauty and subtlety, blending in harmony, and, expressed in some language—verbal, musical, or pictorial—evoke transcendent experiences in others, we have artistic creation of a simple or lyrical kind. To this kind of imagery he would add an entirely different order of image-making which provides the illumination that gives a new insight or understanding. Relative to science, it may take the form of a new hypothesis which embraces and transcends the older hypothesis. As examples of this, he cites Kekule and the benzene ring, Darwin and the theory of evolution, and Hamilton and his equations.

Whereas left hemisphere function is Guilfordian convergent production, right hemisphere function is Guilfordian divergent production. Thus right hemisphere imagery is the vehicle through which incubation produces creativity.

The seat of this imagery appears to be in the Wernicke area of the right cerebral hemisphere (Jaynes, 1976:109). While it was once thought that special means were necessary to elicit imagery, it has lately appeared that the process (like the shining of the stars) goes on all the time, but during our waking hours, under most circumstances, it is overlaid by the more cognitive processes of the generally dominant left hemisphere. These involve the handling of incoming perceptual information and its processing into thought and action via language, and the continual stream of internal discourse which accompanies consciousness. Remove both of these activities from left hemisphere function through relaxation, meditation, hypnosis, fantasy, daydreaming, sensory deprivation, or some similar state, and the imagery of the right hemisphere is brought to focus at once. Since speech and writing are confined to the left hemisphere, most educational processes educate only this half of the brain. Wallas (1926), in his paradigm for creativity, called this aspect "preparation" and

---

[2]J. C. Eccles, "The Physiology of Imagination," in *Readings from Scientific American*, 1972, p. 40.

clearly indicated that it is the necessary but not sufficient condition for creative illumination. The sufficient condition is, of course, incubation, which was Wallas's term for the relaxation which produces right hemisphere imagery.

We have a good repertoire of educational techniques of preparation for creativity (e.g., Williams, 1971; Meeker, 1969), but we lack equally strong techniques for incubation. *Thinking Creatively with Sounds and Words*, a joint product of two of the editors (Khatena & Torrance, 1973) is one of the few devices in this area. It indicates our concern for its importance.

It is obvious that one of the imminent curriculum changes in schools for the gifted will be more attention paid to incubation techniques. The use of art and music education, not only for their own sakes, but to stimulate right hemisphere activity and hence to improve creative function has been mentioned by a number of writers. Williams (1977), in an article entitled "Why Children Should Draw," points out that art stimulates a child's curiosity. He quotes Houston: "Verbal-linear-analytical intelligence is a small part of the intelligence spectrum. There is also visual-aesthetic-plastic (working with the hands) intelligence . . . ." This right hemisphere intelligence is what in an earlier day Lowenfeld called "haptic," and Ferguson (1977) calls "thinking with pictures." Ferguson believes this is an essential strand in the history of technology development, although it is presently neglected in scientific education.

Williams (1977) states that "the differentiation of the brain into left and right hemispheres certainly plays a role in arts-centered learning." According to Houston, Williams says, a child without access to a stimulating arts program "is being systematically cut off from most of the ways in which he can perceive the world. His brain is being systematically damaged. In many ways he is being de-educated." Williams cites a number of elementary schools where an enriched arts program has improved general performance.

Jaynes (1976:364–69) devotes several pages to the importance of music and musical instruction to stimulating the right hemisphere. He cites a number of authorities and facts in support of the special relationship of music to the right hemisphere and hypothesizes (after experiments on neonates) that "the brain is organized at birth to obey musical stimulation in the right hemisphere." Jaynes concludes that the research points "to the great significance of lullabies in development, perhaps influencing the child's later creativity."

It is obvious from the nature of this introduction, and indeed the necessity of a new chapter on this topic, that we are entering the developmental phase of varied, new approaches to the issue of how and why some gifted children become creative. Investigation of the role of imagery and the right hemisphere is too new for assured success, but what research we have is both promising and provocative. If indeed right hemisphere functioning proves the key to creative performance through the production of imagery, the educational results will not be confined to gifted children. Rather, it will signal a revolution in educational curriculums which, by educating both halves of the brain, will come closer to "education of the whole child."

* * * * *

Editor's note: The reader who wishes further update on this developing area, should consult *The Gifted Child Quarterly,* Spring, 1979, (23:1), which issue is on incubation, imagery, and the right hemisphere function in education. *Humanitas* 14:2, May, 1978, also featured a symposium issue on Imagination. Also consult the new *Journal of Mental Imagery* (Brandon House, Box 240, Bronx, N.Y. 10471).

35 Advances in Research on Creative Imagination Imagery

JOE KHATENA

Because of my strong interest in the topic of creativity, and my belief that the study of imagery is a most important key to understanding it, I have chosen to present a substantive message for this special issue linking the two areas.

Imagery is fast growing into an attractive and respected subject of study by American psychologists today. This year has not only seen an upsurge in the relatively great number of papers relating to various aspects of imagery but also the inauguration of the *Journal of Mental Imagery* published by Brandon House, and the founding of an American Association for the Study of Mental Imagery located in Los Angeles, California.

Only a few years ago imagery was readmitted as an appropriate subject of study after 30 years of ostracism following its rejection by Watson and the ascendancy of behaviorism in the 1920s (Holt, 1964; Richardson, 1969). The renewal of interest was probably brought about by the fresh look taken at images as indirect reactivations of earlier sensory or perceptual activity rather than the function of mental mechanism (Bugelski, 1970). However, the study of imagery that followed tended to confine itself to after imagery, eidetic imagery, and memory imagery (Pavio, 1971; Richardson, 1969). Research on imagination imagery related to hypnogogic imagery, perceptual isolation imagery, hallucinogenic drug imagery, photic stimulation, pulse current imagery, and non-drug-induced hallucination. Common to all these studies is the freeing of the individual from the constraints of external stimuli for the purpose of attending to inner stimulus events and experiencing imagination imagery (Richardson, 1969).

From *The Gifted Child Quarterly* 21:4 (1977). Used by permission.

Creative Imagination Imagery

However, the need to study creative imagination imagery has been reiterated by Richardson and Pavio. The two studies they cite as having been the only ones done at the time related to perceptual isolation and its effects on Guilford's creative measures (Kubzanski, 1961) and the facilitatory effects of LSD on creative problem solving (Harman, McKim, Mogar, Fadiman, & Stolaroff, 1966). Other studies done since have been cited in an earlier paper (Khatena 1976a) and include investigations of imagery production under the effects of hypnosis (MacKinnon, 1971), the relationship of aesthetic activities, imagery arousal, and creativity correlates (Leonard & Lindauer, 1973), and the tendency of adolescents and young adults to produce images of unusual visual perspective on the repeated figures activity of the Torrance tests as a predictor of achievement (Torrance, 1972). Further, a study by Krippner, Dreistadt, and Hubbard (1972) summarized and discussed a group of studies that attempted to relate the right or nondominant hemisphere of the brain to the creative person's experience of nonordinary reality through hypnosis, visual imagining processes, psychedelic drugs, dreams, extrasensory perception, and self-actualization. Two comprehensive reviews have documented the area of hypnosis, creativity and the imagination (Bowers & Bowers, 1970; Sheehan, 1972) as well.

Measurement of Creative Imagination Imagery

The lack of objective measures to study creative imagination imagery is a major problem in part alleviated recently by the construction of measures of creative thinking abilities. Of particular relevance to the author's studies of creative imagination imagery have been Onomatopoeia and Images and Sounds and Images, components of *Thinking Creatively with Sounds and Words* (Khatena & Torrance, 1973), though most of the studies reported on the subject have used Onomatopoeia and Images.

In brief, the two components of *Thinking Creatively with Sounds and Words* present either sound or onomatopoeic words as stimuli under free associative conditions which call for the use of the creative imagination to produce original verbal images. The standard scoring procedures award points for originality on the basis of statistical infrequency. The logic of the measures hinge upon the operation of the creative imagination to effect a break-away from the perceptual set of audio-verbal stimuli to produce original verbal images. Since its publication, the author has developed for Onomatopoeia and Images a scoring procedure for analogies and image simplicity-complexity (Khatena, 1976b).

Studies of Creative Imagination Imagery and Analogies

The function of the creative imagination and its imagery-analogy correlates has been explored by the author in several studies that may be grouped as those related to stimulating the creative imagination, effects of time press on production of original verbal images, development patterns in production of original verbal images, original verbal images produced by deaf children, physiological correlates of original images, and autonomy of imagery.

I. *Stimulating the Creative Imagination.* Several studies have attempted to find out the extent to which college adults exposed to a creative thinking program based upon the strategies of breaking away from perceptual set, restructuring, synthesis, and analogy, could be stimulated to produce more original verbal images (e.g., Khatena, 1970a, 1973a; Khatena & Barbour, 1972; Khatena & Parnes, 1974). Generally the results were found to be favorable. This was also the case of another study (Khatena, 1974) where adults were taught to use direct, personal, fantasy and symbolic analogies, figures of speech, and simple and complex image patterns. Those who were taught produced more original verbal images than those who were not. In addition, all subjects preferred the use of direct analogy simple image structure, though the experimentals and controls produced more complex images, and high creative experimentals and controls produced more complex images than low creatives of both treatment groups. Further, it was found that both creative and less creative adults benefit from such training (Khatena, 1973b).

II. *Effects of Time Press.* A second group of studies concerned itself with how adults, adolescents and children were affected in their production of original verbal images by responding to onomatopoeic stimuli at fixed and variable time intervals which served as the agent of "press" (Khatena, 1970b, 1971a, 1972b, 1973c, 1973d). The findings of these studies showed that when the time interval was *fixed* (as in the standard conditions of the recorded text), adults produced more original verbal images given the warm-up of two or four presentations of onomatopoeic stimuli; whereas children and adolescents needed less warm-up and produced more original verbal images in the second of four presentations of onomatopoeic stimuli. In the studies of *varied* time intervals where subjects were grouped as high, moderate, and low creatives, high creative adults and children were found to produce more original verbal images when given moderate time deadlines, while high creative adolescents produced more original verbal images when given as much time as they needed.

III. *Development Patterns in Production of Original Verbal Images.* Two cross-sectional studies explored the production of original verbal images by children between the ages of 8 and 19 (Khatena, 1971b) and 9 and 19 (Khatena, 1972a), and found that in particular children at age 9 and 10 years produced less original verbal images but showed gain at 11 years. A longitudinal study (Khatena & Fisher, 1974) conducted with a group of eight-year-olds over a four-year period supported the earlier cross-sectional findings.

The production of analogies (personal, direct, fantasy, and symbolic) with simple and complex image structures by children, adolescents and adults was also explored (Khatena, 1972c, 1973e, 1975a). The findings showed that high original men and women and boys and girls of all age levels preferred to use the direct analogy form and simple image structure. In addition, as high-original children grew older, they produced more complex and correspondingly less simple images.

IV. *Deaf Children and Production of Original Verbal Images.* A study (Johnson & Khatena, 1975) on the production of original verbal images by deaf and hearing children between the ages of 10 and 19 years found that hearing children produced significantly more original verbal images than deaf children, and that while hearing children did not show any clear improvement as they grew older, deaf children showed significant improvement with age.

V. *Physiological Correlates of Original Verbal Imagery.* A study with adults (Khatena, 1975b) investigating the relationship between vividness of imagery production and creative perceptions found the two to be significantly related, especially to the senses of seeing, hearing and touching. In addition vivid imagers tended to perceive themselves as highly creative. This led to a second study (Khatena, 1976c) that explored the use that college men and women, identified as high, moderate, and low originals, make of visual, auditory, cutaneous, gustatory, olfactory, and organic sense modalities in their production of original verbal images. In general, high originals used their visual, auditory, visual-auditory and other two or more than two sense modalities combined to produce original verbal images.

VI. *Autonomy of Imagery.* Autonomy of imagery, where images appear to follow their course independent of the experiencer's will, often surprise him by their highly creative or unreproductive character (McKellar, 1957), and its relationship with creative perceptions and originality were also investigated (Khatena, 1975a; 1976d). The evidence derived suggests that the more adults perceive themselves as high creatives, the greater the autonomy of their imagery; and the more autonomous imagers appear to produce more original verbal images.

Directions for Further Research

A number of interesting directions that can be taken relative to the study of creative imagination imagery include:

1. Development of more adequate instruments that can measure not only single images but images that fall into complex patterns that will give more clues about the creative person and his mental functioning.
2. Development of creative imagination imagery in continuous or discrete stages after the Torrance (1973) and Gowan (1972) models.
3. Mental health correlates of creative imagination imagery.
4. Research in curriculum application of the findings on creative imagination imagery.
5. Creative imagination imagery of special groups of children (e.g., blind, deaf, and emotionally disturbed) and its educational implications.
6. Cross-cultural study of creative imagination imagery.
7. Effects of intellectual deprivation and enrichment on the quality of creative imagination imagery.
8. Creative imagination imagery as a function of the right or non-dominant hemisphere of the brain.

These are only some directions that may be taken. Other directions may be perceived by scholars as they relate creative imagination imagery to their specialized fields of inquiry. The study of the unknown has always excited the curious and when seriously pursued has led to numerous achievements of our times. To fully grasp the potential dynamics of creative imagination imagery is to extend the boundaries of psychology and education in yet another fruitful direction.

One such direction for future research comes out of recent longitudinal studies of the writer which show a drop in imagery in preadolescent children about age 9 which correlates with the Torrance 4th grade slump in creativity. In children who have eidetic imagery, there is also a similar drop at the same time. Can this be due to a transfer from the right hemisphere processing of images to the left hemisphere processing of verbal material? What would more training in art and other graphic skills do to preserve this precarious balance? The greater complexity of verbal creative imagination may

then be merely due to the need for synergistic cooperation between
right and left hemispheres, the former to pick up the images, and the
latter to translate them into alphanumeric form. How can we in our
education "reconcile analysis with vision"? These are important
unanswered questions which constitute the agenda for the future.

References

Bowers, K. S., & Bowers, P. G. Hypnosis and creativity: A theoretical
    and empirical rapprochement. Research Report No. 11. Unpub-
    lished manuscript, University of Waterloo, 1970.
Bugelski, B. R. Words and things and images. *American Psychologist,*
    1970, 25, 1002–1012.
Gowan, J. C. *Development of the creative individual.* San Diego, Cal.:
    Robert R. Knapp, 1972.
Harman, W. W., McKim, R. H., Mogar, R. E., Fadiman, J., & Stolaroff,
    M. J. Psychedelic agents in creative problem solving: A pilot
    study. *Psychological Reports,* 1966, 19, 211–227.
Holt, R. R. Imagery: The return of the ostracized. *American Psycholo-
    gist,* 1964, 19, 254–264.
Johnson, R. A., & Khatena, J. Comparative study of verbal originality
    in deaf and hearing children. *Perceptual and Motor Skills,* 1975,
    40, 631–635.
Khatena, J. Training college adults to think creatively with words.
    Psychological Reports, 1970, 27, 279–281. (a)
Khatena, J. Repeated presentation of stimuli and production of origi-
    nal responses. *Perceptual and Motor Skills,* 1970, 30, 91–94. (b)
Khatena, J. Adolescents and the meeting of time deadlines in the
    production of original verbal images. *Gifted Child Quarterly,*
    1971, 15, 201–204. (a)
Khatena, J. Production of original verbal images by children between
    the ages of 8 and 19 as measured by the alternate forms of
    Onomatopoeia and Images. *Proceedings of the 79th Annual Con-
    vention of the American Psychological Association,* 1971, 187–
    188. (b)
Khatena, J. Development patterns in production by children aged 9
    to 19 of original images as measured by sounds and images.
    Psychological Reports, 1972, 30, 649–650. (a)
Khatena, J. Original verbal images of children as a function of time.
    Psychological Reports, 1972, 31, 565–566. (b)
Khatena, J. The use of analogy in the production of original verbal
    images. *Journal of Creative Behavior,* 1972, 5(3), 209–213. (c)
Khatena, J. Imagination imagery and original verbal images. *Art Psy-
    chotherapy,* 1973, 1, 113–120. (a)
Khatena, J. Creative level and its effects on training college adults to
    think creatively with words. *Psychological Reports,* 1973, 32,
    336. (b)
Khatena, J. Production of original verbal images by college adults to

variable time intervals. *Perceptual and Motor Skills*, 1973, 36, 1285–1286. (c)

Khatena, J. Repeated presentation of stimuli and production of original responses by children. *Perceptual and Motor Skills*, 1973, 36, 173–174. (d)

Khatena, J. Imagination imagery by children and the production of analogy. *Gifted Child Quarterly*, 1973, 17, 98–102. (e)

Khatena, J. Analogy strategies and the production of original verbal imagery. Paper presented at the 21st Annual Convention of the National Association for Gifted Children, St. Louis, Missouri, 14th February, 1974.

Khatena, J. Creative imagination imagery. *Gifted Child Quarterly*, 1975, 19(2), 149–160. (a)

Khatena, J. Vividness of imagery and creative self perceptions. *Gifted Child Quarterly*, 1975, 19(1), 33–37. (b)

Khatena, J. Relationship of autonomous imagery and creative self perceptions. *Perceptual and Motor Skills*, 1975, 22(2), 180–186. (c)

Khatena, J. Major directions in creativity research. *Gifted Child Quarterly*, 1976, 22(3), 336–349. (a)

Khatena, J. Sabbatical research report on creative imagination imagery and analogy. Unpublished manuscript, Marshall University, 1976. (b)

Khatena, J. Original verbal imagery and sense modalities correlates. *Gifted Child Quarterly*, 1976, 20(2), 180–186. (c)

Khatena, J. Autonomy of imagery and production of original verbal images. *Perceptual and Motor Skills*, 1976, 43, 245–246. (d)

Khatena, J., & Barbour, R. L. Training music majors in college to think creatively with sounds and words. *Psychological Reports*, 1972, 30, 105–106.

Khatena, J., & Fisher, S. A four year study of children's responses to onomatopoeic stimuli. *Perceptual and Motor Skills*, 1974, 39, 1062.

Khatena, J., & Parnes, S. J. Applied imagination and the production of original verbal images. *Perceptual and Motor Skills*, 1974, 38, 130.

Khatena, J., & Torrance, E. P. *Thinking creatively with sounds and words: Norms–technical manual.* Research ed. Lexington, Mass.: Personnel Press, 1973.

Krippner, S., Dreistadt, R., & Hubbard, C. C. The creative person and nonordinary reality. *Gifted Child Quarterly*, 1972, 16, 203–228, 234.

Kubzanski, P. E. Creativity, imagery and sensory deprivation. *Acta Psychologia*, 1961, 19, 507–508.

Leonard, G., & Lindauer, M. S. Aesthetic participation and imagery arousal. *Perceptual and Motor Skills*, 1973, 36, 977–978.

McKellar, P. *Imagination and thinking.* New York: Basic Books, 1957.

MacKinnon, D. W. Creativity and transliminal experience. *Journal of Creative Behavior*, 1971, 5(4), 227–241.

Pavio, A. *Imagery and verbal processes.* New York: Holt, Rinehart &
Winston, 1971.
Richardson, A. *Mental imagery.* New York: Springer, 1969.
Sheehan, P. W. Hypnosis and the manifestations of imagination. In
E. Fromm & R. E. Shor (Eds.). *Hypnosis: Research developments
and perspectives.* Chicago: Aldine-Atherton, 1972.
Torrance, E. P. Tendency to produce unusual visual perspective as
a predictor of creative achievement. *Perceptual and Motor
Skills,* 1972, 34, 911–915.
Torrance, E. P. Cross-cultural studies of creative development in
seven selected societies. *Educational Trends,* 1973, 8(1), 28–38.

36   Creative Imagination and What We Can Do to Stimulate It

JOE KHATENA

Introduction

Have we not often wondered how beautifully and effectively poets
have said things about lovers, while we stand tongue-tied? How
arresting—almost startling—in unexpected relation is the thought of
prayer as "reversed thunder" against the Almighty (G. Herbert:
Prayer) or the awesome brilliance of God flaming out like "shining
from shook foil" (G. M. Hopkins: *God's Grandeur*). How scathing is
the reference to Sir John Falstaff, the degenerate knight of unusual
corpulence in Shakespeare's *Henry IV*, as one who lards the ground
upon which he walks!

Imagination

Imagination articulates, energizes and metamorphoses reality into
dreams and dreams into reality, and by its logic we turn away from
the "soft fetters of easy imitation to soar in the regions of liberty"
(Young, 1759/1959). Coleridge regarded imagination as the most
vital activity of the mind, infinite and eternal, and Blake saw it as a

From *The Gifted Child Quarterly* 21:1 (1977). Used by permission.
For an update, see Joe Khatena, "Creative Imagination through Imagery: Some
Recent Research," *Humanitas,* Vol. 14, No. 2 (1978).

source of energy in whose exercise is experienced in some way the activity of God.

Bowra (1970), in writing about the romantic imagination, observed the imagination to be an agent of illumination in the creative problem-solving process; and in more recent times rich strikes appear to have been made in attempts that operationalize the imagination as functional steps of the creative problem-solving process (e.g., Osborn, 1965; Parnes, 1965). To this may be added contributions like the Purdue Creativity Program (Feldhusen, Treffinger & Bahlke, 1970), New Directions in Creativity (Renzulli & Callahan, 1973), and the Total Creativity Program for Elementary School Teachers (Williams, 1971) that root the activity of the creative imagination to the Structure of Intellect Model (Guilford, 1967). Torrance's (1972) paper, summarizing ways that have been used to teach children to think creatively, not only focuses our attention on both these approaches but also on the use of curricular materials, classroom climate, and educational media, and provides as well a very useful source of information.

My contributions have focused on several dimensions of imaginative functioning, namely, encouraging people to think in creative ways, aided by their understanding and exercise in the use of a number of creative thinking strategies; the role of creative levels and the amount of time given to be productive; creative analogies and imagery; and physiological and other correlates of imagery.

Encouraging the Use of the Imagination

I have worked with a number of creative thinking strategies that I have found to be very useful in encouraging children to use their imagination and think in productive ways (e.g., Khatena, 1971, 1973) —namely, breaking away from the unusual and commonplace, restructuring, and synthesis. Let me share with you some of the approaches I took using these strategies with children.

Breaking Away from the Usual and Commonplace

The thinking strategy breaking away from the usual and commonplace, or what is sometimes known as perceptual set, can be illustrated by presenting the child with a square followed by two drawings, namely, a window and a clock, and he can be told that if he used the square to make these drawings then he would be doing things the way he always did. However, if he drew a large enough circle around the square to, say, make a bubble with a highlight he would be using his imagination to get away from older habits of thought. You can then give him a worksheet containing four rows of three squares each and encourage him to draw interesting and unusual pictures using the square. You will be amazed to see him producing all kinds of interesting pictures from, say, earphones to Martians in Mexico. All along, show you appreciate his attempts, and if he really moves away from drawing objects like windows or doors which are dependent on angular constructions, do not forget to praise him.

As another example, you may give the child the word "roar," with instructions to be imaginative in responding to it. If the child produces responses like "to talk noisily" or "the sound a lion makes," you may regard these as commonplace whereas a response like "blood gushing out of a wound" is imaginative and shows creative strength and may be regarded as such. Illustrate what you want done and follow it with practice exercises that show the imagination at work. Do not forget to give the child appropriate positive feedback relative to imaginative responses.

Restructuring

The second thinking strategy, restructuring, is another way we can use to encourage creative thinking. We are often faced with something whose parts are put together or structured in a certain way to give it an identity. If we are able to pull apart these elements and recombine them or restructure them in a different way we are very likely to come up with something having a new or original identity. It really needs creative energy to free oneself from the bonds of the old order for the purpose of bringing about a new order.

To teach your child to use this strategy you may start with constructing an 8 × 12 inch flannelboard and make cutouts of, say, three geometrical shapes such that you have 10 of each kind. I have preferred the semicircle, triangle, and rectangle. If you like to use these shapes, make circles an inch in diameter and squares that have sides 1 inch long. By cutting the circles into two you will get semicircles, and by cutting the squares into four equal parts you will have rectangles; in addition you can make two right-angled triangles by cutting across the diagonal of a square. These shapes are relatively versatile and allow for all kinds of manipulations and combinations. When you have all these pieces cut, put them in a little plastic bag or envelope ready for use. You should make two sets so that you can freely work with your child on the materials.

Now that these pieces are ready and the flannelboard prepared, give them to your child. Tell him that you are going to construct a figure on the flannelboard and get him to watch what you do. You may begin by constructing a *human figure*: a triangle for a hat, two semicircles for the face, two triangles for the body, two rectangles for the arms and two more for the legs, and two semicircles for the feet. All this requires the use of three triangles, four semicircles, and four rectangles, making a total of 11 pieces. Get your child to do the same, giving whatever help he may need at the time. Then pull apart the pieces you used to make the human figure and reconstruct them into an *automobile*, making sure that only the same 11 pieces are used. The four semicircles can now serve as the two wheels. Place one rectangle on one wheel and a second rectangle on the other such that the long side of the two rectangles are on the wheels and short sides are side by side. Then place two triangles in the shape of a square upon the rectangles on the rear wheel, and the remaining two rectangles upon the one that was first placed on the front wheel. Finally put the remaining triangle against the short sides of the three rectangles above the front wheel such that its base is against them and the apex of the triangle is pointing forward. The car is now ready. Let your child do the same and once again help him build the car. When he has done this, tell him to pull apart the same 11 parts of the automobile and rearrange or restructure them into another object. Of course, with a little practice you will see him producing scenes as well. Your child may try to persuade you to allow him to use some of the pieces in the bag, but do not let him. Encourage him to use his imagination and work within the restrictions of the strategy.

Restructuring can also be used to encourage your child to be more creative with words. For instance, you can show him a picture of the Three Wise Men of Gotham and encourage him to ask questions about it which cannot be answered by merely looking at the picture, and guess why events in the scene are taking place and the consequences of these events, as warmup activities. This may then be followed by getting him to restructure three elements of the picture, namely, the three wise men, the bowl, and the sea, into an unusual and interesting story.

Synthesis

A third strategy called synthesis can also be taught to your child. Unlike restructuring, the act of synthesis provides more freedom of manipulation and expression. This time your child may be allowed to use all 30 elements or pieces that are in the bag. He may use as many of the shapes as he likes to to produce new and interesting pictures on the same flannelboard. You can begin by demonstrating how the pieces can be combined to make a scene of say two boys on a see-saw. Give him a chance to do the same and encourage him to make as many of his own pictures as he can, such that each time he will remember to use his imagination to produce the new and unusual. All along encourage and praise him for self-initiated and interesting and unusual combinations.

You may help him use his imagination still further by encouraging him to talk about the characters and scenes he makes. You may even encourage him to tell a story about them, and if it helps the development of his narrative then suggest or allow him to change details of the scene he has before him.

Synthesis can also be used to encourage children to be imaginative with words in this way as well. For example, you can show your child a picture of, say, the nursery rhyme "Dr. Foster Went to Gloucester" and get him to tell you something about it such that he will ask questions, guess causes, and consequences in much the same way that was described for restructuring, all of which require the use of the imagination. A second picture can then be shown, say, of Tommy Tucker singing for his supper, with similar warm-up activities. He can then be asked to tell a story using a combination of the characters and situations in both pictures with encouragement to use his imagination to make his story unusual and interesting.

Creative Imagination Analogy and Imagery

To move on to the creative imagination and its analogy and imagery correlates, let us note an interesting paper by Jensen (1975) which points to the great value of metaphorical thinking in the problem-solving process, giving many examples of metaphors which we use in our daily lives. Schaefer's (1975) paper on the measurement of metaphorical thinking emphasizes the unique value of metaphor to the creative thinking process, which the Synectics group uses as a potent approach to creatively solve problems (Gordon, 1961) and which has been more recently applied to stimulate creative writing of children and adolescents (Synectics, 1968).

My work in the area of creative analogy has provided some empirical evidence to the analogy mechanisms used with the Synectics system of creative problem solving and to some extent extended their use (Khatena, 1973, 1975a, 1975b). It seems appropriate at this juncture to say something about the nature of analogy and imagery, and the steps that can be taken to encourage their production.

Production of Creative Analogies

We use words with their objective meanings and emotional connotations to convey to others our ideas, feelings, and perceptions about the world. Often we find ourselves trying to communicate thoughts, feelings, or experiences that do not lend themselves to easy expression; we cannot explain or describe what we have in mind, so we search for some familiar situation to which our thought-feeling complex can be related—a process of making the *strange familiar;* sometimes, by reversing this process, whereby we make the *familiar strange,* we allow ourselves insights into relations hitherto concealed to us. Both these mechanisms are operations involved in the making of creative analogies and have been presented to us in the Synectics approach to creative problem solving (Gordon, 1961). Synectics distinguishes four kinds of analogies: personal analogy, direct analogy, fantasy analogy, and symbolic analogy.

Personal Analogy. In personal analogy a relationship is found between yourself and some other phenomenon with which you and others are familiar. Suppose you want others to know how thin you are without having to give a lengthy description; you may say, "I'm as thin as a stick." Or suppose you want to tell someone that you are happy; you may say, "I'm as happy as a lark."

Direct Analogy. Just like personal analogy, direct analogy finds a relationship between two unlike phenomena but without self-involvement. To produce a direct analogy, the "I" of the comparison above may become "he" or "John," to read "John is as thin as a stick." Another direct analogy relative to being fat could be "John is as fat as a pig." And if the activity is focused on his eating habits, the analogy may be "John eats like a pig."

Symbolic Analogy. This form of the analogy uses symbols whereby we try to find a "sign" for a phenomenon we wish to describe that has many related characteristics. For instance, if we come across someone who is dependable, strong, stable, consistent, and so on, and we wish to convey this information about him effectively without having to use too many words, we look around for some phenomenon, animate or inanimate, which has as nearly as possible these qualities. For example, the Rock of Gibraltar has been traditionally known to have such qualities. The Rock then can be used as a "sign" or "symbol" of the qualities possessed by the person in mind. We may then refer to him using symbolic analogy, as "He is the Gibraltar of my life" or "John is as firm as the Rock."

Fantasy Analogy. In fantasy analogy, the comparison object or subject at least must be imaginary. Myths, legends, allegories, fairy tales, and the like are all rich sources of imaginary materials for comparison, as for instance, the Devil, Medusa, Pandora's Box, Ariel, the Rainbow, the Dragon, the Garden of Eden, Paradise, Sugar Candy Mountain, Jekyll and Hyde, and so on. Let us say you wish to convey the information that someone we know is very wicked, evil, and murderous. We may compare such a person to Hyde, like "John is Hyde himself" or like "Leonora's whispers stirred the Hyde in John."

Imagery

Imagery can be described as images or mental pictures that have organized themselves into some kind of pattern. One thing it does is to make sense of the world around for the person making images. He is very much like the artist in the act of creating the world the way he sees it: in the canvas of his mind appear images as he reacts to the world he sees, and, like the artist in the act of painting a picture, he gives organization and meaning to these images. How he depicts his world, the details he includes, the choices he makes of colors, the style he chooses, and the extent to which he allows his emotions to become involved are all dependent upon the emotional-intellectual make-up of the man and the creative energizing forces at work at the time.

I have used analogy to explain imagery, which has been compared to a painting where a person's mind is the canvas on which is patterned his perceptions of the world. I could have just compared imagery to a painting and stopped there, with no attempt to elaborate. Instead, I went on to add further details to the basic comparison where the individual is an artist and his mind the canvas, and by extending or elaborating the comparison, I have combined the images to make a more complex image pattern. To put it in another way, "Imagery is like a painting" is a simple image pattern, whereas "Imagery is a painting on the canvas of man's mind" is a complex image pattern. Simple and complex image patterns can be used in the act of comparison. The more highly imaginative among us tend to use more complex images. Whether we create personal, direct, symbolic, or fantasy analogies, we use imagery, more often than not analogies with complex image patterns as, for instance, "John sings like a crow" compared to "John sings like a featherless crow on a winter's day."

Figures of Speech as Analogy Modes

In the making of analogies we may use any one of several well-known figures of speech based on agreement, similarity, or resemblance such as the simile, metaphor, personification, and allusion.

A *simile* is a form of comparison between two things that are different except in one particular characteristic to which you want to call attention, like "John is as *fat* as a pig" where John and pig are different in kind and yet possess one characteristic in common, namely being *fat*. By focusing attention on John's corpulence in this way we effectively describe *fat* John without lengthy description.

The *metaphor* is a condensed or implied simile. A comparison using this form attempts to relate two things differing in kind as if they were both similar or even identical, like saying "John is a pig." Here John is identified with the pig and with the implication that he resembles the pig not only by being *fat* but also by possessing other piggish qualities. Thus by calling John a pig we are suggesting that John is not only fat but also greedy, filthy, stinking, and so on.

Personification is a form of comparison which attempts to give lifeless objects or abstract things attributes of life and feeling. One well-known example is "Time marches on," in which Time is given attributes of a human being moving forward on foot to indicate the steady passing of time. A variation of this, for instance, "With leaden foot Time creeps along," greatly slows down the pace while still retaining the inevitable forward movement.

Allusion is yet another form of comparison which makes use of familiar phenomena in literature, mythology, legend, present-day happenings and so on. To explain or describe something without having to say much we can often relate this something to something else that is well known, as for example the biblical allusion "She proved to be a good Samaritan," or the literary allusion "David is the Falstaff of our company."

Figures of Speech in Analogies

Each of the four figures of speech described above can be used as comparison forms in the four kinds of analogies. The simile "John is as fat as a pig" or the metaphor "John is a pig" are both direct analogies. As you know, if we wish to use the simile or metaphor in the form of personal analogy, for instance, we will need to involve ourselves in the comparison, like "I'm fat as a pig" or "I'm a pig."

We can use personification in personal analogy and direct analogy, as for instance, "I walked with death in Vietnam," or "Death took her for his bride."

Allusion may also be used in the personal analogy. "I turned him to stone with my glassy stare," or "The bad news struck him down with the force of Jove's thunderbolt" are examples of allusion in the direct analogy form: the first allusion refers to the head of Medusa and the second to the destructive energy of the king of the Greek gods. When I discussed symbolic analogy I illustrated it by giving comparisons in the form of simile and metaphor. You will recall "the Rock" being used as the symbol of dependability, strength, stability and consistency with the simile "He is as firm as the Rock" and the metaphor "He is the Gibraltar of my life." If we wish to use the allusion of *cornerstone* (with St. Peter in mind) as the comparison figure, then by saying "John is the cornerstone of our diplomacy in the Far East" we not only imply that he has the qualities of dependability, strength, stability, and consistency but also that he is the most important single building element upon which we expect to maintain the superstructure of our diplomacy.

We can go on to see that the same figures can be used to great effect in fantasy analogy. For instance, "jealousy" has been described in *Othello* as the "green-eyed monster." In simile form the comparison may read as "His jealousy, like the green-eyed monster, will devour him," and in metaphor form "beware of jealousy, the green-eyed monster that destroys everything in its path."

Other Variables Associated with the Creative Imagination

My explorations of imagination have also involved the study of children, adolescents, and adults as they were encouraged to produce original verbal images under conditions of stress, as well as the role of age and creative level in the production of original verbal images and analogies. A summary of these studies and their findings can be found in two recent papers (Khatena, 1973, 1975b) and under "Verbal Imagery" in Reading 28 in this volume.

Since children in grades 4 to 6, or when they are 9 to 11 years old, and adolescents in the 10th grade, or when they are about 15 years old, seem to find it much harder to use their imagination, we ought to give special attention to their problems and help them overcome some of their inhibitions that prevent their use of imaginative activity and provide them more frequent opportunity for creative behavior. On the matter of training children and adolescents to use their imagination to think in productive ways, you can do this regardless of their creative level. Relative to analogy production, children and adolescents tend to produce direct analogies with simple-image structure most frequently, to show low self-involvement by producing relatively very few analogies, and for the most part do not seem intellectually ready to produce symbolic analogies. This suggests that we teach and encourage them to use their imagination to create more personal and fantasy analogies that have both simple and complex image structures.

Tentative Clues from Ongoing Imagery Research

Some of my very recent research on imagery, its vividness and physiological correlates, may give us some further leads to more effectively plan educational experiences leading to creative behavior, but I offer them now as very tentative for the classroom, and more for the purpose of making you aware of yet other fruitful dimensions of imagination and imagery that you may be able to tap onto in the near future.

One study (Khatena, 1975c) exploring the relationship between vividness of imagery control and creative self-perceptions found that college adults who perceive themselves as highly creative are more likely to have images that are autonomous. A second study (Khatena, 1975d) with college adults investigating the relationship between creative self-perceptions and vividness of imagery production found significant relationship between creative self-perception and vividness of imagery as related to the senses of seeing, hearing, and touching. This was followed by a third study (Khatena, 1975e) which explored as one of its hypotheses the use that college men and women identified as high, moderate, and low originals make of the visual, auditory, cutaneous, kinesthetic, gustatory, olfactory, and organic sense modalities in their production of original verbal images. Generally, it was found that the visual and auditory senses or the visual-auditory senses combined, and the other sense modalities combined, have important relationships with verbal processes as they relate to the imagination, and may have positive implications for learning.

Some Implications for the Teacher

I have tried to say something about the imagination and encouraging its expression through the use of creative thinking strategies, analogy, figurative language, and imagery, and a few variables associated with the proper function of the creative imagination. In addition, some tentative clues from ongoing imagery research were also offered. Let us see what are some of the things you can do or you need to bear in mind in order to encourage children and adolescents to use their imagination more fully and so enhance their creative development.

First, you can set the imagination to work by encouraging the use of the creative thinking strategies I talked about in all kinds of classroom situations, especially as they relate to the learning of reading, mathematics, art, and music.

Secondly, you can teach them to use different kinds of analogies and image complexities prior to creative expression in language programs so as to maximize the quality of imaginative expression.

Third, bear in mind that your students will need their imagination activated prior to creative writing assignments like the imaginative essay, short story, poetry, and the like.

Fourth, deadlines for the completion of assignments requiring the use of the imagination may have to depend upon both the creative and age levels of students, such that high-creative elementary school children may need to be given moderate time deadlines to complete their work, while time restrictions given to adolescents for completing imaginative work may have to be more flexible.

Fifth, adolescents and children can be taught to use their imagination in preparation for productive work and should be reinforced for their productivity.

Sixth, remedial measures need to be taken to alleviate the slumps in the function of the imagination and its verbal productivity correlates in the upper elementary school and 10th grade.

Conclusion

In conclusion, let me reiterate the importance of providing many opportunities for your children to think creatively. Teach them the wonders and mysteries that can follow the use of the imagination. Enthuse them to discover the exciting new and show them how they can transform the familiar into the wonders of production. You can make such a difference to children. Do you not recall the pain and boredom of school with its busy work, mechanical learning, lack of direction, doses of courses, and meaningless credit hours? How often are the same conditions perpetuated! I know that you are faced with a task which is as difficult as it is rewarding, but it is your privilege to unlock their creative potential to its fullest realization.

References

Bowra, C. M. *The romantic imagination.* London: Oxford University Press, 1970.

Feldhusen, J. F., Treffinger, D. J., & Bahlke, S. J. Developing creative thinking: The Purdue Creativity Program. *Journal of Creative Behavior,* 1970, 4(2), 85–90.

Gordon, W. J. J. *Synectics: The development of creative capacity.* New York: Harper & Row, 1961.

Guilford, J. P. *The nature of human intelligence.* New York: McGraw-Hill, 1967.

Jensen, J. V. Metaphorical constructs for the problem-solving process. *Journal of Creative Behavior,* 1975, 9(2), 113–124.

Khatena, J. Teaching disadvantaged preschool children to think creatively with pictures. *Journal of Educational Psychology,* 1971, 52(5), 384–386.

Khatena, J. Imagination and production of original verbal images. *Art Psychotherapy,* 1973, 1, 113–120.

Khatena, J. Creativity research and imagination imagery. Paper prepared for a panel discussion, "Creativity: Where Is It Going?" Presented at the 52nd Annual Convention of The Association for the Gifted and Council for Exceptional Children, Los Angeles, California, April 24, 1975. (a)

Khatena, J. Creative imagination imagery and analogy. *Gifted Child Quarterly*, 1975, 19(2), 149–158. (b)

Khatena, J. Relationship of autonomous imagery and creative self-perceptions. *Perceptual and Motor Skills*, 1975, 40, 789–790. (c)

Khatena, J. Vividness of imagery and creative self-perceptions. *Gifted Child Quarterly*, 1975, 19(1), 33–37. (d)

Khatena, J. Original verbal imagery and its sense modality correlates. Paper prepared for the 22nd Annual Convention of the National Association for Gifted Children, Chicago, October 24, 1975. (e)

Osborn, A. F. *Applied imagination,* 3rd. ed. New York: Charles Scribner's, 1965.

Parnes, S. J. *Creative behavior guidebook.* New York: Charles Scribner's, 1965.

Renzulli, J. S., & Callahan, C. M. *New directions in creativity.* New York: Harper & Row, 1973.

Schaefer, C. E. The importance of measuring metaphorical thinking in children. *Gifted Child Quarterly*, 1975 19(2), 140–148.

Synectics, Inc. *Making it strange.* New York: Harper & Row, 1968.

Torrance, E. P. Can we teach children to think creatively? *Journal of Creative Behavior*, 1972, 6(2), 114–143.

Williams, F. E. *Total creativity program for elementary school teachers.* Englewood Cliffs, N.J.: Educational Technology Publications, 1971.

Young, E. Conjectures on original composition. In E. D. Jones (Ed.), *Critical essays: XVI-XVIII centuries.* London: Oxford University Press, 1959. Originally published 1759.

37   The Role of Imagination in the Development of the Creative Individual

J. C. GOWAN

And, as imagination bodies forth
The forms of things unknown, the poet's pen
Turns them to shapes, and gives to airy nothing
A local habitation and a name.

Shakespeare, Midsummer Night's Dream, V:1

Note: The help of Joe Khatena in the preparation of this paper is gratefully acknowledged.

From *Humanitas* (1978). Used by permission.

Introduction

One evening the young Nicola Tesla was with a friend, quoting poetry, according to his biographers, Hunt and Draper (1964:33):

> As he was walking toward the sunset quoting these words, the idea came like a flash of lightning and the solution to the problem of alternating current motors appeared before him as revelation. He stood as a man in a trance, trying to explain his vision to his friend .... The images which appeared before Tesla seemed as sharp and clear and as solid as metal or stone. The principle of the rotating magnetic field was clear to him. In that moment a world revolution in electrical science was born.

Koestler (1964:118) cites the experience of the Dutch chemist Kekule who was trying to synthesize benzene:

> I turned my chair to the fire and dozed. Again the atoms were gamboling before my eyes. The smaller groups kept modestly in the background. My mental eye, rendered more acute by visions of this kind, could now distinguish larger structures, of minifold conformations, long rows sometimes more closely fitted together, all twining and twisting in snakelike motion. But look! what was that? One of the snakes had seized hold of its own tail and the form whirled mockingly before my eyes. As if by a flash of lightning I awoke.

This imagery granted Kekule a glimpse into noncategorical reality, from which he wrote down the now-famous formula for the benzene ring.

Ghiselin (1952:43) quotes Einstein on the subject of images:

> Words or language do not seem to play any role in my mechanism of thought. The physical entities which seem to serve as elements of thought are certain signs and more or less clear images.

These somewhat spectacular accounts of the power and versimilitude of the creative imagination could be multiplied many times. This power was clearly understood by Wordsworth who, in *The Prelude* (20:1), defines imagination thus:

Imagination, which, in truth
Is but another name for absolute power
And clearest insight, amplitude of mind,
And Reason in her most exalted mood.

These testimonies to the power of creative imagination come from some of the world's geniuses, but how did they get that way? Can any of this awesome ability be taught or stimulated? What is the role of imagination in the development of the creative person? The answer to this question is the task of this article.

This job is not easy, else it would have been performed sooner. It requires analysis of the nature of creativity, the nature of development, and the nature of imagination, and then devising a theory which will relate all three. These diverse inquiries will form the sections of our investigation.

Creativity

The psychological study of creativity is little more than a quarter century old, yet it has borne much fruit and moved into directions not envisioned by its discoverers. Both Guilford (1967) and Osborn (1953) believed that creativity was an outcome of problem-solving aspects of intellect in the Deweyian model and could therefore be taught or stimulated. It was thought to be rational and semantic, consisting essentially of what Hallman (1963) has called "connectedness" (the ability, through the use of verbal analogy, to connect elements which had heretofore been viewed as incommensurable). In Guilford's view (1967:212) imagery is simply figural memory.

In the past few years a newer view of creativity as psychological openness to preconscious or transpersonal sources has emerged. While perhaps part of the zeitgeist, this view can be defended by two rather cogent arguments.

A curious characteristic of creativity which appears to have escaped critical attention is that its variability in individuals far exceeds the variability of other traits and abilities. Wechsler (1974:109), for example, has conclusively demonstrated that the interpersonal variability of such psychological and physiological measures as height, weight, cranial capacity, grip strength, blood pressure, respiration rate, reaction time, pitch, Snellen acuity, intelligence, mental age, and memory span has a limit of $e/1$, where $e = 2.818$, the basis of the natural logarithm system, and in most cases has a mean of 2.3 or less. Yet comparing the creative productions of a genius such as Einstein, Mozart, or Picasso with that of more ordinary mortals, one finds a ratio of 100/1 or over. Obviously the trait and factor theory of creativity cannot account for all of the variance.

The second argument notes that even the most intelligent person cannot be creative at will, and there are many bright people who are never creative. Mastery of a particular discipline is a necessary but not sufficient condition for creative production. To ascertain the missing ingredient, recall the Wallas (1926) paradigm which holds that there are four stages in creative production: preparation, incubation, illumination, and verification. Obviously, if preparation is the necessary condition, it is incubation which is the sufficient one. Incubation consists in relaxing the hold of the conscious mind on the problem, through various techniques such as sleep, reverie, travel, nature, bodily activity, or meditation, so that other parts of the psyche can take over. While it is not too surprising that this sort of "courting the Muse" works for artists, it is quite amazing how often scientific discoveries are made in the same manner. Yet we have the testimony of men such as Archimedes, Newton, Faraday, Agassiz, Hilprecht, Poincaré, Mendeleev, Kekule, Loewi, and others (Ghiselin, 1952; Gowan, 1974) that this is so. Since incubation consists in facilitating the emergence of creative imagery, we find ourselves again dealing with the central idea of this article.

If preparation sets up the mind as a radio receiver, and incubation clears away the static and turns on the power, development may be likened to the fine tuning of the instrument so that what was a howl now becomes a clear and intelligent signal. What we are discussing is similar to a resonance phenomenon in communication theory. Let us look to see how development accomplishes this more precise sympathetic vibration.

Developmental Stage Theory

The time is ripe for a unifying theory about discontinuous developmental stages which will account not only for the different characteristics of each stage but also for the higher and rarer adult stages envisioned by Maslow in his studies of self-actualization (1954). Sullivan (1953) was also prescient enough to write about developmental processes. Piaget (1950), identified cognitive developmental stages. and Erikson (1950), affective developmental stages. Kohlberg (Kohlberg & Mayer, 1972) similarly identified moral growth stages. and Simpson (1966) did the same for the psychomotor. Indeed, the concept of developmental stages seems to be one whose time has come. Says Stephen Bailey (1971):

It seems to me that the most liberating and viable educational reforms of the next several years will come through the building of curricular and other educative activities around some of the developmental insights of men like Piaget, Bruner, Erikson, Bloom, and Maslow. Although much separates these scholars in terms of analytic style and specific fields of concentration, they all seem to hold to the idea that human beings go through fairly discrete stages of development and that each stage calls for rather special educational treatment. And all of these men seem to be united in their belief that the maximization of human potential within the constraints of each life stage is the best way of preparing for succeeding stages.

In *The Development of the Creative Individual* (Gowan, 1972) I stated the new hypotheses as a set of theorems:

1. Developmental process is best understood by conceptualization of the Erikson-Piaget-Gowan periodic table of developmental stages, consisting of triads, thus:

	Latency		*Identity*		*Creativity*
1.	Trust–Sensori-Motor	2.	Autonomy–Preoperational	3.	Initiative–Intuitive
4.	Industry–Concrete Operations	5.	Identity–Formal Operations	6.	Intimacy–Creativity
7.	Generativity–Psychedelia	8.	Ego-Integrity–Illumination		

In this configuration, each stage has a cognitive and an affective characteristic.

2. Each stage has a special affinity for another three stages removed from it. Stages 1, 4, 7 are noticeable for a thing-oriented, sexually latent aspect, dealing with the world of experience. Stages 2, 5, 8 are ego-bound, ego-oriented, and ego-circumscribed. Stages 3 and 6 are times for love and creativity.

3. Within each stage, development occurs through cycles of escalation. Escalation is described as an aspect of developmental process which involves increasing complexity and embraces five attributes: succession, discontinuity, emergence, differentiation, and integration. Succession implies a fixed order within a hierarchy of developmental stages. Discontinuity involves an ordered and discrete sequence of equilibriums like a series of stairs. Emergence involves budding and making the implicit explicit in the flowering of char-

acteristics unseen before. Differentiation refers to the attribute which clarifies, fixates, and metamorphosizes the emphasis in successive developments. Integration summates the other attributes into a higher synthesis with greater complexity.

As a result of this process the environment may have maximum or minimum effect on the individual, depending on his position in the cycle. Continual environmental stimulation, however, is required for escalation into the higher (self-actualizing) levels.

4. There are three cognitive stages higher than those named by Piaget (Flavell, 1963). They go with the intimacy, generativity, and ego-integrity periods, respectively, and are called creativity, psychedelia, and illumination. These stages involve increasing mind expansion beyond formal operations (convergent thinking) and hence are increasingly rare, even in intelligent, healthy adults. Facilitation of escalation into them by various kinds of educational, therapeutic, sensitivity training, meditational, and allied techniques is in the process of becoming a major movement for superior adults.

Although time and space are not available to offer proof of the validity of these hypotheses, some explanatory discussion may be useful to the reader. One immediate question is: Why should there be developmental stages at all; why cannot development, like growth, be one smooth accretion? The answer lies in the critical aspect of energy transformations in the individual. The transformation and focusing of energy is the essence of both the developmental and the creative process. Since the amount of energy available for use is not enough to be expended upon the three areas of "the world, the I, and the thou" simultaneously, it must be focused through attention and expended on first one and then another of these three aspects. This process is what leads to the three-phase periodicity of the developmental stages.

Developmental stage theory can be regarded as the carrying over of the discontinuity principle of the quantum theory to behavioral science. Escalation is a jump from one riser to the next on the developmental staircase; energy from the organism is required for such jumps, but certain freedoms are gained thereby. If we ask, "What is escalating?" one answer appears to be ego-strength, which helps control and develop the creative imagination. This can be seen in comparison of the horrors and dread of night terrors in the child with the beauty and simplicity of a musical or mathematical product in the adult. Developmental process centers around stabilizing and controlling the creative imagination and harnessing it to constructive, not destructive use. We shall later see that this activity is related to the preconscious, the further explanation of which we now consider (see Gowan, 1974).

Development of Creative Imagination: The Gentling of the Preconscious

Theories about creativity and developmental stages are necessary for, and contribute to, understanding of creative imagination. This can also be seen as the "gentling of the preconscious." The process is not one of formulating mental imagery in the usual sense, but of organizing and controlling it so that the experience is not traumatic but can be symbolized and hence usefully employed. Imagery appears to abound in the unconscious mind, ready to rush into consciousness whenever the perceptual flow is stilled. As Wordsworth said:

> For oft when on my couch I lie
> In vacant or in pensive mood,
> They flash upon that inward eye
> Which is the bliss of solitude;
> And then my heart with pleasure fills,
> And dances with daffodils.

But frightening and traumatic images may come too, which is one reason why so few people are willing to be creative enough to entertain a lively imagination.

Merriam-Webster's *New Collegiate Dictionary* defined imagination as "The act or process of imagining; the formation of mental images of objects not present to the senses, especially those never perceived in their entirety; hence mental synthesis of new ideas from their elements experienced separately."

Arieti (1976:37) defines imagination as the ability of the awake mind to produce symbolic functions without effort. These include imagery, ideas, and sequences of words. Imagination is a "precursor of creativity," subsequent elaborations being necessary for it. It is imagery which "plays a crucial role in the process of creativity" (p. 46), and is facilitated by "rest, solitude, darkness and meditation." Arieti's views on the preconscious are handled by means of the construction of the *endocept* (p. 54), a preconscious cognition that occurs without representation, that is, without being expressed in images. As a primitive organization of past experiences, it is the precursor of imagination and is also responsible for the creative intuitions of artists. Arieti goes to some length to explain a theory of creative development in terms of this theoretical construct.

A somewhat different view is taken by Bachelard (1971:1), who sees imagery as an absolute, a starting point of consciousness. He quotes Shelley (p. 13) to the effect that "the imagination is capable of making us create what we see." He concludes, "The phenomenology of perception must stand aside for the phenomenology of the creative imagination." Later (p. 112) Bachelard suggests a method of incubation in the statement that "Reverie is the mnemonics of the imagination."

Koestler (1964:320 ff.) devotes a chapter to the image, which he sees as the basis of analogy. Kretschmer is quoted by Koestler (p. 325) as saying that:

> Creative products of the artistic imagination tend to emerge from a state of lessened consciousness and diminished attention to external stimuli . . . The condition is . . . providing an entirely passive experience of a visual character, divorced from space and time, and reason and will.

The source of this imagery appears to be in the preconscious psyche which by definition is sometimes, though not always, available to the ego. Kubie (1958:104 ff.) traced in detail the relation of a healthy preconscious to creative production. Jung (1934/1954) viewed the "collective unconscious" as the well from which transpersonal material flowed into the psyche. I have used (Gowan, 1975:9 ff.) the term "collective preconscious" to designate an archetypal generating part of the psyche which may be made accessible by various incubative and meditative techniques. When controlled, this results in creativity, and when not, in schizophrenia.

It might be interesting to speculate on a continuum of different kinds of imagery. What might the dimensions of such a continuum be?

One taxonomy (Gowan, 1975:20–1) considers imaginative imagery in terms of the Sullivanian levels of symbolism which it evokes on a developmental scale (Sullivan, 1953:xiv). The lowest, or prototaxic, level consists of experience received before images, the parataxic level consists of experience received as iconic images (as in art), and the syntaxic level consists of experiences received and processed with full verbal cognition.

These constructs without percepts proceed out of the preconscious —that part of the psyche sometimes, though not always, available to the ego. The child's first experience with this sort of thing is a prototaxic and traumatic one, which Sullivan named the "not-me." Sullivan (1953:162–63) defines the "not-me" as follows:

The personification of the not-me is most conspicuously encountered by most of us in an occasional dream while we are asleep; but it is very emphatically encountered by people who are having a severe schizophrenic episode, in aspects that are to them most spectacularly real. As a matter of fact, it is always manifest ... in certain peculiar absences of phenomena when there should be phenomena; and in a good many people ... it is very striking in its indirect manifestation (dissociated behavior) in which people do and say things of which they do not and could not have had knowledge, things which may be quite meaningful to other people, but are unknown to them ... This is a very gradually evolving personification of an always relatively primitive character, that is organized in unusually simple signs in the parataxic mode of experience, and made up of poorly grasped aspects of living, which will presently be regarded as "dreadful," and which still later will be differentiated into incidents which will be attended by awe, horror, loathing, or dread.

It will be seen from this that Sullivan, the expert in the dynamisms of development, identifies the "not-me" as pertaining to that class of experiences which are dissociated and uncanny—outside the pale of rational explanation or control of the developing child. Seen in most children in childish nightmares and night terrors, and in adults in the dissociated experiences of schizophrenia, the "not-me" emerges as a scary, poorly grasped construct evoking emotional horror rather than rational understanding. It is the purpose of normal development to "tame" this "collective" aspect of the psyche, to supplant its parataxic archetypes with an intuitive *modus vivendi* with the preconscious—creativity, and more or less to fully control it in the psychedelic stage.

The continuum in this taxonomy ranges from poorly cognized experiences to well-cognized ones; from affect filled with horror, dread, and fear to one of love, compassion, and delight; from loss of will and lack of ego control to strong will and ego control; from motor automatisms to cognitive representations; from anxiety to mental health; from dissociation and crudity to association and refinement; and from possession to illumination.

The process of development goes through parataxic and iconic imagery drawn from archetype, dreams, myth, and ritual and is expressed in art. The individual feels pressure to express the flood of imagery and experiences psychic relief when this explication is accomplished. Says Collier (1972:35), himself an artist:

The imagination is, in part, dependent upon the capacity of

the mental life to proceed beyond the simple recognition of an a priori objective fact. And the degree to which the subjective consciousness is involved after the first act of recognition determines the level of originality or uniqueness of the imaginative experience. For, after all, to imagine is to do precisely what the word implies—to experience mental images or realizations. These images may be intellectually organized as intuitive or rational ideas, or they may present themselves on the feeling side of consciousness as very positive value judgments, moods or "dream-feelings." If every man possesses some degree of imagination, which we must surely admit, the creative man is distinguished by the intense sharpness and quality of his ideas, by the mental and emotional agitation they cause him, by the urge to relieve the internal pressure through some formative action, and by the ability of the image he creates to illuminate a broader spectrum of consciousness. For those men of powerful imagination, an event which affects the subject consciousness in this way assumes the quality and nature of the revelation . . .

The compulsive yet therapeutic nature of this expression is well described by Schneider (1950:101):

> We can now state more confidently whence comes the juncture of creative thrust and creative mastery in the true artist.
>
> The consistent artist (like the creative scientist) is driven by a vision of the possibility of newer and greater formal interpretation of things. . . .
>
> He knows too the value—not only therapeutically—to himself of an implicitly interpretive "confession," he knows equally well the reward, and enjoys the importance of being an interpreter of power.
>
> When one has such a vision, one is driven to execute it; in that sense, to be an artist, to be creative, is to be compelled. To the creative scientist, it is precisely the same.

The preconscious, like fire, makes a good servant but a bad master. The developing relationship between the individual and the preconscious starts as a scary and traumatic encounter which becomes more humanistic through the parataxic procedures which culminate in art, and finally becomes rational in the syntaxic procedures of creativity. It is like the developing relationship between a young child and a colt. At first the child is afraid of the young horse and cannot ride it; the horse is skittish, unbroken, and unpredictable. Eventually, through many intermediary stages, the child learns to ride the horse and the horse is taught to accept the rider, until finally the man is complete master of the animal, now fully amenable to his commands.

This gentling, humanizing process carried on with the preconscious by creative functions represents both development in the individual and benefits in creative products for society. This "gentling" starts in the Eriksonian "initiative" period (ages 4–7) with efforts by the child and his parents to "totemize" fearsome and irrational elements which contribute to night terrors. Fairy tales are helpful in this respect, especially those such as *Where the Wild Things Are* by Sendak (1963) in which the child protagonist is shown mastering these elements. But any fanciful tale, like *Alice in Wonderland* or *The Wizard of Oz*, helps children picture themselves as in control of this inverse environment instead of being immobilized by it. The aegis of a helpful and loving parental figure is important in producing the boldness to investigate fantasy and so to become creative.

Stewart's description of the Senoi tribe's use of children's dreams (Tart, 1969) is an excellent example of using these initial, frightening aspects of a child's reactions to the "not-me" to develop mental health and conscious control of the preconscious. If the beginning circumstances of the child's encounter with the imaginations of the preconscious is traumatic and uncanny, while the hoped-for ultimate relationship is that of conscious control of creative imagination, then one may well inquire if learning may join with development in hastening this outcome. The answer is a positive yes. For, using Sullivanian terminology, between the initial prototaxic experience and the final syntaxic one, learning and humanizing occur through the various parataxic modes of archetypes, dreams, myth, ritual, and art. These modes are expressed through the creation of Langer's "presentational forms" (1942), that is, through the images and motifs of art. The enhancement of the youth's creative imagination through art forms is therefore a primary objective of education, if we understand art to include music and drama. Such a bridge of helping the youth to become creative through the production of images allows an intuitive relationship with the preconscious, which may later develop into a symbiotic union in syntaxic verbal creativity.

The highest aspect of imaginative imagery comes in the syntaxic processing of verbalization in what we call creative states. (A clear example is *Coleridge's* composition, *Kubla Khan*.) This is a complex process and appears to involve first the production of images and then the substitution of words, music, or mathematics for the images. Consider some very authoritative testimony on this subject:

Coleridge (quoted by Ghiselin, 1952:85), speaking of himself in the third person, says: "All the images rose up before him like *things,* with a parallel production of the corresponding expressions, without any sensation of conscious effort ...." Ghiselin (1952:227) also quotes Gerard, who tells us plainly:

> Imagination is more than bringing images into consciousness; this is imagery or at most hallucination. Imagination ... is an action of the mind that produces a new idea or insight. "Out of chaos the imagination frames a thing of beauty".... The thing comes unheralded, as a flash, fully formed.
>
> Imagination, not reason, creates the novel. It is to social inheritance what mutation is to biological inheritance; it accounts for the arrival of the fittest. Reason or logic applied when judgment indicates the new is promising, acts like natural selection to pan the gold grains from the sand and insure the survival of the fittest.
>
> Imagination supplies the premises and asks questions from which reason grinds out the conclusions....

Abell (1964:19–21) quotes the composer Brahms on his creativity:

> ... I immediately feel vibrations which thrill my being in this exalted state .... These vibrations assume the form of distinct mental images .... Straightaway the ideas flow in upon me directly from God, and not only do I see distinct themes in the mind's eye, but they are clothed in the right forms, harmonies and orchestration.

I have discussed the psychological syndrome of inspiration, emotion, vibrations, images, forms, and creative product elsewhere (Gowan, 1976:378–86). It presently appears that the right cerebral hemisphere may operate like a radio receiver to produce images from the vibrations, which are then transformed by the left hemisphere into verbal or musical form.

.....

Is Imaginative Imagery a Product of the Right Cerebral Hemisphere?

Khatena (1977) has reported a drop in imagery in preadolescent children which correlates with the Torrance 4th-grade slump in creativity. In children who have eidetic imagery, there is also a similar drop. Can this be due to a transfer from the right hemisphere processing of images to the left hemisphere processing of verbal material? Kris's (1965) "regression in the service of the ego" may be no more than a shift from right to left hemisphere dominance. The greater complexity of syntaxic creative imagination may be merely due to the need for synergistic cooperation between right and left hemispheres, the former to pick up the images and the latter to translate them into alphanumeric form.

We are accustomed to think of imagery as something on the order of hallucination because of our implicit assumption that physical reality is "real" and "tangible." But this may be naive. Ferguson (1977) declares that Pribram of Stanford and Bohm of the University of London have proposed theories which, in a nutshell, state that "Our brains mathematically construct concrete reality by interpreting frequencies from another dimension, a realm of meaningful patterned primary reality that transcends time and space. The brain is a hologram interpreting a holographic universe."

If the physical universe has no more reality than the holographic (virtual) image we see in exhibitions, then the subordinate position of imaginative imagery to percepts of "reality" would be removed, and creative imagination would emerge as one of the central building blocks of consciousness. Hence its development, stimulation, control, and perfection would become the aim of both education and the life development of the individual. Such a view, which would elevate the controlled creative imagination to that of co-creator and would raise man from a reactive being to one with control over his future and destiny, would revolutionize both culture and education and enormously actualize the latent potential of mankind.

Now that psychology has centered creativity in human development rather than in divine afflatus, it is obvious that we shall have to increase our prospectus of man's reach and potential. Imagination as the precursor of this creativity and as its means of development seems destined to become far more important in the psychology and education of the future. As Huxley (1962:208) prophesied about that education of the child in his vision of Utopia:

> How does he do his thinking, perceiving and remembering? Is he a visualizer or a non-visualizer? Does his mind work with images or with words, with both at once or with neither? ... Or in more general terms, can we educate children on the conceptual level without killing their capacity for intense nonverbal experience? How can we reconcile analysis with vision?

"This is the life which man should lead above all others, in the contemplation of Beauty absolute," said Socrates, long ago, and he promised us that if man developed this power, "dwelling in that realm alone, he would bring forth not images of beauty, but Beauty itself, and so would become immortal and become the friend of the gods."

References

Abell, A. M. *Talks with Great Composers.* Garmisch-Partenkirchen, Germany: G. E. Schroeder—Verlag, 1964.

Arieti, S. *Creativity: The Magic Synthesis.* New York: Basic Books, 1976.

Bachelard, G. *The Poetics of Reverie.* Boston: Beacon Press, 1971.

Bailey, Stephen. "Education and the Pursuit of Happiness." *UCLA Educator* 14:1:14, Fall 1971.

Collier, G. *Art and the Creative Consciousness.* Englewood Cliffs, N.J.: Prentice-Hall, 1972.

Erikson, E. *Childhood and Society.* New York: Norton, 1950.

Ferguson, M. *Brain-Mind Bulletin,* 2:16 (July 4, 1977). Interface Press, Box 42211, Los Angeles, Cal. 90042.

Flavell, J. H. *The Developmental Psychology of Jean Piaget.* New York: Van Nostrand, 1963.

Ghiselin, B. (Ed.). *The Creative Process.* Berkeley: University of California Press, 1952.

Gowan, J. C. *Development of the Creative Individual.* San Diego: R. Knapp, 1972.

Gowan, J. C. *Development of the Psychedelic Individual.* Buffalo: Creative Education Foundation, 1974.

Gowan, J. C. *Trance, Art & Creativity.* Buffalo: Creative Education Foundation, 1975.

Gowan, J. C. "The View from Myopia." *Gifted Child Quarterly,* 20:4:378–86, 1976.

Guilford, J. P. *The Nature of Human Intelligence.* New York: McGraw-Hill, 1967.

Hallman, R. J. "The Necessary and Sufficient Conditions of Creativity." *Journal of Humanistic Psychology* 3:1, Spring 1963.

Harman, W. W., and others. "Psychedelic Agents in Creative Problem Solving." *Psychological Reports* 19:211–27, 1968.

Holt, R. R. "Imagery, the Return of the Ostracized." *American Psychologist* 19:254–64, 1964.

Hunt, I., and Draper, W. W. *Lightning in His Hand: The Life Story of Nicola Tesla.* Hawthorne, Cal.: Omni Publications, 1964.

Huxley, A. *Island.* New York: Harper & Row, 1962.

Johnson, R. A., and Khatena, J. "Comparative Study of Verbal Originality in Deaf and Hearing Children." *Perceptual and Motor Skills* 40:631–35, 1975.

Jung, C. G. *The Archetypes of the Collective Unconscious.* Princeton, N.J.: Bollingen Press, 1954. Originally published 1934.

Khatena, J. "Imagination, Imagery and Original Verbal Images." *Art Psychotherapy* 1:113–20, 1973.
Khatena, J. "Creative Imagination Imagery." *Gifted Child Quarterly* 19(2):149–60, 1975. (a)
Khatena, J. "Relationship of Autonomous Imagery and Creative Self-Perceptions." *Perceptual and Motor Skills* 22(2):180–86, 1975. (b)
Khatena, J. "Major Directions in Creativity Research." *Gifted Child Quarterly* 22(2):336–49, 1976. (a)
Khatena, J. "Creative Imagination Imagery: Where Is It Going?" *Journal of Creative Behavior* 10(3):189–92, 1976. (b)
Khatena, J. "Original Verbal Imagery and Sense Modalities Correlates." *Gifted Child Quarterly* 20(2):180–86, 1976. (c)
Khatena, J. "Autonomy of Imagery and Production of Original Verbal Images." *Perceptual and Motor Skills* 43, 245–46, 1976. (d)
Khatena, J. "Advances in Research on Creative Imagination Imagery." Symposium presentation, "Educational Creativity: Where Is It Going?" at the American Psychological Association Annual Convention, San Francisco, August 30, 1977. *Gifted Child Quarterly* 21:4:433–440, 1977.
Koestler, A. *The Act of Creation.* New York: Macmillan, 1964.
Kohlberg, L., and Mayer, R. "Development as the Aim of Education." *Harvard Educational Review* 42:449–96, November 1972.
Kris, E. "Psychoanalysis and the Study of Creative Imagination." In H. M. Ruitenbeck (Ed.), *The Creative Imagination.* Chicago: Quadrangle Press, 1965.
Kubie, L. S. *Neurotic Distortion of the Creative Process.* Lawrence: University of Kansas Press, 1958.
Kubzanski, P. "Creativity, Imagery and Sensory Deprivation." *Acta Psychologica* 19:507–8, 1961.
Langer, S. *Philosophy in a New Key.* New York: Mentor, 1942.
Leonard, G., and Lindauer, M. S. "Aesthetic Participation and Imagery Arousal." *Perceptual and Motor Skills* 36:977–78, 1973.
MacKinnon, D. W. "Creativity and Transliminal Experience." *Journal of Creative Behavior* 5:4:227–41, 1971.
Maslow, A. *Motivation and Personality.* New York: Harper Bros., 1954.
Osborn, A. *Applied Imagination.* New York: Scribners, 1953.
Piaget, J. *The Psychology of Intelligence.* London: Routledge & Kegan Paul, 1950.
Richardson, A. *Mental Imagery.* New York: Springer, 1969.
Schneider, D. *The Psychoanalyst and the Artist.* New York: Farrah & Strauss, 1950.
Sendak, M. *Where the Wild Things Are.* New York: Harper Bros., 1963.
Simpson, E. J. *The Classification of Educational Objectives: Psychomotor Domain.* Urbana: University of Illinois Press, 1966.
Sullivan, H. S. *The Interpersonal Theory of Psychiatry.* New York: W. W. Norton, 1953.

Tart, C. (Ed.). *Altered States of Consciousness.* New York: John Wiley, 1969.

Torrance, E. P. "Tendency to Produce Unusual Visual Perspective as a Predictor of Creativity." *Perceptual and Motor Skills* 34:911–15, 1972.

Wallas, G. *The Art of Thought.* London: Watts, 1926.

Wechsler, D. *The Collected Papers of David Wechsler.* New York: Academic Press, 1974.

Chapter Thirteen

New Horizons

Introduction

Lewis Terman, the father of the gifted child movement, was such a leader that for the next 40 years after he began his genetic studies of genius in 1922 there was little if any substantive advance. But no discipline can call itself a science if it does not make progress and cultivate new ideas. As indicated in Reading 1, a proper appraisal of Terman's work marks it as a forerunner of a much larger gestalt of humanistic psychology, whose ultimate development represents the expanding powers of man and whose boundaries are much wider than any dreamed of formerly. The study of giftedness, creativity, and development is bound together with a dawning appreciation of mankind's immense potential.

It is appropriate to remember that, as Herman Hesse said, "A genius is always a forerunner." The brightest minds of this age fore-shadow what might be the norm in a golden age to come. Nature first reveals in the divergent genotype the plan for the evolution of the phenotype. Performance attained first by a few superior individuals in a culture should be reached progressively by more people, until eventually it is representative of the culture.

In an age when all institutions are being put to the test of usefulness and scientific breakthroughs are becoming monthly occurrences, we need to direct our attention toward the future. This will not only help us keep up with the escalating pace of civilization but also ensure that the social changes which result are gradual and hence peaceful, not revolutionary or violent. In this second edition we have attempted to update coverage of the discipline, and a great deal of new material has been introduced. A guideline in selecting this material has been: Does it contribute new or advanced ideas? Will it speak to the *zeitgeist* of the eighties?

In the three selections which comprise this chapter, the final one in the book, two of the editors, J. C. Gowan and E. P. Torrance, as well as Stanley Krippner, have taken looks at the future and made some educated conjectures about where our discipline is going. Whether these realms are within the grasp of the gifted youth of tomorrow may be debatable, but they are certainly within their reach.

* * * * *

The *zeitgeist* favors very rapid development of new ideas and discoveries in the areas of giftedness and creativity. Hence educators need to keep on their toes to stay abreast of the times. Reading confined to the area of special education has ceased to be adequate, for more and more research continues to come from other fields, such as psychology, sociology, history, anthropology, physiology and noetics. One way of keeping track of these many changes is to join the *National Association for Gifted Children* (217 Gregory Dr., Hot Springs, AR, 71901), receive the *Gifted Child Quarterly* and attend the national convention each year. Another is to join the Creative Education Foundation (State University College, 1300 Elmwood Ave., Buffalo, 14222), receive *The Journal of Creative Behavior* and attend the Creative Problem-Solving Institute held there each June. A third is to subscribe to the *Brain/Mind Bulletin,* a bi-weekly newsletter edited by Marilyn Ferguson at Box 42211, Los Angeles, 90042.

38 Images of the Future of Gifted Adolescents: Effects of Alienation and Specialized Cerebral Functioning

E. PAUL TORRANCE AND CECIL R. REYNOLDS

For some time the senior author (Torrance, 1976a, 1976b) has contended that an emphasis of differentiated programs for gifted and talented students should be to help such students enlarge, enrich, and make more accurate their images of the future. There are several compelling reasons for such an emphasis. People's images of the future influence their ability to live, cope, and grow in a high-change society. Images of the future are important in their search for their identity. They also write in advance a considerable part of the history of the future.

Although schools can do much to help all children enlarge, enrich, and make more accurate their images of the future, the problem is different for gifted and talented students. Images of the future of gifted and talented students are immensely different from those of their less gifted and talented peers—so different that different methods, materials, and procedures are required. This is one point about which educators of gifted and talented students should probably be willing to risk charges of elitism. Such a position has been championed by a number of eminent scholars of history, such as Arnold Toynbee (1964) and Fred Polak (1973).

Polak, in his provocative book entitled *The Image of the Future,* has maintained that throughout history, advances in civilization have been spurred and guided by the images of the future of its gifted and talented members. He made a special point of the fact that "images of the future are always aristocratic in origin" (p. 12). He argued that the authors of images of the future that change the world and make it better come from a creative minority. The formation of images of the future, Polak contends, depends upon an awareness of the future that makes possible conscious, voluntary, and responsible choices among alternatives.

From *The Gifted Child Quarterly* 22:1 (1978). Used by permission.

Initially, the senior author and his associates (Torrance, 1976a, 1976b; Torrance, Kaufmann, Gibbs, & Torrance, 1976) were concerned only about what kinds of images of the future gifted and talented students have and whether differentiated programs for them can enlarge, enrich, and make more accurate their images of the future. Much useful data have now accumulated concerning these matters (Torrance, Kaufmann, & Hallford, 1977), and we can proceed to a second stage of trying to understand the role of such psychological variables as alienation and style of learning and thinking on the development of images of the future. A first study in this area was conducted by the authors during the summer of 1977 in connection with their evaluation of the Career Awareness Component of the Georgia Governor's Honors Program. The initial results of this investigation will be described herein.

Procedures

The gifted and talented students studied were 200 participants in the 1977 Career Awareness Component of the Georgia Governor's Honors Program. This is a six-week summer program for gifted and talented students and emphasizes interdisciplinary studies of careers and futures. The participants were selected on the basis of outstanding achievement in the visual arts, music, science, social science, mathematics, French, industrial design, management, home economics, and the communication arts.

As a part of the program, these 200 students were administered the *Allen Adolescent Alienation Index* (Allen, 1973), a posttest soliloquy of their future careers, and Torrance, Reynolds, and Riegel's *Your Style of Learning and Thinking* (1976). Brief descriptions of these instruments will be given.

The *Allen Adolescent Alienation Index* (Allen, 1973) was developed by Walter R. Allen for studying feelings of alienation among black and white, advantaged and disadvantaged students. Satisfactory test-retest reliability, internal consistency, and construct validity have been established for this 50-item inventory of a wide range of adolescent experiences. Alienation scores are significantly related to degree of economic and cultural disadvantagedness and to race, with blacks scoring higher on alienation than whites.

The essential instructions for the posttest soliloquies are as follows:

> Now, try to imagine yourself as you approach the end of your career. Write a soliloquy describing what you have accomplished in your life. In a soliloquy, one reminisces not only about what he/she has done but also about how he/she has felt about

those accomplishments, those secret feelings, hopes, and dreams. Your soliloquy should reflect not only what you are doing at this future time but what is happening in the world at the time, how you have changed, and how the world has changed.

Write your soliloquy in the first person, using present and past tenses. Write as though you are looking back on your career.

Your Style of Learning and Thinking (Torrance, Riegel, & Reynolds, 1976) is a 40-item self-report, multiple-choice inventory of styles of learning and thinking derived from research and theory concerning the specialized functions of the right and left hemispheres of the brain. It is easier to use than most of the performance tests that have been devised for this purpose and has more useful feedback properties. Considerable evidence has been accumulated concerning test-retest reliability and validity. On the basis of their patterns of scores, the 200 participants were classified as predominantly right, predominantly left, integrated, and mixed styles. The distribution among these four patterns is as follows: right = 66; left = 48; integrated = 54; and mixed = 32.

Results

Alienation

The alienation scores of the participants of this study were generally quite low, significantly lower than those of high school students in general. In order to obtain data for 20 high alienation subjects, it was necessary to establish the cutoff at the mean for the general high school sample. For comparison, a random sample of 20 was selected within the range used in classifying participants in the first study as highly alienated.

The results of the analyses of variance are presented in Table 38.1. None of the differences in means was significant at the .05 level of confidence. Also, none of the chi squares on the checklist items was significant at this level. Several differences, however, approached significance at this level. These differences included strong trends for the occurrence of unconventional future careers among the high alienation group (50% compared with 25%), concern for the use of the environment to meet man's needs (30% compared with 10%), and concern about the exhaustion of natural resources, energy, etc. (20% compared with 5%). However, the low-alienation group tended to portray significantly more optimistic future images and skills in resolving conflicts in positive ways than the high-alienation group.

TABLE 38.1
Means and F-ratios of High and Low Alienated Gifted and Talented Students and Images of the Future (Posttest Soliloquies)

	Means		
Variable	High Alienated (N=20)	Low Alienated (N=20)	F-ratio
Words	286.4	348.2	3.8867*
Satisfaction with career	6.9	7.3	1.0083
Perception of self as changed	5.4	6.5	3.0414
Perception of world as changed	3.2	4.5	2.4952
Work for better world	4.9	5.4	0.4258
Awareness of future problems	3.4	4.1	0.8257
Proposed future solutions	3.5	4.1	0.6221
Perception of self as a creative person	5.5	5.4	0.0037

*F is significant at .1 level

Although the participants classified as high alienated are not extreme in their alienation, the results are provocative. Going back to the raw data, it becomes clear that many interesting dynamics have been developed by these gifted alienated students. After all, they have been successful—successful enough to be nominated by their schools as outstanding and to be selected for the Governor's Honors program.

The following soliloquies will illustrate some of the strategies that gifted students display in their soliloquies of future careers. The first soliloquy is by an alienated white male gifted in mathematics:

Dear World:
I was born on January 29, 1961, in S————, Ga. As any ordinary person, I went through grade school. My grades were only slightly unbelievable. When I graduated, I went to the University of Georgia as a third-quarter sophomore. I graduated and got my Ph.D. in business management. Living in Athens, I had come to hate large cities. Therefore, I came back to the small town of S———— and got a job at the Bank of S———— as a teller. Within 13 months I had worked my way up. Through the next 25 years I continuously improved myself and steadily rose the ladder of authority.

At age 42, I became vice president of the Bank of S————. This position paid quite well and I enjoyed the advantages. I not only enjoyed my job but also my social life. . . . I died at age 42, when, making a trip to ———— College as a speaker for the 25th anniversary of the GHP experience, I made the mistake of eating in the cafeteria. I died within the hour. I suppose the only way I had survived 25 years ago was that my stomach was younger and stronger then. The death was painful but quick, and though I am sorry to go this way, I am looking forward to meeting many of you in the great beyond.

Love,
Tom

P.S. World, if you're wondering how I'm writing this now that I'm dead, it's because I'm using my telepathic powers. I have always had them, but never used them on earth because it may have embarrassed you.

Many alienated gifted students use the type of humor seen in this soliloquy as a way of dealing with their feelings of being alienated and at the same time maintaining their productivity and high level of achievement.

A number of gifted students accept their alienation and plan productive careers in accord with this acceptance. The following soliloquy by a white girl in the visual arts area illustrates this strategy:

I look back on my life and see all of the mistakes that I made, all of the goals I reached (and did not reach). As a child and adolescent, I never was outgoing or extroverted. All my expressions of feelings were given an outlet only in my art work and poetry. I knew, even as a child, that I must be an artist in order to be my complete self....

My senior year of high school, I entered Gainesville Junior College under the joint-enrollment program and gained enough honors to enter the University of Georgia as a sophomore majoring in art. I learned in high school that I could not expect to make a living as an artist, and I began thinking of teaching....

I don't know, after I got out of college, I taught and it was nice but I wasn't fulfilled. After two years, I went back to college for my master's degree and became interested in art therapy. I've always loved children and felt that I could relate to them much better than to adults. I am now working as an art therapist ... with retarded and emotionally disturbed children and I feel that it is the best and most fulfilling job that I could ever want. In the future I plan to travel more and go abroad for a while, but I couldn't leave these children now. They are really opening up and letting go of serious problems through their art work and I'm glad to be part of their lives.

Other favorite strategies of alienated gifted adolescents seem to be through a computerized world or the creation of a retreat in outer

space. In the following soliloquy, a white male combined these two
strategies:

A Computerized World

Here it is—the year 2000. I'm sitting at my desk remembering
how it used to be. How when I was in school the computer was
just a simple tool like a hammer, and only people with special
training could operate them. I never knew how much value
would be set on the computer then, but I went into the business
of computers.

Now computers have taken over the world. This was caused
by putting too much importance on the computer. When man
saw how the computer made his work easier, he started using
computers for everything. He put them in cars, houses, air-
planes, etc. This seemed good for a while. We became richer
and richer until young technicians were trained. Now I have my
own computer store. These are very common today. In computer stores, you have all kinds of computer-operated devices. Instead of fuses these days we have rechargeable computers to
program lighting, heating, cooling, etc.

Yes, I made good money, being one of the rich technicians.
I was the first to start computer stores, so I am known as the best
and it's a blooming business. I employ about three million
people in the United States and about 20 million in other countries. I still test and install equipment but this is for the very rich
or when I am experimenting with a new device.

My apartment is a ranch style house. It has electric windows,
doors, etc. We don't have to worry about power because the
computer has solved all of the energy problems. I have two
computerized cars and a computerized space mobile. On week-
ends I go to the moon on a restful retreat trip. It's very lovely
up there ...

A search for identity also characterizes the soliloquies of gifted
adolescents. Such a search is quite explicit in the following excerpts
from a soliloquy by a member of this group, a white male:

I am 40 years old now and though I am no longer a young
man, I still feel as though I am only 21. I still enjoy the things
that I once did, perhaps even more since I have *finally found
myself* amidst the mass confusion and harshness of the world.

When I was younger I was incessantly searching for idealistic
principles, and thank the Lord for that. For had I not committed
myself to the ultimate good of finding one's own self and of

understanding one's own feelings as well as motivations, I most certainly would not be the happy and successful human being that I perceive myself to be.

After describing his career, he closes with a final statement which helps illustrate the search for identity of the alienated gifted adolescent:

Reading this, one might think that I lived in a Utopia of some sort. This is not true; I too have my problems. But all I have to do is sort through my experiences and relate them to the present problem. If that doesn't work, I just use my own best judgment and hope things come out for the best (and they almost invariably do).

Style of Learning and Thinking

Because of possible difficulties in interpreting results, the mixed pattern of learning and thinking was eliminated from the study dealing with the specialized cerebral functions and images of future careers. Scores obtained from the posttest soliloquies were analyzed in the same way as the data in the alienation study.

The results of the analyses of variance are presented in Table 38.2. Significant F-ratios were obtained for all of the variables studied except for number of words written. Those having the right hemisphere specialized functions and the integrated functions expressed greater satisfaction with their projected future careers, perception of self as changed, perception of the world as changed, commitment to working for a better world, awareness of future problems, proposed future solutions, and perception of self as a creative, problem-solving person. There was a fair degree of consistency for the right hemisphere group to excel the integrated group.

On the checklist items, statistically significant chi squares were obtained for: unconventional careers, the effects of ideas on life and culture, the use of the environment to meet human needs, educational problems, optimism about the future, and strategy of resolving conflicts. The results concerning strategies of conflict resolution are especially provocative and are presented in Table 38.3.

The differences are quite impressive, with those claiming an integrated or a right hemisphere style of thinking and learning sharing greater ability to grapple with the conflicts of the future and to resolve them hopefully. When one begins to write a scenario soliloquy of the future, one almost invariably encounters forces headed in

TABLE 38.2
Means and F-ratios for Cerebral Specializations and Images of the Future (Posttest)

	Means			
Variable	Right N=30	Left N=30	Integrated N=30	F-ratio
Words	319.6	324.1	328.0	0.003
Satisfaction with career	7.8	6.0	7.7	17.709**
Perception of self as changed	7.5	4.8	6.9	21.641**
Perception of world as changed	5.7	3.1	4.8	7.875**
Work for better world	6.0	4.1	6.1	7.635**
Awareness of future problems	5.1	3.2	4.4	4.311*
Proposed future solutions	5.3	2.6	4.7	12.65**
Perception of self as creative person	7.6	3.6	6.2	31.75**

*F is significant at .01 level
**F is significant at .05 level.

TABLE 38.3
Chi Square Analysis of Effects of Cerebral Specialization on Conflict Resolution in Posttest Soliloquies of Future Careers

	Number		
	Right	Left	Integrated
No conflict, optimistic or neutral outcome	2	12	5
Conflict, optimistic outcome	15	7	22
Conflict, neutral outcome	2	4	2
Conflict, pessimistic outcome	1	2	1
No conflict, pessimistic outcome	0	5	0

$X2 = 23.652$
$p. < .001$

a collision course. It is seldom possible to resolve this type of conflict through logical means (a specialized function of the left hemisphere). Such solutions require creative thinking and the simultaneous processing of many kinds of information (a specialty of the right hemisphere). This could be the most important finding of this study, as it helps define an important problem in helping gifted students with a left hemisphere style of learning and thinking become more effective problem solvers.

The following excerpts from the soliloquy by a white male with a left hemisphere style of learning and thinking describe the struggle to pull away from a left hemisphere style of learning, thinking, and living:

> Yet as another day goes by I feel myself as the median between past and future. Up to now, I was mostly future. Tomorrow, I will be mostly past. I reflect upon my ever increasing past as a broth which has been stirred until it became today .... I see myself looking for another challenge, another hustle, another adventure. Yes, as I went to college, I knew I wasn't brilliant or extremely talented, but I knew myself. I knew I could handle anything anyone could throw me with the thought of George Orwell's *Animal Farm:* "I will work harder!" Indeed I did....
>
> My first engineering job was one of little prestige but I used it as a springboard for more promising opportunities. But when I went home at night, I took my job with me. Then I met my future wife. The relationship was stormy. I had been wrapped up in myself and my work for so long that I just didn't know how to deal with myself, but I worked at it. I was fortunate that she was patient.... She helped me develop hobbies and other amusements which I had not experienced since I was a teenager. She taught me about a part of myself which I had never known....
>
> Recently, however, I have been getting into trouble. My goals have become tougher and tougher and my endurance is lessening. I have caught myself losing concentration, getting hopelessly tired, and just a little dazed. Half my life is over. I am worried....
>
> I may die young because of my life style, but it is not that of which I am afraid. If I die young, I will have lived a life well lived. Of what I am afraid is the loss of independence and brain power. Being prisoner of my body is that of which I am afraid.

Some of the gifted students claiming a left hemisphere style of learning and thinking are aware that this dominance is robbing them of a completeness that they desire. Yet they seem unable to change to a more balanced or integrated style. The following excerpts from the soliloquy of a very successful civil engineer in the year 2037 illustrates this phenomenon:

> ... Yet if I could do it over again, there are things I would do differently. I would, in the words of another writer, "take time to smell the flowers." For I feel that my life has been too hurried, too rushed, for me to really enjoy some of the better times. I regret not having savored the quieter moments, and always being too busy to truly enjoy myself. My career has been very fulfilling and satisfying, yet I see now that I was too absorbed

in it to take time off for much else. The good times that I had together with my family were few and far between. Not that I feel I've neglected my duties as a father—both of my sons have grown into fine young men—yet I still feel uncomfortable, uneasy, as though some vital element has been missing from my life.

Some members of this group of gifted adolescents with a dominant left hemisphere style of learning and thinking continued their soliloquies on a collision course to death. This is illustrated in the following closing excerpt from a soliloquy of a Marine who places himself in conflict with those who denounce military force:

> . . . It is an irony that I will die to save the right of free speech, the right that is used to denounce me and what I am doing. Ah, the fighting seems to pick up. The shield of West Point says, "Duty, Honor, and Country." I am proud to say I have all three, Duty in my wo— I have been retired—

Many of the members of this group described successful future careers but failed to find meaning in them. The final paragraph from the soliloquy by a successful lawyer in the year 2022 illustrates this point:

> The world continues around us. Politicians, social problems, fads, all change, but human nature remains the same. I look back to a comforting busy life and seeing myself doing what is right to do. I ask myself, "Was it right?" If it was, why doesn't American success fill the empty spaces in my soul?

It will take a great deal more incubation concerning the data we have and a great deal more data to fathom the real meaning of these findings. While it is very important that we do this, we do not think we should wait before trying to develop materials, methods, and procedures for helping students enlarge, enrich, and make more accurate their images of the future. At this point, we shall only identify the major ideas under development.

Enriching, Enlarging, Making More Accurate

Interdisciplinary Studies

It seems rather certain that many occupations of the future will require interdisciplinary skills. In fact, it has been interesting to note the interdisciplinary nature of the future careers described by gifted and talented students in their scenarios and soliloquies. Some of the models developed in the Career Awareness Component of the Georgia Governor's Honors Program seem to be quite successful. The methodology of both the futures and career education components have been thoroughly interdisciplinary, and they have meshed at many points. Students were taught to use many of the research methodologies of the futurists as well as more traditional methods such as survey research and bibliographic techniques. A variety of simulation methods were used, including game analogs with role playing, metaphorical analogs, mechanical analogs, and mathematical analogs.

Considerable use was made of the Delphi technique as a method of consensus attainment. The 100 students in one cluster group made future predictions. These were compiled into a master list and subjected to Delpha procedures to establish the characteristics of future communities. Students in groups of 25 then created future communities, using the resulting data. In order to receive a charter, these future communities had to demonstrate how they would deal with a variety of government, family, economic, religious, and educational problems.

Our Interscholastic Future Problem Solving Program (Torrance, Bruch, & Torrance, 1976; Torrance & Torrance, 1977) has also been quite interdisciplinary in nature. In fact, some coordinators and resource teachers in programs for the gifted and talented have used the Future Problem Solving Program as a device for helping such children "put their curriculum together." A future problem which begins as one in geography (such as our cooling of the earth problem in October 1976) rapidly moves into problems in psychology, politics, communication, physics, economics, and the like.

While we have many indications from students, teachers, and parents that participation in this program does enlarge, enrich, and make more accurate students' images of the future, we have not conducted formal evaluations, as we have done of the Career Awareness Component of the Governor's Honors Program. We expect to do this in 1977–78.

Children Teaching Teachers and Other Adults

In recent years, considerable attention has been given to the idea of children teaching children. It has just been announced that a new NBC TV program entitled "Junior Hall of Fame," using this idea, will be introduced on Saturday mornings. For several years Torrance has experimented with and advocated programs through which children teach teachers and other adults (Torrance, 1973a, 1974). This procedure has seemed especially appropriate for culturally different and disadvantaged children and has given teachers and other adults important learning experience otherwise inaccessible to them.

Educators have not yet given attention to this idea but I believe they will, as they develop a better understanding of futures studies. Margaret Mead (1970) predicted this trend at least a couple of decades ago. She has suggested that we have shifted from a "post figurative" culture, in which the young learn from the old, to one which is "cofigurative," in which both adults and children learn chiefly from their peers. She believes that we are already beginning to shift to the next stage, a "prefigurative" culture in which the old learn from the young. In a prefigurative culture, the future dominates the present, just as in a postfigurative culture the past (tradition) dominated the present. In our evaluations of the 1976 Career Awareness Program, we found interesting evidence of Margaret Mead's theories.

Throughout the evaluation of the 1976 program, learning from peers was rated by these gifted and talented students as the most exciting feature of the program. Ninety-eight percent of them rated "learning from peers with similar interest" as one of the most exciting features of the program, while only 75% rated "exciting, helpful teachers" in this category. In April 1977 when we (Torrance, Kaufmann, Ball, & Torrance, 1977) conducted follow-up study, 96% of them reported that they had continued to maintain contacts with their peers from the program. Already they had had three reunions, something unprecedented in the Georgia Governor's Honors Program. Thus, it seems clear that what Mead calls a "cofigurative" culture was operating. In the follow-up it was also found that these gifted students had done a great deal of teaching of their peers. Seventy-four percent reported that they had taught skills learned in the program to their peers or had helped them solve problems or raise consciousness concerning problems; 66% of their nominating teachers verified this claim. More striking, however, is the report that 31% of them reported that they had taught their teachers or adult leaders some new method, skill, etc., and 25% of the nominating teachers verified this. We expect that this tendency will show an increase with the participants in the 1977 program. We believe that this will be facilitated by our sending to their schools a self-report detailing their learnings and suggesting how they might be used in their schools. This may be the only way that teachers can really learn about the future. As the pace of cultural change accelerates, people recognize that the younger members of society have absorbed the latest aspects of the culture and are in closer contact than they with the future.

New Production Techniques in Sociodrama

About four years ago, Torrance (1973a, 1975, 1976c) proposed sociodrama as a problem-solving approach to studying the future. Many of the production techniques created by Moreno (1946, 1969) are admirably suited to this purpose—the future projection technique, dream techniques, the Magic Shop technique, etc. I have renovated these and some of the basic production techniques to facilitate the goals of enlarging, enriching, and making more accurate the future images of participants. For example, I invented the "Up the Cherry Tree" soliloquy technique to help the protagonist in a future conflict to escape from the restraints of his ordinary environments and to think in the future tense. This production technique was inspired by an event from the life of Robert Goddard, the rocket pioneer. It was while sitting aloft in a cherry tree which he was pruning that he became convinced of the idea that interplanetary travel was possible.

Perhaps a better illustration, however, is the Future Double Technique, a variation of Moreno's Double and Multiple Double techniques. In the Multiple Double variant, one double serves as the future self and another as the past or present self, depending upon the time perspective of the protagonist. This set of production techniques is based upon the belief that each person has a future self, as well as a present and past self, which influences thinking and feeling. Involving the future self in the confrontation frequently helps resolve the conflict in a satisfactory way. The underlying theory is very much like that behind the transactional analysis idea of the Parent, Child, and Adult selves.

Sociodrama itself is an effective technique for teaching skills of conflict resolution when the conflict involves two forces on a collision course. This can be demonstrated by having participants construct scenarios involving protagonists on a collision course. The conflicts should be such that the authors can think of no logical solution. Each scenario is then given to a different team for sociodramatic enactment. Almost invariably a solution emerges from the action, one that the authors of the scenario had been unable to think of. I am not yet certain how well this will work for persons having a left hemisphere style of learning. However, it may provide a vehicle for escaping from this type of dominance.

Conclusion

We hope that some of you may share our excitement in these emerging insights concerning the development of images of the future of gifted students and educational methodologies for enlarging, enriching, and making more accurate our images of the future. The challenge is great.

References

Allen, W. R. *Preliminary technical-norms manual: Allen Adolescent Alienation Inventory.* Athens, Ga.: Georgia Studies of Creative Behavior, University of Georgia, 1973.

Mead, M. *Culture and commitment.* New York: Doubleday, Natural History Press, 1970.

Moreno, J. L. *Psychodrama.* Vol. I. Beacon, N.Y.: Beacon House, 1946.

Moreno, J. L., & Moreno, Z. T. *Psychodrama.* Vol. III. Beacon, N.Y.: Beacon House, 1969.

Polak, F. L. *The image of the future.* Amsterdam, Holland: Elsevier, 1973.

Torrance, E. P. What gifted disadvantaged children can teach their teachers. *Gifted Child Quarterly,* 1973, *17,* 243–249. (a)

Torrance, E. P. *Notes on sociodrama as a creative problem solving process to study the future.* Athens, Ga.: Georgia Studies of Creative Thinking, University of Georgia, 1973. (b)

Torrance, E. P. Readiness of teachers of gifted to learn from culturally different gifted children. *Gifted Child Quarterly,* 1974, *18,* 137–142.

Torrance, E. P. Sociodrama as a creative problem-solving approach to studying the future. *Journal of Creative Behavior,* 1975, *9,* 182–195.

Torrance, E. P. Career education of the gifted and talented: Images of the future. Paper presented at the Commissioner's Conference on Career Education, Houston, Texas, November 7, 1976. (a)

Torrance, E. P. Images of the future of today's gifted and talented students. Paper presented at the Western Symposium on Learning, Bellingham, Washington, October 8, 1976. (b)

Torrance, E. P. *Sociodrama in career education.* Athens, Ga.: Career Education Project, College of Education, University of Georgia, 1976. (c)

Torrance, E. P., Bruch, C. B., & Torrance, J. P. Interscholastic futuristic creative problem solving. *Journal of Creative Behavior,* 1976, *10,* 117–125.

Torrance, E. P., Kaufmann, F., Ball, O., & Torrance, J. P. *Evaluation of career awareness component, Georgia Governor's Honors Program.* Athens, Ga.: Department of Educational Psychology, 1977.

Torrance, E. P., Kaufmann, F., Gibbs, S., & Torrance, J. P. *Preliminary report: Evaluation of the 1976 Institute of Career Develop-*

ment of the Governor's Honors Program. Athens, Ga.: Department of Educational Psychology, 1976.

Torrance, E. P., Kaufmann, F., & Hallford, M. Effects of a career development institute on the images of the future of gifted adolescents. Paper presented at annual meeting of the Association for the Gifted, Council on Exceptional Children, Atlanta, Ga., April 15, 1977.

Torrance, E. P., Reynolds, C. R., & Riegel, T. R., Jr. *Preliminary norms-technical manual for Your Style of Learning and Thinking.* Athens, Ga.: Georgia Studies of Creative Behavior, University of Georgia, 1976.

Torrance, E. P., & Torrance, J. P. The 1976–77 future problem solving program. Unpublished paper, Georgia Studies of Creative Behavior, University of Georgia, 1977.

Toynbee, A. Is America neglecting her creative minority? In C. W. Taylor (Ed.), *Widening horizons in creativity.* New York: John Wiley, 1964.

39   The Creative Person and Non–Ordinary Reality

Stanley Krippner, Roy Dreistadt, and C. Clark Hubbard

When I watch that flowing river, out of regions I see not, pour for a season its streams into me, I see that I am a pensioner, not a cause, but a surprised spectator of this ethereal water; that I desire and look up and put myself in the attitude of reception, but from some alien energy the visions come.

—Ralph Waldo Emerson

From what source do creative individuals derive their original ideas? Is it possible that at least part of their giftedness reflects time that they spend at different levels of reality? If so, are they able to return from non-ordinary reality with ideas that they can translate into the terms and forms of the ordinary reality with which most people interact?

These questions cannot be dismissed as mere theoretical speculation. The answers which a society gives to them will affect the kind

From *The Gifted Child Quarterly* 16:3 (1972). Used by permission.

of education, training, and nurturance which it advocates for gifted children, and the type of reinforcements it provides for talented adults.

The Creative Person

Many writers have theorized that the creative person's originality derives, in part, from his ability to perceive the world differently than do other persons (Progoff, 1963). It is also stated that the creative individual is less bound than others by cultural conditioning (Krippner, 1968). Furthermore, it is felt that the creative person retains a childlike capacity to open-mindedly experience the world in a personalized, innovative manner (Kris, 1965). He also possesses a childlike ability to fantasize, to imagine, and to express curiosity (Torrance, 1962), along with the tools of structure and discipline which maturity brings (Pearce, 1971).

In addition to these abilities, the creative individual typically is more emotionally stable and self-confident than his peers (e.g., Kneller, 1965; Witty, 1930). In a study of creative adolescents, Schaefer (1969: 72, 233–242) found, in general, that creative adolescents viewed themselves as independent, unconventional, and iconoclastic, as well as creative, imaginative, and ingenious.

In other words, not only do creative people perceive their world differently, but they also have confidence in the validity of their perceptions. There are many exceptions to this generalization, but the fact that a creative person produces an original idea, design, or product gives witness to his confidence that his perception of reality is true and genuine, no matter how divergent and unconventional it may appear to others.

Non–Ordinary Reality

There are numerous levels at which one can perceive the reality of the universe. Many of these levels apparently are beyond the scope of the human sensorium. For example, some mammals respond to sounds at too high a frequency for discernment by the human ear and brain. Creative individuals are in somewhat the same situation; they perceive nuances of color, space, emotion, rhythm, etc., to which most people remain oblivious (Kneller, 1965). Thus, for all practical purposes, the creative man or woman often finds himself at a level of reality so unusual it could be referred to as "non-ordinary reality."

These non-ordinary realities are not the exclusive product of the creative individual. A primitive tribesman coming into a civilized country would notice things which most of the people of that culture would disregard. His behavior would seem strange to others—but would be quite understandable from the tribesman's frame of reference. As Pearce (1971) notes, "People from different cultures not only use a different language, but inhabit a different sensory world." Similar instances of varying perceptions would characterize a tourist in a foreign country, a slum dweller who finds himself in a penthouse apartment, or a rather overprotected adult who has wandered into a children's playground.

A similar situation characterizes the level of reality at which many schizophrenic individuals exist. Their perceptions, too, are divergent and unconventional. However, they function very poorly in society— if at all—as a result of their non-ordinary reality, and find it a handicap rather than a gift. An exception is the rare creative person who is also schizophrenic and who has managed to put his bizarre experiences to use in art or literature. At one time it was felt that creativity and mental illness were closely linked (e.g., Lombroso, 1891). Research data (e.g., Witty, 1930) has largely dispelled this notion, and it is generally felt that psychopathology distorts and blocks creativeness rather than serving as a facilitator (e.g., Kubie, 1966).

Many creative persons enter and emerge from various non-ordinary realities with very little effort. Others seek for special techniques by which these unusual perceptions can be attained. Examples would be the use of hypnosis, psychedelic drugs, and dream recall to obtain creative fantasies which can be utilized in the creative work of gifted people. When the gifted person returns from non-ordinary reality with an idea which he can apply to his work, he creates a product which often assists other people to transcend ordinary reality as they read his poem, watch his film, see his painting, or use his invention. If a large enough number of people have positive contacts with these creative products, the nature of that society's reality structure will be changed. In this way, non-ordinary reality can eventually become ordinary reality for a small group of people or for an entire culture.[1]

Hypnosis and Creativity

A number of individuals have used hypnotic suggestion to enhance creativity. Sergei Rachmaninoff, the great Russian pianist and com-

---

[1] One example of this phenomenon would be musical composition. When a new musical style is introduced (e.g., syncopation, atonality, ragtime, jazz, rock-and-roll) it is rejected by most people who hear it. Over the years, however, repeated playings accustom individuals to the innovation, and it gradually becomes a standard part of the cultural musical repertoire.

poser, plunged into deep depression at the age of twenty-one because his first piano concerto was received unfavorably (cited by Krippner, 1969). His depression and misery continued for so long a time that his friends became alarmed and persuaded him to visit Dr. Nikolai Dahl, who specialized in hypnotic treatment. After some preliminary instructions, Dr. Dahl repeated over and over such statements as, "You will begin to write another concerto; you will work with great facility." The treatment continued for one half hour per day over a period of three months.

Rachmaninoff's depression was removed by the hypnotic suggestions and he began to compose again, working with speed and inspiration. Musical ideas flowed from his pen, were elaborated, and became his Concerto Number Two in C minor for Piano and Orchestra. It was first performed in 1901 by the Moscow Philharmonic Orchestra and was a great success. Rachmaninoff openly acknowledged his debt to Dr. Dahl and dedicated the concerto to him.

Experimental Studies

Recent experimental studies appear to throw some light on the relationship between hypnotic induction and the creative act by showing that as children grow older they seem to become less susceptible to hypnosis and also less creative. London (1962) studied 57 boys and girls aged five and older. He found that children are significantly more susceptible to hypnosis than are adults. Torrance (1962) found that the children he studied showed declines in originality—as measured by creativity tests—upon entering kindergarten, fourth grade, and junior high school. It appears that when the growing child learns to perceive the world through the eyes of his culture, he surrenders his individualistic outlook, becoming less open to new experiences, less original, less imaginative, and more stereotyped in his thinking. However, the highly imaginative person may be less likely to give up his interest in creative activity and more likely to react quickly to hypnotic suggestion (Krippner, 1969); both behaviors depend on retaining certain childlike qualities. Pearce (1971: 115) explains this phenomenon by noting that the adult who can freely abandon his ordinary world-view and retreat to an unformed, childlike world-view is the one who can feel secure with a hypnotist as he was once secure with his parents in a similar function. What takes place is a reproduction of the natural developmental processes of early experience.

. . . . .

McCord and Sherrill (1961) reported an experiment using one subject—a professor of mathematics. McCord hypnotized the mathematician and gave him the suggestion that after the hypnotic session ended, he would be able to solve calculus problems with a higher degree of accuracy and more rapidly than he had ever solved them before. The hypnotic episode was then terminated, the mathematician was given the calculus problems, and he was asked to solve as many as possible in 20 minutes. The subject worked with great speed, skipped steps in the mathematical processes, performed some of the calculations "in his head" which he would normally have written out, and wrote other more complex calculations down at a rapid rate of speed. In 20 minutes he accomplished without loss of accuracy what would normally have taken him two hours. He reported that he enjoyed doing these calculus problems and that he felt his unconscious mind had participated more than usual in the calculations.

Mental Modalities

Creative people often report solving complex problems rapidly by using visual imagery without resorting to verbal behavior. Thus, Mysior (1971) performed an experiment to determine whether subjects could do additions and multiplications to solve mathematical problems by purely visual processes. Mysior had previously observed that one type of mentally retarded person, referred to as a "calendar idiot," could determine within a few seconds on which day of the week any past or future date would fall. Attempts to find a *simple* formula to solve this problem have been unsuccessful, although a *complex* formula is known.

The hypothesis occurred to Mysior that access to mental functions like the method supposedly used by "calendar idiots" is inhibited by other functions to which most people have become conditioned. He had also observed people who had taken "speed reading" courses and could read at the rapid rate of 350 to 1,500 words per minute. In learning "speed reading," a "pacer" is often used which covers the printed page line by line at an increasing speed. This forces the person to read faster subvocally, then to leave out words, and eventually to reach the point where he no longer translates visual sensory input into conceptualized sound but derives the meaning directly from the printed material. Mental functions are then converted from one mental modality to another. Mysior (1971: 98) concluded that people usually "cannot extract any meaning directly from the visual input because their earlier conditioning to sound-language acts as an inhibitor."

These observations led Mysior to perform an experiment which he began by training subjects to multiply four digit numbers by four digit numbers. They did this by utilizing a method involving a single operation in which the answer could be written digit by digit on one line from right to left. The subjects were then hypnotized and instructed to clearly visualize the numbers written on the blackboard, to close their eyes, and *to forget the names of the numbers*. They were then asked to "multiply" the numbers by visually transforming them as they had been taught. In this procedure, hypnosis was utilized as a "pacer" to prevent the subjects from verbally multiplying the numbers, and to force them to "multiply" the numbers by the purely visual process they had been taught.

His results tended to confirm his hypothesis that if conditioned inhibitions produced by verbalizing processes are removed, mental functioning can be altered, making it easier to multiply and add by a purely visual process.

Time Distortion

The capacity of accomplishing a large amount of work in a short period of time, as in "speed reading" and in the calculus problem-solving experiment under hypnosis, appear to be related to the findings of hypnotic time distortion experiments.

Cooper and Erickson (1954) did the pioneer work on hypnotic time distortion. They used hypnosis to slow down the subjective perception of time in 14 subjects. Three to 20 hours of training were required (depending on the subject) to develop the ability to lengthen one's experience of time. Cooper and Erickson found that a subject's ability to experience time distortion depended on his attaining a high degree of immersion in the world which was suggested by the hypnotist, and on an accompanying inattentiveness to his actual surroundings. In other words, he temporarily abandoned ordinary reality and entered non-ordinary reality.

They reported that the subjects in this condition could accomplish in a short time interval far more work than usual. In one experiment, for example, a college student who had clothes-designing talent designed a dress in 10 seconds when she was hypnotized but experienced the session as being an hour in length. She said that she ordinarily took several hours to design a dress. Cooper and Erickson suggested that time distortion could be utilized for creative mental activity in those fields in which a person is highly skilled.

Most creative persons accomplish a larger amount of work than others during the same amount of time. They, no doubt, accomplish this feat in various ways—time distortion may be one of their techniques.

Reduced Defensiveness

Bowers (1965) noted that previous research had suggested that creative persons have greater access to fluid, undeveloped realms of conceptualization than non-creative persons. Furthermore, creative persons are also less defensive than others. She wanted to study the role of lowered defensiveness in fostering creativity and surmised that hypnotic trance induction would lower defenses temporarily. Thus, she executed an experiment with two groups of students; one group was hypnotized and the other was given a program of relaxation training that lasted the same length of time as the hypnotic induction period of the hypnotized group.

All the subjects were given the same instructions. They were told that they had the ability to be creative if they would allow themselves to make use of all their relevant experiences. They were also told to perceive in unconventional ways, to notice aspects of problems overlooked previously, to ignore the possibility of criticism, to recall past moments of insight and the emotional feelings associated with these moments, and to feel confident about their ability to do well on the tests.

Before the instructions were given, the two groups of subjects had taken a number of creativity tests; a comparable series of tests were given to them after the instructions. It was found that there were no significant differences between the test scores that the two groups attained in the pre-instruction period, but after the instruction period the hypnotized subjects did significantly better on the creativity tests than did the non-hypnotized subjects. The hypnotized subjects also obtained higher scores on the creativity tests after the instructions than they did before the instructions, while the non-hypnotized subjects did not. Bowers concluded that instructions administered under hypnosis can facilitate creative thinking.

Bowers also administered clerical ability tests (which are noncreative in nature) to both of these groups before and after the instructions, and since the hypnotized subjects did not raise their scores on *these* tests to a significant degree it indicated to Bowers that increased motivation under hypnosis was not the main factor accounting for their superior performance on the creativity tests.

She also gave a set of instructions to hypnotized and non-hypnotized subjects in which she encouraged them to be clever, original, flexible, and fluent, *but did not mention attitudes that would reduce defensiveness*. The results were not as dramatic in this case, but the hypnotized subjects still scored significantly higher on the creativity tests. Bowers concluded that reduced defensiveness is not the only factor in creativity.

It can be proposed from the findings of these various experiments that hypnosis enables a person to use more of his abilities than are ordinarily accessible to him. This conclusion has been reached by Kupriyanovich (1970), who has stated that the brain has "huge reserves," and that people generally use only a small portion of their mental ability.

Hemispheric Differences

There is some evidence that creative people make more use than others of the right hemisphere of their brain which is "non-dominant" for right-handed persons.

Bakan has investigated this possibility using a saccadic eye movement laterality index that was developed by Day (1964). Bakan (1971) found correlations between the direction in which a subject looks while he is thinking and various personality and physiological variables. Individuals who look to the right ("right-movers") scored higher on the mathematical than on the verbal scale of the Scholastic Aptitude Test, were more likely to major in the physical sciences and mathematics in college, and reported having less vivid visual imagery than do "left-movers." He also found "right-movers" to be less hypnotizable than "left-movers" (1969).

More recently, Harnad (1972) did a study at Princeton University with 10 professors of mathematics and 24 graduate students in mathematics to determine what would distinguish the "left-movers" from the "right-movers" within the mathematics field. His hypothesis was that "left-movers" would use more visual imagery in problem-solving, have a more esthetic attitude toward their work, and be more creative than "right-movers." The subjects were asked questions about their work, and the drift of their eye movements was noted. The "left-movers" reported significantly more imagery and more outside artistic activities than did "right-movers." In addition, Harnad administered a creativity measure, finding that "left-movers" among the professors were more creative.

In a study with 20 subjects with a college education or higher, Harnad (1972) found that "left-movers" scored higher on the Mednik and Halpern Remote Associates Test and were more esthetically responsive in evaluating pieces of prose for "pleasingness" and "unpleasingness."

Harnad (1972) theorized that during reflection there is a predominance of activity in the cortical hemisphere which is contralateral to the direction of the eye movement. Therefore, "left-movers" tend to make more use of their non-dominant (i.e., right) hemisphere. He supports this view by citing neurophysiological evidence regarding the contralateral control of conjugate saccades. He also cites evidence about the correspondence between inferences about hemispherical asymmetry of function made on the basis of the eye movement index and inferences made from sources such as unilateral cortical lesions, split-brain, and dichotic-listening experiments. All these data indicate that "left-movers" are more creative and make more use of their non-dominant cortical hemisphere.

Therefore, Harnad (1972) is of the opinion that since creativity seems to involve a random combinatory play of ideas, it is aided by the non-dominant hemisphere. This hemisphere is less bound by ordinary reality (based on sensory data and reasoning processes) than is the dominant hemisphere. He concludes the results of altered states of consciousness, such as dreaming, psychedelic drug states, mystical experiences, perceptual deprivation experience, esthetic experience, the subjective world of the young child, and psychoses, involve the non-dominant hemisphere.

Psychedelics and Creativity

There have been many highly creative persons who have used consciousness-altering drugs (e.g., opium, alcohol, LSD, hashish) though one can only—at this time—speculate as to whether or not any of these drugs increased their creativity. Samuel Taylor Coleridge, a poet and philosopher, habitually used a preparation of opium. Charles Baudelaire, a nineteenth-century writer, lavishly described his sensations after eating hashish. William James (1902), the famous psychologist and philosopher, tried using nitrous oxide— commonly known as laughing gas—to "stimulate the mystical consciousness." Aldous Huxley, the novelist and essayist, took mescaline and LSD on frequent occasions. Even Sigmund Freud, the founder of psychoanalysis, ingested cocaine for several years and recommended it highly.

In recent years, psychedelic ("mind-manifesting") drugs have often been used for creative purposes. In 1965, the psychiatrist Humphry Osmond and the architect Kyo Izumi announced that they had designed a new mental hospital with the aid of psychedelic drugs. Izumi (1968) took LSD when he visited traditionally designed mental hospitals to determine their effects upon persons in altered states of consciousness. In this condition, the long corridors and pale colors appeared bizarre and frightening to him; the corridor "seemed infinite, and it seemed as if I would never get to the end of it." He and Osmond assumed that the hospital would look similarly unpleasant to the mental patients. As a result of Izumi's experiences, he and Osmond designed a decentralized series of unimposing buildings with pleasant colors and no corridors.

Barron (1963) administered psilocybin to several highly creative persons and recorded their impressions. For example, one of Barron's subjects, a composer, wrote, "Every corner is alive in a silent intimacy." Barron concluded, "What psilocybin does is to ... dissolve many definitions and ... melt many boundaries, permit greater intensities or more extreme values of experience to occur in many dimensions." However, some of the artists in Barron's study were wildly enthusiastic about their seemingly increased sensitivity *during* the drug experience but later when the effects of the drug wore off they found that the artistic work they had produced had little artistic merit. For instance, a painter recalled, "I have seldom known such absolute identification with what I was doing—nor such a lack of concern with it afterwards." It appears that an artist is not necessarily able to evaluate his psychedelically inspired work while he is under the influence of the drug.

· · · · ·

Dreams and Creativity

There are records of many instances of artistic, scientific, and philosophical insights occurring during dreams. However, an important question has never been resolved: Does the creative dream represent a consolidation of ideas attained while one is awake (and in ordinary reality), or does it represent insights gained from experiences attained within the non-ordinary reality of the dream itself?

It can be noted that the content of some creative dreams is used literally (directly), whereas the dream content of other creative dreams is used analogically (symbolically) in the creative work. Artists, for example, generally use the content of their creative dreams literally. Leo Katz and Martin Baer are two twentieth-century painters who occasionally recalled dreams which were so esthetically exciting that the artists represented them directly on canvas.

Richard Wagner (cited by Hock, 1960), describing his opera *Tristan and Isolde* to Mathilde Wesendonck, wrote, "For once you are going to hear a dream, a dream that I have made sound .... I dreamed all this; never could my poor head have invented such a thing purposely."

Giuseppe Tartini (cited by Porterfield, 1941: 9), the eighteenth-century composer and inventor of the modern violin bow, dreamed that the devil had become his slave. In his dream, he tried to fool the devil by giving him a dream violin to play. To his surprise, Satan played a "sonata of such exquisite beauty as surpassed the boldest flights of my imagination." After Tartini awoke he tried as best he could to recall the music and wrote "The Devil's Sonata."

Robert Louis Stevenson (cited by. Woods, 1947: 871–879) wrote that he learned early in his life that he could dream complete stories and that he could even go back to the same dreams on succeeding nights to give them a different ending. Later he trained himself to remember his dreams and to dream plots for his books. He wrote that his dreams were produced by "little people" who "labor all night long," and set before him "truncheons of tales upon their lighted theatre." Stevenson described how he obtained the plot for his short story, "The Strange Case of Dr. Jekyll and Mr. Hyde":

> For two days I went about racking my brains for a plot of any sort; and on the second night I dreamed the scene at the window, and a scene afterwards split in two, in which Hyde, pursued for some crime, took the powder and underwent the change in the presence of his pursuers. All the rest was made awake, and consciously .... All that was given me was the matter of three scenes, and the central idea of a voluntary change becoming involuntary.

Jean Cocteau (1952) dreamed he was watching a play about King Arthur; he later noted that it was "an epoch and characters about which I had no documentary information." The dream was so challenging that Cocteau was led to write his *The Knights of the Round Table*. He concluded, "The poet is at the disposal of his night. He must clean his house and await its visitation."

Sometimes dream states and drug states are combined in creative dreams. One can cite Samuel Taylor Coleridge's creative dream that occurred after he took laudanum, an opium preparation. He described the dream in his "Preparatory Note to Kubla Khan" in the third person, as follows (from Ghiselin, 1952: 85):

> ... he fell asleep in his chair at the moment that he was reading the following sentence ... in *Purchas's Pilgrimage:* "Here the Khan Kubla commanded a palace to be built, and a stately garden thereunto. And thus ten miles of fertile ground were inclosed with a wall." The author continued for about three hours in a profound sleep... during which time he has the most vivid conference, that he could not have composed less than from two to three hundred lines; if that indeed can be called composition in which all the images rose up before him as *things*, with a parallel production of the corresponding ex-

pressions, without any sensation or consciousness of effort .... On awakening he appeared to himself to have a distinct recollection of the whole, and taking his pen, ink, and paper, instantly and eagerly wrote down the lines that are here preserved.

Coleridge recorded the beginning of the poem which he remembered from his dream; this became the celebrated work *Kubla Khan.*

Do these creative dreams of artists consolidate old material, or do they find and explore a new reality? It appears that these dreams do both; they find and give expression to non-ordinary reality by giving better insight into people and events, and they do so by consolidating or integrating past material. Conversely, we can also say that by giving expression to a non-ordinary reality these dreams synthesize a great deal of material.

Dreams of Science

Scientists, philosophers, and inventors also have creative dreams and use the content of these dreams either literally (directly) or analogically (symbolically) in their creative work. (It will be recalled that artists, musicians, and writers generally use the content in a literal manner.)

Herman V. Hilprecht (cited by Woods, 1947:525–530) attempted to decipher two small fragments of agate which were believed to belong to the finger rings of a Babylonian and had cuneiform writing on them of the Cassite period in Babylonian history. After midnight he was weary and exhausted, went to sleep, and dreamed the following:

> A tall thin priest of old pre-Christian Nippur, about forty years of age and clad in a simple abba, led me to the treasure chamber of the temple .... He addressed me as follows: "The two fragments which you have published separately on pages 22 and 26, belong together, are not finger rings and their history is as follows: King Kurigalzu (Ca. 1300 B.C.) once sent to the temple of Bel ... an inscribed votive cylinder of agate. Then we priests suddenly received the command to make for the statue of the god Ninib a pair of earrings of agate. We were in a great dismay, since there was no agate as raw material at hand. In order to execute the command there was nothing for us to do but cut the votive cylinder into three parts, thus making three rings, each of which contained a portion of the original inscription. The first two rings served as earrings for the statue of the god; the two fragments which have given you so much trouble

are portions of them. If you will put the two together you will have confirmation of my words. But the third ring you have not found in the course of your excavations and you never will find it." With this the priest disappeared. I woke up....

Hilprecht later verified this interpretation by actually putting the fragments together at the Imperial Museum of Constantinople, thereby showing that they had once belonged to one and the same votive cylinder.

In his creative dream Hilprecht combined identically shaped "rings" (association by similarity) and thereby reconstructed the votive cylinder. He also combined other bits of information that agreed with this reconstruction. All this represents a process of consolidation. Hilprecht's dream thus integrated a great deal of material, but by synthesizing the material correctly the dream also gave him a picture of a non-ordinary reality—a *past* reality. It is conceivable, too, that Hilprecht's close contact with the "rings" helped give him imagery of the past events he saw in his dream in the same manner as the touch of an object purportedly gives a psychic paragnost accurate imagery of the past history of the object.

The naturalist Louis Agassiz (cited by Krippner & Hughes, 1970) attempted to transfer the image of a fossilized fish from a stone but found the image too blurred. He gave up the project only to dream a few nights later of an entire fossilized fish. He hurried to the laboratory the next morning, but the image was as obscure as before. The dream returned the next night. When he examined the slab the next morning, the vague image appeared unchanged. Hoping to have the dream a third time, Agassiz put a pencil and paper by his bed. The dream returned and he drew the image. The next morning when he looked at what he had drawn, he was surprised that he had produced so many details in total darkness. He returned to his laboratory and used the drawing as a guide to chisel the slab. When the stone layer fell away, Agassiz found the fossil in excellent condition and identical to the image he had seen in his dream.

Agassiz' creative dream of the fossilized fish may have been induced by having perceived unconsciously a clue in the stone slab which he had ignored while awake. If so, the dream could have emphasized and drawn his attention to stimuli he had perceived subliminally while he was awake. Perhaps Agassiz also perceived the fossil fish clairvoyantly by extrasensory perception (e.g., Krippner, 1963). If this is true, subliminal perception and extrasensory perception helped Agassiz experience non-ordinary reality which quickly turned into ordinary reality once the slab was cut.

The creative dreams of Hilprecht and Agassiz gave the solution to a problem literally or directly. One can cite as well creative dreams of scientists and inventors that gave the solution of a problem analogically or symbolically.

The chemist, Friedrich August Kekule (cited by Koestler, 1964: 118) had a tendency to make theoretical discoveries in hypnagogic reverie states. Kekule wrote:

> I turned my chair to the fire and dozed. Again the atoms were gambolling before my eyes. The smaller groups kept modestly in the background. My mental eye, rendered more acute by visions of this kind, could now distinguish larger structures, of manifold conformations; long rows, sometimes more closely fitted together, all twining and twisting in snakelike motion. But look! What was that? One of the snakes had seized hold of its own tail, and the form whirled mockingly before my eyes. As if by a flash of lightning I awoke.

The dream image of a snake holding its tail in its mouth led Kekule by analogy to his discovery that benzene has a ringlike structure (usually represented by a hexagon) and to his "closed-chain" or "ring" theory which showed the importance of molecular structure in organic chemistry. The imagery granted Kekule a glimpse into a non-ordinary reality of molecular structure.

Another period of reverie by Kekule was responsible for additional theoretical developments in organic chemistry (cited by Sturdevant, 1962–1963):

> One beautiful summer evening I was riding on the last omnibus through the deserted streets usually so filled with life ... I fell into a reverie. Atoms flitted before my eyes. I had never before succeeded in perceiving their manner of moving. That evening, however, I saw that frequently two smaller atoms were coupled together, that larger ones seized the two smaller ones; that still larger ones held fast three and even four of the smaller ones and that all were whirled around in a bewildering dance. I saw how the larger atoms formed a row and one dragged along still smaller ones at the end of the chain ... Thus arose the structural theory.

In 1869, D. I. Mendeleev went to bed exhausted after struggling to conceptualize a way to categorize the elements based upon their atomic weights (cited by Kedrov, 1957). He reported, "I saw in a dream a table where all the elements fell into place as required. Awakening, I immediately wrote it down on a piece of paper. Only in one place did a correction later seem necessary." In this manner, Mendeleev's Periodic Table of the Elements was created.[2]

In the field of invention the creative dream of Elias Howe provided an analogy for solving a puzzling problem. Howe had worked unsuccessfully for several years to invent a lock stitch sewing machine when he had a dream in which he was captured by a tribe of savages. Kaempffert (1924:385) tells the story as follows:

> ... Howe made the needles of his early failures with a hole in the middle of the shank. His brain was busy with the invention day and night and even when he slept. One night he dreamed ... that he was captured by a tribe of savages who took him a prisoner before their king.
>
> "Elias Howe," roared the monarch, "I command you on pain of death to finish this machine at once."
>
> Cold sweat poured down his brow, his hands shook with fear, his knees quaked. Try as he would, the inventor could not get the missing figure in the problem over which he had worked so long. All this was so real to him that he cried aloud. In the vision he saw himself surrounded by dark-skinned and painted warriors, who formed a hollow square about him and led him to the place of execution. Suddenly he noticed that near the heads of the spears which his guards carried, there were eye-shaped holes! He had solved the secret! What he needed was a needle with an eye near the point! He awoke from his dream, sprang out of bed, and at once made a whittled model of the eye-pointed needle, with which he brought his experiments to a successful close.

The new reality Howe found through this analogy in his creative dream was the possibility of a properly working lock stitch sewing machine. Once again, an idea obtained in an altered state of consciousness had applications which proved to be extremely practical.

While he was still a student, Niels Bohr (cited by Krippner & Hughes, 1970), the physicist, had a dream in which he saw himself standing in the boiling gaseous center of the sun while the planets revolved around the sun to which they were attached by thin filaments. The planets whistled as they passed by him. Then the burning gas cooled and solidified the sun and planets crumbled away, and

---

[2]Noting that hypnagogic and reverie states are frequently associated with theta brain wave rhythms, Green, Green, and Walters (1971) have instigated a biofeedback project to train individuals to enter these states through EEG brain wave training. The association between theta production and creativity will be explored among the subjects who can successfully produce the theta rhythm.

Bohr woke up. The dream stimulated him to use the solar system as an analogy to help analyze the structure of the atom. This gave Bohr the first picture of the atom as consisting of a nucleus with electrons revolving around it.

Sriniwasa Ramanujan (cited by Newman, 1948), a self-taught mathematician from India, claimed that the goddess of Namakkal inspired him with mathematical formulae in his dreams. After awakening in the morning, Ramanujan frequently wrote down mathematical ideas and verified them.

It can be seen that creative persons in their dreams sometimes appear to experience non-ordinary reality, and at the same time make different types of consolidations. Finding a new reality in a creative dream gives the person a novel slant or direction for consolidating his information, and the consolidation enables him to see the details and structure of the new reality more clearly. In some cases, finding a new reality not only gives the person a new direction for consolidating his information, but even involves finding additional information to be included in the consolidation.

The Role of Extrasensory Perception

Aside from the possibility that extrasensory perception (ESP) may have played a part in some of the creative dreams just described, there have in general been many unusual and puzzling creative achievements in which ESP may have played a role.

When Igor Sikorsky was ten years of age, he dreamed of coursing the skies in the softly lit, walnut-paneled cabin of an enormous flying machine. Sikorsky later became an eminent aircraft designer and inventor of the helicopter. Three decades after the dream, he went aboard one of his own four-engine clippers to inspect a job of interior decorating done by Pan American Airways. With a start, he recognized the cabin as identical to the one in his boyhood dream.

Max Planck, the physicist, first spoke of his "constant" when he was twenty-three years of age; however, he did not understand its implications for wave theory until much later. Indeed, he had to convince himself of its correctness; it varied so greatly from the logic of his time that he could not comprehend it when the idea first came to him.

Hadamard (1945:116–123) has discussed a number of interesting "paradoxical cases of intuition" among great mathematicians. In the nineteenth century, Evarist Galois produced a manuscript that signified a complete transformation of higher algebra. The paper projected a full light on what had been only glimpsed thus far by the greatest mathematicians. In a letter Galois wrote to his friend during the night before he died, he stated a theorem on the "periods" of a certain type of integral. Hadamard comments that although his theorem is clear to mathematicians of today, it could not have been understood by scientists living at the time of Galois. These "periods" acquired meaning only by means of some principles in the theory of certain functions that were found about a quarter of a century after the death of Galois. Hadamard concludes that Galois must have thought of these principles in some way before he could arrive at the "periods," but that they must have been unconscious in his mind since he made no mention of them.

Another example of a nineteenth-century mathematician cited by Hadamard (1945) concerns Bernhard Riemann. When Riemann died, a note was found among his papers that read: "These properties of S (the function in question) are deduced from an expression of it which, however, I did not succeed in simplifying enough to publish it." Hadamard himself has since proved all the properties except one with the help of facts that were unknown in Riemann's time. Hadamard added that in regard to one of the properties that Riemann enunciated, "It is hardly conceivable how he can have found it without using some of these general principles, no mention of which is made in his paper."

Yet another instance of this type concerns Pierre de Fermat who, in the seventeenth century, contributed to the development of the infinitesimal calculus, to the calculus of probabilities, and to the theory of numbers. He was also a co-founder of analytic geometry. After Fermat's death, it was discovered that he had a copy of Diophantes' book and that he had written this statement in the margin: "I have proved that the relation $X^m + Y^m = Z^m$ is impossible in integral numbers (X, Y, Z different from 0; m greater than 2); but the margin does not leave me room enough to inscribe the proof." Since then, three centuries have passed and mathematicians are still trying to prove it. Hadamard (1945) believes that Fermat was not mistaken because partial proofs have been found, though by an immense amount of work that "required the help of some important algebraic theories of which no knowledge existed at the time of Fermat and no conception appears in his writings."

Hadamard theorized that these mathematical discoveries were made intuitively and imaginatively with the aid of deep unconscious processes. According to Freud's psychoanalytic theory (Freud, 1933) the primary processes involved an imaginative intuitive thought derived from the unconscious. And, according to recent parapsychological speculation, the unconscious is also where ESP originates. If this is true, it seems that any thought processes deriving from this mental level readily have access to information obtained by ESP (Anderson, 1962).

Koestler (1963:75) mentions some interesting discoveries made by great astronomers such as Pythagoras, Ptolemy, Copernicus, Galileo, Kepler, and Newton, and writes, ". . . the manner in which some of the most important individual discoveries were arrived at reminds one more of a sleepwalker's performance than an electronic brain's." Regarding Kepler, Koestler (1963:394) writes, "Unlike his First and Second Laws, which he found by that peculiar combination of sleepwalking intuition and wide-awake alertness for clues—a mental process on two levels, which drew mysterious benefits out of his apparent blunderings—the Third Law was the fruit of nothing but patient, dogged trying." Koestler (1963:502) continues, "With true sleepwalker's assurance, Newton avoided the booby traps strewn over the field: magnetism, circular inertia, Galileo's tides, Kepler's sweeping brooms, Descartes' vortices—and at the same time knowingly walked into what looked like the deadliest trap of all: action-at-a-distance."

Although most of Koestler's sleepwalking insight can be explained as initially information acquired by normal perception which was subsequently used in imaginative thinking, it is likely that some of the "sleepwalking" in these scientific discoveries also involved using information acquired by ESP. Data acquired through ESP, as well as the activities of his imaginative thought processes, may enable a scientist to explore non-ordinary reality.

Perhaps one of the most interesting cases of this kind is that of Michael Faraday (cited by Koestler, 1964), one of the greatest physicists of all time. Faraday was a visionary even in a literal sense. He "saw" the stresses surrounding magnets and electric currents as "curves of force in space," which he called "lines of forces." He visualized the universe as patterned by narrow curved tubes through which all forms of "ray-vibrations" or energy-radiations are propagated. This vision of curved tubes which "rose up before him like things" led him to the ideas of the dynamo and the electric motor. It also made him discard the concept of the ether and to postulate that light is electromagnetic radiation. Did Faraday enter these new realities through his imagination, or was he also assisted by ESP?

The case of Jonathan Swift (cited by Haefele, 1962), the writer of *Gulliver's Travels* and other novels, combines artistic and scientific creativity. When Gulliver reaches Laputa, the astronomers state that the planet Mars has two moons quite close to the planet. One completed its orbit every ten hours, the other every 21.5 hours. It took astronomers in ordinary reality 150 years to discover that Mars did, indeed, have two moons which completed their orbits around the planet every eight and every 30 hours.

A final instance of the possible association between ESP and creativity concerns *Futility*, a popular novel written by Morgan Robertson in 1898. It described the wreck of a giant ship called the

Titan. This ship was considered "unsinkable" by the characters in the novel; it displaced 70,000 tons, was 800 feet long, had 24 lifeboats, and carried 3,000 passengers. Its engines were equipped with three propellers. One night in April, while proceeding at 25 knots, the Titan encountered an iceberg in the fog and sank with great loss of life.

On April 15, 1912, the Titanic was wrecked in a disaster which echoed the events portrayed in the novel 14 years previously. The Titanic displaced 66,000 tons and was 828 feet long. It had three propellers and was proceeding at 23 knots on its maiden voyage, carrying nearly 3,000 passengers. There was great loss of life because the Titanic was equipped with only 20 lifeboats.

Thus, the role played by ESP in creativity demands further study. Anderson (1962) is convinced that the association exists because both ESP and creativity have their roots in deep, unconscious levels of the psyche. She concludes that creativity "by a process of purely conscious calculation seems never to occur. Scrutiny of the conscious scene for the creative end never reveals it; it is never there."

Self-Actualization and Creativity

Roberts (1971) utilizes a provocative conception of consciousness in developing a holistic theory which emphasizes the relatedness, interplay, and interdependence of all parts of a social system. Roberts' theory is especially useful in understanding how one's pattern of consciousness may lead him into contact with non-ordinary reality.

Roberts describes five major characteristics of human social systems which also become hallmarks of the variations in consciousness which permeate the activity of both individuals and groups.

The five types of consciousness, as Roberts describes them, are survival, stability, sociability, expertise, and self. He asserts that these types of consciousness pervade man's ideas of his universe, as well as his characteristic ways of perceiving the world.

These five types of consciousness, on the individual level, relate to the hierarchy of human needs described by Maslow (1970). The lower order needs (e.g., physiological drives, safety and security, love and affection, esteem and status) must be satisfied to some extent, according to Maslow, before the higher or self-actualization needs (e.g., curiosity, understanding, appreciation of beauty, creativity) can fully emerge. Roberts has associated a type of consciousness with each of Maslow's need categories:

An inspection of Roberts' typology reveals why creative behavior is more frequently associated with consciousness of self than with the other types.

Types of Consciousness	Hierarchy of Needs
Survival	Physiological drives
Stability	Safety and security
Sociability	Love and affection
Expertise	Esteem and status
Self	Self-Actualization (e.g., creativity)

In survival consciousness, the person, group, or society is concerned with avoiding physical pain and satisfying needs for food, water, and warmth. Day-to-day subsistence is the overriding motive, and there is no time or interest for high-level creative pursuits.

In stability consciousness, a person or persons go beyond day-to-day needs by trying to insure that the future will also be secure. The need for continuity and order produces discipline and structure; however, it may also produce rigid rules, dogmatic belief systems, authoritarian personality types, and a dominance-submissive mode of interpersonal relations. A modicum of structure is essential to lay the groundwork for creativity, but the presence of dogma and authoritarianism can stifle originality and divergent thinking.

In sociability consciousness, there is a seeking for affection, a giving of affection, and, eventually, a joining together with other like-minded persons for mutual action, protection, and benefit. The social values of congeniality, egalitarianism, and democracy have developed in this stage. However, some people expend most of their energy attempting to enter this type of consciousness (e.g., the persons who feel starved for love) and have no time available for creative endeavors.

In expertise consciousness, the person or group attempts mastery of specialized knowledge, skills, and abilities to insure his continuity. Esteem is won as each skill is mastered or as a society evolves technologically. Many of these abilities may be used creatively; yet, most persons never break through the narrow limitations of this type of consciousness to engage in original pursuits on a broader level.

In the consciousness of self, the individual or society places a great emphasis upon the development of human potentiality. One's consciousness at this stage differs considerably from those at other levels of development. Roberts cites Thomas Jefferson as an individual who had attained full consciousness of self. His ideas were frequently divergent from those of his contemporaries and were often far advanced for his time. This presumably occurred because he lived and moved in non-ordinary reality much of the time. As people become more self-actualized, their consciousness changes as does their perception of the world. This shift in perception brings with it new conceptualizations which permit a person to engage in what is referred to as creative behavior.

In other words, the altered states of consciousness which often stimulate original thinking need not be induced by hypnosis or psychedelic drugs. Development of the total personality through satisfaction of basic needs and personal growth toward self-actualization produce a dramatic change in awareness, perception, and concept-formation. These changes often result in an increased ability to recall dream and reverie states. Furthermore, they may equal or even surpass in usefulness the temporary alterations in consciousness which characterize hypnosis and drug states.

The attainment of creative behavior is described by Gowan (1972: 53) as the outcome of the proper functioning of an individual's development.

> ... creativity ... is emergent in the personal unfoldment of the individual as part of his developmental process. This unfoldment is as natural as the budding and blossoming of a rose, if proper conditions of sunshine, soil and moisture are present. Once a certain developmental stage has been reached, creativity is a direct outcome of self-awareness.

Essential to creative behavior is the ability to transcend the limitations set by one's cultural conditioning and to be aware of more of one's universe than would be possible if the world-view imposed by one's society were strictly followed (Pearce, 1971). The Dutch psychologist Herman Cohen (1971) has described how various types of mental discipline, such as meditation, can assist this process. Through various types of self-development, one can rise above the culturally conditioned tendency to rigidly categorize experience into predetermined slots and to isolate one's ideas from one's emotions, and one's concepts from one's perceptions. Cohen goes so far as to state, "Realizing one's potentialities, whether these potentialities are interpreted in terms of creativity, psychological vitality, or spiritual growth, means exactly the same as overcoming dualistic thinking."

The association between self-actualization and creativity has also been stressed by Barron (1968:4) who writes:

> A person may be said to be most elegant, and most healthy, when his awareness includes the broadest possible aspects of human experience, and the deepest possible comprehension of them, while at the same time he is the most simple and direct in his feelings, thoughts, and actions.

Barron's emphasis on simplicity and directness is important because the self-actualized person has little trouble behaving in child-like ways if this will enhance his ability to perceive and conceptualize in creative ways.

This type of awareness is the goal of some psychotherapists (e.g., Rogers, 1961) who try to lead their clients from rigidity to flow, from fixed behavior to change. Roberts (1961:154) notes that when a client has discovered the type of psychotherapy which emphasizes self-actualization, he finds himself in "a new dimension."

> The client has now incorporated the quality of motion, of flow, of changingness, into every aspect of his psychological life, and this becomes his outstanding characteristic. The ways in which he construes experiences are continually changing as his personal constructs are modified by each new living event. His experiencing is process in nature, feeling the new in each situation and interpreting it anew; interpreting in terms of the past only to the extent that the now is identical with the past. He perceives himself as responsibly related to his problems. Indeed he feels a fully responsible relationship to his life in all its fluid aspects. He lives fully in himself as a constantly changing process of flow.

Maslow (1967) interviewed a large number of self-actualized people and found creative behavior to be one of their most salient characteristics. He further noted that self-actualizers experienced little or no conflict in situations that other people found difficult because self-actualizing individuals were better able to transcend dichotomies and avoid the traditional conflicts between duty and pleasure, work and play, individualism and social involvement, and egoism and altruism.

Bugental (1965:277) insists that self-actualization *must* become transcendence, which he views as the broadened state of consciousness which enables man to cognize reality in dimensions which are above and beyond traditional dualities and multiplicities. Needless to say, an individual must possess certain ego-strength before he can successfully transcend the ego; the ability to relinquish ordinary reality must wait until a fairly firm reality picture is built up (Pearce, 1971:115).

People engaged in dualistic thinking tend to regard difference only as a reversal point and are totally unaware that it is both reversal point and equalizing point. From this fixed reversal point the person does not see the counterparts as distinguished components of a oneness, but as hostile opposites. Under the influence of his cultural conditioning he selects one and rejects the other, thereby building up his rigid set of beliefs and values.

The core principle is that the creative person *learns to deal with a oneness.* The so-called counterparts are not divided parts or opposites, but distinguished parts of a unity, a oneness. Thus when one compares short and long lines one compares, in a sense, lines of *equal lengths,* because what is not equal in comparing them is the *difference.* It can be said that the difference between the lines comes into being while comparing equal lengths. The difference makes one aware of the equalness of the counterparts. And the counterparts bring the difference into being by becoming equal. In this way the difference reaches a zero-point and the whole oneness-of-three—that is, the counterparts plus difference—disappears.

This core principle can be applied to some of the pairs of opposites which restrict thinking and growth: dualisms of body and mind, matter and spirit, being and non-being, God and man, life and death, the one and the many, good and bad, individual and society, freedom and determinism, form and formless, and time and eternity.

The Western concept of time is dualistic. Discrimination of past, present, and future is made by regarding the present as a reversal point. But the present should be experienced as both the reversal point and the equalizing point of past and future. In this way the past and future merge into the present, and present thereby becomes the Here and Now—the liberating concept of both time and eternity.

This principle is implicit in much of Eastern philosophy (e.g., Satprem, 1964; Suzuki, 1964). Ben-Avi (1959:1819), while discussing Zen Buddhism, counsels that illumination and growth "must be rooted in the immediate, the concrete experience of the individual" because abstract formulations often encourage dualistic thinking and intellectualizations that retard one's development. Further, it is significant that most Zen masters and Yogis are extremely critical of psychedelic drugs, are mildly critical of hypnosis, and deemphasize the role of dreams in fostering creativity. For these practitioners of meditative disciplines, who spend most of their adult life in altered conscious states, one's creativity emerges naturally as one's life develops. The creative person produces items of great beauty just as a flower creates a magnificent spectacle of color as it unfolds. For them, creativity is viewed as a process rather than a product.

As the gifted person attempts to experience non-ordinary reality for creative purposes, he may be tempted to utilize shortcuts for attaining temporary insights. However, he should not ignore the more central role that his growth and development as a self-actualized human being can play in creativity.

There is a growing body of evidence (e.g., Maslow, 1967, 1970; Witty, 1940) that to be fully human is also to become creative. This position can not help but assume importance as a society begins to pay attention to the needs of its gifted children and talented adults.

References

Anderson, M. L. The relations of psi to creativity. *Journal of Parapsychology*, 1962, *26*:277–292.

Bakan, P. Hypnotizability, laterality of eye-movement and functional brain asymmetry. *Perceptual and Motor Skills*, 1969, *28*:927–932.

Bakan, P. The eyes have it. *Psychology Today*, 1971, *4*:64–67, 96.

Barron, F. *Creativity and Mental Health*. Princeton, N.J.: Van Nostrand, 1963.

Barron, F. *Creativity and Personal Freedom*. New York: Van Nostrand, 1968.

Ben-Avi, A. Zen Buddhism. In *American Handbook of Psychiatry*. Vol. II. Ed. S. Arieti. New York: Basic Books, 1959.

Bowers, P. G. The effect of hypnosis and suggestions of reduced defensiveness on creativity test performance. Unpublished doctoral dissertation, University of Wisconsin, 1965.

Bugental, J. F. *The Search for Authenticity*. New York: Holt, Rinehart & Winston, 1965.

Castaneda, C. *A Separate Reality*. New York: Simon & Schuster, 1972.

Cocteau, J. The process of inspiration. In *The Creative Process*, edited by B. Ghiselin. Berkeley: University of California Press, 1952.

Cohen, H. What the "here and now" really means. Paper presented at the Second International Invitation-Conference of Humanistic Psychology, Wurzburg, Federal German Republic, 1971.

Cooper, L. F., and Erickson, M. H. *Time Distortion in Hypnosis*. Baltimore: Williams & Wilkin, 1954.

Day, M. E. An eye-movement phenomenon relating to attention, thought and anxiety. *Perceptual and Motor Skills*, 1964, *19*:443–446.

Emerson, R. W. *Selected Prose and Poetry*. New York: Rinehart, 1950. Page 126.

Freud, S. *New Introductory Lectures on Psychoanalysis*. New York: Norton, 1933.

Ghiselin, B. (Ed.). *The Creative Process*. Berkeley, Calif.: University of California Press, 1952.

Gowan, J. C. *The Development of the Creative Individual*. San Diego, Cal.: Robert Knapp, 1972.

Green, A. M., Green, E. E., and Walters, E. D. Psychophysiological training for creativity. Paper presented at the annual convention, American Psychological Association, Washington, D.C., 1971.

Hadamard, J. *The Psychology of Invention in the Mathematical Field*. Princeton, N.J.: Princeton University Press, 1945.

Haefele, J. W. *Creativity and Innovation*. New York: Reinholt, 1962.

Harnad, S. R. Creativity, lateral saccades and the non-dominant hemisphere. 1972.

Hock, A. *Reason and Genius.* New York: Philosophical Library, 1960.

Izumi, K. LSD and architectural design. In *Psychedelics: Their Uses and Implications,* edited by B. S. Aaronson and H. Osmond. New York: Doubleday, 1968.

James, W. *The Varieties of Religious Experience.* New York: Collier, 1961. Originally published, 1902.

Kaempffert, W. *A Popular History of American Invention.* Vol. II. New York: Scribner's, 1924.

Kedrov, B. M. On the question of the psychology of scientific creativity (on the occasion of the discovery by D. I. Mendeleev of the periodic law). *Voprosy Psiklologii,* 1957, 3:91–113.

Kneller, G. F. *The Art and Science of Creativity.* New York: Holt, Rinehart and Winston, 1965.

Koestler, A. *The Sleepwalkers.* New York: Grosset and Dunlap, 1963.

Koestler, A. *The Act of Creation.* New York: Macmillan, 1964.

Krippner, S. Creativity and psychic phenomena. *Gifted Child Quarterly,* 1963, 7:51–61.

Krippner, S. The psychedelic artist. In *Psychedelic Art* by R. E. L. Masters and J. Houston. New York: Grove Press, 1968.

Krippner, S. The psychedelic state, the hypnotic trance, and the creative act. In *Altered States of Consciousness: A Book of Readings,* edited by C. T. Tart. New York: Wiley, 1969.

Krippner, S., and Hughes, W. Dreams and human potential. *Journal of Humanistic Psychology,* 1970, 10:1–20.

Kris, E. Psychoanalysis and the study of creative imagination. In *The Creative Imagination,* edited by H. M. Ruitenbeck. Chicago: Quadrangle, 1965.

Kubie, L. S. *Neurotic Distortion of the Creative Process.* New York: Noonday Press, 1966.

Kupriyanovich, L. Reserves of memory. *Nauka i Zhirn',* 1970, 37:65–72.

Lombroso, C. *The Man of Genius.* London: Scott, 1891.

London, P. Hypnosis in children: An experimental approach. *International Journal of Clinical and Experimental Hypnosis,* 1962, 10:79–91.

McCord, H., and Sherrill, C. I. A note on increased ability to do calculus post-hypnotically. *American Journal of Clinical Hypnosis,* 1961, 4:20.

Maslow, A. H. A theory of metamotivation: The biological rooting of the value-life. *Journal of Humanistic Psychology,* 1967, 7:93–127.

Maslow, A. H. *Motivation and Personality.* 2nd. ed. New York: Harper and Row, 1970.

Mysior, A. Shifting from conceptual to visual problem-solving facilitated by hypnosis. *American Journal of Clinical Hypnosis,* 1971, 14:97–101.

Newman, J. R. Sriniwasa Ramanujan. *Scientific American,* 1948, 178:54–57.

Pearce, J. C. *The Crack in the Cosmic Egg: Challenging Constructs of Mind and Reality.* New York: Julian Press, 1971.

Porterfield, A. L. *Creative Factors in Scientific Research.* Durham, N.C.: Duke University Press, 1941.

Progoff, I. *The Symbolic and the Real.* New York: Julian Press, 1963.

Roberts, T. B. Toward a humanistic social science: A consciousness theory outlined and applied. *Journal of Human Relations,* 1971, *18*:1204–1227.

Rogers, C. R. *On Becoming a Person.* New York: Houghton Mifflin, 1961.

Satprem. *Sri Aurobindo: The Adventure of Consciousness.* New York: India Library Society, 1969.

Schaefer, C. E. The self-concept of creative adolescents. *Journal of Psychology,* 1969, 72:233–242.

Sturdevant, W. D. ESP and creativity. *Parapsychology,* 1962–1963, 4:107–112.

Suzuki, D. T. *An Introduction to Zen Buddhism.* New York: Grove Press, 1964.

Tart, C. T. Scientific foundations for the study of altered states of consciousness. *Journal of Transpersonal Psychology,* 1971, 3:93–124.

Torrance, E. P. *Guiding Creative Talent.* Englewood Cliffs, N.J.: Prentice-Hall, 1962.

Torrance, E. P. *Rewarding Creative Behavior.* Englewood Cliffs, N.J.: Prentice-Hall, 1965.

Witty, P. A. A study of one hundred gifted children. *Educational Administration and Supervision,* 1930 (entire).

Witty, P. A. Some considerations in the education of gifted children. *Educational Administration and Supervision,* 1940, 26:513–521.

Woods, R. L. *The World of Dreams.* New York: Random House, 1947.

40 Some New Thoughts on the Development of Creativity

J. C. GOWAN

One of the most curious characteristics of creativity, and one that generally appears to have escaped critical attention, is the fact that its variability in individuals far exceeds the limits of variability characteristic of other traits and abilities. Wechsler (1974), for example, has conclusively demonstrated that the interpersonal variability of such psychological and physiological measures as height, weight, cranial capacity, grip strength, blood pressure, respiration rate, reaction time, pitch, Snellen acuity, intelligence, mental age, and memory span has a limit of $e/1$, where $e = 2.818$, the basis of the natural logarithm system, and in most cases has a mean of 2.3 or less. Yet comparing the creative productions of a genius such as Einstein, Mozart, or Picasso with those of more ordinary mortals, one finds a ratio of $100/1$ or over. Obviously the trait and factor theory of creativity cannot account for all the variance.

It is the thesis of this article that the remaining variance can best be accounted for by the concept of "psychological openness" akin to the mental health concept of Maslow (1954). Certainly this trait is consonant with Maslow's concepts of high mental health, since it was one of the characteristics he identified in self-actualizing persons.

Both J. P. Guilford (1967) and Alex Osborn (1953) believed that creativity was an outcome of certain problem-solving aspects of intellect; that it could therefore be taught or stimulated; and that it was rational and semantic, consisting essentially of what Hallman has called "connectedness"—that is, the ability, through the use of verbal analogy, to connect (by common ratios or otherwise) elements that heretofore had been viewed as incommensurable or disparate.

If this view is correct, then the obvious way to stimulate creativity in the classroom is to facilitate the child's ability to make such connections via the Williams Cube material, the Meeker method, or by similar curriculum procedures. But while the Structure-of-Intellect and the creative problem-solving methods are certainly useful, it is perhaps time to ask whether we are putting all of our educational eggs in one basket. This is especially pertinent since two other theories as to the genesis of creative ability have gained currency, and

From *The Journal of Creative Behavior* 11:2 (1977). Used by permission.
Copyright © 1976 by John Curtis Gowan.

each has important educational applications.

The first of these new theories is, of course, Maslow's view that creativity results from mental health. To the extent that this theory is true, we ought to be strengthening the mental health of children, primarily through developmental guidance procedures along lines set down in Blocher (1966) and Bower and Hollister (1968). When the author was director of a summer workshop in creativity for gifted children, this aspect proved to be so important that a full-time counselor accompanied the children to every class (at a 1/25 ratio).

A second theory, in some minds even more important, is that creativity is nothing but psychological openness to preconscious sources. A careful perusal of Ghiselin (1952) will certainly do much to make this theory palatable, and there is considerable other evidence for it besides—in particular, the above-mentioned fact that creative production does not obey the Wechsler law of interpersonal variance less than e. If this is true, then we need to learn how to rub Aladdin's lamp to get the genie to come, and it appears that meditation, reverie, fantasy, and the like are the most promising methods. Outside the Khatena and Torrance *Sounds and Images,* however, there are few facilitations in this area.

But if psychologists are in doubt about which theory of creativity contributes the most variance to the whole, let us turn to an even better set of witnesses—namely, the creative geniuses themselves, in the rare moments when they reveal the workings of the creative process. Consider Mozart:

> The whole, though it be long, stands almost complete and finished in my mind, so that I can survey it ... at a glance. Nor do I hear in my imagination the parts successively, but I hear them, as it were, all at once. . . . What delight this is I cannot tell! (Vernon, 1970)

And Tchaikowsky:

> The only music capable of moving and touching us is that which flows from the depth of a composer's soul when he is stirred by imagination ... it takes root with extraordinary force and rapidity, shoots up through the earth, puts forth branches, leaves and finally blossoms. I cannot define the creative process in any other way than by this simile. (Vernon, 1970)

And finally Poincaré on his discovery of Fuchsian functions (among the most complicated in higher mathematics). Having labored a long time in vain, he had the following revelation:

At the moment when I put my foot on the step, the idea came to me, without anything in my former thoughts seeming to have paved the way for it, that the transformations I had used to define the Fuchsian functions were identical with those of non-Euclidean geometry. ... Most striking at first is this appearance of sudden illumination, a manifest sign of long, unconscious prior work ... it is only fruitful if it is on one hand preceded and on the other hand followed by a period of conscious work ....
(Vernon, 1970)

What each of these geniuses is doing is confirming the correctness of the Wallas paradigm, which states that preparation and incubation must precede illumination and that verification must follow it. But what is the exact mechanism by which such creative ideas may be induced to occur? It is obvious by the sudden uprush of new ideas which seem to break into consciousness with a shock of recognition that we are here dealing with material that has somehow accumulated at subconscious levels of the mind. Since such ideas are generally not accessible to the ego, but appear to be so under the creative impetus, it is evident that they belong to the preconscious, which has been defined as consisting of just such occasionally accessible material. Moreover, there is a *collective* aspect about the knowledge, as if we were all drilling into a common underground aquifer for well water. Indeed, many great scientific discoveries have had more than one discoverer—Leibnitz and Newton in the case of the calculus, and Darwin and Wallace for the theory of evolution.

We theorize that the collective preconscious is best compared to the terminal of a giant computer which is in another realm, outside time and space, and contains an infinity of potentialities; all are real in that realm but only one will eventuate in our dimension. Under conditions of relaxation, meditation, incubation, and the like, messages in the form of images manifest in the printout of that cosmic computer and collator. But with all that random dissociated infinity in the machine, why is it only the creative ideas that are brought through to consciousness?

Poincaré explains the subliminal self's activities as follows:

All the combinations would be formed in consequence of the automatism of the subliminal self, but only the interesting ones would break into consciousness. ... Is it only chance which confers this privilege? ... The privileged unconscious phenomena ... are those which affect most profoundly our emotional sensibility. ... The useful combinations are precisely the most beautiful .... (Ghiselin, 1952)

As the recovery process proceeds from the germ of a creative idea down deep and rises like an expanding bubble through successive layers of consciousness, various individuals become cognizant of the nascent creativity in different modes. Some feel it first prototaxically, like Houseman:

> Experience has taught me, when I am shaving of a morning, to keep watch over my thoughts, because, if a line of poetry strays into my memory, my skin bristles so that the razor ceases to act. This particular symptom is accompanied by a shiver down the spine; there is another which consists in a constriction of the throat and a precipitation of water to the eyes; and there is a third which I can only describe by borrowing a phrase from one of Keat's last letters, where he says, speaking of Fanny Brawne, "everything that reminds me of her goes through me like a spear." The seat of this sensation is the pit of the stomach. (Ghiselin, 1952)

Others feel it parataxically through images and emotions; for example, Einstein:

> Words or language do not seem to play any role in my mechanism of thought. The psychical entities which seem to serve as elements in thought are certain signs and more or less clear images .... (Ghiselin, 1952)

Wordsworth:

> Poetry is the spontaneous overflow of powerful feelings: it takes its origin from emotion recollected in tranquility. (Ghiselin, 1952)

Coleridge, speaking of himself in the third person:

> All the images rose up before him as *things*, with a parallel production of the corresponding expressions, without any sensation of conscious effort. (Ghiselin, 1952)

The major question is how to transfer these images/emotions to the alphanumeric syntaxic level, and this analysis is the source of considerable testimony. But the prime secret is relaxation of the conscious mind. Says Kipling: "When your daemon is in charge, do not try to think consciously. Drift, wait, obey" (Ghiselin, 1952).

The reason why it takes higher ability to be verbally creative is that the crossing of the successive discontinuity of psychic layers during the bubble's trip upward to full consciousness requires a complex level of verbal analogy fitting each stage; for one must both see that a proportionate ratio exists below, and also intuit the same ratio in the higher elements which may be semantically very different. This correspondence of a ratio across a semantic chasm from the known to the unknown is the secret of transferring creative affective images to full verbal creativity at the syntaxic level. Amy Lowell says of the poet:

> He must be born with a subconscious factory always working for him or he can never be a poet at all, and he must have knowledge and talent enough to "putty" up his holes.... Here is where the conscious training of the poet comes in, for he must fill up what the subconscious has left, and fill it in as much in the key of the rest as possible. Every long poem is sprinkled with these *lacunae*. Let no one undervalue this process of puttying; it is a condition of good poetry. (Ghiselin, 1952)
>
> . . . . .

Figure 40.1 indicates the symbiotic relationship between the conscious mind and the collective preconscious which produces creative products. On the left, the conscious mind has taken over completely, and only convergent production ensues. The part played by the preconscious, then, gradually increases and that of the conscious decreases, until in the middle of the figure they are both equally present. This represents the acme of creativity. As we move toward the extreme right the preconscious assumes a larger and larger share until eventually it becomes all, and the product is analogous to automatic writing. In the middle of the diagram creative products would be distinguished from one another by the amount of each which they contain. Mathematical and physical discoveries might be toward the left of center, and abstract artistic productions such as *Kubla Khan* or surrealistic paintings would be toward the right.

Because all this "psychological openness" is so much more bizarre and less "respectable" than, say, the Structure-of-Intellect theory with its solid dependence on statistics, it is desirable to reinforce this testimony with other, even more credible witnesses describing even more incredible processes and events.

Recognizing the importance of preconscious inspiration, many creative persons have intuitively derived individual mechanisms for throwing themselves into this mode of knowledge.

Gerald Heard says:

> To have truly original thought the mind must throw off its critical guard, its filtering censor. It must put itself in a state of

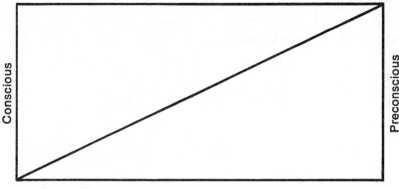

FIGURE 40.1

depersonalization.... The best researchers when confronting problems and riddles which have defied all solution by ordinary methods, did employ their minds in an unusual way, did put themselves into a state of egoless creativity, which permitted them to have insights so remarkable that by means of these they were able to make their greatest and most original discoveries. (Weil, Metsner, & Leary, 1971)

Lord Tennyson was accustomed to pass into "an ecstatic state" and had a formula for inducing it. Tennyson says in a letter written in 1794:

I have had ... a kind of walking trance ... when I have been all alone. This has often come upon me through repeating my own name to myself silently, till, all at once out of the intensity and conscious of the individuality, the individuality itself seems to dissolve and fade away into boundless being .... (Prince, 1963)

Prince (1963) similarly describes the inception of *Uncle Tom's Cabin,* quoting from the biography of Harriet Beecher Stowe:

Mrs. Stowe was seated in her pew in the college church at Brunswick, during the communion service.... Suddenly like the unrolling of a picture scroll, the scene of the death of Uncle Tom seemed to pass before her.... She was so affected she could scarcely keep from weeping.... That Sunday afternoon she went to her room, locked the door and wrote out, substantially as it appears ... the chapter called "The Death of Uncle Tom."

But no matter how eminent or noteworthy are writers and authors, creative persons in the sciences carry the most weight of evidence. We are indebted to Krippner, Dreistadt, & Hubbard (1972) for the following: "One can cite as well creative dreams of scientists and inventors that gave the solution of a problem analogically or symbolically."

The chemist, Friedrich August Kekule (cited by Koestler, 1964), had a tendency to make theoretical discoveries in hypnagogic reverie states. Kekule wrote:

I turned my chair to the fire and dozed. Again the atoms were gambolling before my eyes. The smaller groups kept modestly in the background. My mental eye, rendered more acute by visions of this kind, could now distinguish larger structures, of manifold conformations; long rows, sometimes more closely fitted together, all twining and twisting in snakelike motion. But look! What was that? One of the snakes had seized hold of its own tail, and the form whirled mockingly before my eyes. As if by a flash of lightning I awoke.

At this juncture, it is instructive to break into the narrative to ask a searching question: "What did Kekule see?" While you are thinking of the answer, it may bₑ helpful to tell a baseball joke.

Three umpires were arguing about calling balls and strikes. The first said: "I calls 'em as they are."

The second said: "I call 'em as I sees 'em."

The third said: "They ain t nothin' 'till I calls 'em."

Kekule said that what he saw was a ring. Despite what Kekule *concluded* (which was a concept), let us persist in analyzing what Kekule *described*. To do so, please reread his description. In the light of what we know now about molecular structure, the "long rows, sometimes more closely fitted together, all twining and twisting" clearly describes the DNA molecule. Kekule was in the presence of a noncategorical numinous archetype in a nonordinary state of reality —in other words, in the cave of Aladdin. He went in looking for a dollar, and he came out with a dollar. Had he been prepared by prior discipline to look for a thousand dollars he could have found that also. An orchestra can play only the symphonies for which it has the men and instruments. One is reminded of George Kelly's phrase: "One is constrained to experience events in the way one anticipates them."

The numinous archetype presented in hypnagogic dreams and creative reveries is a noncategorical image, and is hence as capable of as many interpretations as there are percipients (e.g., the smile on the *Mona Lisa*). Each participant will interpret the numinous archetype idiosyncratically, in accordance with his level of development (like the seven blind Indians who went to see the elephant). The archetype hence acts as a generating entity, which may produce a number of art forms or alphanumeric scientific statements. Since this nonordinary experience may occur in many persons, the key concept of creativity is to possess the previously prepared matrix of verbal or mathematical analogy which will catch the ephemeral vision and preserve it in concrete form.

> In 1869, D. I. Mendeleev went to bed exhausted after struggling to conceptualize a way to categorize the elements based upon their atomic weights. He reported, "I saw in a dream a table where all the elements fell into place as required. Awakening, I immediately wrote it down on a piece of paper. Only in one place did a correction later seem necessary." In this manner, Mendeleev's Periodic Table of the Elements was created. (Krippner et al., 1972)

We have stated earlier that the collective preconscious seems to be in a realm of nonordinary reality, outside time and space, which of course gives it access to the future. In curious reinforcement of this hypothesis, many creative discoveries have an element of precognition about them. When Kekule saw the whirling forms, he may have glimpsed the DNA molecular structure. When Mendeleev dreamed the atomic order of the elements, he left a hole, where later helium was discovered, and still later his open-ended model had places for all the radioactive and transuranium elements such as plutonium.

In the preceding article (Reading 39), Krippner and others (1972) have documented case after case where scientific discoveries were made in dreams or other states of non-ordinary reality. Similar accounts may be found in Ghiselin (1952) and Koestler (1964). Indeed, we will go so far as to guess that nearly every such discovery has come out of some creative vision, rather than from cogitation alone. Ferguson (1977) is especially convincing in regard to this matter, stating:

> It is non-verbal thinking ... that has fixed the outlines and filled in the details of our material surroundings. ... Pyramids, cathedrals and rockets exist not because of geometry, theory of structures or thermodynamics, but because they were first a picture—literally a vision—in the minds of those who built them.

If all this sounds wild to you, listen to the most famous aviator of our day, Charles Lindbergh (1969):

> ... I think the great adventures of the future lie—in voyages

inconceivable by our 20th century rationality—beyond the solar system, through distant galaxies, possibly through peripheries untouched by time and space. I believe early entrance to this era can be attained by the application of our scientific knowledge not to life's mechanical vehicles but to the essence of life itself: to the infinite and infinitely evolving qualities that have resulted in the awareness, shape and character of man. I believe this application is necessary to the very survival of mankind ... will we discover that only *without* spaceships can we reach the galaxies ... I believe it is through sensing and thinking about such concepts that great adventures of the future will be found.

Perhaps we have labored the point too long, but these concepts are so new and unusual that it is very important to impress them firmly on minds unused to such views. We have long thought of man's brain as a problem-solver; perhaps an even better model would be that of a radio receiver. When the set has been properly assembled through preparation and discipline, the static in the locality has been cleared through relaxation and incubation, and the power is on, then we may hear the faint calls of distant stations—signals which are always in the air, but are only received with the best equipment under the best and clearest operating conditions. Such a simile tells us why high giftedness enhances the creative range and why the easy production of verbal analogies (like the proportion between radio frequency and audio frequency) facilitates high-fidelity reception.

These ideas are so new that all we can do in turning from theory to practice is to sketch some ways in which such views may affect the classroom in the future. It would be a grave error to conclude that we should abandon all that has gone before and delve into divination and the occult; indeed, such a procedure would be disastrous. The Wallas paradigm still holds true and useful. Mental discipline and scholarship are still required for the preparation phase. What we are talking about is more conscious attention to the incubation phase.

Moreover, to look at the end product in highly creative geniuses at their best hardly tells us much about how to induce creativity consciously through educational procedures. What they gained in flashes of creative intuition may come to lesser lights through longer and more painstaking efforts. Inducing creativity in the classroom may not be the same as observing it in the field.

There are, however, some procedures we can begin to make use of. I should like to list a few for you now:

1.   We should study creativity directly in high school and university classes. Almost no schools at the present time have courses

on this subject. The 21st century will find this lack incomprehensible.

2. We can help young children learn techniques of relaxation and incubation. This does not mean that we should teach them any particular form of meditation, but it might be useful for all children to know what meditation, relaxation, and other types of unstressing are.

3. We should help children practice imagination and imagery during such relaxed periods. The Torrance and Khatena record, *Sounds and Images,* is only one of several devices on the market for this purpose. As a consequence of such periods we should encourage the production of poetry, art, music, etc.

4. As long as the child is in the concrete operations phase, the images will tend to be static and not particularly creative; but when he enters the formal operations phase one can expect and should push for more finished artistic creations, especially in poetic form. Children at this stage should be strongly encouraged to keep a journal and put their poetry and other thoughts into it. The development of the easy ability at this level helps the child to become truly creative in the next stage, and this is where (in upper high school and in lower division college) most gifted children do not make the transition to creative production. I think the most important facilitation which can take place at this time is a seminar-type home room where the adolescent can be with others of the same persuasion, for (because of the strong gregarious needs at this stage) nothing does more to inhibit creativity than group sanctions against it in other adolescents.

It might be prudent of us to listen to the last testament of a prophet and sage on educational objectives in a Utopia:

How does he do his thinking, perceiving, and remembering? Is he a visualizer or a non-visualizer? Does his mind work with images or with words, with both at once or with neither? How close to the surface is his story-telling faculty? Does he see the world as Wordsworth and Traherne saw it when they were children? And if so, what can be done to prevent the glory and freshness from fading into the light of common day? Or in more general terms, can we educate children on the conceptual level without killing their capacity for intense non-verbal experience? How can we reconcile analysis with vision? (Huxley, 1962)

Few orthodox teachers will agree with Huxley's tripartite prescription for accomplishing this educational miracle, which consisted of *maithuna* for the psychomotor level, *moksha*-medicine (drugs) for the affective level, and meditation for the cognitive level. But let us remember that Huxley was a visionary, and that many of the predictions in *Brave New World* have come true. Certainly his ideas are worth thinking about, if only to trigger our own.

About 9,000 years ago, prehistoric man was suddenly catapulted into history as the result of an astonishing social discovery. Previous to this, small bands of nomadic tribes had roamed a large hunting area looking for game and gathering live fruits and vegetables wild. Then someone found out that if one domesticated animals and plants, one could have a ready supply of food always at hand in a confined space. Thus were agriculture and civilization born, and man escalated into history, and to the possibility of a far greater population on a given land mass. We are still reaping the benefits of that change, but our continuing ecological crises show us that we are nearing the end of that period. Fortunately we are on the brink of another momentous discovery which will have even greater impact on cultural and personal escalation.

Heretofore we have harvested creativity wild. We have used as creative only those persons who stubbornly remained so despite all efforts of the family, religion, education, and politics to grind it out of them. In the prosecution of this campaign, men and women have been punished, flogged, silenced, imprisoned, tortured, ostracized, and killed. Jesus, Socrates, Huss, Lavoisier, Lincoln, Gandhi, Kennedy, and King are good examples. As a result of these misguided efforts, our society produces only a small percentage of its potential of creative individuals (the ones with the most uncooperative dispositions).

If we learn to domesticate creativity—that is, to enhance rather than deny it in our culture—we can increase the number of creative persons in our midst by about fourfold. That would put the number and percent of such individuals over the "critical mass" point. When this level is reached in a culture, as it was in Periclean Athens, the Renaissance, the *Aufklarung*, the Court of the Sun King, Elizabethan England, and our own Federalist period, there is an escalation of creativity resulting, and civilization makes a great leap forward. We can have a golden age of this type such as the world has never seen, and I am convinced that it will occur early in the 21st century. But we must make preparations now, and the society we save will be our own. The alternative is either nuclear war or learning to speak Arabic and bow down four times a day toward Mecca.

In conclusion, if we may be permitted a peep at the future, we see an integrated science of human development and talent. The gestalt we are talking about there is at present at best a shore dimly seen, but it is the coming science of man of the 21st century. A genius is always a forerunner; and the best minds of this age foresee the dawn of that one. All of these branches of humanistic psychology will be welded together in a *structure d'ensemble,* greater than interest in the gifted, greater than interest in creativity, greater, in fact, than anything except the potential of man himself. We may come from dust, but our destiny is in the stars. Thoreau, that rustic seer, prophesized in the last sentence of *Walden:* "That day is yet to dawn, for the sun is only a morning star."

Toynbee tells us that each civilization leaves its monument and its religion. Our monument is on the moon, and the "religion" our culture will bequeath is the coming science of man and his infinite potential. This potential is truly infinite because man may be part animal but he is also part of the noumenon. And as Schroedinger correctly observed in *What Is Life,* "The 'I' that observes the universe is the same 'I' that created it." The present powers of genius are merely the earnest of greater powers to be unfolded. You need not take my word for this. Listen instead to the words of the greatest genius of our age—Albert Einstein:

> A human being is a part of the whole, called by us "Universe"; a part limited in time and space. He experiences himself, his thoughts and feelings as something separated from the rest—a kind of optical delusion of his consciousness. This delusion is a kind of prison for us, restricting us to our personal desires and to affection for a few persons nearest us. Our task must be to free ourselves from this prison by widening our circle of compassion to embrace all living creatures and the whole nature in its beauty. Nobody is able to achieve this completely, but the striving for such achievement is, in itself, a part of the liberation and a foundation for inner security (cited in Gowan, 1975).

References

Blocher, D. *Developmental counseling.* New York: Ronald Press, 1966.

Bower, E. G., & Hollister, H. G. *Behavioral science frontiers in education.* New York: Wiley, 1968.

Ghiselin, B. (Ed.). *The creative process.* New York: New American, 1952.

Gowan, J. C. *Development of the creative individual.* San Diego: Knapp, 1972.

Gowan, J. C. *Trance, art, and creativity.* Northridge, Cal.: J. C. Gowan, 1975.

Guilford, J. P. *The nature of human intelligence.* New York: McGraw-Hill, 1967.

Huxley, A. *Island.* New York: Harper, 1962.

Koestler, A. *The act of creation.* New York: Macmillan, 1964.

Krippner, S., Dreistadt, R., and Hubbard, C. C. The creative person and non-ordinary reality. *The Gifted Child Quarterly,* 1972, *16,* 203–228.

Lindbergh, C. A. *A letter from Lindbergh.* New York: Harcourt-Brace, 1969.

Maslow, A. *Motivation and personality.* New York: Harper, 1954.

Osborn, A. *Applied imagination.* New York: Scribner's, 1953.

Prince, W. F. *Noted witnesses for psychic occurrences.* Hyde Park, New York: University Books, 1963.

Vernon, P. E. *Creativity.* Baltimore: Penguin Books, 1970.

Wechsler, D. *The collected papers of David Wechsler.* New York: Academic Press, 1974.

Weil, G. M., Metsner, R., & Leary, T. *The psychedelic reader.* New York: Citadel Press, 1971.

References

Arieti, S. *Creativity: The Magic Synthesis.* New York: Basic Books, 1976.

Biondi, A., & Parnes, S. *Assessing Creative Growth.* Vols. 1 & 2. New York: Creative Synergetic Association, 1976.

Bloom, B. S. (Ed.). *Taxonomy of Educational Objectives: Cognitive Domain.* New York: David McKay Co., 1956.

Blosser, G. H. "Group Intelligence Tests as Screening Devices in Locating Gifted and Superior Students in the Ninth Grade." *Exceptional Children,* Vol. 29 (1963), pp. 282–87.

Bonsall, Marcella, and Stefflre, B. "The Temperament of Gifted Children." *California Journal of Educational Research,* Vol. 6 (September 1955), pp. 162–65.

Bowra, C. M. *The Romantic Imagination.* London: Oxford University Press, 1950.

Brandwein, P. *The Gifted Student as a Future Scientist.* New York: Harcourt Brace, 1956.

Bruch, Catherine B. "Increasing Children's Creativity through a Combination of Teacher Training Approaches." *The Gifted Child Quarterly,* Vol. 9 (1965), pp. 24–29.

Bruner, J. S. *Toward a Theory of Instruction.* Cambridge, Mass.: Harvard University Press, 1966.

Duncan, Ann Dell Warren. *Behavior Rates of Gifted and Regular Elementary School Children.* Cincinnati, Ohio: National Association for Gifted Children, February 1969.

Eccles, J. C. "The Physiology of Imagination." Reprinted in *Readings from Scientific American.* New York: Scientific American, Inc., 1972, pp. 31–40. Originally published 1958.

Erikson, E. "The Eight Stages of Man." *Childhood and Society.* New York: Norton, 1950.

Feldhusen, J. F. "Programming and the Talented Pupil." *The Clearinghouse,* Vol. 38 (1963), pp. 151–54.

Feldhusen, J. F., and others. "Teaching Creative Thinking." *The Elementary School Journal,* Vol. 70, No. 1 (October 1969).

Feldhusen, J., and Treffinger, D. *Teaching Creative Thinking and Problem Solving.* Dubuque, Iowa: Kendall/Hunt Publishing Co., 1976.

Ferguson, E. S. "The Mind's Eye: Nonverbal Thought in Technology." *Science,* Vol. 197, No. 4306 (August 1977), pp. 827–36.

Flanagan, J. C. "The Identification, Development and Utilization of Human Talents." *The Gifted Child Quarterly,* Vol. 4 (1960), pp. 51–54, 58.

Flavell, J. H. *The Developmental Psychology of Jean Piaget.* New York: Van Nostrand, 1963.

Gage, N. L. *Handbook of Research on Teaching.* Chicago: Rand McNally & Co., 1963.

Gallagher, J. *Teaching the Gifted Child.* Boston: Allyn & Bacon, 1975.

Gear, G. "Effects of Training in Teacher's Accuracy in Identifying Gifted Children." *Gifted Child Quarterly,* Vol. 22, No. 1 (1978).

Getzels, J. W., and Jackson, P. W. *Creativity and Intelligence.* New York: John Wiley & Sons, 1962.

Gowan, J. C. "The Gifted Underachiever, A Problem for Everyone." *Exceptional Children,* Vol. 21, No. 7 (1955), pp. 247–49.

Gowan, J. C. "The Dynamics of Underachievement in Gifted Students." *Exceptional Children,* Vol. 24, No. 3 (1957), pp. 98–101.

Gowan, J. C. "The Factors of Achievement in School and College." *Journal of Counseling Psychology,* Vol. 7 (1960), pp. 91–95. (a)

Gowan, J. C. "Self-Report Tests on the Prediction of Teacher Effectiveness." *School Review,* Vol. 66 (1960), pp. 409–419. (b)

Gowan, J. C. "The Guidance of Creative Children." *Journal of the National Association of Women Deans and Counselors,* Vol. 31 (1968), pp. 154–61.

Gowan, J. C. *The Development of the Creative Individual.* San Diego: R. Knapp Co., 1972.

Gowan, J. C. *The Development of the Psychedelic Individual.* Buffalo, N.Y.: Creative Education Foundation; 1974.

Gowan, J. C. *Trance, Art, and Creativity.* Buffalo, N.Y.: Creative Education Foundation, 1975.

Gowan, J. C., & Bruch, C. B. *The Academically Talented and Guidance.* Boston: Houghton Mifflin Co., 1971.

Gowan, J. C., and Demos, G. D. *The Education and Guidance of the Ablest.* Springfield, Ill.: Charles C Thomas, Publisher, 1964.

Gowan, J. C., and Demos, G. D. (Eds.). *The Guidance of Exceptional Children.* New York: David McKay Co., 1965, 1972.

Gowan, J. C., Demos, G. D., and Torrance, E. P. (Eds.). *Creativity: Its Educational Implications.* New York: John Wiley & Sons, 1967.

Gowan, J. C., and Groth, Norma Jean. "Development of Vocational Choice in Gifted Children." *California Educational Research Summaries,* 1968.

Gowan, J. C., and Winward, M. E. "Costs of Special Education Programs for Gifted Children." *The Gifted Child Quarterly,* Vol. 4 (1960), pp. 33–36.

Guilford, J. P. *The Nature of Human Intelligence.* New York: McGraw-Hill Book Co., 1967.

Guilford, J. P. *Intelligence and Creativity: Their Educational Implications.* San Diego, Calif.: R. Knapp Co., 1969.

Guilford, J. P. *Way Beyond the IQ.* Buffalo, N.Y.: Creative Education Foundation, 1977.

Hallman, R. J. "Techniques of Creative Teaching." *Journal of Creative Behavior,* Vol. 1 (September 1966), pp. 325–30.

Hanson, L. F., and Komoski, P. K. "School Use of Programmed Instruction." In Robert Glaser (Ed.), *Teaching Machines and Programmed Instruction, II, Data and Directions*, pp. 657, 664, and 669. Washington, D.C.: Department of Audio-Visual Instruction of the National Education Association, 1965.

Hauck, B. B., and Freehill, M. F. (Eds.). *The Gifted: Case Studies.* Dubuque: William C. Brown Co., 1972.

Jaynes, J. *The Origin of Consciousness in the Breakdown of the Bicameral Mind.* Boston: Houghton Mifflin Co., 1976.

Keating, D. P. (Ed.). *Intellectual Talent: Research and Development.* Baltimore, Md.: Johns Hopkins University Press, 1976.

Khatena, J. "Children's Version of Onomatopoeia and Images: A Preliminary Validity Study of Verbal Originality." *Perceptual and Motor Skills*, Vol. 33 (1971), p. 26. (a)

Khatena, J. "A Second Study: Training College Adults to Think Creatively with Words." *Psychological Reports*, Vol. 28 (1971), pp. 385–86. (b)

Khatena, J. "Something About Myself: A Brief Screening Device for Identifying Creatively Gifted Children and Adults." *Gifted Child Quarterly*, Vol. 15, No. 4 (1971), pp. 262–66. (c)

Khatena, J. "The Use of Analogy in the Production of Original Verbal Images." *Journal of Creative Behavior*, Vol. 31 (1972), pp. 565–66.

Khatena, J. "Imagination and Production of Original Verbal Images." *Art Psychotherapy*, Vol. 1 (1973), pp. 113–20. (a)

Khatena, J. "Imagination Imagery by Children and the Production of Analogy." *Gifted Child Quarterly*, Vol. 17, No. 2 (1973), pp. 98–102. (b)

Khatena, J. "Facilitating the Creative Functioning of the Gifted." *Gifted Child Quarterly*, Vol. 21, No. 2 (Summer 1977), pp. 218–226.

Khatena, J. "Creative Imagination through Imagery: Some Recent Research." *Humanitas*, Vol. 14, No. 1 (1978). (a)

Khatena, J. "Some Advances in Thought on the Gifted." *Gifted Child Quarterly*, Vol. 22, No. 1 (b)

Khatena, J. *The Creatively Gifted Child: Some Suggestions for Parents and Teachers.* New York: Vantage Press, 1978. (c)

Khatena, J., and Torrance, E. P. *Thinking Creatively with Sounds and Words: Norms-Technical Manual.* Research ed. Lexington, Mass.: Personnel Press, 1973.

Khatena, J., and Torrance, E. P. *Khatena-Torrance Creative Perception Inventory.* Chicago, Ill.: Stoetting, 1976.

Kornrich, M. *Achievement: A Book of Readings.* Springfield, Ill.: Charles C Thomas, Publishers, 1966.

Krathwohl, D., and Bloom, B. S. (Eds.). *Taxonomy of Educational Objectives: Affective Domain.* New York: David McKay Co., 1966.

Lehman, H. C. *Age and Achievement.* Princeton, N.J.: Princeton University Press, 1953.

Maccoby, E. E., and Jacklin, C. N. *The Psychology of Sex Differences.* Palo Alto, Calif.: Stanford University Press, 1974.

Maslow, A. *Motivation and Personality.* New York: Harper Bros., 1954.

Meeker, Mary. *The SOI: Its Uses and Interpretations.* Columbus, Ohio: Charles E. Merrill Publishing Co., 1969.

Meeker, Mary. *Advance Teaching Judgment, Planning and Decision Making.* El Segundo, Calif.: SOI Institute, 1976.

Montour, K. "Three Precocious Boys: What Happened to Them." *Gifted Child Quarterly,* Vol. 20 (1976).

Montour, K. "The Marvelous Boys and Modern Counterparts." *The Gifted Child Quarterly,* Vol. 22, No. 1 (1978).

Parnes, S., Noller, R., and Biondi, A. *Guide to Creative Action.* Rev. ed. *Creative Actionbook.* Rev. ed. (workbook for above). New York: Charles Scribner's Sons, 1977.

Patterson, C. M. "Counseling Underachievers." In C. M. Patterson, *Counseling and Guidance in Schools: A First Course,* Chap. 1. New York: Harper & Row Publishers, 1962.

Pegnato, C. C., and Birch, J. W. "Locating Gifted Children in Junior High School." *Exceptional Children,* Vol. 25 (1959), pp. 300–304.

Renzulli, J. S. "A Curriculum Development Model for Academically Superior Students." *Exceptional Children,* Vol. 35 (April 1970), pp. 611–15.

Renzulli, J. "The Enrichment Triad Model." Part I: *Gifted Child Quarterly,* Vol. 20, No. 3 (1976), pp. 303–26; Part II, abstract, *Gifted Child Quarterly,* Vol. 21, No. 2 (1977), pp. 227–34.

Renzulli, J. *The Enrichment Triad Model.* Wethersfield, Conn.: Creative Learning Press, 1977.

Roth, R. M., and Meyersburg, H. A. "The Nonachievement Syndrome." *Personnel and Guidance Journal,* Vol. 42 (February 1963), pp. 535–40.

Rothenberg, A., & Hausman, C. R. (Eds.). *The Creativity Question.* Durham, N.C.: Duke University Press, 1976.

Ryans, D. G. *Characteristics of Teachers.* Washington, D.C.: American Council on Education, 1961.

Seagoe, M. V. *Terman and the Gifted.* Los Altos, Calif.: William Kaufmann, 1975.

Simonton, D. K. "Sociocultural Context of Individual Creativity." *Journal of Personality and Social Psychology,* Vol. 32, No. 6 (1975), pp. 1119–33.

Simonton, D. K. "Creative Productivity, Age, and Stress." *Journal of Personality and Social Psychology,* Vol. 35, No. 11 (1977), pp. 791–804.

Simonton, D. K. "The Eminent Genius in History: The Critical Role of Creative Development." *Gifted Child Quarterly,* Vol. 22, No. 2 (1978).

Spaulding, R. L. "Affective Dimensions of Creative Process." *The Gifted Child Quarterly,* Vol. 7 (1963), pp. 150–57.

Stanley, J. C. "The Case for Extreme Educational Acceleration of Intellectually Brilliant Youths." *The Gifted Child Quarterly*, Vol. 20, No. 1 (1976).

Stanley, J. C., George, W. C., and Solano, C. H. (Eds.). *The Gifted and the Creative: A Fifty-Year Perspective.* Baltimore, Md.: Johns Hopkins University Press, 1977.

Stanley, J. C., Keating, D. P., and Fox, Lynn. *Mathematical Talent: Discovery, Description and Development.* Baltimore, Md.: Johns Hopkins University Press, 1974.

Terman, L. M. "The Discovery and Encouragement of Exceptional Talent." *American Psychologist*, Vol. 9, No. 6 (1954), pp. 221–30.

Terman, L. M., and Oden, Melita. *Genetic Studies of Genius.* Vol. V, *The Gifted Group at Mid-Life.* Stanford, Calif.: Stanford University Press, 1959.

Torrance, E. P. *Guiding Creative Talent.* Englewood Cliffs, N.J.: Prentice-Hall, 1962. (a)

Torrance, E. P. "Ten Ways of Helping Young Children Gifted in Creative Writing and Speech." *Gifted Child Quarterly*, Vol. 6 (1962), pp. 121–27. (b)

Torrance, E. P. *Rewarding Creative Behavior.* Englewood Cliffs, N.J.: Prentice-Hall, 1965.

Torrance, E. P. *Gifted Children in the Classroom.* New York: Macmillan Co., 1965.

Torrance, E. P. "Career Patterns and Peak Creative Achievements of Creative High School Students Twelve Years Later." *Gifted Child Quarterly*, Vol. 16 (1972), pp. 75–78.

Torrance, E. P. *The Torrance Tests of Creative Thinking: Norms-Technical Manual.* Lexington, Mass.: Ginn & Co., 1974.

Torrance, E. P. *Discovery and Nurturance of Giftedness in the Culturally Different.* Reston, Va.: Council for Exceptional Children, 1977.

Torrance, E. P., and Myers, R. E. *Creative Learning and Teaching.* New York: Harper & Row, 1970.

Upton, A. *Creative Analysis.* New York: E. P. Dutton & Co., 1961.

Walker, W. J. "Creativity in the High School Climate." *Gifted Child Quarterly*, Vol. 10 (1966), pp. 139–44.

Wallas, G. *The Art of Thought.* London: C. A. Watts, 1926.

Williams. F. E. *Classroom Ideas for Encouraging Thinking and Feeling.* Buffalo, N.Y.: D. O. K. Publishing Co., 1971.

Williams, R. "Why Children Should Draw." *Saturday Review*, September 3, 1977, pp. 11–16.

Contributing Authors

Nicholas Colangelo. Assistant Professor of Counseling, Iowa State University, Iowa City.

Marvin Dice. Fontbonne College, St. Louis, Mo.

Roy Dreistadt. On staff of Maimonides Hospital, Brooklyn, N.Y.

John Feldhusen. Professor of Educational Psychology, Purdue University, West Lafayette, Ind.

Juliana Gensley. Professor of Education, Emerita, California State University, Long Beach.

John Curtis Gowan. Professor of Educational Psychology, Emeritus, California State University, Northridge; Executive Director, National Association for Gifted Children; Editor, *The Gifted Child Quarterly.*

J. P. Guilford. Professor of Psychology, Emeritus, University of Southern California, Los Angeles.

C. C. Hubbard. On staff of Maimonides Hospital, Brooklyn, N.Y.

Joe Khatena. Professor and Chairman, Department of Educational Psychology, Mississippi State University, Mississippi State, Miss.; President, National Association for Gifted Children.

Charlotte Malone. Extension Coordinator, University of California, San Diego.

Jean Morse. Professor, Georgia State University, Atlanta.

Philip A. Perrone. Professor, Department of Counseling and Guidance, and Director, Research and Guidance Laboratory, University of Wisconsin—Madison.

Lawrence R. Pfleger. Formerly with Research and Guidance Laboratory, University of Wisconsin—Madison.

Charles J. Pulvino. Professor, Department of Counseling and Guidance, University of Wisconsin—Madison.

Joe Renzulli. Professor of Education, University of Connecticut, Storrs.

C. R. Reynolds. Assistant in Educational Psychology, University of Georgia, Athens.

Judith Rodenstein. Ph.D. candidate, Department of Counseling and Guidance, and Research Assistant, Research and Guidance Laboratory, University of Wisconsin—Madison.

D. K. Simonton. Assistant Professor of Psychology, University of California, Davis.

Julia Simpson. Counselor, Westlake Village, Cal.

Julian Stanley. Professor of Psychology, Johns Hopkins University, Baltimore, Md.

E. Paul Torrance. Chairman and Professor, Department of Educational Psychology, University of Georgia, Athens.

D. K. Treffinger. Chairman, Department of Educational Psychology, University of Kansas, Lawrence.

Frank E. Williams. Former Director, Creativity Project, Macalester College, St. Paul, Minn.; now a consultant at 3760 Dallas Rd., N.W., West Salem, Ore. 97304.

Ronald T. Zaffrann. Assistant Professor, Marquette University, Milwaukee.

Name Index

Subject Index